A. C. Wood.

July 1934

A MODERN HISTORY OF THE ENGLISH PEOPLE

A MODERN HISTORY OF
THE ENGLISH PEOPLE
1880–1922

By

R. H. GRETTON

LONDON
MARTIN SECKER
NUMBER FIVE JOHN STREET
ADELPHI

BIBLIOGRAPHY

Volume   I, 1880 to 1898, first published 1912
Volume II, 1899 to 1910, first published 1914
Volume III, 1910 to 1922, first published 1929
First issue of the single-volume edition, 1930

C

PREFACE

A WRITER who set himself, in 1930, to give an account of English life between 1880 and 1922 could hardly escape having his whole view affected by the Great War. He would find it very difficult to recover in mind, or to present, an England entirely unconscious of that terrific experience ahead of it. On this ground, if on no other, the reproduction, without any rewriting, of volumes, two of which were published just before the war, and the third ten years after it, may be excused. For the suddenness of the impact of war, which is thus revealed, is a genuine historical fact.

It is a piece of good fortune, for the point of view from which this work was undertaken, that the first part of it was being written in 1912 and 1913. For one of my objects has been to try to represent a people living its life (as in fact it must live it) in ignorance of the future ; and nothing could effect that purpose more dramatically than this reprinting. Our absorption in the problems that were under our eyes, our complete unconsciousness of the impending horror that was to make all these problems trifling, could not be better displayed. A review of this kind may not be " History "; indeed, but for the cumbrousness of the title, the book should have been called " Materials for " — or even " Correctives to "—" a Modern History of the English People." History, no doubt, has to move by the large and sweeping events, and for that purpose to read them back into the years before they happened. It has to trace causes, observe tendencies. Yet in that process how much falsification may there not be ? Can generations

5

who lived up to and through the war continue to accept the smooth and reasonable accounts of how other wars in our history came about—the neat and continuous tracing of national policy, and the precise linking of one stage to another ?

Or, to take other examples, we can hardly think of Pompeii except as a tragic city, of Elizabethan England except as stirred by Shakespeare's plays or excited about Drake's voyages. Yet in fact Pompeii must have been a pleasant and happy little town ; and as for Elizabethan England, when " the red glare on Skiddaw roused the burghers of Carlisle," probably it roused most of them to wonder what all the fuss was about.

To say this is not to decry the writing of history in the large sense. On the contrary, if any general reflection emerges from the pages of such a volume as this, it is that the kind of attack upon formal history which bases itself upon an exaggeration of the principle of John Richard Green's *History of the English People*—the view, namely, that the real history of a nation is not its diplomacy and its wars and its high politics, but the daily life of the people — is unsound. What becomes clear, surely, from an attempt to follow day by day and year by year the normal, casual life of the ordinary man is that, while it is perfectly true that his life as he lives it seems to make up a record which is almost startlingly different from the record of formal history, the fact remains that it is high politics, and not the ordinary man's life, which make his destiny. A review of English life in the forty years from 1880 to 1922 is neither misleading nor frivolous if it finds the vogue of a music-hall song sometimes more significant of national temper than an Imperial Conference, or gives as much space, on occasion, to a sensational crime as to international relations. Yet the songs and the crimes were taking place in a world changing steadily, not because of them, but because Free Trade and Protection had come to grips again, because the great Dominions were changing their status, because the Great War was looming, because the Irish Free State was in the throes of birth. And therefore formal history also will not be misleading if, when the time comes for it to be written, it makes these and the like subjects the thread of its record.

In that case, it may be asked, is the ordinary man's casual life worth depicting at all ? To put that question would be to take a line as one-sided and unsound as the other extreme view that diplomacy and wars are not national history. Anyone who goes back over the events of his own time must be aware of how much a mood of frivolity or seriousness in a nation has at times affected political decisions ; still more aware of how general changes of mental habit, loosening of prejudices, modifications of the moral fibre of a people, affect in one way or another the events that shape its history. And these are aspects of national life which only a narrative of the ordinary man's existence can fairly represent. There is, it may be pleaded, real value in such an attempt. Some of the critical stages of our past history might be much more comprehensible if we had, for those periods, more knowledge of the ordinary man of the time. How was it, for instance, that the accession to power of Henry VII. so soon and so markedly stabilised both the throne and the nation ? What was it, exactly, that made England of the Restoration so suddenly an almost " modern " kind of England, in comparison with the England of Charles I. and the Protectorate ? Most people who read history, and all who teach it, must have been struck by these and other changes ; they seem to be at once so profound and so swift. But the history of high politics alone cannot explain them. Indeed, the case is rather the other way round ; we feel that the casual ordinary details which we know so imperfectly would, if we could get at them, do much to explain the politics.

Or to take an even later period, and a rather different point of view. The period of the Industrial Revolution, the Combination Laws, the Six Acts and so on, was for many years treated in terms of unrelieved gloom and shame. Only of quite recent years have patient and sensible researchers begun to remind us that sweated cotton-spinners, handloom weavers slowly starving to death, and child-slaves in the mines and mills, were, after all, but a part of the industrial population, and that, in all this inky time, a hundred other trades were flourishing, and their workers contented and prosperous. This is a case in which the need of formal history to move by the light of large changes had gravely distorted the truth. Beside the immense reconstruction of industrial organisation, history should have been able to place, for the truth of its colour and its comment, some current account of the ordinary life of the time. At least it may be hoped that those who read this volume, and recover from it something of the way in which they and their world have lived up to and through great changes, may bring a different mind to the history not only of war and diplomacy, but also of economic and social "revolutions." We are too apt to forget that a Frenchman of 1789 or 1790 knew no more of the Terror than we knew in 1912 and 1913 of the Great War ; and that, to the people of a hundred years ago, the Industrial Revolution was no more clear or one-sided in its aspects than is the problem of unemployment to us to-day.

A word may perhaps be said as to the dates with which this volume opens and closes. The year 1880, to some extent, of course, as arbitrary a choice as any such beginning date must be, does nevertheless serve not amiss. For it marks in several ways the transition to modern highly democratic politics ; and it is near enough to the first appearance of many things—electric light and chemical explosives, steel ships, agricultural depression, aggressive Trade Unionism, and so on—which have made the English world of to-day. As to the closing date, 1922, the end of the Coalition may be held to mark nearly enough the transition in England from a world which was still, up to that time, mainly the world of the war-time, to the very different " post-war " state of mind. It has been suggested by one critic that 1926 would have provided a more reasonable close, on the ground that the failure of the General Strike in that year will be seen finally as the end of the whole period of industrial relations, of a complete phase of Trade Union principles and conceptions, and so of a very important chapter of the social life of our time, and this, moreover, the very chapter which can be discerned as opening at the beginning of the book. But it would have been impossible to treat of the General Strike except in the light of the English world in which it took place ; and that world was already not the war world, but the post-war world.

R. H. GRETTON.

CONTENTS

BOOK I: 1880–1898

CHAPTER I

THE BEGINNING OF THE EIGHTIES

THE year 1880 opened in the midst of a fog unparalleled in our annals, which almost without intermission brooded over London from November 1879 to the following February. This gloom—bad for the health, depressing to the spirits, obscuring the outlook— might well have been an emanation of the feelings of Englishmen; for in nearly every department of the national life at that moment were lowered health, depression and uncertainty. Trade, which for several years past had been struggling with falling prices, had reached a point approaching stagnation. A soaking and inclement summer in 1879 had ruined the crops; in every cornfield the shocks had stood blackened and sprouting, till the farm-hands could scarcely tear the sheaves apart. The complete failure of the harvest, coming after years of steady decline in the price of corn, brought to a head the discontent of agriculturists. It immediately made itself felt in London, where the season of 1880 was marked by a shrunken list of entertainments; one ball a night, instead of two or three, showed that rent-rolls had been affected. Agricultural depression, as a social grievance, may be said to date from this bad summer. In Ireland such a summer had brought its inevitable result; famine had taken cruel hold before the Duchess of Marlborough's relief fund was instituted. Hyde Park saw already those gatherings of the unemployed which in the next years were to force upon public attention a problem to which no year brought the solution. In South Wales the ironworks were battling

with a market in which, between 1873 and 1879, the price
of sheet-iron had fallen from £18 to £9 a ton. In Sheffield
a survey of the condition of fifty-one limited liability
companies showed that only sixteen of them had
their shares above par; fifteen had either compounded
with their creditors or been wound up; and the total
depreciation of their share capital was put at three and
a half millions.[1]   The Potteries were witnessing disputes
about wages; in Lancashire there were despondent
attempts to set on foot great emigration schemes, or to
devise " short time " agreements for working three weeks
of the month.

Affairs of State presented no more cheering aspect.
The two political parties were wrangling over embroilments
abroad that, while heavily burdening the national finances
and demanding attention which should have been occupied
at home, were beginning to appear to the bulk of the nation
as gratuitous and perverse. In Afghanistan our arms
were engaged in a war that looked like involving us in all
the cost and blood of a permanent occupation.   In South
Africa we were confronting the resentment roused by that
first annexation of the Transvaal which was to prove so
inadequately considered.   In South-Eastern Europe we
were entangled in a diplomatic situation which might at
any time issue in war.   Meanwhile the national finances
showed a deficit of six millions; Lord Beaconsfield's
Government had increased warlike expenditure from
twenty-five millions to thirty-two and a quarter millions
a year; the Revenue accounts betrayed gravely decreased
spending power in the nation; customs receipts had
fallen by a million, excise by nearly two millions, and
income tax by a quarter of a million.

Socially, too, though the world of the great did not
lack brilliant figures, the season of 1880 was overcast by
the prevailing dullness, and was one which put to its record

[1] *The Times*, 23rd December 1880.

no great event, "none of the accustomed star progresses
of Shahs, Sultans and Emperors," [1] no great work of art,
and no great novel; for Beaconsfield's *Endymion*, though
its publication was an exciting event, did not, in a
literary sense, redeem the year's reputation.   Society
was still adorned by Lord Houghton, and occasionally by Lord Beaconsfield and Bernal Osborne; Sir
William Harcourt and Sir George Trevelyan were at the
height of their dinner-party fame, Mr Gladstone was
"talking shop like a tenth Muse," and Lord Salisbury
was sharpening conversation with his cynicism.   This
world was moreover in the very process of being widened,
alike in its interests and its outlook, by that falling of
barriers which, admitting first of all poetry in the persons
of Tennyson and Browning, painting in the persons of
Leighton and Millais, and less defined artistic gifts in the
fascinating and erratic Laurence Oliphant, was on the
verge of something like surrender to the coruscations of
Whistler and Oscar Wilde.   The process was not yet
complete, though it had advanced speedily, as anyone
may see who compares Thackeray's *Book of Snobs*
with *Punch* for 1880.   The direct advance of the middle-
class tide did not appear very great; its real advance was
by creeks and inlets.   Sir Gorgius Midas, returning home
late to find only six footmen awake to open the door to
him, is as easy game for *Punch* as De Mogyns, with
his flunkeys in peach-coloured liveries and pea-green
plush breeches, had been to Thackeray.   Frontal assault
by huge wealth and bad breeding had not advanced far;
but in subordinate ways change was appearing.   A generation had come up in which not only were the sons of
tradesmen sent to great public schools, but the tradesmen
themselves had been there; *Punch* could portray a
duke dining with his tailor, and complaining of the fit of
his trousers, to which the tailor replies that the duke,

[1] *The Times*, 30th July 1880.

ever since he had been the tailor's fag at Eton, had been a whimperer. Then again, the old narrow circle of the well-born was growing bored with itself, and if a woman like *Punch's* Mrs Ponsonby de Tomkyns, a social climber, but a shrewd, decent, capable body, liked to give great parties, and angle desperately for guests, society had no objection to providing the guests. A certain awkward period of transition was past. The old days, in which the great world had moved on an exalted stage— its normal doings, its gambling, its passions canvassed by all the town—had passed away, with its outward signs of rich dress, ornate vehicles and footmen on the board. In those days men of the great world made all kinds of excursions into other worlds—spent nights in the London dancing gardens, hours in furtive cockfighting pits, were patrons of prizefighters, mingled in all the raffish under-life of jockeys, horse-copers, night-houses, and West End bars. They disported freely, because their world was unapproachably theirs; and there were no means of un-locking its doors from outside. Since those days changing ideas, growth of immense middle-class wealth, had practi-cally made an end of the old " high life." It may, in fact, be said to have died with the sixties. There had followed a period in which society had still tried to oppose on-coming forces ; but it had had traitors within its camp. Men like Lord St Aldegonde in *Lothair* had begun applying ancient self-confidence in new ways. No one could ever really rival them ; so why should they, for the sake of separating themselves in appearances, be missing new openings for pleasure ? A fresh element had been introduced into national life by the development in the middle classes on the one hand of a new athleticism and on the other of an exquisiteness of their own. Society, looking over its barriers, saw that with its old-fashioned " lions of a season," its beards and moustaches of the Crimea, its exclusive traditions of sport, it was really engaged in things that were *vieux jeu*. By now, rowing had travelled far outside the universities, and the veriest Cockney could laugh at Ouida's dandy flinging away his cigar, leaping into an eight, and stroking it to victory. Lawn tennis, which has done more for the mental enfranchisement of the middle class than has been recognised, was at the height of its first popularity in 1880 ; and *Punch's* title-page for the year shows the Four Seasons carrying racquets, with Toby tightening up a net. Cycling was making headway, football clubs were increasing rapidly. The very sneers which aristocracy aimed at these forms of athleticism show how completely the ordinary people were developing a world of their own ; and were able to forget recent days in which any proclivities towards sport involved for them either pretentiousness, or the parasitic life of a " Mr Sponge." As for the new exquisiteness, society had waked to the spectacle of clean-shaven young men, and women in gowns with no waists but much embroidery, cultivating " intenseness " and " living beautifully." These were the new amusements open to society. The set called " the Souls " came into being, brilliant figures like Mr Arthur Balfour and Lady Granby moving in languid grace, and acquiring " the Grecian Bend," neighboured by the Cimabue Browns, Postlethwaite, and Maudle of *Punch*. At this time *Patience* was presented to a delighted world ; and Gorgius Midas Junior complained that his millions brought him less deference in great houses than was shown to "some artist feller." Even a short list of those present at an evening party in 1881 includes the names of Mr Whistler and Mr Oscar Wilde with that of the Prince of Wales.[1]

Nevertheless in 1880—perhaps because there was so much to make the year a grave one—the tone of the season seems to have been set, not by the new " intensity," but by the old seriousness of that " evangelising " group

[1] *The Times*, 4th June 1881.

which was still so strong and occupied a position strange to modern eyes—Lord Shaftesbury, Lord Harrowby, Lord and Lady Mount Temple, Lord Kinnaird, the Buxtons and Samuel Morley.[1] Mention of this group is a reminder that, even in the sphere of the Church, the year 1880 was one of gloom and embroilment. The tedious proceedings against ritualistic practices at St Alban's, Holborn, were still, after five years, dragging on ; the Rev. T. P. Dale was haled to prison in November for not complying with the requirements of the Court of Arches in regard to his church in the City ; and in the same month prosecutions were set on foot in respect to St Vedast's, London, Bordesley, and Miles Platting. The strength of the Evangelical party at this date was seen also in the appointment of Dr Ryle in March to the vacant Deanery of Salisbury ; this choice of a notable parish priest and writer of tracts, for an office hitherto associated with scholarly and donnish rather than with pastoral distinction, being regarded as a striking departure from custom. It is a mere coincidence, though an interesting one, that in this year, in May, the Young Men's Christian Association purchased for £25,000 Exeter Hall, the very name of which had already become a synonym for Evangelicalism. Indeed the cursory eye regarding the appearances made by the Church in records of current events finds them hardly less out of humour than those of other national activities. Beyond the ritual question the only matter in which the Church bulked largely in the newspapers was in its resentment of the Burial Act ; in September the papers contained long controversies as to the power of parish clergy to charge increased fees to Nonconformists, to refuse the use of the church bells at Nonconformist funerals, and other such pettinesses.

However, when we have recognised all the depression that existed, all the grounds for anxiety, and all the lack

---

[1] Lady St Helier's *Memories of Fifty Years.*

of inspiration, it has to be said that the time was certainly not one of paralysis. At least two inventions of the foremost importance made in this year their first advances in England, and made them with great rapidity. The year had hardly opened before it was announced that Mr Edison's "carbon electric lamp" had reached the stage of practical serviceableness the world had been awaiting.[1] At the end of February Dr Lyon Playfair had partially lighted his town house by electricity; in April the new light was at work in Aldersgate Street Station, and in December thirty-four lights were installed at Paddington Station. But although this year first established electric lighting in England, and though its development was immediate, some years had to elapse before it became a really practical method of lighting. As yet every installation was an affair of a separate producing plant, with the result that, besides being too expensive for private houses except as a hobby, it was also too tiresome. Thus, when installed in Her Majesty's Theatre in July it annoyed the audience by the persistent "thrumming" of the dynamo. Its other uses in this year were chiefly on the sea. An Orient liner, the *Chimborazo*, was equipped with it in June, the lights used, though described as "incandescent," being not what were later called incandescent lamps, but arc lights of 70 c.p. The more significant development at the moment was the use of the light for naval purposes; the potentialities of its high power were at once perceived, and by the middle of April two warships, the *Minotaur* and the *Agincourt*, had astounded the dwellers at Gibraltar by suddenly turning upon the Rock beams of a light hitherto unknown. The name of "searchlight" had yet to be invented, and the general opinion among the garrison officers was hardly favourable to the new invention; it made, they thought, the ships themselves an excellent mark.

[1] *The Times*, 5th January 1880.

The second invention, which equally found its development somewhat checked, though in a different way, was the telephone. It had already gained so much ground in England that in January 1880 there was talk of action by the Postmaster-General to restrain an enterprise which was likely to cut into the profits of the telegraph service. It was doubtful if he could establish his case that a telephone message was a kind of telegram, and therefore an infringement of monopoly ; but it seemed to be certain that he would make the attempt—certain, indeed, that he could not afford to do otherwise. For at this time the telephone was expected to render telegrams as obsolete as the electric light would make gas ; there was not any idea of the extent to which the two earlier inventions would continue to exist alongside the two new ones. The Postmaster-General's action was entered, and came on late in November, the Attorney-General, on his behalf, suing the Edison Telephone Company. At the same time the Post Office Authorities could not fail to perceive that it was impossible to deprive the public of the new facilities ; if the telephone were a kind of telegraph then the public would have a right to demand a telephone service from the telegraph authorities. Consequently in December the Post Office was ordering 200,000 Gower-Bell telephones. Meanwhile a good deal of interest was being taken in the first working uses of the invention ; in April, for instance, lines were run from several chambers in the Temple to the Law Courts (then still at Westminster) and the Houses of Parliament, the wires being carried along the District Railway. In some other large towns the new idea had been more extensively taken up ; early in July there were cries of alarm about the danger and inconvenience of the network of overhead telephone wires in Liverpool and other places.[1]

The Post Office had real ground for anxiety in face of

---

[1] *The Times*, 9th July 1880.

this invention. The State purchase of the telegraph
system had just succeeded, after ten years, in proving
itself a good bargain. The telegraph revenue for 1879
had been £1,452,489, and the expenditure £1,111,547.
But the demand for postal facilities was ever growing.
A favourite scheme at this time was one of pneumatic
despatch-boxes to be set up in the streets, whereby the
public could shoot its telegrams into the post offices.
Then there was a demand for a parcel post, transmitting
small parcels " at uniform rates payable by adhesive
stamps " ; and another demand was in process of being
met by the Money Order Bill before Parliament this year.
It is interesting to note that this last proposal had no small
opposition to encounter. Several Chambers of Commerce,
including so important a chamber as that of Manchester,
lodged petitions against it on the ground that the issue
of postal notes would damage certain private enterprises,
like the Cheque Bank, which had hitherto supplied a
form of easily negotiable paper money. Another point
of interest—a side-light on new commercial methods
which we shall have to consider later—was that some
advocates of the demand for money orders argued
that they would promote shopping with big firms, and
give people in the country the chance to avail themselves of the lower prices which the large stores then
coming into existence were able, by the size of their
dealings, to offer. In view of the ever-growing requirements of the public the Post Office may well
have been disturbed by anything which threatened its
one source of trading profit. It may be noted here,
though it is not strictly a Post Office matter, that the
" newly opened line of telegraph to South Africa " had
begun working in January 1880. Its first important
message conveyed the news of the arrest of the President
of " the Committee of Boers in the Transvaal " which had
been concentrating the local resentment of annexation—

a message ominous of the kind of work which was to fall on that cable in later years.

An invention of a different kind, which in the end affected the spending powers and prosperity of the poorer classes in England to a degree not foreseen at the time, also reached in 1880 the point of practical working. It was announced on 3rd February that the steamship *Strathleven* had arrived in London from Australia with 70 bullock carcasses, 500 sheep carcasses, and two tons of butter. She had left Sydney and Melbourne in December and had arrived with the supplies in " perfectly sound condition." Now the importation of meat preserved by low temperatures was not a new thing. For some time carcasses had been brought from America, but the chambers in which they had been conveyed were kept cool with blocks of ice. The system of chambers refrigerated by machines practically dates from 1880.[1] However, in spite of new methods of storage, the trade would not have developed so rapidly as it did but for a curious and almost accidental circumstance. By enabling meat to be brought from Australia and New Zealand (distances over which ice-cooled chambers could not have been made to pay) refrigeration tapped an astoundingly cheap market. Till this time the great sheep-runs of those colonies had been worked on the wool-profits entirely ; the carcasses were regarded as practically worthless. Consequently when sheep carcasses first became, thanks to the new refrigeration, of marketable value, there was no difficulty in obtaining them cheaply enough to allow the importers to face a long period of prejudice and experiment. For some time the meat was criticised, and even abused ; the first shipment showed an adverse balance to the importers of £19 on the cargo, the beef having been sold at an average of 5¼d. a lb., and the mutton at an average of 5d. Never-

---

[1] *Encyclopædia Britannica*, article on Refrigerating, by T. B. Lightfoot.

theless in November an " Australian Fresh Meat Company " was floated, with a capital of £300,000 ; and the keenness of the sheep-owner in the Antipodes for a source of profit hitherto undreamt of was at work to break down the prejudices of Smithfield Market, and to give the English workman more butcher's meat in a month than his fathers had in a year.

Nor was it the workman only whose resources were enlarged. The daily menu of comparatively well-to-do families had been extremely limited. The occasion of a trade exhibition in Germany, at which a display of American " canned goods " was made, served *The Times* for a homily on the lack of variety in English catering. It wrote [1] : " No nation in the world has so narrow a code of clean articles of food as ours." Householders of moderate means rarely afforded fish, mutton was " suspected and avoided," poultry " lacked flavour and strength," and pork was " less acceptable above stairs than below." Vegetables, moreover, must have been a luxury in small houses. An indictment of the greengrocer's profits reveals the fact that the retail price of a cucumber in September 1880 was 10d., of a pound of runner beans, 6d., and of a cauliflower, 8d. Even so, the housekeepers had not complained ; the indictment came from the grower, who felt himself to be getting an inadequate share of the profit.[2] Dairy produce was hardly procurable at a more reasonable cost, fresh butter being normally at 1s. 7d. a pound. It is probable, however, that many town families felt this pinch less, since the Margarine Act was not yet in existence, and much must have passed for butter which was not butter at all. It was, for instance, noted as curious that, though oleomargarine never had a price quoted in the market reports, and was not displayed in shop-windows, a lawsuit about patent royalties elicited the fact that the sale of this

[1] *The Times*, 22nd April 1880.   [2] Ditto, 18th September 1880.

compound amounted to 98,000,000 lbs.[1] But whatever may have been the facts about other foods the question of the meat supply was the only one formulated. The general supply had been restricted by severe Government prohibition imposed on the importation of live animals owing to fears of cattle disease [2]; and drastic regulations as to the movement of live cattle from the Metropolitan Meat Market had caused real shortage of food in seaside places and country towns.[3] It was high time that a new traffic in dead meat should be established ; and it is not difficult to see that the security for a new venture lay in the middle-class demand. There is no mistaking the calibre of the letters on the subject to the newspapers. Certain persons complained of the toughness of the meat, its bad colour ; others wrote of the precise way to treat it, especially the necessity for long and slow thawing ; and in their phrases describing the excellences of the meat when so treated, how it " cut firm and tender under the knife," " the quality of the gravy in the well," there is all the ponderous interest in eating, all the detailed affection for a joint, that Dickens portrayed in his middle-class fathers.

" Sweetness and light " had, as we have seen, affected the upper strata of the middle class with unhealthy violence in the shape of the æsthetic movement. It had led also to advances in education, which were in some respects slightly fevered, and ladies of very distinguished learning—Dr Sophia Jex-Blake, Dr Garrett Anderson, Miss Lucy Harrison, for instance—were becoming perturbed by what they considered to be over-pressure in girls' schools.[4] There was sanity enough, however, in the way educational advances were affecting the business man's idea of his business ; and Matthew Arnold might have

[1] *The Times*, 28th April 1880.
[2] Ditto, 20th July 1880.
[3] Ditto, 23rd May 1881.
[4] See, e.g., *The Times*, 15th April 1880.

begun to feel he had not preached to deaf ears when Professor Huxley, speaking at the opening of Mason College, Birmingham, on 1st October, in this year, celebrated the passing of the day when the men and the methods of science were pooh-poohed by the men of business. On 13th July the court of the new Victoria University held its first meeting, the characteristics of the University being, first, that for the attainment of its degrees it required attendance at prescribed courses of lectures, thus differing from the University of London ; and secondly, that it was designed to federate a number of colleges—Manchester, Liverpool, Leeds and Sheffield. Akin to the spirit of these matters was the announcement, on 30th July, of the first instance of an offer which was to become in time a familiar, almost a national, institution. Mr Andrew Carnegie had written from New York to the Provost of Dunfermline, offering to present the town with a free library. It is not difficult, again, to trace the growing concern for reality in education in the deputation which waited upon the Board of Education in July from the Manchester Kindergarten Society, and other such societies, urging the adoption of kindergarten methods in elementary schools. The Board, however, had too much other business on hand. It had not yet succeeded in perfecting its machinery. School Boards had had ten years of existence, but though they had done much they were still far from the ideal of provision for every child. In London the total child population of school age was reckoned in 1880 at 740,377. The voluntary schools had accommodation for 269,469, the Board Schools for 225,236, a total of 494,705. But the average attendance was as yet only 373,701—just about half the juvenile population.

The expansion of provincial university education is a subject which will confront us again later. It was one aspect of that growing civic activity which, though it might be despised by the fastidious and the æsthetic as a mere exaltation of the material and the parochial, was a very genuine piece of middle-class self-assertion. Such cities as Glasgow, Manchester, Liverpool, and especially Birmingham, had for some time before this history opens been developing their resources and enlarging the scope of the services they offered their citizens. Gas companies, water companies, tramway companies had been made aware that no monopoly would be allowed to remain in private hands; the principle of ultimate right of purchase by the Corporation was well established. Yet, great as previous developments had been, the year 1880 serves none the less well in this matter too as a fresh starting point. It witnessed the first successful flotation of Consolidated Municipal Stock; and this was a very important departure, for hitherto the capital expenditure of corporations had had to be met by loans from the Public Works Loan Commissioners, from banks, insurance companies and private lenders. These arrangements involved varying rates of interest, from 5 per cent. to $3\frac{3}{4}$ per cent., the keeping of separate sinking funds, and separate approaches to Parliament or the Local Government Board for powers for new works. In the early seventies some corporations had adopted the idea of a Suspense Account, into which money borrowed at low rates was paid to be used for the liquidation of loans. Then arose the idea of a Corporation Debenture Stock, the Birmingham Finance Committee drawing up a scheme for such an issue in 1876,[1] and although the Local Government Board considered itself unable to sanction the proposal, an attempt was made in the following year to raise a million and a half of debenture stock. Prospectuses were published, but only £300,000 were subscribed, and the attempt failed. The first success in the venture was achieved by the Liverpool Corporation, which issued on

[1] For this subject I have drawn largely on Mr J. T. Bunce's *History of the Corporation of Birmingham.*

1st September 1880 two millions of stock, under the Liverpool Loans Act. Sir W. B. Forwood, who had been chiefly responsible for the Act, told the Corporation that " it had been a difficult and intricate matter to get the Bill through, because the Liverpool Corporation were the first in the kingdom to obtain powers to fund their debt in the way proposed." [1] But Birmingham was close on Liverpool's heels with its second attempt. Instead of proceeding by a Loans Act, with all the cost of a private Bill, the Corporation applied to the Local Government Board for a provisional order to amend and partially repeal some local Acts and Orders, so as to enable the Corporation to issue a consolidated stock in which trustees who were empowered to invest in Government securities might invest. This method of procedure nearly wrecked the enterprise, for although the Board, after public inquiry, made the Order, the Bill confirming it was opposed by Lord Redesdale on the ground that the Board was exceeding its powers. However he finally withdrew his opposition on condition that the question of the Board's powers was raised in Parliament. The Bill passed. It had cost the Corporation only £70, and it would save thousands. The calculation in the case of Liverpool was that £25,000 or £30,000 a year would be saved by the raising of a large sum at a single, comparatively low, rate of interest. What was more important from the public point of view was, first, that municipalities had discovered a new form of financial power in the exercise of which the Local Government debt of the United Kingdom rose to six hundred millions in 1910 ; and, secondly, that they had found a way of attracting the general investor, and had no longer to borrow, in the old sense of the word.

The provision of a new field for investments could not have come at a better time than this. The possibilities

[1] *The Times*, 2nd September 1880.

of the new field were not, however, fully perceived at the moment, and its opening did nothing to cure the special source of depression in this depressing year—the state of the money market. The year, as it progressed, brought a revival of trade; the signs were hopeful as early as February, and another summer of rain and flood could not disguise the fact that business was recovering. Yet revival brought with it a new uneasiness. The money market was not comfortable. Not only were Consols very high, but all good stocks were high with them. There had been for long, *The Times* remarked,[1] no war to cause new issues, no great economic changes, such as the invention of railways, or extensive measures of colonisation. The general result was an accumulation of privately held capital which might, on a recovery of trade, be a temptation to the reckless floating of new enterprises, and consequent financial disturbance. Fears were expressed later on in the year that some of the new impulsion of business was really—in the iron trade, for instance—only speculative. Other conditions, besides prices and production, were affecting the market. It was never decided beyond question, even in all the discussions of the great period of bimetallism, precisely how the shortage of gold, which became so serious between 1880 and 1890, affected trade and industry. That it had some direct effect may be taken for granted, since otherwise the bimetallic theory would never have gained ground. One indirect effect is certain. The " tightness," so to speak, of the coinage, while producing a nominal lowering of prices, tended to keep wages from rising; and was thus responsible for some of the force which at this time the agitations of working people assumed. Masters of industry in every part of the country were nervous about the strikes that might be expected to accompany a revival of trade.

Not that the working class agitations were entirely a

[1] 29th July 1880.

matter of wages. In one of the great industries, then as now the most highly organised on the side of the employees —the cotton industry—observers already thought they saw signs of a spirit which we shall find at its full activity later. As yet the idea was only expressed in a vague and obviously prejudiced form, *The Times* venturing the opinion, when labour troubles in Lancashire became serious in the autumn, that the real cause at the back of the agitation was not a matter of wages but " a struggle for mastery." [1] The opinion, though crudely expressed, was shrewd. The trade unions had attained to such numbers that they felt the day within sight when they should command practically all the working hands of the country. At the Trade Union Congress in September of this year the delegates represented an aggregate of 600,000 members, the strongest unions being the miners, with 50,000 members ; the engineers, with 45,000 ; the boiler-makers, with 20,000; and the railway workers, with 15,000. They were already strengthening themselves by alliance with the Co-operative Societies, a meeting between representatives of the two movements taking place later in September. The wages question, arising more acutely from the shortage of gold coinage, was undoubtedly an immediate cause of strikes (the cotton trade dispute ended in December with the masters " risking " an advance in wages), but there was a predisposing cause of a more far-reaching nature. We shall have to record, under 1881, the foundation of the Social Democratic Federation in London. Whether or no it be true that the British working man had been affected by contact with the refugees fleeing to England from the repressive measures taken in France after the Commune, and by Bismarck a few years later in Germany, it seems at least certain, as William Morris put it,[2] that " there was no longer, among the mass

[1] *The Times*, 18th September 1880.
[2] Mackail's *Life of William Morris*, ii. 81.

of the working class in London, any decided hostility to Socialism." But whatever suspicions may have been growing of a spirit among workmen that was looking for more fundamental advances than in wages, nothing seems to have been less present to the minds of politicians in 1880, as they approached and passed through a General Election, than uneasiness about the conditions of the temper of the working man. Yet it is fair to add that the broadly determining influence in that election was such a revulsion of feeling in the direction of domestic and internal politics that the nation might well have looked forward to having its house drastically set in order.

CHAPTER II

THE GENERAL ELECTION, 1880

YET to speak of the General Election of 1880 as offering a prospect of national spring-cleaning is to give a positive description to what was mainly a negative movement. The distinction is necessary, because in the following five years the prevalence of a habit of confounding different matters under the common title of " Beaconsfieldism " was to lead the reforming party into disaster ; dislike of the positions in which Beaconsfield had left Great Britain in various parts of the world was to become, in more than one case, a refusal to deal with those positions, hardly distinguishable from carelessness.

The tone and pitch of this election were entirely set by Mr Gladstone ; the campaign which was to bring the Liberals triumphantly to power being really begun at the close of 1879. The events of 1878, the Russo-Turkish War, the subsequent inflaming of bellicose spirit in England, and the secret agreements with Russia and Turkey that accompanied the Berlin Conference—had all touched Mr Gladstone in one of his tenderest spots : Turkey and her dependencies in Europe. He had used a phrase very significant of the line his thought was taking —" the people want a little more experience of Beaconsfield Toryism "[1]—before the occurrence of two events which fitted exactly into his case. Affairs in South Africa, already made ticklish enough by the annexation of the Transvaal, were rendered more depressing by a campaign undertaken, as it seemed even to the Government,

[1] Morley's *Life of Gladstone*, ii. 583.

2

somewhat wantonly against the Zulus.   More serious still, the Ameer of Afghanistan having failed to accede to what the Government demanded of him by way of recognition of the weight of British influence in his affairs, war had been undertaken in Afghanistan also.

To these developments, which wore to Mr Gladstone's mind the true Disraelian stamp of cynical disregard of righteousness, add the inevitable corollary of the burden on the national finances, and what more burningly inspiring text could a man of Mr Gladstone's political tradition have found to his hand ?   When the Liberal Committee of Mid-Lothian invited him in 1879 to contest that division, and he accepted the invitation, he was, by a sure political instinct, giving himself at once an inspiring audience and the stimulus of a difficult fight.   He had declined in the previous year to stand again for Greenwich, his seat at that date ; he had remained unpersuaded by the offer of a safe seat in Edinburgh.   The Mid-Lothian suggestion gave him the chance of striking the blow at his own time, and not at what time Lord Beaconsfield might choose to dissolve.   Towards the end of November 1879 he went into Scotland, and the next fortnight witnessed the historic " Mid-Lothian Campaign."   In these days of far more widely spread newspaper reading, and the consequent organisation of reporting from outlying centres, it is necessary to remind ourselves of the violently outstanding methods of this campaign.   Political platform-speaking then was restricted within limits generally recognised and accepted.   Such speeches as were reported were placed under the rather odd heading " Parliament Out of Session," which by itself is enough to suggest that these efforts were regarded as mere aftermath.   There was one other form in which they were recognised.   It was tacitly admitted that the ordinary practice of members of the House in addressing themselves to their constituents once a year or so had in some instances an interest beyond the bounds of the constituency. Reports of the speeches of such men appeared under the heading : " The Member for Oxford," or " Westminster," or " Birmingham," a form of title which made even Mr Chamberlain's Radical pronouncements somewhat muffled. Nothing approaching the present mobility of notable speakers, or the frequent platform appearances of leading figures outside their own constituencies, existed in those days. In a general election such appearances were made, but not often. Mr Gladstone lived to deplore our modern fashion ; but his Mid-Lothian campaign was largely responsible for its origin.[1]

Further, it was not only the unusualness of such a series of speeches which roused the public mind ; it was also the fact that Mr Gladstone was making them. He had retired from the leadership of his party in 1874 ; he had even intimated that he did not intend to face another general election ; and here he was taking the field in a way so marked and so far out of the ordinary political course that the public could only draw one conclusion. Mr Gladstone himself never displayed his intellectual peculiarities more strikingly than in the absence of any such conclusion from his own mind ; for some months to come he spoke of the question of the leadership as out of his own hands, in a manner that must have been exasperating to less subtle-minded colleagues. The British public entertained no doubts. The crowds at the principal stations at which his train stopped on the way to Edinburgh, the enthusiasm in Scotland, and the reception of what Beaconsfield called " this drenching rhetoric," all meant one thing—the ushering back of Mr Gladstone to leadership.

Mr Gladstone's tone, then—his choice of subjects during the Mid-Lothian campaign—set the tone of the election. It was, in spite of its trumpet-call appearance, essentially

[1] See *Saturday Review*, 29th November 1879.

negative.[1] The Government's foreign policy, the Government's bad finance and growing deficit, might, indeed, in Mid-Lothian speeches, be the text of the plea for righteousness among nations and a restoration of national resources ; but practically the appeal was only for that result which Mr Gladstone himself described after the triumph as " the downfall of Beaconsfieldism." [2] He might tell one of his audiences that " he had come down expressly to raise effectually before the people of the country the question in which manner they wished to be governed " [3] ; but in fact the General Election amounted to no more than asking whether they wished to be governed in the Beaconsfield way, or not. Sir William Harcourt, addressing a great meeting in January, devoted himself entirely to denouncing the Government for "recklessly pursuing an Asiatic policy " ; and a week later, in Birmingham, the heart then of Radicalism, devoted his speech to the evils of jingoism (still a new word) and the Afghan War.

This was, obviously, the soundest fighting policy. And as no campaign can be purely negative, in the background of this one were certain promises of domestic legislation. Chief among them was a proposed equalisation of the county franchise with the borough franchise—the charter of the agricultural labourer. There were also schemes for the establishment of representative County Government, amendment of the laws of land transfer and settlement, and a system of municipal government for London. It is plain from this list that the favourite phrase of economic writers of this time, " the era of administration has come," was influencing the politicians. Still it was the negative rather than any positive line of attack which kept—perhaps alone could keep—the Liberal leaders

[1] *The Times*, 1st April, had a leader expressing concern lest the election should be taken by Continental nations as expressing complete repudiation of concern in European interests
[2] Morley's *Life of Gladstone*, ii: 615.
[3] Ditto, ii. 588.

together.   Lord Hartington, the leader of the party in
the Commons, was very cool on the extension of the
franchise ; Lord Granville, the chief, as an ex-Foreign
Minister, was little interested in domestic affairs ; Harcourt was already Mr Gladstone's staunch lieutenant, and
had his faithful eye mainly on Turkey.   The franchise
question, in any case, was one with which the Tories had
coquetted ; and though it may have carried some votes
it can hardly have counted heavily.   Beaconsfield, with
his extraordinary prophetic gift, raised in his manifesto to
the country in March 1880 the question of the government
of Ireland, and sought to fasten upon the Liberals five years
before its time the odium of a separatist policy.   Ireland,
however, was not as yet a real problem to English electors.
Battle was joined on the ground Mr Gladstone had taken.

Some surprise was felt at its coming when it did.   The
Mid-Lothian campaign had lighted such a flare that men
expected Beaconsfield to wait for some chance of damping
it, even if slightly, before a dissolution of Parliament.
The dissolution was announced on 6th March ; and the
accepted explanation of that early date is that Beaconsfield was misled into a false estimate of the feeling of the
country by the results of two bye-elections, in February,
at Liverpool and in Southwark.   In both the Liberal
candidate had been beaten, and Southwark moreover was
a seat gained to the Tories.   It seems possible, however,
in view of the fact that Beaconsfield's manifesto attempted
to divert the minds of the electors to the Irish question,
that what influenced him was not so much the mere
return of Tories for these seats as the fact that in Liverpool
the Home Rule cry had been employed in the fight.   The
Irish had made the Liberal candidate commit himself to
a promise to vote for " an inquiry into the nature and
extent of the Irish demand for self-government." [1]   A
storm had been raised at the bare possibility of treating

[1] *The Times*, 5th February 1880.

Home Rule as a valid question. Lord Hartington, moreover, had taken the line that it was a matter for the individual decision of members; and this indication of uncertainty in the Liberal ranks may have appealed to Beaconsfield as a useful opening for driving in his wedge. Unfortunately for him this occurrence of the Home Rule demand was an isolated case. The brief month during which Parliament sat, from 6th February to 6th March, had not been long enough to give the Irish members the chance for which, under Parnell, they were ready; and the strategy Beaconsfield attempted proved impracticable. The elections went heavily against him. On the first day's results, on 31st March, the Liberals had a net gain of 15 seats in 69 constituencies; by the end of the second week of the election their net gains stood at 99; and finally the new Parliament showed itself composed of 347 Liberals, 240 Conservatives and 65 Irish Nationalists.

Mr Gladstone's own election was, as his speech-making had been, the centre of importance. The interest taken in it gives us a sidelight on what must have been the last of old electoral methods—a survival due to the absence of reform from the county franchise. One of the first points that occurred to him in taking up the candidature for Mid-Lothian was the matter of " faggot " votes. The qualification in those days for the county franchise was the possession of a 40s. freehold, or a £10 copyhold, or a £50 leasehold, or an occupation valued at £12. It was not difficult, with sufficient money at command, to manufacture these votes; and Mr Gladstone, franchise reformer though he was, was too old a hand to be a purist; he had fought his first election before the Reform Bill. So now the answer to Conservative faggotting was Liberal faggotting; and *The Times* of 27th January 1880 contains a curious and interesting article on the running-up of houses in Edinburgh, but just over the county border, to give one hundred and sixty new owner and occupier votes on the Liberal side. The work went on night and day, and men stood at dusk in the light of the flares cheering for Gladstone. His majority at the declaration of the poll on 5th April was two hundred and nineteen.

Another feature of the election, though not one that was prominent in the newspapers, was that new ideas in party organisation were on trial on the Liberal side. In this, rather than in his legislative projects, is to be found the basis of the dislike and fear of Mr Chamberlain as a demagogue. A generation more accustomed than our own to exalt a classical education used its words nicely, and " demagogue " to it meant less the producer of measures appealing to the masses than a man who organised the masses. Judged merely by his legislative proposals Mr Chamberlain showed no terrifying face. The Employers Liability Bill, of which he was in charge as President of the Board of Trade, was, after all, very much a corollary of the Factory Acts ; and for the rest Mr Chamberlain's own programme, as announced by him at Birmingham in October of that year, was devoted to such eminently middle-class questions as the reform of railway rates for goods traffic, of the bankruptcy laws, and of the patent laws. But his organising schemes were a different matter. In 1877 he had inaugurated a new means of handling electoral forces. Hitherto the choice of candidates and the management of electoral affairs had been in the hands of local committees, who corresponded, when necessary, with the party whips, but were essentially independent. Mr Chamberlain aimed at making organisation more democratic and more co-ordinated. The local associations were to be much larger, and to be popularly elected ; and, secondly, they were to be federated under a central organisation which would give general orders, provide candidates, have a sanctioning voice in any local

choice of candidates, issue literature, and wield an army
of speakers. This was perhaps the first matter in which
his future Cabinet colleagues felt Mr Chamberlain's
determination and force. He invited Lord Hartington
to become the nominal head of the new system. Lord
Hartington did not much take to it, and declined.[1] Mr
Chamberlain went on his way, with a warning to his
leader that he could not afford not to be associated
with it. By 1880 the idea was so well advanced that
after the election the " new democratic machinery " became a subject for letters to the newspapers from the
more timid Liberals and the more bitterly disappointed
Conservatives.   One of the effects most dreaded was
the enhanced power which such organisation might
give to wealth in an election.   Party funds would,
it was thought, unduly turn the day, when they acted
through a highly drilled system.

Lord Beaconsfield resigned on 21st April. The processes
by which Mr Gladstone returned in actuality to that leadership which, in everyone's opinion but his own, he had
assumed five months earlier, need not be set forth.
They have been given to the world in the words of those
who were concerned in them.[2] It is sufficient to say here
that Lord Granville and Lord Hartington were so im-
movably agreed upon the impossibility of carrying on a
Government without Mr Gladstone, and the equal impossibility of his occupying any but the chief place in a
Government, that Queen Victoria had to give way. Mr
Gladstone's Government[3] met the new Parliament on
20th May 1880.

It was a meeting full of enthusiasm, full of hope—and
almost tragic to look back upon now. So fine a career

[1] Holland's *Life of the Duke of Devonshire*, i. 244-249.
[2] See Morley's *Life of Gladstone*, ii. 620-628; Holland's *Life
of the Duke of Devonshire*, i. 273-293; Fitzmaurice's *Life of Lord
Granville*.

seemed to open before a Government with a majority clear of the Irish vote, pledged to end the policy which distracted politics with foreign adventure, and headed by a man who was a popular idol. Yet at the very threshold the new House met with a difficulty which, wasting its time, exasperating its temper, and dislocating its procedure, was typical of the barren wrangling in which the new forces were to expend themselves like a river trailing amid a waste of sand. Before it came to work, the House was suddenly divided by the question whether one of the new members for Northampton, Mr Charles Bradlaugh, who had, as an avowed atheist, declined to take the oath, could be allowed to take his seat. Mr Bradlaugh then professed himself ready to take the oath; but it was easy to rouse the House against the cynicism of such an attitude. The prolonged controversy which followed—continued debates in the House, discussions in the press, proceedings in the law courts, to which Mr Bradlaugh took the question of his rights—may in one respect be passed rapidly over. In this parliament he never sat. So curiously was the House cut asunder by this unforeseen problem that even when, in 1883, an Affirmation Bill, designed to relieve the difficulty, had the eloquent support of Mr Gladstone, it was thrown out by a majority of three. Removed more than once from the House by physical force, Mr Bradlaugh turned to great meetings in public halls and in the parks of London to try to break down the opposition that had such bewildering obstinacy. It was not until eight years later that he may be said to have won the case of principle, and eleven years later the personal case. In 1885 he was allowed to take the oath without any comment. But this silent passing-over of the tempest naturally did not satisfy him. In 1888 he secured the passing of an Affirmation Act, and in 1891, when he was on his death-bed, the resolution of 1881, by which the House had finally asserted itself in the original controversy, was expunged from the records. But though the facts should be stated as briefly as possible, their significance must not be missed. In the House itself the most striking feature of the controversy was that it revealed the existence of a group on the Tory side which was to attain much notoriety during the life of this Parliament. For the first time members saw the co-operation between Lord Randolph Churchill, Mr Arthur Balfour, Sir John Gorst and Sir Henry Drummond-Wolff which earned them the name of " The Fourth Party." Dissatisfied with the leadership of Sir Stafford Northcote, who seemed to them dull and slow in action, formal in his methods, a slave to the conventions of politics, this group were as ready to scoff at their own Front Bench as to attack the other Front Bench. The formalities of Opposition would not have admitted the seizing of the opportunity offered by the case of Mr Bradlaugh; it exactly suited Lord Randolph's purposes. The existence of the Fourth Party affected the Government seriously throughout its career. The attacks of clever men, who had none of the traditions of holding office, had always to be met after the official answer on any question had been given to the Opposition leaders, and accepted by them in the official spirit which, as ex-Ministers, they were ready to display. Moreover, as was very soon noticed, Lord Randolph Churchill had a peculiar gift for "drawing" Mr Gladstone. The position which the Fourth Party attained was due not only to the scandalous notoriety attaching to a revolt against constituted leaders, but to the fact that Mr Gladstone's colleagues could never induce him to treat the group as irresponsible interlopers. However, the taste of their quality was a comparatively minor aspect of the Bradlaugh controversy. That had also a deeper significance.

It is true that the persistence of the House was largely due to the mere tactical value to the Opposition of a question in which the Government could not command its majority. Sir Stafford Northcote refused in 1881 overtures made to him by the Speaker with a view to reaching the solution of silence that was accepted in 1885. But it is beyond doubt that at the time that solution would only have left open the door of bitterness. We have to face the spectacle of a House, not without the approval of a very great part of the country, quite assuming its right to demand some form of religious conviction in a member ; the spectacle, moreover, of intelligent men convinced that to be an atheist was to be morally untrustworthy, that to deny the existence of God was worse than " that form of opinion which would teach us that, whatever may be beyond the visible things of this world, whatever may be beyond this short span of life, you know and you can know nothing of it, and that it is a bootless undertaking to attempt to establish relations with it."[1] Perhaps after all the Bradlaugh controversy did no less in the end for genuine religious conviction than for the freedom of those who have no such conviction. It was one of the occasional shocks which force the pace of the whole-hearted in either direction.

But at the moment the effect of the controversy was one of barrenness and discouragement. The Radicals in the country perceived their great majority already " jockeyed." The position of Mr Bradlaugh himself can now be disentangled from the discussions, and estimated at its worth. The deep bewilderment of the moment arose from the almost diabolical cleverness with which the question was twisted in the House to a problem of religious liberty. *The Times* saw what had happened ; " Mr Bradlaugh, admitted to the House, will be of just whatever account the House pleases. But Mr Bradlaugh and

[1] Mr Gladstone on the Affirmation Bill, 26th April 1883.

religious liberty together are not thus easily to be dealt with." [1] This was the first baiting of a Government which was to pass so much of its time with its head down to attacks in the House that it could rarely get a real outlook. In no matter was this lack of outlook more disastrous than in the question of the Transvaal. In alarm at the danger involved by the Boers' apparent inability to cope with native attacks in 1877—the danger that native successes against them might light an appalling conflagration—Sir Theophilus Shepstone had formally placed the Transvaal under British sovereignty. He had exceeded his instructions, which gave him no authority to proclaim annexation except on assurances that the step was in consonance with the wishes of the majority of the Boers. It was immediately made apparent that practically the whole Boer community was against it; yet the Conservative Government held to the annexation. Mr Gladstone expatiated on the wickedness of this in his Mid-Lothian denunciations; even Lord Hartington asserted that annexation in those circumstances could not be maintained; and public opinion must have been in some degree represented by *The Times* which wrote [2]: "We have to consider the welfare of the whole of the South African colonies, as well as the interests of the inhabitants of the Transvaal, and neither of these can be weighed in the balance against a mere reluctance to abandon a policy which was justified at one time by circumstances which have now passed away. . . . Englishmen will find it difficult to reconcile themselves to the forcible occupation of a country whose people declare that they have never been and do not wish to be her Majesty's subjects." The question was forced upon the Liberal Government's attention publicly in May by a memorial demanding the recall of Sir Bartle Frere, who

---

[1] Leading article, 29th June 1880.
[2] Ditto, 17th January 1880.

was identified with the policy of annexation. The sum
of the Government's action in the matter during this year
is that two months later Sir Bartle Frere was recalled ;
but the annexation was not cancelled. What does this
contradictory conclusion mean ? By itself it is astonishing ; but taken in connection with those affairs in Egypt
which will confront us later it appears susceptible of
explanation. It may be thrown out here as a suggestion,
to be supported hereafter, that this Cabinet more than
once undertook the more difficult, in preference to the
point-blank, solution of a problem; and then had not time
or sufficient freedom from immediate worries to carry out
adequately the task it had set itself. The Cabinet certainly undertook a complicated solution of the Transvaal
difficulty, the reasons for which may perhaps be sought
in the Prime Minister's character. Mr Gladstone in
Mid-Lothian might thunder flat opposition to certain acts
of state, to certain lines of policy ; Mr Gladstone in
office felt the habit of office close round him, a habit in
which there are no violent and fundamental reversals.
It may also have been, as matters turned out, somewhat
unfortunate that the Turkish difficulty—to the almost
laughable surprise and glee of Mr Gladstone—collapsed
instantly on a tentative application of precisely the kind
of pressure that Beaconsfield might have used ; Mr Gladstone was capable of being attracted by the prospect of
showing his great rival that mere reversals of policy were
not the only way of governing better than he. At all
events, it is certain that the reversal of the annexation
was set aside in favour of a complicated series of moves
whereby, federation having been first established in South
Africa, local independence should follow ; and the Boers
be thus ultimately satisfied.[1] The federation schemes
failed ; Frere, whose retention in South Africa was for
some weeks justified largely on the ground of his associa-

[1] Morley's *Life of Gladstone*, iii, 30.

tion with the federation plans, was recalled. The complicated moves crumbled at the first stage. To judge by the later analogy of Egypt, it would appear safe to assert that Mr Gladstone's interest was diverted, and the matter was all disastrously left drifting.

What was the diversion of interest? For one thing, Mr Gladstone was extraordinarily—one might say, for a Prime Minister, almost deplorably—interested in the daily proceedings of the House.[1] It was not a great session, but it bore some fruit : the first Employers Liability Act, establishing a system of compensation to workmen for injuries inflicted by defects in works, or machinery plant, or stock connected with the business, or by default of fellow-servants having superintendence or direction ; the change of the Malt Tax into a Beer Duty, effected in the Budget ; the Burial Bill, establishing the right of Nonconformists to inter their dead with the services of their own sect in parish churchyards. Another measure, introduced in this year, both gave the Prime Minister trouble in the Cabinet and, being ultimately rejected by the Lords, brought on, after the session had closed, the first acute stage of that Irish struggle which in the next few years was so to drain the energies of both the Government and the House of Commons. This was the Compensation for Disturbance Bill. Mr Gladstone had passed an Act in 1870 to meet the case of hardships suffered by tenants in Ireland who, on being turned out of their holdings, received no allowance for improvements they had made. But the Act had never worked well ; there was no provision in it for valuing the improvements, and no provision that the rent should be a fair one, and it did not apply in cases in which the tenant owed as much as a year's rent. The case for an improved Act was strengthened by the bad harvests of 1878 and, especially, 1879,[2]

[1] Morley's *Life of Gladstone*, iii. 7, 8.
[2] *Cf. supra*, p. 15.

and the new Bill entitled the tenant to compensation if
he could prove to the court (1) that he was unable to pay
the rent ; (2) that this was not from pure thriftlessness
or idleness, but from the bad harvest of the current year,
or of two preceding years ; (3) that he was willing to
continue his tenancy on just and reasonable terms as to
rent and otherwise ; (4) that these terms were unreasonably refused by the landlord.

There were not a few in the House of Commons
who during the passage of this Bill perceived a warning in the person of a certain silent man. The new
Parliament saw at the head of the Irish party a new
leader, Charles Stewart Parnell. The House had some
knowledge of his fighting power, and some reason to
be disturbed by his accession to leadership. In the
previous Parliament a profound change had come over
the behaviour of the Irish party. Under Isaac Butt's
leadership the Irish had for years pursued the patient
course of introducing measures on Ireland's behalf and
seeing them set by. They produced Bills for some form
of Home Rule year after year, and were told : " Parliament will not, cannot grant Home Rule. The utmost
favour which the House of Commons can show to its
advocates is to listen to them with patience and courtesy
once a year." [1] When the prevailing mind of important
people in England could be stated in that form, something
was bound to happen. Biggar and Parnell happened.
When the latter entered the House in 1875 the former had
already discovered the principle of obstruction ; the new
recruit, practically ignorant of politics [2] but full of hatred
of England's attitude towards Ireland, swiftly seized the
rudiments of the new methods, and there followed those
famous all-night sittings in which four or five Irish
members held up the whole business of the House by

[1] *The Times*, 20th April 1877.
[2] Barry O'Brien's *Life of Parnell*.

incessantly moving that progress be reported, or that the
chairman leave the chair.   But when the new Parliament
met, there was in the minds of those who had eyes to see
much more than the fear of mere repetition of these scenes,
which in the old Parliament the leader of the party had
disliked and disavowed. The fact that Butt had now ceased
to be the leader was more than a menace to Parliamentary
order.   Hitherto Irish agitation had had two wholly
separate currents.   The Parliamentary agitation was a
steady-going plea for self-government on a federal basis.
The absolute separatist agitation, working through the
Fenian methods, was carried on by the Clan-na-Gael
in America and the Irish Republican Brotherhood in
Ireland, Michael Davitt being the chief link between the
two.[1]   The leaders of this agitation wholly despised and
repudiated the Parliamentary party.   Now between the
appearance of obstructive tactics in the House and the
meeting of the new Parliament these two currents had
ceased to be disconnected.   That it is necessary to use
so indefinite an expression is a tribute to the extreme
strategic skill of which Parnell was master.   All the
enmity he aroused in England, all the watchfulness to
catch him tripping, never succeeded in proving that he
was a Fenian, or that Irish Nationalism and Fenianism
were now one ; and yet it was patent that they were no
longer two.   In December 1877 Michael Davitt had been
released from prison on ticket-of-leave from the end of the
sentence passed upon him for complicity in the Fenian
outrages of 1867.   Parnell met him in Dublin in January
1878.   By that time the Clan-na-Gael had marked the rise
and the effectiveness of the new spirit in the Irish Parliamentary party, to which Mr Barry O'Brien bears testimony : " ' Had Davitt come to America in the beginning
of 1877,' said a member of the Clan-na-Gael to me, ' he
would have found a few men ready to discuss the new

[1] Parnell Commissioners' Report, p. 30.

departure and to favour it. But neither he nor we would have dared broach it at a public meeting of the League.' But a change had taken place in a twelvemonth. Parnell's action in Parliament had made people think that something might be done with Parliamentarianism after all." [1] Davitt went to America after that change, in August 1878. Moreover he went with a plan which provided a channel whereby the two currents of agitation might communicate. He had already devised the Land Campaign.

We shall miss the strength of this move if we do not recognise that the land question in Ireland was, if not actually different, susceptible of being made very different from any such question in England. In England land nationalisation is a political ideal on exactly the same footing as other political ideals. In Ireland the possession of land by the landlords could be represented as a form of English garrisoning. Parnell more than once spoke of the destruction of English landlordism as the key to Home Rule. The landlords were indeed for the most part English, and their relations with their tenants had in general none of that idealism which even at the worst has never been absent from these relations in England. Too often the landlord's attitude suggested that the Irish lived on a conquered land, and had no rights save such as the landlord chose to allow. This had been so obvious that there had been sufficient strength of feeling in England to carry more than one Land Act. " The landlord," wrote a chief secretary in the middle of last century, " had a monopoly of the means of existence. . . . ' The landlords in Ireland,' said Lord Donoughmore in 1854, ' have been in the habit of letting land, not farms.' " [2] These words sum up the problems of Irish land tenure—exorbitant rents, and eviction without

[1] Barry O'Brien's *Life of Parnell*, i. 165.
[2] Thomas Drummond's *Life and Letters*

compensation. Therefore the land agitation could be intimately associated with Home Rule ; a subject— and this was the brilliant point of the conception— which the Clan-na-Gael could approach from one side, and the Parliamentary party from another, meeting no doubt in the middle, but never marching to it along the same line. The conception had immediate success. While Davitt was in America in 1878 a telegram was sent to Parnell offering the support of the Clan-na-Gael for the Parliamentary party on the conditions : (a) of the party's abandoning Butt's federal proposals and making a general declaration for self-government ; (b) of the party's agitating the land question on a peasant proprietary basis, while accepting concessions tending to abolish arbitrary eviction ; (c) of the party's voting together on all questions, adopting an aggressive policy, and energetically resisting coercive legislation.[1] Was not such a proposal, it may be asked, a complete conjunction of the two currents of agitation ? It might have been—but Parnell never answered the telegram. It was the first occasion on which his famous gift of silence came into play. He did not accept the Clan-na-Gael's offer overtly. But on 7th June 1879 he appeared on a platform in Ireland with members of the Land League, which Davitt had founded at a meeting at Irishtown on 20th April, and on 21st October 1879 he was at the Dublin Conference at which the League was organised finally into the National Land League. Its main working clause set up an organisation among tenant farmers for defending those who might be threatened with eviction, for facilitating the working of the Land Act of 1870, and for obtaining such reform as would enable the tenant to become owner of the land by paying a fair rent for a limited number of years. Parnell was at first reluctant to accept the scheme ; he saw, much as he disliked the

[1] Parnell Commissioners' Report, p. 9.

purely constitutional spirit of Isaac Butt, that the party's effectiveness in Parliament depended in no small degree upon not coming into contact with the law. But he decided that he must " take the risk," [1] and it is a point of some importance that the Land League constitution contained no demand for the self-government of Ireland. That made it merely a weapon, and not, so to speak, a different impersonation of the Parliamentary party. The last point for this brief summary is that Parnell himself went to America in December 1879, and was hurriedly recalled for the General Election of 1880.

When the new Parliament met, there must therefore have been every ground for regarding the Irish party, thirty-five members of which were pledged Parnellites, with new apprehension. Yet it may be doubted whether actual apprehension was felt. The intervention of the Home Rule question in the Liverpool bye-election had, as we have said, been without any parallel in the General Election. Liberals had beaten Home Rulers in some Irish constituencies—Dundalk, Athlone, and Mallow, for instance. One cause of possible discomfort, which had been foreseen, was avoided by the fact that the Liberal majority did not depend upon the Irish ; and no uneasiness was shown in the summary statement that " the Government may even approach once more the question of Irish university education ; and it will certainly be expected to deal effectively in some way with the present condition of Ireland." [2] The serene reliance of the Ministerial party on Mr Gladstone's confidence in his own mission floated the Compensation for Disturbance Bill successfully through the House, and there were none but momentary qualms in face of Parnell's silence. That silence was obstinate. He was ready to see what the

[1] Parnell Commissioners' Report, p. 15.
[2] *The Times*, leading article, 17th April 1880.

new Government would do, but he would take no single step towards it. He would not answer the Clan-na-Gael's telegram, but he would equally not answer any signals from the English. He took practically no part in the proceedings on the Bill. It was thrown out, as has been recorded, by the House of Lords. Then the new force for which Parnell stood revealed itself. Nothing could have done more to strengthen the new Land League than this event. The League was instantly at work in every case that offered it a foothold. Rents were refused above the " valued rent " scale, any man who paid more was banned. Every farm where there had been an eviction became a centre of activity, and any man who took such a farm, or did anything for the landlord or the agent concerned, was banned. On 15th September 1880 Lord Mountmorres was murdered near Clonbar. A week later an agent—whose name came afterwards to stand for the campaign, Captain Boycott—was put under the ban. The police could get no information, and the banning of men was accompanied by the shooting of those who held on their way in spite of the League, by the maiming of cattle placed on evicted farms, and by all sorts of minor violences. Parnell and Biggar denounced all violent action, and the Parnell Commission, examining later all the evidence that was brought by Parnell's most convinced and determined opponents, had to conclude that these denunciations were not insincere.[1] The other current of agitation was operating, and the figures of cases of agrarian crime rose from 863 in 1879 to 2589 in 1880, although the acute agitation had not begun until September in the latter year ; evictions rose from 6239 in 1879 to 10,457 in 1880. The figures of crime for separate months in 1880 show that from 67 in May the cases rose to 165 in September, 269 in October, 559 in November, and 865 in December. The crimes thus scheduled were

_____
[1] Parnell Commissioners' Report, p. 76.

chiefly those of sending threatening letters, killing or maiming cattle, arson, firing into houses or at the person, and murder.[1]

In face of this onrush of events the first thought of the executive in Dublin was one of regret that the new Government had allowed the Coercion Act of the late Government to lapse. Lord Cowper, the Viceroy, and Mr Forster, the Chief Secretary, were insistent with the Cabinet to promise renewal of the Act, and all through the later months of the year were threatening resignation unless the Habeas Corpus Act were suspended. Meanwhile Lord Cowper was urging that the Land League should be treated as an illegal conspiracy and its leading members arrested. Mr Gladstone, who had already lost the Duke of Argyll from his Cabinet, and Lord Lansdowne from a minor place in his Government, over the Compensation Bill, and who knew that Lord Hartington had never liked it, was not disposed to see much reason at the moment to be at the pains of dissociating the Irish party from these disturbances. He announced at the Guildhall banquet on 9th November that the Government would stipulate that order must be restored in Ireland before grievances could be considered, returning thus to the old over-logical position that England cherished. A week earlier, with dramatic effect, the Government in Ireland had arrested five Irish members, Parnell, Biggar, Dillon, Sullivan and Sexton ; and nine other Land Leaguers, including Patrick Egan and Brennan. So the year ended with the Government deeply into the first of its quagmires.

[1] These figures are taken from the Parnell Commissioners' Report.

CHAPTER III

1881 : COMMON SENSE

IN reviewing the events of 1880 there was occasion to make allowance for a general depression. In 1881 it is possible to trace, as a prevailing influence, a tendency towards " common-sense " views, which may be the natural British reaction from a period of self-pity.

The return to sturdiness arose primarily from a revival of trade. The railways gave the first distinct note of the improvement, the half-yearly dividends declared in February being much better than had been anticipated. The favouring conditions recorded were " lowness of wages and prices coupled with a good steady trade." [1] Sheffield's exports to America had in the previous year risen to over a million pounds in value ; and there seemed to be no serious prospect of strikes to disturb output. The year 1881 was, in fact, fairly free of such troubles. Strikes occurred in the month of June among the colliers in some districts, the blast-furnace men and the nail-makers; but, though 30,000 men were out in the last case, the only real menace came from the colliers ; and as they were conferring on the extension to all districts of the sliding scale, already at work in the northern districts, Staffordshire and Yorkshire, there was no great alarm. The general confidence must have been well restored ; for the early part of 1881 saw that large call for capital which the financial experts had been foretelling in 1880. In the first three months of 1881 about a hundred companies were floated, and the capital asked for was thirty-three and a quarter millions

[1] *The Times*, 8th February 1881.

sterling. Two millions of this were in Birmingham Corporation 3½ per cent. Stock ; and the changed conditions since that corporation's last attempt [1] were sufficiently indicated by the subscription of the whole amount at an average of £98. 2s. 1d.[2] Over twelve millions were in railway issues of preference stock, bonds and debentures. But it is evident that the City believed the public to be in a mood now for more than solid disposal of savings, for the remaining nineteen millions were asked for in more speculative ventures. Still the timidity of the orthodox observer of the money market remained very great. *The Times*, for instance, considered that only about six millions of real capital were called for beyond the corporation and railway issues. The Stock Exchange was not as yet a normal field for middle-class savings, which were " as a rule invested as they are made in houses or land, new plant, increase of stocks, etc." [3] In accordance with this state of things we find the stock and share list of the chief daily papers at this time no more than a column long— a typical instance showing, besides home and foreign Government securities, twenty-four mining companies, twenty-six Colonial securities, eighteen industrial companies, twelve tram companies, five gas companies, three shipping companies, and one land company. Even this moderate compilation was not regarded as quite healthy. Seventeen gold-mining companies appeared among these early prospectuses of the year, and a month or two later *The Times* was commenting on the " inundation of gold-mining companies since 1879." [4] To modern eyes it hardly looks like an inundation : the total capital of all the companies amounted to only three millions, and of those floated in the year now under discussion only two asked for as

[1] *Cf.* p. 28.
[2] Bunce's *History of the Corporation of Birmingham*, ii: 34.
[3] *The Times*, 4th April 1881.
[4] Leading article, 5th May.

much as a quarter of a million; the majority were
floated at from £50,000 to £80,000. It is curious and
interesting to follow in these years all the effects
of the shortage of gold, all the complicated projects for
meeting the shortage, all the puny efforts to increase the
supply, knowing, as we do now know, what an immense
source was all the time awaiting exploitation in South
Africa. Both from the political and the financial point
of view it should be borne in mind, in reading of the events
of the succeeding three years, that the British public as
yet knew practically nothing of the mineral wealth of the
Transvaal ; and the world of high politics and high finance,
some members of which must have had the information,
did not believe in it. The public knew no more than the
occasional rumours of a nugget having been found here
and there—" a fine little nugget from the north side of the
Tugela," or " undoubtedly payable gold in the Lydenburg
district "—and the rumours were generally accompanied
by a warning that opinion in. Pretoria was very wild, and
that there was nothing to warrant a gold " rush." In
fact, similar rumours from the head waters of the River
Yukon, in Alaska, were much more hopefully regarded.
That ministers had more knowledge than this is certain ;
Sir Garnet Wolseley, the Administrator of the Transvaal,
in a despatch to Sir Michael Hicks Beach on the question of
annexation, at the end of 1879, had written : " The Transvaal is rich in minerals ; gold has already been found in
quantities, and there can be little doubt that larger and
still more valuable goldfields will sooner or later be discovered."   Yet this emphatic statement appears to have
made no more impression on the Cabinet than the newspaper rumours had made on the public. Goschen, for
example, laboured long at the Exchequer to devise solutions of the gold problem without any apparent expectation of relief from a new supply. Scientists worked at

[1] Morley's *Life of Gladstone*, iii. 26.

new methods of treating auriferous ores, which had been
sent to them from South Africa—one of such methods, the
use of hydrochloric acid, for refractory ores, was exhibited
in London on 19th August 1881. But did even they
know the significance of the task they had been set ? At
any rate, for the present no new supply was in contemplation ; and the prevailing consciousness of the problem is
sufficiently indicated by the meeting in Paris in May of this
year of an international conference to deal with it. But
as the bimetallic theory did not attain its full height in
England until a year or two later we may leave that
conference with the bare mention of its meeting. In this
country the more active economic theory was of another
kind. Early in May the question of the new French tariff
became acute. Existing commercial treaties with France
had determined by lapse of time ; and the new proposals
of that country showed a considerable, and even grave,
enhancement of import duties. The cotton and woollen
trades were the most seriously disturbed, the previous
taxes on their products having been 20 per cent. *ad valorem*,
and the new taxes being 44 per cent. The Protectionist
party, numbering still many of the surviving opponents
of Repeal, was not slow to take this opportunity. By
the month of September the Fair Trade League was in
existence, with a programme singularly like a famous
programme of twenty-two years later. It opened its
campaign with emphasis on " retaliation " against high
duties in other countries ; and, again as happened later,
the idea of enabling these detached islands to take as
downright a line as countries with large and varied resources by the formation of an Imperial Bund was early
affixed to the programme, and in the end became more
prominent than the original idea. The movement attracted
the politically roving spirit of Lord Randolph Churchill ;
and on 18th September he was laying before an audience
at Oldham the desirability of taxing all foreign manu-

factured goods to relieve the burdens on land, and dilating
on " the antagonism set up by the Liberal party between
manufacturing and agricultural interests." In November
he was even so near the later spirit as to be expending his
sarcasm on " the commercial edifice constructed by the
immortal Cobden and the divine Bright." In October
the movement was being presented less aristocratically
to the working man, a meeting at Sheffield passing a
resolution to deplore " the failure of the present system
of free trade so called . . . endangering the steady employment, the fair wages, and the future well-being of
our working classes."

However, such trade problems as there were in this year
did not disturb the general sense of restored comfort.
The great middle class, convinced of its mission as the
repository of " progress," had enough to engross it.
Electricity was the new god of progress, and it continued
its advances. Among public buildings two more railway
stations, Charing Cross and Liverpool Street, installed the
new light in January; the General Post Office began
using it in the same month ; in June the Prudential Assurance Company had nine lights of 150 c.p. in its offices ;
and the House of Commons first did its work under electric
light. Among great private houses Trentham was fitted
with the light in November. But the novelty in this year
was the application of the invention to street lighting.
Bristol appears to have been the first town to make the
experiment, which it did in some of its principal thoroughfares in January; and Brighton followed with an installation on the sea-front in February. Liverpool set up sixty
lamps over two and a half miles of its streets in April.
London, more able to command the rivalry of inventors,
offered the lighting of the City to be divided between three
companies for an experimental period of twelve months,
with a view to selecting one of them at the end of the
period. Great interest was taken, even from the artistic

point of view of " seeing London in a new light," though
a sarcastic person wrote to the Press to remark that the
City was the worst part of London for the experiment,
since 685,000 of its 800,000 inhabitants were not there at
night, and only " the cats and the caretakers " would enjoy
the fun. For the first time the gas companies took alarm ;
they had somewhat unwisely raised their charges at the
beginning of the year, and the best comfort that could be
offered them was that there was still a great future for
gas as a heating and power agent. Their panic subsided
later owing to an unexpected slowness of pace in the
development of the new illuminant. Meanwhile one of the
most useful applications of electricity was in its extreme
infancy. In May Mr Alexander Siemens was lecturing
at the Society of Arts on the transmission of vehicles by
electric power. The system he lectured upon was the use
of a positive and a negative rail, replacing the customary
tram-rails : after consideration, Mr Siemens told his
audience, the authorities had decided to class the vehicle
as a tramcar. But this was obviously too dangerous a
method to last ; " live " rails would be impossible on the
road surface. For several years yet invention failed at
this problem. An " electric railway " was opened at the
Crystal Palace in April, and towards the end of the year
an electric tram was running on the Giant's Causeway and
Portrush line ; but both these were worked with live rails.
The latter, however, must have stimulated the inventors,
for it was announced that it could be worked at a cost of
a penny a mile, whereas the steam-trams, to which, in
spite of their noisiness and dirt, corporations in large
centres of population were finding themselves forced to
consent, cost from 1s. to 1s. 9d. a mile. It may be added
here that the general advances in electrical invention were
summed up in an Electrical Exhibition opened in Paris
in September of this year. Beyond its more common uses
the delicate developments of electricity were attracting

the medical profession.   An " induction balance " had been
used in the case of President Garfield in August to locate
the bullet that had been fired at him ; and at the end of
the year experiments were made with a needle fitted with
a kind of telephone attachment fixed to the surgeon's ear,
which might, it was hoped, supersede the old probe.

The particular medical interest of the year, however,
so far as general knowledge went, was the new theory
of bacteria.   The researches of Pasteur had for some
time been closely watched from England ; and although,
as we shall have occasion to see later, it was chiefly the
immediate and palpable cause of his researches, the treatment of hydrophobia, which interested the public mind,
yet incidentally the more profound results were known
even to the newspapers.   In February telegrams from
Paris stated that in investigating a case of hydrophobia
Pasteur had found " a small organism or microbe," and
the question had been raised whether this was a new form
of disease, or whether rabies was caused by a microscopic
organism.   The ensuing months saw much discussion,[1]
the existence of these small organisms being admitted,
but one school of medical thought maintaining a theory of
" spontaneous generation," and holding that if water were
put into a bottle living organisms would be " evolved "
by putrefaction, but were not themselves the putrefaction.

Again, the idea of progress was at the root of all the
interest taken in ballooning at this time.   Some of it,
indeed, was merely a matter of fashion.   The gatherings
at Hurlingham and Ranelagh nowadays to see the start
of balloon races had their origin in 1881 in a garden-party
given by the new Balloon Society at Lillie Bridge ; the
company was content with the spectacle of a single
balloon, and its passengers made the report that London,
owing to the people in the streets being indistinguishable,
looked like a city of the dead.   On 1st June two Guardsmen

[1] See, for instance, *The Times,* 18th March and 9th August 1881.

went to the Derby by balloon, starting from the Crystal Palace and landing at Epsom, in a field a quarter of a mile from the grand stand. But the real impetus of the balloon craze of these years was the serious middle-class enthusiasm. It was most ingeniously enlisted. A scheme would be propounded for reaching the Pole by triple balloons " lashed together for mutual aid," and launched on a " wind-curve " calculated to carry them in eighteen hours from a ship's chosen winter-quarters to the Pole. There would be devices for using balloons for army signalling; for sending them up in fogs to explode dynamite and blow off the vapours; for employing them to illuminate large surfaces with electric light.

It is all rather solemn; and indeed the middle-class of England, conscious of itself as a class for some time now, had not yet been penetrated by self-consciousness in the subtler sense. Sport and the worship of exercise never filled more than a couple of columns of the daily papers; there were considerable intervals between race meetings; the word " polo " was printed in inverted commas; there was no golf; football was still open to antagonism, for the Mayor of Southampton issued in September 1880 an appeal to the heads of families and schools to prevent the game of football " being played according to Rugby Union, Association, and other rules of a dangerous character," and the winter of 1881 brought another outcry, accompanied with specimen lists of casualties. The appearance of cycling in the sporting columns marks the first approach of a new era. Yet however distinctly we may see the middle-class as still ponderous and solid, it is no less a shock to come upon a perfectly grave notice in *The Times* [1] to this effect : " Fashion seems to have decreed that photographic albums are in future to be ornamented on each page. We have the ' Mikado ' album with Japanese scenes, the ' Language

[1] 4th February 1881.

of Flowers,' and the ' Picturesque ' with copies of etchings
of quaint and pretty places." We are indeed in the days
yet of albums ; and it was not a hopelessly old-fashioned
member of the aristocracy who had presented to the
Princess Frederica of Hanover at her wedding "a plush
table."

The most depressing circumstance, however, was not
the impenetrability of the middle-class, but the fact that
when penetrated, as on some matters of taste it was
beginning to be, by new ideas, it sucked them up in a
thoroughly wrong-headed way. The laying of the foundation stone of the City and Guilds of London Institute at
South Kensington was accompanied by the reflection that
the time of shoddy and bad work was over. "Think,"
wrote the impassioned leader-writer, " what a museum of
horrors a furniture shop was before 1851. That was the
beginning of our renaissance." And a month or two
earlier we find *papier-maché* imitations of stamped leather
seriously commended by the same newspaper as a form of
decorative art. The death of Decimus Burton in December
of this year called forth genuine and not ill-balanced
appreciations of his architectural work in London—the
Athenæum Clubhouse, the Hyde Park Corner screen, and
the Constitution Hill Arch—yet at the same time the
beautiful and dignified old building in Lincoln's Inn Fields,
which our own generation rejoices to have seen saved from
demolition, was described as "that large, dull, heavy-
looking mansion, Newcastle House." A still more deplorable tendency is seen in a sarcastic leading article of
this year on the conference of master builders, in which
the builders are implored to consider " the pitiful elevation
of the lengthy roads from the market gardens of Tyburnia
or South Kensington " and to reflect " how very far its
monotonous doors and windows fall short of the ideal
street in which each dwelling shall look as if it could stand
by itself with a character of its own." So lamentably was

the middle class taking at a gulp its own interpretation
of what " artistic " meant, and longing to translate the
genuine town architecture of London—the not unworthy
attempt to treat the street, rather than the house, as the
essential consideration in massed centres of population—
into prettiness and picturesqueness. This was the year
which saw the formation of the Bedford Park Company in July, with a capital of £125,000, to develop that
estate.

The most forceful influences in matters of taste at this
time—influences destined in the end to spread through
every social level—had turned their backs upon the
middle class. One voice that had long raised itself against
that class in this year fell silent. In February Thomas
Carlyle died : the world lost in him not only a writer of
history, but even more a prophet of the social conscience,
a man of genius to whom the masses of the people were real.
A teacher yet with years of life before him who had in
no small measure reached his democratic feeling by way
of revolt against the lack of a sense of responsibility, the
lack of light, in the middle classes, was John Ruskin ; he
was by now addressing himself almost entirely to the
working man. Matthew Arnold, starting from yet a third
position, was reaching the same end, and in carrying his
gospel of the humaneness of education to the working
men's colleges he was taking part in the new movement.
We are at the period of conjunction between art and
socialism, of which William Morris is the typical exponent.
In May 1881 various Radical clubs of working men in
London combined, forming the Democratic Federation :
and, although the working man's circumstances in the
ensuing years would in any case have endued such an
organisation with power, it is none the less true that
the presence in the movement of such men as Morris made
it more formidable. He had a voice that was unwearying
and was listened to. No one has expressed more tersely

than he the theory that was behind the alliance of art
with socialism. " I know," he said, referring to a recent
demonstration by working men, "what these men want :
employment which would foster their self-respect, and
win the praise and sympathy of their fellows, and dwellings
which they could come to with pleasure, surroundings
which would soothe and elevate them ; reasonable labour,
reasonable rest. There is only one thing that can give
them this—Art." [1] The self-respect of the workman
coming from labour that was reasonable was the heart of
Morris's social creed ; and it had this soundness—that
he had come to it not from a theoretical consideration of
the workman, but from his own experience in dealing with
the world. He wanted to have, and to make for other
people, beautiful things. He was roused to fury, not by
blank impenetrability on the part of the middle class, but
by the quality of its susceptibility. It allowed itself to
be told that many of its surroundings were ugly, and it
substituted for them others of a different taste with exactly
the same superficial attention. In his own work as
a craftsman he was " confronted everywhere with the
double barrier of material that would not take good colour,
and colour which in its own substance was uniformly bad."[2]
Worst of all, he saw his gospel running to waste among
people who bought things made in that inadequate way
and were satisfied with them. It was to his mind the same
spirit that showed itself in lack of regulation of employment ; in the blundering semi-charitable movement for
workmen's dwellings ; in such groping efforts on the
workman's behalf as the Coffee-house movement, now
very active.

In this spirit art as the gospel of genuineness, of reasonableness and of reality was being preached to the workman.
In 1881 the first Whitechapel art show was held in a school-

[1] Speech delivered at Burslem, 13th October 1881.
[2] Mackail's *Life of William Morris*, i. 311.

room, with pictures by Leighton, Watts, Burne-Jones
and Walter Crane, and an exhibition of pottery and
embroideries. More directly the building of the City and
Guilds of London Institute was heralding a fresh era in
industrial art ; the new Natural History Museum, opened
on Easter Monday in this year, began to put order into the
educational chaos of South Kensington ; and the Ruskin
Museum at Sheffield was far advanced. The opening of
the University College at Nottingham on 28th June led
to a gratified survey of an educational movement which,
beginning with the University of London, had expanded
to the Queen's Colleges of Ireland, the University of
Durham, with its offshoot in the Science College at Newcastle, the Victoria University, the Science College at
Leeds, Mason College at Birmingham, and the most recent
university colleges of Liverpool and Nottingham. The
vigour of educational interest in the provinces was matter
for comment. The School Boards were making progress
towards secondary education, and, though the teaching
of domestic economy had as yet but limited support, the
movement for including in the code such subjects as
cooking, heating and ventilation had come into existence.

We may see the effect of the year's access of common-
sense in the state of ecclesiastical controversy. Mr Dale
was transferred from the conspicuousness of his city church
to a country living ; and early in the year an attempt was
made, by means of a memorial to the Archbishop of Canterbury, to set up a policy of "live and let live." The
memorial pleaded for " recognised toleration of even wide
diversities of ceremonial," and also petitioned that the
courts for ecclesiastical causes should be " such as to secure
the conscientious obedience of clergymen who believe
the constitution of the Church of Christ to be of divine
appointment." The memorial was signed by five deans :
Dr Church of St Paul's, Dr Lake of Durham, Dr Cowie of
Manchester, Lord Alwyne Compton of Worcester, and Dr

3

Purey Cust of York ; by several archdeacons ; and among
the canonry by Gregory, Liddon and Stubbs of St Paul's,
and Dr King of Christ Church. What, again, could be
more sensible than the comment made upon that notoriety
which the attacks of street roughs were bringing upon the
Salvation Army ? The disturbances had produced a
question in Parliament, to which Sir William Harcourt,
as Home Secretary, had replied that, if the Salvation Army
complained of attacks, it was fair to remind the Army that
its methods were somewhat provocative. The comment
made on this was that such a doctrine might easily go
too far. "We need not assist the roughs to put the
Salvation Army down. Another course lies before us all.
It is to do the Army's work in a better way."[1] These
disturbances became more deliberate and more organised
later on ; but they are mentioned here because, although
the Army had been in existence since 1865, this
year was the first in which it attracted widespread
attention.

Even the world of fashion seems to show us in 1881 the
working of common-sense. It is a small but not quite
insignificant fact that "Evans's" this year ceased to be
even a name. It had previously come to the end of its
too lingering career as the only survival of the "night
houses" of the sixties ; and now the last familiar name
of that rowdy high life of Lord Hastings and his friends
disappeared, and the place became the Falstaff Club. An
event, however, of more importance is the indication that
the great world was changing its habits in regard to the
old-fashioned London season. The idea was being mooted
that the time had come to be done with the old sharp
distinction between "the season" and "out of season."
The modern comfort of railway travelling—dining cars,
for instance, had appeared this year on the Great Northern
and Midland railways—was making it unnecessary, and

[1] *The Times,* 13th October 1881.

indeed almost silly, to keep up a fashion due to a time
when the journey to London of a great household was too
large an affair to be undertaken more than once a year.[1]
Common-sense seemed too to be colouring very strongly
the relation of great families to their territories. Rents
had had to be reduced on account of the combination
of general agricultural depression with particularly bad
harvests ; and while on the one hand this led to a perverse
and peevish kind of common-sense in the deliberate turning
of some large tracts into rabbit warrens,[2] it led also to a
new hardheadedness in the forwarding of agricultural
associations to make experiments in crops, fertilisers and
soils. Rectors complained that their glebe could find no
tenants ; yet land could hardly have been valueless when
a farm of 190 acres in Sussex fetched £7200, and 103 acres
of marsh pastureland fetched £7500. It is significant also
of a new feeling in society that the sale of game by great
landlords was taken quite calmly. Preserving was already a business.

The season of 1881 was again chronicled as one devoid
of notable interest. It had its " lion," of the kind usual in
those days, in the shape of the King of the Sandwich Islands,
who came to Claridge's in July, and was at all the parties
in London and elsewhere for a month. A " lion " more
interesting to us now was Ivan Turgenieff, who came, as
was fitting for the writer of *A Sportsman's Sketches*,
in the autumn, and was shooting partridges in Cambridgeshire in October. The season had its mild sensation in
the marriage of the Baroness Burdett-Coutts in February
to an American ; and it is a coincidence that one of the
marks of the season was a new impulse of friendliness
between this country and the United States. The lingering soreness of the Alabama claims was dispelled by the

[1] *The Times*, 30th July 1880.
[2] *Cf*. the case of a large estate of a thousand acres in Hampshire;
The Times, 23rd July 1881;

feelings of sympathy aroused by the assassination of President Garfield. New York became once more a subject of interest free of afterthoughts, and the British public read this year of the "costly house" of Mr Vanderbilt, which had absorbed only the sum, petty to a millionaire of these days, of £300,000 ; and of the advance of high buildings, which now sound equally petty ; houses were being put up actually of seven or nine storeys high, and the New York correspondents prophesied that in a few years the streets would "tower to the height of ten or eleven storeys."

Early in the year the season had been overcast by two events. In March the papers began to contain intimations of Beaconsfield's failure of health. On 19th April he died; and modern generations, to whom his domination appears to have been absolute, will find the leading articles at the time of his death singularly reserved, and not obscurely tinged by a mistrust that he never surmounted. Perhaps the reason was that, as an old man, he had relapsed into those characteristics of the alien—the avowed alien—which were partly racial and partly the Dæmon of his genius. That strange figure, with the dyed hair, the sunken, smouldering eyes and parchment cheeks, which only broke its silence at London dinner-tables to launch some levin of an epigram, must have reminded the great world that, after all, the new spirit of Imperialism, the new regime in India, and almost all such power as the Tories had of appealing to the working man, were the achievement of an individual whom people yet alive could remember in a fringed waistcoat and green velvet trousers, affronting in person and manner every canon of their tastes. Perhaps, too, in the later years of his power the absorption of English energies in foreign affairs, the apprehension that it raised of entanglement in European disputes, had savoured of a cosmopolitanism not English in the great man, a quality, it may be, which his eminence had kept out of sight, until age brought back the ineradicable trait of his race. At any rate the strangeness of him sounded its note at the end as at the beginning; at the sale of his effects three months after his death people crowded the house in Curzon Street to stare at the bedroom walls hung with blue silk embroidered with roses in bloom, the crimson satin damask dining-room, the brocades of the drawing-room. Even in the formal tributes of the Press the strangeness is more commented on than anything else : " His secret lay perhaps," *The Times* wrote, " in the magnetic influence of a dauntless will, in his unrivalled power of patience, in his impenetrable reserve and detachment." " Magnetic " and " impenetrable " were curious epitaphs for a Prime Minister of England.

The other shadow on the year was one which afterwards became so heavy that it is somewhat difficult to recall the spirit in which it was first met. On 28th February the telegrams announcing the British defeat on Majuba Hill were published in London. Bitter as the news was, prompt as the outcry was in some sections of the community, yet the country did not as a whole forget how ready it had been in the previous year to accede to the Boer demand for the withdrawal of the annexation. On the whole it was conscious that it had slipped into this disaster by something' approaching carelessness. True, the outbreak of hostile operations by the Boers had at the beginning of the year somewhat dimmed that consciousness ; and there were not lacking signs of a very different kind when, on Lord Roberts's departure to take command in South Africa, ladies strewed his path from his carriage to the train with flowers. But prevailing influences were in the main for the steadying of opinion. It was affected partly by the old spirit towards Colonial responsibilities—the pre-Disraelian spirit   " There are," *The Times* wrote, " some thirty-five millions of people in these islands. . . . Can it be said that any one of these is benefited by the sacrifices that all

have made on behalf of South Africa ?   We cannot but be
proud of the heroism displayed by Englishmen at Rorke's
Drift, or at Ulundi, but can we honestly say that a quarrel
with Cetewayo or the Boers of the Transvaal is one in which
it is worth while for a single Englishman to shed his blood ?
. . . Are we indeed the weaker or the stronger, the richer
or the poorer, the happier or the reverse, for our vast
Colonial possessions ? " [1]   Of course after Majuba, opinion
underwent modification.   But the attitude even then was
not one of reasserting annexation, but only of insisting on
a considerable measure of control of the Transvaal's affairs.
The doctrine of suzerainty, appearing in answer to this
demand, was but coldly received.   The word, it was felt,
was virtually invented for the occasion, and had no real
meaning.   " To style the Queen suzerain is not to specify
her relations to the feudatory republic." [2]   What was
required was " a practical reconciliation, which to some
persons seems at present impossible, between the liberty
of a population of sequestered farmers to select their own
magistrates and determine their own taxation, and their
privation of right to irritate the sea of native life on their
borders into periodical storms and tempests of war." [3]
Most important of all is it to realise that the Government's
announced policy of not pursuing the war, and of meeting
the Boers to decide the status of the Transvaal, had strong
support.   The idea was placed beside the withdrawal from
Candahar, which had taken place quietly early in this
year, as the most sensible course to pursue.   In the month
of June Mr Chamberlain, speaking at Birmingham, exposed some of the errors of the preceding months.   Even
to the beginning of December 1880, in spite of all that had
become publicly known about the Boer hatred of annexation, Sir Owen Lanyon, the Administrator, was still telling

[1] *The Times*, 6th January 1881;
[2] Ditto, 8th March 1881.
[3] Ditto, 5th April 1881;

the Government that three-quarters of the Boer population
had ceased to care about it.　After the insurrection had
broken out there were more blunders.　Mr Kruger had
spoken of submitting the question to a Royal Commission,
and Sir George Colley had been instructed to arrange a
settlement on the first condition that the Boers must lay
down their arms.　" While the correspondence was going
on," said Mr Chamberlain, " and in the midst of the negotiations, the British troops unfortunately on three several
occasions marching in inferior numbers to attack the
strong position of the Boers met with a repulse."　In
the midst of rumours, disquieting and reassuring, as to
the progress in South Africa of the commission which had
been appointed to arrange the terms of settlement, the
persistent story of error was recalled.　" We know now
that we were wrong, that the annexation was unpopular
from the first, and that the injudicious way in which it
was carried out only served to fan the smouldering discontent.　It is not the fact that they have defeated us
that has opened our eyes, for that taken by itself would
rather have tended to keep them closed, but the fact that
they have satisfied us of the substantial justice of their
case. . . . Nor is it possible to acquit the present Government for declining to do a year ago what it had subsequently admitted the justice and necessity of doing. . . .
We were misinformed and misled from the outset." [1]
There was a genuine wish that the settlement now should
not be hedged about by conditions that could only lead
to spite and irritation.　Nothing, in fact, it was thought,
could be better than to have done with the whole matter,
and the news that the Convention was signed was received
with relief.　" England can now have no desire to intrude
herself upon the Transvaal.　The more completely its
people can get on without interference of any kind the
better pleased we shall be. . . . The fact is that between

---

[1] *The Times*, 12th July 1881.

England and the Transvaal there is no natural connection
whatever." [1]　" I am sure," Mr Gladstone said, speaking
at the Mansion House two or three days after the signature,
" that there are no rival interests between us and the
Boers." Lord Salisbury, who had been elected at a
meeting at Lord Abergavenny's house on 10th May to
succeed Lord Beaconsfield as leader of the Tory peers,
might make speeches about the loyal minority in the
Transvaal, and say that everything in South Africa would
now happen " under the shadow of Majuba Hill " ; but
the question practically dropped out of English political
life for some years.

Indeed only with difficulty could it have continued to
occupy a place. Parliament had found itself reduced to
a lamentable barrenness. After the turn that events had
taken in Ireland, men knew what to expect in England ;
and before Parliament met there was much discussion
about the forms of closure of debate (the idea was still so
new that the word for it retained its French form—*clôture*) [2]
in operation in the parliaments of other countries. The
blow struck by the executive in the arrests of Parnell,
Biggar and others in November 1880 was mistimed ; the
accused were brought for trial in January, and on the
disagreement of the jury were all discharged. Lord
Cowper and Mr Forster, backed by Lord Hartington, had
never relaxed their demand for renewal of the Coercion
Act ; and they could now bring to bear on the Cabinet
discussions the effect of this futile trial. Yet it was not
believed that the Government would agree ; they were
supposed to be too much under the control of the Radical
wing. " Mr Chamberlain and Mr Bright will not vindicate
the law ; they will dismember the Empire, and Mr Gladstone and the rest will consent to register their decrees." [3]

[1] *The Times,* 5th August 1881.

[2] It was Matthew Arnold who first pointed out that the English
language contained the word " closure," which quite met the need.

[3] *Quarterly Review,* January 1881.

That view was mistaken. The Queen's speech at the opening of Parliament hinted at suspension of the Habeas Corpus Act; and almost immediately Mr Forster introduced a Coercion Bill, giving power to arrest suspected persons and keep them in prison for any period up to 30th September 1882. Irish obstruction met this at once in such force that the first stage, the leave of the House to introduce the Bill, was only attained by a course of action which remains one of the historic incidents of Parliament. When the debate had lasted several days the Speaker cut across all forms of procedure by putting the question on his own responsibility. The House was taken by surprise, and the debate was ended. The Crimes Act became law in March, and the old attitude towards Ireland was in full sway in Mr Gladstone's idea of producing, concurrently with the Coercion measure, a Land measure, establishing the " Three F's "—fair rent, fixity of tenure, and freedom of sale. The Bessborough Commission had just reported in favour of such legislation; but it was unfortunate that it had not reported a year earlier. In 1880 the Bill might have changed the face of the Irish situation; in 1881 it was doggedly wrangled over by Irishmen infuriated by the revival of coercion, Conservatives displeased with any land legislation, and Liberals sore and angry at the conditions which had driven them into coercion. Moreover, the moment the Land Act was passed it was cleverly taken over by the Land League. Instead of weakening that body it strengthened it. Parnell contrived that no one should apply to the Land Court without consulting, and obtaining the consent of, the local branch of the League.

These two measures, and bewildered discussions of the paralysis of debate and the forms of procedure in the face of obstruction, occupied almost the whole of a very long session. The Judicature Act, taking the opportunity of the approaching transfer of the Law Courts from West-

minster to their new site at Temple Bar, made changes
in the organisation of legal administration ; and the Chief
Baron, the Serjeants at Law, and other dignitaries were
abolished. The Bankruptcy Act did away with old
methods of liquidation, which had led to much corrupt
bargaining with creditors and to fraudulent arrangements ;
and provided for the establishment of a new Bankruptcy
Court, for public examination of debtors, and an audit of
accounts in liquidation.

The place Ireland had been taking during the session
was not in the least out of proportion to the urgency and
gravity of the Irish problem: Already the Land League
was achieving the end set before it by Irish newspapers,
notably *The Irish World* and *The Irishman*, which had
been fond of saying that Ireland could not hope to beat
England in battle, but she might render the work of government " nervous and distracted." [1] The House of Commons
had cheered the announcement early in February that
Michael Davitt had been arrested on his unexpired ticket-
of-leave ; but those who cheered expected a counterstroke
in the shape of dynamite, and the precautions adopted
are exemplified in the care taken when a heavy parcel
addressed to Sir William Harcourt was delivered at the
Home Office. Removed by the police and opened by them
it was found to contain an old pistol. Davitt's arrest
itself was a sign of the confusion of thought that had set
in. He had been the first and the most energetic in the
condemnation of the violence that broke out in 1880 [2] ;
but his name stood in the popular mind for Fenianism,
and Government followed the popular mind. For some
months no other spectacular step was taken. But agrarian
crime in Ireland was making another great increase ; the
figures for 1880 were 2590 ; for 1881 they were 4439.
Boycotting was rife, with its accompaniments of shooting,

[1] *Cf.* Parnell Commissioners' Report, p. 70.
[2] *Ibid.*, p. 88.

cattle-maiming, and murder. For a while the Government hesitated on the subject of the Land League. Their law officers had given opinions on its vulnerability as a conspiracy ; but there were other considerations summed up in a letter of Lord Cowper's to the Cabinet. "If," he wrote, " the restraining influences of the central body were withdrawn, and the local branches driven to become secret societies, crime, particularly assassination, might increase, for though the central body gives unity and strength to the movement it does to a certain extent restrain crime." [1] This is very close to what Parnell himself had said in a speech at New Ross, co. Wexford, in September 1880, when he took the line that violence was a corollary of lack of organisation, and that if the Land League were completely organised no man would dare abuse his rights as a landlord.[2] But the Government could see only one step to take. In October 1881 it suppressed the Land League, and under the Crimes Act lodged Parnell, Sexton, O'Kelly, O'Brien and Dr Kenny in Kilmainham gaol. The Land League, its responsible heads removed, transferred its headquarters, under Patrick Egan, to Paris, and left in Ireland the Ladies' Land League, which had been founded, in February 1881, under the command of Miss Anna Parnell. Mr Forster had had his way, and one incident of this autumn must have gratified him. Parnell, against the advice of Dillon, issued from Kilmainham the " No Rent " manifesto, urging tenants to refuse all rent until constitutional rights were restored. But the priests were against this open defiance of law, and the manifesto " fell absolutely flat." [3] The arrests may therefore have seemed for the moment to be a successful move. Yet Mr Gladstone admitted in after years that the policy of the Government had been a mistake ; and John Bright confessed that

---

[1] Quoted in Barry O'Brien's *Life of Parnell*, i. 287.
[2] Parnell Commissioners' Report, p. 88.
[3] Barry O'Brien's *Life of Parnell*, i. 320.

the mistake was due to a misapprehension of the forces of the Land League.[1]

The brewing of another storm was at present unnoticed by the British public. In August rumours began to reach England of disaffection among the native troops of Egypt. These rumours were denied by the Khedive; and even when, a month later, circumstantial reports followed of an *émeute* in Cairo, in which the palace had been surrounded by troops and guns, and demands had been made on the army's behalf by one whose name was given as " Achmet el Ourabi," the ordinary Englishman was not much stirred. He knew only vaguely of Egypt as a country whose ruler by extravagant expenditure and reckless borrowing had run his nation into hopeless debt, and had had to submit to the appointment of a joint French and English control, which worked badly owing to mutual jealousies. He saw these jealousies breaking out now, French newspapers suggesting that the military rising was in some way engineered by England as a step towards intervention, English newspapers suggesting, when (in exercise of her supremacy) Turkey sent commissioners to investigate the outbreak, that this was some Machiavellian stroke of Bismarck's, and that there might be worse things than anarchy in Egypt. The year ended with the Turkish commissioners, whose arrival had caused immense excitement in Cairo, going peaceably to dinner-parties, but doing little else; and with an interview in which Arabi, now arrived at the familiar spelling, protested to Sir William Gregory his loyalty to the Sultan, his faithfulness to religion, his sole desire to improve the conditions and efficiency of the Egyptian army, and his lack of any intention to undermine the joint control.

[1] Barry O'Brien's *Life of Parnell*, i. 331 ; ii. 360.

CHAPTER IV

1882 : IRELAND, EGYPT—AND JUMBO

THE Liberal Government of 1880-1885 was itself conscious of carrying certain handicaps. The worship of Mr Gladstone, useful though it may have been in holding the party together, was apt to become a dead weight when problems arose in which he took but a perfunctory interest. Mistrust of Mr Chamberlain caused such members of the Cabinet as Lord Hartington and Lord Granville to feel uncomfortable and uncertain in their work. In Parliament the Irish disaffection and the harassing activity of the " Fourth Party " incessantly hampered the progress of public business. But there was a heavier handicap than any of these. The forces of idealism in the national life—the forces making for reconsideration of social duties, for readjustment of social conceptions—were to a very large extent divorced from politics and political creeds. They had been drained off along several channels. There was the Socialist view, that Parliament was in the hands of the professional and manufacturing middle class, and worked solely from the standpoint of that class. There was the view of the ardent social reformer, who, though he may be said actually to date from a famous piece of Parliamentary action — the Factory Acts — had grown impatient, and preferred almost any nostrum to the hope of reforming legislation. There was the somewhat chilly ethical enthusiasm, born of the new religion of science, which held that sanitary inspection could cure more evils than the most drastic Act of Parliament. There was the

Christian zeal, whether of the type of Charles Kingsley or of Father Dolling, which, seeing with new eyes the terrible state of its vineyard, called aloud for labour that would never have time to look beyond the immediate day's work. All this diversion of idealism the Government did not number among its handicaps ; yet it was certainly the heaviest. The bad effect was twofold. On the one hand social problems accumulated such a force of highly educated opinion that they became exasperatingly thorny to handle ; and on the other hand much of the Radical strength in the country was sapped by the easy habit of looking on, detached from the necessity of distinguishing between right and wrong, so long as one Government was as good or as bad as another. So far the Government had displayed no capacity for drawing to itself the vitality of all that independent enthusiasm.

At the beginning of 1882 it nearly achieved, however, a great clearing of its path. Mr Gladstone never showed more brilliant political instinct than in the masterly conception of a stroke of Irish policy by which he could sweep influences, apparently hostile at the time and weakening to his power, into a single whole-hearted purpose. Within the Cabinet his own disappointment at having been obliged to revive coercion coincided in some measure with the Radical feeling of Mr Chamberlain. Coercion was also, for very different reasons, the especial object at the moment of the attacks of the " Fourth Party " in the House. Mr W. H. Smith was hinting at the possibility of a Conservative scheme of land purchase for Ireland ; and Lord Hartington was in a mood which he expressed thus to Lord Granville : " It seems to me that an effort ought to be made to unite the two great parties on an Irish policy. . . . Though we go on talking about local government, and about the county franchise and redistribution of seats, and though Chamberlain thinks that we are on the eve of great political changes, I do not believe that one of them will be made while the Irish difficulty lasts." [1] All these influences were at sixes and sevens. Hartington's union of the two parties would have been rather repressive than otherwise, so the idea had no reality ; Smith was only making the kind of remark which is safe and comforting out of office ; the " Fourth Party " was merely scoring debating points about the inconsistency and failure of Ministerial professions. But, whatever the separate intentions, they all expressed one opinion—that the present situation of the Irish question was hopeless. The day-to-day method of meeting it had produced such a tangle that it was time to attempt a wider and longer view, if Government was to escape suffocation. Mr Gladstone's brilliance lay in seeing that these very different lines of criticism made a kind of current on which he might set floating a policy of genuine advance in Ireland : and it fell out that an opportunity was not unwelcome to the Irish leaders. Parnell in gaol was feeling that the direction of events in Ireland was in danger of slipping from his hands. The co-operation between the extremist section and the Parliamentary party was his work, and nobody but he could manage it ; his silence, his refusal to be " drawn " either by the extremists or by his own party, his capacity for locking up the precise threads of co-operation in his single mind, and keeping that mind impenetrable, were the only conditions on which the co-operation could be safely worked. In gaol he was out of touch, and was growing nervous. He mistrusted the Ladies' Land League and lived in dread of the party's being publicly and irredeemably associated with Fenianism. He was therefore in a mood not to hold off from the intimations which presently reached him of Mr Gladstone's desire to make a fresh start. Intimations had previously reached Mr Gladstone of Parnell's state of mind.[2] These exchanges (never acknowledged as such by

[1] Holland's *Life of the Duke of Devonshire*, i. 344.
[2] Morley's *Life of Gladstone*, iii. 64.

either of the two men) took place in April 1882; and to
Parnell they must have been strengthened by the fact
that the Arrears of Rent Bill, introduced originally by
an Irish member, Mr Redmond, to supplement and ameli-
orate the Land Act of 1881, had been taken up by the
Government, and passed into law on 18th April. It provided that, in cases in which the tenant could satisfy the
legal tribunal of his inability to pay the whole of his
arrears of rent, he should be called upon to pay the rent
for 1881, but only half the arrears of preceding years, the
State paying the other half. Mr Gladstone, as his nature
was, having seen a piece of rectification to perform, moved
very rapidly in his opinions. There is a famous letter of
his to Mr Forster, dated in this month (it became famous
later in the discussion of whether the trend of his mind
towards Home Rule could have been foreseen by his
party), in which he showed this rapidity very clearly. He
asserted that, until there were seriously responsible bodies
in Ireland, every plan framed by the Government came
as an English plan, and was as such condemned, and that
there must therefore be some form of local self-government.
This was the passage afterwards most canvassed; but
the passage most to our immediate purpose, as showing
how far Mr Gladstone had moved, was this: "If we say
we must postpone the question till the state of the country
is more fit for it, I should answer that the least danger
is in going forward at once. It is liberty alone which fits
men for liberty. This proposition, like every other in
politics, has its bounds; but it is far safer than the
counter-doctrine, wait till they are fit." [1] This was a
fairly swift change in eighteen months from the position
he had taken at the Guildhall Banquet on 9th November
1880, that order must be restored before grievances could
be considered.

As Gladstone and Parnell never admitted the exchange

[1] Morley's *Life of Gladstone*, iii. 58.

of preliminary intimations in April 1882, so neither of them would ever admit the implication contained in the words " The Kilmainham Treaty." But when. Parnell and the others were released from gaol, on 2nd May, it was fairly well understood that, if the Government would continue to consider sympathetically the difficulties of the Irish tenant, there would be a diminution of agrarian crime. Parnell's side of the bargain was variously stated. The fact probably was that he merely meant to prove the truth of what he had said in 1880, that violence was really lack of organisation, and that the Land League, if he were free to control it, would neither murder men nor maim cattle. Though on the release of the prisoners Lord Cowper resigned the Viceroyalty, and Mr Forster the Chief Secretaryship, the Cabinet on the whole was with Mr Gladstone, even Lord Hartington holding the opinion that enough had been done to reassert the law, and that no danger was involved in the release.[1] A new hopefulness pervaded the political atmosphere. Lord Spencer succeeded to the Viceroyalty and Lord Frederick Cavendish undertook the Chief Secretaryship.

Before a week had passed, the Phœnix Park murders took place. Lord Frederick Cavendish was walking with Mr Burke, the Under Secretary, across the park on 6th May, after a long consultation with Lord Spencer at the castle, when they were set upon and stabbed to death. " It has been said," Lord Morley writes, " that the nineteenth century had seen the course of its history twenty-five times diverted by actual or attempted crime. In that sinister list the murders in the Phœnix Park have a tragic place." [2] For one horrified moment every eye turned to Parnell ; but there could be no mistaking his innocence. He bore too obviously the marks of having received from the crime a blow which seemed to him nothing less than

[1] Holland's *Life of the Duke of Devonshire*, i. 353:
[2] *Life of Gladstone*, iii. 68.

fatal ; prostrated and despairing he called on Mr Gladstone on the morning after the murders to tell him that he felt unable to do any more for Ireland ; he was with real difficulty restrained from resigning his seat. That first horror relieved, there emerged from the inevitably re-newed conflict of political views a dignity of spirit which forbade any bandying to and fro of the tragedy. Whether in the bearing of those whose personal loss was cruel or of those whose political work was for the time ruined, whether in the language of the Press or of the House of Commons, there was no reckless accusation, no bitterness of re-crimination. Years afterwards it could even be written that " the crime cleared the air like a disastrous storm, and made possible the beginning of better relations be-tween the English and Irish." [1] That is not true of the state of feeling at the moment. The murders did certainly produce a softening, even a wonderful softening, of hearts, in which no wild words were permitted ; but English feeling returned at once to its fixed point. On 11th May Sir William Harcourt introduced a new Crimes Bill, and Ireland was put back under coercion and abnormal pro-cesses of law for the detection of the murderers. Irish members fought the Bill, even with violence in the House, but it was quickly passed. Indeed, the condition of Ireland seemed to justify the most stern Tory view. Parnell's worst fears of what might happen while he was in prison were realised. He had lost control, and for the time being was too bitterly stricken to attempt to regain it. The Land League without his guidance plunged help-lessly. The Invincibles, a Fenian organisation which hardly affected to conceal its responsibility for the murders, " roved with knives about the streets of Dublin. Dis-content had stirred in the ranks of the Royal Irish Con-stabulary. . . . Over half the country the demoralisation of every class, the terror, the fierce hatred, the universal

[1] Holland's *Life of the Duke of Devonshire,* i. 353.

distrust, had grown to an incredible pitch. . . . The power of random arrest and detention under the Coercion Act of 1881 had not improved the moral of magistrates and police." [1]

In such conditions vaguely informed public opinion concentrated upon Ireland could only do harm. It happened fortunately that popular interest was suddenly drawn off, by the discovery that a riot in Alexandria on 12th June was an affair of the utmost seriousness. Fifty Europeans had been killed, and the troops under Arabi were raising new batteries round the harbour. The great mass of commonplace people in England never penetrated, during the ensuing events, much beyond the figure of Arabi himself. He was a rebel of some sort, and the reason for our being engaged in suppressing him gave no pause to the ordinary man. He knew that three years earlier, in June 1879, the Khedive Ismail of Egypt had been deposed in order to make way for a complete reconstruction of the financial position of his country. He knew also that in this reconstruction England had taken a leading part among the European Powers ; and it was obvious that the work could not go forward if the peace were disturbed. Roughly speaking, such a simplification of the facts had actually occurred by this time ; but for the authorities both in England and in Egypt the progress of events during the past eighteen months had been extremely baffling. The International Commission of Liquidation, whose main work had been to unify at a fixed rate of interest the immense mass of irregular unrelated loans raised by Ismail, had naturally been obliged, in securing the administration of the finances, to overhaul some departments of the public life of the country. The army, for very good reasons, had not been dealt with. For one thing, it was more unequivocally a Turkish affair than most of the questions in Egypt. The suzerainty of Turkey,

[1] Morley's *Life of Gladstone*, iii. 70.

a mere shadow in most respects, had been maintained over the army, and the permission to keep a standing army of 18,000 men was specifically given in the Sultan's new firman after Ismail's deposition. Any attempt, therefore, to bring the army into relation with the new life of Egypt was bound to be a delicate matter; and unluckily, when the attempt was made, it was unwisely handled. The presentation to the Khedive in January 1881 of a petition from the army seems to have been such an attempt, since it complained not only of arrears of pay, but also of a system of promotion based on anything but merit. But the petition further demanded the dismissal of Osman Rifki Pasha, the Turk who was Minister for War in the Egyptian Government, and showed generally so much anti-Turkish feeling that Riaz Pasha, the Khedive's Prime Minister, treated it as mutiny. Technically, no doubt, it was mutiny, but the plain course in that case was to take steps to secure some part of the army, and arrest the ringleaders. Riaz took the foolish step of sending for the two officers known to be chiefly responsible for the petition to appear before a Council of Ministers, hoping that his intention of conveying them from the council to prison would not be divined, and that the army, left leaderless, could then be reduced to discipline. Of course, the troops saw through the device, broke into the room where the Ministry was sitting, and rescued the two officers. They were Arabi Bey and Ali Bey Fehmi. The Khedive, caught with no force at his back, was compelled to overlook completely the rescue of the two colonels, and the army was given a sudden new sense of .power. In fact, the collapse of authority was so thorough that the army itself was scared, as people are apt to be when a door which they were making ready to force suddenly opens from within. The question arises : what is behind the door ? This nervousness, the fear of retribution at any moment, had produced the *émeute* of September 1881, which had vaguely brought

Egypt back to the mind of the English public.   An order
issued to the 3rd Regiment of Infantry—Arabi's regiment
—to proceed to Alexandria had been interpreted as a first
step towards punishment, by separating the leaders of the
movement.   Arabi with 2500 men and some artillery
marched to the Abdin palace, demanding to see the
Khedive.   The Khedive was at another palace, but under
the advice of Sir Auckland Colvin, the British Agent in
Cairo, he returned to Cairo—displaying no little courage—
and met Arabi, who dictated to him the dismissal of the
Ministry, the summoning of a parliament, and the raising
of the army to the full establishment allowed by the Sultan's
firman.   The Khedive acceded at once to the first demand,
on the condition that the two others were referred to
Turkey.

It will be noticed that in these demands a new element
appeared.   The phrase about summoning a parliament
was an open profession of co-operation between the army
and the Nationalist party in Egypt ; and this brings
us up to the year of our present survey—1882.   The
Nationalist party was not strong ; it was a group which
had come together in the days when Ismail's rather crude
interest in European progress had created an expectation
of experiments in constitutional government.   At the
beginning of 1882 the group had, however, attained some
importance, because, on the dismissal of the Riaz Ministry,
Cherif Pasha had been appointed Prime Minister, and he
had imbibed deeply the idea of constitutional experiments.
He had therefore persuaded the Khedive to agree to the
summoning of a Chamber of Notables, one of Ismail's
schemes, and it met in 1882.   The question of how far
Arabi's movement was a Nationalist one is at the root
of much of the controversy that has since taken place in
England.   Mr Wilfrid Blunt was in Egypt at this time, and
he wrote a letter to *The Times*, published on 6th February,
in which he asserted that the army had not made a political

move, and did not intend to make one. At the same time
the two movements could hardly be kept apart. Arabi
himself had remarked in a statement of his case that " the
army was the only power able to protect the growing
liberty of Egypt "[1]; and before many months were past
Mr Blunt was championing Arabi on the widest Nationalist
grounds. There was indeed some fusion of the two movements ; and it is traced by Lord Cromer to an unfortunate
mistake by the British Government.[2] In January 1882
Gambetta was still in power in France, and his ambition led
him to try to keep pace with British energy in Egypt.
He suggested a Joint Note to the Khedive, in which Lord
Granville, agreeing after some demur to its presentation,
let pass a phrase harmless enough in appearance but disastrous in effect. It was this : " The two governments,
being closely associated in the resolve to guard by their
united efforts against all cause of complication, internal
or external, which might menace the order of things
established in Egypt . . ." etc. Now the Chamber of
Notables had just met for the first time when the Note was
presented, and inevitably it saw the word " internal " in
the phrase just quoted as aimed at itself. In the resentment thus aroused the Arabists and the Nationalists were
thrown into one another's arms ; and the tone of the whole
Note, as thrusting back the Sultan's prerogative in
Egyptian affairs, took on a deeper colour. At that
moment Gambetta fell, and confusion was made worse
confounded by a sudden reversal of French policy. Under
M. de Freycinet, his successor, the party which believed
the whole Egyptian question to be a device of Germany's
for locking up French troops in Egypt prevailed ; the propulsion due to Gambetta in the direction of an Anglo-French
occupation ceased, and was replaced by a policy of inviting
Turkish intervention. It was a policy singularly difficult

---

[1] *The Times*, 3rd January 1882.
[2] *Modern Egypt*, i., cap. 13.

to direct at a time when the earlier policy had been carried far enough to irritate the Porte; but the British Government did its best. A conference of the Powers was invited to meet at Constantinople, to enter into consultation with the Porte with a view to military action by Turkey against Arabi under Anglo-French instructions. But the Porte at first refused to take part in the consultations; and when at length it did agree to do so, it wasted weeks in considering, altering, accepting, and withdrawing from the Anglo-French proposals. Meanwhile it had sent two more commissioners to Egypt with contradictory instructions, one to repudiate Arabi and the other to intrigue with him. Not unnaturally the " nerves " of the leading spirits in Egypt grew worse and worse under the delay.

Arabi, suspecting plots against himself, had forty-two officers and men arrested on a charge of conspiracy, and had Osman Rifki Pasha and forty others exiled to the furthest Soudan. The army was out of hand, its pay had been increased with no reference to the ability of the Budget to provide the money, and officers were being promoted absurdly. The riots in Alexandria in June, and Arabi's feverish entrenchment of himself in the forts, showed that the nervousness had become uncontrollable. The Powers, not being possessed of nerves, continued to confer, but a message was sent from the Sultan ordering discontinuance of work on the forts, and England invited the Powers generally to send ships to make an international demonstration off Alexandria, from which and from all the Delta the Christians were taking flight. The invitation was not accepted; and when, a month later, Arabi was defying the Sultan and mounting guns again in new forts, only a British squadron lay off the port.

The public at home, little concerned as to the origin of such a situation, waited on the tiptoe of excitement. It was not disappointed. At daybreak on 10th July Admiral Seymour, in command of the squadron, gave notice that, failing Arabi's compliance with the Sultan's orders and surrender of the forts within twenty-four hours, he should open fire. A night or two before, the ships had suddenly turned their electric lights upon the forts, and the startled gunners, not knowing but that the new flash might be some deadly form of gunnery, stampeded from the batteries.[1] When the bombardment began on 11th July they were far from stampeding, and their reply from the forts was not ineffective ; they had big and powerful guns to handle. But by five o'clock in the afternoon the bombardment had done its work, and Arabi's troops were in flight. A certain irresoluteness on the part of the British Government showed itself in the absence of any orders to the fleet beyond the bombardment. No force was landed, and in the general disaster of the flight Alexandria was set on fire, and immense damage done. However, on the whole the policy of merely taking each question as it arose was for the present not unsuccessful. When it became clear that Turkey's suspicions and dilatoriness were unsurmountable, the British Government made ready more *ad interim* steps. Sir Garnet Wolseley was sent out to Egypt before July was over, with an expeditionary force, the line taken now being the necessity of protecting the Suez Canal, as the Egyptian troops were practically at large in the Delta. Arabi had in fact written a letter to Mr Gladstone, offering him an allied Egypt which would keep open England's road to India, but threatening, if he were attacked, to bring about a general.Mohammedan rising and the destruction of the Canal.

In little more than two years this Government, which had come into power to end foreign embroilments, had become engaged in war, and involved in a conflict of interests as hazardous as any of Beaconsfield's. France,

[1] *The Times*, 10th July 1882.

at the time of Wolseley's operations, " resumed her liberty of action in Egypt," and England recognised the end of the Dual Control [1] ; so that a very present source of international disagreement had definitely opened. The measure of this distortion of the hopes and intentions of Liberals in 1880 was given by the resignation of John Bright from the Government. He declined on his Quaker principles to be a party to the prosecution of war ; and though Mr Gladstone felt that Bright had shown insufficient appreciation of the " facts of the case with the obligations that they appeared to entail," [2] it is not difficult to see the general justification of his action. The mind of England was running again on the barren glorifications that he hated. The rare spectacle of a fleet in action had stimulated popular imagination, and the armoured train with its Gatling guns, which was used for reconnaissances from Alexandria, was almost like a new toy to the public. Later in the year there was great disappointment because the authorities refused a request from the City of London that British and Indian soldiers from Egypt might be allowed to take part in the Lord Mayor's Show. It was a condition of popular temper which might well be too much for John Bright. Nor could it but confirm that detachment of idealistic forces from politics which has been mentioned. This Government seemed indeed indistinguishable from any other Government ; and Parliament had at the same time a curiously helpless aspect. A peculiarity of its work just now, which was commented upon with some gloom, was the number of temporary measures of legislation.[3] The Employers' Liability Act of 1880 was to terminate in 1887 ; the Corrupt Practices Acts were all limited in duration ; the powers of the Railway Commissioners were not perpetual ; a measure to

[1] Cromer's *Modern Egypt.*
[2] Morley's *Life of Gladstone,* iii. 83.
[3] *The Times,* 12th July 1882.

remove restrictions on the negotiation of promissory notes was valid for only three years ; a measure dealing with habitual drunkards was to remain in force until 1890. Parliament seemed to mistrust its own efforts. Moreover it did its work with great difficulty, and had to face this year a profound alteration of its procedure. Closure of debate, so much discussed in the previous year, took shape in a new Standing Order permitting the Speaker or Chairman of Committee to bring debate to an end by putting the question on a motion being made to that effect, provided that division on the motion showed not less than two hundred members for the closure, or not less than a hundred when the opposition to the motion showed less than forty members. It was not a severe resolution, in view of later steps of the same kind. Yet it was much disliked ; and Lord Randolph Churchill found it a good stick for beating the Government. That it was necessary is clear enough, when we find the Government programme again " carrying over " such measures as the Bankruptcy Bill, the County Government Bill, and the Municipality of London Bill. Other questions, too, were accumulating for Ministers. For instance, several great inland towns were pressing for an assimilation of excise procedure with that of customs, the grievance being that, whereas at ports the customs arrangements allowed " bonding " on a large scale, there was no such possibility in inland towns, except in some " wet " trades. A few towns—Manchester, Leeds, Halifax and Bradford—were by a fiction treated as ports ; other big places like Birmingham, Sheffield and Wolverhampton had no way of " bonding " dry goods.

However, while idealists were standing so far aloof from the proceedings of Parliament, an Act was passed which was to give them the widest possible scope in that sphere of " administration " which they so much affected—the Municipal Corporations Act 1882. It did not attract notice at the time, being nominally designed for the consolidation of all the amending and supplementary Acts which had been passed since the Municipal Corporations Act 1835. Some such consolidation was indeed necessary, owing to the perpetual accretion of duties under laws like the Public Health Act of 1875, the Contagious Diseases (Animals) Act 1878, and the Weights and Measures Act 1878. Moreover reform was still called for in the matter of old, sometimes corrupt, corporations which had survived the Act of 1835. There were still bodies like the Mayor and Burgesses of Dunwich, an almost extinct village, who were entitled to receive copies of all public documents from the Stationery Office; the Mayor and Barons of Corfe Castle, who had the patronage of a number of sinecure salaries; and the Corporation of New Romney, who disposed among themselves of an income of £800 from municipal lands. The new Act, by making burgess-ship purely a franchise, and not an office, effected a final reform. The important feature of the Act, however, was that, while specifying the obligatory work of a municipality (such as the provision of necessary establishments, the maintenance of local police, etc.), the Act did not circumscribe its functions. In other words, while setting forth what a corporation *must* do—not on any exacting scale—it refrained from putting any statutory limit to what it *might* do. The limitations in that respect were judiciously left to the natural human objection to paying heavy rates. This stroke of peculiarly English genius arouses the enthusiasm of a foreign observer like Professor Redlich.[1] The things that a corporation might do, instead of being subject to the approval of a bureaucratic department, remained in the sphere of private bill legislation; and thus Parliament, and not a department, is the final authority. The wide democratic franchise under the Act, including all ratepayers of twelve months' residence before 15th July in any year, and not excluding women, pro-

[1] In his book, *The Local Government of England.*

vided both a stimulus and a check ; the corporation would
be anxious to retain the support of the citizens by progressive measures, and at the same time any overloading
of the town with debt would show its result in the ballot
boxes.   " Rate collectors far more than any central Boards
of Control are the real schoolmasters of municipal policy." [1]

In the national life generally the year was marked by a
return of better temper.   Trade was good ; reconsideration of rents had somewhat eased the farmer ; the cereal
harvest was fair, and the root harvest good.   The social
world was enlivened by a greater disposition on the part
of the Queen to be seen.   It may be mentioned in passing
that the last of the few attempts on her life took place on
2nd March, when a man, who was subsequently adjudged
a lunatic, fired a pistol at her as she was driving out of
Windsor station.   There was, it is true, a singularly heavy
death-roll of notable men.   On 3rd January Harrison
Ainsworth died, out of humour with a world which his
later novels had failed to attract, and in which he had not
succeeded as the man of fashion he wished to be.   On 4th
January Bernal Osborne made his exit from a London
where he had kept alive the witty traditions of the days
of Alvanley.   Dante Gabriel Rossetti died on 11th April,
in the midst of the period when the Pre-Raphaelite movement was being violently spread abroad by the general
æsthetic craze.   The death of Darwin on 20th April
brought from abroad such unprecedented appreciations
of an Englishman's work that this country became conscious in a new way of the achievement represented by the
evolutionary theory ; and this may account in some degree
for that outbreak of extreme antagonism between scientific
research and orthodox theology which reverberated
through the middle eighties.   Dr Pusey died on 17th
September ; and the occasion served for articles reminding
a generation much entangled in Ritualist controversies,

[1] Redlich's *Local Government*, i. 393.

in the imprisonment of recalcitrant clergymen, that only
a vulgar confusion could have made the word "Puseyism"
synonymous with advanced ritualism; his mystical
conception of the Church and her work, founded on a
wonderful knowledge of early Christian writers, remained
throughout his life indissolubly linked with a piety of the
Wesleyan rather than the Tractarian spirit. On 4th
December died a very different Churchman, Archbishop
Tait. He had had stormy years of rule, yet he preserved
to the end that belief in a sweet reasonableness which
he was always ready to apply. His last application of it
came before public notice within a week of his death.
He had effected a compromise in the St Alban's case,
by which Mr Mackonochie was transferred to St Peter's,
London Docks. It did not in the least conciliate anti-
ritualists.

In the revival of trade the shortage of gold grew more
troublesome. Some of the responsibility for it was put
down to the prosperity of the working classes, which caused
"a large absorption of gold"; and it was this aspect of the
problem which brought to the front this year a proposal
for issuing one-pound Bank of England notes. Another
aspect which worried the financial authorities was the
question of meeting the wear and tear of the gold currency.
Short supplies of the metal caused the coins to remain
long in circulation; and the result was that the currency
was falling dangerously in real value. This point, however,
may be postponed until the time when the Treasury at
last attacked it. The South African goldfields were coming more into the public eye; there had been a "rush"
to the De Kaap fields, and "placer" mining was not unsuccessful. But the men with money were showing themselves more cautious than the men without, although it
was pretty well known that only mining on a large scale,
with heavy machinery, could work the deposits thoroughly.
For the time being fortunes were made in other ways.

Nitrates just then were making millionaires ; and the experience of American farmers in fattening stock was causing almost a boom here in oilcake, and new speculations in cotton-seed oil works.

It is not, after all, these signs of a solid prosperity that most give the year its air of better spirits. That is to be found rather in such a revelation as is provided by the immense and serious interest taken in the removal of Jumbo to America. Jumbo was the great elephant at the Zoological Gardens—the largest that had ever been seen out of the native lands of elephants—but he might have been thought to be otherwise an ordinary elephant until it was suddenly announced at the end of January that Barnum, an American showman, had bought him for £2000, and was going to transport him across the water. The whole nation was stirred. Some disputed furiously as to whether he had or had not been a difficult animal to handle, and whether his keeper's statement that his temper had grown queer was or was not a mere excuse to cover his removal. Others, equally serious, called in question the legal right of the " Zoo " to dispose of animals without obtaining in some way the consent of the nation. Lighter-hearted folk jested, often as ponderously as the subject could require ; songs sprang up in the streets, and Jumbo practically filled the ordinary man's mind until, two months later, the departure took place. It was described as fully as if it had been the departure of a prince. The adventures of the enormous crate in which Jumbo was drawn to the docks by a long string of horses, the quarters provided for him on board ship, were all set forth by every newspaper in the land ; and Lady Burdett-Coutts went on board to give him his last London bun. The public's cheerful readiness to be amused had another opportunity in August, when Cetewayo came to England. Responsible people were shaking their heads about his visit, and it had, in fact, been once postponed ; it was not long since he and his Zulu people had been in arms against us, and the question of his restoration to the chieftainship, which he undoubtedly hoped to forward by his visit, caused some nervousness. But London only saw in him a stout, genial, black potentate, whose bellicose prestige they could pardon because, if it had cost the English something to beat him, he had at any rate very handsomely worried the Boers. So people gathered in crowds at Melbury House, Kensington, where he stayed, to see him drive out. He paid visits to both the Queen and the Prince of Wales ; and he managed to keep up his imperturbability until he was taken to Woolwich Arsenal, and then he confessed that he had really been overwhelmed with astonishment at the sights and sounds and resources of England ever since he had landed.

The newest marvels of civilisation were continuing their advances. The year is notable in the history of electric lighting for the fact that a new step, described by Professor Sylvanus Thompson in a scientific lecture in March, had been taken by the invention of " little electric lamps made by enclosing in glass bulbs thin wires of platinum or thin strips of carbon which on the passage of an electric current grow white hot "[1] ; the importance of the invention for domestic lighting was at once seen. The immediate sequel was a series of disputes as to patents between rival inventors, chiefly Mr Edison and Mr Swan. The use of arc lamps for street lighting had meanwhile so thoroughly established itself (Birmingham, Brighton, Canterbury, Newbury, Sheffield and East London had installed it) that the great corporations, led by Manchester, were on the alert against possible monopolies; and the Government had in hand an Electric Lighting Bill designed to regulate the foundation of companies. The Bill ultimately included a clause giving local authorities power of compulsory purchase of electric light undertakings at the end of twenty-

[1] *The Times,* 18th March 1882.

one years. The telephone was conquering long distances ; in July experiments were made in speaking from Brussels to Paris, and in December a line was working between Brighton and London. But as yet the National Telephone Company's revenue was no more than £27,000 in the year, and its profits £4217.[1] Tramway experiments moved more slowly ; a car, worked from accumulators under the seats, was tried at Leytonstone in March. A minor invention of the year which should not miss a place in this record is the fountain pen ; the stylograph had been in use for some time, but late in this year descriptions were published of the application of the reservoir principle to a pen with a detachable double-pointed nib.[2] Nor need one hesitate to attach to the march of progress the tentative prominence attained this year by the advocates of " rational dress." A lecture in February by Mr Frederick Treves on the unhygienic dress of women was followed in March by an exhibition organised by the National Health Society of hygienic dresses, the patterns being gathered chiefly from America and Germany ; they included " divided skirts," but the mocker was not yet aroused.

So much indeed was progress in the air that the Londoner's dissatisfaction with his own local government grew acute. A month could not pass without some complaint either against vestries or against the Metropolitan Board of Works ; of the former this one or that was slow to lay down wooden paving (1880 had seen much activity in that work), while the latter was attacked because of the smell of sewers, or petty interference with private building projects. From this atmosphere of complaint about the merest trivialities of local control the Londoner looked out and saw the provincial corporations, not niggling over petty duties, but launching out into all sorts of public services. He found himself under a form of government

[1] *The Times*, 19th August 1882.
[2] Ditto, 6th December 1882.

which derived no fresh strength from the new Municipal Corporations Act, because it was not a corporation ; and for the same reason had but the meanest responsibility towards the citizens. The demand for a municipality of London becametherefore one of the items of regular appearance in political speeches of this time. It happened that the autumn provided two striking examples of the courage of provincial corporations. In October the Manchester Ship Canal project first became of interest to the country at large ; Alderman Bosdin Leech, of that city, was writing letters to the Press to enlist the public attention. The scheme was unanimously approved at a town's meeting held in Manchester on 14th November, and although there was naturally some apprehension as to the cost of the undertaking, the prospect of direct importation of goods to Manchester was a powerful argument, especially as only in the previous year the cotton trade had been seriously hampered by a " cornering " of cotton in Liverpool, and a period of gambling which had raised the price of raw cotton by 10 to 20 per cent. The other piece of remarkable municipal energy was the progress of the scheme for supplying Liverpool with water from the Welsh hills ; the laying of the great mains through Delamere Forest at the end of this year was a picturesque period of the work. But the provincial corporations were by now influencing the community in more subtle ways than these. A great Art and Industrial Exhibition was held this year in Manchester ; and William Morris, speaking at the opening ceremony, was able to point to a general improvement in industrial art. The work of all the local schools of manual art, which had slowly been established in the large industrial centres, of the Workmen's Institutes, the Athenæums, and other such places, was beginning to tell. A Royal Commission was sitting, which, imperfectly appreciated though it was at the time, ended by altering entirely the aims and scope of national education

4

—the Commission on Technical Instruction. It was the recognition of all the local schools, and so the first step towards their expansion into a system of higher education.

General Wolseley did not keep the nation waiting long for news from Egypt. Moving rapidly, he attacked Arabi at Tel-el-Kebir on 13th September—one of the notable night attacks of military history—inflicting a complete defeat on his troops, and taking him prisoner, with other leaders of his army. No memory remained now of a Nationalist character in the movement ; Arabi was called a mere military adventurer, Egypt had had to be " rescued from him," his foot had been " on her throat " ; and a general impression that the war was over led to the commutation a few months later of the sentence of death passed upon Arabi by the court martial in Cairo on 3rd December. He and six of his associates left Egypt for exile on 26th December. It seemed that the Government, pottering on from point to point, had come out of the business fairly well after all. They directed their agent in Cairo, now Lord Dufferin, to proceed with a rehabilitation of Egyptian finances in view of a speedy withdrawal of the British troops. But their lack of a clear purpose in Egypt showed itself now in the fact that, while speaking of withdrawal, they were lending an ear to considerations which could not possibly be reconciled with withdrawal. Upper Egypt was the last great stronghold, it was thought, of slavery, and the licences to trade in the Soudan, which were issued by the Egyptian Government, were more or less open licences for slave-raiding. Consequently even those Liberals who had been least inclined to continue a policy of interference in Lower Egypt now began to confuse Mr Gladstone's mind by pressing upon him duties in Upper Egypt. We miss much of the difficulty of the Egyptian struggles of the next few years, and the true nature of Gordon's mission to Khartoum, unless we see that Mr Gladstone's lack of any real interest in the Egyptian question rendered him peculiarly open to conflicting impulsions from different sections of his followers. The suppression of slavery was an old ideal, and the zeal to pursue it in the Soudan is one of the reasons why Tel-el-Kebir is the beginning, and not the end, of a story. Another reason had recently been causing anxiety in Egypt itself. Just at the time when Arabi's movement had been growing strongest in Cairo, in August 1881, a man in the Soudan had proclaimed himself Mahdi—an assumption of direct spiritual kinship with Mohammed, and divine inspiration—and the universal hatred there of the Egyptian Government secured him an immediate following. But no real knowledge of what was going on in Upper Egypt prevailed among those well-intentioned people who were pressing the slave trade upon Mr Gladstone's attention.

On the whole the year ended not amiss for him and his colleagues, and the foundation of the National Liberal Club at a large meeting on 5th November was an enthusiastic mustering of new forces. In Ireland the Crimes Act, putting an end to those activities of the Land League which had survived in the Ladies' Land League, had been helped in its effect by the loss of heart in the Irish party after the Phœnix Park murders. It may be mentioned here, since Patrick Egan rendered his accounts of the Land League funds to Parnell in October of this year, that the League had handled the sum of £244,820. Of this, in round figures, £50,000 had gone to relief of distress ; £15,000 to the expenses of trials ; £148,000 had been spent by the League and the Ladies' League in support of evicted tenants, the erection of wooden houses for them, defence against ejectments, etc.[1] The cases of agrarian crime now fell from 4439 in 1881 to 3432 in 1882 ; but the true state of the case is better shown by the fact that for 1883 the figures dropped with a run to 870. We see

[1] Parnell Commissioners' Report, p. 96.

Mr Gladstone himself, according to one of his Cabinet,
taking a " *couleur-de-rose* view " of the condition of Ireland.[1] Egypt appeared to have been successfully dealt
with ; and the summing up of the Government's position
on the traditional occasion of the Guildhall Banquet was
that they had done well, and that the Conservatives had
no good fighting ground ; Lord Randolph Churchill's
" Balaclava charges " were magnificent, but not war.[2]
The autumn and winter were singularly free from labour
troubles. In the early part of the year there had been
some anxiety in London; a large deputation of unemployed
men waited upon the Lord Mayor, representing printers,
carpenters, bricklayers, painters, warehousemen, navvies
and smiths. Except in its combination of a number of
unrelated trades, this deputation hardly amounted to the
faintest mutter of the storms of a few years later ; and the
winter brought no distressing signs of lack of employment.
The vitality of the Socialist movement was, however,
apparent in the revival of the newspaper *Freiheit*, in spite
of a general refusal of printing firms to publish it. At the
same time the prosecution of a paper called *The Free-
thinker* on a charge of blasphemous libel was attended by
comments which showed that even the respectable world
was inclined to think that it was a mistake to aim at
suppressing such organs of opinion. " Whether from
growth of charity, or indifference, or perplexity, or experience of the mischievousness of persecution," *The
Times* remarked, " most men are not inclined to put in
prison the apostles of the views which they most detest,
and they are rather at a loss what to do with persecuting
laws which remain unrepealed." [3] The socialists, fighting
for their own freedom of speech, have often since fought
for freedom in other than political matters ; and in the

[1] Holland's *Life of the Duke of Devonshire*, i. 369.
[2] *The Times*, 10th November 1882,
[3] 19th July 1882.

struggles of the eighties for the liberty of street-corner meetings socialism and irreligion were confused together, as we have already seen them confused in the case of Mr Bradlaugh's seat in Parliament.

A subject which attained no little public discussion in the autumn of 1882 was the idea of cremating the dead. Two persons who died about that time had left instructions in their wills that their bodies were to be burned. No facilities existed for carrying out the instructions ; nevertheless the bodies were burned, and the subject continued to be so much written about that within a few years the difficulties experienced in regard to these early cremations were entirely removed.

CHAPTER V

1883 : A YEAR OF GROUNDSWELL

AS the Government's tenure of office extended, it became more and more clear that the Liberal victory of 1880 had been due rather to a revulsion from Disraelian policy than to any arraying by the Liberal leaders of the progressive forces of the country. By this time the temporary bond had fallen asunder, and the year was marked in every direction by a futile restlessness. The Egyptian question had brought about a coolness with France, an atmosphere in which any subject of dispute might become very dangerous. The Irish question reeked once more of dynamite. The forces of social reform and moral effort moved in a world agitated by strikes, and those of material reform saw the spectre of cholera looming across the waste of bad housing and sanitary deficiencies.

The " resumption of liberty " in Egypt, which had been the French attitude towards the bombardment of Alexandria, revealed itself in certain respects at the beginning of the year in Cairo as a complete breaking up of the Control. Unfortunately Baring, who had displayed a peculiar gift for investing the Control with a loose working equipment in which points of punctilio could not arise, was in India.[1] He did not return to Egypt until June 1883. Meanwhile a quarrel was brewing in regard to the Suez Canal. The irritation of shipowners at what they regarded as excessive levies for the passage of the Canal had issued in a proposal that application should be made to the Khedive for a concession for a second canal, parallel with the existing one,

[1] He was Financial Member of the Viceroy's Council.

the idea being rendered plausible by the argument that in any case the amount of the traffic demanded a second waterway. This, however, did not help the shipowners, for M. de Lesseps, the builder of the existing canal, claimed a monopoly for his enterprise, and a prior right to any concession for a second ; he had a draft agreement in readiness for its construction at a cost of eight millions.[1] The French authorities saw in the proposal another sign of England's determination to secure to herself every advantage in Egypt, by tricking them out of their chief remaining source of power there. Towards the close of the year the dispute took a different direction, the English demand being now for the acceptance by the Suez Canal Board of an advisory committee of shipowners. De Lesseps was himself in England at the time, and was being entertained in Manchester, where the citizens hoped for the support of his name for the Ship Canal project. He avoided committing himself to that ; and took instead every opportunity of insisting upon the autonomy of the Suez Canal Board. It was, indeed, a period of bad blood between the two nations in which an amicable settlement of such a question, however much either side may have had its legitimate grievances, was impracticable. In July there was an ugly outburst of feeling in England, caused by rumours that the French flag had been hoisted in the New Hebrides ; the demand was instantly raised that the New Hebrides should be formally annexed to Australia, and that, to make complete use of the opportunity, New Guinea should be annexed at the same time. Barely a week later reports reached England of the arrest of a British subject by a French admiral at Tamatave, in Madagascar. The island had been under French influence for two hundred years, but this treatment of it as a French possession was not to be allowed to pass. Luckily the British subject, who had been deported to Réunion, was released six weeks later,

[1] *The Times*, 24th July 1883.

and that incident was closed.[1]   It may be noted here that the state of our relations with France in 1883 settled a question which of late years had agitated a good many minds.   Early in 1881 the scheme for a tunnel under the Channel to connect England and France by railway had made a sudden advance.   Borings had been undertaken at Dover, and as a result detailed estimates of cost had been made possible.   Now the English military authorities, headed by Sir Garnet Wolseley, declared against the project ;   they said they could not assure the country against invasion by the tunnel, and an Anti-Channel-Tunnel Association was formed.   The promoters, however, went forward, and introduced a private Bill into Parliament, which came before a Joint Committee of the two Houses in April 1883.   It reported in July against the Bill, though not unanimously.   The military evidence had carried the day.[2]

The distortion which had been given to the Irish situation by the Phœnix Park murders only became fully apparent in this year.   In Ireland itself difficulties diminished ;   the statistics of agrarian crime fell, as has already been mentioned, to 870 ;   evictions fell from 5201 to 3643 ;   and agitation by speeches and all the forms of boycotting diminished greatly.   But alarm and panic shifted to England ;   dynamite explosions occurred in London, and there were a number of seizures of explosives by the police.   The " Kilmainham Treaty " had been disliked by the Clan-na-Gael ;   and Parnell's attitude after the Phœnix Park murders would have led to an open repudiation of him but for his useful gift of never being agreeable to the English.[3]   We have seen that he had felt in Kilmainham gaol the danger of leaving the field to less cautious persons ;   and the helplessness that overwhelmed

[1] *The Times*, 1st September 1883.
[2] Ditto, 19th July 1883.
[3] Barry O'Brien's *Life of Parnell*, i. 377.

him at the news of the Phœnix Park murders prevented his recovering his influence over the Clan-na-Gael. Therefore, while he could and did moderate the pace of agitation in Ireland, he had lost for the moment his general hold on violence ; and the London explosions were the result. It was the Invincibles' year, and it opened with one of the most famous dramatic moments in criminal records. The Crimes Act of 1882 had rendered possible processes of arrest which had placed under lock and key a number of men suspected of complicity in the Phœnix Park murders. By the middle of January nineteen men were in detention. Two informers had given assistance to the police, but the prisoners did not really fear the evidence of these two. Then, as they filed into the dock one day during the preliminary proceedings, they saw one of their own number divert his steps, and their defiant confidence was over. The scene when James Carey took the witness-stand has been described by more capable pens, and need not be retold here. His evidence convicted six men, and two pleaded guilty. Six were sentenced to death, but the sentence on one was commuted. Five men were hanged, Brady, Curley, Fagan, Kelly and Caffrey ; and Delaney, Mullet and Fitzharris were sent to penal servitude for life. The Invincibles were not men to sink into obscurity after such events. Throughout the first half of the year they were the bogey at which suburban England continued to shiver. The newspapers canvassed the identity of the terrible " Number One," who had appeared in the Kilmainham evidence to be a power horribly supreme. The British Government made friendly representations to the Government of the United States on the hatching of Irish-American plots in that country ; Fenian brotherhoods were reported to be devoting Sunday excursions up the Hudson River to the amiable purpose of experimenting with explosives. The Home Office stimulated local authorities in England to a more vigorous search for dynamite, and more alertness to

its possible manufacture in their districts ; and prohibited
in the public interest an exhibition of explosives which
was to have been held in all innocence in Sheffield. On
the top of all this the Invincibles showed that the popular
notion of their organisation was not exaggerated. On July
30th a man, who had attracted no notice among his fellow-
passengers, was shot dead on board a liner which had just
reached East London, Natal. He was Carey the Informer.
The police protection which had sufficed to screen him
entirely from the eyes of the world at large, and ship him
off in complete secrecy to South Africa, had not saved him
from the Invincibles. Beside this *coup* their other violences of the year seemed almost tame. On 15th March
an explosion took place at the Local Government Board
offices ; it caused no loss of life or serious injury, and not
much damage to any part of the building beyond the
windows ; but it remains a famous explosion, because it
was the return of a terror that men had begun to forget.
On 30th October two explosions occurred on the Underground Railway, one at Praed Street Station, and one
between Charing Cross and Westminster. In both cases
some persons were injured, but no one was killed.

If Parnell had lost his grip on this current of Irish
agitation, he had certainly not lost the confidence of Ireland. It became known during this year that in his zeal
for the cause he had let his family estates and his own
financial position become heavily encumbered. A public
subscription was set on foot, and it acquired a more than
passing interest, because it was the means of bringing into
public notice what has been known as the Errington
incident. In 1881 the English Government had had the
curious notion of getting aid from the Vatican in dealing
with Ireland. At first the idea was only that the Vatican
might restrain priests in Ireland from supporting agitation ;
and Mr Gladstone, in a letter to Cardinal Newman,
expressed the opinion that it was the Pope's positive duty

to exercise this restraint.[1] With that object, documents
detailing the attitude of certain priests had been conveyed
to Rome by Mr George Errington, an Irish Roman Catholic
gentleman, who had gone there for the purpose. He was
not, Mr Gladstone was careful to explain, an official
emissary, but a volunteer in the matter. However, as he
had gone with letters from Lord Granville, and as his
despatches were deposited in the Foreign Office, the distinction is insignificant. It would be hard to find any real
difference between the position of Mr Errington at Rome
in 1881 and the position of, say, Lord Odo Russell in the
late sixties. No representative of the British Government
could be acknowledged an " official " representative at the
Vatican, since that would have implied a recognition of the
temporal power of the Pope. But just as Lord Odo Russell
was to all intents and purposes a Minister Plenipotentiary,
so Mr Errington was an Envoy Extraordinary in all but the
name. Cardinal Newman had held out little encouragement to Mr Gladstone to look for Papal intervention, and
none came at that time. It did come in 1883, in connection
with this national tribute to Parnell, and the result of it
showed that the Vatican's first decision had been the wiser.
A Papal rescript against the tribute was issued. Up to
that moment the sum collected had been £7000, and six
months after the rescript it was £37,000. Mr Gladstone in
after days told Mr Barry O'Brien that the acceptance by
the Government of the Errington mission had been chiefly
due to Lord Spencer.[2]

The influence of the Irish question on the Parliamentary
year of 1883 was rather indirect. The obstruction of recent
years had been met for the moment with the Closure
resolutions ; but the effect of it had gone deeper than the
immediate result. The House, in long and trying sessions,
had been feeling that it must strike out some new lines of

[1] Morley's *Life of Gladstone*, iii. 52.
[2] Barry O'Brien's *Life of Parnell*, ii. 26.

dividing its work, if it was to have time for real discussions of policy. It had the high ideal of not bounding its view by the legislative necessities of the day : " Parliament is not merely a legislative body. It is the Grand Inquest of the nation charged, in addition to its legislative duties, with the custody of Imperial interests, and called upon to lead and to form the public opinion of the time.[1] " The institution of Grand Committees, to relieve the House of some of its work, was the first attempt of Parliament to keep its head, so to speak, above water. These Committees, empanelled by the Committee of Selection, were two in number—the Grand Committee on Law and the Grand Committee on Trade.[2] They were sanctioned by the Commons in 1882, but went to work for the first time in 1883, relieving the House of the necessity under which it had hitherto laboured of forming itself into committee on every Bill other than a private Bill. By the new arrangement a considerable quantity of work was delegated. Two other attempts to save time were now in progress. In 1882 a Department of Agriculture had been proposed, and in 1883 a Department for Scotland was a prominent subject of discussion. Both were the butts for somewhat easy sarcasm ; the Board of Agriculture, it was said, would not know what to do with itself, and as for a Department for Scotland, there was not more logical reason for setting it up than for setting up a Department for Yorkshire. However, the scheme went forward ; and Lord Rosebery's assistance in working out the details was perhaps his first important public service. For the rest Parliament had but a stale bill of fare. Bankruptcy legislation was still before it, a reforming Act being passed this year ; County Government (with its attendant subjects of London Municipal

---

[1] *The Times*, 6th January 1881.

[2] The committees were not altogether invented at this time. Sir T. Erskine May found precedents, upon which the committees were designed.

reform, and especially a reform of the water supply authority) and the county franchise had not yet been touched.
The last was the most vital of the subjects, for Lord Randolph Churchill was devoting himself to it. He was arguing that the enfranchisement of the agricultural labourer
was not called for, even by the labourer himself, and that
a rearrangement of boroughs and a redistribution of seats
would be the truer franchise reform at the moment.[1] The
failure of the Affirmation Bill of this session has been
recorded [2]; it was the last expenditure of the time of this
Parliament on the controversy that had arisen about Mr
Bradlaugh's right to take his seat. In spite of Mr Gladstone's eloquence, in spite of a widely spread feeling that it
was unwise to mix dislike of Mr Bradlaugh's opinions with
the general question of preserving in Parliament a religious
test which had elsewhere disappeared, the Bill was rejected
on 3rd May. But at least this particle of good resulted—
that there was agreement henceforth to leave time to do
the work—time and the ultimate disappearance of conditions in which the question was useful to an Opposition
somewhat poorly equipped. How ready the Opposition
was to adopt weapons from any quarter is seen in their
immediate following of the Liberals' idea of a huge political
club, which should give the social amenities of such institutions to men of political inclinations who could not hope
for admission to the older clubs. Two months after the
meeting for the promotion of the National Liberal Club,
one was held by the Conservatives to found the Constitu-
tional.Club. Both places may be, and have been, regarded
cynically by those of Pall Mall and St James's Street.
The historian's interest in them is that they were the first
clubs in which considerations other than those of social
fitness were recognised in the election of candidates, and
in which political opinions became a qualification.[3]

[1] *The Times*, 12th April 1883. [2] See p. 41.
[3] The Carlton and the Reform, though broadly Tory and Liberal,
do not technically require the holding of certain political opinions

It is remarkable that the year saw no fewer than eight Sunday Closing Bills before Parliament, three of them applicable to the whole country and five to separate localities. This, like the growing strength of the Local Veto movement, is an interesting reminder that the Blue Ribbon Army was at the time making great strides. It had been founded in 1878 on the model of an organisation which had been very successful in the United States. Mr William Noble, who had for some years before that date been a prominent platform speaker in the cause of temperance, on returning from a tour in the States enlisted the interest of several philanthropists and took the Standard Theatre, Shoreditch, which was then untenanted. His ardent zeal was so contagious that for nearly two years, from February 1878 till January 1880, he continued to fill that place with audiences ; and when he was compelled to leave it, because of its approaching demolition, the Blue Ribbon Army was already a great force, and the pledge cards used by Mr Noble were in demand all over the country. English distaste for the parading of opinions must have been undergoing curious modifications when it was possible to note, among the striking events of a year, the spread of two such organisations as the Blue Ribbon Army and the Salvation Army.[1] The latter, indeed, was fighting its way in a very literal sense. We have already had occasion to note the hostility it called forth, and an actual organisation of a sort had arisen to combat it. The " Skeleton Army " has been forgotten now ; it appeared in 1883, fighting the Salvation Army outside the Eagle Tavern in the City Road, and these encounters occurred persistently, Sunday after Sunday. Both the Salvation Army and the Blue Ribbon Army (and we may perhaps

as a qualification. Brooks's, again, is broadly Liberal, but that is a survival of its original character as the Whigs' Club, and Whiggism was always as much a social as a political qualification.

[1] *The Times*, 30th December 1882.

mention with these the missions of Moody and Sankey, who returned to England in 1883, and were in Liverpool and Manchester in March and in London in November) were elements in that reconsideration of a nation's duty towards its less fortunate members, which was replacing the individualism of the great industrial expansion. Crude as the Salvation Army's methods appeared, the way for educated people to meet them was seen to be by doing the work better ; and this was more than an intellectual retort. The death of Arnold Toynbee, on 11th March 1883, served to bring to light suddenly a whole world of sociological enthusiasm, of zeal and affection for the unfortunate, which had been steadily modifying the trend of politico-economical thought; and when the knowledge of Toynbee's own efforts turned men's minds to the poorer parts of our great cities, it was with the result of making them conclude that the Church of England was not behindhand in the new spirit, and that " in forty years the clergy had advanced immensely in public esteem," by their devotion to the practical as well as the spiritual work at their doors. Two distinct lines of thought were, in fact, tending towards the same end. The spiritual revival which began with Wesley and Whitefield, as an evangelising movement not parochial in its scope, had been followed by the more parochial, because more strictly canonical, revivalism of the Oxford Tractarians. While the religious spirit of the universities had been thus modified, the philosophical outlook underwent a change almost as profound under the domination of T. H. Green. He had but lately died—on 26th March 1882—and his lectures had been spoken of at his death as "the very heart of the philosophical education of Oxford." [1] The effect of his work had been to quicken the sense of social responsibility, and to raise up a school which both hastened the distrust of the old individualism, and presented a very guarded front to the new theories which the

[1] *The Times*, 27th March 1882;

popular mind was summing up in the phrase " the survival
of the fittest." The forces that came into view on the
death of Arnold Toynbee therefore were combined forces
of religious and secular impulse, and this dual character
has continued to be displayed in the Social Settlement
movement that arose with the foundation of Toynbee
Hall in 1884. There was, indeed, an earlier settlement
in existence. The Ancoats Brotherhood had been founded
in 1877 in Manchester by a devoted citizen, Mr Charles
Rowley. It was not specifically a University settlement,
but drew upon the services of any one who could be
attracted to the work. It was an isolated enterprise,
and not until after the death of Toynbee can there be
said to have been a Settlement movement. The movement crystallises for us several of the somewhat inchoate
aspirations of a new day. The settlements were to be
centres in the poorest parts of great cities for the dissemination of that humaner education without which
the improved conditions that were the workman's goal
would be but a barren achievement. They were to
help the educated classes to see that a sound Liberalism
must hope, not to raise the working man out of his class
but to produce a community of mental outlook between
classes. They were to help the masses of the poor to see
in knowledge their truest leadership, and to learn to
distinguish between knowledge and frothy acquisition
of political dogmas. Thus the Settlement movement
was partly, at least, the reply of the intellectual middle
class to the attitude of the artist-socialists. "Radicalism," William Morris wrote in this year, "is made by
and for the middle classes ; they will have no objection
to its *political* development, if they think they can
stop it there ; but as to real social changes they will
not allow them if they can help it." And again : "It is
obvious that the support to be looked for for constructive
socialism from the working classes at present is nought

. . . What we want is real leaders, themselves working men, and content to be so till classes are abolished. But you see when a man has gifts for that kind of thing he finds himself tending to rise out of his class." [1]   University settlements were the denial of both of these positions. Such advances as the Socialist movement made in 1883 were not spectacular. Some knowledge of the propagandist work that was being done may be gathered from the fact that late in August the question of the power of public authorities to prohibit meetings in such places as the London parks was being raised. Nervousness about these meetings was certainly growing, assisted perhaps by the dynamite explosions, which had nothing to do with them; for, when it was announced that the site of the disused Tothill Fields prison at Westminster had been bought by the Roman Catholics for their cathedral, the Government was sharply criticised for not keeping the site as a central depot for troops in case of rioting. Something of the same nervousness is visible also in the withdrawal of several members from the Cobden Club this year, because of the admission of one or two foreign politicians " of an advanced, not to say revolutionary, character." [2]   But though the socialists were clearly mustering some of the unemployed waste lives of London streets, they were not yet definitely mobilising them. In January Louise Michel came to England to lecture on the oppression and sweating of women in France, and to urge English people not to let the education of the girls of the working classes fall behind that of the boys. She spoke, as it happened, at a moment when women in this country had achieved a notable amelioration of their status. The Married Women's Property Act came into force at the beginning of this year, abolishing the old system under which a woman's property passed on her marriage into

[1] Mackail's *Life of William Morris*, ii. 103, 111
[2] *The Times*, 18th June 1883.

her husband's control. Henceforward a married woman could hold property and carry on business in her own right. One of the minor effects of the measure was to give particular interest to the debate on a Woman Suffrage Bill introduced by a private member in July. The question arose whether married women were also to have this form of liberty, but the mover of the Bill repudiated any such intention, confining his proposals to single women who would be able to qualify as householders. The Bill was rejected by a majority of 16 in a House of 245 members. Meanwhile the advanced woman was interested in a subject which came to be attached, like a kind of label, to the feminist movement—a Rational Dress Association, with Lady Harberton as a moving spirit, offered prizes for a design of a suitable knickerbocker costume for women.

One of the most prominent items in the programme of social reform, the better housing of the poor and the destruction of insanitary areas, was forced upon public attention this year by a scare which was to be repeated in ensuing summers. Early in July the ravages of cholera in Egypt grew alarming. The disease did not on this occasion spread as far north in Europe as it did in a later year ; but our traffic with Egypt was sufficient to cause the issue of most stringent regulations in this country. These were aimed less at setting up quarantine than at making the amplest provision for dealing with any cases that might make their appearance here, the idea being that, if energy went too much to quarantine preparations, which could hardly be relied upon to exclude infection absolutely, we might be caught behind the barriers with inadequate isolation arrangements. A Cholera Bill was hurriedly passed through Parliament ; in effect it constituted the local managers of the Metropolitan Asylums Board separate authorities under the Public Health Act, and it suspended certain Acts of Parliament and extended others so as to give the fullest powers everywhere for making hospital provision.   The more lasting result of the alarms was a new concern in this country for sanitation in every town, and especially in the ports.   In November Sir William Forwood was calling the attention of the Liverpool Corporation to the fact that there were at that moment 15,000 houses in that town, containing 60,000 people, which were all unfit for human habitation.   At this time no section of the community was under any responsibility in the matter of house sanitation, nor was any authority charged with enforcing a general standard.   In 1880 there was a proposal to set up in London a society which should provide for its members, at a subscription of a guinea, expert inspection of the drainage of their houses ; and peculiar point was given to the proposal a few months later by a doctor, who related the disastrous processes by which he had discovered that his own house, in one of the wealthy quarters of London and on an estate which had been developed not haphazard, but deliberately as a region of the well-to-do, was actually not connected with the main sewers, but was built over old cesspools.[1]   Medical men generally were disturbing the public apathy in such matters.   The bacterial theory was a fresh and forcible ally ; and in 1883, even before the cholera alarm spread, the problem of housing and sanitation was being attacked from a new angle—that of the infectious nature of tuberculosis.

One reason, no doubt, for the advance which medical opinion was making in affairs of public health was the feeling—a somewhat complacent feeling, perhaps—that this was a scientific age.   The same spirit which put Agnosticism and Religion into the lists, and watched them fight out their battles in the public prints, predisposed men to attend to the gospel of the doctors.   The theory of the survival of the fittest justified every exhortation to being on the side of the fit.   Incidentally it sent the Londoner and his country cousin to gaze at a creature exhibited this

[1] *The Times*, 20th April 1881.

year at the Westminster Aquarium, a very hairy child
brought from the territory north of Siam and said to have
a slight tail ! To call this creature " the missing link "
was enough to make it the talk of the town. The Aquarium
was still prospering in the curious career which made it
in itself a historical link.   Some of the old free promenad-
ing and some of the old impropriety of Ranelagh and
Vauxhall lingered in its large spaces and its vague
atmosphere of side-shows ; while the performances of
such people as " Zaeo," who was much advertised during
1880 and 1881 in the programme on the central stage, was
a sign of the changes that were turning the old cellars
and halls of song into the modern variety music-hall.   The
Aquarium clung to its character, and thereby to its public,
even though the music-halls had developed entirely on
their own lines.   Mere singing no longer sufficed for their
programmes.   They had even a public which made them
rebel, at this date, against the restrictions preventing them
from producing stage plays [1] ;   and which caused the
observant to reflect on the division of classes which was
growing up in amusements as in everything else.   It was
a somewhat superficial reflection, but at the moment it
was easy to think that there were divisions, just because
the places to which people of any class might go were easy
to single out.   One of them was St James's Hall, and its
chief entertainment in this year was of a kind that had
taken a curious hold of the public caprice.   It was a
thought-reading performance ; and the exposures in previous years of the fraudulent character of the grosser forms
of " spiritualism " had caused those who made their living
out of this kind of interest to turn to the less material
devices.   In 1881 there had been two prosecutions on
charges of false pretences arising out of the older sort of
performance ;   one an affair of " slate-writing," and the
other of crystal-gazing and table-turning.   The thought-

<hr>

[1] *The Times,* 3rd February 1883:

reading which succeeded those exposed tricks did not long go unattacked ; the performer at St James's Hall was challenged by Mr Labouchere to " read " the number on a banknote deposited by him in an envelope held by a certain Member of Parliament. The thought-reader demanded conditions on his own side, and for weeks the fairness or unfairness of the challenge, and the real nature of the performance, were under discussion in the newspapers, even scientists like Professor Ray Lankester coming forward with theories. The challenge never developed beyond a contest of wits as to the conditions. Another event in the amusement calendar of this year was the Fisheries Exhibition, the first of a series of specialised exhibitions which had great success, and became annual London entertainments. The Fisheries Exhibition was said at the time to have done much to popularise the eating of fish, but probably its success could be attributed to the exhibition of strange kinds of boats and boating gear. The centre of attraction was the display of equipment for Arctic exploration, which at this time shared with ballooning the first place in the popular admiration of adventure. It was even a craze which could be mildly scoffed at, for *The Times*, writing in April of the opening of the Arctic " season," said it had become as regular as the University Boat Race or the Twelfth of August.[1] Exploring parties of various nationalities were annually engaged in taking observations round the Polar basin.

Aeronauts, perhaps fired with a desire to be taking the popular eye with definite performances, were devising oversea flights. An attempt made in 1881 had been disastrous, Mr Walter Powell, M.P., having lost his life in the Channel while crossing to France. It was not until 1883 that the first success was achieved. On 13th June of this year the news arrived that a Frenchman had made an ascent, and at first it was thought he too had perished ;

[1] 4th April 1883;

but a few days later he was landed by a fishing boat, having been picked up in the Channel ; he had come near enough to the English shore to hear the waves breaking. On 1st August a voyage was at last accomplished, Sir Claude de Crespigny and others crossing from Maldon in Essex to Flushing ; and in September the English Channel was crossed twice—on 10th September by a Frenchman who landed near Folkestone, and a week later by an English party which started from Hastings and landed at Cherbourg. To the year's record of adventure belongs also the news published in London on 26th July that Captain Webb had been drowned in attempting to swim the rapids below Niagara Falls. It was a foolhardy enterprise, but the world could anticipate anything from the man who had achieved the feat of swimming the English Channel, with its baffling tidal currents. On that former occasion Webb had been in the water for twenty-one hours and three-quarters, and the distance he swam was estimated variously at from thirty-nine to forty-five miles.

Mention may be made here of the death of another man who stood in a different way for daring and romance. Captain Mayne Reid died in London on 23rd September. He was the last writer of those immense and fluent tales of adventure, of which he and Fenimore Cooper and G. P. R. James had the secret. Their works were already " books for boys," and taste for the long novel in masculine hands had gone back into the main channel of English fiction, from which the writers of adventure stories had for a time partially diverted it. *John Inglesant* had been published in 1881, and won its instant success ; the work of George Meredith had certainly accomplished no insignificant advance when it was spoken of, not as obscure, but as " dazzling with excess of light " ; Mr Henry James's art was already classed as " exquisite." [1]

A survey of the state of trade at the beginning of the

---

[1] *The Times,* 13th August 1883.

year gave rise to the warning that a time of restricted profits was at hand [1] ; and there can be no doubt that the warning was based largely on the uneasiness of the labour market. The Trade Unions took a new step this year by joining in an International Congress of workmen's organisations. In one sense the Congress was not taken very seriously ; it was thought that there could be little real co-operation between labour movements in this country and those in other countries, since the latter aimed rather at producing direct State action upon industrial problems than at assisting sectional efforts of the workmen for better conditions. But even without international agreement there was enough to make employers anxious, and Mr Henry Fawcett, urging them to take up profit-sharing as a means of steadying the industrial situation, expressed the opinion that it was " vain to expect any marked improvement of general economic conditions as long as the production of wealth involves a keen conflict of opposing pecuniary interests." What effect any wide adoption of the profit-sharing principle might have had at this time, before Trade Unionism underwent the vigorous development of the later eighties, it is vain to conjecture. It was not attempted. In January the year saw its first strike, a serious one on the Caledonian Railway, in which long hours and an exacting system of fines were the chief complaints of the men. The passenger traffic was carried on with difficulty, and the goods traffic was practically suspended, a state of things which was bound to lead to an early settlement. The strike was over before the end of the month. The autumn brought other strikes. Late in August the weavers in Lancashire came out, and their dispute lasted over a month. The Darlington iron and steel workers were also out, and so were the Sunderland engineers ; and by the end of November there was daily expectation that the cotton spinners and the Yorkshire

[1] *The Times,* 10th January 1883.

miners would strike. Masters and men were at logger-
heads as to the reality or otherwise of the trade revival,
the latter demanding a share of increased profits, while the
former denied that the revival had brought any real profits.
The coinage problem was a baffling element in such disagreements. For the moment the bank rate, which had
been 6 per cent. at the beginning of 1882, had gone down
to 4 per cent., though no one believed it could long remain
there. The lightness of gold coins, owing to wear and tear,
was becoming too serious to be set aside, and in February
there was talk of a steady calling-in of sovereigns. However, this year saw the first distinct expectation of relief
from a new supply of the metal. In May Mr Goschen
suggested that the Treasury authorities could perhaps
afford to wait, in view of " the rumours, apparently well-
founded, of a great discovery of gold in the territories
north-west of the Transvaal." This shows how curiously
the real area of mineral wealth—the Rand—was still in
the background ; and a communication a few weeks later
from South Africa shows the same thing. It spoke at
large of the " Transvaal goldfields," but the details were
all of nugget-mining in the Lydenburg and Spitzkop
districts, and on certain farms where old Portuguese
workings, long overgrown, were being opened up. The
scale of mining which was in the public eye can be judged
from the statement that two claims worked quietly for
twelve months past had actually yielded £6000 worth of
gold ; and that claims owned by Cape Town adventurers
had gone up in value from £24 to £50. Yet before the
year closed, telegrams from South Africa were beginning to
be couched in terms which can easily be seen, in the light
of subsequent developments, to give the first hints of the
truth. A Transvaal mining law was promulgated on 18th
August ; and in November it was announced that certain
" rotten quartz leads " were being opened, and crushing
operations commenced. The " placer " miners had been

throwing away quartz that would have crushed out at four
ounces to the ton. Their day, and the day of four-figure
annual returns, was almost over. Naturally, however, there
was some reluctance to risk money in mines situated in the
territory of the Boers. No friendliness on their part could
be relied upon to protect mining rights, or to encourage the
production of gold to the profit of British shareholders.
It happened that delegates from the Transvaal were in
England at the end of the year, laying before the Government a request for the abolition of the indeterminate
" suzerainty " of Great Britain, and the establishment of
the absolute freedom of the Transvaal. Their presence
was put to service by the exploiters of one or two gold
companies, floated in December. The delegates were
appealed to on the subject of the Transvaal Government's
attitude, and they replied in some indignation that that
Government had no desire with regard to the goldfields
except " to see the mineral resources of the country developed to their fullest extent." But as yet only some
rather shoddy enterprises made their appearance, with
so much accompaniment of quarrelling as to the real
vendors and the real owners of claims that the public
remained cautious.

In a year of restricted business spirit new ventures were
not likely to advance far. Electric lighting was checked
by the non-existence as yet of any system of supply from
a central generating station ; the inventors were for the
time being in their laboratories again, trying to work out
such a system. The only event of the year worth recording under this head is the first use of the light in a church ;
it was installed at St Matthew's, Brixton, in September.
No advance was made in the use of electric power for
propulsion, though a tramcar working on storage batteries
was put into service on the Acton lines, and did regular
duty among the horse cars. The extent of the field open
to the inventor of a practicable method of propulsion was

seen to be great; trams had become so general that London now had seventy miles of line working, Manchester and its suburbs had forty-two miles, and the total length of tram lines in the kingdom was four hundred and forty-four miles.

Almost at the end of the year came a piece of news which was the opening of a most unsatisfactory chapter in Egyptian affairs. On 22nd November information reached Cairo that Hicks Pasha, the British officer who was in command of the Egyptian forces in the Soudan, had been completely overwhelmed by the Mahdi, and his army destroyed, during a march undertaken by him from Khartoum to attack the Mahdi. He ought never to have been in the Soudan; but the English Government were now displaying the foolish attitude of supposing that, when they had said they did not intend to be drawn into difficulties in Egypt, they had settled their part in the matter. They had thought this enough when, in the spring of 1883, General Hicks had been appointed to the Soudan army. The dangers in the Soudan were obvious to the English authorities in Egypt. It was a vast territory of provinces with widely separated headquarters under various governors; it was garrisoned by an army undisciplined, unpaid, thoroughly unsoldierly; its provinces were nearly all cut off from one another by the Mahdi's forces; one province, Kordofan, had fallen completely into his hands in February 1883. Darfur, under Slatin Bey, was practically beyond defence. What could there be, it might well be asked, to entangle the British Government in a war in the Soudan, when the utmost that could reasonably concern them was the existence of sufficiently stable conditions in Lower Egypt to keep the Canal open and the bondholders' interest regularly paid, and when even to preserve that minimum they had become impatient of maintaining military responsibility? After the annihilation of Hicks Pasha's force it was too late to ask that question. It was indeed possible even then to determine upon withdrawal of the Soudan garrisons, and the establishment of a firm frontier against the Mahdi between Upper and Lower Egypt. But it was not possible for the Government to leave the work to either the Egyptian or the Turkish authorities. The Mahdi had seized the popular imagination. Ministers had put off determined consideration of their duty until the humanitarian pressure not to leave the field to slave-raiding—a pressure which they might, with a little clear sight and plain speaking, have overcome —was reinforced by public outcry against the supremacy of a barbarous ruffian. The Government moved now in a series of jerks, communicated by successive outcries, having missed once for all the opportunity to establish a purpose of their own.

The record of this year may be coloured by mention of a curious phenomenon which filled many evenings with beauty. The sunsets of the summer and autumn were so magnificent that they became the general topic of conversation. The reason for them appeared to be an eruption of the volcano Krakatoa, in the South Pacific. This, according to the scientific view of the phenomenon, had loaded the whole atmosphere of the globe with impalpable dust, which caught brilliantly the level rays of the setting sun.

CHAPTER VI

ON 8th January 1884 it was announced in the
London newspapers that General Gordon was
leaving England for the Congo to take up an appointment offered him by the King of the Belgians; and
there ensued gratified comments on the possibility that the
slave trade through Upper Egypt might be checked at its
source by a firm hand in the Congo territory. But there
were other comments, far from gratified, on allowing
Gordon of all people to pass into the service of a foreign
state at such a time, when, if anything was to be done in
Upper Egypt itself, he was, in the popular opinion, the
man to do it. By 18th January the Congo appointment
had been declined, and Gordon and Colonel Stewart left
London for Egypt.

In the ten days' interval there had been another public
outcry, vigorously gathered to a head by *The Pall Mall
Gazette*. It has an interest beyond the immediate circumstances, because it was probably the first occasion on
which a newspaper set itself, by acting as the organiser
of opinion on a particular detail of policy, to change a
Government's mind at high speed. However strongly
newspapers had spoken before this on political subjects,
they had not adopted the method of hammering, day
in, day out, at a single detail, and turning policy into
a catchword. That was almost what happened now. The
cry of " Gordon for Khartoum " was raised to such a pitch
that the Government decided they had after all been right
in their first idea. For they had been thinking of him a
month earlier. In December 1883 they had suggested to

Sir Evelyn Baring in Cairo that Gordon might be sent to Khartoum. Baring had rejected the suggestion, and he rejected it again when it was repeated. He was for withdrawal from the Soudan, establishing the Egyptian frontier either at Berber or at Wady Halfa ; and was maintaining that attitude in the face of the resignation of Cherif Pasha, the Egyptian Prime Minister, and the refusal of Riaz Pasha to form a ministry ; and he did not wish anyone to be appointed to carry out the withdrawal who might be moved by conflicting ideas. He mistrusted Gordon in that respect. But unfortunately the Belgian appointment brought Gordon's name into prominence at the moment. He had been in the Soudan before, having only retired from command at Khartoum in January 1880, with a fine record of energetic action against the slave dealing along the White Nile [1] ; he was a hero both to the general public and to the Anti-Slavery Society ; and as the Government had not previously adopted the only indefeasible line, that of forbidding any English officer to go to the Soudan, it failed to stand up against the clamour for sending Gordon. The Cabinet had had its warning from its representative in Cairo. Baring had been perfectly explicit against sending any Englishman to the Soudan at this crisis, and especially against sending Gordon. No Englishman could be left unsupported at Khartoum, so that to send one was bound to mean a Soudan expedition ; and to send a popular hero would mean also an unmanageable heat of feeling in England.[2]

Mr Gladstone's reputation has suffered heavily for the blunder. His great age, which he seemed to bear so easily, inevitably appeared in his inability to deal with subjects that failed to interest him, in over-absorption in the subjects that did interest him. One member of the

[1] See an article on his work there in *The Times*, 22nd January 1880.

[2] Lord Cromer's *Modern Egypt*, i. 428.

Government used to say afterwards that Mr Gladstone took virtually no notice of public affairs between the Irish Land Act of 1881 and the Home Rule Bill of 1886 ; in the House he often appeared quite torpid during debates on any subject remote from Ireland.   At the same time his great reputation and popularity with his party made the state of his thoughts and feelings the final consideration in the Government.   He disliked having any responsibility to Egypt ; the undertaking of it was to his mind the worst piece of " Beaconsfieldism."   The result of this was that those who saw the gravity of the situation—saw that Mr Gladstone was neither turning his back on the whole question, nor facing it clearly—could not against the weight of his personality compel the Cabinet to consider the question.   In the critical months of 1882 Lord Hartington . had written : " I wonder whether any human being (out of Downing Street) would believe that not a word has been said in the Cabinet about Egypt for a fortnight, and I suppose will not be for another week, if then " ; or again : " I am afraid that there is no chance of a Cabinet or of getting Mr Gladstone to pay any attention to Egypt while the Arrears Bill is going on." [1] The same conditions existed in 1884.   In the summer, directly after the preliminary credit for the Khartoum expedition had been voted, the Cabinet dispersed over the country, even though no one definitely knew the facts of Gordon's situation ; and a few days earlier Mr Gladstone, drawing nice distinctions between Khartoum " surrounded " and Khartoum " hemmed in," had blandly proposed " to collect the sum of the evidence as to Gordon's position " [2]—a position as to which some of Mr Gladstone's colleagues had for months been in correspondence with the Government's representative in Cairo.   The passionate resentment against Mr Gladstone after the death of Gordon was not quite justly based.   It

[1] Holland's *Life of the Duke of Devonshire,* i. 363, 365.
[2] *Ibid.* i. 477.

was not the single—and to some extent debatable—
question of the delay in the Khartoum expedition which
provides the most serious charge ; it was the extent to
which a Prime Minister allowed his distaste for the whole
Egyptian complication to prejudice his mind against
dealing with detail.

The situation in the Soudan was in itself complicated
enough to demand steady attention ; it demanded more,
once Gordon had been despatched. Possibly the considerable amount of service which he had undertaken for
foreign Powers, in circumstances which had emphasised
his personal responsibility, combined with a strongly
marked religious strain which in any case made his sense
of that responsibility high, had rendered him by this
time ill-fitted for the mere carrying out of orders. It is
at any rate certain that before he was finally shut up in
Khartoum he had virtually refused to act on orders, and
was pursuing a policy of his own. The apprehension
which Lord Cromer had felt in regard to the appointment
was to be fully justified. Even on the way out to Egypt
Gordon had procured the first modification in his instructions. He had in his interview with the Cabinet in
London undertaken no more than the duty of reporting
upon the situation in the Soudan, with a view to evacuation.
While on the voyage he thought that he could do the work
better if he had definite official status, and he induced
the British Government to secure from the Egyptian
Government his nomination as Governor-General of the
Soudan, believing the evacuation could be carried out
with more dignity if it were accompanied by a restoration
of the petty sultans of the Soudan provinces, instead of
leaving the country openly to the Mahdi. This was not in
one sense a great change of policy, especially as Gordon,
on receiving his written instructions at Cairo, himself insisted on the insertion of a most emphatic clause binding
him to evacuation ; but it was a great departure from the

British Government's previous determination. An Englishman as Governor-General was far from a noncommittal attitude.

On his way up to Khartoum Gordon made a strange and serious mistake. At Berber he proclaimed the intention of evacuating the Soudan. It was characterised by Lord Wolseley as " a fatal announcement " ; he wrote to Lord Hartington (13th April 1884) : " This has prevented all men of any influence from helping. . . . Knowing that anarchy, or possibly anarchy *plus* the Mahdi, must follow upon Gordon's departure, every one thought only of his own safety. . . . To help Gordon under such circumstances would have been suicidal on any man's part."[1] The proclamation was particularly ill-timed, since the Mahdi's influence was being extended by Osman Digna dangerously close to Berber. Valentine Baker Pasha, who had been sent to reinforce the Suakin garrison when the defeat of Hicks Pasha threatened the Suakin-Berber route, had moved out rather hastily with Egyptian troops against Osman,[2] and his force had been cut up on 5th February. Consequently when Gordon reached Khartoum, on 18th February, the surrounding of that place had become more than a possibility. Luckily the Egyptian Government was able to send up to Suakin at once 4000 British troops under General Graham, whose two defeats of Osman Digna at El Teb on 29th February and Tamai on 13th March kept that warrior for a while from assisting in the isolation of Khartoum.

The news of these battles, with all the picturesque detail of fighting in squares with Gatling guns at the corners, and of the wild charges of the " Fuzzies," as the Mahdi's troops were being called, was followed by the first of the eagerly awaited news from Khartoum itself, messages reaching London on 21st March from Khartoum by way of Berber.

[1] Holland's *Life of the Duke of Devonshire.*
[2] Lord Cromer's *Modern Egypt,* i. 400.

They were dated 14th and 15th March, and conveyed the information that Gordon had been engaged in small military operations round Khartoum, chiefly for the purpose of extricating the garrison of Halfiyeh ; it was also intimated that Khartoum was practically surrounded by the enemy.   To the British public the affair was already a war ; they had in their own simple view pitted Gordon against the Mahdi ; and in the constant meetings held throughout the summer to protest against the " abandonment of Gordon " (for as early as the month of May the situation was so regarded) there was one continuous note of bewildered amazement at the Government's failure to conceive the position in this plain sense.   Unfortunately to Gordon also it was by that time a war.   He had passed through another of the changes of mind which so perplexed the Government at home, and their representative in Cairo.   He had not yet entirely declined (as he was to do before long) the policy of evacuation which he had so emphatically accepted in the beginning ; he had only got as far as a new and more complicated version of " evacuation, but not abandonment."   He was asking in March that an Egyptian Governor-General with a British Commission (his own being technically an Egyptian Commission) should be appointed ; and he asked for a particular man—Zobeir Pasha.   Now although to the general public in England this was an incident of no such vividness as battles in the desert, it is not too much to say that it made the Government gasp.   Moreover it upset that humanitarian opinion which had worked so ardently for Gordon's appointment Zobeir had been the greatest and most unscrupulous of the slave traders of the Soudan and had been deported for that reason to Cairo ; and here was the idol of the Anti-Slavery Society demanding his appointment as Governor-General !   As a matter of fact this was exactly one of those strange quixotic pieces of fearlessness which had made Gordon a popular hero.   In his former period of office in the Soudan he had had occasion to approve of the execution by one of his lieutenants of Zobeir's son. Yet believing now that Zobeir was a man who could hold Khartoum against the Mahdi, and even recover a large part of the Soudan, he declined to be influenced by any possible danger to himself in bringing Zobeir up to Khartoum. He was, no doubt, right in his belief. The experiment would, indeed, have been a risky one. Zobeir might join the Mahdi ; or, if he did not, he might become as troublesome to Lower Egypt as the Mahdi could. But of his warlike reputation in the Soudan, of his ability to rally the natives to him and hold Khartoum if he chose to, there could be no possible doubt.[1] However, Gordon's wish never got beyond the stage of suggestion. The general proposition that the Soudan should not be abandoned had support in England ; Khartoum left to be the capital of a slave-trading state was not a pretty picture. But the difficulty was that no one could think of any person capable of holding it except Zobeir ; and the only practicable policy was that of sending him. The Anti-Slavery Society hotly opposed it, and they found the Government especially ready to listen to them, since Gordon's proposal involved a direct British Commission to Zobeir and a subsidy of money. At the same time it was distinctly implied that the policy of evacuation was beginning to slip into the background in Gordon's mind. Two or three weeks after this Gordon finally abandoned the idea. Towards the end of March two of his pashas were defeated, by the treachery of their own troops, in engagements near Khartoum ; Berber was seized with panic, and all who could left the place. The fighting spirit in Gordon was roused, and those in England and in Cairo whose minds had been wholly set on withdrawing from the Soudan to a point of safe defence for Lower Egypt were staggered by receiving from him furious telegrams in which he announced his intention of " smashing the Mahdi "

[1] Lord Cromer's *Modern Egypt*, i. 450.

before considering anything else. His change of mind was complete. It is fair to pause here for a moment to consider how differently the situation must have appeared to him and to the Government at home. It is probable that only he knew the extent to which the Soudan provinces were at that moment mere detached headquarters amid a sea of Mahdism, islands incapable of communication. It may be doubted whether even before Gordon arrived the garrisons of the southern provinces—Darfur, under Slatin Bey, Bahr-el-Ghazal, under Lupton Bey, and Equatoria, under Emin Pasha—could possibly have made their way north. Their predicament weighed heavily on Gordon's mind ; he could see no way of saving them and at the same time saving the garrisons of the eastern and northern provinces, Sennar, Kassala, Berbera, Khartoum and Dongola. The Soudan was cut in two halves by the Mahdi ; and this explains the historic telegram despatched by Gordon on 7th April 1884, announcing his intention of retiring to the Equator, and leaving to the British Government "the indelible disgrace " of abandoning the northern and eastern garrisons. He intended evidently to gather up Lupton, Slatin and Emin on his way, and withdraw by the Congo, since he could see no possibility of conveying them northwards. It could hardly be of much profit now to speculate on what might have been done. Gordon, as we have seen, began by a proclamation which set the whole disaffected population of the Soudan on the alert for withdrawal movements, and went on to a misleading distinction between evacuation and abandonment. By the time that he sent the telegram of 7th April the situation had changed as completely as his own mind had changed. Khartoum was cut off from Dongola and Berber, and no relieving movement towards Berber from Suakin could be undertaken, because the weather was too hot for the marching of troops. The only thing that had not changed was the attitude of the British Government ; and the result was a hopeless interplay of cross purposes for two or three months. Gordon, feeling himself shut up in Khartoum, was confident that, as his isolation was known, a relief expedition would be on the way to him, and he issued, therefore, whenever opportunity offered, intimations of his ability to hold out. The Government, never having had any intention of sending British troops to the Soudan, and interpreting Gordon's messages in a wholly different spirit from that in which they were sent, held to instructing him to withdraw, and awaited his appearance. Mr Gladstone's view, as late as 31st July 1884, was that to send an expedition either to Dongola or to Khartoum would be " to act in the teeth of evidence as to Gordon, which, however imperfect, is far from trivial." [1] That Lord Hartington was as much bewildered as anybody by Gordon's behaviour and his contradictory telegrams may be seen from his letters to Lord Granville. " I have read Gordon's telegrams again," he wrote, " and I confess that I am utterly unable to understand them. . . . I think that all we can do is to look at the position as it is known to us from other sources, and to pay no attention to what he says." Granville was inclined to conclude, from the fact that messages were passing from Gordon to the Mudir of Dongola, that the Cabinet's messages were equally reaching Gordon and that he would not answer them.[2] In the end it was " looking at the position as it is known from other sources " which at last moved the Government to undertake an expedition. The preliminary credit was voted on 8th August ; and Lord Wolseley drew up a plan of campaign. This did not commend itself to General Stephenson, who was then in command at Cairo, and Lord Wolseley had to be sent out to take command. He left Cairo with his force on 5th October. By that time there had been no communication with Gordon for six months, except that on two or

[1] Holland's *Life of the Duke of Devonshire*, i. 477.
[2] *Ibid.* i. 489, 492.

three occasions in June and July messages had come from
him asking as to the whereabouts of the relief expedition.
It had been a long delay ; but, as we have said, the blame
which the Government has to bear should be placed further
back than these events, and on more general grounds. The
confusion of ideas at the time must have been extreme,
and the blame must rest on the mistakes of omission and
commission alike which led up to the events of 1884. It
is, for instance, worth recalling that Mr H. M. Stanley,
who happened to reach London in July of this year from
the Congo, expressed himself in an interview as perfectly
confident about Gordon. He derided the whole idea of a
Nile expedition in the summer (for which popular opinion
in England was pressing), saying that the men would die
like flies; and he asserted that Gordon could leave
Khartoum when he liked, and withdraw by the Congo—
that he only needed " to act like a soldier," and rescue
would be unnecessary.[1]

With the undertaking of the expedition popular attention slackened. Little news was coming through from
Egypt, and what came was not of importance. It is more
interesting to us now than it was to people then to know
that Major Kitchener was at Dongola, whence there was
some hope of his making communication with Gordon.
If in the pause that ensued English people looked at
affairs nearer home, they must have decided that, if their
attention had not been so taken up with Egypt, they would
still have had a sufficiently exciting year. An earthquake
had occurred, which was distinctly felt in London and the
Midlands, but was quite serious in Essex, where so much
damage was done in the villages that a fund had to be
started for rebuilding houses. There was a succession of
dynamite explosions, generally occurring two or three at a
time in different places, which gave the appearance of a
regular campaign. The long-expected County Franchise

---

[1] Interview published in *The Times*, 29th July 1884.

Bill had been produced, and over it Lords and Commons were flatly at war. The dynamite explosions began with a railway station series : on 27th February there was one at Victoria Station; fortunately it occurred in the small hours of the morning, and there was no loss of life. A day or two later infernal machines were discovered, before they went off, at Charing Cross and Paddington. On 31st May there were explosions at Scotland Yard, the Junior Carlton Club in Pall Mall, and a frustrated attempt at the Military Education Office in St James's Square; at the same time a bag of dynamite was found near the Nelson Column in Trafalgar Square. In September the alarm spread outside London, a quantity of dynamite being found at Sunderland on the 13th, and an explosion taking place in the Council Chamber at Salisbury on the 29th. Nervous as the public had become, there was by good fortune so little loss of life, or even injury, in these explosions that there was no panic ; nevertheless black bags without obvious owners were for a year or two regarded with extreme disfavour and suspicion.

The County Franchise Bill, which would in any case have given the Government plenty of work, found itself early in the year dragging an unexpected weight. On 7th February a meeting of members of Parliament was held at the House of Commons to consider the moving of a Woman Suffrage amendment to the Bill. One was drawn up, and the moving of it was undertaken by Mr Woodall ; it proposed to enfranchise women householders. The movement for enfranchising women was at this date influential, but limited. It had been in existence for some twenty years, and was almost exclusively a movement of educated women who, having found their own careers hampered by the absence of arrangements for admitting women to university courses and examinations, to professional diplomas and professional practice, naturally went on to contemplate the general position of women under the law and under social custom ; and came thence to the conclusion, expressed for them most efficiently by J. S. Mill, that until women had the same political status as men they must continue to labour under disabilities in any society politically constituted. Theoretically the movement was not confined to the more highly educated classes of women ; but practically, although its leaders spoke and wrote to some extent of the wage-earners, the active suffragists were women who had had a university training, or had qualified as doctors, or were distinguished writers. The pledged supporters of the movement were not very numerous, the annual income of the principal suffrage society being about £350[1] ; but its members were mostly women of proved capacity, and the suffragist cause did not lose by the limitation. Mr Woodall's amendment gave the movement an occasion such as it had not yet enjoyed. Since it had attained force and publicity its only opportunities, and they but rare ones, had been in the shape of private members' Bills, which no one took seriously. Now, however, an opening of a different kind presented itself, and frequent public meetings were held in support of Mr Woodall's amendment. Whether it was a genuine opportunity is questionable ; it could hardly in cold blood be considered possible that a measure dealing only with a certain class of constituencies, and proceeding on lines already tried, should be the vehicle for an experiment in a wholly new principle over the entire kingdom. Moreover the subject fell instantly into the vortex of party. A good many Conservatives were said, indeed, to be convinced supporters of the movement—Lord Salisbury, Sir Stafford Northcote, Lord John Manners and Sir Michael Hicks Beach among them—and it is interesting to find *The Times* speaking of a Woman Suffrage measure as " the trump Conservative card which Lord Beaconsfield kept

[1] See, *e.g.*, report of the annual meeting of the society, *The Times*, 10th July 1889.

in his hand." [1]   But the honesty of general Conservative
support for the amendment was deeply suspect. Mr Gladstone had announced that if the clause were carried he
would throw up the Bill, and thus a great deal of the
Opposition vote for it was purely opportunist. On 12th
June the amendment came up for discussion, and was
rejected by 271 votes to 135.

This adventure was speedily lost sight of in the gathering
of a far more considerable storm in regard to the Bill.
By assimilating the county franchise to that created in
the boroughs by the Acts of 1832 and 1867, the Bill
swept away the old property limitations of the vote in
country_ places, and gave it, as in boroughs, to the
occupiers of rated dwelling-houses. It thus enfranchised
the labourer; and the change, both in the number and
in the educational level of the electorate, was great. In
July the House of Lords rejected the Bill, some warning of
such an event being perhaps conveyed by the action of the
Opposition in the Commons who, on the third reading, did
not go into the Lobby at all, but walked out of the House.
The ground which the Lords alleged for their rejection of
the measure was that it was only half a scheme, and that a
redistribution of seats should have accompanied so large
an alteration of the electoral basis. Mr Gladstone, while
agreeing that the two operations should come into action
together, asserted roundly that to have grappled with them
in one Bill would have been an insane attempt. He
informed a party meeting, held at the Foreign Office
immediately after the vote in the House of Lords, of an
offer made to the Tories that, if the Bill passed, both Houses
should adopt an identical resolution saying that they had
passed the Franchise Bill in reliance on a promise that the
accompanying Redistribution Bill should be introduced
and passed the next year. The offer was characteristic
of the moderation with which Mr Gladstone handled the

[1] 13th June 1884.

whole situation. There was not lacking a quantity of strong feeling against the House of Lords which might, if he had chosen, have been worked into passion. Indeed, the summer and autumn saw some very downright meetings in the country—in Chatsworth Park, at Leicester and Manchester especially—and some violent ones ; there was a regular riot at Bournemouth at the end of July, and another at Birmingham in October, when Sir Stafford Northcote and Lord Randolph Churchill were refused a hearing, and their platform was stormed after a free fight. A Democratic Committee for the Abolition of the House of Lords was established in London, Sir Wilfrid Lawson, Mr Labouchere, Professor Beesly and Mr Bradlaugh at its head—and it absorbed no doubt an earlier body quaintly named " The Society for Removing Bishops from the House of Lords." But all this feeling did not in the least hustle Mr Gladstone out of his chosen path. He had set his mind on carrying his Bill, and he did not intend to have it swamped in a general campaign between the two Houses, or a general test of the constitutional privileges of the Peers. The Tories were not in a strong position ; whatever may have been their real dislike of the new franchise they had paid too much lip-service to it to confront easily the indignation the Peers had roused. " The Conservatives," Mr Goschen wrote about this time, " never pronounce against the Franchise ; they have never had a meeting against it ; never spoken except as regards the time of yielding." [1] Moreover Mr Gladstone had a valuable ally in Queen Victoria, who, dreading as she always did the Radical element in the Cabinet, was only too ready to assist Mr Gladstone in any course alternative to a wholesale attack upon the House of Lords. She feared above all things the attitude expressed by a most interesting new recruit of the Ministerial benches in the House of Commons, Mr John

[1] Elliot's *Life of Lord Goschen*, i. 277.

Morley,[1] who had said to a political audience : " Be sure that no power on earth can henceforth separate the question of mending the Commons from the other question of ending or mending the House of Lords." [2]   The Queen's influence was active throughout the months of recess, and Mr Gladstone made handsome acknowledgment of its patient and prosperous application.[3]

A session which had opened with the expectation that it would be entirely concerned with Egypt and the Franchise ended by fulfilling that prophecy. Various Bills were discussed; a Merchant Shipping Bill, extending the Employers' Liability Act to shipping, and setting a limit upon insurance of ships and cargo; a London Government Bill, setting up a single Municipality (a Common Council of 240 members to take over the powers of the City Corporation, the Metropolitan Board of Works, the Commissioners of Sewers, the magistrates for Middlesex, Kent and Surrey within the limits, and the Burial Boards and Vestries, reserving only the poor law, education and the police for other control, and enjoining the acquisition by the new body of the undertakings of the gas and water companies) ; and finally a more curious Bill, designed to relieve the gold shortage by turning the half-sovereign, which suffered more than the sovereign from wear and tear, into a token coin, and making sovereigns the only legal tender on Bills of Exchange. But all three proposals were dropped. A considerable measure, however, was the attempted conversion this year of the National Debt. The scheme was to convert six hundred millions of 3 per cent. stock into $2\frac{3}{4}$ per cent. stock, by issuing £108 of the new for every £100 of the old. The high price of Consols for so many years justified the belief that the interest was more than the nation need pay, and a lower price would, it was argued,

---

[1] He had been elected for Newcastle in 1883.
[2] *The Times*, 31st July 1884.
[3] Morley's *Life of Gladstone*, iii. 138.

have the advantage of making the security more marketable. The conversion scheme was gazetted on 8th August,
but did not attain any great success ; the public converted
about nine and a half millions, and twelve millions which
the Government held were also converted, but this was a
very small proportion of the total.[1]

It was not altogether a happy year for such an attempt.
The stock markets, disturbed by the uncertainty of our
foreign relations, and by a heavy selling of Suez Canal
shares, were too nervous for experiments. The bank rate
had been reduced to 3 per cent., but only by a strictness
on the part of the bank in fixing definite occasions for making advances to bill brokers. Trade was slack, except in
the woollen industry ; an abundance of shipping had depressed freights and checked shipbuilding ; railway traffic
returns were poor, and a coal strike was threatening in the
Midlands. The competition of foreign manufactures was
growing with the growing solidity of the German Empire
and the growing immigrant population of the United
States ; the militant Tory spirits in England were
divided between abusing foreign imports and abusing the
demands of Trade Unionism.[2] The new Bankruptcy Act
was a source of some uneasiness ; for while working well
on the whole, and putting an end to the vicious private
compositions with creditors, it was also keeping in existence
firms of a somewhat shaky solvency, which shrank from the
publicity of the new arrangements. The cotton strike
begun in 1883 overshadowed the beginning of 1884. It
may even have had some damping effect upon the progress
of the Manchester Ship Canal scheme, which came before
Parliament in a private Bill this year, and was discussed by
a Select Committee of the House of Lords in the spring.
The scheme had to meet the opposition of Liverpool, which

[1] *The Times,* 18th October 1884.
[2] *E.g.* Lord Dunraven and Sir E. Beckett (Lord Grimthorpe) in
The Times, 4th November 1884.

was expressed in the form of anxiety as to the possible effect of the new waterway upon the existing channels of the Mersey. The Bill passed its second reading in the Commons; but came to grief in the general abandonment of legislation during the Franchise controversy; though the determination of Manchester in the matter was seen in the decision, taken later in the year, to promote another Bill in the following session.

Manchester figured also in a remarkable controversy which arose in the early autumn. It was said that the corporation wished to undertake the management of a hotel in the city. The truth at the back of the story was that a hotel built on some land leased from the corporation had been suddenly thrown on the corporation's hands by the financial failure of the lessee, before its completion; and, rather than leave the place idle, a licencee had been put in as the corporation's tenant. Birmingham had, however, attempted before this to obtain the leave of Parliament to carry on the business of a licensed victualler, so that it was natural to suppose that Manchester was on the same track. The controversy on the subject, which was raised by a licensed victuallers' organisation, is chiefly interesting because it revealed no intellectual objection to municipal trading, as such; the only argument was that to include hotel-keeping was going rather far. Meanwhile the enormous impulse given to municipal affairs by the new power to issue stock may be judged from a report published early in 1884 of the towns which had already obtained the power [1]; they numbered no less than twenty-seven, and the amount of authorised municipal stock had gone up from five and a quarter millions to about seventy-five millions. The local government debt of the country at this time was already over a hundred millions.

In the region of social reform the year is notable for the appointment of the Royal Commission on the Housing

[1] *The Times*, 18th January 1884.

of the Poor, which was gazetted on 4th March. The presence on the Commission of the Prince of Wales as chairman expressed strikingly the degree to which the general national conscience was aroused on the subject. The housing conditions in London were most prominently discussed (in January the Local Government Board had sent round a circular to the local authorities of London, pointing out their powers and duties under various Acts, as to the inspection of houses, the abatement of nuisances, and the demolition of unsuitable dwellings) ; but the public was well aware that sanitary conditions in country places were exceedingly bad.   Some committees of private people in the richer parts of London had been investigating conditions in such districts as Southwark ; so that in every way the commission came at a time likely to render it fruitful.   It coincided with an event which, if as much designed for pleasure as for business, was likely in a small way to be of some assistance, the Health Exhibition, the successor to the Fisheries Exhibition of the previous year. Conferences on sanitary matters were held in connection with the exhibition ; and both to them and to the housing question a renewed alarm of cholera gave great importance. The first anxiety arose from a case discovered at Port Said on board a homeward-bound troopship in April ; at the end of June the disease appeared at Toulon, and spread to Marseilles, to Spain and to Italy ; it continued to ravage the south of Europe almost until the winter set in.   The precautions taken in England still followed the principle of improved sanitation, cleanliness, etc. ; and out of this attitude grew the sharp attacks made in this year on the Duke of Bedford on account of the shameful condition of Covent Garden Market, where vegetables lay about rotting, and no standard of cleanliness had ever been enforced. " Mud-Salad Market " was the name *Punch* gave to it at this time.   A somewhat odder, and yet no less lasting, result of the Health Exhibition was the sudden impulsion it gave to the consideration of healthy clothing. From this year dates the rise of Dr Jaeger's teachings in England ; and *The Times* somewhat rashly committed itself to the assertion that Englishmen would not be ashamed of wearing a comfortable coat because it was ugly.[1] But healthiness does not necessitate the colours in clothing which the enthusiasts adopted ; and they remained, therefore, when the first ardour of the movement waned, a somewhat conspicuous snuff-brown band. The ordinary man had not as a whole displayed much interest in the sanitary conferences of the Health Exhibition ; but it was some consolation to record that by its means he had learned again to walk in gardens of an evening and listen to a band. Indeed the ordinary man's pursuit of health was opening up everywhere fresh avenues. Cycling was giving access to country places, and the National Cyclists' Union and the Cyclists' Touring Club were in their second year of existence. Swimming was much in vogue, and the Beckwiths' entertainment had for a season or two been one of the most popular in London ; it was announced in the summer of 1884 that Miss Beckwith was going to attempt to swim the Channel. The family visit to the seaside in the summer had ceased by now to be a subject for superior jokes ; and *Punch's* butt had become the Cockney tourist at " Bullong." However, Boulogne had no objection to receiving him, and was in this year dredging its harbour to allow of a fixed-hour steamship service across the Channel, Lord Radnor at the same time being approached for foreshore rights for a corresponding deep-sea harbour at Folkestone.

At a great demonstration in July against the House of Lords, after the rejection of the Franchise Bill, there was a small group which, while joining in the demonstration, preferred to have its own platform. It was a group of socialists, and it attracted little attention until a speaker

[1] 4th October 1884.

referred contemptuously to John Bright (who had been roused to battle again by the action of the Peers) ; whereupon the group was broken up by wrathful bystanders. Yet though socialism was as yet contemptible to the London populace it was already giving rise to some anxiety. Henry George was lecturing in London in January of 1884 on Land Nationalisation ; and the frequent references to him, spiteful or humorous, in newspapers and comic prints throughout the year give some measure of the great impression he had made. His theories coloured the whole of the Radical programme. The first number of a new socialist paper, *Justice*, was published on 9th January 1884.

Meanwhile middle-class attempts to do what was just by the poor and the oppressed were increasing. There was some inclination to perceive the rise of a " new Radicalism," humanitarian and courageous, but distinctly inclined to interference ; trade unions were warned that it was not wise to invoke too much State interference. But this was a misreading of the signs. The fault of the trade unions was rather, as Mr Chamberlain saw, a more marked tendency to exclude politics from their sphere of work. In a letter to a correspondent published early in the year Mr Chamberlain deplored this tendency, as " a practical abnegation of the most vital interests of the working classes." There is in this an interesting indication that the disjunction of official Liberalism from the main current of social change was causing some anxiety to Radical leaders. But the latter had no opportunity of keeping their minds with any continuity upon a restoration of understanding. They missed such chances as were offered them, for instance, by the prolonged discussion of the condition of the Friendly Societies, some of which were not financially above suspicion ; they did not see in the earnest work of the societies' most prominent critic, Canon Blackley, the nucleus of a scheme of national insurance for workmen. They missed even such chances of action in the socialist direction as were offered by the middle-class themselves ; the railway companies, exhausted by competition, were tentatively expressing, through some of their chairmen, the opinion that increased control by the Board of Trade would not be unwelcome, if it would limit the competition. The Government had, in fact, come to office with an imperfect appreciation of the spirit of advanced sections of the community, and it never had leisure to obtain a clearer view. Meanwhile the sense of the increased power of the working classes in the community, their improved economic and, consequently, civic weight, so to speak, is shown by a certain tendency to call in question the whole basis of taxation. It was urged that the corollary of all the efforts being made for a social amelioration should be a greater union in responsibility ; and the debates on the County Franchise Bill were accompanied by the criticism that we were multiplying the voters without increasing the number of taxpayers. Hence arose the plea that there should be less reliance on indirect taxation ; the days had passed when we " drank ourselves out of the Alabama indemnity " ; and that there should be no exceptions from direct taxation. Another idea was that the Income Tax should be abolished, and money raised by stamps on every sale of goods. However, social ideas of any kind failed to penetrate into the rather narrow circle of the politicians' outlook, and remained in the region of private effort, where the benevolent spirit was more active than the critical. New ideas, for instance, in connection with elementary education showed to what astonishing lengths the departure from the old individualism was proceeding. Thoughtful people had begun to perceive in the elementary schools not mere machines for giving knowledge, after the operation of which children must sink or survive, as they could, but also fresh opportunities for dealing with poverty and the inadequacies of poor homes. Thus we find a New Education Code showing

signs of an inclination to lay less stress on examination
results, and more on a classification of children with
proper regard to their health, and at the same time a
movement of private philanthropy for providing the
children of the very poor with decent clothing and with
cheap meals at school. Compulsory education was having
its indirect effect in bringing to the light of day children
whose lack of clothing and nourishment would otherwise
have been concealed in the swarming courts of town slums.
It is curious to find that an early difficulty in the way of
feeding children was the distrust they showed of such food
as macaroni, lentils, haricot beans, and even of soup [1]; so
strong remained the British feeling that only meat made
a meal, even among those who could hardly ever have
meat. The fact that other forms of food were being used
in this work may be an indication that the more well-to-do
people were becoming aware of that narrowness of range
in catering which was remarked a year or two earlier.
The limitation of the meat supply by the embargo on imported cattle was still very great ; but the chilled meat trade
was steadily advancing. The largest cargo yet landed in
England arrived on 26th September in a shipment of 22,000
carcasses, and 1000 pieces of beef, from New Zealand ;
cold storage warehouses had been constructed under
Cannon Street Railway Station in order to handle large
consignments. It was fortunate that the leaders of this
enterprise were persistent, for the impossibility under the
existing regulations of moving live cattle was leading to
some atrocious experiments in conserving dead meat ; thus
a system had been devised of injecting boracic acid into an
animal before killing it, the circulation of the blood conveying the preservative over the body ; and other experiments were made with carbonic acid.[2] The new inventions
which had so enlivened the past three or four years were

---

[1] *The Times*, 13th December 1884.
[2] Ditto, 31st January and 26th July 1884.

in 1884 a little at a standstill. Electric lighting had not yet reached the stage of central supply stations, and to install it still meant buying a complete producing plant. The slowness of development was put down in some measure to the provisions of the Electric Lighting Act ; it was beginning to be felt that empowering local authorities to purchase lighting undertakings at the end of twenty-one years was rather too drastic, since the companies could not expect to cut out the gas companies with such speed as to recoup themselves within that period. In electric traction the year witnessed a distinct change of method. The " live rail " was replaced by the first practical " feed " system for street use, the employment of a sunk conduit carrying the current rail. It was tried at Blackpool, and with no small success. But it was expensive, and so many other experiments were being made in America that most of the tramway companies preferred to hold their hands for the present.

The opening of the new University College for Wales in September carried on the advance of provincial university education. About the same time the question of over-pressure in girls' schools, which had become a somewhat heated item in a general discussion of the emancipation of women and their entry into occupations hitherto ex-clusively masculine, came up again in the form of a report by Dr Crichton Browne. The report was considered somewhat rhetorical, and weak in evidence, and likely therefore to put an end to genuine discussion.

Autumn brought an unprecedented return of life to London. Instead of an adjourned session, such as had previously been the means of finishing a heavy year's work, the Government opened a new session in November. The reason, of course, was that the Franchise Bill, having been rejected by the Lords, could only reappear in a new session, and as a Redistribution Bill was ahead it was necessary to take at once the chances of a new attempt with the

Franchise Bill—chances which the Queen's influence had, as we have said, rendered much brighter. The great world made the best of the business, decided to have an autumn season, and to amuse itself in London until Christmas— a thing it had never done before. In any case, the relations between the two Houses were exciting enough to make hostesses sure of vivacious dinner-tables and gossipy evening parties. The Tadpoles and Tapers came back to town discussing the propriety or otherwise of a creation of peers to pass the Bill, a course Mr Gladstone preferred to avoid [1]; and meanwhile two men from the opposing sides who could hardly have been better chosen—Lord Hartington and Sir Michael Hicks Beach—were parleying on possible means of adjustment. Outwardly there was to the last minute uncertainty as to the attitude of the House of Lords, Lord Salisbury still demanding the actual production of the Redistribution Bill before he would undertake to pass the Franchise Bill. But on 18th November the crisis was passed. The Franchise Bill was read a second time in the Lords, the committee stage being postponed for the Tory leaders to see in private the Redistribution Bill. All went well ; on 27th November the Franchise Bill passed its committee stage ; the Redistribution Bill was introduced in the Commons on 2nd December, and on the 6th Parliament adjourned until the following February. The Redistribution Bill, discussed as it had been in private between leaders of the two parties, promised an easy passage ; but it, like the other Bill, raised at the outset a kind of corollary discussion. The advocates of Proportional Representation saw their opportunity, just as the advocates of Woman Suffrage had seen theirs, and held meetings in December to commend their views to the electorate. But they did not succeed in persuading Mr Gladstone; and Mr Courtney, the chief advocate of the new idea, resigned his post in the Government.

[1] Morley's *Life of Gladstone*, iii. 130.

The Redistribution Bill, in order to bring about the proper digestion of a large accession of voters, had to readjust drastically the electoral areas. Boroughs of less than 15,000 inhabitants were disfranchised, and thrown into county constituencies, to balance the new rural vote. Towns with a population of less than 50,000 were to have only one member; and in general, save for the very large towns, the constituencies were all to be single-member areas. By these means 160 seats were set free, to be allotted to the new constituencies produced by the re-division of the county areas.

Mr Gladstone had steered his Bills through after his own fashion. Only the boldest members of the party ventured to remark that he had done exactly what he said he would not do; he had let the Lords see the Redistribution Bill as a condition of passing the Franchise Bill. So unquestioned was his supremacy that his party accepted what he had done; indeed, they hardly realised it. But the true Radicals in after years put down to Mr Gladstone's action on this occasion the confidence with which the House of Lords rejected Liberal Bills. No other business had occupied Parliament, though there was at this time some discussion of our naval strength, and a demand for extensive building of torpedo boats. This class of boat, with its swiftness and deadliness of attack, was at the moment the idol of a navy which only four years before had seen the disappearance from the active list of the last of the wooden armour-clads.

Yet even the political excitement about the Franchise Bill could not conceal the more general anxiety about Gordon. In September news of gloomy omen had come. Colonel Stewart, Gordon's companion in Khartoum, on whose cool judgment the British authorities in Cairo had relied much in their bewilderment about Gordon himself, left Khartoum on 10th September, with some other Englishmen, in an attempt to reach Lower Egypt by way

of the Nile.   Their steamer was wrecked sixty miles below
Abu Hamed, and Stewart and his companions, having been
lured into a village, were murdered there.   After this another long silence ensued.   Wolseley was making his way
up the Nile, but was not ready until December for the move
across the desert from Korti.   There he divided his force
into two columns, one under Sir Herbert Stewart starting
to take the desert route, and the other under General Earle
to take the Nile route.   On the day that Herbert Stewart
set out a message arrived from Gordon, on a scrap of paper
about the size of a postage stamp :   " Khartoum all right.
14. 12. 84.   C. G. GORDON."   A verbal message accompanied
it to the effect that Khartoum was in great straits.   But at
least Gordon was still alive, relief was approaching him,
and the year ended in good hope.

CHAPTER VII

1885 : THE DEATH OF GORDON, THE GENERAL ELECTION, AND THE RISE OF SOCIALISM

IT was a remarkable stroke of Fate which placed the Government at the beginning of 1885 in the position of not having to "meet Parliament." As the session had been opened in November, and only adjourned over Christmas, the reassembling in 1885 was not accompanied with the formalities of a Speech from the Throne, an Address in either House, and a general engagement of forces. On the contrary, there was at the critical moment all the natural instinct of the politician to carry through a large piece of half-finished work ; and, as the holding-over of the important stages of the Redistribution Bill provided that condition, the Government did not actually have to go to the country until the popular mind had undergone no slight change from a temper on the subject of Gordon, which would beyond a doubt have wrecked the Liberal party at the beginning of the year.

The first news of the year from the Soudan was cheering. On 16th January it was announced in London that Herbert Stewart had reached Metemmeh, and on the 22nd the papers had the news of the battle of Abu Klea. The story of the fight was one to soothe ruffled popular pride ; the British square had been broken in the battle, but by sheer fighting courage, sheer pluck, the troops had restored their formation, and it was reported that when the enemy had drawn off 1100 of their dead had been counted on the field. Nevertheless the battle cost the life of one who was a hero of adventure, Colonel Burnaby. The next piece of news was a blow. Herbert Stewart himself had been shot on 18th January, while his force was advancing through bush the day after the battle, and his wound was grave. But the force pushed on, and on 21st January reached the Nile at Gubat. Here it met four steamers, the river fleet which Gordon had had at Khartoum, and with them was one more tiny scrap of paper. It bore the words : " Khartoum is all right. Could hold out for years. C. G. GORDON. 29. 12. 84." The decision to use the steamers for a hasty advance to Khartoum was instantly taken, but Sir Charles Wilson, who had succeeded Herbert Stewart in command, ordered certain reconnaissances to be made before they moved. They actually started up the Nile again on 24th January.

On 6th February England had the news that Khartoum had fallen, and the relief force had been too late. In official quarters it had been known twenty-four hours earlier. Sir Charles Wilson's little advance force, steaming up the Nile, had come in sight of Khartoum, and simultaneously under heavy firing from the river-sides, on 28th January. Their eyes searched for the flag that should have been flying. A man had shouted from the bank on the previous day that Khartoum had fallen, and Gordon was killed. The flag was not there. After satisfying himself by other observations that Khartoum was wholly in the Mahdi's hands Sir Charles Wilson turned his steamers and went downstream. For a few days England refused to believe the worst ; rumours about Gordon were rife among the natives around Wolseley's camp at Korti, and for ten days England remained in suspense. Then on 16th February was published a telegram from Wolseley, saying that Gordon had been killed. Just before sunrise on 26th January, with the steamers so close at hand, he had faced at the entrance to his residence the spears of the Mahdi's horde, and died as fearlessly as he had lived.

The angry excitement in England was intense. From the Queen herself, who sent her Ministers a sharp telegram of rebuke without observing the ordinary custom of putting the message in cypher,[1] down to the humblest of her subjects, the outcry against Mr Gladstone and his Government arose. Gordon had indeed become almost a figure of legend in the popular mind ; men told how he had gone through the whole of the campaign of the Ever-Victorious Army in China with no weapon but a cane, how little he had cared for danger in his earlier days in the Soudan. His religious fervour, his disregard for himself, his missionary enthusiasm, all contributed to produce a kind of idealisation of him against which no amount of knowledge of the inner history of his last mission could have prevailed. Be this at least said to the honour of those most bitterly attacked on account of his death—that no word was uttered by them to destroy the character which the prevalent hero-worship built up. It is true that no contrary word would have been likely to carry weight; but the many that might have been said in heat or exasperation by those who were now held responsible were left unsaid.

In the nation's hour of bitterness the news published on 21st February that Herbert Stewart had died of his wound was a real additional grief. Gallant, frank and sweet-natured, he was in the opinion of many the finest soldier of them all. Parliament had just met again ; and in spite of its not meeting with the usual discussion of the Government's work in a debate on an Address, it could not of course proceed far without an opportunity for arraigning Ministers. On 27th February a Vote of Censure was moved, and was only defeated by 302 votes to 288. The Government had to face a double disaffection among its followers, the greater one contained in the reason for the motion of censure, and a lesser one arising from the hostility of one group of Liberals to the announced policy of not allowing

[1] Morley's *Life of Gladstone*, iii. 167.

the Mahdi to hold Khartoum. The latter led to a number of abstentions from the division. But, as we have said, the existence of a great piece of work, half-accomplished, tided the Cabinet over the internal dissensions which followed such a vote. It was agreed in the Cabinet that the Redistribution Bill should be carried through. There was also reason to believe that the Conservatives were not at the moment very anxious to come into office, and shoulder the thankless task of taking secondary decisions about the Soudan.[1] Indeed the Conservatives were in no sense in a strong position ; the reproaches for the death of Gordon had not been aimed entirely in one direction, and Conservatives were reminded that they had at no period in the past year displayed the possession of any policy of their own which might have helped to guide events ; their work of criticism and of extracting from the Ministry at any given moment its intentions had been so ill-done that there was even room for asking, with what would in easier circumstances have been comical bewilderment, whether we were actually at war, and if so, with whom.[2]

For one half of England these were the events that shadowed and embittered the opening of 1885. There was another half which had not at this time heart or strength to look beyond its own urgent need. The winter was full of distress and unemployment. Early in January three or four thousand men in Birmingham presented themselves, orderly, quiet, but near starvation, before the mayor, asking for work. From every great town came a similar cry, and in London the distress was as much greater as the poor streets spread further. Deputations had gone to the Lord Mayor in earlier years, and a few thoughtful people had paid attention to them. Now with the more bitter need came a new and more menacing frame of mind among the men. On 16th February a deputation of unemployed went to the Local Government Board, where

[1] *The Times*, 2nd March 1885.　　[2] Ditto, 14th February 1885.

they were received by Mr George Russell, the Parliamentary Secretary. He could make them no more than an official reply; the problem they represented could hardly be said officially to have any existence. That fact was, to the men concerned, the heart of their reproach; and this was what they meant when they asserted at the end of their fruitless visit that the Board and the Government would be responsible for the deaths that destitution would bring in the next few weeks. " Responsible for murder " was the exaggerated phrase they used; but they saw strong and willing men being pushed out of life, and if it were not a deliberate process, such as might fairly be called murder, then the sooner someone began to deliberate about it the better. As the men left the Local Government Board they distributed a manifesto fiercely worded against a Government which had acknowledged its helplessness; the manifesto bore the names of John Burns, J. E. Williams, William Henry, and James Macdonald. Round the corner in Downing Street they held a defiant meeting before the police had gathered force to stop them, and a man spoke hanging to the cross-bar of a lamp-post. We may picture him there—the first portent of a series of troubled years.

The problem of the unemployed had, we have remarked, no official existence. Yet at this very moment it came nearer to having one than it was to come again for some years. At the end of January a conference, extraordinary to look back upon, took place in London. It was called the Industrial Remuneration Conference, and it had been rendered possible by an anonymous gift of £1000 for the purpose. The fact is significant of how much the social unrest had begun to impress thoughtful people, however little appearance it made on the surface of things. The proceedings of the conference are a most interesting index of the state of sociological opinion at the time of the dissolution of the old individualism. The intellectuals of

the official and political world met face to face the teachers
of socialism, and those leaders of the trade unions who were
introducing profound changes into the theory of trade
combination. Sir Charles Dilke presided over the meeting.
Lord Bramwell read a paper against socialism ; Mr
Bernard Shaw joyously defended a thesis that the landlord,
the capitalist and the burglar were equally damaging to the
community. Mr Arthur Balfour criticised Henry George's
Progress and Poverty ; Mr Shaw Lefevre spoke of the
English land system as " relics of feudalism " which should
be swept away ; Mr Williams, of the Social Democratic
Federation, retorted that when Mr Chamberlain spoke of
nationalising the land, but avoided saying anything about
manufactures, he was but an " Artful Dodger." Mr John
Morley, with a watchful eye upon the proceedings of the
Fair Trade League, warned the Conference of the fallacies
of the Imperial Zollverein school, and of the hopelessness
of expecting any colony to give up its tariff. In the less
controversial hours of the conference the Rev. H. Solly
preached the doctrine, more familiar to our day than to
his, of avoiding congestion of labour by the institution
of industrial villages ; and Mr John Burns, with no little
common-sense, pointed out how much the principle of
socialism was already embodied in the normal activity of
great and advanced municipalities.

There was leaven enough here, and some of it seemed to
be already at work in the community. Mr Shaw Lefevre's
references to the land had this additional point—that he
had been Chairman of a Departmental Committee which
had reported in the middle of January in favour of an
allotment system for labourers ; and Mr Jesse Collings was
at the height of his advocacy of small holdings, while Mr
Chamberlain was making speeches which were thought to
point not obscurely to a special taxation of landed property
such as might advance a break-up of big estates.[1] Again

[1] *The Times*, 5th February 1885.

the hostility visible on one side of the conference to the middleman and the capitalist had its practical counterpart in the advancing work of the co-operative movement. It was already including both production and distribution, though it was more engaged in the latter. Mr Burns's reference to municipalities was also full of significance. The opinion of the social reformers of the period that " the era of administration had come " issued in January 1885 in the formation of the Fabian Society, whose principle was the advancement of socialistic ideals at every opportunity afforded by the existing machinery of the State, in contra-distinction to those socialists who wished to begin by recreating the machinery. Mr Bernard Shaw had appeared at the Industrial Remuneration Conference as a representative of this new society. The Fabians based their hopes mainly on Local Government. The great municipalities had at the moment not much further to expand ; the chief project of the year, that of Manchester's water-supply from Thirlmere, had been really settled when parliamentary powers for the work had been obtained in 1879, though six years had intervened before the Water Committee of the Council resolved to commence the undertaking. But the lesser municipalities might still be aroused ; and in any case there remained the prospect of reorganisation of county government, which was still an unfulfilled promise.

Once again, just when a domestic problem had gathered force and impetus which might have moved Parliament, an urgent distraction intervened, and again it was a bequest of "Beaconsfieldism." It came this time from Afghanistan. Russia, advancing her possessions in Central Asia, had annexed Turcoman territory; and the necessary conse-quence had been a commission to delimit the frontier between that territory and Afghanistan. The British relations with the Ameer were such that the commission consisted of British and Russian diplomats. While they were at work Russian troops came into conflict with Afghan troops at Penjdeh, routed them after a heavy fight, and occupied the place. On this question Mr Gladstone showed none of the lack of interest which had been so fatal in Egypt. Partly, no doubt, this was due to the detached sharpness of the incident ; there was no ambiguity as to England's position. But at the same time, however serious the matter was at the moment, however anxious the diplomatic problem, the fact remains that the Penjdeh incident could be looked back upon afterwards as " a perfect godsend " from a Liberal politician's point of view.[1] England was so much roused that a vote of credit was passed with no difficulty, the reserves were called out, and every eye was turned upon the possibility of war with Russia. Mr Gladstone, seizing the opportunity to deplore a distraction of our forces, was able to abandon quietly the whole of the Khartoum problem, and in addition to meet the remaining costs of the Soudan expedition, amounting to four and a half millions, out of a vote of credit already obtained, instead of having to move a separate vote and thereby definitely raise the question of abandoning Khartoum. Thus Mr Gladstone achieved the feat of satisfying at one and the same time the Radicals, by removing the possibility of more bloodshed in Egypt, and the Whigs, by opposing Russian aggression. The result rewarded his admirable party skill. The Russian menace subsided, and by the beginning of May an agreement had been reached which removed all danger. Wolseley was ordered home from Dongola, the decision was taken to establish the Egyptian frontier at Wady Halfa, and the hot fit in England passed as opportunely as in one sense it had arisen. Baring's despatches from Egypt were to the effect that, while he could not pretend to agree in all the decisions that had been taken, he was sure that the general lines of the Government's policy were perfectly practicable, and

[1] Holland's *Life of the Duke of Devonshire*, ii. 31.

would, if persevered in, lead to success. On 30th June the Mahdi died, and his place in the Soudan was taken by the Khalifa.

A minor interest brought out by the return of the troops was the fact that, for the first time, colonial troops joined the British regular forces in an affair in which their colony was not directly concerned, and took, as it were, Imperial status. An Australian contingent had been landed at Suakin, and had taken part in operations under Sir Gerald Graham. With this development of colonial spirit may be linked a speech made by Mr Goschen at Manchester in February, which marks the beginning of the most striking change of our time in the hierarchy of Government departments. He pointed out that colonising, both by the British and by other nations, had now spread so widely that in every part of the world Britain had civilised neighbours; therefore statesmanship, which had never found a home at the Colonial Office, would have to be brought to bear upon our colonial relations and upon the foreign relations springing out of them. For the moment this pronouncement lost its value amid the difficulties of the year, but it deserves to be recorded in its place.

The Government appeared now to have ridden out another storm. But the Cabinet was working uncomfortably; Mr Chamberlain was making speeches which his less Radical colleagues disliked; coercion was holding Ireland down; and the question of relieving its severity and at the same time introducing some measure of local self-government was a constant source of friction amongst Ministers. On 8th June the Government fell, being defeated on an amendment to the second reading of the Budget, dealing with the proposed increase of the beer duty. It was common knowledge that the Government Whips had deliberately permitted the defeat. Mr Gladstone resigned. His action has a place in constitutional history, since it had not hitherto been customary for defeat on a minor point to involve resignation, while a government had a majority for its general policy.[1] But on the other hand the smallness of the majority on the Vote of Censure would have been sufficient cause for a change of government, if the desire to pass the Redistribution Bill had not operated. The step that was now taken caused some difficulty. A dissolution of Parliament was impossible until both the new franchise and the new distribution of seats were in operation ; and it became necessary therefore for Lord Salisbury to consider taking office without a majority in the Commons. Not unnaturally he began by stipulating for a promise of support from the outgoing Liberals. In the end he took office without any definite promise, but with an understanding that necessary matters, such as supply, would not be contested. Yet the brief remainder of the life of this Parliament was not to be devoid of interest or importance. Now that the party balance was again in question the Irish vote recovered that power of swaying the scales, which since 1882 it had largely ceased to possess. For some time coercion, which at the period of the Phœnix Park murders had been restored without compunction, had been afflicting Radical consciences ; though the revival of dynamite outrages had blurred sensitiveness on the subject. Those outrages had not ceased. At the very beginning of January 1885 there was another explosion on the Underground Railway, this time between Gower Street and King's Cross stations ; only slight personal injuries resulted. On 24th January there was another group of simultaneous explosions, such as the previous year had seen, and these were the most notorious explosions of this period of Fenianism. They occurred in Westminster Hall, in the House of Commons itself, and in the White Tower

[1] See an article on English Public Life in *The Edinburgh Review*, July 1911.

of the Tower of London. In Westminster Hall two policemen were very seriously injured, but practically no damage, save to the stone flooring, was inflicted on the building; the concussion had the extraordinary effect of shaking down from the timbers of the roof the dust of ages, and those who entered the hall directly afterwards walked on a thick grey carpet of it. Parliament had not yet met; consequently the explosion in the House of Commons, beyond half-wrecking the seats and galleries, had no result, except the natural alarm at the thought that dynamite could be deposited in a spot normally so well policed. In the Tower of London several people were injured, and damage done by a fire which followed the explosion. Yet when party exigencies required it, politicians did not find that difficulty in keeping their minds clear of a confusion between Fenianism and the Home Rule movement, which they were equally ready on other occasions to indulge. Some of them displayed certainly after the change of government a suppleness which those who were not politicians found unaccountable. The spectacle of Lord Randolph Churchill supporting, and even Sir Michael Hicks Beach regarding benevolently, a motion by Parnell calling attention to Lord Spencer's " maladministration of the law " under the Coercion Act, was bewildering to most, and repugnant to many. Lord Randolph Churchill's reputation stamped his share in the matter as being purely tactical. But what was to be thought of the speech delivered in the House of Lords by the new Viceroy of Ireland, Lord Carnarvon ? [1] He had been Governor-General of British colonies, and in his speech he remarked that, as he had seen those communities living in loyal obedience to the law and the Crown, so he could not see at home " any irreconcilable bar to the unity and amity " of English and Irish. It was a hint, rather than a statement; the only positive part of the speech was

[1] *The Times*, 7th July 1885.

its repudiation of coercion. But since it was a speech made by the new Viceroy in the presence of the new Prime Minister (and a speech by a viceroy was in any case so unusual that it had had but two precedents since the Union) [1] no slight interpretation of its meaning could easily be formed. It was not an unfair conclusion that the precedent of the self-governing colonies was in the Ministry's mind. What had the Liberals to set against it ? The answer is, a policy of local self-government, for which at this moment Mr Chamberlain stood most prominently. He was taking a strong line, and in June 1885, just after the defeat of Mr Gladstone's Ministry, had shown his sense of the suddenly restored importance of the Irish vote by making the famous speech in which he compared the existing rule of Ireland to the rule of oppressed Poland ; an Irishman " could not move without an official controlling him." At the same time his policy amounted not to a separate government for Ireland, but only to a system of local councils, under a central board in Dublin. Even that degree of Irish independence had not been accepted by most of his colleagues ; and meanwhile on the Conservative side Lord Randolph Churchill's fair words to Ireland were so much disliked that at a great meeting at Liverpool, which he addressed at the end of July, the two members for the constituency in which he spoke took the serious step of declining to appear on the platform. The Irish party was thus confronted with a situation in which two conciliatory policies were being expressed, but neither with such authority that it could be definitely selected at the expense of the other. Strong as Lord Carnarvon's speech had been, it could not be used to pin the new Government down. As soon as Liberals began to formulate the idea that between Lord Salisbury, Lord Randolph Churchill, and Parnell there was an understanding as to the support of the Irish vote, it was seen that

[1] Morley's *Life of Gladstone*, iii. 211.

6

nothing had happened to render impossible a flat denial of any such understanding.[1]

A summer of most unusual heat interrupted political warfare. The thermometer more than once reached 90° in the shade ; and trade, which had begun the year somewhat slackly, had no chance of recovery when the heat combined with the collapse of the session to send people at an early date out of town. The sight of the unemployed at the beginning of the year had given some measure of the commercial conditions. There were those among business men who thought that one cause of weakness was that means of production had outstripped means of distribution ; this was a Lancashire view. Trade was bad not only in England, but all over the world, largely because of the appreciation of gold ; and at the same time, although capital was cheap, there was little encouragement towards speculation.[2] A Royal Commission on Trade had been asked for, and was believed to be in process of formation ; but its actual appearance was delayed, and many people felt that after all, with the various nostrums then in the market—Bimetallism, Fair Trade, and the repeal of the Bank Act, for example—a commission might be but a hotbed for faddists. Its best work would probably lie in inquiring into the relations between British traders and foreign customers, and into the possibility of more assistance to those relations from the Foreign Office. Meanwhile so much change was beginning in the banking world that it seems to be fair to conclude that the struggle of trade with enlarged competition and narrowed coinage supply was leading to a reconsideration of the principles of banking. In 1885 Glyn, Mills, Currie & Co. decided to register themselves under the Companies Acts (though not with limited liability), and so undertake the statutory duty of publishing a balance sheet ; this was thought to be

---

[1] See *The Times*, 8th and 10th August 1885.
[2] See a speech by Mr Goschen, *The Times*, 24th June 1885.

a good example for private banks to follow. An equally important change is seen in the commencement about this time of the absorption of small banks into larger combinations; the Capital and Counties Bank took over the Gloucestershire Banking Company in 1885; and there had previously been one or two amalgamations in the Birmingham district. The relief of the gold supply had not yet begun, though the progress of events in the Transvaal is marked by the description of the new "slimes" process for dealing with gold from deep levels.[1]

Early in the summer the Royal Commission on the Housing of the Poor issued a first interim report. It recommended for the time being a more active enforcement of the existing law; but it proposed also the purchase of three prison sites—those of Coldbath Fields, Pentonville and Millbank—and setting them free for housing purposes by demolishing the prisons. That at Coldbath Fields was already out of use, and Millbank was shortly to be abandoned as a place of detention. A Bill to forward these recommendations was passed by Parliament after the change of Government. It also strengthened and made applicable to the whole country certain powers of the Local Government Board hitherto confined to London, and contained a provision that anyone letting a house to a tenant without taking reasonable precautions for the health of the inmates would be liable for any death due to his negligence. A more remarkable provision (especially as events had placed the Bill in Tory hands) was a stipulation that the two prison sites which it had been decid d to take over should not be taken at their market value; this was regarded as a step towards State socialism.[2] Still more curious in the mouth of Lord Salisbury, who moved the second reading of the Bill in the House of Lords, was a clause deciding that the price of land

[1] *The Times*, 12th August 1885.
[2] Ditto, 17th July 1885.

for housing purposes was not to be the best that could be got, but the best that in all the circumstances could reasonably be obtained. So easy a thing was the Fair Rent principle when its field of operation was not Ireland ! Oddly enough, there was less comment on the clause empowering the Local Government Board to set Housing Acts in operation, a duty hitherto left to local authorities.

Society lost in this year two or three notable figures. Lord Houghton died in August with one of the most famous and most charming of death-bed sayings on his lips : " Yes, I am going to join the majority, and, you know, I have always preferred minorities." Both the charm and the truth of the saying were characteristic of him ; he was never prone to take the facile view of things ; and under his typically English appearance there lay an essentially un-English nature, alike in his ease of manner and in his wide tolerance. At the beginning of October died Lord Shaftesbury, a man whose natural goodness directed him, as perhaps natural goodness seldom does, into the very paths where he could most fulfil himself. He was proud, somewhat intolerant of opposition, unyielding in principle, and for those reasons unlikely to have made his life success-ful in the normal paths of office ; but, diverted by his passionate sympathy and eager mind into philanthropic paths, he found every quality he had work together for good.[1] He died before he had seriously to measure his zeal for doing what he thought right by the working poor against the working men's new inclination to judge what they themselves thought to be their due from the community. But his advocacy of the Factory Laws had been the first assault upon individualism—an assault made much more effective by the support of his great name. A person socially less lofty, but none the less a real figure of the

[1] For the characters of Lord Houghton and Lord Shaftesbury see Mr G. W. E. Russell's *Collections and Recollections,* chapters iii. and v.

London world, was Sir Moses Montefiore, who died in July, well past his hundredth year; he was associated with the Rothschilds, and had been the second Jewish sheriff of London, just after the days of Emancipation.

Of material progress the year offers little to record. The Manchester Ship Canal Bill at last was law, after having had to be promoted three times. The enormous cost of these preliminary stages raised the whole question of the oppressiveness of private bill procedure, and the futility of a separate inquiry before a committee of each House; but the criticism died down in the face of more stirring parliamentary events. Before the end of the year it was said that the project had already reduced railway freights between Manchester and Liverpool from 9s. 2d. a ton to 8s. a ton.[1] Naval experts were excited by the trials of the first submersible boat. It had been invented by Nordenfeldt, the gunmaker, and it was sixty-four feet long, constructed of steel plates varying from five-eighths of an inch in thickness at the centre to three-eighths of an inch at the ends. It was submerged partly by filling water-tanks and partly by the action of vertical propellers, and when under water its fire-box was sealed, and pressure was obtained from tanks previously heated. Its best performance was staying down for six hours with a crew of four men.[2] The invention gave fresh point to the advocacy of liquid fuel for the navy, which Admiral Selwyn started this year. But a steam submarine was not a very practicable machine, and the idea made no real advances till electricity had become much more potent. A new electric locomotive made its appearance in November, the fresh principle being a revolving motor rendering belt transmission unnecessary, which was one more step toward electric trams. Meanwhile the steam tram at last invaded London, and one was running on the North

[1] *The Times,* 30th October 1885.
[2] Ditto, 1st October 1885.

Metropolitan lines. A strange new method of propelling vehicles must be modestly recorded at this point. A Mr Butler constructed a vehicle, in the form of a tricycle, which was driven by an internal combustion engine. Ever since the days of Trevethick's steam carriage, in 1802, mechanical propulsion of carriages had interested inventors. Against a dead weight of opposition they pursued their schemes, and for heavy haulage steam traction engines had long been in use, under the strict limitations of the Act of 1865, which forbade a speed of more than four miles an hour, and enjoined that every such vehicle must be preceded by a man carrying a red flag. Even this discouragement did not wholly extinguish invention, and in 1881 an attempt, though a vain one, had been made to prove that the Act did not apply to a steam tricycle. Mr Butler's was a completely fresh start. He applied to his machine the principle of exploding vapour—benzoline vapour was the one he used—inside the piston cylinder by means of an electric spark. At the same time Gottlieb Daimler in France was applying the same principle, but using petroleum spirit to provide the vapour.[1] As far as England is concerned the subject has to be left for the present, with Mr Butler's isolated idea useless in face of the Act of 1865, and commercially still-born.

The demand for sixpenny telegrams had been acceded to,[2] but the details required no little arrangement, since under the old minimum of a shilling the names and addresses of the receiver and the sender had been transmitted free of charge, and the Post Office declined to continue this practice with a sixpenny minimum. This year also saw the completion of the Revised Version of the Bible, the version of the Old Testament having been finished on 1st May, after fifteen years' work. The New Testament version had been finished and published two or three years

[1] See the article on Motors in the *Encyclopædia Britannica*.
[2] The new system came into force on 1st October 1885.

earlier. The Church of England was at present in smoother water, and the Ritual controversy had largely declined. Evangelicalism, indeed, had not weakened ; for a year or two earlier the Church Army had been founded (it held its first large annual meeting on 28th May 1884) to take up in the streets and byways the same kind of work as the Salvation Army was doing. The latter still met with strong opposition ; dragoons had to be called out to quell a fight between it and the Skeleton Army at Worthing, and there were savage riots at Derby, in which stones flew and the band instruments were used as weapons. A somewhat old-fashioned outbreak of morality in this year was the discussion of the nude in art which accompanied the course of the Royal Academy Exhibition in the summer.[1] A more important event in the history of art is that in 1885 was founded the New English Art Club. There had been until now hardly any opportunity for an artist not in accord with the theory and practice of the Royal Academy to set his work before the public. The Grosvenor Gallery had, indeed, attached to itself the Pre-Raphaelite group and the æsthetic movement. But it had no inclination to pass outside the safe financial ground provided by a craze. Meanwhile there had been growing up in England a school of painters, trained for the most part in Paris, whose work, not so mannered as to take the ecstatic fancy of the æsthetic, nor so consciously original as to have a public of its own, like Whistler's, was nevertheless vital and revolutionary enough to fail altogether of entrance to the Academy. The work of this school had been the most notable feature of the Glasgow Exhibition of 1881, and it was high time that it should be seen in London. The New English Art Club gathered genius and talent which has ever since sapped the reputation of the Royal Academy.

In the world of education the year 1885 is significant as showing the first signs of a general acceptance of

[1] *The Times*, 22nd May, and other dates, 1885.

new duties. At a conference in Manchester it was stated with some pride that Owens College was in a position to offer to the working man a choice of three hundred lectures, the cost of which was voluntarily met by Manchester residents. Towards the end of the year the People's Palace scheme took shape, the object again being the provision of advanced education for working men and women ; and something of the same sort is to be traced in the movement for making the London University a teaching body, instead of a merely examining body. The year saw also a notable step forward in science, photography being for the first time successfully applied to astronomical purposes. The value of this was promptly seen in the proposal, emanating in the first instance from Dr Gill, Astronomer Royal at the Cape, for international co-operation in a great work of charting the heavens.

The autumn brought with it the uproar of a general election, in which one great issue was obscured by conflicting half-lights. Over the field of politics there were issues enough. Mr Chamberlain's speeches outlined the whole range of the Radical programme, including bankruptcy reform, a reform of the Charity Commission with a view to enlarging the social area of educational endowments, county government reform, free education, cottages and land for labourers, shipping measures, a graduated income tax; and some form of self-government for Ireland, and disestablishment of the Church of England. Mr Gladstone's manifesto was naturally less far-reaching. On his own side critics called it a " rather weak production," and opined that " if it was not that the party are ready to take anything from him, it would fall rather flat." [1] He placed first reform of the procedure of the House of Commons, and on county government reform avoided committing himself to a definite scheme ; on the land question he proposed the

[1] Lord Hartington to Mr Goschen : Elliot's *Life of Lord Goschen*, ii. 2;

abolition of entail and a system of freer transfer, adding
that he " would rejoice if these or other means in themselves commendable led to a large increase in the owners
of the soil"; on disestablishment he spoke oracularly, and
seemed to regard it as but a distant possibility ; on free
education he was careful to point out the disadvantages ;
on Ireland he expressed himself in favour of the greatest
possible extension of self-government consistent with
maintenance of the authority of the Crown and Parliament.
Of these proposals one—that of county government
reform—was as prominent in the programme of the other
side. The existing confusion of the spheres of local
authorities was extreme, the justices administering some
Acts, the local Health Boards others, the Guardians of the
Poor and the School Boards still others. Disestablishment
had appeared somewhat unexpectedly as a very forcible
item in the election ; apparently there was some hope that
the newly enfranchised might be moved on the subject,[1] and
it was at any rate found, as the polling time approached,
that nothing more interested the electors. Mr Chamberlain had by this time rather drawn in his horns ; he had had
an interview with Mr Gladstone at Hawarden on 8th
October, and by the end of the month was saying that
disestablishment could hardly be dealt with in the coming
Parliament. But many candidates were already committed to it, and churchmen were roused in every constituency. Against the general Liberal programme the Tories
had not, beyond county government, much positive line
of their own. But they made a good fight out of the
differences between Mr Gladstone and the advanced
Radicals. Lord Randolph Churchill vastly increased his
reputation at this sort of warfare, and did not shrink from
competing with Mr Chamberlain on his own caucus ground.
He became president of the Conservative News Agency,
an organisation for supplying caricatures and pamphlets

[1] See, *e.g.*, *The Times*, 11th April 1885.

to candidates in all constituencies, and for supplementing the resources of local newspapers. The mistake of raising the disestablishment question enough to irritate the clergy, and then dropping it enough to discourage Nonconformists, was a notable score for the Tories. It may be added here that the Woman Suffrage movement had been so far forwarded by the opportunities it had received for debate in the House that it had been able to exact after the General Election more precise information of the position occupied by the question in the opinions of the new House. Out of 495 members for England and Wales 253 were in favour of Woman Suffrage and 102 against ; of the 72 Scottish members 24 were in favour and 18 against ; of the 86 Irish members 25 were in favour and 3 against.

Behind all the electoral conflict was that issue which we have described as obscured by half-lights. The Liberals offered Ireland local government by councils. The Tories made no specific offer ; but it was fairly well known that Parnell had spoken of having got " something better " than the Liberal offer.[1] He himself had declared outright for national independence in a speech at Dublin in August 1885 ; but no one in England supposed the " something better " to amount to this ideal. The final disposal of the Irish vote in English constituencies turned on a matter that involved no revelations. Mr Gladstone in a speech at Edinburgh had spoken of the " dangers of a situation in which either party would be liable to be seduced from the right path by the temptation which might be offered to it by the vote of the Irish members," and exhorted the electors of Great Britain to return one party or the other by a majority which would make it independent of the Irish vote. Some of his followers were dismayed ; they expected Parnell instantly to denounce Gladstone as insincere in his promises to Ireland, if he was so anxious for an independent majority. But Parnell still used no language

---

[1] Barry O'Brien's *Life of Parnell*, ii. 137.

but that of attempting to persuade Mr Gladstone to formulate precisely his proposals with regard to Ireland. Mr Gladstone replied with a rather bantering speech, to the effect that he was not in office, and that it did not lie with him to make proposals. This it was that stirred Parnell to fury, and he issued the sharp manifesto by which the Irish vote went to Conservative candidates.

It did not, however, carry the day in Great Britain : the result of the election showed a return of 333 Liberals against 251 Tories. But the pledged Home Rule party, the unquestioning adherents of Parnell, who had been but 35 in 1880, were now a solid block of 86 ; they had carried every seat in Ireland that was not Conservative. As for the newly enfranchised electorate, analysis showed that the Tory fears had been singularly unfounded, and their opposition to the Franchise Bill, as a piece of party legislation, singularly foolish. Of a county electorate of 2,303,133 voters no less than 1,837,088 had gone to the poll, and of these votes 1,020,774 had been Liberal, and 816,314 Conservative. It was a fair deduction that party divisions ran now to the bottom of English life, and that there was no such class feeling as had made the sweeping results after the Reform Bill of 1832. A minor interest of the election, but one which closes for the time a subject of prominence in the few previous years, was the general defeat of the " Fair Trade " party. Its leader, Mr Ecroyd, had been beaten in Lancashire ; Mr James Lowther lost his seat in Lincolnshire, and four or five other candidates committed to the policy had been beaten. A general criticism of the results on the Tory side was that apathy among their leaders on domestic questions, and the activity and force of the trade unions, had largely turned the election.[1]

Almost immediately, however, this second start for the Liberals was gravely compromised. On 18th December was published the famous rumour that Mr Gladstone was con-

[1] *The Times*, 15th December 1885.

sidering a scheme of complete Home Rule for Ireland ; the denial which followed was cautious, amounting to no more than that the statement was unauthorised. It was enough to set at work the liveliest speculations as to the position of Lord Hartington, Mr Chamberlain, Mr Goschen, and other Liberal leaders, whose repudiation of any measure of real independence for Ireland had been emphatic ; and the political year ended in uncertainty and disturbance.

Socially, too, it ended in apprehension. The approach of winter revived all the distressing evidences of unemployment, and a new militant atmosphere had been aroused by the determined campaign of the police against street meetings. In September occurred the first of the cases to attract much attention. The police arrested a bannerbearer in the midst of a socialist procession, and in the police-court case which followed William Morris was fined for interference. This drew attention to the Social Democratic Federation, which in April had hardly succeeded in interesting even the casual crowd of a Hyde Park meeting. The free speech campaign grew before the end of the year to a size which caused *The Times* to pronounce upon it as very dangerous and ominous, when it was taken in conjunction with the Irish agitation, the Crofter movement in Scotland, and the whole programme of advanced Liberalism.[1] Within twelve months its ominousness depended on no conjunction with other movements. In general elections labour had as yet no large direct share ; but the Trade Union Congress issued in September an election address to the trades bidding them demand of the candidates promises of land for allotments, of free elementary education, and of the removal of " all unnecessary obstacles to civil and magisterial work." In this last direction a step had already been taken by the appointment of the first working-men magistrates [2]—a printer,

[1] 31st December 1885.
[2] Announced by *The Manchester Guardian* in May 1885.

a spinner and a weaver, all secretaries of trade unions, being appointed to the Bench of the Duchy of Lancaster in May, and a miners' agent being appointed in June.

In the closing days of 1885 occurred the last Soudan fight that was to take place for some years. The withdrawal to Wady Halfa was not quite completed when, on 30th December, the Khalifa attacked the troops at Ginniss. He was badly beaten, 800 of his men being killed ; and the chief satisfaction growing out of the battle was that Egyptian troops had been engaged, as well as British, and had thus had some of their fear of the dervishes removed. The general policy in regard to the Soudan had been carried on by Lord Salisbury without alteration.

CHAPTER VIII

1886 : HOME RULE, THE NAMELESS PARTY, AND THE LABOUR RIOTS

EVEN at the very dawn of 1886 the great Home Rule "split" was in the making. The published rumours of Mr Gladstone's intentions were as much an effect as a cause of popular speculation about them [1]; speculation had begun, because everyone was sure that he must have intentions ; and assurance arose from the fact that everyone was pretty certain Lord Salisbury had some. However, the actual publication of the ideas which Mr Gladstone was said to have in his mind did undoubtedly create a new situation ; and the excitement it caused was not in the least out of proportion to the gravity of what was taking place behind the scenes. Lord Hartington and Mr Goschen were already half alienated. At this crisis, as at the time of the Mid-Lothian campaign, Mr Gladstone displayed his curious custom of regarding the real factors in a situation as materially affected by the formal political factors. He was not in office, and Lord Salisbury was ; therefore the circumstances of the election results warranted an understanding between the Tories and the Nationalists, in order to keep the former in office ; therefore Mr Gladstone felt himself justified in awaiting a Tory plan of Irish legislation, and his own ideas were not a project in the real sense. This was an attitude much like his conviction that even after the Mid-Lothian Campaign he was free to accept or refuse the Premiership. To Lord Hartington both these

[1] Morley's *Life of Gladstone*, iii. 265.

cases were equally an empty adherence to forms. Whatever might be the political theory of the situation, the truth was that Mr Gladstone was considering a plan of Irish self-government. This fact dominated the situation. If the Tories had any intentions of concession to Ireland, they could not now be known ; whenever Mr Gladstone moved, his unrivalled position in politics and in the public view gave him the field, and the other party merely reacted automatically in the opposite direction. Mr Gladstone did not himself recognise this ; he made an offer to the Tories, in December 1885, of leaving the field to them ; and the argument was used on the Tory side that the Irish were Conservative people, only accidentally thrown in 1880 on to the Liberal side.[1] But in truth the return of the importance of the Irish vote had revived as much of old prejudice as of new energy ; and there were already complaints of the Irish question being " thrust to the forefront," when local government in England, land transfer, and the procedure of the House of Commons were the questions awaiting decision.[2] Besides, the nature of the exchange of opinion among Liberal leaders must have been shrewdly gauged by the Tory leaders, for by the time Parliament met the latter had decided upon a course in which no glimmer of their last year's temper of tentative concession to Ireland was to be found. Not only were they leaving the field to Mr Gladstone, but they were going to drive him into it. They must have known the instant cost to him. Parliament met for the Queen's speech on 21st January ; on 26th January notice was given in the House of Commons of the Government's intention to introduce a Coercion Bill for Ireland, and on the same day the Government fell. Mr Jesse Collings carried an amendment to the address on the

[1] See a letter by Mr Wilfrid Blunt in *The Times*, 1st January 1886.

[2] *The Times*, 1st January 1886:

subject of Labourers' Allotments—the " three acres and
a cow " amendment—on which the Irish party voted with
the Liberals. But the significant point was that eighteen
Liberals, including Hartington, Goschen, Courtney, Henry
James, Lubbock, Arthur Elliot and Albert Grey, voted
against the amendment; and more than fifty Liberals,
including John Bright, abstained from the division.
Governments have often been overthrown by more or
less irrelevant votes ; but what was there in Mr Collings's
victory to cause *The Times* at once to start the idea that
"a sagacious Liberal Leader"—Lord Hartington, for choice
—should seize the opportunity to construct a new party
out of equally dissatisfied Liberals and Conservatives ?
To that degree had the " split " already become notorious.
Meanwhile, on 28th January, Lord Salisbury resigned
office, and on 1st February Mr Gladstone became Prime
Minister for the third time.

As if the year were not opening in sufficiently unusual
circumstances, a thoroughly startling event now interrupted the bent of public attention. The troubles and
distress of the unemployed had failed to attract notice
amid the political excitement. On 8th February a meeting
was being held in Trafalgar Square, which appears to have
been chiefly an occasion taken by the Fair Trade speakers
to call attention to unemployment as a product of Free
Trade. Suddenly the meeting was invaded by men from
branches of the Social Democratic Federation, headed by
Hyndman, John Burns, and Champion. To them such
a gathering seemed a mere exploiting of the sufferings of
the unemployed for a political purpose, and they captured
it. In an instant its temper was wholly and violently
changed. A seething mob left the Square, marched
through Pall Mall, St James's Street, and Piccadilly,
smashed the club windows from which men were looking,
as they had looked before, at the woeful procession, over-
turned and smashed broughams and other private carriages

and then divided into raiding parties, which went breaking
windows and doors along South Audley Street, Oxford
Street and Regent Street. For a couple of hours the
mob held these sacred precincts in terror. The police
had been entirely taken by surprise, and could not muster
in time. No life was lost, no personal injuries were inflicted ; the crowd was admitted next day to have had
" forbearance," and to have included a large proportion
of men who though poor and distressed had no thought of
crime [1] : but all the same London at large felt that it had
had its glimpse of revolution. This, it said to itself, was
at the back of the vague mutterings it had heard about
street-corner meetings and the right of free speech ; and
it proceeded to draw the distinction, which has always
comforted the respectable classes, between the genuine
unemployed and the agitator. The latter was pronounced
a " moral dynamiter," and the former class was said to
be made up of the " inevitable " products of casual labour,
bad housing and laziness. Yet fright remained strong
enough to cause the ventilation of some rather vague
plans for undertaking " public works " to give employment ; and from letters written to the newspapers by
various employers it is plain that they at least knew better
than to blind themselves by drawing facile distinctions
in regard to the temper of labouring men. While no
one was arrested on account of the startling incidents
in London, trouble was brewing elsewhere. There was
rioting in Bristol ; and in Gateshead, Glasgow, Manchester,
Norwich, Nottingham and Sheffield there was such acute
distress that at any moment outbreaks might occur.[2]
In Manchester, indeed, there was a small riot, which had
a curious origin ; it began not with the mere holding of a

---

[1] *The Times*, 10th February 1886.
[2] In Leicester, where the battle between vaccination and its
opponents was raging, prosecutions were suspended at this time,
because of the prevailing distress.

socialist meeting one Sunday at the end of February, but with the gathering of a crowd after the public-houses closed in the afternoon, to attack the socialists.

Those menaces, however, died down again for a time. They had not yet, so far as could be seen, affected the trade unions; and the trouble was regarded as merely an unfortunate conjunction of theories in themselves negligible with the existence of an unusual degree of destitution. Interest swung back to politics, but practically to only one subject in politics. The annexation of Burma, announced on 2nd January, passed almost unnoticed; a military expedition from India had occupied Mandalay early in December 1885, and King Theebaw and his army had surrendered; the stories of his cruelties and excesses made him for a short time a kind of popular ogre. On the same date it was announced that an envoy had started for Abyssinia, with autograph letters from the Queen, a mission which, issuing first in the withdrawal under agreement with King Menelik of the Soudan garrisons near his frontier, established relations with him important to many British interests. On the same date, again, were published rumours that Bishop Hannington had been killed by the King of Uganda. But Central Africa could not attract any attention while Mr Gladstone was gathering a new Cabinet about him. Of his old colleagues, Lord Hartington, Lord Derby, Lord Northbrook and Mr Bright were absent from it; and Mr Goschen had not taken that place in it which a few months before would certainly have been his. Mr Chamberlain had joined; but both he and Sir George Trevelyan allowed it to be known that they committed themselves no further than to an examination of proposed legislation for Ireland; it was the public belief that Mr Chamberlain intended to try for his own solution of local councils for Ireland; but no one knew whether he had still in mind that Central Board in Dublin which had previously been the suspected

feature of the scheme.[1] Cabinet meetings throughout
February and March were of unprecedented frequency.
The public speculated on the possibility of Mr Gladstone's
resignation, and the construction of a new Liberal Cabinet
under Lord Hartington, with Lord Wolseley as Lord
Lieutenant of Ireland, to carry out a policy of severe
repression, with local government to follow. Then on
26th March Mr Chamberlain and Sir George Trevelyan
resigned ; Mr Gladstone remained in office, and the nation
knew that it would have to consider a full Home Rule
proposal. The death of Mr W. E. Forster, occurring on
5th April, caused at this moment a recalling of recent
Liberal relations with Ireland, which may well have confirmed in their opinion both those Liberals who were
determined to make a new effort, and those who felt that
for the present there could be no new way. Each group
read in its own fashion the life-story of the most bitterly
disillusioned of them all.

The concentration of interest on the one subject was
assisted in some measure by proceedings which for the
time being held the socialist movement in suspended
animation. Four of its leaders—Hyndman, Burns,
Champion and J. E. Williams—were put on their trial
for sedition. The failure of the authorities to make any
arrests after the riotous proceedings of 8th February
in London had produced a newspaper agitation, which
finally forced them into taking such steps as could be taken
to meet the pressure of opinion. Socialist meetings were
continually going on, and the speeches at them provided
sufficient excuse for some Government action. But not,
as proved, sufficient evidence to support a heavy charge.
The trial was a long one, the defendants being, of course,
committed to the Old Bailey. They were acquitted,
though the jury allowed themselves the expression of a
rider to the effect that Burns and Champion had used

[1] Morley's *Life of Gladstone*, iii. 194.

language inflammatory and greatly to be condemned. The importance of the trial lay in the new view that it gave to people of superficial thought of the quality of these leaders of socialism. Such men as Morris and Edward Aveling, indeed, the respectable world had heard of ; it dismissed the rest as " ranters." But four men who could conduct their own case at the Old Bailey to an acquittal, men of whom only one was in the middle-class sense educated, were a new portent ; and from that day the ordinary view of working-class disaffection took a different turn. In general, the trial, by removing the whole matter from the streets to courts of justice, took it for the time out of the foreground of the popular mind.

The House of Commons at the moment practically marked time, awaiting the Home Rule Bill ; but it had one interesting incident when a Woman Suffrage Bill came up (of course, a private member's Bill) at the very end of the sitting on 19th February. Only an hour of time remained, and that was largely occupied by the protests of members against the mere idea of considering such a Bill in such a way. But it ended in the Bill being given a second reading ; and, though a vote taken in the small hours of the morning in a more than half empty House could not be regarded as of genuine importance, the supporters of Woman Suffrage were jubilant at having established the fact that a second reading for their Bill was not an impossibility. This was the first time one had ever been given. An academic triumph scored by the movement this year was the qualification of the first woman surgeon ; Mrs M. E. Dowson, the wife of a London engineer, obtained her diploma from the Irish College of Surgeons in June.

The long and frequent Cabinet meetings achieved a result which, whether politically good or bad, was beyond cavil remarkable ; for they had in six weeks constructed from the keel-plate a Bill of the utmost magnitude and the

very first order. In the early days of April it was sufficiently advanced for Parnell to be privately in consultation with Mr Morley, the new Irish Secretary; and on
8th April it was introduced upon a stage in every way
worthy of it. The House of Commons was crowded to the
doors, and even the floor space between the table and the
Bar was covered with benches; every gallery was full;
and many members had come at daybreak to secure their
seats. Mr Gladstone rose magnificently to the occasion,
and spoke for three and a half hours. The Bill as it stood
set up a legislature of two Houses in Dublin [1] to deal with
Irish, as distinct from Imperial, affairs, and as a corollary
excluded Irish members from Westminster; it left the
control of customs to the Imperial Parliament, fixing the
Irish contribution to Imperial funds at one-fourteenth of
the total sum collected, the rest being handed over to the
Irish Parliament; it left the control of the police for two
years in British hands; the Viceroy was to continue to
exist, but not as a party appointment, and in his Privy
Council was to be formed a Cabinet which, as in Great
Britain, would be the real executive, and would be responsible to Parliament.

The first reading of the Bill took place without a division
on 13th April. Before it reached its next stage the effect
of its policy on party balance was given an unexpectedly
swift propulsion. Mr Chamberlain, with that instinct for
handling the electoral machine which had so distinguished
him in 1880, went down to Birmingham on 25th April to
discuss the new situation with the Liberal Two Thousand;
they wished to delay their vote, but Mr Chamberlain
induced them to decide at once, with the result that, by an
overwhelming majority, they refused their support to the

[1] The Upper House was to consist of 28 representative peers and
75 elected members; and the Lower House of 206 elected members.
The two were to sit together, but either House might demand
a separate vote.

Home Rule Bill. The cleverness of this move lay in its
preparation of the way for the compact whereby the seats
of Liberal Anti-Home-Rulers might be left unattacked by
Conservatives ; this course was, in fact, propounded before a month had passed.[1] On 10th May the second reading debate on the Bill opened, and Lord Hartington moved
an amendment of simple rejection. Parnell, speaking for
his party, expressed his intention to attack in committee
certain points of detail, such as the control of the police,
and the exact amount of Ireland's contribution to Imperial funds. This may have given a vague sense that
after all the Irish might not be satisfied, and may have
turned a few waverers. Others quailed before the proposals contained in the Bill for buying out the landlords ;
and Mr Chamberlain had given notice of moving the
rejection of the Land Purchase Bill which was introduced
on 16th April to carry out these proposals. Finally,
Lord Randolph Churchill in the middle of May was inciting
Ulster to take arms against the Bill, and the position of
the " loyal minority " was turning yet other votes. For
a month the fight went on ; calculations of the result
grew more and more tense, and the most sanguine hope
on the day before the division was that the Bill might have
a majority of about six. In that case the presumption
was that it would be carried no further on such a slight
majority, but would be taken merely as an assertion of the
principle of autonomy for Ireland ; the session would be
prorogued, and the Cabinet would set itself to drafting a
new Bill which might conciliate some of those who at the
present stage were objecting only to details. Parnell
disliked this prospect, which he thought would discourage
Home Rule Liberals. It never became a practical question.
In the small hours of 8th June the Bill was rejected by
341 votes to 311. In effect the vital decision had been
made a week earlier, when a meeting of dissentient

[1] *The Times,* 17th May 1886.

Liberals, with Mr Chamberlain in the chair, decided not to abstain from the division, but to vote against the Bill ; this decision gave 93 votes to the Opposition. The meeting was finally swayed by the influence which, outside as well as inside Parliament, most deeply affected Liberals who had an uncertain mind on the question—the influence of John Bright. When he declared against the Bill he greatly sharpened the immediate issue.

London was at the height of the season, and a season of such excitement as it had not known for years. In every drawing-room the split had made itself felt. One of the greatest Liberal peers, the Duke of Westminster, ostentatiously sold the portrait of Mr Gladstone, which Millais had painted for him ; and Birmingham Radicals were guests in great Whig houses. Men were blackballed at clubs for no other reason than their opinions on Home Rule. Hostesses had a new terror to face, for they hardly knew from day to day what old friends would no longer sit at the same table. To a large part of society Home Rule was not only a political tenet : it became a social barrier ; and the tendency to regard differences in political opinions as implying differences of class—a tendency entirely the product of the last hundred years—was considerably enhanced. For Mr Gladstone himself, even in the first outbursts, there was some pity, and some kindly feeling. That so unrivalled a political life should end in such a scattering of his own forces had an obvious touch of melancholy. But on the other hand it was clear that only Mr Gladstone could have raised Home Rule to the pitch of a party test, and therefore there was little room for pity in the general view. Meanwhile, from the standpoint of commercial London, the net result of the struggle was that town had not for a long time been so full or so busy ; and that across the middle of the money-making fell dissolution and a general election, the second within seven months. The resolution to dissolve was taken by the

Government on 10th June, but the agreement of Queen Victoria to a somewhat tiresome course was only obtained with some difficulty ; she yielded finally to Mr Gladstone's representations that a year of embittered Home Rule controversy would do more harm than a second dissolution. Complaints from the public were loud ; Mr Gladstone was accused of "springing the election on an absolutely unprepared country," and was warned that he would find Scotland and Wales, those Liberal strongholds, far less in his favour than he supposed. Some Liberals were complaining that the production of the Home Rule Bill had rendered any alternative policy of peace towards Ireland extremely difficult [1] ; others wailed in a barren controversy as to whether or no Mr Gladstone had done wrong to the party by "concealing his thoughts." [2] The truest word came, as so often, from a looker-on ; Professor Goldwin Smith, writing from Canada to chastise a Liberal Government for bringing in a Bill with no reasoned defence of it, but only sentimentalities about Ireland and the "G.O.M.," remarked also that there was a suspicion, "which, unfortunately, after what has taken place, cannot be said to be fantastic," that the Conservatives had not been far from a Home Rule Bill of their own. [3] The recalling of that suspicion was the best answer both to those who talked of the election being "sprung" upon the country, and to those who complained of Mr Gladstone's silence. Events had moved so fast that politicians had forgotten how much Home Rule had been talked in the previous year, and the rumours of Tory intrigues, as well as of Liberal manœuvrings. The election went rapidly forward ; in spite of some acrimony the general compact that the seats of dissentient

[1] See, *e.g.*, Mr Goschen in *The Times*, 18th June 1886.
[2] See, *e.g.*, the correspondence between Bright and Gladstone in *The Times*, 3rd July 1886.
[3] *The Times*, 7th July 1886.

Liberals should not be attacked by Tories held good ; the party was so divided that, although the central electoral organisation declared for Mr Gladstone, its big new club, the National Liberal, promoted a subscription for candidates standing against Home Rule.. Before the end of July the new House had been returned with 196 Liberals instead of 235, 316 Tories instead of 251, and 74 dissentient Liberals. Only against Home Rule could there be said to be a majority ; and the question was how far that meant a majority against a Liberal Cabinet in general—how far, in other words, Home Rule in future was to be a permanent Liberal attitude.

It is more than likely that the damage done to trade by a dissolution at the height of the season had some slight effect upon the polls. To business men it was peculiarly exasperating, since their affairs were not in a condition to bear disturbance. The smallness of the bank reserves was a standing cause of uneasiness ; and the stock market had been restless in face of a railway-rate war in America and the " capturing " of line after line by financial magnates there. Copper had been a badly falling market, too, but was felt by this time to have reached a level which, if low, was probably healthier than its recent heights ; the tin market had had a revival, and so had the sugar market, which throughout the early eighties was never in quite a normal condition owing to the disturbing effects of the bounty system.[1] The shipping trade, if not at the moment prosperous, was looking forward more cheerfully, since it had just passed through a period of change, and triple-expansion engines had now established themselves firmly.[2] When business men took a rather wider view of commercial conditions than those afforded by the London exchanges they could not help seeing that, although in their own narrower sense business was not yet good, there

---

[1] Deputations to Ministers on this subject were frequent.
[2] *The Times*, 2nd January 1886.

had been a great change since 1880. The consuming power
of the people had distinctly improved ; the consumption of
tea and sugar had risen strongly, and the income-tax
assessments were also rising. People began in fact to
ask in some bewilderment, as they faced these signs, what
was the trade depression ? It is possible that some of the
apparent depression throughout these years may be traced
to the steady growth of the limited liability principle in
trading. In every town businesses were being put upon
this basis, and with the increased capital thus obtained
were absorbing or squeezing out of the market the smaller
middlemen. Great department shops, like the Army and
Navy Stores, the Civil Service Supply Association,
Whiteley's, Lewis's, were at their busiest expansion in the
early eighties. The result was a diminution in the number
of the channels of trade, without diminution of the volume.
The bankruptcy statistics were depressing, and individual
traders in almost every part of the country could speak
of bad times ; but the broad statistics of the nation's
housekeeping showed at any rate more financial elasticity
than it had possessed for years previously. Much might be
hoped from a period of political steadiness; and the amount
of capital which was waiting for employment may be
gathered from the fact that in October, when Guinness's
made the first of that series of brewery flotations which
we shall have to deal with later, the capital offered was so
much over-subscribed that no less than 13,000 letters of
regret were posted.

Every trade undertaking seemed in this year to be
busy at turning itself into a limited liability company.
Punch described the tendency as a new fashion. At the
same time capitalists were not losing their caution ; the
first attempt to float the Manchester Ship Canal, which
was made in this year, met with failure. The prospectus,
backed by Rothschilds', was issued on 21st July. The
contractors, Lucas & Aird, undertook the work for five

and three quarter millions, which was less than the
engineers' original estimates ; the estimated gross revenue
was put at £885,000 a year ; and interim dividends of
4 per cent. payable out of capital had been allowed by
Parliament.[1] But the public proved shy ; Lancashire
was already full of expensive means of transit, and the
cotton mills had been built everywhere in accordance with
railway facilities, and might not, it was thought, easily
adjust themselves to the canal. The apparent coolness
of Lancashire investors was remarked, and for the present
the flotation failed. A trade problem which attained some
prominence this year, but waited long for a solution, was
the absence of any power to compel the working in this
country of patents taken out by foreigners ; the only
possible procedure was to issue a *mandamus* to compel the
patentee to grant licences for manufacture of his patent ;
but as the *mandamus* could not reach him the power was
useless. As for the gold problem, it still sought solution.
The bimetallists' theories began to gather more force.
Lord Grey in February of this year brought the whole
subject forward again, relating it to the most startling
difficulties of the moment by arguing that the labour
troubles were largely due to the shortage of gold, since the
wages bills of employers were in fact going up by the appreciation of the sovereign, and the masters, without knowing the real reason, felt only that they must cut wages down;
while the workman, whose sovereign bought him no more
than before, could not see why he should be paid less. The
bimetallist proposal which Lord Grey revived was for the
issue of one-pound notes payable in silver; and that for a
limited period these notes should be issued at the bank in
exchange for sovereigns, whatever the weight of the latter.

[1] This method of tempting capitalists to put their money into
large projects was noted by the socialists, who suggested, in
deputations to Ministers, that it might be applied to relief works
set on foot for the unemployed.

But there were two objections to this—the first that, if you were to escape the ultimate necessity of reconverting the silver into gold, you must come to an international agreement that gold should cease to be the only valid exchange ; and the second (a serious objection which the bimetallists never really overcame), that there was no unanimity as to the basis of calculation of the relative value at which silver was to be coined. The knowledge of the gold supply in South Africa was still wide of the mark. The air was full of rumours: about one thousand Europeans were said to be at the goldfields, and Delagoa Bay and Cape Town were alike full of adventurers. Yet the most authoritative article of the moment on the goldfields [1] dealt entirely with the Barberton and James Town districts, with the operations of companies no one of which had a capital of more than £200,000, and most had only £25,000 or £30,000; and the article concluded with the opinion that the whole industry was insignificant in comparison with the great days of the Australian fields. The Rand was still being kept out of sight by those who knew of it. In the autumn a Currency Commission was appointed, with Mr Balfour, one of the foremost bimetallists, as its chairman.

A striking feature of the year was the interest aroused by the announcement that Pasteur had discovered a cure for hydrophobia. The England of to-day, to which rabies is unknown, has forgotten the recurrent horror of deaths from the bites of dogs, for which no alleviation had appeared until Pasteur's system of injection was believed to have provided one. Fortunately, in this matter, as in that of cholera, medical opinion was by now so sane that reliance upon cure was not allowed to weaken the arguments for preventive measures. The public was warned that, until the first element of novelty had passed away, it would be impossible really to sift the evidence of cures, or to be certain that in the cases treated the dogs had been actually

---

[1] *The Times*, 23rd September 1886.

rabid ; and meanwhile the wisdom of muzzling orders was being steadily emphasised.

It was not, on the whole, a year of great interest in science ; the æsthetic movement was beginning to have the effect of shifting middle-class interest from progress to literature. Electricity had fallen upon dull times. A slight fillip was given to the ballooning craze by the voyage across the Channel of a French balloon fitted with steering gear, wherewith the aeronauts had manœuvred over ships in the Channel, and dropped imitation torpedoes. But a controversy between rival publishers about their respective libraries of cheap literature showed the true tendency just then of middle-class culture. The controversy revealed how large and profitable a sale there was for cheap standard books. The originator of this form of enterprise, Mr H. G. Bohn, had died two years before (on 25th August 1884), just as his idea was becoming a popular success. The contrasts presented to the world in *Patience* were being repeated in the less exalted ranks of the community. In society they had already begun to fade, and women, instead of hanging on the utterances of the exquisite, were filling the schools of arms, and devoting themselves to boxing and fencing. Young ladies were distressing their parents by travelling on the tops of omnibuses ; and playing the banjo was the most desirable accomplishment in Mayfair drawing-rooms. The elegant pale poets and the massive heavy dragoons of *Patience* were now being repeated *ad infinitum* at suburban tea-parties, in young men who conversed with a finger to the brow, and other young men who played lawn tennis, and rode high bicycles, and were muscular and obtuse. Theosophy began this year to have a rather large and ill-informed following, with the result that " astral bodies " became a current joke ; and telepathy and phantasms occupied the smatterers in science, as well as the Psychical Research Society.

The promoters of annual exhibitions in London were again as successful as they had been with the " Fisheries " and the " Healtheries " in attaching their provision of mere amusement to a serious subject. This year the exhibition was of Colonial and Indian products and industries; and it fitted very cleverly with that new view of the importance of the Colonies to which Mr Goschen had given expression.[1] The Secretary for the Colonies announced that he would be At Home in his department on certain days to Colonial representatives ; and the latter, arriving in England in July in connection with the exhibition, were given an official round of entertainments, the Queen receiving them at Windsor, the Admiralty giving them a day with the fleet at Portsmouth, and various banquets being arranged. Permanent results followed ; at the end of the year the Colonial Secretary (Mr E. Stanhope) made proposals for a Colonial Conference, to be attended by the Agents-General in London, and any leading public men from the colonies who might happen to be able to come to England—a more informal affair than the later developments of the kind ; colonial defence and telegraphic and postal services were the subjects proposed for discussion. It was also largely due to the Colonial and Indian Exhibition that, when interest in Queen Victoria's approaching Jubilee began to be strong, the Prince of Wales suggested the foundation of the Imperial Institute, to give permanence to the kind of presentation of colonial activities this year had achieved. The main sporting event of the year was the racing for the America Cup, for which, after a long interval, a challenge had been sent from England. The British representative was the *Galatea*, and the winds proved far too light for her. Her rival, the *Mayflower*, had been given the " skimming-dish " form, which was then so new that it had not been ventured upon for the boat that had to

[1] See p. 158.

cross the Atlantic before the contest; the *Galatea's* beam
was 15 feet, the *Mayflower's* 23·5 feet, and the *Galatea's*
draught was 13·5 feet, while the *Mayflower's* was only 9 feet.

The sporting world was shocked later in the year by the
suicide of Fred Archer, the most popular jockey of his
day.[1] He rode in the course of his career no less than 2746
winners, and his great gift was in riding horses that could
not possibly have won with any other jockey. The sensation caused by the news of his suicide has, too, more than a
personal importance ; it marks, and was felt at the time to
mark, the enormous increase in the popularity of racing,
which had been growing up almost unobserved. The
interest in Fred Archer reached households which twenty
years before would have paid no attention to his death ;
and his pleasant steady character had done much to break
down the old view of the turf as a disreputable interest
for anyone but owners. His suicide was attributed to
depression of spirits caused by the incessant " wasting " to
keep down his weight.

When the new Parliament met there was in it a party
which as yet was no party. What were dissentient
Liberals to do ? The Liberal headquarter organisation had
exiled them ; and indeed after the results of the election
they were not likely to want to attach themselves to a
party standing for Home Rule. Yet were they going to
abandon all Liberal principles ? The only answer to this
question was that when asked, towards the end of July,
to formulate a new Radical programme of reform, and
found a new club upon it, Mr Chamberlain replied that
after such an upheaval it would be better to wait a few
months before taking any definite steps.[2] Mr Chamberlain,
there can be little doubt, was feeling solitary at the
moment. He had political satellites, but no political
friend. Lord Hartington acted with him in regard to
Home Rule, but the gulf between the two on other topics

[1] 8th November 1886.   [2] *The Times,* 28th July 1886.

was too great to be easily bridged. It happened unfortunately that at the same time Mr Chamberlain, by another current of events, lost the help of a genuine political friendship. Sir Charles Dilke, whose own entrance into the Government of 1886 had been, owing to his great ability and wide democratic sympathies, combined with an unusual knowledge of foreign affairs, quite beyond question, had secured Mr Chamberlain's presence in that Government by refusing to serve himself unless Mr Chamberlain were invited to join. Now at the crisis of the latter's career, Sir Charles Dilke withdrew from Parliament, his personal honour and morality having been brought into question by a case in the law courts. Thus isolated, Mr Chamberlain decided to travel abroad for some time, leaving politics and Liberal Unionism behind him. The Government had in the end been formed on a purely Conservative basis. Lord Salisbury had offered (though at the time this was not definitely known) to stand aside in favour of Lord Hartington, and to serve under him if he would form a Government. But Lord Hartington was not a man who moved at that speed, and the offer was declined. A Cabinet was formed in which there was only one appointment that excited comment. Lord Randolph Churchill, the bane of his leaders, the rash apostle of Tory Democracy, the incalculable element in the party, was made Chancellor of the Exchequer, with the leadership of the Commons. No wonder men thought that old political traditions were perishing, if the path to office was to make yourself obnoxious to your leaders, and a will-o'-the-wisp to your constituents. At the same time no one doubted Lord Randolph's brilliancy ; and as it was now evident that the Conservative working man was a reality, there might be less temptation to embark on " Tory Democracy " as a policy. The only doubt was whether he would manage well the somewhat delicate relations with the dissentient Liberals. For some weeks the latter were too much taken up with

their own difficulties to be critical. By August they had
acquired a name. The Liberal Unionist Association had
been formed outside Parliament; but it was ultimately
announced that Mr Chamberlain and all the dissentients
were joining it.[1] During the autumn sitting the new party
were sufficiently established to be showing signs of offence
at their treatment in the House of Commons; there were
complaints that the Tories howled them down, but were
afraid of the real Home Rulers. A sign of very strained
relations was given in the Birmingham municipal elections,
where the Liberal Unionists supported Gladstonian Liberal
candidates, with Mr Chamberlain's approval, because of
the Tory attitude in the town.

These ins and outs were supposed to be the only
legitimate interest of politicians. The heavy hand shut
down again upon Ireland, the new Government's first step
being pretty sharply criticised even by many of their
friends. Sir Robert Hamilton, the Permanent Under
Secretary for Ireland, was removed from his post, because
he had been identified with Mr Gladstone's proposals.
It was felt that this was a serious blow at the principles
of public service. An agitation for a revision of judicial
rents in Ireland was being pressed upon the Government,
partly because the summer of 1886 had seen another
failure of harvest, and partly on the more general plea that
the appreciation of gold made the judicial rents unfair;
it was pointed out that even in England the rent-roll was
calculated to have dropped from sixty millions to forty-
five millions a year, and the evidence before the Royal
Commission on Trade had tended in the same direction.[2]
The Government refused to take any steps; evictions
increased; "moonlighting" began once more to aggravate

[1] The name was in existence some years earlier (see, for instance,
an article in *The Fortnightly Review*, vol. i., 1880), but it was now
first definitely adopted, as a party name.

[2] See *The Pall Mall Gazette* " Extra " on Irish Rents, 1886.

the figures of agrarian crime ; and the Plan of Campaign
was launched in November.

Party difficulties blinded politicians once again to the
very serious trouble at their doors. The temper which
had broken out in the brief street fury of 8th February,
and had been suspended for a while by the trial of the
socialist leaders, was bad enough in June to cause people to
say that the excitement of elections in London was really
to be dreaded. Nor was the nervousness confined to
London ; at Cardiff, for instance, the police were so
perturbed that, having had to deal with a crowd which had
given them some difficulty, they went on to fall upon a
perfectly harmless one, listening to speeches at the Liberal
Club, and very nearly batoned the new member ; and in
Liverpool socialist meetings were acting as sparks to the
magazine of Orange fever which is always in store there.
Nevertheless London was naturally the centre of anxiety.
When a big socialist demonstration was held in Trafalgar
Square at the end of August no less than 2000 police were
on duty : they had warning enough then to be ready. But
a new danger was revealed when the socialists took to
invading other meetings, such as a demonstration in
favour of Free Education at the beginning of October,
which had naturally appeared to call for less policing.
Nor was London allowed to forget the real misery
which was issuing in these disturbances. A manifesto was
published by the Social Democratic Federation calling on
the destitute and unemployed to follow the Lord Mayor's
Show, silently, in thousands. This was, of course, instantly forbidden by the police, and the result was that,
after the Lord Mayor's Show had turned as usual from the
Strand down to the Embankment, there was a sudden rush
of men to Trafalgar Square, and a defiant meeting began.
But troops were at hand which had been on duty for the
procession. Suddenly a line of Life Guards appeared
trotting round the square to a strategic position, and with

this force in reserve the police marched into the crowd and
set to work to scatter it. The energies of the leaders of
upper-class opinion at this time were turned to attempting
to separate the distressed from those who were organising
and leading them. The accepted point of view was that
open-air meetings were wholly unnecessary, and that the
socialist demand for free speech was only being craftily
attached to a genuine trouble, and should be firmly
handled.[1] The distress, at any rate, had been so pressed
upon public notice that the closing months of the year were
full of suggestions for meeting it. There were appeals for
charity, signed by men of such different views as the Bishop
of London, Cardinal Manning and Mr Spurgeon; there
were requests for a mitigation of the rules of outdoor
relief, and appeals for funds to enable public bodies to
set on foot relief works; a Mansion House Committee was
appointed to collect information as to the unemployment,
and to consider schemes to meet it. But as a political
question the trouble was not allowed to rank; it was held
to be " undignified " to expect any reference to it at the
Lord Mayor's banquet; and the single exception to this
attitude, which can be quoted as of any importance, is the
plea by one whose early death deprived the poor of a good
friend, Lord Sydney Godolphin Osborne. He was busy in
October urging the Government to attend as a Government
to the matter. Though not strictly affairs of the unemployed, the trouble at this time in Skye, where the military
were called out against the disaffected crofters, and the
tithe riots in Lancashire and Wales, should have added
to the general uneasiness about the temper of the working
people. It was a time too much disturbed by poverty and

[1] An interesting side-issue was that large new hotels, such as
the Grand, opened in 1880, and the Metropole, opened in 1885,
were attracting many visitors, especially Americans, to the neighbourhood of Trafalgar Square, which was therefore peculiarly
unsuitable for public meetings.

hardship for any very immediate interest to be taken by
working men in their representation on the benches of the
House of Commons.   Joseph Arch was returned as the first
agricultural labourer in the House, and the Labour
members at the beginning of the year numbered nine—
Messrs Abraham, Arch, Broadhurst, Burt, W. R. Cremer,
Fenwick, Leicester, Pickard and J. Wilson.

At the end of the year the party problem was suddenly
galvanised again into prominence.   To everyone's amazement, Lord Randolph Churchill resigned the Chancellorship
of the Exchequer.   His reason was that he had been unable
to carry his declared policy of economy against the demands of the Admiralty and the War Office.   Even those
who sympathised with him felt his resignation, before he
had so much as produced a Budget, an extraordinarily
hasty step.   It is known now that he calculated on the
Government being obliged to ask him to resume his post,
and so give him a vastly strengthened position.   But he had
been too sure that the Liberal Unionists were not yet ready
for coalition—he had considered his possible Conservative
successors alone.   He can hardly be blamed for this.
On the very day of his resignation, for instance, Mr Chamberlain had been asserting himself " unchanged " on such a
Radical proposal as that of Disestablishment ; and although
on 17th December Mr Chamberlain had a great meeting in
Birmingham, as a counter-blast to a Home Rule meeting
in November at which Morley and Parnell had spoken,
it was rumoured on 23rd December that he was considering a *rapprochement* with the Liberal leaders.   The
revival of coercion had held the dissentient Liberals at a
distance from the Conservatives ; and the truth at which
the rumours guessed was that Sir William Harcourt, Lord
Herschell, Mr Chamberlain, Sir George Trevelyan and
Mr Morley were meeting quietly at Sir William Harcourt's
house.   But the most important person was not there ;
Lord Hartington had refused to attend ; and meanwhile

the Conservatives, really anxious about their position in the Commons, were moving heaven and earth to get him to accept the leadership there. He would not consent to that, but he would do what was at the moment almost as much help to the Tories—he would persuade Mr Goschen to take the Exchequer. The results were considerable; the Tories got a Chancellor of the Exchequer who as a financier commanded everyone's respect, and were really better off in that regard than before Lord Randolph Churchill resigned; but they also got what they valued still more, an admission that Liberal Unionists could serve under a Conservative Prime Minister.

The public mind slipped back comfortably into those varied plans for celebrating the Queen's Jubilee which largely occupied the newspapers in December 1886; and expended some of its leisure in speculating about Emin Pasha. News had filtered through that he alone of all the provincial governors of the Soudan was still holding out; and proposals were being made for sending him relief.

CHAPTER IX

1887 : THE JUBILEE

THE report of the Royal Commission on Trade, which was one of the first events of the New Year,[1] proved to be a much more balanced attempt to diagnose industrial difficulties than had been anticipated at the time of the Commission's appointment. The "Fair Trade" remedy was, indeed, recommended by a small minority of four commissioners ; but was dismissed by the majority on the ground that it was " hardly worth while to discuss a scheme which involves at once a total upset of our present Budget arrangements, a reversal of our trade policy, and a breach with our foreign customers." The report dwelt upon some of those inconsistent features of the trade situation which had already puzzled the observant. There was no falling off in the volume of our foreign trade, or in the amount of capital engaged in it, or in the accumulation of capital throughout the country, or in the aggregate of production. Yet something certainly was amiss. The commissioners put part of the responsibility down to over-production ; they also suggested, but only in tentative terms, that the rise in the value of gold was a source of difficulty ; they asserted more confidently that the workman was getting wages which were perhaps too little affected by falling prices. Their recommendations moved, as was to be expected, on extremely official lines ; they advised, for instance, that traders should be exhorted to cheapen production and so widen the market, and should realise that as competition became keener business methods

[1] Published on 17th January 1887;

must become better; higher education, and a more
attentive collection of statistics were corollaries of this
proposition. But some of the recommendations were
rather less academic; they called for re-examination of
railway traffic rates, for the freeing of canals from railway
ownership and control, for light railways to assist agriculture and make possible an industrial decentralisation; and
for legislation against counterfeit marking, and for some
improvement of the Limited Liability Acts.

Such a document could not mean much to the thousands
out of employment; and what it meant to their leaders
was not conciliatory. Kindly people were ready enough
to feel sympathetic, and hold drawing-room meetings to
discuss whether the distress was exceptional or chronic;
that distinction was at the time a favourite method of
attacking the " agitators," the argument being that there
was always inevitable distress, as a sort of "waste product"
of an industrial age, and that the prominence given to it
was only a move of the socialists. The latter were represented as objecting to philanthropic inquiry, and resenting
" inquisition "; this was, no doubt, one way of describing
the socialist's impatience at seeing the whole question
shuffled off into a philanthropic atmosphere against all
their endeavours to keep it in a political one. But it is
possible that, like most reformers, they had their eyes so
firmly set upon the goal that they failed to observe how
many laps in the race they had already run. It was Lord
Salisbury, to continue the metaphor, who rang the bell in
one of those moments of frankness with which he was apt
to disturb his friends and allies. He was replying to a
correspondent on the subject of State-aided emigration—
a favourite project of the time for relieving industrial
congestion; private effort had already established a settlement of East Londoners in Manitoba. Lord Salisbury
wrote that until this remedy was more demonstrably a
success Parliament would not adopt it; but when it was,

Parliament would not be frightened by any socialist quality in the scheme. " If it is convinced that a measure is likely to answer," he said, " it never troubles itself about the school of thought from which the measure is drawn."[1] This is in its way a version of the Fabian position ; but the socialists, in contact with the problem of the unemployed, demanded for it a political formulation ; and the apparently impregnable habit of treating trade questions as a middle-class affair exasperated them into making their demand one for separate formulation. They pursued their campaign of street meetings, and early in February there was more rioting, not only in London, where windows were broken in Clerkenwell and up Goswell Road, but also at Blantyre and Coatbridge; in April John Williams was arrested again, with some others, after a socialist meeting at the Marble Arch.

One immediate effect of the report of the Commission on Trade makes this year peculiarly notable. The insistence upon the need for better trade methods and higher education provided a rallying point for all the energy which had been going into municipal art schools and training classes. Here was a piece of work which Parliament might well undertake for the business community, the more easily as that community had already created the skeleton of a system. Lord Hartington, to whom technical education in this country owes more than to anyone else, was the first prominent public man to take up the idea. In a speech at the London Polytechnic on 16th March he urged the great municipalities to organise technical education on a large scale in subjects suitable to the industrial needs of their districts ; as yet, no suggestion was made of any other than private provision of the necessary funds. On 21st March a deputation waited upon Lord Cranbrook at the Education Department to ask for departmental action ; he, too, attributed the duty of taking action to the local

[1] Letter published in *The Times,* 22nd February 1885.

authorities, on the fairly sound principle that they could go on to " that real secondary education which can never be reached by the Elementary Education Department " ; he added a quotation from a speech some years earlier by Mr Mundella, to the effect that the idea of giving technical education to the whole working class was an entire mistake, the inference being that local authorities could move in a partial way that would be impossible to a public department. Meanwhile the stirring of a new spirit in education was seen in a growing revolt of teachers against " the Juggernaut of percentages " ; they wished for a little more flexibility in method, and a little less rigid judgment by examination results ; there was, perhaps, something in the dry comment that their revolt was from one point of view a confession that the system got a great deal of work out of them.

The death of Sir Joseph Whitworth on 23rd January may have helped to awaken men to some understanding of what modern trade exacted—what alertness, what high degree of technical knowledge. For he had made his immense fortune by certain mechanical inventions which were thoroughly of the new movement—accurate measuring machines, true planes, standard gauges, and other such implements. He himself had had no technical education beyond that which he picked up in engineering shops ; personally he was in the tradition of the story-book men of business who build up a fortune on a foundation stone of half-a-crown, and was to the end of his life a rather rough man, with a passion for trotting horses. But his work made such education more than ever necessary for other men. In the end, he also made it more attainable in his own city, for he left the greater part of his huge fortune on trust for public purposes in Manchester, and the first expansion of technical education there was due to his bequest.

The greatest fillip of all to technical education was given

by the fortunate association of it with the great affair in all men's minds this year—the Jubilee. When the celebration was only a month away, and popular enthusiasm for the Queen at its height, she went down to open the Queen's Hall of the People's Palace in Mile End Road, and to lay the foundation stone of the Technical and Handicraft Schools of that institution. It had grown from a long-buried seed. In 1841 Mr Barber Beaumont left a large sum of money " for the intellectual improvement and the rational recreation and amusement of the people of the East End." There had been no organised means of applying the bequest, and for forty years it lay practically idle. Then a novel by Walter Besant, *All Sorts and Conditions of Men*, drew an imaginary picture of a great palace of education and recreation in East London ; men recalled the dormant bequest, and the scheme for the People's Palace sprang to life. Besant worked hard for it ; Mr Beaumont's money did not suffice for the purpose, and subscriptions were raised, the great City companies, especially the Drapers' Company, contributing largely ; and the project was sufficiently advanced by May 1887 to be able to gather to itself some of the Jubilee enthusiasm. Besant was presented to the Queen after she had laid the foundation stone. Meanwhile the City justifiably reminded the world that it was doing a good deal already. The City and Guilds of London Institute at South Kensington was advancing towards completion ; the Finsbury Technical College was teaching 169 day students and 764 evening students, a large majority of whom were artisans, and 200 of whom were apprentices ; the South London School of Technical Art had 187 pupils ; and the guilds also made grants to the schools of engineering and chemical technology at University College, and the school of metallurgy at King's College.

The public was ready to be interested in social affairs. The uneasiness among the Conservative leaders at the

time of Lord Randolph Churchill's resignation was one of
those curious political alarms which belong to pure politics
and not to real life at all.   In point of fact, although people
were startled and interested by that event, there was in
the nation at large none of that canvassing of its effect
upon party relations which Lord Salisbury seemed to fear.
The nation had had its fill of politics for a while.   The new
Franchise and the quarrel between the two Houses of
Parliament, the death of Gordon, and the Home Rule Bill
had given it two years in which political subjects were
the prime interest.   The ordinary man was quite ready to
let them slip into the background.   One event, however, of
the beginning of the year touched him.   On 12th January
Lord Iddesleigh died suddenly in an ante-room while waiting to see Lord Salisbury.   It was sad even from the most
casual point of view.   As Sir Stafford Northcote, Lord
Iddesleigh had had to see his position in the House of
Commons slowly but remorselessly weakened ; he had been
too old, too slow, too formal in his leadership of the Opposition from 1880 to 1885 to hold his own in a Parliament fresh
and active.   Lord Randolph Churchill's gadfly activities
had been as damaging to Sir Stafford Northcote as to
Mr Gladstone; and in the brief Government of Lord
Salisbury from June 1885 to February 1886 Northcote
found no place at all ; his leadership in the Commons
was taken away, and he accepted the consolation of
a title, going to the House of Lords as Lord Iddesleigh.
When Lord Salisbury returned to power in July 1886
he made Lord Iddesleigh Foreign Secretary ; but in the
disturbance caused by Lord Randolph Churchill's resignation Lord Salisbury changed his mind again, and did
it somewhat unkindly.   Lord Iddesleigh read in the newspapers one morning that Lord Salisbury had decided to
take his place at the Foreign Office.   It was no wonder
that when the news came that the old man, tired, disappointed, but patient and loyal to the end, had died in a

chair in Lord Salisbury's ante-room, people who had never known him felt grieved.

His last piece of work at the Foreign Office had been in connection with the expedition for the relief of Emin Pasha. Mr H. M. Stanley left London towards the end of January to reach the Soudan by way of the Congo.

With the approach of the Queen's Jubilee, the national pride in her was reviving the feeling that the British were a fine race, and their Empire a noble achievement. Perhaps because this form of patriotism had but poor sustenance in recent affairs, it grew somewhat self-conscious and aggressive, and a little inclined to " trail its coat." It made much of the Colonial Conference which assembled early in April. Imperial Federation was proposed as a subject for debate, but beyond a rather empty discussion of the types of ship that colonies might keep up in a general system of Imperial Defence little was accomplished, except that Australia definitely undertook a payment for the maintenance of a British squadron on her coasts. Other debates of the conference were on the desirability of making colonial guaranteed stocks legal trustee investments, and on commercial relations, and postal and telegraphic facilities. The last point had already been adopted as his own by Mr Henniker Heaton, and his advocacy of an Imperial Penny Post was well under way. These were the kind of assertive but not immediately pressing affairs for which the ordinary man was in the mind. His view of the political situation was simple : Gladstone had been beaten, Salisbury was in, therefore there would be nothing searching or subversive to bother about, and he might, politically speaking, take a spell off. He was suddenly wrenched from his security in April by a newspaper bombshell.

To those more vitally concerned political parties were still in no small confusion. When the first flush of Goschen's acceptance of the Chancellorship of the Exchequer had passed off, men asked, What, after all, would his position exactly amount to ? They felt that, whatever might be the readiness for a coalition among some of the dissentient Liberals, there was a strong Conservative feeling against it ; Mr Chamberlain had not ceased to be regarded as a dangerous Radical. Yet on the other hand it appeared with some suddenness that he would never again be a Gladstonian ; the Round Table conference which had met in December to attempt to patch up the Liberal split had not achieved its object. An article from Mr Chamberlain's pen, speaking of the Irish people as " disloyal," [1] revealed a temper which was so remote from that of the Gladstonians that the hopes of a *rapprochement* were extinguished. Yet, again, Mr Chamberlain was believed to entertain still his own scheme of concession to Ireland—some fair rent proposals and a system of local governing bodies, without any control of the administration of justice or of the police— and was not likely, therefore, even if his general Radical views did not stop the way, to pull in harmony with the Government. The Crimes Bill was a serious obstacle to coalition; its production was a reply to the Plan of Campaign. The Plan was another stage in the disintegration of Parnell's control of Irish agitation. It was that tenants in Ireland, carefully organised by estates, and acting under committees for each estate, should cease entirely to deal with the landlord's agent as individuals ; should offer as a body, through the committee, the halfyearly rent subject to the reduction they demanded ; and, if this were refused, should fund the money, drawing upon it for relief when the agent had put in force all the tedious and objectionable processes of eviction, sale, and distress. Parnell condemned the Plan, which was first published as a supplement to *United Ireland* on 20th November 1886 ; it was over that border of obvious illegality which he had always refused to cross. But it went forward in spite of

[1] Published in *The Baptist*, February 1887.

him ; and he was driven back to fighting in the House
of Commons against the inevitable coercion measures.
Practically he was where he had been before 1880, with
the two currents of Irish agitation again wholly separate,
and the Irish party handicapped by the odium of
violences with which it had no connection. Moreover he
was now often ill, and he moved about the precincts of the
House carelessly dressed, with lank hair, a wild dark figure,
his old silence and reserve turned into a new and more
mystifying habit of disappearing entirely from sight for
days or even weeks at a time ; no one knew where he was
at such times, but there were already many who suspected
in what company he was. Both his own circumstances
and the political circumstances of the moment must be
taken into account as we come to the sensational blow
struck in April of this year. In politics we have the only
hope of a stable and continuous Government held in
check by the delay of the coalition, a great cause of
delay being the reluctance of dissentient Liberals to accept
the Government's Irish policy; at the end of March separate
meetings of Conservatives and Liberal Unionists were being
held on the Crimes Bill. On the personal side we have
Parnell still in control of his party, but clearly, by reason
of the persistence in the Plan of Campaign, less able to
maintain his old attitude of aloofness from violence ; and
also, for other reasons, in a position which might be
reckoned on as making him less ready to resent attack.
It was a tempting occasion for a stroke which should so
deeply discredit him as to brush away the last reluctance
of Liberal Unionists, and also render co-operation with the
Irish Nationalists a killing handicap to the Liberals. So
the stroke was dealt. *The Times* began publishing a series
of articles entitled " Parnellism and Crime," in which
extracts from speeches by members of the Parnellite party
were so conjoined with the story of agrarian crime in
Ireland as to make the parliamentary agitation and Fenian

lawlessness one thing. But these articles would not have accomplished the object in view. The final attack was the publication on 18th April of a facsimile of a letter purporting to have been written by Parnell soon after the Phœnix Park murders. The text left no doubt of the insinuation. The letter—dated " 15/5/82," a fortnight after the murders —ran thus :

" DEAR SIR,—I am not surprised at your friend's anger, but he and you should know that to denounce the murders was the only course open to us. To do that promptly was plainly our best policy. But you can tell him, and all others concerned, that though I regret the accident of Lord F. Cavendish's death, I cannot refuse to admit that Burke got no more than his deserts. You are at liberty to show him this, and others whom you can trust also, but let not my address be known. He can write to the House of Commons. Yours very truly,

" CHAS. S. PARNELL."

No one who at this interval of time opens that famous number of the newspaper, and sees the middle of one of its central pages occupied by the facsimile, can fail to respond to the thrill that its publication caused, especially in days when in the normal course nothing interrupted the plain typography of newspapers, when there were no photographic illustrations or any other efforts of " process " reproduction. It was the sight of the handwriting which swept away all suspension of judgment. To the world at large it was clear enough that at the very time when he had been denouncing and repudiating completely the Phœnix Park murders, Parnell had been writing to a Fenian leader to say that these repudiations were merely diplomatic—that he only regretted Lord F. Cavendish's death as an accident, and had less than no regret for the death of Mr Burke.

The publication of the facsimile was carefully timed. The day of its appearance was the day of the second reading division on the Government's Coercion Bill. No one could say that Parnell lacked occasion for an immediate denial, and members of Parliament, who had brought to the Lobby that excitement which had run like wildfire over the country during the day, clustered silent in the House when Parnell rose immediately before the division. He gave the most downright denial to the authenticity of the letter; he was as calm as ever, and he put his denial in the plainest, simplest terms. But even in this assembly the power of the reproduced handwriting was strong, and the high standing of the newspaper concerned was a considerable element in the estimation of the worth of the denial. The Conservatives openly derided it; the Liberal Unionists, if less jubilant, felt it so inadequate that they could act as if the letter were genuine. They had been assisted over their scruples, and the Coercion Bill got its second reading. It was a measure severe even in the history of coercion; for its operation had no time-limit. It gave the usual powers to the executive to proclaim disturbed districts and dangerous associations, to order inquiries upon oath even when no one was actually on trial, and to suspend trial by jury for a list of offences that practically covered all the operations of the Plan of Campaign. Yet once again the old rule held good, that with a Coercion Bill a Land Bill should pass. So great had been the hurry for coercion that the Government did not appear to mind what variations of purpose it went through on the land question. In 1885 it had refused all reconsideration of judicial rents; in 1886 the Cowper Commission and the Government's own envoy, Sir Redvers Buller, alike reported that the demand for a reduction of rents was an honest demand, and that the Irish tenants, as a whole, genuinely could not pay the old rents. Still the Government held to its refusal, evictions went forward (the famous Woodford evictions on the Clanricarde estate took place in the winter of 1886-1887) ; and then in July 1887 Lord Salisbury calmly accepted the evidence he had been steadily refusing, and established new judicial rents under a land court. These two Bills, it may be remarked in passing, were Mr Balfour's introduction as a member of Government to the House of Commons. He had succeeded Sir Michael Hicks Beach as Chief Secretary at the beginning of March.

The Coercion Bill is memorable as having led to one of the most drastic alterations of procedure in the House of Commons. It was the first Bill to which " guillotine " closure was applied. Curiously enough, the Bill had not been subjected to the purely obstructive tactics of the Irish party. But on 10th June the Government carried a resolution that a week later the committee stage of the Bill should end, and clauses still undiscussed should be put forthwith without debate. This was a violent answer to the growing bewilderment, which was expressed at the opening of this session (and at the opening of every session for the past six or seven years), as to how the House of Commons was to get through its work. Before the guillotine closure was adopted the House had already made the existing closure resolutions more readily applicable. The stipulation in the resolution of 1882 for a majority of a certain size was abolished, and closure of debate by a bare majority was authorised, provided the chairman accepted a motion to that effect and not less than two hundred members supported it. Parliament made very little progress this year with anything but its Irish legislation. The Government accepted from a private member a Truck Bill dealing with certain methods of paying workmen in kind, which had escaped earlier Acts ; it was still, for instance, the custom in some districts to pay agricultural labourers partly in supplies of cider. The passing of the First Offenders Bill, introduced by Sir Howard Vincent, not for the first time, was a good piece of work rather hastily done ; gloomy critics predicted that it would lead to such espionage as this country had never tolerated. A Technical Education Bill was introduced, giving power to local authorities to set up technical schools and to combine for this purpose with other localities in order to save overlapping and spread the cost ; but the Bill was dropped to make way for other legislation. An Allotments Bill was more fortunate, and became law ; the authority to administer it was the Local Sanitary Authority, appealing to Quarter Sessions, but there was a strong disposition to eliminate the latter and set up the Local Government Board as the supreme authority. This disposition (and indeed the production of the Bill itself) indicated that the legislation on County Government, long promised by the Liberal Ministry of 1880 but always postponed by the various complications of that Ministry's career, was going to be taken up by their opponents. One of the reasons given by Mr W. H. Smith (who had succeeded Lord Randolph Churchill as Leader of the Commons) for the abandonment of certain Bills in August was the necessity for passing a Local Boundaries Bill to clear the way for a Local Government Bill in the following year.

Nothing shows better the suspension of public interest in politics than the curious history of the Government's Irish legislation of this year. A Coercion Bill for the first time permanently at the disposal of the Executive, a Land Bill which was a bland " doubling " on all Lord Salisbury had said the year before, and incidentally a drastic innovation in the procedure of the House—all accomplished without any disturbance. Mr Gladstone could not have attempted one quarter of such changes without rousing the country. Partly this was due to his great personal position. What he did stood in the popular mind for the fiery, the exalted, the-breath of the future. His defeat had been enough to make men settle down in their normal ways again ; and the men who defeated him were free to do almost anything without risk of disturbance. Partly too the supposed Parnell letter in *The Times* had had on the normal Englishman the effect it was intended to have on the Liberal Unionists. Parnell had always despised English public opinion, and, as we have seen, part of the secret of his power in Ireland was his avoiding any friendliness from England. His curt denial of the authenticity of the letter therefore was taken to be his usual contemptuous way of treating this country, the result being that in the general sense no one felt himself called upon to have any conscience about the Irish party or the Irish. The public after a week or two dropped the letter as it had dropped all politics, and gave itself to a summer of heightened gaiety, a holiday summer.

Everything was done—even to the appropriation of a Parisian popular tune for street and barrel-organ use—to make people think of the Jubilee and nothing else. Shops placarded it, villages feasted it, errand-boys whistled it. Last of all the weather rose to it. On 20th June the Queen proceeded to a great thanksgiving service in Westminster Abbey, where her venerable figure was enthroned upon a dais on the very spot on which fifty years before she had received the homage of her realm. Her procession to the Abbey was such as had never in the world's history accompanied a crowned head. Three kings were in it—the King of Denmark, the King of the Belgians, and the King of the Hellenes—and the Crown Princes of every throne in Christendom, and of some outside Christendom. Three sons, five sons-in-law, and nine grandsons and grandsons-in-law rode behind her carriage ; midmost in the line of sons-in-law rode the tall Crown Prince of the German Empire, his silver helmet, his long fair beard, and his white tunic making him the princeliest figure of the whole. The day was a universal holiday, and there was not a town or village which had not the means of making festival, and of giving it lasting commemoration in some monument, however modest. At nightfall bonfires were lit on all high hills. A new coinage was struck, chiefly remarkable, after the first novelty had passed away, for the fact that the sixpence was identical in design with the half-sovereign, so that a little gilding was sufficient for the perpetration of frauds.[1]

The Jubilee was an occasion which prompted retrospects, and every newspaper and review fell to taking stock of England's progress during fifty years. Developments of machinery and means of communication belong in the main to a period earlier than that of this history. They provided ground for almost unmitigated satisfaction. Yet the social condition of the country gave some pause ; it hardly seemed to express the results of a general advance, except in the broadest kind of material well-being. Even in that respect, though the country as a whole was vastly richer, there seemed to be forms of poverty more acute than the old days had known ; and there were still horrible slums, horrible corners in country villages, hovels on the thresholds of mansions. Wealth had indeed been more widely distributed; but the distribution had run in channels. The growth of industrialism had, since the passing of the Limited Liability Acts, begun to carry the profits of industry out into the professional middle classes, as a return for the investment of savings. Professor Leone Levi, one of the greatest political economists of the day, writing soon after the publication of the Report of the Royal Commission on Trade, to contest the view that the fall in prices was due to the shortage of gold, pointed out that the fall might easily be an apparent one, due to the fact that the increase of Limited Liability Companies diminished apparent profits, spreading them more widely ; private shareholders looked for less return on their money than the manufacturing capitalists. Again, that same growth, by calling for

[1] These sixpenny pieces were called in.

a corresponding expansion of means of distribution, had profoundly affected the middleman class ; and here also the Limited Liability Acts came into the field. Large "Stores" were in existence ; and the shareholders in them were a kind of sleeping middlemen. This feature of English commercial life was already important enough to have attracted the notice of the taxation experts of the country.[1] Industrialism had not adjusted itself to the new weights it had to carry ; and its periods of production were being governed rather by the call for dividends than by considerations of steady trade. It could not fail to be remarked at the same time that, as the spread of wealth had increased, the standard of living had gone up. In education, in material comforts, in amusements, the upper middle class were now approximating to the habits of Society; and the lower middle class, the smaller professional men and the shopkeepers, were coming into the position of the upper middle class. The consciousness of this, working in the artisan and the labourer, who had not yet shared as much in the growing wealth as in the spreading intelligence of the community, was no small element in the new uprising of labour, the new demands for something more than mere advancement of wages.

It is interesting to find in this very year of the Jubilee signs of another change, incalculable in effect. Compulsory education and the abolition of the stamp duty on newspapers had begun to make England a newspaper-reading nation. This had been seen in one respect in the influence which a newspaper agitation had had in the sending of Gordon to the Soudan.[2] In 1887 it disturbed the minds of the respectable by its obvious fruitfulness in new forms of gambling. In January one cheap print had set on foot the

---

[1] Elliot's *Life of Lord Goschen*, ii. 158.

[2] See page 124 ; and Mr G. W. E. Russell's *One Look Back*, p. 246.

form of competition which has ever since been readily
worked into a craze; it offered prizes for discovering
certain easy words in a series of pictures, the prizes to go
to the first correct solution which happened to be opened.
Other kinds of gambling due to the spread of newspapers
appeared in the autumn. There was a riot at Lillie
Bridge on 19th September, where a crowd of five or six
thousand had gathered to see a race; the race did not take
place, and the crowd wrecked the stands and railings of the
ground, and burned the fragments. It was pretty well
known that the stoppage of the race was really brought
about to suit some betting-books[1]; and the riot drew
attention, first, to the immense crowds which were
attracted to sporting events, and, secondly, to the cheap
newspapers which sent them there. The riot was followed
by a police raid on a gambling club in London; and these
were the first steps in a somewhat ineffectual attack during
the late eighties and early nineties upon the betting
tendencies of the workman. Another effect of cheap
newspapers on ideas of sport was observed about this
time. A famous old cricketer, signing himself "F. G.,"
wrote to *The Times*[2] to complain of a new school
of cricket reporting which classified counties into first
and second class counties, and talked of "championships"
and "premierships"; the cricket enthusiast, he thought,
was becoming a mere statistician, with "records" at his
fingers' ends. The football mania had not yet begun; but
the same spirit was evidently at work to create it.

The Jubilee, not overshadowed by parliamentary battles,
was equally free of social shadows. The palpable existence of unemployment was rendered less pressing by the
warmth of the summer weather; yet in various minor
ways a certain financial pinch left its marks. Thus
the trade in meat was slack, and the importers of the

[1] *The Times*, 24th September 1887.
[2] 5th September 1887.

chilled supply found it a depressing year; however it may
be mentioned that even a depressed market now took
76,000 cwt. a month, which gives some measure of the
growth of this industry in seven years. While we are on
the subject of food, it may be mentioned that 1887 saw at
last the passing of the Margarine Act, by which the word
" margarine " had to be stamped on all packets containing
that substance; the makers and purveyors had fought hard
to alter the legal description to " butterine." If the meat
market was not as good as a festival year seemed to imply,
there were other means of jollity; and when the Chancellor
of the Exchequer introduced his next Budget he commented
gratefully on the large increase in the product of the beer
and spirit duties, which the Jubilee festivities had put into
his pocket. Tobacco duties also were becoming more
productive, and for this there was an interesting reason.
Anyone who turns over the newspapers for 1887 will be
struck by an outbreak of advertisements of cigarettes.
Of course cigarettes had been smoked in England for some
time previously, but they were still looked upon as rather
outlandish. Mr Labouchere's incessant smoking of them
was enough to mark him out, and the æsthetes affected
them as a piece of elegance. It was not until about 1887
that their use became common; and the change had been
caused by the Soudan expedition. Officers and men alike
had learned to enjoy cigarettes in Egypt, and as they
brought their new habit home it spread among people,
both high and low, who would never have picked it up
from the æsthete or the dandy.

An event of the summer which was almost as popular
as the Jubilee was the " Wild West " Show at Brompton.
Colonel Cody, with his romantic past of fighting Indians
and his troupe of picturesque cowboys, became the rage.
Even the most grown-up persons recalled their boyhood
and went to see the show. Meanwhile a sign of some
uneasiness about the standing amusements of London was

seen in the strong opposition to the application made
this year by the Empire Theatre for a music-hall licence in
place of its previous theatre licence ; the application was
granted, but not without a great deal of public criticism
of the condition of music-hall entertainments.

Parliament had an unusually long session, and had not
risen when, in September, a sudden violent occurrence took
place in Ireland. But again the withdrawal of public
interest showed itself in the comparative coolness and ease
with which the Government were able to take the affair.
A meeting at Mitchelstown, co. Cork, at which Mr Dillon
was speaking, was turned into a riot by the determination
of the police to force their official note-taker through the
midst of the crowd. In the end three men were killed
by rifle fire from the police barracks. Yet so little was
the British public inclined to care for such things at the
moment that Mr Balfour was able to answer indignant
questions in the House by merely giving the police version
of the affair ; and even Mr Gladstone's cry, " Remember
Mitchelstown," roused no one who would not have been
ready to be roused by less tragic events.

Mr Balfour was able to carry out through the executive
in Dublin the severest kind of repression. Some two
hundred branches of the National League were suppressed ;
the Lord Mayor of Dublin was prosecuted for publishing
in a newspaper, owned by him, reports of League meetings ;
Mr William O'Brien was sent to gaol as a common criminal
for speaking at proclaimed meetings ; Mr Wilfrid Blunt
was similarly treated for trying to address a gathering
on the Clanricarde estate. Mr O'Brien's refusal to wear
prison dress drew some flippant attention, for his own
clothes had been taken away, and his demand for their
restoration was echoed in British jests about " O'Brien's
trousers." Mr Blunt's arrest also caused a slight stir, because, being an English squire, he was appalled into strong
language by the discovery that a policeman could positively

prevent him from making a speech. But otherwise no
one in England paid much heed to Mr Balfour's rule ;
even though the Irish problem took one of its curious
twists when in August there came loud complaints from
Ulster because the large London Livery Companies, taking
advantage of the Land Purchase Act, were clearing out of
their Irish estates, and leaving to their fate all religious
and charitable institutions to which, as landlords, they
had hitherto subscribed. Private landlords were not
clearing out in quite this conscienceless way ; and indignant Ulstermen were inclined to question whether under
the terms of the Plantation it was legal for the Livery
Companies to act as they were acting. In any case Mr
Balfour's policy did not interfere with the progress of the
Conservatives and the Liberal Unionists towards coalition.
One prominent Unionist, Sir George Trevelyan, had
returned to the Gladstonians in May, when he knew that
Mr Gladstone was not of fixed mind on the question of retaining Irish members at Westminster. Lord Hartington,
on the other hand, was speaking more strongly than ever
against all the proposed or hinted forms of self-government
for Ireland, and against the Parnellite party. A flicker of
the spirit of the previous year arose upon a speech by Sir
George Trevelyan in July, which caused Liberal Unionists
to ask him by what right he " took upon himself to
excommunicate Bright, Hartington and Chamberlain."
But the plain man's view of the situation was the true one :
the coalition would take place by a process of driftings,
and letters were even being written to the papers to prove
that before common opposition to Home Rule united the
two groups they had had a bond of union in a common
policy, Mr Chamberlain and Lord Randolph Churchill being
almost as near together in democratic schemes as, say,
Mr Goschen and Sir Michael Hicks Beach were in distrust
of such schemes. Before the end of the year the Liberal
Unionists held a great meeting which virtually amounted

to adherence to the Conservative side ; and when Mr
Chamberlain left England in December for New York, to
act as British Commissioner in the Canadian Fisheries
dispute, he was not only taking a post offered by Lord
Salisbury, but was also arranging a convenient absence,
on the further side of which he might with less emphasis
take the final step of severance from his old party.   It is
curious, considering how events developed sixteen years
later, that at this time one of the reasons given by the Tory
newspapers for welcoming Mr Chamberlain was that he
and his Liberal Unionist allies might be expected to
counteract a tendency towards Protection in the Conservative party.   The Fair Trade cry had been, after all, less
damaged by its defeats at the polls than many people
thought, and it was vigorous towards the end of the year.
The papers which deplored it as a reactionary movement
looked to the democratic ideas of Mr Chamberlain as a
useful influence against it.

Nothing that modern retrospect can add would make
the Home Rule split more serious, more damaging, than
it was at the time.   Yet we can perceive now concurrent
effects of it unperceived at the time.   Events had so
fallen that both Lord Randolph Churchill and Mr
Chamberlain were out of office, and out of influence, at
a time when a politician in any sort of touch with the
working poor might have diverted the whole course of
social history.   As it was, the world at large continued to
satisfy itself by mentally separating the socialist speaker
from the mass of working people.   The latter, politicians
thought they understood.   When in May a deputation
of pit-brow women waited upon the Home Secretary to
protest against the attempt which was being made to put
a stop to the work of women at colliery pit-mouths, he
expressed his readiness to accede to their views, and rejoiced in the opportunity of showing that a Conservative
Government was open to the reasoned requests of labour.

When the Parliamentary Committee of the Trade Union Congress decided in June against taking part in an International Conference of Labour they were commended for maintaining the independence of the British artisan, and keeping him clear of associations with foreign workmen who founded their programme upon more State intervention than men in this country demanded.[1] Nor was there any misgiving about the conference in the autumn on the conditions of working women, when a strong committee, on which Miss Maude Stanley, Mrs Barnett, Mrs Hickford, Mrs Allison, Mrs Verney, Canon Barnett, Lord Meath, Mr G. R. Sims and Professor Stuart served, met to consider the relation of women's work to social life, and more specifically the hours, wages and conditions of women's work. This conference, again, was largely due to a novel of Walter Besant's, *Children of Gibeon*, which had depicted the circumstances of sweated women in the East End; Besant served as honorary treasurer of the committee. All these movements were supposed to be separable from London street meetings, which again began to be troublesome in October. In one sense they were separable; even William Morris himself was thinking at this time that the free speech campaign was beginning to take on an importance of its own, apart from the subject of the speaking. He thought he discerned in the leaders of the campaign a desire to figure as heroes.[2] But in the deeper sense there was no line of division. What was happening was the birth of a new school of labour aspiration, which was not satisfied to see all political economy brushed aside, because the individualist form of it had been dethroned. The tendency of even thoughtful men in other classes just now was to replace political science by a humanitarian spirit in administration; and the knowledge that such a spirit was abroad made men the more ready to be

---

[1] *The Times*, 15th June 1887.
[2] Mackail's *Life of William Morris*, ii. 179.

impatient with the London street meetings. As these meetings had become a battle-ground the socialist leaders were disposed to keep them going; they could not be blamed for seeing the opportunity. Having tried to hold one in Trafalgar Square, and caused the authorities to take action on the somewhat absurd legal point that the Square was Crown territory, and could therefore be arbitrarily closed, the socialists called a large meeting in Hyde Park on 20th October, and thence led a mass of men as a deputation to the Home Office; the police devoted themselves to riding constantly through and through the marching men, and breaking up the ranks. Two or three days later, on a Sunday, there was a march of the unemployed to Westminster Abbey. Some months earlier they had similarly attended service in St Paul's; on both occasions the men sat for the most part quite quietly amid the nervous congregation, though one or two shouted remarks during the sermon. The closing of Trafalgar Square was rescinded, and a meeting was held there on 24th October, after which men paraded the West End streets, but nothing occurred beyond the excusable panic of the shopkeepers. Hyndman had issued a programme of demands, including an eight hours' day in all Government workshops, the opening to cultivation of all waste lands in Crown or Government possession, and the establishment of relief works at State or local charges. For the moment the reopening of Trafalgar Square appeared to have had its effect in causing the demonstrations there to dwindle by the removal of a grievance. But some arrests in the Square early in November for using threatening language led to a fresh prohibition of meetings there, and the result was the fight of " Bloody Sunday," 13th November. The unemployed and their leaders made a determined attack on the Square, which was held by a strong barrier of police. Police vedettes met the oncoming processions from every direction, and had broken them up before they reached the main cordon. The chief fight took place at the corner of the Strand. "No one who saw it will ever forget the strange and indeed terrible sight of that grey winter day, the vast, sombre-coloured crowd, the brief but fierce struggle at the corner of the Strand, and the river of steel and scarlet that moved slowly through the dusky swaying masses, when two squadrons of the Life Guards were summoned up from Whitehall." [1] Before the columns of the unemployed were finally headed off, the upper side of the Square was lined by a battalion of Foot Guards with bayonets fixed and ball cartridge in their pouches. After the affray two of the stoutest fighters remained in custody—Cunninghame Graham, then a Member of Parliament, and John Burns. For weeks the alarm caused by this wild scene lasted; special constables were enrolled as for a revolution, and Trafalgar Square was held daily by pickets of police. There was no further attack; but there was one other socialist manifestation. In December a man named Alfred Linnell, who had been injured in the fight, died. His funeral on 18th December was attended by a huge but perfectly orderly crowd, and William Morris and Henry Quelch, of the Social Democratic Federation, spoke at the graveside. Cunninghame Graham, John Burns, the Rev. Stewart Headlam, and Mrs Annie Besant were in the procession. No one knew what effect a man's death might have on the agitation; it made an anxious close to the year. Moreover in the Western Isles of Scotland the crofters were raiding the deer forests, declaring they were starving, and the tithe riots in Wales had not ceased.

In December the British public learned for the first time where the real wealth of gold in the Transvaal lay. A Board of Trade report on the Witwatersrand district was published on 15th December. The Rand had been pro-

---

[1] Mackail's *Life of William Morris,* ii. 191.

claimed a goldfield in March, but for all effective purposes the secret had been kept until the industry was under way ; and by this time eighty or ninety companies had been registered in connection with the Rand, and 1400 stamps were already working. The discovery of the gold there was attributed to a Mr Struben, an Englishman long resident in Johannesburg.[1] Smaller fields still continued to be opened up, as at Luipaard's Vlei ; and altogether the export of gold from South Africa was expected to approach £200,000 in this year ; in 1885 it had been £69,543. A hint of the monopolising of wealth by a large ring at work in South Africa was given by the announcement in August 1887 that the De Beers Company were buying out the French Diamond Mining Company at Kimberley. A mining subject of a somewhat different kind had caused scandal in political quarters in the summer. The recent annexation of Burma had brought under British control the rich ruby mines which had belonged to King Theebaw. It became known that a lease to work these mines was being granted, and there were circumstances connected with the grant which caused Lord Cross, the Secretary for India, to cut short the pending negotiations, and reserve the subject for inquiry.

Late in the year the final stage of an undertaking, which has made several appearances in these pages, was inaugurated. The first sod of the Manchester Ship Canal was cut on 11th November at Eastham Ferry by Lord Egerton of Tatton. Shares to the value of five millions had been issued in the summer, three millions having been taken up in Lancashire before the prospectus was published for the second time,[2] and Barings and Rothschilds had underwritten a considerable amount. The raising of the three millions was a fine piece of local patriotism.

[1] It has also been attributed to Sir J. B. Robinson.
[2] See p. 186.

CHAPTER X

1888 : THE SOCIAL CONSCIENCE

IN the year 1888 it seemed that the many currents
of restlessness—the restlessness not only of working
people and the people on the " starvation line," but
of educated and thoughtful people also in regard to the
responsibilities of citizenship—were producing a genuine
effect. The body politic of England stirred uneasily, and
could not quite go to sleep again. There was no cause
for anxieties abroad. For the moment our relations
with France were patched up ; in October 1887 the
Government had announced simultaneously the conclusion of an agreement neutralising the Suez Canal in time
of war, and the withdrawal of all French claims on the
New Hebrides.[1] Germany lay under a double oppression :
her famous old Emperor William, first wearer of the crown
of a united Germany, was at the end of his long life (he
died on 9th March) ; and his heir, the Crown Prince who
had taken all London's eyes in the Jubilee procession, was
a stricken man. He only reigned three months, dying on
15th June, of cancer in the throat.

So England practically spent the year with its own
conscience. In January the horrors of sweated labour
were for the first time systematically revealed by a
Board of Trade report, coinciding with the work of
the private committee investigating the conditions of
women's industry. The subject was approached without

[1] See page 103. The subject of the New Hebrides had provided
the liveliest passages of discussion at the Colonial Conference.
See *The Times*, 27th July 1887.

any sentimental excess. Sweating was diagnosed as an evil largely due to the extreme subdivision of labour in certain trades ; for instance, a single subdivision of the tailor's trade, coatmaking, was further subdivided into the work of cutters, basters, machinists, pressers, fellers, buttonhole makers, and general workers. It was urged on behalf of the various sub-contractors in trades so divided that they worked as hard as any of the grades below them, and that care should be taken to distinguish between a system itself and excesses in a system. When Lord Dunraven a month later raised the question in the House of Lords, and obtained the appointment of a Select Committee, the same careful spirit was at work ; the mere system of manufacture of cheap clothing (which was the trade mostly impugned) was, after all, it was said, the same as the system in other industrial work ; cheap pens and cheap cotton goods were equally made possible by subdivision of labour ; and with an export trade of four millions a year in clothing it behoved reformers to be cautious. An increase of inspectors might be desirable. But was it not a matter in which a general improvement of tone in the community would be the only valid method of reform ? So sharply was public attention roused that the Salvation Army was attacked for producing, by its charitable system of providing work for those in need of food and shelter, an undercutting of the market in laundry-work and match-making ; the accusation was strenuously denied. The subject ran off into all sorts of side-issues. Was the middleman to be blamed ? But the middleman must be a necessary and not uneconomic link in the social fabric. Was alien immigration a chief source of sweating ? But, if that were stopped, would the underpaid work be refused by English people ? Was not the fault as much with the purchaser as with anybody else ? No direct legislation against sweating would avail, if the purchaser insisted on extreme cheapness. The private committee on women's work formed itself into a larger and more immediately philanthropic body, called the Women's Protective and Provident League, which was active in collecting evidence for the Select Committee. A more important step was taken in July, when the match-making girls of a large factory in the East End were encouraged to strike by the outcry against sweating ; Miss Clementina Black at once devoted herself to forming a Match-makers' Union ; the girls won their fight themselves, and wrote a new chapter in the history of women's labour. It was altogether no wonder that in the autumn Lord Sydney Godolphin Osborne should express rather sombre gratification in the reflection that at last some knowledge of the awful conditions of the East End and of provincial slums was penetrating an England which with these horrors at its doors went on subscribing half-a-million a year for foreign missions, spent its money lavishly on the building of a Church House,[1] and its time on a Pan-Anglican conference of bishops from all over the world.

The sarcastic implication of this reflection, as well as its main purport, was thoroughly in the spirit of the year. In religious matters too the nation was singularly stirred. A focussing point for much new thought, some of it very yeasty, was provided by the publication early in April of a novel, *Robert Elsmere*, by Mrs Humphry Ward. Reference has been made to that conflict between divines and men of science, which arose out of enthusiastic acceptance of the evolutionary theory, and was sharply revived in the eighties by the death of Charles Darwin and the consequent recapitulation of his achievements. As it happened, the controversy found the Church of England in a phase of slight, perhaps too slight, attention to purely doctrinal and historical work. That had become associated chiefly with the Tractarians ; and in the reaction against

[1] The Church House at Westminster was begun in 1887, after a great deal of discussion.

High Church methods and practices, which centred in
F. D. Maurice and Charles Kingsley, there had been a
tendency to feel that ecclesiastical learning was not altogether a healthy pursuit. To show to the world that
passion for the poor and afflicted, devotion to parish work,
and zealous care of souls were not necessarily bound up
with a sacramental interpretation of priesthood and an
ascetic life tending to monasticism, was the object of the
Maurice group ; and as the priestliness and asceticism were
founded on the historical teachings of the Tractarians, the
group had a tendency to avoid learning which was, so to
speak, technical Church learning. The muscular curate
was the prevailing type of young clergyman. When the
attack came, when new scientific schools of thought, new
theories of the origin of life, assailed the whole Christian
cosmogony, and thereby raised the searching problem of
Christian evidences, men of religious faith retired into
more than one camp. The High Church, secure in its
own mysticism, held no parley at all from its citadel.
Churchmen of the Maurice and Kingsley type became the
Broad Church, and started throwing up earthworks to
enclose a portion of the debatable ground, from whence
they might answer the shots aimed at them ; in other
words, they rationalised certain regions of evidence, especially in the Old Testament. Meanwhile a strong intellectual
movement among lay churchmen rationalised the whole
body of Christianity, and these people, ceasing thereby in
mere honesty to call themselves churchmen, yet called
themselves Christians. The Evangelicals, with a section of
Nonconformity (one portion of which was in the broadest
Church position), rejecting the extreme ground of the
mystics, battled faithfully with the exponents of the higher
criticism, and gave not the least convincing proof of the
reality of their religious feeling in the firmness with which
they refused to yield an inch of ground. A controversy of
some fame took place just at this time ; Dr Henry Wace,

Principal of King's College, London, engaged in an argumentative duel with Professor Huxley in the pages of *The Nineteenth Century*, and this type of discussion never received a better summing-up than on this occasion. The question of the origin of life seriously disturbed dinner-parties, and protoplasm was a word that could destroy the friendships of years. If the theologians' position showed some obstinacy, the scientists on their side laid themselves open to the biting comment that " nothing is infallible now, except science." Floating somewhat vaguely in the welter was the recent school of taste in art and life. Æstheticism in its worst aspect offered a cynical kind of support to the Ritualists ; in its best it held a large part of the intellectual world aloof from destructive criticism and from an exaggerated emphasis on the exercise of the intellect.

Matthew Arnold, who had, if often indirectly, borne so large a part in this drastic reconsideration of belief, hardly lived to see it become (though the phrase is rather inappropriate) a popular affair. He died on 16th April, just after Mrs Ward, whose uncle he was, had published her novel. Mr Gladstone found himself at leisure to take up the ecclesiastical discussions which always interested him even more than politics ; and an article by him on this novel [1] set all the country talking. It is ancient history now ; the modern world would not be stirred by the spectacle of a parish priest, who has resigned his living owing to an inability to believe in miracles, founding in the East End a sect based on an indeterminate mixture of Positivism, social enthusiasm, and sacramental phrases without the Sacraments. But the appearance of the book remains a monument of that searching of the social conscience which had so strikingly come to light every now and then in the early eighties, and in 1888 was the predominant influence.

Housing reform was at work. Large private benefactions

[1] In *The Nineteenth Century*, 1888.

were being projected to supplement the work of public bodies, and at least one great ground landlord, whose leases were falling in, was setting aside, in his plans for rebuilding, sites for workmen's dwellings.[1] Educational reform was advanced a stage in this year by the Report of the Royal Commission on the Education Acts. It had nothing to say about making education entirely free, though Mr Chamberlain in his new surroundings maintained that ideal more frankly than any other part of his former Radical programme. The commission was indeed Conservative in essence, a majority of fifteen supporting the voluntary school system and recommending a development of religious education, from which a minority of five, including Sir John Lubbock, Mr Lyulph Stanley and Dr Dale dissented. But on more general topics some useful recommendations were made, as, for instance, that teachers' salaries should be fixed, instead of being dependent on the grant ; and that, while the system of payment by results in the Government grant could not be entirely abolished, it might be subject to much relaxation. An improvement of the training colleges was also recommended. A movement was on foot earlier in the year to ease the conditions under which elementary schools might enter on technical education. It was beginning to be felt that it would be difficult to lay down the line at which elementary education ends and technical instruction should begin, so that the sounder policy might be a wide and deep improvement of elementary education. The Associated Chambers of Commerce, on the other hand, preferred that the two forms of teaching should be kept separate. The subject in general had a year of helpful ventilation and discussion.

Events had so fallen out that the chief parliamentary work of 1888 was also in the spirit of the year. The Local Government Bill gave the representative principle a new sphere hitherto occupied by non-elective authorities.

[1] Lord Cadogan, on his Chelsea estates.

Not only had " the era of administration " come, but the
power of administration was placed within reach of all.
Until this time the authority in the counties had been the
justices in Quarter Sessions ; it was now to be a body
similar to the great popular municipalities, elected on
the same household suffrage, with some modifications,
such as the removal of the disqualification of clergymen
and ministers. But more important still from the
democratic point of view was the amount of delegation
of work which the Bill was framed to permit. Practically all county work might be delegated to committees,
with the provision that they must report to the council,
and that the council had the sole power of expenditure.
Two committees were compulsory under the Bill—the
Finance Committee (which was not only a watching
committee, as in the existing municipalities, but an
estimating committee, without whose sanction no sum over
fifty pounds could be expended) ; and a Standing Joint
Committee, formed of councillors and justices, for police
purposes. But any number of other committees might be
formed, and in order to save wasteful expenditure from
overlapping in such matters as drainage, roads, etc., a
council might unite with other councils in setting up joint
committees with delegated powers. The result of all the
delegation was that the council as a whole need not meet
often (four meetings a year was the statutory minimum),
and thus membership was open to men who had not much
time to spare from their work, and at the same time county
business was not hampered with incessant debating. A
general county rate was authorised by the Bill. The
Bill did not apply to Ireland ; but Liberal Unionists
congratulated themselves on having an instrument the
possible extension of which might undermine the Home
Rule movement. Conservatives indeed regarded the
measure as savouring far too strongly of Liberal Unionism,
and the Government had to face much resentment among

their supporters in the country. Tory critics pointed out
that administration by Quarter Sessions had been econ-
omical, fairly efficient, and, above all, free from jobbery.
Other critics, while more friendly to the principle, objected
that much more ought to have been done to unify rating,
that interference with the old control of the police might
endanger the efficiency of the service, that triennial elections were not frequent enough to keep up local interest,
and so on. Liberals regretted the exclusion of Poor Law
administration from the work of the new councils ; but
the creation of a County of London, with the consequent
abolition of the Metropolitan Board of Works, was no
small consolation to them. 'All was going well with the
Bill, when suddenly a controversy sprang up on the
clauses detailing the licensing powers of the new authority.
The councils were to be allowed to refuse the renewal of
licences to public-houses, on payment of compensation
to the licence-holder. Temperance reformers detected
danger in the implication contained in this clause, that an
interest in a licence was a valuable interest ; they maintained hotly that a licence was an annual grant, and that
the licensing authority had a right in any year to refuse
renewal. Less extreme men were puzzled by the absence
of any basis for computation of the value of a licence.
Brewers and licence-holders for their part disliked any
change which would place them under new and popularly
elected bodies. So great an outcry arose from all these
conflicting interests that the Government decided to
withdraw the licensing clauses altogether. The Bill
then made a prosperous passage, and was law before the
House rose in August.

The licensed victualling trade was at a critical point in
its history. We have recorded the first large brewery
flotation, that of Guinness's, in 1886. Others followed,
notably that of Samuel Allsopp & Sons, in February 1887,
with a capital of £1,100,000 ; and that of Bass, Ratcliff

& Gretton, in January 1888, with a capital of £2,720,000. For some time breweries all over the kingdom had been buying public-houses, in order to avoid the expense and uncertainty of constant competition for the custom of licensed victuallers. The possession of a large number of licensed premises gave a brewery a regular and steady trade. But the acquisition of them was an extremely expensive affair, and the standard of price for such premises constantly rose. Brewing firms had therefore been obliged to raise a large number of mortgages and loans, and had only been waiting for an easy investment market to come to the public for capital to consolidate these liabilities. It was natural that they should at the same time decide to put their businesses under the Limited Liability Acts ; the old private partnership was apt to be a tiresome arrangement in businesses so large in scale. But apart from the legal and financial convenience of limited liability the only object which it was wise to have in view was the consolidation of the mortgages and loans. Even a moderate call for new ordinary capital would not have done any harm. But the Guinness flotation had been so eagerly taken up, and brewing profits at the moment were such a temptation to the investor, that some breweries put their whole capital on the market. The two courses of action were exemplified in the cases of Allsopp's and Bass's. The former brewery offered all classes of its shares for subscription ; the public demand was almost entirely for the ordinary and preference shares. Bass's on the other hand kept the ordinary and preference shares in the possession of the old shareholders, and offered the public £910,000 of debentures. They were taking the course that really represented the actual requirements of breweries at the time ; Allsopp's were using the opportunity of those requirements for a wholly different operation.

The amount of money waiting for investment was enormous. The application for Allsopp's shares amounted to something like a hundred millions, and Bass's debentures were issued at 107 per cent. The rush of prospectuses was becoming so lively as to cause a fresh scrutiny of the limited liability laws, and a fear that the company promoter was not sufficiently under control. Suggestions were made that the law should demand two registrations, an initial one, which might be easy enough to keep the ball rolling, and a final one of a much more stringent kind in respect to paid-up capital and the proportion borne to it by preliminary expenses. Besides brewery flotations, this year saw also the formation of several Trusts, the chief one being the Cheshire Salt Trust, with a capital of three millions ; and—a more exciting affair—the beginning of the South African gold "boom." The industry on the Rand was going ahead fast. The gold exports for a single month (February) were £75,647—more than the whole year's export in 1885 ; and from the Rand alone the export for March was 14,706 oz., and for April 15,853 oz. There seemed to be no cloud on the promising outlook. An article in *The Times* [1] on the Rand conditions dwelt on the absence of any disturbance such as the inrush of capitalists and labour had been expected to produce. President Kruger had appointed as Landrost of the district not a Boer unlikely to be in sympathy with the work, but a naturalised Austrian " of agreeable manners " ; and the Englishmen on the Rand were saying that they were better off than at Cape Town. The monthly output by the end of the year was about 21,000 oz., though it was believed that for private reasons a good deal of gold was being kept back.[2] The connection which has already been spoken of between the new goldfield and the immensely wealthy diamond mines of South Africa came out clearly at a meeting of the Goldfields of South Africa Ltd. in

[1] 22nd May 1888.

[2] Board of Trade Report on the Witwatersrand. Published 17th December 1888.

October, when the shareholders expressed themselves as so confident in the gold industry that they wished to get rid of their De Beers shares, and put the money into the Rand.   De Beers had in May amalgamated with the Kimberley Central Diamond Mining Company, and was now a virtual monopoly.

The already prolific output of the Rand took the wind from the sails of the Currency Commission's report, which was published in November.   The commission was equally divided in its recommendations, neither of which was original.   One half recommended the issue of banknotes of small values ; the other half were for the bimetallist solution, and for an international agreement fixing the ratio at which coins of either metal should be available for the payment of debts, at the option of the debtor. No action was taken on the report.   The Treasury was otherwise occupied, for Mr Goschen, the Chancellor of the Exchequer, had decided to carry out compulsorily the conversion of the Three-per-cents., which Mr Childers had attempted on voluntary lines in 1884.   That attempt had not been useless.   The twenty millions or so of stock, which had since that time borne $2\frac{3}{4}$ per cent. interest instead of 3 per cent., afforded an extremely useful in-dication of the real position of public credit ; they stood at 102.   It was obvious that, if the lower rate of interest could still command a premium, it was absurd for the country to be going on paying 3 per cent.   The fact that municipalities had been reconsidering their rate of interest must also have influenced Mr Goschen.   In 1887 the Bir-mingham Corporation found its $3\frac{1}{2}$ per cent. stock standing at a premium of 3 to $4\frac{1}{2}$; and decided that the issue it was about to make should be at 3 per cent. only.   It had obtained for an issue late in the year an average price of £98, 15s.   Consequently Mr Goschen had double reason to feel confidence in the lowering of the national rate of interest, and he did not hesitate to apply it to the whole of the national stock. His Budget of 1888 contained a scheme by which five hundred and fifty-eight millions of Three-per-cents. were to fall after the current year to $2\frac{3}{4}$ per cent., and after a further fourteen years to $2\frac{1}{2}$ per cent., at which they were to stand for twenty years. Some portion of the stock could legally be converted without notice ; and in order to induce stockholders who were entitled to notice to bring their holdings rapidly into the scheme, Mr Goschen offered a premium of 5s. per £100 on stock converted before 12th April, and also a brokerage of 1s. 6d. per £100 to brokers converting before that date. The result was that by 12th April the new stock amounted to four hundred and fifty millions, and the success of the scheme was assured. It too had profited by the better business conditions.

To say, as we have said, that this was a year in which the public conscience was stirred must not be allowed to carry too sombre an implication. The passion of the year for coster songs (" 'E's all right when you know 'im, But you've got to know 'im fust " was of this date) reveals depths of innocent ease. Strenuous ideas, social conventions, had in many directions been relaxed. People of exalted birth were going almost ostentatiously into trade ; impoverished younger sons were taking positions in city businesses, and noble ladies were opening millinery shops. With the decline of fashionable æstheticism, artists had taken to dressing in the ordinary smart clothes of men about town, and velvet and long hair were no more the mode. The New Gallery, opened this year, found itself taking over from the Grosvenor Gallery a school of taste in art which had already become respectably traditional ; and Mr Whistler had so far ceased to infuriate the ordinary citizen that he had become to *Punch* " the licensed Vistler." Advanced artistic taste was now occupying itself with William Morris's special gospel of " reasonable labour," and work in which the workman could take interest. The Arts and Crafts Guild, which had been founded in 1884, held this year its first exhibition. The restoration of the individual hand and brain to the chief place in manufacture was destined, in Morris's view, to chasten industrial art, wherein the domination of the machine was producing a gulf betwixt utility and ornamentation ; the latter was becoming an excrescence, and increasingly meaningless in design.

The great excitement of the summer was the railway " Race to the North." It began in July, when the London & North-Western and Caledonian Railways announced an eight-and-a half-hours run to Edinburgh. As the journey had been one of ten hours this was an effective advertisement ; but the Great. Northern and North-Eastern Railways promptly replied by announcing an eight-hours run. The North-Western and Caledonian did the same early in August ; and the race hit the public fancy. Men surrendered like children to the fascination of railway engines ; and rejoiced in this colossal duel of locomotive monsters, hurtling across England through the night, and pantingly comparing times in Edinburgh in the morning. After the respective routes had shaved down their difference to a matter of a minute or two, the rivals took a rest, and the public travelled by whichever route it had backed. Historically the principal interest of the struggle lies in the obvious deduction that the passenger traffic to Scotland was becoming very valuable ; which is another indication of the spread of wealth in the middle classes, and the readiness to expend it. Scientifically too the race had a special interest. Such tremendous rates of speed with such heavy loads meant firstly that the modern engineering tools had succeeded in producing large surfaces with a minimum of liability to destructive friction, and secondly that Bessemer steel rails would bear an astonishing amount of shock and strain.

The other craze of the summer was neither useful nor scientific. It was in 1888 that Mr Baldwin first performed the feat of dropping from a balloon with a parachute, which opened as he fell and floated him to earth. It gave a fresh impetus to the rather failing interest in ballooning.

Electric lighting had at length made the advance which enabled it to take its share in the busy company-promoting of the year. House-to-house supply had been rendered possible, and at the same time an Act was passed extending the duration of Provisional Electric Lighting Orders to forty-two years. This made the enterprise commercially profitable, and two companies were at once formed in London. They prudently undertook districts which contained enough theatres, clubs, and large hotels to secure a steady consumption—the districts of Pall Mall, St James's and St Martin-in-the-Fields. A new process for making aluminium, reducing the cost from forty shillings a pound to about fifteen shillings a pound; more experiments with a " spirit motor "; and a successful employment of wax instead of tinfoil for the cylinders of phonographs, were minor activities of the inventors. Phonographs of the new kind were a great interest of the year.

The Local Government Bill was the only parliamentary business to which the public paid much heed. The movement for setting up a Department of Agriculture was revived, and, as was natural, began to have more weight under a Government strong in the landed interest. Reform of the House of Lords was in the air. The case of a peer who had been warned off the turf late in 1887 had led *The Times* to remark that such a case brought us " nearer to the highly necessary reform of the House of Lords "; but a motion in the House by Lord Rosebery proposing a Second Chamber of 200 members, some elected by the Peers, others by the town and county councils, others provided by an increase of life peerages, was but tamely debated, and was rejected by a majority of more than two to one. However, a few Conservative peers and several Liberal Unionist peers voted for it. The real interest of the session, after the Local Government Bill, was a vivid re-crudescence in the House of Commons of Irish controversy. Since his complete denial of the authenticity of the letter published in *The Times* in April 1887 Parnell, true to his constant disregard of English opinion, and little inclined, in a state of poor health, to give himself trouble, had taken no further steps in the matter.   He had declined all advice to proceed against *The Times* for libel.   But at the end of 1887 a member of his party, finding what he considered to be ground for action on his own part in the articles on " Parnellism and Crime," had entered a libel suit.   It came on for trial in July 1888, and a verdict was given against him.   The trial was used to strike another blow at Parnell. Counsel for *The Times* was the Attorney-General ; and in consequence, when he produced and read in court further incriminating letters alleged to have been signed by Parnell, his speech was not far removed from an official indictment. Even Parnell could hardly treat this with contempt, and he moved in the House of Commons for a Select Committee. The Government offered him instead a commission of three judges, set up by an Act of Parliament.   Feeling in the House ran very strong [1] ; it was said by the Liberals and the Irish that the proposal to set the Bench to work meant the hope of a prejudiced English verdict, and when the Bill was found to empower the commission to consider charges against " other persons " besides Parnell there was great indignation at the idea of placing virtually the whole question of Irish government before a legal tribunal. Mr Gladstone was in his most impassioned mood, and the committee stage of the Bill was marked by violent scenes in the House.   The temper of Irish Nationalist members had been rather hot throughout the year.   They were indignant at what they considered an insulting nonchalance in Mr Balfour, and from the beginning of the session they had accused him of deliberately absenting

[1] *Cf.* Morley's *Life of Gladstone*, iii. 390.

himself from the House when Irish questions bulked largely on the notice paper. This smouldering resentment was partly responsible for the violence that accompanied the Parnell Commission Bill debates. The world outside cannot be said to have cared very much about the details of the affair, and when the commission met, in October 1888, no one paid great attention to the immense production of evidence. The terms of reference to the commission practically necessitated an examination into the speeches of Irish members and all disturbing events in Ireland for years past. Nor was there even as much popular interest as there would have been a few years later, when it was announced that Mr Cecil Rhodes, an ex-Cabinet Minister in Cape Colony, and a principal shareholder in De Beers, had been in correspondence with Parnell, and, in order to mark his view of Home Rule as a possible commencement of Devolution and Imperial Federation, had subscribed £10,000 to the Irish party funds. Mr Rhodes expressed his own conviction, from his experience with the Dutch in Cape Colony, that the difficulty of the loyal minority in Ulster was one that would settle itself.

Parliament assembled for an autumn sitting. It had an Employers' Liability Bill to deal with, modifying the doctrine of "common employment" in the workman's favour, introducing the responsibility of sub-contractors, and extending the benefits to seamen. Mr Chamberlain was evidently making his presence felt in the Coalition, for this was one of the measures of his Radical days. The session was also notable for some changes in procedure; the House began meeting at three o'clock in the afternoon, instead of at four o'clock, and the Standing Committees on Law and Trade, which had been allowed to lapse, were again set up. This revived the idea of an Estimates Committee, but a Conservative Government was not likely to take so new a step. Its advocates found some cogent arguments in the agitation which was beginning about the defences of the country. It was clear that there would be strong pressure to increase the Naval Estimates, and an Estimates Committee might, it was pleaded, bring about that co-ordination of naval and military expenditure which was surely to be desired. The pressure was fully at work in a meeting at the Mansion House in May, when Admiral Hornby asked if England was really able to keep the sea ; and gave as his own reply 'the opinion that she would require 186 cruisers for the purpose. A committee had reported upon the state of the defences of our naval ports, and, cautious as its official phrases were, men discerned in the report a real concern about the existing circumstances. In every suburban railway carriage of a morning the navy, new battleships, new men, new methods, were the pre-vailing topic of conversation ; and Lord Charles Beresford, who had made a fighting reputation for himself at the bombardment of Alexandria, and Lord Randolph Churchill raised the subject on every possible occasion. The celebrations of the tercentenary of the Armada were a rallying ground for the agitators ; they were also an early instance of the local pageant, for the historic game of bowls on Plymouth Hoe was re-enacted, and was followed by a procession of all the sovereigns of England. The discussion of our defences gave some prominence also to an agitation persistent throughout these years for giving better atten-tion to the Volunteer movement, which was feeling itself neglected and very inadequately supported in funds by the War Office. This year saw it in peculiar difficulty owing to the necessity of abandoning its old training and shooting ground at Wimbledon. A year or two passed before it was in possession of new ground at Bisley. Volunteers, it may be remarked, were introducing cycling into their service, but the high bicycle did not lend itself well to such uses.

In the world of labour there was a singular lull. To some extent, no doubt, the better trade conditions had absorbed unemployed labour ; and street meetings were not so severely under the ban of the police. Organisation was taking the energies of the most prominent labour leaders, and the Independent Labour Party was set on foot. The removal of all restrictions upon combination was the one item of the International Trade Union Congress upon which there was harmony. But the year is chiefly remarkable in this connection for the appearance of a newspaper which, though not formally associated with the labour movement, aimed at becoming a power among working men. This newspaper was *The Star*, a halfpenny evening paper, first published in January 1888. Several towns in the north had had such papers for some time ; and London had one, *The Echo*, designed like *The Star* to be a democratic organ. But *The Echo* displayed a rather undiluted idealism, which tended to limit its public to men already possessing energetic political opinions. The purpose of *The Star* was rather, by providing an attractive and readable staple of news, to instil politics and other interests of the mind into readers who would never buy a paper for such things in the first place. It appealed also to the new generation at large, by starting with a galaxy of subversive talent in its staff of critics. Mr Bernard Shaw contributed the musical criticism, Mr Walkley, the dramatic, Mr John Davidson, and later Mr Richard Le Gallienne, the literary criticism.

December brought round again a deputation of unemployed men to the Lord Mayor, but no one expected a very anxious winter. Public alarm about the East End was given a very different, and a much more gruesome, turn ; the notorious Whitechapel murders began this autumn. A woman was found murdered in the backyard of a house in Whitechapel on 31st August, and another on 8th September ; two more similar murders took place on 30th September, and on 15th October the incident occurred which introduced a peculiar horror, the police receiving postcards and letters signed " Jack the Ripper." The mutilations which accompanied the murders were atrocious, and seemed to prove that they were all the work of one man, and that he must have had a training in surgery. It was incredible that such things should continue with the hue and cry that was raised, and yet a fifth murder took place on 8th November. They even continued into 1889, and then the terrible series suddenly came to an end. The perpetrator was never brought to justice.

At the end of the year news arrived of Stanley's progress on the expedition for the relief of Emin Pasha. The news was a whole year late ; the messages received from him reported the expedition safe and well in November 1887. As a matter of fact, reports had already reached England which rather dimmed the satisfaction. Stanley had left part of his force under Major Barttelot encamped at a certain point, to maintain his communications. He had trusted to a well-known chief of an Arab tribe, Tippoo Tib, an old slave-raider, to supply the camp with provisions, and Tippoo Tib had undertaken to do so. He failed to keep his word, and in July rumours had come to England that Barttelot and his force were in the greatest straits. In October word came of Barttelot's death, and no one knew then where Stanley was. The messages from him in November were followed by some in December, from Zanzibar, to the effect that the meeting between Stanley and Emin had taken place in January 1888, and that both were safe.

Just at the time when this happy appendix was being placed to the history of the Soudan war, there was fighting once more at Suakin. Sir F. Grenfell was in command in Egypt, and he inflicted a defeat upon some dervish forces which had been inclined to press Suakin too closely. The battle revived in England discussion of our position at Suakin, but Lord Salisbury made no declaration of policy beyond the determination to retain the place.

CHAPTER XI

IT was natural that after a year such as 1888 men should come to the next with good heart. Trade was cheerful, and may for the moment stand personified in jolly Colonel North, then at the height of his fame, spending his money on his great house at Eltham, on his greyhounds, and on large genial benefactions—a millionaire playing up to his character. The Stock Exchange found the way to middle-class pockets, and the investors who had surrendered to the fascinations of the brewery boom and the gold boom were ready for all sorts of further adventures. An underground railway from St James's Street to Holborn Circus, with a capital of £750,000 ; a tramway, working on the conduit system in an experimental stage at Northfleet, Kent ; a number of electric light companies ; an amalgamation of the two chief telephone companies—the National and the United—into one concern, with an enlarged capital; and an incessant conversion of private trading companies into limited liability concerns—all flooded the market with prospectuses, but did not exhaust the money awaiting investment. Another sign of the greater distribution of wealth is to be found in Mr Goschen's Budget speech of the year, when he pleaded for a new policy of taxing a much greater number of articles of consumption, since the old policy of taxing a small number no longer spread taxation fairly according to wealth.[1] There were also indications of prosperity, however deplorable from the strictly ethical point of view, in the steady increase of the return from duties on intoxicants, which helped to keep up the Budget surpluses of

[1] Elliot's *Life of Lord Goschen*, ii. 158.

these years, and in the growth of betting and gambling. This latter subject greatly exercised respectable minds at this time ; raids upon gambling clubs by the police were frequent ; the Convocation of Canterbury had a report on the subject made to it by a committee ; and legislation was vaguely demanded. It was felt that clubs were not the only point at which the police might strike. Cheaper newspapers had produced so large a betting population that a regular professional class of bookmakers had sprung up to meet the requirements of those who were from their circumstances unable to go to race meetings, but found in betting from newspaper reports the kind of excitement which could colour their monotonous lives by being crammed into factory dinner-hours. Meanwhile one of the countless prospectuses of the year can be seen now to have been a promise of yet more cheap newspapers to come ; it asked for a capital to run wood-pulp paper-mills in Norway.

Some moralists, contemplating this result of news-paper reading, were inclined to deplore the teaching of so many people to read. But on the whole the movement for free education advanced strongly, with the argument that, if education had led to difficulties, this only meant that education must be fuller. The Technical Education Act was passed this year, with very little discussion ; its provisions have been already noted.[1] In this year also University " Extension " teaching took a new form ; a meeting of Extension Students at Oxford had been tried as an experiment in the summer of 1888, and had been so successful that it was now decided to establish the idea on a more complete and definite scale. Courses of lectures were to be so arranged that students could come into residence for either a fortnight or a month at choice ; and in the more continuous association of tutors and students the extension system would acquire, as it were, the additional value of a brief university term.

[1] See page 210

An unfortunate incident in the general revival of cheerful interest in all kinds of subjects was that ecclesiastical controversies also revived. Dr Benson was now Archbishop of Canterbury, and he allowed himself to be induced to cite the Bishop of Lincoln, Dr King, before him for ritualistic practices. No one had much belief in this restoration of a form of procedure, the validity of which was more than doubtful, and the enforcing power *nil*. Dean Church described the precedents as " fishy." The " Lincoln Judgment " which issued from the case remained, failing appeal to a tribunal which had enforcing power, an expression of opinion from which each side was free to extract what it liked and neglect the rest. But the proceedings served to irritate a number of old sores ; and, as it happened at the time that the new and very elaborate reredos in St Paul's Cathedral had been attacked as papistical, another centre was provided for disagreement. How radically general public opinion had altered since the old days of ritualistic prosecutions may be seen in the tendency to be more interested in æsthetic than in doctrinal criticism of the reredos. The change may also be seen under another aspect in the report of a joint committee of both Houses of the Convocation of Canterbury, which recommended the establishment of brotherhoods of celibate clergy as the most useful way of supplementing the work of the Church in large towns.[1]

The elections to the first county councils took place in the spring, and, although the social stirrings of the previous year had given some indication of the new spirit, no one was prepared for the astonishing energy aroused by the elections to the London County Council. It may in some lights be seen as pathetic that London should thus confess its backwardness in municipal development, should be genuinely excited by the prospect of activities which were

[1] One brotherhood, called the Order of St Paul, was founded, but came to a premature end.

an old story in every other large centre of population ;
Manchester and Glasgow men might have smiled as a
grown man smiles at a child.   But at least, when the
elections were over, London had such a council as probably
had never been gathered for municipal work anywhere in
the world.   Some of the most capable members of the
House of Lords were on it—Lord Hobhouse, Lord Rosebery, Lord Monkswell ;   Radical scions of great houses,
like Mr George Russell and Mr Richard Grosvenor ;
philanthropists like Mr Quintin Hogg ;   some of the most
notable economists, such as Sir Thomas Farrer, Sir Reginald
Welby, and Sir John Lubbock;   men of letters like Mr
Frederic Harrison ;   City magnates, barristers and, above
all, a very powerful force of working men, among them John
Burns, who had shown in fighting his election at Battersea
that his recent exploits in London streets were not those
of a mere ranter, but those of a man whose power with
workmen was almost what he chose to make it.   Altogether the elections blew a blast of new air into every
corner of London.   The doctrine that the working man had
little to expect from the ceaseless strife of party in Parliament was hasty;   but it did far more good than harm in
turning the minds of the labouring men to the possibilities
of the London County Council.   " Practicable Socialism "
was the motto with which Burns entered the council.
The novel which we have already mentioned as having
borne a great share in the foundation of the People's
Palace, Walter Besant's *All Sorts and Conditions of Men*,
gives us the real key to the enthusiasm with which
the first London County Council was elected.   One of
the characters in that book is pleading with a club of
working men to turn from barren political theories :
" Has any Government," he cries, " ever done anything
for you ?   Has it raised your wages ?   Has it shortened
your hours ?   Has it protected you against rogues and
adulterators ? . . . Listen.   You want clean streets and

houses in which decent folk can live. The Government has appointed sanitary officers. Yet look about you. Put your heads into the courts of Whitechapel—what has the sanitary officer done ? You want strong and well-built houses. There are Government inspectors. Yet look at the lath and plaster houses that a child could kick over. You want honest food. All that you eat and drink is adulterated. How does the Government help you there ? . . . You want your own Local Government. What every little town has you have not." [1] Seven years later London had its Local Government, and rose to the occasion as keenly as the most ardent reformer could desire. There is no more important landmark for the social historian of the last thirty years than that election. The point is not that there was a large majority on the more democratic side—the Progressives, as they were ultimately called—but that the keenness displayed is a measure of the quantity of thought and activity which was at this time deliberately diverted from parliamentary politics, because of the opinion that better work could be done elsewhere. The deliberateness must be borne in mind, because when that activity returned at last into political channels it was in some quarters mistaken for a new force.

Another event of the early months of 1889 which sprang from the introspections of 1888 was the foundation of the Christian Social Union. Its aim was to take full account of the changes which were occurring in the social system, the immense nexus which was replacing the old relations of employer and employed, of salesman and purchaser, and to awaken a new kind of responsibility. In a word, it asked afresh the question, Who is my neighbour ?—and suggested that only the widest possible answer could now satisfy a Christian.

The parliamentary session of 1889 was chiefly interesting for the triumph of the party which had been agitating the

[1] *All Sorts and Conditions of Men*, chapter xxviii.

question of our naval defences. The naval estimates
provided for a new construction programme of the
enormous size of twenty-one and a half millions, ten of
which were to be drawn from the Consolidated Fund over
a period of seven years, the remaining eleven and a half
to fall on the estimates over a period of five years. Ten
new battleships were to be laid down under this programme,
the truth being that one of the great changes in ideas of
naval construction was taking place. The introduction
of armour-plating had, quite naturally, turned the minds
of naval constructors rather to the defensive side of shipbuilding; armour was to protect the ship from destruction. It now occurred to the authorities—or perhaps
especially to Mr White, the Chief Constructor—that the
offensive duties of a fleet had fallen too much into the
background; and these ten battleships were to inculcate
the new doctrine of offensive power. The voice which
might most honestly have been raised against this great
expenditure was stilled. On 27th March John Bright died,
after a long illness. He must for years have felt himself
but little in accord with political developments; and the
support his name gave to the Unionist Coalition must have
been as sad to him as his own inability to remain in the
Government which bombarded Alexandria. It was by an
impulse little short of inspiration that *The Times* applied
as his epitaph the words written by Matthew Arnold of
Byron :

" He taught us little, but our soul
Had felt him like the thunder's roll."

Beyond naval affairs the session had only minor
interests. The long-talked-of Department of Agriculture
was at length set up, with Mr Chaplin as its first President.
The Scottish Local Government Act, extending the
establishment of County Government to Scotland, was
found to be more remarkable than had at first sight

appeared, since it gave permission to apply part of the
Exchequer grant to the county authority for the payment
of school fees, and so established the principle of free
education. Mention must also be made of the Cruelty
to Children Act, passed this year, since it extended the
protection given under the old Act so as to include the
exposure of children for begging purposes in the streets,
and also added an improvement by permitting the issue
of a search warrant by a magistrate on sworn information,
instead of leaving the duty of prosecution to Poor Law
Guardians only. There was some hope that Parliament
might also face in this year the problem of the light gold
coinage, by applying part of the Budget surplus to the
calling-in of light gold coins at no loss to the holders of
them, provided they were paid in before a certain time.
It was fairly clear by now that if once the gold coinage
could be restored to its value there was every prospect
of such a supply from the Rand that for a very long
time to come there would be bullion enough to maintain
the value. Any man may see for himself to-day what the
new supply meant. Out of every ten sovereigns that he
receives in ordinary transactions he will probably not
find one more than fifteen years old ; it is quite possible
that no one of any given ten would be more than eight or
nine years old ; and three or four of them would be only
a year or two old. In 1889, when the Light Coinage Bill
was introduced, it was quite a common thing for people
to have sovereigns of more than one previous reign in their
pockets—and the nearest previous reign was fifty-two
years away. There had been such a shortage of bullion
that new coinage had fallen hopelessly behind the demand.
But the Bill was dropped. Even in 1889 the solution provided by the new supply of gold was of course less of a
certainty than it afterwards became ; and the bimetallists
held their ground, while those who were against them felt
it necessary to express, as that conservative financier, Mr

Gladstone, did at this'time, a readiness to permit the issue
of small banknotes. Meanwhile the Rand output rose
until it reached a monthly average in this year of some
35,000 oz. ; the white population of the Transvaal was
about 100,000, but the Boers were said to be treating the
new industry fairly, and no ominous sounds came from
that part of the world. The relations between the two
groups of the Ministerial Coalition were still uneasy. Mr
Chamberlain was difficult for the Conservatives to absorb.
He was advocating the production of some " substitute
for Mr Gladstone's rejected Bill," [1] when the Government
preferred to let the grass grow over the whole question of
alternative measures for Ireland ; his idea was the production of a large and final scheme of land purchase, by
which the difficulties in the way of a generous grant of
local government would be, he thought, much lessened.
The Tories, on the other hand, were talking of abolishing
the Viceroyalty, as the logical conclusion of the Act of
Union, and were drawing careful distinctions between the
state of things on the Clanricarde estate—the extreme
case of an absentee landlord—and that on the Massereene
estate, where the Plan of Campaign had, they said, been
" worsted at close quarters," and boycotting had failed.
A Cabinet Committee did indeed sit on the question of
land purchase at the end of the year ; the price of coalition
had to be paid, and Mr Chamberlain possessed the means
of enforcing payment. He returned during the year to
his old occupation of constructing electoral machines. A
Central Organising Committee for the Liberal Unionist
party, on which representatives from all portions of the
country were to sit, was formed in March. A Liberal
Unionist van campaign over the country, with speech-
makers, magic lanterns, and pamphlets, was opened in
October ; and a Government which had lost five seats at
bye-elections could not afford to offend the master hand

[1] Letter to his constituents in Birmingham, 20th March 1889.

at campaigning. A quarrel between Mr Chamberlain and Lord Randolph Churchill over the question whether the latter had, or had not, the first reversion of John Bright's seat in Birmingham showed that.there was plenty of touchiness in the Coalition ; and Lord Salisbury's speech to the conference of Conservative Organisations, in which he again offered to make way for another Premier, if that would advance the progress of the Coalition, was a significant confession. The quarrel mentioned was afterwards looked back upon as the beginning of the end of Lord Randolph's career ; Mr Chamberlain had his way in the matter completely.

But all this was, to the general public, taking place comparatively behind the scenes. Its only interest in Ireland had more spectacular opportunities. The Parnell Commission suddenly turned dramatic at the beginning of the year. After weeks of evidence the judges came to the question of the letters alleged to have been written by Parnell, and demanded the production of the man who supplied them to *The Times*. The moment he appeared Irishmen were on the alert ; he proved to be a broken-down journalist named Pigott, whom every Irish member knew as ready to do anything for money. To Englishmen the sensation came a few days later, when Sir Charles Russell, who was counsel for Parnell, made Pigott write certain words in the witness-box, confronted him with the same misspellings in the notorious letters as he now made in court, and thundered him into a total breakdown and a confession. He had forged the letters. He made a full confession next day, and fled to Madrid. Detectives followed him, and the news published on 2nd March that he had shot himself in a hotel there on the arrival of the detectives was, for the ordinary man, the end of the drama. The Parnell Commission might again relapse into the patient taking of evidence ; it had at least provided a genuine excitement. However, there was another small excitement of a different kind to come. A warrant was out for the arrest of Dr Tanner, an Irish member, on account of a speech he had delivered in Ireland. He had escaped the police for some time, and suddenly appeared in the House of Commons, when no one but his friends had for weeks known where he was. London enjoyed the comedy of his Jack-in-the-box appearance enormously, and when he left the House in the middle of a close bodyguard of members the group grew into a kind of hilarious procession to a neighbouring hotel. There Dr Tanner submitted to arrest; and the whole affair was too much of a joke for anyone but Radical members to labour the point that this kind of execution of an Irish warrant was a new piece of Mr Balfour's tyranny. It was to the Londoner a gay beginning to a season which brought him visits from General Boulanger, who flaunted himself as a Republican hero; the Shah of Persia, who got himself instantly into street songs; and Barnum's show.

The summer brought also one of those baffling criminal trials which have the power of absorbing the whole nation's attention. Early in August Mrs Maybrick was condemned on a charge of poisoning her husband, and it was said at once that "not one in three of the thousands who have followed the case expected a verdict of guilty." [1] Mr Maybrick was a man who had taken all sorts of drugs—eighteen different kinds within a single fortnight—and the doctors called during the case differed hopelessly as to the cause of death. A great popular agitation followed the verdict, and public meetings were held all over the country. The sentence of death was commuted, and very distinguished lawyers devoted themselves to the task of trying to secure Mrs Maybrick's release. The agitation was unsuccessful. The case must find a place in history because it focussed anew all the strong feeling in favour, first, of a reform of procedure which should allow prisoners to be put on

[1] *The Times,* 8th August 1889.

oath and give evidence, and, secondly, of the establishment of a Court of Criminal Appeal.

Thus in a full tide of interests the country swept on to a
profound shock. On 14th August 2500 dock labourers at
the East and West India Dock and South London Docks
struck work. For a day or two no interest was taken in
the matter. Then the large but orderly crowd at the West
India Dock gates began to draw people's attention, and,
as an uneasy temper manifested itself in other docks,
the cause of the strike became known. The men, working
at the most casual kind of casual labour, attending daily at
the dock gates, getting perhaps an hour's work one day, and
no work for three days, and then two or three hours again,
had struck on a demand that hiring of labour should not
be for less than four hours at a time, and that there should
be a uniform rate of pay of sixpence an hour. A necessary corollary of these demands was that the " contract "
system of work at the docks should be abandoned—that
is to say, instead of letting out separately the job of loading
or unloading this or that ship to a contractor, who then
hired men as he needed them, the dock companies should
themselves be responsible for the labour in their docks,
and by not splitting up the various jobs should be
able to hire men for a decent period, transferring them,
as needed, to different ships. Dock labour was an
extreme case of unregulated interaction of supply and
demand. It was unskilled labour, crowds of men
were always ready for it, and the dock companies had
acted accordingly. By letting out the work on contract
they made their money without any responsibility,
and the contractor made his profit on the basis of the
overwhelming supply of the labour he needed. The
men's demands amounted to a minimum wage of two
shillings a day for those who were lucky enough to be taken
on. This implied no weekly minimum, because no man was
sure of being taken on two days running, much less for

a week. It implied no general wage-earning standard, because no man could be sure of being taken on at all. There can be little wonder that a strike begun by men of such casual employment was not expected to last long.

On 17th August 2000 men marched from the docks to the offices of the West India Dock Committee in the City, and a deputation of them saw the chairman, Mr Norwood, a Member of Parliament, who told them that their demands should have attention, but that he could promise them nothing until they were in a different state of mind. He made the great mistake of miscalculating not only the possibility of organisation among the men, but also the change in public opinion about the operation of laws of supply and demand. The organisation began to show at once what had been happening in the past few years at those street meetings, which had from time to time broken the surface routine of London ; men of the most casual type of workman had come to recognise certain leaders and to be accustomed to listen to them. In other parts of the country, where a single industry was dominant —on the coalfields, in the cotton towns in Lancashire, the engineering towns of the Tyne and the Wear and the Clyde—workmen had for years had their leaders. But in the great welter of London, where there were so many small industries that there was no common industrial feeling, there had been no opportunity for such concentration, until the lack of employment, due to a period of depressed trade, threw together in the streets workmen of all kinds ; and men of force and capacity seized the chance to give a general basis to labour movements. The fact that this had been accomplished was of immense importance now when a specific case arose. John Burns instantly came back upon the East End scene, and found ready to work with him a dock labourer with an extraordinary hold on his fellows, Ben Tillett.

By 20th August the strike had extended to all the docks.

Pickets from Millwall, Victoria Docks, and Albert Docks reported that all the men there were out, and from Tilbury 1000 had come out. The dock companies had attempted to get the work done by coolies from the ships, but these men had refused to do it. More important still was the announcement which Burns was able to make to the men, that he had received virtual promises from other great ports—Liverpool, Glasgow, Grimsby and Hull—that the dock labourers there would support the London men by striking for an equivalent rise in wages, if ships were sent round from London to those ports for loading or unloading. Next day the dock directors placarded their docks with posters offering men twenty shillings a week to come in behind the strikers' backs. The average wage of a London dock labourer had rarely reached ten shillings a week. But the strike leaders were confident that "blacklegging" would be impossible on a large enough scale to break the strike. They picketed the docks; and then another procession went to the City, with 20,000 men in it this time, quiet, and giving no trouble to the police. Not the least remarkable fact about the whole affair is that already it was clear that the general feeling in the City was on the side of the men ; the dock companies' attitude had been so careless an exploiting of the mass of unskilled labour that even the City man felt uncomfortable.

When another large procession marched up, on 22nd August, various business men brought pressure to bear on the dock directors, to induce them to meet the men's leaders again. On this occasion the directors said they would agree to a four-hours minimum engagement, when as much as four hours of the working day were left ; but they would not give up the right to engage men at any hour they chose (which meant that the minimum wage would not always be earned), nor would they agree to the payment of sixpence an hour, except with the maintenance of the contract system. The interview therefore came to nothing.

The companies now tried importing labour from other places, and a number of men were hired from Liverpool. But the pickets successfully brought them out next day, and telegrams from the strike leaders stopped an attempt to get men from Southampton. Two shillings an hour was now being offered to " blacklegs," but the picketing was effective, and although a few men were smuggled into the docks, and kept there continuously, being fed and lodged in the sheds, the companies were baffled. Meanwhile the lightermen on the river, whose services might have been used to unload ships out in the stream and land the cargoes at wharves, had also come out on strike for better conditions. By 25th August, when a great meeting took place in Hyde Park, it was clear that public opinion was very largely with the men, the contract system having been one of the recognised forms of sweating condemned by the House of Lords Committee; the " docker's tanner " made its appearance in music-hall songs, always to a burst of applause ; and a fund was set on foot—Dr Liddon taking a large share in the work—to provide food for the wives and children of the men on strike. More important still, the shipowners were against the dock companies, who charged shipping companies heavy prices for handling cargoes, and then proved themselves such inefficient middlemen that they lost the means of doing the work. The organisation of the strike now included a regular daily programme. There was always a huge meeting of men on Tower Hill, a procession to the City with collecting boxes, which never came back empty, and a meeting afterwards at the West India Dock gates. Money was shared out by the leaders in the evening. Before the end of August the streets around the docks had been emptied of almost all traffic ; there was no work for waggons or carts to do. The Corn Exchange and the Coal Exchange were practically idle, the wool salerooms and the Mincing Lane rooms were idle too. On 26th August a new element came into the struggle, Mr Sydney Buxton, Member of Parliament for Poplar, the dockers' division, joining in the interviews between the dock directors and the strike leaders.

On 28th August the directors said that, if the sixpence an hour was not insisted upon, they might meet the other demands; but the men kept firmly to that minimum. If the directors had believed in the men's power of continuing the fight, they might by this time perhaps have taken warning from the sound of the cheers which greeted Burns and Tillett as they left the dock offices after that interview. The two leaders had come this time without the customary procession; the cheers were from sober City men in the street, who had happened to recognise them as they left the dock offices. Mr Buxton now suggested that the shipowners might deal with the men directly, engaging the labour to handle their own cargoes, and Sir Thomas Sutherland, chairman of the Peninsular & Oriental line, was ready to take up the suggestion, if the dock companies would stand aside altogether. But some shipowners, chiefly men in a small way of business, did not care for this solution.

September opened with a new interposition of negotiators. Cardinal Manning, whose father and brother had been chairmen of dock companies, had been to see the Lord Mayor, and to suggest an attempt at intervention. The two of them went to interview Mr Norwood, and spoke to him plainly of "the isolated and untenable position of the dock companies"; Mr Norwood now argued that it was impossible in the existing state of the dock finances to accede to the men's demands. It may be noted that a sidelight on this view of the question can be gained from the angry comment of the shipowners, to the effect that the "stupid rivalries" of the dock companies had caused them to overweight themselves with capital. For a day or two after the intervention of the Cardinal and the Lord Mayor public opinion was in suspense, and the proceedings of the strikers were more critically watched The issue of a manifesto by Burns and Cunninghame Graham, threatening a " general strike," was condemned as a rather hectoring proceeding ; and the work of the strikers' pickets was so jealously scrutinised that accusations of incitement to violence began to be made. Then the dock directors foolishly threw opinion against them once more by refusing to recognise Burns and Tillett at all in the negotiations, which had now narrowed themselves down to the single question of the extra penny an hour.

On 6th September a new move was made. A conference was called at the Mansion House, consisting of the Lord Mayor, Cardinal Manning, the Bishop of London, Mr Sydney Buxton, John Burns and Tillett. There seemed to be a possible line of negotiation in a resumption of work at fivepence an hour, on condition that within a certain period the rate should rise to sixpence an hour. Burns and Tillett refrained from pressing for recognition by the dock directors, and the Lord Mayor, the Cardinal, and Mr Buxton conducted interviews with the directors. This led to an unfortunate hitch. By some misunderstanding the three negotiators thought that, if the sixpence an hour were granted on 1st January, the men would accept those terms, and they succeeded in making the dock directors agree to this. But as the extra penny was not, in this agreement, applied also to overtime payment, the men refused to accept so long a delay, and the terms were rejected at a mass meeting. The negotiators, who had believed that they could on their part offer the definite adherence of the men, were offended, and it seemed likely that public sympathy would be alienated. Probably one thing that prevented such a change of opinion was the unswerving energy which the leaders of the strike were devoting to the suppression of tendencies to violence. Burns, interposing his sturdy shoulders and fists between strikers and blacklegs whenever a fight seemed imminent, deserved all the credit he got for riding the storm. Moreover the sharing-out of relief had been admirably organised; the pickets were on the whole showing excellent discipline; and the strike was altogether being conducted with no little dignity.

On 13th September, when it had lasted four weeks, settlement at last began to appear within sight. The conference of negotiators had begun again on 9th September, and Cardinal Manning and Mr Buxton were in communication with the dock directors. The announcement that the lightermen were willing to return to work, pending arbitration in their case, was the first real relief; and it was accompanied by a rumour that the dock negotiations were proceeding on the basis of the payment of sixpence an hour beginning on 1st November. On Saturday, 15th September, the dock settlement was signed on those lines. The men had won practically all their demands, and a huge triumphant meeting was held in Hyde Park. The dock directors undertook not to discriminate against strikers, and the strikers not to discriminate against blacklegs. The latter undertaking had behind it, as everyone knew, the strength of the fact that the strike had organised at last some of the most casual labour in the country. The Dock, Wharf, and Riverside Labourers Union had grown out of it, and under one of the most prominent of the strike lieutenants, Tom Mann, it grew rapidly into a body formidable enough to be sure that the ground gained would not be lost. Within a month many of those who had been blacklegs in the strike were members of the union. The dock directors held a peevish meeting, complaining of the attitude during the strike of the clergy and the big shipowners, and even of the public. The Strike Committee published their accounts, duly audited,[1] and showed the world that, out of £46,499 re-

[1] *The Times*, 4th December 1889.

ceived in subscriptions (£4000 had come in one sum from
Australia, and large sums from Germany and France)
there was only a sum of £192, 11s. for which the auditors
could not account. This minute failure was due to a
natural difficulty in keeping accounts at the beginning of
the strike. That it was so minute, in an average distribution of over £11,000 a week to a great number of men not
at the time bound together in a regular organisation, is
an astonishing tribute, alike to the leaders who carried it
out, and to the men's acceptance of their leaders' control.

London had at last seen organised labour at war ; and,
because things that happen in London have the newspapers
at their service, the whole country had seen it too, in a
way in which it had never yet seen a strike. This may
partly account for the friendliness of the London public
to the strikers ; London is always ready to be carelessly
genial towards something that is fresh. In one sense
indeed the strike did inaugurate a new chapter. The
trade unions all over the kingdom had supported men as
yet unorganised, and that unrest in London, which had
appeared to casual observers so vague and so easily to
be distinguished from the recognised—even, by contrast,
respectable—labour movements, had coalesced with Trade
Unionism. For the most unskilled and casual labour the
laws of supply and demand were no longer to be in control
of the market. The dock strike had done effectively for
men what the Committee on Sweating was trying to do
for women ; and political economy as the elder generation
understood it had been dethroned. The organised
strength of the workmen, with public opinion acting to
some extent as the " governor " on the engine, had introduced the new element of regulation. As long as strikes
were confined to skilled trades the change was not so
apparent, for, after all, the willingness of the skilled
men was a vital feature of the supply; it could not be
regarded as such in an unskilled labour market.

Barely had the dock strike been settled when another serious one occurred in London, at the South Metropolitan Gas Works. Then came a regular crop of strikes : the workers at the Silvertown Rubber Works came out, and so did bakers, omnibus men and tramcar men. The engineers at the Maxim-Nordenfeldt Works followed, and the employees in the gas department of the Manchester Corporation. Philosophical observers noted two distinct forms of strike among those going on in the last portion of the year. One form—that, for instance, of the strikes of bakers, omnibus men and tramcar men—was for the lightening of a heavy load of work ; the other—that of the gas employees and the engineers—arose from the men's claim to a voice in the control of the work, on such points as the abolition of overtime and the regulation of piecework. The latter came to be called the " New Trade Unionism," and people, who had never had enough bitter things to say of the old straightforward strikes for more wages, began now to think of them as almost praiseworthy in contrast with the new kind of strike. The South Metropolitan Gas Strike was rendered notable by the policy which the directors adopted ; they offered to apply the co-operative principle to the work, the men to participate in the profits on a sliding scale, receiving 1 per cent. on their wages for every penny by which the price fell below two and eight-pence per thousand cubic feet.[1] The Union objected to this arrangement, as likely to weaken the men's allegiance to the Union, and the dispute went on. It lasted until well into the new year, and then in February 1890 ended in the complete surrender of the men, who accepted the profit-sharing principle, and returned to the hours in force before the strike. The serious outbreak of strikes caused considerable discussion of the possibility of setting

[1] The price of gas in London is regulated by an Act of Parliament, under which a fall of price accompanies every advance of a certain magnitude in profits.

up conciliation boards. They had been working well for twenty years in the north of England,[1] and the London Chamber of Commerce appointed a committee to consider the introduction of the principle as part of the chamber's work. A Blue Book on strikes, published in November, showed that, out of 509 strikes in 1888, 332 had been settled by arbitration.

One or two other interests at the end of the year diverted the public mind from industrial experiences. Late in October a meeting was held at St James's Hall to urge the Government to action in the matter of rabies among dogs. In 1870 eight counties had been affected by it ; in 1889 thirty-three were affected, and the number of deaths from hydrophobia had amounted in thirty-eight years to 939. There was a movement for founding a Pasteur Institute in London for the treatment of cases ; but the desire for prophylactic treatment was kept subordinate to a demand for a general muzzling order to be enforced for twelve months. Even Pasteur himself was strong on the point that by such regulations hydrophobia could be entirely stamped out. Moreover prophylaxis by inoculation was at the moment somewhat on its trial in England. There has always been a strong opposition to the vaccination laws, and so many people had been going to prison rather than conform to them that the Government had this year to set up a Royal Commission on the subject.

In November Stanley and Emin Pasha were at last approaching civilisation, and in December they reached Zanzibar. Emin had been ill, but his health was improving, and it seemed likely that his long years in the Soudan, his extreme danger, and the anxieties he must have suffered when the fall of Khartoum left him utterly alone, would not lastingly have injured him. Stanley was returning, not only with the rescued man, but with new geographical

[1] See a letter by Dr Spence Watson in *The Times,* 5th October 1889.

knowledge as to the extent of the great Victoria Nyanza. There was, however, reservation in the enthusiasm over the news of the arrival in Zanzibar. The affair of Major Barttelot and the rearguard of the expedition was still awaiting elucidation.

In the closing days of the year Robert Browning died in Venice. A well-known and well-liked figure in London society, he was in advance of his day in his refusal to play the poet, and his taste for passing among his fellow-men as one of themselves. Yet those with whom he had least association—the over-earnest and the over-intense—had done most to foster admiration of his work.

CHAPTER XII

1890: A YEAR WITH A STORMY ENDING

TEN years of the new social spirit, of the revolt against political economy, may not have achieved much for the poorest and most oppressed forms of labour. Sweating, the knowledge of which had gone to the hearts of decent people, remained almost undiminished, though here and there workgirls had combined. Yet those who could see further than their own pet remedies (and pet remedies abounded to a degree that makes the innocence of the eighties almost as remarkable as their warm heart) had cause to rejoice. Labour had not grown tidier in its habits, more elevated in its amusements, more thoughtful in its leisure. On the contrary it was betting and drinking rather faster than before. But it was far on the road to being able to bargain for its wages ; and, slow though the visible differences may have been, it was none the less a vast change that has put the great majority of labouring men in the position formerly occupied by the most skilled and most intelligent alone. Moreover even among the intelligent and the well-organised workmen there was new force of will. One of the strikes of the early part of 1890 was a coal-mining strike in the Midland district. It lasted only four days, the men obtaining their demands ; but it aroused its share of comment. " Twenty or even ten years ago," said *The Times*,[1] " it would have been out of the question for 300,000 workmen to combine so perfectly as to stop work at one given moment and to resume it at another." The importance

[1] 21st March 1890.

of a big strike having occurred in London is nowhere better seen than in the greatly enlarged interest which was now taken in all labour disputes. Much of it ceased to be a sympathetic interest. The world, pursuing its custom of making distinctions satisfactory to itself, was careful to separate sweating and bad housing conditions from the general labour movement; it thought it could hold up its hands at the latter while devising remedies for the former. But at least it was more aware of the general movement than it had ever been, and the summer brought it sufficient reason to hold up its hands.

Financially the year opened with the " cold fit " which not unnaturally followed the company-promoting booms of the past year or two. After three years of its new existence Allsopp's brewery was in difficulties, and a shareholders' committee was appointed in February; the committee decided that there had been no misrepresentation in the prospectus, but a large body of shareholders adhered to their opinion that the goodwill had been greatly over-estimated. In any case the policy followed in the flotation, of placing all the ordinary and preference stock on the market, had thrown a heavy burden on the profit-making, which owing to increased agency charges from the severity of competition had failed to respond to the need. But apart from the rights and wrongs of the case, the mere fact of the discontent of shareholders was enough to cool the speculative mood. One of the principal business activities of the year was the advance in the amalgamation of the banking companies. The Capital and Counties, the Birmingham and Midland, the Union, and Prescott Dimsdale's carried out several absorptions in 1890; Williams Deacon's combined with the Manchester and Salford Bank; and Lloyd's Bank, which had taken up several local banks in Worcestershire and Warwickshire in 1889, was growing into a widespread business. The reasons for these amalgamations were, no doubt, sound

enough.   The shortage of gold made the maintenance of a
number of separate bank reserves increasingly difficult,
while the advance of wealth depending more and more
upon paper exchanges made the burden of disjointed responsibilities much heavier.   Moreover one bank depended
so much upon the solvency of another that the separate
stability of each had almost ceased to exist, and large
amalgamations hardly altered the reality of the situation.
At the same time they undoubtedly lessened the elasticity
of local trade.   Personal character ceased to be valid
security for loans and overdrafts when the old local
bankers, with their individual knowledge of all their
clients, were replaced by distant directors whose lack of
such knowledge compelled them to confine their loan
business within hard and fast rules.   Many a merchant
and tradesman, who could once have pulled through a
difficult time by the help of a banker who knew his recti-
tude, fails under the present system, which demands more
formal securities.   Meanwhile, the gold difficulty brought
about a vigorous revival of bimetallism, and of discussion
of the true relation between money and gold and prices.
The Rand continued to enlarge its output, reaching in
this year 43,000 oz. a month.   But the Treasury proposals
to deal with the coinage still hung fire, and made no
appearance in Parliament this year.

The London County Council, if late in the field of municipal enterprise, distinguished itself in its very first year of
existence by a policy new in conception.   This became
famous in private Bill controversy a little later as " the
betterment principle."   The principle, for which opportunity was given by the necessity confronting the council
of making up the deficiencies of the Metropolitan Board
of Works in the sphere of street improvements, was that
enhancements of the value of premises, such as might
accrue from better frontages, better means of approach,
and better surroundings, should go by rights not to the

owner, who had done nothing to bring about the new conditions, but to the public body, which had done all. The principle was an old one in America, but there the enhancement of value was paid down by the owner in a lump sum ; the London County Council proposed to make it a tax on the premises. The idea was at once assailed, the Duke of Argyll being its most prominent critic ; and it appeared that not the least drawback to the scheme was going to be its distortion of the English tongue. " Betterment " was bad enough ; but the duke did worse when he wrote that the tax was illogical and unjust because the " goodment " of a house in a small street was no more due to the owner or occupier than the " betterment " of a house in a big new street. Other critics followed with a further atrocity of language, arguing that if " betterment " applied to some houses, " worsement " might be claimed against a municipal authority by the owners of premises unfavourably affected by the diversion of traffic to new streets, or by tradesmen compelled to move elsewhere. The opponents of the scheme as a whole treated the affair as one of the property market ; the council's experts, notably Sir Thomas Farrer, took the higher and less disputable line that a public authority had a right of taxation, and, as street improvements cost money, taxation should fall to a special extent on those benefited by the expenditure. An attempt, however, to introduce the principle in the Strand Improvement Bill, promoted by the council this year for pulling down Holywell Street and opening up the " bottle-neck " of the Strand at that point, failed ; the clause was thrown out by the House of Commons Committee, chiefly owing to the objectors' arguments that the council made no estimate of the amount of " betterment," and that the definition of the principle and the limitations of its application were arbitrary.

Before the session opened, one of the heroes of the

Irish conflict had passed from the scene.   On 19th January
J. G. Biggar, the inventor of obstruction, died.   On 22nd
April 1875 he had first baffled the House of Commons,
holding back an important debate by the simple process
of reading enormous extracts from volumes bearing more
or less remotely on the subject, and adding brief
comments of his own.   Later on he invented the more
subtle method of endlessly moving the Chairman out of
the Chair in Committee.   His name stood for fifteen years
of constant fear of parliamentary paralysis.

Hardly had the House met in February when the
Report of the Parnell Commission was published.[1]   Lord
Morley has given us a vivid picture of the members during
a dull debate all poring over the Blue Book just put into
their hands [2]; but, hard as both sides tried, with cheap

---

[1] The chief findings of the commission were, briefly :

(a) That the Invincibles were not a branch of the Land League,
nor organised nor paid by the League ; nor did any of the Irish
party associate with known Invincibles.   The Pigott letters were
all forgeries.   Parnell and the rest of the party had no knowledge
beforehand of the Phœnix Park murders and were not insincere
in condemning them.

(b) That there was no ground for the charge made by *The Times*
that the leaders of the Land League based their scheme on a system
of assassination, or, even in the case of the most dangerous
language, intended to procure murder ; though such language did
cause an excitable peasantry to carry out the Land League's laws
even by assassination.

(c) That the Land League leaders never denounced boycotting
and intimidation, and never took any steps to assist the police in
detecting crime.

(d) That there was ground for suspicion that Land League funds
were used to compensate persons injured in the commission of
crime.

(e) That the Irish Party funds had received large sums of money
from the Irish National League of America, which was controlled
by the Clan-na-Gael, the dynamiters' organisation.

[2] *Life of Gladstone*, iii. 408:

annotated editions of the report, to whip up feeling on the
subject, it cannot be said that outside the political world
anyone cared very much for detailed decisions of the
commission as to whether Parnell and his followers
had in this, that, or the other way sanctioned or been
encouraged by violence and the party of violence. The
ordinary man's interest was only aroused when, in the
debate on the report, a month later, Lord Randolph
Churchill electrified everybody by roundly attacking the
Conservative Government. He was at this time rather
erratic in his political appearances, and the remonstrance
which his constituents at Paddington addressed to him
shows no little anxiety.

Parnell himself was hardly ever seen during the session.
Since his illness in 1886 he had grown more and more
mysterious, and the piles of letters and telegrams awaiting
him from time to time at the House of Commons were a
strange spectacle. In his absence—and in the uneasiness
which his absence caused to those who knew the circumstances—the Irish party were faced with the necessity of
making up their minds about what looked like a large instalment of Mr Chamberlain's alternative to Home Rule.
Mr Balfour introduced in March an Irish Land Purchase
Bill, setting up a scheme of voluntary transfer of ownership from landlord to tenant, purchase money being
advanced to the latter from a Government loan at $2\frac{3}{4}$
per cent., the total amount being limited to thirty-three
millions. At the same time Mr Balfour proposed to set
up a Congested Districts Board, with power to create
small holdings, and to promote migration within Ireland
or emigration from it.

Fortunately for the practically leaderless Irish members
the two proposals were not pressed forward at the time.
The House was engaged on other matters—notably the
Tithe Rent Charge Bill, which removed the duty of paying
tithes from the occupier of land to the owner, and the

Employers' Liability Bill ; amending Bills on this subject
were, it was said, becoming a " hardy annual," but the
need for this one was shown by the fact that on an average
62 per cent. of the workmen's claims under existing Acts
failed on some technical point. The present Bill made
the great step of placing the liability entirely on the
employer, removing sub-contractors out of the case. The
work of the Royal Commission on the Housing of the Poor
was finally met this year by a Housing of the Working
Classes Act, which for twenty years was to govern the
activity of public authorities in this direction.

The final report of that commission had been a fairly
drastic document. In the sphere of administration it
recommended that a statutory duty should be laid upon
local authorities of enforcing the powers they possessed in
the matter of insanitary dwellings ; that medical officers
of health should reside within, or within a mile of, their
districts, and give their whole time to their work ; that
the staffs of sanitary inspectors should be increased,
and should consist of men acquainted with the principles
of building construction ; that for London the Home
Secretary should appoint special inspectors to report at
once ; and that any vestries and district boards which
had not made by-laws should be obliged to do so immediately. Secondly, the report recommended the consolidation and amendment of existing Health and Housing Acts.
Thirdly, in the direction of new proposals, it recommended
that local authorities should have greater facilities for the
erection of workmen's dwellings, and compulsory powers
for purchase of land for dwellings ; that vacant sites should
be rated at 4 per cent. of their selling value ; that compensation for land acquired under Housing Acts should be
reduced to market value and no more ; that there should
be a system of cheap Government loans for municipal
housing schemes ; that railway companies destroying
houses in extending their lines should be obliged to provide

accommodation for the number of persons so displaced, and to provide it concurrently with the destruction of the original houses ; and that cheap transit to outlying districts should be facilitated, the Government initiating provision of cheap trains. There were also some recommendations as to easier methods of securing damages against owners of property by those who had suffered from the owners' neglect in sanitary matters ; as to small holdings ; and as to Mr Chamberlain's new doctrine of loans to enable workmen to become owners of their houses.

The report was too sweeping to be embodied all at once in legislation, but the Act of this year was quite energetic. The first part re-enacted and consolidated earlier Acts, and the second part created new powers of buying up insanitary areas, demolishing unfit dwellings and obstructive dwellings (so as to permit the opening of closed courts and culs-de-sac), and of erecting new houses on those sites. Power was given in this part of the Act to deal with smaller areas than those for which powers were given by the Artisans' Dwellings Act.

Two Acts dealing with infectious diseases should also be mentioned. That of 1889 empowered local authorities to make by-laws for the notification of infectious diseases by the head of the family concerned and by the doctor attending the case. That of 1890 gave powers for stopping the sale of milk from dairies notified as infectious, and for undertaking the disinfection of houses. To some Conservatives all this social legislation seemed excessive, and again the Liberal Unionist influence was blamed. Even those who were not of this mind felt that Parliament was overloading itself. Its real difficulty, however, lay in none of these things, but in a second attempt to create a policy of extinguishing public-house licences with payment of compensation. Mr Goschen in the Budget proposed to allot a sum raised by extra duties on beer and spirits to the local authorities. The ground was prepared by

a return of licensed houses, showing that the proportion
of them to population ranged in county districts from
2·2 per thousand inhabitants, in Cornwall, Middlesex,
Northumberland, Surrey and the West Riding, to 7·9
per thousand in Cambridgeshire ; and in boroughs from
1·6 per thousand in Jarrow to 7·6 per thousand in
Canterbury and 10 per thousand in St Pancras. The
statistics had many curious features, but the whole
subject was fought out again on the broad question of
whether a licence was really and actually an annual thing,
or included a genuine presumptive value.

It happened that at the moment a suit was in progress
which brought the question to the proof of law—the
famous case of Sharp v. Wakefield. It was a case in which
the renewal of a licence had been refused point-blank by
licensing authorities on the evidence of the police, and
the licence-holder based a claim for compensation on the
argument that, though a licence was nominally only
given for a year, it carried implicitly the expectation of
renewal, since without that no one would spend money
on a public-house, or have any interest in maintaining it
decently. The brewers (who were of course behind the
case) had made a tactical mistake. They had chosen to
fight on the claim of a public-house remote from any
ordinary population that might need it, far from police
supervision, and suspected of being a haunt of poachers
and bad characters. Consequently when the Court of
Appeal upheld the magistrates' decision—as in the end
the House of Lords also upheld it—the party which refused
to recognise any right to compensation had been given a
handsome weapon. Mr Gladstone pronounced that the
annual power of non-renewal was " the one healthy spot
in our licensing law " ; and the Liberal Unionist wing of
the Ministerial party refused to admit the compensation
principle except subject to a ten years' time-limit, after
which the absolute power of non-renewal should hold

good.[1] The net result was that the Government dropped the whole proposal; but, as the extra tax on liquor was established, the money had to be used. It was therefore attached to technical education. In the latter subject the year was not without importance. The Act of 1889 had proved to be obscure on certain points, and a conference between local authorities and the education authorities was held to clear up doubts. It had the great result of establishing the right of local authorities to grant scholarships, which infinitely increased the value of the Act. An Act securing this point, and also definitely including manual instruction under the terms of the earlier Act, was passed in 1891. It is not without interest to note that the London School Board caused an outcry in 1890 by providing pianos for its schoolgirls.

With the summer came the sequel to the dock strike of 1889—a stirring among wage-earners. Profit-sharing schemes succeeded to conciliation board projects as the most widely discussed methods of meeting the new unrest, but the workmen, as they had already shown in the South Metropolitan Gas Strike, were extremely suspicious of any weakening of their attachment to their unions. The Labour Electoral Association, which had been founded a year or two earlier, was beginning to receive the adherence of the large trade unions, and this political tendency puzzled the kindly people who had been telling the workman that Parliament was useless to him. The association opened a special fund to support candidatures of labouring men for Parliament; and the idea of paying salaries to members of Parliament, which was brought forward from time to time during these years, received additional argument. Dismissal of the idea took usually the grimly brief form that few young men of parts and ambition would be tempted

[1] See a statement by Mr W. H. Smith in *The Times*, 24th June 1890.

by £400 a year, and no working men were worth it. As
May day approached, it looked as if the old struggle with
the police might revive ; the socialist bodies arranged
a demonstration, which the police prohibited ; but the
affair proved in the end too small to fight over. Two
books just at this period were the means of conveying
socialist visions to the public outside the socialist
ranks. Bellamy's *Looking Backward*, a presentation of
the *phalanstère* system in its logical completeness, was
published in 1889 ; and William Morris's *News from
Nowhere*, a charming fiction of an England without capitalists or landlords, pervaded with the golden afternoon light
of the wide meadows of the Upper Thames, where he had
made his home, was published in 1890. But neither book
had any relation to the working activities of the moment.
John Burns was extraordinarily energetic, addressing
meetings of workmen almost every day, and enlarging the
number of trade unions ; while Ben Tillett, his colleague
of the year before, was upholding the need for keeping
all the unions national in scope, so that in any given
case not the local men alone would have to be dealt
with. Women workers were also on the way to vigorous
combination. Certain associations of ladies in various
towns for the care of friendless girls had been developing
under pressure of the growing concern for working women
into local unions of women workers. In 1890 the Birmingham Union held a conference at which papers on
various subjects connected with the industries of women
and girls were read. It was an important conference,
because it led to a succession of others, from which in the
end the National Union of Women Workers arose. In one
of the hardest of women's trades, that of chain-making,
there was an endeavour to set up a trade union. Unfortunately the Sweating Committee was ending in disappointment. On the Conservative as well as the Liberal
side there was some indignation when it was announced in

the summer of 1889 that the committee was postponing its report ; and when, early in 1890, Lord Dunraven discharged himself from the chairmanship, because his draft report had been unanimously rejected, there was little hope of light or help from the inquiry. The report was a cautious document, which made no proposals for legislation. The state of public feeling, however, prevented the disappearance of the subject, now that it had been effectively raised.

At the Trade Union Congress of the year Burns triumphed in the mingling of the new men with the old in the labour movement, the new men being wholly and solely working men ; and in the fact that in 1889 forty-five new unions had been established, and seventy-two more in the nine months of 1890. The total income of trade unions in 1890 was very nearly a million pounds. The gospel of the Eight Hours' Day largely occupied the congress ; and even prominent politicians like Mr Courtney and Mr Morley—nay, Mr Gladstone himself—had to weigh very seriously their opposition to it.

Strikes were frequent. Boot and shoe makers, brick makers, railway porters and quay labourers, Liverpool dock labourers and bargemen were all out in April ; and ironworkers and colliers in South Wales during the summer. Such manifestations aroused much more than purely local anxiety. But at the height of that anxiety, relief was given by an event which could only be taken as vastly diverting—the police struck ! They demanded in June more wages and allowances, and although a month later their strike had collapsed to an affair concerning some forty men, the story had roused such hilarious excitement that Life Guards had to be called up to disperse the mob which hung about Bow Street. Less amusing, but equally shocking to the official mind, was a strike of postmen which followed. In this the principle of Union labour in a Government department was at stake, and the authorities only won a temporary victory, after great inconvenience to the public, by the dismissal of 400 men. Though probably without relation to labour troubles, an outbreak of insubordination in the Grenadier Guards added to the respectable citizen's indignation at the general spirit of revolt ; the matter was at any rate serious enough to cause the second battalion of the regiment to be ordered to Bermuda as a punishment. It must be added that the new Trade Unionism showed that it had no small control of its men in the case of a strike at some of the London docks in September, concerned with the unloading of grain ships. Tom Mann and the Dockers' Union ordered the men back to work, and they went. It is interesting to find the British Association at its meeting this year diagnosing the social condition very shrewdly ; in a discussion on " Some Typical Economic Fallacies of Social Reform " its members gave the first signs of knowledge that the humaneness which had usurped the place of political economy was not the force of the future ; and there was an astonishing tendency to accept the doctrine that the problem of socialism was only one of degree, and not of kind. One of the greatest of the older political economists, Professor Thorold Rogers, was just at the end of his life ; he died on 13th October.

At one moment in the summer foreign policy laid hold of the public mind in such a way as it rarely does in England during peaceful times. In June an agreement between Great Britain and Germany was published, by which, in return for recognition of our status in various parts of Africa, we ceded Heligoland. The cession was violently criticised, and there was a momentary recrudescence of Jingoism. The young Kaiser was not popular in England, as his father had been. He was regarded as over-ambitious, impatient, self-willed ; and his acquiescence in Bismarck's retirement from the Imperial Chancellorship this year was thought to have been rather too ready. The British public,

crediting the Kaiser with self-assertion and dreams of
German expansion, was in no mood for cessions of territory.
However, Lord Salisbury's reputation survived the
momentary outburst. Our profit from the German agreement was the establishment of our interest in Zanzibar,
Somaliland, and Uganda. When the Anglo-Portuguese
agreement followed, later in the year, it was remarked
that Africa was now "pretty well parcelled out." It was
not quite. Trouble was brewing in the Transvaal, where
some Europeans at Johannesburg in March pulled down
the flag of the Republic, and three arrests were made for
high treason. A reminder that the filling up of the map
of Africa did not necessarily mean the end of adventure was
afforded by the life-story of Sir Richard Burton, who died
in October. Whatever might happen to the map, Arabs
remained on the earth, and a man who could live with
them, as Burton had lived, need never want for romance.
Virile, emphatic, impatient, uncontrolled, Burton was
one of the most picturesque figures of his day. Outside
Arab life and literature his great interest was swordsman-
ship ; and he was the first to stand out in England against
the over-elaboration of style in fencing.

Among the domestic interests of the year the most
remarkable was a wave of self-consciousness in regard to
British art. The æsthetes had themselves to blame, but
they must have shuddered when they saw the newly aroused
sensibility of England expressing itself as a John Bull
kind of appreciativeness. In one art this new sort of
Jingoism did not advance very far. The announcement
in 1890 that Sir Arthur Sullivan was engaged in the composition of grand opera on the subject of *Ivanhoe* marked
one of the least happy moments of British art. But
British painting was a different affair, and it had recently
followed a trend genuinely national. There was therefore
much enthusiasm behind the proposal to found a
National Gallery of British Art ; the movement first

acquired force in March and April 1890 ; and in June Mr Henry Tate, a millionaire sugar merchant, offered his collection of modern British pictures, fifty-one in number, as the nucleus for the Gallery. But he had stipulations to make. He maintained that the authorities of the National Gallery were not to be trusted with a new collection of pictures, since they kept buried out of sight in the basement of the Gallery a large number of paintings, especially the Turner water-colours, which ought to be in the public view. He would therefore only offer his pictures on the understanding that satisfactory arrangements should be made for keeping them on exhibition. This was bound to mean a new building ; and the whole project was for the time held back by negotiations between the Government and Mr Tate.

The Church of England mourned in 1890 the loss of Dr Liddon, who died in September. His preaching in St Paul's was one of the most powerful instruments in that restoration of the cathedral to a living agency in the life of London, which had been proceeding under Dean Church. But, great as his preaching had been, his influence upon young men at Oxford and in London was greater. A little earlier the Roman Catholics in England had lost Cardinal Newman, who died in August. He had always been rather a great convert than a great Roman Catholic. The story of his spiritual struggle was so intimately the story of many souls of his time, whether the goal reached had been the same for them or not, that he became a figure almost of legend. For the greater part of his life he failed to find favour at the Vatican for any of his plans or his ideas for extending the Roman Catholic influence in England. Manning appeared to suspect him of Liberalising tendencies of thought. But late in his life a change came at the Vatican, and from Leo XIII. Newman received the cardinal's hat; Manning, who had received his from Pius IX., may have felt that Newman's was easily earned.

The national concern, which had expressed itself so largely in 1889, about the increase of betting, showed no diminution. It was augmented by the very natural readiness to point an obvious moral, from the fact that, while on the one hand the workmen were fighting for more wages and more control of their lives, they were at the same time spending more money on gambling, and more of their hours in a barren form of excitement. The real secret of the spread of betting on horse races was rightly discerned to be the originating of the " Starting Price " idea. It was impossible for bookmakers not on the course itself, and therefore unaware of the run of the betting at the last moment, to make a profitable business of betting until there was some fixed form of the odds to be laid.   The invention of a starting price provided this. The chief sporting papers arranged that their reporters at races should establish, just before each race started, the most commonly offered odds in the ring, and these were telegraphed to London as the starting prices of the horses named.   Then all that the backer had to do was to pay his money to the bookmaker, the understanding being that he took these odds. The publication of the odds by the evening papers completed the setting up of a regular racing system for those who need never go near a race. Nor was this the only form of popular gambling. Prize competitions in newspapers, which had already attracted the attention of the police, were enormously enlarged by the violent rivalry of two penny weekly papers just at this time.   The proprietors, or their advisers, made the ingenious discovery that all the advantages of a lottery—namely, the temptation of an enormous prize, drawing so many small sums that handsome profit would still be left—could be gained by a penny publication with this extra advantage, that the sale of tickets was the sale of the paper. A prize of several hundred pounds, a freehold house and garden, even of "£1 a week for life." sounded magnificent;

but hundreds of thousands of sixpences would cover the cost several times over. A bald lottery being illegal, prizes were offered for some competition easy enough to make hundreds of thousands of persons enter for it. But as the early efforts of this kind were so easy that the selection of a winner had to depend upon pure chance, the authorities had ground for action under the Lottery Acts, and the papers concerned took alarm. Not, however, before the main popular demand for amusement had been attracted into this new channel. Outdoor pursuits took one or two new turns. In 1890 golf had become so popular that for the first time it seemed to challenge the supremacy of lawn tennis; golf clubs rather than tennis racquets were the smart thing to carry on a Saturday afternoon. " Safety " bicycles too were making their way fast. They had been invented in Coventry in 1885, but had not at first displaced the high machine. Now they were beginning to be seen everywhere. In regard to more passing interests of the ordinary man it may be mentioned that the famous forty days' fast of Succi was successfully completed this year, and drew crowds to the Westminster Aquarium, where Succi sat in a glass-sided room, melancholy and nervous-looking, and smoked cigarettes. An old craze of the early eighties was revived by Dr Nansen's plans for reaching the North Pole; he proposed to give up the earlier plan of establishing the ship in winter quarters somewhere out of the ice-pack, and to shorten the sledge-marching, by having the ship built with a V-shaped hull, so that she could be taken right into the ice-pack, and would, when the pack closed, be merely lifted up and wedged, instead of being crushed. A glance at other scientific interests shows us that the telephone was by now so greatly improved that lines were opened this year from London to Birmingham, Liverpool and Manchester. The frozen meat trade, too, had issued finally from its probation; the New Zealand traffic, which in 1882 had amounted to £19,000 in value, touched in 1890 a million sterling. Nor was the meat market the only gainer. Whereas there had formerly been no direct service of steamers to New Zealand, there were in 1890 ten mail steamers and twenty-two cargo steamers all on the New Zealand service, and all buying coal and stores there as well as their cargoes.

The year is also memorable in science as having seen the publication of Dr Koch's theory of tuberculosis and its remedy ; in the closing months of the year a most vigorous discussion of it took place in the British medical profession. The clinical use of hypnotism attracted some attention ; experiments at the Salpetrière Hospital in Paris were being watched carefully.

The year had a strange and wild ending. Early in November the contests of employers and workmen threatened to rise into a savage war in the shipping trade. Everyone was expecting at this time a labour war on a great scale—railways, mines or shipping seemed most likely to provide the battlefield ; and shipping gave the first menace. The establishment of unions had spread to it, and under J. H. Wilson the Seamen's and Firemen's Union had been set up. Inevitably there had followed an objection on the part of union men to working with non-union men ; the microcosm of a ship could not but intensify differences. The shipowners not only expressed their feelings with more violence than most employers, asserting that they would " lay up " all British shipping at need, but also immediately formed a combination of their own, the Shipping Federation. For the time being neither side fired the first shot ; but a dock strike at Southampton, issuing in disorder and riotousness, which had been markedly absent from the London strike, kept uneasiness very much alive.

Then the affair of the Stanley expedition to relieve Emin broke out into that bitter controversy which had long

been vaguely in the air. Stanley had come to England in
the summer, and gave public lectures to crowded audiences.
For a time he was the lion of the season. Then his
popularity cooled a little on the discovery that he did
not at all take the ordinary Briton's view of Germany's
ambitions. Emin Pasha, after having been rescued, had
actually entered the German service ; and Stanley not
only failed to see any fault in this, but even revealed a wish
to behold German enterprise at work in different parts of
Africa. People remembered that the fate of his rearguard
still called for explanation. In November he made the
first move himself by attacking his critics ; he accused
Major Barttelot and his companion, Mr Jameson, of having
resorted to cannibalism and cruelty to the natives round
their camp. His critics replied by a plain charge against
him of carelessness and gross mismanagement, amounting
to sheer abandonment of his rearguard, in order to push
on to the personal glory of relieving Emin.

Stanley had published an account of his journey under
the title of *In Darkest Africa*. At the time when the
quarrel arose England was being stirred by a book
which, cleverly taking a cue from this title, was called
In Darkest England. It was written by General Booth,
the head of the Salvation Army, and was an extreme presentation of that misery of poverty and sweating in great
towns which had had so many presentations of late years.
Booth's plea was that the Salvation Army was able to reach
lower strata than any other organisation had attempted
to reach ; and he wrote the book as an appeal to the
country to provide him with so large a sum of money that
his Army could set on foot what amounted to permanent
relief works, refuges, night shelters, and a whole network
of institutions. He threw over all economic considerations, to a degree which even the most ardent reformer
had as yet shrunk from ; his relief work had already been
accused of doing more harm than good by undercutting the

market. His present challenge was instantly taken up ; prominent people pointed out his ignorance of the work that was already being done, his failure to guarantee adequate administration of the funds he asked for, and the danger of diverting to one object, and that largely untried, the money which at present was flowing in many useful channels. His statistics were disputed too. But before the year closed his fund had reached £90,000.

The scheme was unfortunately launched. It had small chance of public attention against the two shattering events of November 1890. When men opened their newspapers on the 14th all the mysteriousness of Parnell's recent life, all the hints and suggestions which had gathered round his first refusal to bring *The Times* to trial, fused to a thunderclap in the report of the divorce case of O'Shea *v.* O'Shea and Parnell. The case was undefended. Parliament, as it happened, had met again this month, and by a stroke of Fate Irish business was the work before the House. The Irish Land Purchase Bill, postponed from the summer, and the Irish Relief Bill, setting up the Congested Districts Board, were resumed. The Irish party was not in the House to discuss them ; it was sitting upstairs, in Committee Room 15, which those days rendered famous, with Parnell in the chair presiding, sometimes cynically, sometimes tyrannously, over discussions of his retention of the leadership. His constant absences from London had led to a confusion at the beginning of these sittings. Mr Gladstone, acting on the unmistakable sense of the Liberal party organisations, had intimated that, while Parnell remained leader, he could not himself lead a party whose chief work, as long as he led it, would be Home Rule ; therefore either Parnell must resign, or he must. This intimation could not be conveyed to Parnell immediately ; it was the moment of one of his disappearances. It could hardly be conveyed first to anyone but him ; and so it fell out that the Irish party met, and expressed confidence in him as leader, before Mr Gladstone's attitude was known. The party had met far too hastily, and their resolution was rather an expression of their feelings towards British reception of the disastrous news than a considered decision. No party largely Roman Catholic, and representing a country preponderantly Roman Catholic, could have remained under a Protestant leader in such circumstances. But the resolution delivered them into Parnell's hands. He fought his ground in a way which was the final revelation of his contempt for public opinion in England. He refused sympathetic and influential advice to retire for the moment, and trust to the storm blowing over. He drove his party into such a position that, in order to avoid the ultimate reproof to him, the majority, forty-four in number, at last walked out of the committee-room. Then he dashed over to Ireland, suppressed an issue of *United Ireland* which would have been fatal to his position, and made speeches in Dublin as if he were still leader. He fairly took his opponents' breath away. Parliament only sat for a fortnight, and in that time the two Irish Bills were passed. The effect of the O'Shea case on the demeanour of the House was extraordinary. All spirit seemed to have gone from it, and it was spoken of as " The Long-faced Parliament." The affair was such a complete disaster, and was ending in such a desperate struggle, that the men not immediately concerned felt it like a cloud upon them.

In consequence Parliament had perhaps too little attention to spare for the other shattering event. On 15th November financial London was shaken to its foundations by the news that the great banking firm of Barings had come to grief, its difficulty being attributed to imprudent commitments for public loans and private enterprises in Argentina and Uruguay. The one hopeful element in the situation, to which tottering credit clung, was that the announcement of the disaster was not made until it could

be accompanied by intimations that the Bank of England
had the firm's affairs in hand, with a guarantee of twelve
millions to meet the liabilities. Everyone. trusted that
this meant that in the last resort the Treasury would be
behind the bank. As a matter of fact it was not. Mr
Goschen had been summoned to town by the governor of
the bank directly the danger became known, but he had
seen no course to pursue except to throw the responsibility
of meeting the crisis entirely on the City. He could not
run the risk of pledging the Treasury to a guarantee, and
then perhaps having to defend in Parliament the use of
public money in support of a private firm. Yet he was
much distressed, and some of the visits he paid to financiers
in the City did not encourage him; he found most of them
near panic. But the governor of the Bank of England
rose to the occasion, and gathered sober men around him.
He borrowed a million and a half in gold from Russia,
Rothschilds' secured the assistance of the Bank of France
to the extent of three millions, and the bankers and
merchants of London guaranteed seven millions. Thus the
Bank of England was able, when the announcement of
Barings' situation had to be made, to convey reassurances.
The firm's liabilities were about twenty millions, and the
whole object at stake was to give time for the realisation
of assets without such a panic as would have depreciated
them beyond remedy. This the guarantee fund did.
Immediate liquidation was stayed off, and the firm was
quietly reconstructed as a limited liability company, and
registered on 21st November. Consols dropped to 93,
but that was a small penalty to pay. If the shock had
added to the storminess of events, it had at least been
prevented from ending the year in chaos.

CHAPTER XIII

1891: THE ISOLATION OF TRADE UNIONS

ONE of the most baffling difficulties of the Home Rule question was that, while on the one hand it provided an ideal capable of calling out all that was high-minded and devoted in the Liberal forces, it was at the same time so entirely a question by itself, and so detachable from all normal social advance in Great Britain, that a party committed to it was not thereby committed to anything else. More—Mr Gladstone was an old man, and the enormous plan for Irish self-government had not been constructed until he was old. The result was that he frankly remained in leadership for that single purpose only, so that the Liberal party stood committed to a policy which not merely did not include, but positively precluded, other activities. The downfall of Parnell, disturbing as it was, did not affect the Liberal party's position altogether adversely. No harm was ever done to an ideal by events which force its supporters to uphold its righteousness beyond and above all personal failings. It was of little concern in the end that opponents of Home Rule should now be saying that the O'Shea divorce case amounted morally to a reversing of the Parnell Commission's Report. But that Parnell should have refused the Liberal party's tactical decisions, that Home Rule should no longer be the united demand of a homogeneous force in Parliament, but a bone of contention between two groups, who were capturing and recapturing one another's newspapers, one another's platforms, one another's seats in Parliament— all this was of serious concern. The cause was further weakened by statements which Parnell was making, to the effect that he and his party had never really liked the Home Rule Bill of 1886, and only accepted it on Mr Gladstone's threat of resignation.   The Unionists were able to gain much ground by pointing out what a serious difference it made if the Irish party had not genuinely accepted the Bill of 1886, and the Liberal party were not really in accord with their supposed allies.   From the Liberal point of view the worst of these recriminations was that, since Mr Gladstone remained where he had been for Home Rule, and Home Rule alone, these wrangles demanded the best brains of the Liberal party to overrule them.   This in turn meant that the party was not taking its share in other affairs, and had too little attention for social reform.   Trade Unionism was left to fight its battles alone.   Whether, if circumstances had been other than they were, the development of the labour movement would have been different—whether any politicians would have been ready at this time to see that the purely social consideration of wages and labour conditions was now as impossible as the old purely economic consideration, and that the problem was becoming political—must remain an open question.   At any rate one example on each side in politics can be quoted as showing a perception of the new conditions.   Mr Courtney, speaking in February of this year, remarked upon the change in labour aspirations from an inclination towards isolated socialistic experiments to a conviction that the goal must be reached by legislation. Lord Dunraven, a little later, was expressing himself in favour of a State Department of Industry.

That industrial conditions formed a very large and insistent question was admitted in the establishment in 1891 of a Royal Commission on Labour Problems.   Wage disputes were for the moment in the background.   Trade union leaders believed in the power of organised labour to mend many flaws in the industrial system, which employers

had so far failed to cure. Unemployment and irregularity
of employment came, they thought, largely from the fact
that labour was almost as helpless as raw material ; a
master could pour both alike into his factory at high speed
in a time of demand, and leave both alike outside when the
demand was slack. Fully organised labour, on the other
hand, could secure that an employer's prudence for his
own profits should necessarily imply prudence also for his
employees' wages and conditions. Consequently, practically all the labour struggles of this time were rather on
questions either of working conditions or of the recognition of unions than on questions of wages. There were
not a few of such struggles. In January the miners in the
Silksworth Colliery struck on a demand that the "deputies"
should be union men. The managers refused to have
union men in that position, and for two months the fight
went on. It was complicated by the decision of the
managers to evict men on strike from cottages owned by
the colliery, a course which caused a sympathetic strike
to spread in pits which had taken no part in the original
dispute. The settlement reached in March was that while
the men would not insist on the " deputies " being union
men, the managers would not forbid them to be. A railway strike in Scotland, affecting the Glasgow & South
Western Railway, the North British Railway, and the
Caledonian Railway turned on complaints of overwork
and heavy overtime exactions. It failed, because although
the business community agreed that the men were overworked they would give no support to the strike. The
companies held out against receiving any representatives
of the men's union as such, and against entering on any
negotiations before the men returned to work. At Cardiff
the Seamen's and Firemen's Union struck against the issue
by the shipping firms of a " ticket " which insisted on
union men not refusing to work with non-union men.
This also failed, partly because the dockers, stevedores,

and coal-porters were not in alliance with the seamen and firemen. In London tailors struck on three points— better workshops, a uniform " time-log " (the existing system of payment being a complicated one) and the abolition of partnership in a piece of work ; the masters conceded the first and third points, reserving the second for consideration, and the men returned to work after a ten days' strike distinguished by the elaboration of its picketing. In June there was an omnibus strike in London, and again the picketing was good—hardly a 'bus was on the streets for a week. Overwork was the chief complaint, and the men won a seventy-hours week, a minimum wage of six-and-sixpence a day for drivers and five shillings a day for conductors, the right to a day off in the week at their own charges, and an understanding that if the companies' dividends rose there would be an advance in wages. An interesting effort of the year, apart from strikes, was the attempt made by the Dockers' Union, which was also a General Labourers' Union, to bring into its ranks the agricultural labourer. The idea was that a pooling of interests might lead to an improvement of conditions in the country—an increase of allotments, as well as advances in wages—and that this, in turn, would react on the dockers' conditions, by diminishing the flocking of rural labour to the towns, where it became for the most part casual labour at the dock gates.

It was no wonder that Trade Unionism of this nature roused fresh opposition. It was denounced as an attempt to set up a new monopoly, and the special point of attack was the policy adopted by Trade Unionists of intimating to employers their intention not to work with non-union men. This was described as " intimidation," and was actually held to be so in a county court judgment delivered this year, but overridden by a decision of the Queen's Bench in July. Other opponents argued that the attempt to set up a monopoly would have a bad effect on prices ;

that, for instance, higher wages in trades which were absolutely necessary to the public, such as shipping, docks, railways and collieries, would only mean that less money would be spent in other directions in which there was no compulsion for the public to spend, so that wages in the cotton and other such industries would decrease. A more curious criticism was that, if men by successful development of their unions forced their wages up, women's wages would suffer, because, being outside unions, they would get no work unless they consented to take a poor wage. On the whole the first feeling in the labour world when it became known that the Government contemplated setting up a Royal Commission was one of anxiety; it seemed probable that the object of the commission, whether acknowledged or not, would be a restriction of the rights of combination. The commission was appointed in April. It was said at the time that the Prince of Wales, who had been deeply interested in all the sidelights on life in great towns which the Housing Commission had produced, would have liked to serve on this new commission, but had been persuaded that it would be unwise. The members of the commission were: Lord Hartington, Lord Derby, Sir M. Hicks Beach, Sir John Gorst, Mr Mundella, Mr Courtney, Sir H. Fowler, Mr Jesse Collings, Mr Gerald Balfour, Mr T. Burt and Mr W. Abraham, from the two Houses of Parliament; Mr Harland, of the Belfast shipbuilding firm, Mr Bolton of the Caledonian Railway, Sir F. Pollock, Professor of Jurisprudence at Oxford, Professor Marshall, Professor of Political Economy at Cambridge, Sir W. Lewis, of the Cardiff Docks, Mr T. H. Ismay, of the White Star Line, Mr David Dale, an ironmaster, Mr G. Livesey, managing director of the South Metropolitan Gas Works, Mr Tunstall, a cotton employer, and Mr Hewlett, managing director of the Wigan Coal and Iron Company—for the masters of industry; and for the men, J. Mawdsley, of the Operative

10

Cotton Spinners, Tom Mann, of the Dockers' Union, E. Trow, of the Conciliation Board of the Iron and Steel Trades, H. Tait, of the Glasgow United Trades Council, S. Plimsoll, and M. Austin of the Irish Democratic Labour Federation. The reference to the commission was wide and simple; it was "to inquire into questions affecting the relations between employers and employed and the conditions of labour, which have been raised during the recent trade disputes in the United Kingdom, and to report whether legislation, and if so what, could be directed to good ends." The commission divided itself into three groups; Group A undertook inquiry into mining, iron-works, engineering, shipbuilding, and cognate industries. Group B undertook, roughly speaking, the transport industries; and Group C undertook the textile and chemical industries, and building, and other miscellaneous trades. In the last group two women "sub-commissioners" were appointed late in the year to investigate the conditions of women's labour. The work was enormous, and it was difficult for the commissioners, in the mass of detailed complaints and petty vexations brought before them, to keep any general view of their task. But some main lines of Trade Union policy were prominent enough to provide landmarks. At the Trade Union Congress, for example, which now represented over a million and a quarter workmen, the most prominent subjects were an eight-hours day, and an amendment of the law of conspiracy so that technical conspiracy should only be if directed to an object criminal in itself, and intimidation should only consist in actual threats of violence. The plea for limitation of work, in particular, provided a rallying-point for the evidence of employers before the commission.

One of the strongest proofs of a prevailing unconsciousness of the reality of the new forces at work is provided by the comments on the doings of the London County Council.

When the first council came into existence the comments even of Conservative organs were wholly favourable. So incredible had it been thought that the new social movement, the new labour forces, should actually issue in any administrative act. Barely twelve months later the tone had changed completely, and by 1891 hardly anything was too bad to say of the council. It proposed to set up bands in the parks, and was stormed at for wasting money on pastimes for the poor ; it proposed to purchase tramways, and to take over the London Fire Brigade, and was told that its career was a long succession of " absurdities which have humiliated London." Yet there was so little objection in principle to any of these proposals that the real offence of the council seemed to be that it proposed to do things for itself, instead of waiting to be given what the governing classes thought good for it. This was the worse offence, since these classes at the moment were in a liberal mood. The Conservative Ministry had set up County Government, they had passed a great Housing Act, and in 1891 they accomplished another of the tasks which the Liberal party had for years promised to undertake : they made elementary education free of charges. It was done by a simple process of adding ten shillings a year per pupil to the capitation grant. This sum was based on an average school fee of threepence per week. If any school charged more than that, it was at liberty to go on charging the difference. But in effect this was a Free Education Bill ; and so the Liberal party's committal to Home Rule was made still more exclusive of other interests by the removal of another traditional item of its programme. The Bill was not such as a Liberal Government would have introduced ; there would almost certainly have been some provision for increased public control over voluntary schools in a Liberal measure.[1] But in the discussion of the Bill the Opposition were content not to

[1] See *The Daily News*, 24th April 1891.

press that point. The Act came into operation in September of this year. Mr Goschen had a sufficient surplus in his Budget to provide at once the half-year's cost of the change, so that there was no need to delay its introduction. He had also enough money at last to press through the reform of the gold coinage which had been projected two years earlier. The Light Coinage Bill allotted a sum of £400,000 to the cost of withdrawing light gold coins at their face value. Parcels of gold coin of not less than £100 in value were to be received at the Bank of England without any light-weight deduction. It was decided that the average life of a sovereign before falling " below the remedy " was twenty years, and that of a half-sovereign about ten years ; so that, if the South African gold supply proved to be as good as was said, the object of the Treasury would be in future not to allow gold coins to return from the bank into circulation after they had served for those periods.

The Factory Act of this year, though it had nothing to do with current labour movements, was an important piece of work. By setting up the local authorities as the inspecting power for sanitary purposes in connection with workshops, a position from which the appointment of factory inspectors in 1871 had deposed them, it created a dual supervision of industrial places, the inspectors being still charged with the supervision of hours of labour and age of employment ; the inspector and the local authority were put into a situation in which there was bound to be a good deal of intercommunication, with a chance of excellent results.[1] Provision was made for the Home Secretary to have power to enforce the law, in the case of inaction on the part of a local authority ; and workshops where adult men only were at work were brought under regulation. The Home Secretary was also given powers for certifying dangerous and unhealthy trades—a provision

[1] Cf. *The Factory System*, by R. W. Cooke-Taylor, p. 121.

which year after year proved more fruitful of good ; and
an echo, somewhat feeble, but important, of the increased
concern for sweated industries was to be found in the
clause requiring every occupier of a workshop, and every
contractor for work, to keep lists of their outworkers..
The same kind of influence too may be seen in the provision
that all piece-workers in textile factories should be supplied
with information to enable them to understand their scale
of payment.   These regulations were, however, the work
of the social conscience, and in the tradition of the last
twenty years, rather than in the spirit of the coming time.
That spirit may perhaps be detected in the restoration of
important work to the local authorities, through which,
as we have seen, the socialists hoped to operate most
effectively.   The new Act paid no attention to one popular
demand : it appointed no women inspectors.

Parliament was prorogued at the beginning of August,
which gave a comfortable sense that the national affairs
were at last returning to a normal high-water mark.   The
London season had not been a very cheerful one.   Influenza,
which had hitherto been only a winter scourge, attacked
London in May, and as a summer fever it caused nervousness.   Dinner-parties failed, because people were really
afraid of infection ; the after-effects of the disease seemed
to be worse than they had been in previous years.   In addition to this, the notorious " Baccarat scandal " had
damped society's spirits, because when the name of a very
great personage, almost the highest in the land and quite
the highest in active social life, was brought into the case,
there was an uneasy feeling that society had better tread
gently for the moment.   It was pretty generally known
before the case came to trial that the Prince of Wales was
concerned in it.   Sir William Gordon Cumming brought
an action for slander against Mr and Mrs Arthur Wilson
of Tranby Croft, and against others members of a house-
party there, for having said that he cheated at cards.   The

Prince was called as a witness. He appeared in the box, the packed court gazed breathlessly, counsel in the case were appropriately submissive and respectful, and the law emerged from the ordeal of a wholly unprecedented event without a stain on its reputation for inimitable blandness. Outside the courts the results of the case were rather more lasting. Even those little inclined to notice such gossip as had long been current about the Prince of Wales felt the difference made by such a public revelation that " his ' set ' was a baccarat ' set.' " [1]

Materially, as well as morally, the season was damped. Though the Baring disaster had been staved off, the effect of the strain was visible in a general contraction of financial activity. Flotations decreased; the Bankers' Clearing House returns fell 12¼ per cent. The Baring crisis had raised again in Mr Goschen's mind the question of the country's gold reserves ; and he took up once more the suggestion of banknotes of small values. He let it be known that he was ready to consider authorising the Bank of England to issue twenty-five millions in one-pound notes against a reserve four-fifths in gold and one-fifth in Consols. But the hint was not favourably taken ; and the banks pursued their own policy of entering into amalgamations ; Parr's in 1891 became one of the prominent absorbing banks. In spite of the financial stringency the general purchasing power of the people remained good, as far as official figures showed. But there was no enterprise in amusements, no cheerful craze. When a new music hall in London, the Tivoli, was put up to auction, the reserve was not reached ; however, as the bidding rose to £100,000 there must have been sufficient belief in the popular support for such places. In the autumn the gambling mania received an encouragement which must have seemed deplorable to those who were trying to wean the workman from betting. This was the year of the famous " man that broke the bank at

[1] *The Times*, 10th June 1891.

Monte Carlo," and he was hymned on every barrel organ. He was a Mr Wells, and he first rose to fame by winning £20,000 at roulette within a week. When his luck at that table stopped he turned to *trente et quarante*, and in a few stakes made £6400 more. He was playing for months, and his success gave rise to a great discussion of gambling " systems." In November his net winnings were said to be £30,000, and occasionally he " broke " a table in half-an-hour from the opening of play. His career relieved a somewhat dull year.

Hardly even in science is any notable event to be found. Electric light had made at last its final stride ; and it was said in 1891 that the number of incandescent lamps in London was greater than in any one of the five largest cities of America. One or two events of engineering history may be recorded. In August the last of the old broad-gauge lines of the Great Western Railway were taken up, and replaced by lines of the standard gauge. At the beginning of the year naval experts were greatly interested by a system of tubular boilers which Yarrow's had fitted in a torpedo boat built for the Argentine navy ; the firm had been for three years experimenting with them as a rapid means of getting up steam, and also, it was hoped, a safer method of keeping up the high pressures demanded ; but this Argentine boat was the first practical trial of the system. The Manchester Ship Canal was well advanced ; in June water was admitted to the section from Ellesmere Port to Eastham, and a second section, making a total of eleven miles, was open by the end of September. The first attempt to bring the Manchester, Sheffield and Lincolnshire Railway—now the Great Central Railway—to London was also made, but the private Bill for the purpose was rejected by the Select Committee of the House of Commons.

We come this year for the first time in our period upon a really popular demand in fiction. The field since 1880 had been held by writers more or less established, more or less conscientious artists—Meredith, Hardy and Henry James; Besant and Mrs Humphry Ward ; Edna Lyall, Mrs Lynn Linton, Miss Braddon and Wilkie Collins. But when we read in a review of a new book by Mr Rudyard Kipling, *The Light that Failed*, a protest against " his apparent power—the affectation of barbarity," and the remark that " the public read him, so his dissatisfied critics must wait to be justified by an unborn generation," we recognise that here was a demand wholly beyond the normal guides of literary taste. It was a new impulse, a new British self-consciousness. The story told of battles of the Egyptian campaigns, and although the phrase had yet to be invented (by that same author) the idea of " the white man's burden " had been initiated. It had an impulsion of a practical kind this year in the first annual meeting in December of the British South Africa Company, which in a halo of romance was beginning its pioneer work north of the Transvaal. Mr Cecil Rhodes was already a figure of note in the London world, a figure lacking in social flexibility, positive, greatly given to argument, but wielding a large fortune, tireless, not afraid of the social sin of being a bore with his schemes of advancing British frontiers in the land of his adoption. He had by now made the British South Africa Company so important a body that the whole question of the position of chartered companies was being discussed. Some of those who most strongly approved of the existence of such companies thought that they should be set up by Act of Parliament rather than by Royal Charter, and should be compelled to keep their commercial and their administrative accounts separately. The informality of this method of governing uncivilised races was naturally popular with a generation which, through Mr Kipling's Indian stories, was learning to see itself as peculiarly gifted for the shouldering of responsibility in remote places of the earth.

Drama, as well as literature, has an important date in 1891. During the autumn Mr J. T. Grein set up the organisation which he called " The Independent Theatre." He asked for two hundred subscribers of £2, 10s. each, for the production of plays of serious interest, which, from lack of elements of popular appeal, were unlikely ever to appear in the English theatres of the time. The theatrical advertisements in newspapers of the eighties had been certainly barren reading. At the head of the profession Irving was playing chiefly Shakespeare, varying it with somewhat disastrous experiments in Tennyson's verse plays, and with frankly money-making productions of popular pieces, like Wills's *Charles I.*, or *The Bells*, or *The Corsican Brothers*. Other leading actors confined themselves to old-fashioned comedies, such as *Money* and *Caste*, to new melodramas, to farces, generally taken from French originals. The Bancrofts, Charles Wyndham, John Hare, William Terriss, Toole and Edward Terry rang their changes on a paltry list. Mr Grein's object was principally to produce plays by Ibsen, and the Independent Theatre did in fact first introduce those plays to British audiences. But the venture was regarded askance by most of the London world. To many, Ibsen stood for an unhealthy analysis of subjects better left unanalysed ; to others he stood for a foreign impropriety, different from the old kind, but still not to be encouraged ; to the advanced æsthetes he stood for a deplorable solemnity, very hampering to the gracefulness of life. But a sufficient appeal could be made to the middle-class culture, which somewhat heavily pursued the difficult life of appreciative enjoyment, and the Independent Theatre might perhaps have lasted longer if its efforts had not revealed the fact that the field of drama it affected was not a very wide one.

Educated taste at this time was much engrossed with "applied art." Furniture, wall-papers, hangings were all subjected to anxious, even over-anxious, canons of

beauty; the great period of the " hand-made " was being
ushered in with rather barbaric chairs and tables, and
silver implements speckled with little hammer-marks.
In 1891 William Morris added printing to his many ac-
complishments, and set up the Kelmscott Press, working
with founts of type designed by himself, after a laborious
study of early models of typography.

During the parliamentary recess the Liberal party
made up its mind to overhaul its electoral banners.
How dilapidated they were we have already seen. That
the great leader should have devoted himself exclusively
to one overmastering purpose would have been less serious
if he had not been at the same time, by belonging to a much
earlier generation, incapable of estimating new conditions
in domestic politics. There is no evidence that Mr
Gladstone in these years took any interest in the new
forces and the new mind of labour. He had made Mr
Broadhurst a member of his short-lived Government in
1886, but Mr Broadhurst was not, in the official view, a
Labour representative; he was only a Liberal with an
unusual and interesting career. A Member of Parliament
of a democratic turn, who was not a Liberal in name as
well as outlook, would have had no meaning whatever for
Mr Gladstone. But it might have been thought that this
disability on Mr Gladstone's part was rendered less serious
by his very frank and constantly repeated declaration
that he had now only one object in political life. Did not
this lay upon other important members of the party the
duty of keeping the party in the forefront of advanced
thought on social questions ? In their defence it must
be said, first, that Mr Gladstone was apt to be masterful
in regard to the formation of public opinion by his
colleagues. Moreover, most of those colleagues went back
to the days when schemes of social reform were usually
coupled with the name of Mr Chamberlain, and regarded as
impracticable Radicalism. Therefore when Mr Chamber-

lain took himself and his programme elsewhere no heat was left among the leaders in which new ideas might germinate.

Consequently, when the approach of the next General Election became imminent the party managers had to take that most futile step, the construction—not the selection—of a programme of legislation. County Government, Factory Legislation, Employers' Liability, and even Free Education had been taken away. What could be put in their place? One prominent item, indeed, of Mr Chamberlain's programme had not been even nibbled at by his new friends—Disestablishment of the Church. But Mr Gladstone would never lead a general assault on the Church he loved and magnified, and any wholesale measure of disestablishment must commit him at least to countenancing accusations against that Church. But he had shown in the case of the Irish Church that he could make distinctions. Statistics and local grievances could plausibly be used to make distinctions in the case of the Church of England in Wales, and perhaps also in that of the Presbyterian Church in Scotland. The disestablishment of those two Churches therefore was a possible item in the programme. Next, a backward glance over the career of the Conservative Government discovered its weakest moment in the licensing proposals which it had tried to attach to the duties of the new Local Governments.[1] The decision in Sharp v. Wakefield had given the sanction of the highest legal tribunals to the opponents of those proposals. Here then was another possible party advantage. In a non-party way the legal decision had already had its effect. No less Conservative a person than Sir Michael Hicks Beach had announced at the licensing sessions in his part of the country—Fairford, in Gloucestershire—that the licensing magistrates would be ready to hear testimony as to any public-house which was felt to be unnecessary; in other words, that they were prepared to

[1] See pp. 230, 270.

enforce the purely annual existence of a licence, by refusing it on grounds other than those of misconduct. He also revealed a less direct result of recent controversies in an announcement that in future managers of "tied" houses, when asking for renewal of licences, must produce their agreements with brewers—a sign that public opinion was not at the moment friendly to the idea of licence-holders as the mere nominees of brewers. But stronger stuff was needed for a programme *in vacuo* than for processes of administration. The idea of Local Veto had already been made familiar by the apostles of total abstinence; it was now seen to combine the question of licensing with the new spirit of Local Government in a way that qualified it for a prominent place in party politics, and it became another element in the programme. Extension of the Local Government principle by district and parish councils with considerable powers for acquiring land for allotments, erecting cottages, and establishing small holdings; electoral reforms, including the abolition of plural voting, the payment of members, and State payment of returning officers' expenses; land reforms, with the abolition of primogeniture and entail, and the taxation of land values; and lastly, reform of the House of Lords—these miscellaneous proposals completed the party outfit.

Mr Gladstone was to speak at Newcastle on 2nd October. He accepted his conventional duty, and enunciated the *doctrinaire* list which had been evolved from the minds of party organisers. It fell flat. No one had any difficulty in deciding that Mr Gladstone cared about none of the speech, until he came to Home Rule.[1] The mass of Liberal agents saw the Church roused against them on Disestablishment, the brewers against them on Local Veto; and no real force roused for them. The Programme could only command the habitual and traditional

---

[1] In Morley's *Life of Gladstone* (iii. 462) the whole speech is dismissed with a dozen lines of distant reference.

Liberals, and such enthusiasm as might exist would be personal enthusiasm for Mr Gladstone. He after all was their beacon, and the programme only a disagreeable necessity. Home Rule was a reality; the other proposals were not. Nor was a minor factor in the speech, which was Mr Gladstone's own. He insisted on an early evacuation of Egypt. On the old lines of policy in regard to Egypt he was justified. Early in this year a battle fought by Sir Francis Grenfell at Tokar, in which Osman Digna was totally defeated, put the finishing touch to that restoration of confidence and security which had been decided upon as the governing consideration after the fall of Khartoum. Three battles had now had the result of establishing the frontier and relieving it from dervish pressure, and also of giving confidence to the Egyptian soldiers and making them into a real army. The battle before Suakin in 1888 has been mentioned.[1] In 1889 Grenfell defeated at Toski a threatening force under a warrior named Wad El Nejumi, who was believed by those qualified to know to be the really great soldier of the Mahdi's and the Khalifa's power.[2] The defeat of Osman Digna completed this stage of our work in Egypt; and Mr Gladstone therefore had some ground for reintroducing the question of evacuation. But of recent years temper in England had changed. The new sentiment for the British burden of responsibility was in the air; Mr Kipling was inflaming recollections of the Soudan campaigns; and Egypt under Baring and Grenfell was a satisfactory subject for national contemplation. Mr Gladstone had better have left it alone.

Even in that portion of his speech which dealt with Home Rule some observers thought that Mr Gladstone was troubled and embarrassed. He was indeed distressed by the spectacle of Parnell fighting, in a way he thought

[1] See p. 241.
[2] Lord Cromer's *Modern Egypt*, ii. 64, 65.

mad, for control in Irish affairs. Bye-elections had occurred in Ireland, and Parnell had put up candidates against other Home Rule candidates ; they had been beaten disastrously, but he would not give in. On his marriage with the lady who had been Mrs O'Shea the last powerful force in Ireland, which had not yet declared against him, *The Freeman's Journal*, submitted to the Roman Catholic view, and threw him over. He was to and fro between England and Ireland almost every week ; each time his return showed him more haggard, more hoarse. Suddenly, a few days after the Newcastle speech, it was announced that he was lying desperately ill of pneumonia in his house at Brighton, having taken to his bed on his latest return from Ireland. The next day it was announced that he was dead. He was only in his forty-sixth year. The desperate strain and effort of the last twelve months of his life, the struggle, not against England directly, but against his late colleagues, seemed to the normal English mind to be aptly summed up by *The St James's Gazette*, in a quotation from the scene of Brian de Bois Guilbert's death in *Ivanhoe* : " Unscathed by the lance of his enemy, he had died a victim to his own contending passions." Some time afterwards, when the Irish party became once more united under one leader, the enduring work of Parnell could be perceived. He had roused Ireland to a single enthusiasm, which, though centred in himself while he yet led the party, was so burningly alive that it could centre finally in the party as a whole. His tactical work failed, because it depended too much on his own cast of mind ; it was a balancing of policies which no one else could successfully imitate. But his conception of his work, his unwearying refusal to present the Home Rule case as other than a demand, built up a spirit in Ireland which neither fell with him nor died with him. Not by the party as he left it, any more than by the party as he found it, could he be judged ; but by the crystalline compactness

with which for twenty years past the main Irish question
has been kept free of all the legislation that was once
supposed to be alternative to Home Rule.

On other benches too Parliament was to see gaps, when
it met. On 6th October died Mr W. H. Smith, a more
perfect type of the *bourgeois* than England has since produced. Methodical, capable, not without solid dignity, he
left a stronger tradition behind him than his contemporaries
expected. His upbringing made him less sensitive than
his almost as solid predecessor, Stafford Northcote ; but
he also suffered less from the goading of Lord Randolph
Churchill, who had in the later eighties begun to fall
out of parliamentary life, and in this year left England
for a hunting tour in South Africa. Another great figure
passed out of the House of Commons upon the death, late
in December, of the Duke of Devonshire, Lord Hartington
succeeding to the title. Had he remained in the Commons
he would have had to face the strongest pressure to identify
himself finally with the Conservative party by taking the
leadership there ; as it was, he was able once more to move
as deliberately as he always liked to move.

The lapse of a year since the inception of the Salvation
Army scheme, known as the *Darkest England* scheme,
provided an occasion for further criticism of it. It appeared that the year's expenditure of £17,000 had been
taken from the capital sum subscribed ; and the work had
not been regulated on the basis of an income from the sum.
General Booth had asked for much more, and was proceeding on the assumption that the larger sum was assured.
He was considering a method of assisted emigration to
South Africa, and here also was somewhat hampered by
fairly direct intimations that the class of persons he proposed to send would not be welcomed in the Colonies, or
in the British South Africa territories. His scheme,
instead of being launched complete, had grown into
little more than an enlargement of the Army's charit-

able work, which might or might not be prolonged, according as its power of appeal to the public was maintained. Meanwhile the Army was in the midst of some of the worst —and some of the last—of its street battles. It had been received with violent resentment in Eastbourne, a town which prided itself upon its manners and its social amenities. Every Sunday the Salvation Army fought with rowdies in the streets, and another kind of hostility confronted it in an attempt by the town authority to enforce a section of a local Improvement Act against street processions. The warfare raged undiminished through the winter.

London at the same time saw a revival of police action against socialist meetings. In Chelsea, Hoxton, Peckham, Southwark, Mile End, and Wanstead meetings of the Social Democratic Federation were broken up, and speakers were arrested. But this singling out of one form of meeting among the many that were held every Sunday had now no public opinion to back it. The winter was passing without any serious strikes, or grievous distress. But the insistence with which unemployment had been kept in the eye of London, and the new spirit of investigation of labour problems, had secured a patient and genuine interest for a great work which at this time was being published, Mr Charles Booth's *Life and Labour in London*. Mr Booth had himself been led on by his investigations into pauperism to propose, in a paper read before the Statistical Society in December, a system of Old Age Pensions of five shillings a week, which would not, in his opinion, be enough to discourage thrift, but enough to keep the deserving aged poor from the workhouse. It is characteristic of the Liberal paralysis of the time that, within twenty-four hours of that paper being read, Mr Chamberlain was adopting the subject as an urgent piece of domestic reform, and that no prominent Liberal seized upon it as a more vital appeal to the country than anything in the Newcastle Programme.

CHAPTER XIV

1892: A HALF-HEARTED ELECTION

THE year in which "Ta-ra-ra-boom-de-ay" over-ran the streets of our towns may well give pause to the observer of English habits. The tasteless and irrepressible air was at the time a universal annoyance; it appears now almost a portent. It was such an affront to English respectability as had never yet been administered, not only because it flaunted a vision of a high-kicking dancer on a music-hall stage, but because the very sound of the tune was jeering, as well as ludicrous. The sudden absurd jolt of its high note became a grin at the gait and carriage of a respectable man. Its penetrating shrillness warned people that nothing was going to be taken seriously. The street boy whistled it; the junior clerk sang it in suburban drawing-rooms; the gay dog went to see Lottie Collins dance it; even the cashier and the junior partner thought it. It was essentially different from any popular song which had from time to time ruled the pavement. The wildest of comic songs hitherto had been something said, which might appeal to you individually as funny, or be dismissed as nonsense. This one said nothing; it was a mere conspiracy against gravity of deportment, which every errand boy challenged you to join. It had no individual interest whatever; it was the voice of the crowd asserting itself. That overriding of the British self-consciousness of behaviour which had begun—and had been resented—in the Blue Ribbon Army and the Salvation Army, and had been forced forward by circumstances in the struggles of the unemployed, and the

more flamboyant side of socialist street meetings, now
invaded the mass of the careless.   Cheerful blatancy was
as ready to parade the streets as profound conviction was ;
and the year of "Ta-ra-ra-boom-de-ay" contained the
germ of the "Mafficker." The origin of the tune was
gravely discussed in a law suit concerning copyright in it ;
it came from America, where it was said to have sprung
either from lower-class negroes, or from disreputable
haunts in St Louis.   Certainly in its peculiarly idiotic
quality of sound it has never been equalled.

To say that a street tune substantially modified the
course of politics would be, in spite of Fletcher of Saltoun,
to treat popular melody rather too gravely.   Yet there
certainly was at this time a tendency on the part of the
plain average man, without much interest in politics or
social reform, to make a little more of his own interests,
and rather less of the labour revolt, the state of Ireland,
the blessings of education, than he had been obliged to
make in recent years.   He advanced his own amusements
with vigour.   Golf attained in this year so much of a
position in England that for the first time the Amateur
Championship competition was held outside Scotland ;
it took place in May at Sandwich.   The popularity of the
game was felt to be "bewilderingly sudden." [1]   Cycling
had been receiving an immense impetus from the invention
of the safety bicycle, which, besides being far handier, and
easier to ride, than the old high bicycle, had rendered
cycling practicable for women.   In its evening hours half
England was crazily intent upon "missing word" competitions ; later in the year, when it was decided at Bow
Street that these were lotteries, it appeared in the evidence
that the coupons sent in by competitors ran into hundreds
of thousands every week.   The world of art was diverted
by the publication of Whistler's *Gentle Art of Making
Enemies* ; but found some more serious interests in the

[1] *The Times*, 14th May 1892.

successful issue of the negotiations with Mr Tate for the
foundation of the National Gallery of British Art, and in a
considerable protest against the growing disfigurement of
towns by sky signs, and of country districts by advertisement boards.   In literature the publication of *Tess of
the D'Urbervilles* awoke a livelier interest in modern
novelists ; and the work of William Watson encouraged
people to believe that the death of Browning and Tennyson
would not leave the nation without a poet of the grand
scale.   Tennyson's death occurred in October of this
year.   Even the heavy ground of the drama was stirred ;
comedies by Oscar Wilde and J. M. Barrie blew over it a
breath of wit and native high spirits such as England had
not been known to possess.   Finally, Paderewski's first
appearances in London created a wild enthusiasm which,
if at the time exaggerated, and often lacking in genuine
appreciation, did nevertheless make music a subject of
common interest, and prepared the way for a removal of
the reproach that England as a nation cared nothing for it.

The year opened with sorrow.   A form of influenza, apt
to lead on to pneumonia, was again prevalent during the
winter months ; and on 14th January the Duke of Clarence,
eldest son of the Prince of Wales, died from it.   On the
same day Cardinal Manning died.   He had filled for a
long time with tact, but with unflinching assertion, a
difficult position in a society which could not admit the
claim to princely rank, which he could not forgo.   Every
opportunity of position and power was to him a means of
advancing the ends of his Church.   His secession from
the Church of England had been at the time more alarming
than that of Newman, because he was a greater preacher
and a greater administrator.   His intervention in the dock
strike of 1889 was part of an increased activity during his
later years in the cause of reform at home.   This activity
has been attributed to the decline of his influence at
Rome, which had, under Pius IX., been considerable ;

with Leo XIII. he was less in sympathy.[1] The Free Churches also lost this year a very prominent figure by the death of the Rev. C. H. Spurgeon. His preaching at the great building in Newington, known as the Metropolitan Tabernacle, had for many years attracted enormous crowds to the place ; and his sermons, being always reprinted in pamphlet form, probably reached a wider public than was in the compass of any other popular preacher. Homely, positive, charged with an amazing vigour of appeal and of denunciation, and delivered with marvellously effective control of the voice, these sermons were profoundly satisfying to Free Churchmen. They did not at this time look for such direct political quality in their preachers as the later fashion demanded.

The Church of England was involved in the final bout of controversy with the Agnostics on Biblical inspiration. From the staid pages of monthly reviews the battle had spread to the newspapers ; and the Duke of Argyll, Mr Gladstone, and Professor Huxley were solemnly debating whether men should or should not believe in God, since the Book of Genesis shows no knowledge of the existence of kangaroos, and the story of Creation is demonstrably unsound in the matter of the greater saurians. This kind of controversy was doomed by the approach of a new spirit, which, if in many respects too light-hearted, was sane in its inclination to think that a Church stood or fell by other tests than those of reason, just as it had learned to feel that a social structure stood or fell by other tests than those of strictly logical principles.

One of the most striking instances of this spirit was provided now by the second election for the London County Council, which took place in March. All the criticism which the council's work had brought upon it from Conservatives, from irritable rich householders, from any who disliked and feared democratic administration, was con-

[1] See Mr G. W. E. Russell's *Collections and Recollections*, chap. iv.

centrated in a great attack during the early weeks of 1892. The strange result was that resentment of carping criticism was expressed not only by the advanced side of the council, but by the whole body of members. Even the leaders of the Moderate party complained of grumblings and growlings which were meant to " crab " the council, and might have the effect of frightening useful men from joining it. It was a Moderate member, too, who went so far in his admiration for the council as to say that it had in London so great and important a charge that it ought to have a permanent organisation, somewhat on the scale of Government departments. This was exactly the kind of large view of the council's duties which fussy ratepayers detested. At any rate, the attacks proved futile, and the new body elected this year had almost as large a Progressive majority as the original council had had. It made the first attempt to run trams along the Embankment, but failed to obtain powers from Parliament. Late in the year it accomplished an advanced piece of administration by setting up a works department of its own, and thus giving itself a strong hand against the contractors for public works. This was distinctly the most socialistic step that any municipal authority had yet taken, and was on quite a different plane from the provision of public services, such as gas and water, which in their day had made stir enough. Discussion of the water-supply, which from time to time was a pressing subject in London, when a dry summer revealed the inadequacy of the Water Companies' services, arose this year in a new form. The Birmingham Corporation promoted a Bill for powers to obtain a water-supply from certain mountain valleys in Wales, at a cost of six millions. The question whether London did not need that particular source of supply was raised. But it was not a matter on which there was as yet any commanding force of public opinion, and Birmingham secured the right to the valleys. The water-supply of all large towns was becoming a more serious problem, not only from the perpetual increase of domestic demands, but from at least two other demands. One was the demand for public swimming baths and washhouses, and the other was the great extension of the use of lifts in big buildings. To take one example alone : in Birmingham the requirements of water for the latter purpose had amounted to 30,000 gallons daily, even in 1885, and by 1890 the amount had risen to 80,000 gallons. Another municipal interest of the year 1892 was the first instance of an electric tramway worked by a municipality.[1] At Blackpool the local authority took over the lines of tramway which had for some years been working on the conduit system. In this year Mrs Rylands, the widow of an immensely wealthy cotton-spinner, bought complete the famous Althorp Library, belonging to Lord Spencer, a library rich in every kind of treasure of book-collecting, and gave it to the citizens of Manchester.

Early in the year events began to be coloured by the prospect of a parliamentary election. · The Government, having been in office for six years, had come to the customary time for a dissolution. The London County Council election was considered by the Liberal party organisers to be of good omen, and Liberal leaders talked County Council politics (Mr Gladstone even going so far as to suggest that the council might have control of the police), until the other side scoffed at them for " throwing Imperial questions into the background," though no one seemed very clear as to what Imperial questions there were at the moment. The advocacy of Old Age Pensions remained chiefly with the Conservatives, and was cautiously handled ; Mr Chamberlain had persuaded both Lord Salisbury and Mr Balfour that it was not a matter to be neglected, and they wrote letters supporting the idea of a contributory scheme

[1] See *The Municipal Journal*, 2nd September 1910 : article on the Jubilee of Trams.

of pensions, in which the State would have no concern beyond the setting-up of the machinery. Liberals were critical, both of this and of more general schemes of industrial insurance, which had been brought into the political atmosphere of the moment by the recent establishment of the German system of workmen's insurance. Allotments again provided matter for speech-making, and here, too, with the Act of 1887 to their credit, Government speakers took a high line. Mr Chamberlain asserted that 100,000 labourers now had allotments; and the Duke of Devonshire, going as usual to the root of the matter, even when the root was rather deep digging for a noble landlord, advised his party, besides making efforts to increase the effectiveness of the Allotments Act, not to neglect "those other and older objects of Liberal policy that were directed towards the freeing of the land from those encumbrances and difficulties under which our existing laws place it, as to inheritance and transfer." In the end this matter turned less to Conservative advantage than was expected; but in the preliminary rounds it was of more value to them than to Liberals. For a short time Woman Suffrage came to the front again. During the brief session before the dissolution Sir Albert Rollit introduced a Woman Suffrage Bill, and the question was discovered to have a new kind of vitality, when the platform at a meeting in St James's Hall in support of the Bill was stormed by a section who objected to the class limitations in the Bill. Hitherto Woman Suffrage measures had been so remote from practical politics that precise terms of enfranchisement had never been in dispute. The Bill was defeated in the House by 175 votes to 152. The most direct pronouncement on the position of labour from either great party came from Lord Randolph Churchill, who had returned to England in January. He upheld once more that form of democracy which consisted in trying to excise the middle class from the body politic.

In a letter to a candidate he remarked that political power had passed from the landlords and the landed interest to the capitalist and the manufacturer, who made laws to suit themselves ; why, he asked, should not the Conservatives combine regulation of all conditions of labour by the State, under the guidance of the Labour vote, with " a foreign policy which sought to extend, by means of tariff reforms, over our colonies and even over other friendly states the area of profitable barter of produce ? " But Lord Randolph Churchill had already ceased to be a real force in politics, and newspapers no longer made much of any suggestions from him. Besides, Labour had completed the turn of thought by which it had come back to faith in parliamentary work, and a determination to signalise in that, as well as in municipal affairs, the coming of the era of administration. Leaders on both sides had to take account of a new kind of Labour candidature. Mr Balfour took account of it, genuinely enough, by asserting that Liberals were always more interested in political reform than in social reform, and were therefore not the truest friends of labour. Mr Gladstone took account of it, not altogether happily, by deprecating independence of candidatures on the Labour side, as distinct from independence of action in Parliament ; in other words he preferred a member nominally Liberal, whose votes might occasionally go against the party, to a candidate whose poll must inevitably weaken the Liberal poll in any constituency. But indeed, whatever had been said on either side, the Labour candidatures would have remained detached from both. Two or three times in the spring and early summer the power of trade unions shook the country. Early in March there was a strike of colliers, and although it only affected one-third of the coalfields it caused a panic at the thought of the possible laying-idle of factories and furnaces everywhere. Fortunately that strike was over in a fortnight, though it was followed by a more serious one on the Durham coalfields, which lasted for twelve weeks. The two strikes were on wages conditions, the masters claiming the right, in view of the state of the market, to reduce wages by 13½ per cent. The men won a point in getting the reduction put at 10 per cent. In each case the working of the Union organisation was of a kind to make Labour little inclined to rely on any party but itself.

Amid all these political excursions Home Rule lost none of its party importance. Even in 1891 there had been lively discussion of whether Mr Gladstone should or should not be giving the country some details of the shape that Home Rule was then taking in his mind. One of the most prominent of the young men of his party, Mr Asquith, was pressing him on the point in public speeches. In 1892 all that was known was that the retention of a considerable number of Irish members at Westminster had been decided upon. The Conservatives, besides boasting of the effect of their five years of " resolute government " of Ireland, introduced this year an Irish Local Government Bill. But it was not very seriously intended ; the elective nature of the bodies it set up was " bulwarked," as the ingenious phrase had it, in every possible way ; and the Bill in the end was dropped. It had never been worth while for Liberals to give it serious opposition. Yet they went to the country in the end with their own policy to the last degree vague in such vital points as the control of the police and the judiciary and the treatment of the land question ; and relied to no small extent upon attacking Mr Balfour's coercion, instead of explaining their own proposals.

Coercion, indeed, and the comparative failure of the Allotments Act proved in the end the two most pointed weapons for the use of Liberals. The employment of them, combined with a certain weakness in Conservative, as distinct from Liberal Unionist, electoral organisation, provided the Tories' excuse for their defeat. Parliament was dissolved in June ; and although the Government had been losing seats continually at bye-elections, probably no one on the Liberal side, except Mr Gladstone, had expected a complete Liberal victory. He expressed the most extravagant anticipations. In an article published in *The Nineteenth Century*[1] he tried to persuade the country to expect a Liberal majority of at least 100, and to be prepared even for the possibility of a Tory "landslide." Not only was he wrong, but his disillusionment took a peculiarly personal turn ; his majority in Mid-Lothian, which had been over 3000 in 1885, and unassailed in 1886, fell to 690. In the country generally the only sign of opinion which could be called at all striking was the comparative failure of the Liberal Unionists. They had numbered 74 after the election of 1886 ; they numbered after the election of 1892 only 47 ; it seemed therefore that the attachment of the word "Liberal" to a position which did not include Home Rule was of no value as an appeal to electors ; and to that extent Home Rule became a more firmly settled point of Liberal policy. The new House, which assembled in August, contained 274 Liberals, 81 Home Rulers (72 Anti-Parnellites and 9 Parnellites), 268 Conservatives and 47 Liberal Unionists. This gave a Home Rule majority of 40. It was not a strong majority, but it was remarkable, if the purely political circumstances alone be considered, that there should have been such a majority at all. The Conservative Government had passed a very considerable quantity of democratic legislation, and their record in that respect was far more satisfactory than that of the Liberal Government of 1880. One of their final pieces of work was a Shop Hours Act, prohibiting the employment of young persons under eighteen years of age for more than seventy-four hours in a week, including meal times. The Act required amendment later, as no provision was made in it for the

[1] September 1891.

expenses of administering it.   But it was another instance
of the kind of social legislation of these five years.
Much of this, no doubt, was due to Mr Chamberlain's
influence.   But Lord Salisbury was quite as much alive
to democratic demands as anyone of his time, for all
the cynicism with which he occasionally presented them
to his party.   He was probably more alive to them than
Mr Gladstone, who never successfully separated in his mind
constitutional reforms and social advancement.   Lord
Salisbury had but little patience with the rights of man or
the rights of citizenship ; but he could see any given claim
when it was presented to him apart from abstractions.
Thus he had been able to move far in social reform since
1886.   But he could not move in the spirit of the rights
of democracy, and this spirit was what most distinguished,
next to his own legislation, the past six years.   Herein we
may find some part of the reason for the defeat of the
Conservatives.   Much though they had done, they held
themselves capable of either giving or withholding ;   and
political Trade Unionism was bent upon breaking down
that attitude.   The fact that the Conservatives and
Liberal Unionists failed to obtain against the Liberals
alone a majority sufficient to counterbalance the Irish vote
may be attributed firstly to the personal popularity of
Mr Gladstone, and secondly to the new Trade Unionism.
Incidentally new journalism had its share in the result.   It
is beyond doubt that *The Star* already wielded a formidable
power ;   and in the spring of 1892 it was followed by the
establishment of two halfpenny morning papers, *The
Morning Herald* and *The Morning Leader*, the latter being
published by the proprietors of *The Star*.   These were the
first halfpenny morning papers in the kingdom, and they
came in time to help sway the election.   The working man
could not yet return many members of his own class to
Parliament.   His sense that Tories, even when they had
passed Factory Acts and a Local Government Act and a

Free Education Act, were still Tories, could for the most
part only express itself in voting for Liberals. This, with
the persistent Liberalism of Scotland and Wales, just
defeated the Unionists. Lord Salisbury did not immediately resign ; he was not, until a vote was taken,
in a minority. But the vote came speedily. Mr Asquith
moved a motion of No Confidence on 8th August, and it
was carried by 350 votes to 310. Then Lord Salisbury
resigned, and Mr Gladstone formed his fourth Government.
It included some new men, Mr Asquith becoming Home
Secretary, Sir H. H. Fowler, President of the Local Government Board, and Mr James Bryce, Chancellor of the Duchy
of Lancaster.

There were new men in the House also. In some
respects newness was perhaps unnecessarily self-conscious.
The brass band which accompanied Mr Keir Hardie to
Westminster when he took his seat gave some offence ; his
tweed cap hardly less. He was elected for South-West
Ham ; and if the band and the cap were intended to
announce that a Labour member had arrived who did not
call himself a Liberal, expected no favour from Liberals,
and did not want the patronising kindliness which had
been shown to previous members from the ranks of labouring men, they were not altogether out of place. Mr John
Burns, too, was returned to Parliament, sitting for
Battersea. These two stood for a change in the political
spirit of labour, not unlike that which Parnell had made in
the case of Ireland. The other Labour members had, like
Isaac Butt, accepted the forms of the House, and parliamentary action to them meant all the old forms ; they
sat with the Liberals, and their hope lay in moving
Liberals to action.

Meanwhile outside the House advanced Labour men,
in the same way as the Clan-na-Gael, had begun to despise
parliamentarianism, and preferred to rely upon their own
organisations acting directly on the social body. The

Independent Labour Party proposed now, as Parnell had done, to have at its back all the energy of these outside forces, while employing parliamentary action. At the moment, indeed, the outside forces showed some tendency to become as detached from all normal and lawful methods of agitation as the Clan-na-Gael was. Some members of the Social Democratic Federation developed anarchist leanings, abolished the chairman at their conferences, and held frankly revolutionary meetings in Hyde Park. Four men were arrested at Walsall, for manufacturing bombs, and were sentenced to penal servitude. The publisher and proprietor of *The Commonweal*, the organ of socialism, were indicted for publishing a violent article, after this trial, denouncing the Home Secretary, the judge who tried the case, and the inspector of police who conducted it. They were sentenced to eighteen months' hard labour for incitement to murder.

But on the whole the Labour forces outside Parliament were not likely to become as embarrassing to their leaders as Irish dynamiters had been to Parnell, and the Trade Union Congress in the autumn, while it showed the vigorous influence of the new movement, confined itself to an effective and not at all extravagant programme. It instructed its Parliamentary Committee to prepare a scheme for Independent Labour representation ; and it passed resolutions demanding an easier franchise qualification (of three months' residence, instead of a year's) ; the appointment as factory inspectors of men who had worked not less than five years in factories ; and an eight-hours day. The last demand received an unexpected encouragement from a vote in favour of it given by the cotton operatives' trade unions. This was a great surprise, because the cotton hands had never hitherto favoured the movement ; there were some who were inclined to attribute the vote less to conviction on a Trade Union theory than to a knowledge that there had been a good deal of over-production in the trade, and that an eight-hours day would be a form of short time convenient to the operatives.

Unfortunately the winter in Lancashire was to pass under the shadow of something worse than short time. Affairs there had not been going well. The Ship Canal was proving disastrously costly; instead of the eight and a half millions which were to have covered all the cost of construction and the purchase of other undertakings, ten millions had already been spent, and it seemed likely that fourteen millions would be swallowed before the work was finished. Then depressed trade turned the cotton-masters to thinking of bimetallism, and seeking in that a cure for ills that had no connection with currency. Finally at the beginning of November the masters decided that they must make a 5 per cent. reduction in wages, and the operatives struck, asking for a short-time agreement instead. Fifty or sixty thousand operatives were out before the first week of the strike was over. It was expected to be a tough fight, because for some years the alternatives of short time or lowered wages in a trade crisis had been in dispute between masters and men, and now had come to trial; but that it would be a fight through the whole dark winter no one supposed. The strike added a sharper interest to the Conference of Women Workers at Bristol in November, which gave much of its time to the consideration and advocacy of womens' trade unions; the Women's Trade Union Association, meeting about the same time, had to confess to a year of poor results, although great efforts had been made.[1] The Bristol Conference, a sequel to the Conference of the Birmingham Union of Women Workers in 1890, also pressed forward the question of the appointment of women factory inspectors; and one of the first services of the new Liberal Government was to accede to this pressure,

[1] This was the Association's third yearly meeting.

Mr Asquith as Home Secretary appointing several women inspectors.

Naturally the new Government also went to work early in Ireland. Mr Morley, who had again taken the Chief Secretaryship, set up in October a Royal Commission to investigate the conditions induced by the steady course of evictions under the recent " resolute government." The bitterness of feeling was seen in the assertions of landlords that they would have nothing to do with the commission. The first petulance passed away, and the work seemed likely to proceed fairly smoothly, when a breeze between the judge who presided over the commission and certain lawyers who appeared for landlords brought ill-feeling back again ; and in the end the landlords carried out their original threat, and declined to appear. Another matter in which the Ministry seized its new opportunities was the question of allotments. So much of their Social Reform programme had been taken from them that any point in which the arrogance of the other side might be pricked was of no small value. A return was at once prepared, and was published in August, showing how poor a thing the Allotments Act of 1887 had proved to be in the working. Instead of Mr Chamberlain's 100,000 men, it appeared from the returns that only 2891 tenants had been set up under the Act ; and the perfunctory character of the Act was shown by the discovery that only fifty-six rural sanitary authorities (the local bodies which administered the Act) had acquired land, while five hundred and eighteen authorities had taken no steps at all.

There was some apprehension of distress as the winter approached. But in one sense the worst struggle of the unemployed appeared to be over ; they no longer had to rouse the comfortable world to the fact of their existence and their starvation. The new Home Secretary speedily removed one of the old grievances by opening Trafalgar Square to meetings on Sundays, Saturdays and Bank

Holidays; though he ventured on ground which might have been provocative when he spoke of the mischief of holding meetings there day after day—the very thing which in extreme states of popular feeling was the most impressive means of action. But the concession was well received; all the energy of those who concerned themselves with the problem of unemployment could go to trying to devise remedies, and the Local Government Board was urged again to relax the rigidities of the Poor Law, and to sanction some form of relief organisation. It was at last being admitted that a neglected state of unemployment brought a terrible train of consequences, in that it finally submerged workmen who could never recover from a fortnight's failure of work, and were thrust down into pauperism beyond remedy. The official response was not very fruitful, but it was some acknowledgment of the difficulty. A Royal Commission on the Poor Law was set up. It was less concerned with immediate labour problems than with the subject of Old Age Pensions, to which it was obvious that the new Government must pay attention. The commission's work gradually narrowed itself down to this, and no effort was made to devise modifications of the Poor Law to meet the case of the unemployed. The commission did not represent in any way the new labour forces; John Burns declined to serve on it. The only Labour members were of the old school—Joseph Arch, and Henry Broadhurst. Mr Chamberlain was one of the commissioners; he had lately promulgated a "labour programme" which showed him for the first time out of real touch with those democratic movements which ten years before he had pre-eminently represented. He proposed to shorten hours of labour in mines and other dangerous employments; to set up arbitration tribunals; to found a system of contributory insurance for compensation for injuries, and for old age pensions; to limit pauper immigration; to increase the powers of local

authorities in matters' of housing and town improvements ;
and to empower such authorities to advance money to
working men to enable them to become owners of their
houses.   This last item, curious as it sounds now, was
ardently advocated by Mr Chamberlain for a year or two.
He had in fact undergone the inevitable change from his
environment.   He had not become a Tory ; but he had
missed the contact with the new element in democratic
feeling by which such a man as he would have profited,
if he had remained on the Liberal side.   Even on his
present side he did not overlook the existence of the new
element ; but he could have no contact with it, and the
result was that he miscalculated it.   He denied that the
new Labour members represented any real force in the
labour world, and that led him to mistake an advanced
programme in the spirit of 1880 for an appeal to advanced
labour.

Meanwhile the Salvation Army scheme was showing
itself as founded rather on experience of destitution than
on a proper understanding of the problem of unemployment.   The honesty of the administration of the fund,
and the adequate keeping of accounts, were established
by the investigations of a committee which had undertaken the work at General Booth's request.   But the
committee found that the relief works of the Army were
really underselling the market in lines of cheap labour,
and were thus creating as much destitution as they relieved.
It may be added here that the Salvation Army's years of
street struggles now came virtually to an end ; the clause
in a Local Act, under which the Eastbourne authorities
had repressed the Army's activities, was repealed by
Parliament in this year; and when the Town Council
tried to make by-laws permitting repression the Home
Secretary refused his sanction.   Active persecution of the
Salvation Army may from this time be said to have ceased.

By the end of the year it was becoming terribly evident

11

that distress of a grievous kind, even if it did not amount
to starvation, was at thousands of doors where no such
visitant had been expected. In October a business with
vast ramifications, called the Liberator Building Society,
went into bankruptcy. The small savings of an immense
number of people were in it ; it had, indeed, never been
an affair for large investments, but had acquired practically
all its capital from the artisan and the small shopkeeper.
The first announcement of its failure left, perhaps,
some hope ; the announcement in November that the
Public Prosecutor had been approached in the matter
began to put a different complexion on the state of the
society's business.

As for the large investor, a bad trade year in Great
Britain had kept his new interest in South Africa alive.
The gold boom continued in a milder form, and Mr
Rhodes was a stalwart figure to give the investor confidence
in the possibilities of the territories he so largely controlled.
He was in England again in the winter, rousing a great
meeting of the British South Africa Company to enthusiasm for his schemes, which were now being revealed
at their height. He spoke of telegraph lines from south
to north of Africa by way of Uganda and Wady Halfa, and
of an advance of civilisation by that route, which should,
so to speak, take the dervishes in the rear, and remove
the necessity of having to fight them. The idea was that
other interruptions of the magnificent whole might also
be removed without fighting. Complaints about the
Boers' treatment of the gold industry, which had been
making a slight appearance from time to time, were
growing rather more loud. However, the hope was
expressed that the backward nation which occupied the
Transvaal might be removed from it ultimately without
war ; though references to " gratuitous germs of race
bitterness " betray glimpses of the real feelings at work.

Alarm about cholera, from which England had been

free for some years, returned in the summer, when the
presence of the disease at St Petersburg and Hamburg
led to fears that it might be introduced into this country
by immigrants. In the autumn there were a few cases
in the ports on the English as well as on the French
side of the Channel. The authorities had the more
reason to be uncomfortable since a fever epidemic in
London in the summer, 4000 cases being under treatment
in September, had shown once again the prevalence of
insanitary conditions. However, the cholera was successfully kept within bounds. The cases in England were
limited to thirty-five, and the isolation arrangements
were so good that in no single instance did the disease
extend to other persons than those who landed in
England with it upon them. That is to say, there was
no spread of infection at all.

CHAPTER XV

1893: MR GLADSTONE'S LAST FIGHT

ALTHOUGH the Liberal majority was unreal for any purpose but that of Home Rule, the Government entered on its first serious session amid as much obloquy and fear from Conservatism as if it were a revolutionary junta in command of absolute power. Mr Gladstone was the sole cause of this attitude. In the clash of violent feeling roused during the Home Rule controversy of 1886 the personal dislike of him, active enough in the late seventies, had assumed an almost superstitious form. For a few years before the election of 1880 it was actually difficult for a London hostess to gather a dinner-party to meet Mr Gladstone, unless she was content to confine herself to his known adherents. His power of moving great audiences, his desire to move them, and the directions in which he wished to move them, appeared as a terrible break with the old gentleman-like politics in which he had been reared. Dread of his power grew to be a very large element in Queen Victoria's obvious mistrust of him; and she was only reflecting the feelings of the higher social ranks of the country. When he took up the cause of Home Rule, dislike was inflamed into hatred. He alone at that time could have created and held together a party against the furious attacks of the Tories and the Unionists; therefore the fact that he was there to do it focussed upon him the intense bitterness of feeling. A yet more amazing stage remained. That adoration of him on his own side which took such affectionate pride in the vigour of his old age, which gloried

in his capacity at eighty-three to lead one more Government to attempt Home Rule, which pinned its faith so
fiercely to him as the " Grand Old Man," was answered
on the other side by a belief, ridiculous as it might seem,
that such a spirit in so old a man could only be attributed
to some form of demoniac possession.   Numbers of people,
otherwise sensible, actually believed that there was something satanic in Mr Gladstone ; and, once that superstitious feeling was aroused, his constant expression of his
deeply religious convictions only made the case worse.
The working of his mind, often involved, and showing
such expertness in mental processes that the result was
frequently a balanced pronouncement, in which simpler
minds could see no finality, became in the eyes of the
superstitious another sign of " possession " ; they took
it as a form of gathering into his toils those who, if they
had read his real thoughts, would have ceased from following him.   In the two Mr Gladstones of popular fancy—
the Grand Old Man who would perform a miracle, and
the Terrible Old Man who would ruin the Empire—the
ordinary person's interest in politics was centred, not
upon the new Government as a Government.

The times were not propitious.   The great strike in
Lancashire, which had begun in November, showed no
signs of coming to an end, and hunger stalked through the
cotton towns.   Other industries were in a nervous, irritable condition which portended more strikes.   At the
same time the full effects of the Liberator bankruptcy
began to be apparent ; early in January it was said that
the examination of the society's affairs was leading to the
conclusion that the shareholders would lose everything,
and the depositors would be fortunate if they got three or
four shillings in the pound.   Angry discussions raged as
to the responsibility of prominent persons who had allowed
their names to figure on the prospectus ; but there were
individuals upon whom it soon appeared that direct

punishment would fall. The man who was supposed
to have been chiefly responsible for fraudulent handling
of the funds, Jabez Spencer Balfour, had fled the country
at an early stage of the disaster, and no one knew where
he was. But three men were put on their trial, Hobbs,
Wright and Newman, and though the evidence of the
financial juggling which had gone on—the interweaving
of building speculation with private borrowings which
had, for instance, the prosecution alleged, transferred two
millions sterling to the pockets of Hobbs from the
Liberator's funds—was extremely complicated, the end
of the trial was plain enough. Hobbs and Wright were
sentenced to twelve years' penal servitude, and Newman
to five years. In April, a month after the trial was over,
news at last arrived of Balfour ; he had been recognised
at Buenos Ayres, and application had been made for his
extradition. He was regarded as the real villain of the
piece. Hobbs had only aspired to be Mayor of Croydon ;
but Balfour had posed as a financial magnate, with a great
extravagant country house, a seat in Parliament, and a
reputation for benevolence. He proceeded now to prove
that at any rate the cleverness at the back of the Liberator
frauds had been largely his contribution. His extradition
was formally granted by the Argentine authorities on
17th April ; he invented ingenious processes of the law by
which he delayed for two whole years the carrying out of
the extradition order, and almost caused his victims to
despair of his ever being brought to justice. But meanwhile some vengeance had been taken ; and energy was
now turned to setting on foot a Relief Fund for those who
had been ruined.

The cotton strike terminated on 24th March in the
famous Brooklands agreement, which has ever since
governed the relations of employers and employed in
that industry. It provided that the immediate reduction
of wages should be, not 5 per cent., against which the mill-

hands had struck, but 3 per cent. The more important feature of the agreement was that in future no changes should take place at intervals less than a year from the date of the last change, and that no single change should exceed 5 per cent. either of advance or of reduction ; machinery for consultation and arbitration was also set up, and an arrangement made for establishing committees of the masters' and the men's organisations, two committees on either side, a lower and a higher, each of which should have not less than seven days, in a case of dispute, to consider its attitude. The agreement was hailed as a credit to Lancashire ; it was also a remarkable sign of the new relations which labour was setting up with its employers. A strike was no longer an isolated affair, and no longer a simple affair ; it contained various possibilities ; it was almost always now a declaration of unity of which masters might take account, if they wished. The statistics of strikes showed an increasing number of disputes which were not about wages ; thus in 1890 wages disputes were 62 per cent. of the whole, and in 1891 were 54 per cent. An equally significant fact was that in strikes undertaken purely to defend Trade Union principles, although the masters won rather more than half the battles, the cases which the strikers won were the far more important ones. These statistics of the industrial world had been published for several years past, and in this year the work of collecting and presenting them was put under a special branch of the Board of Trade, the Labour Department, which Mr Mundella, President of the Board, created.

During the winter the new education was of as much interest as the new Unionism. The two subjects were not devoid of a remote connection, because upper middle-class people, seeing prices disturbed, and conveniences of life affected, by the demands of workmen, began to question why they should at the same time be paying more for the education of those workmen. It was not a very reasonable

train of thought, but it was an enticing one.   Local taxation, according to a Local Government Board report
published in April of this year, was certainly tending
to fall more heavily on the house-occupier and less
on the landowner.   Sometimes the grievance was
put differently ; the ratepayer complained that he was
being mulcted for the education of the working classes,
who then used their education to form unions, and
endanger dividends.   People grumbled increasingly at the
effect of compulsory education in making the educated
less content with their station in life ; to meet them with
more education was in this view deplorable.   A time of
uncertain trade and a wet, depressing winter made these
grievances louder, so that it behoved the champions of
education to bestir themselves.   It was useless to blink
the fact that the new education would not only go on
making demands upon the national pocket, but would make
ever-increasing demands.   There was already a dearth of
teachers in technical schools, and the state of the teaching
staff of elementary schools cried aloud for more and better
training colleges.   The Duke of Devonshire, in his level-
headed way, attacked the most prevalent ground of complaint ; he argued that, instead of increasing the attempt
to migrate from one class to another, technical education
would diminish the " black-coat fetish," would set up an
ideal of workmanship in place of the feeling that the desk-
worker was a more respectable person than the skilled
artisan, and so would diminish the tendency to congestion
in the world of clerks and shop assistants.   The answer
made to this argument was that technical schools showed
a danger of turning out bad artists rather than good crafts-
men.   It fell to Mr Balfour, speaking at Manchester, to
remind the country that, after all, a progressive and
energetic community like Manchester had had a
Mechanics' Institute twenty years ago and a School of Art
fifty-six years ago ; the Technical Education Act had

only put upon a national basis work which the great
industrial towns had found so desirable, that they had
instituted private efforts to set it on foot long before anyone dreamed of it as proper work for public authorities.
Meanwhile other speakers like Lord Justice Bowen reminded the public that education (which he called " the
cultivation for market-purposes of brute brain power ")
was not thought of by its best supporters as supplanting
morality and religion ; a leaven had been set to work, and
time must be given for its operation.

Parliament met on 31st January for what became the
longest session that had ever been known. It sat till the
third week in September, and then, with only five weeks'
recess, sat again until the beginning of March 1894—a
session of thirteen months. The Government introduced
rapidly three large measures. The Home Rule Bill was
produced in February, the Welsh Disestablishment Bill
in the same month, and the Local Veto Bill at the beginning
of March. But of these only the Home Rule Bill counted
for the moment in the Liberal forces. The introduction
of the other two might have been thought to have been
designed, in some extraordinary failure of judgment, to
serve as irritants during several months in which the
Liberal party would be too much occupied to defend
them in the country. The licensed victualling trade at
once organised meetings against the Local Veto Bill ;
and even people well affected towards licensing reform
were cooled by the production of a measure, which made
no alterations in the system of licensing, but was devoted
solely to such projects as establishing polls of districts,
to be taken on the demand of ten persons, on the question
of prohibiting the sale of liquor in the district, and setting
up a form of public management of licensed houses with a
bonus to the resident manager on the sale of non-
intoxicants. It was little wonder that Mr Chamberlain
saw as much profit in attacking this measure as in com-

bating Home Rule.[1] The Welsh Disestablishment Bill
also provoked meetings against the Government all over
England ; and, as neither Bill was advanced a single stage
in all this year, their production seemed a gratuitous
rousing of opposition. Practically the whole of the time
until the adjournment for the short recess in September
was taken up by the Home Rule Bill. Its only novel feature
as compared with the previous Bill [2] was the retention
at Westminster of Irish members, their numbers being
reduced from a hundred and three to eighty. But exactly
what their position was to be, whether they were to vote on
all subjects or only on Irish subjects, and what was to be
said in the former case of a situation in which Irishmen
might govern England, by holding the balance between
parties, but Englishmen could not govern Ireland—
these were the points of hottest dispute in the interminable debates in Committee. The second reading
debate was a long one, and at the beginning of it the
Opposition were not wholly united in their policy. A
party meeting had to be called at the Carlton Club (it was
notable as marking Lord Randolph Churchill's return to
the fold of the orthodox on Irish questions) ; and, though
some strong differences of opinion as to the method of
fighting the Bill were expressed, the decision was ultimately
taken for a solid vote against the second reading on 22nd
April. Then the long Committee stage began ; it occupied
sixty-three sittings, and Mr Gladstone himself was not
free from some responsibility for the inordinate length of
the proceedings. The concentration of the past seven
years upon the subject of Ireland had so preserved his
energy, besides enlarging his store of knowledge, that he
brought to these debates an incredible vigour. Unfortunately vigour with him meant copiousness ; he maintained,
in a House of Commons which had learned obstructive
arts, the tradition of a day when these were unknown,

[1] *The Times*, 7th April 1893.   [2] See p. 181.

and the result was that his speeches offered a thousand
points of petty debate, in sentences which he threw in
merely for purposes of illustration or amplification.[1]
Dull though the whole debate became to the world
outside the walls of Parliament, there was little else to
talk about. The introduction of the Bill had intensified
the animosities in society, which were so bad for the spirit
of the London season.

Then the business world was depressed by a disastrous
failure of credit in Australia. In March banks began to
suspend payment there, and the whole structure of credit
in the colony was found to depend to a dangerous degree
upon land speculation, which at a time of crisis dropped
with a run. Banks had also been engaged in direct trading,
and their capital was insufficiently paid up. Moreover,
though the gold reserves were larger than in England,
being on an average 20 to 25 per cent. of the deposits, as
against an average of about 12 per cent. in England, they
were not large enough for a country in which, owing to
its isolation, securities were necessarily almost impossible
to realise in a moment of difficulty. Out of fifteen large
banks in Australia seven had suspended payment in April,
and the crash had the more serious effects in England,
because, oddly enough, there were few British shareholders,
but a very large number of British depositors ; one bank
alone, the Commercial Bank of Australia, held British deposits to the amount of five or six millions. Such a disaster
as this, following on the disaster to a less speculative class
in the Liberator Society's downfall, disposed the country
very ill to the reception of a Budget showing a deficit of a
million and a half, and demanding an extra penny on the
Income Tax. The alcohol revenue, which had been so
strong a support of Mr Goschen's management of national
finances, had fallen off heavily, as was usual in years of
bad trade ; and that enhancement of revenue which Sir

[1] Morley's *Life of Gladstone*, iii. 502.

William Harcourt was known to have in mind, the Death
Duties, could not be proposed in a session so overwhelmingly occupied as this was by the Home Rule Bill.
At this moment, too, a strike occurred which was
more menacing and disturbing than recent strikes had
been. It was a dock strike at Hull, and it arose out of
unionists' refusal to work with non-unionists. We have
had occasion to remark that the first threat of a shipping
strike on these lines had been accompanied by peculiarly
sharp exchanges from either side.[1] It was now to be seen
that such appearances were not empty. The struggle at
once became a severe one. The Seamen's and Firemen's
Union joined the dockers ; the Shipping Federation, now
a virtually complete organisation of shipowners, would not
yield an inch. The careful keeping of order which had
distinguished other strikes gave way, and fires occurred at
the docks which could hardly have been caused by anything but incendiarism. The military were called out.
But the strike never became a widespread movement
affecting other ports, and it ended after six weeks in the
defeat of the men.

In June a trouble of a different kind descended upon
the nation. While the fleet in the Mediterranean was
carrying out some tactical exercises, the flagship, the
Victoria, was rammed broadside by the *Camperdown*, and
sank so rapidly that the Admiral in command, thirty-three
officers, and three hundred and twenty men were drowned.
The reason for the accident appeared to be that orders
given for a certain turning movement of the two lines, in
which the fleet was being handled, had been based on an
error in calculating the distance between the lines, and
the *Victoria* and the *Camperdown*, the leading ships,
instead of clearing one another in the turn, came into
collision. The news appalled the country, and was a
grievous spot in a somewhat sorry year.

[1] See p. 280.

In July temper in the House of Commons grew pugnacious. The committee stage of the Home Rule Bill was placed under the operation of a closure resolution, bringing discussion to an end on successive sections of the Bill at certain hours. Considering the time that had been spent on the Bill, the Government seemed to have no alternative; but the resentment shown was far greater than in the previous applications of that kind of closure under the late Government. It flamed up at the end of the committee stage into a free fight on the floor of the House. Words had been used which created an uproar, and a Nationalist member, who had been shouting at an Ulster member, and could not make him hear in the noise, went to sit by him, to make sure of his hearing. A neighbour of the Ulster member pushed the Nationalist away, and that let loose the fight. The Speaker was sent for, and, as his dignified presence fortunately caused the fighting to die down, the incident terminated there and then. But it seemed to many people in the country characteristic of a misguided session, and of a year of irritable feelings. The summer witnessed a second strike which led to rioting, and this time with more serious results than had occurred at Hull. The prices of coal had been adversely affected by the prevailing weakness of trade, and the masters demanded a reduction of 25 points of the 40 per cent. advances in wages which had been conceded between 1880 and 1890. The strike against the reduction was not universal; the Northumberland and Durham miners never joined it, and the South Wales miners were only involved for a time. The Midlands, Yorkshire and Lancashire were the heart of the strike, and it was in Yorkshire that its most deplorable incident occurred. Men had been imported to work mines in South Wales and South Yorkshire, and the determination of the strikers to prevent this led to violent riots. Soldiers were drafted into those districts, and it happened that at Featherstone in South

Yorkshire a fight against blacklegging occurred on a day
during Doncaster Races, The authorities had unwisely
pursued their usual method of mustering police at Doncaster from other districts, making no special allowance
for the disturbed state of the colliery regions. The result
was that the strikers were able to move far too rapidly,
and did so much damage to the colliery that, when the
military arrived, the mob was completely out of hand.
Orders were given to fire, and two men were killed. This
brought a sharp attack upon Mr Asquith from Mr Keir
Hardie, and an official inquiry was opened. But of course
no blame could be attached ; the colliery was in danger of
being entirely wrecked, and the action of the mob, whatever its excuse, was not technically defensible. The
report made by the committee of inquiry was that the
soldiers were justified in firing ; and the whole matter
could only survive as one more grievance of the socialists
against capital. Capital on its own side was not blind to
the suggestions of counter-combination which the strike
conveyed. In September there was no little talk of the
formation of a huge Coal Trust, which should maintain
the prices of coal. The ordinary point of view was that
it was all very well for the miners to talk about a living
wage, but, if the public would not buy the commodity,
how could an artificial standard of wages be kept up ?
This gave a very plausible argument for a coal trust;
by controlling prices, and establishing a sliding scale of
wages in relation to the market, the trust could secure
the men's position. But in point of fact the coalowners
were so far from a spirit of combination that they could not
even stand together during the strike. As the dispute
lengthened out, and the price of coal rose, some of the
masters found the temptation too much for them, and
broke away from their own side, conceding the miners'
terms, in order to have their pits at work. Those who
did so were said to have made fortunes ; but incidentally

they embittered the dispute on both sides. It dragged on throughout the autumn, with various side-issues. A Labour Disputes Bill was introduced at the end of July, to enable the Board of Trade to appoint a conciliator or inquirer in a dispute ; no power was given to enforce any award that might be made, and the Bill was therefore regarded as bloodless. The great work that might be done by an official, inquiring into the two points of view, and acting as a channel of communication, was hardly likely to be foreseen at a time when strikes were at their sharpest. A more curious concomitant of the present strike was the spirit displayed at the annual meeting of the Chambers of Commerce in September. Never before had the gradual change from the old idea of free competition to a desire for State interference shown itself so clearly. The resolution in favour of compulsory arbitration boards had a fairly obvious connection with recent events. But it was curious to see the same spirit which animated working men moving now in the trading classes, in resolutions in favour of a State system of secondary education, of a reduction of railway rates, of graduated taxation designed to relieve the trading middleman, and of the creation of a department of Government for commercial affairs. It was small wonder that the philosophical economists, looking on, should say that socialism was now only a question of the degree to which State action was invoked, and was no longer a battle-ground between classes. This kind of comment was rendered much more possible by a change in the attitude of the leaders of professed socialism, a change which corrected the somewhat violent swinging of the pendulum during the disputes of the late eighties in London. May day of 1893 was made the occasion for the issue of a new socialist manifesto. It was the work rather of Mr Bernard Shaw, Mr Sidney Webb, and the Fabians, than of William Morris and the older school. It formulated definitely the return to political economy in its pronouncement that moralisation of the conditions of a capitalist society would not serve as an ideal. Complete ownership by the community of the means of wealth, and the end of the wage-system, must be the goal. At the same time the manifesto repudiated the anarchist tendencies which had made their appearance, not so much in actual violence, as in the doctrine that all tinkering reform should be opposed, in order that the flood might gather for revolution. The new manifesto, on the contrary, urged that all ameliorative measures should be accepted, as giving the workman more leisure and more equipment to work for a new social order. In practice, therefore, socialists would use their efforts for an eight-hours day, for the establishment of a minimum living wage, for the suppression of sweating and sub-contracting, and for universal suffrage. In other words, the socialist would not stand outside politics, but would be in the midst of them, distinguishable from a Radical only by the end he kept in view, and not at all by his conduct at any given time. Fifteen years later it was to be difficult for many Liberals to say whether they were socialists or not.

An immediate sequel to this new attitude on the part of the socialists was the formation of the Independent Labour Party. An earlier attempt to form such a party in 1888 had failed. In 1893 a conference was held in Bradford, with better results, and the I.L.P. was constituted, "with the object of securing the collective ownership of all the means of production, distribution and exchange, by means of direct Labour representation in Parliament and on local authorities." It was the natural outcome of the arrival in Parliament of the new spirit infused into trade unions during the eighties—of Mr Keir Hardie's tweed cap and brass band. He was elected the first President of the party.

When the Home Rule Bill at last went to the House of

Lords, at the beginning of September, its course was speedily run. There had already been one small brush between the two Houses. The London County Council, in its Bill for constructing a proper approach to the south side of the Tower Bridge, attempted once more to establish the " betterment " principle. It had asked for the support of other corporations, and so much ground had been won for the idea since its inception that its advocates in the House were not confined to one side. The clause, after passing the Commons, was cut out of the Bill by the Lords. But on the return of the Bill, the Commons insisted by a majority of 221 to 88 on the retention of the clause, many Unionists voting for it, although the stronghold of Unionism—Birmingham—had not been persuaded to support the principle. The Lords, however, were in no mood for agreement, and again struck out the clause. For the Irish Bill they mustered in astonishing force. Lord Spencer moved the second reading on 5th September ; the Duke of Devonshire moved the rejection of the Bill ; and on 8th September the House divided. There were 41 votes for the Bill, and 419 against it. The division has certainly one feature of interest. Some measure of the almost passionate feeling against Home Rule is given by the great size of the vote. That in September, sacred month of sport, the House of Lords should have felt it necessary not only to reject the Bill—fifty men could have done that—but to overwhelm it, to obliterate it, to stamp it out of existence, shows what kind of opposition had been aroused.

Mr Gladstone had let it be known, before the Bill was introduced, that he did not intend to make its inevitable rejection by the House of Lords a ground for immediate dissolution. The Commons had turned to other work. They took up, not the two large and controversial measures which had been formally introduced early in the session, but two of a sound popular appeal. One was the Parish

Councils Bill, extending the system of local government to smaller areas than the counties, and the other, which chiefly occupied the remainder of the year in Parliament, was an Employers' Liability Bill, one more amendment of the existing Acts. It brought domestic servants under the Act; and it also cleared away the last confusions about "common employment," making the employer liable for accidents due to the negligence of a fellow-workman. A more doubtful provision was that allowing the removal to the High Court of a claim for more than £100; the value of compensation to a workman's family would be seriously diminished by months of delay. The real point of struggle, however, was in the repeal of the power of "contracting out" of liability. The chief justification for "contracting out" had been the existence in very many cases of accident insurance societies, maintained by large firms for the benefit of their workmen; it was reasonably argued that, if employers were to be liable, without distinction, to actions for compensation, none of them would add to their burden the maintenance of such societies.

In October the distress and disturbance of the coal strike grew so serious that the mayors of the Midland towns met to try to arrange a settlement. As this was just the period at which some of the masters were giving way, the opportunity was hardly favourable, and the attempt failed. For another month the dispute remained as it was. Then the Government was moved to intervene, and was able to arrange a conference of fourteen coal-owners and fourteen representatives of the miners, to meet at the Foreign Office under the chairmanship of Lord Rosebery. Not only did the conference succeed in coming to terms, but it laid the foundation of a system which was to prove as lasting an instrument of negotiation between masters and men as the Brooklands agreement in the cotton trade. Their immediate point the men won;

they were to return to work at their old wages, not subject
to the deduction the masters originally claimed, until 1st
February 1894 ; and meanwhile a Conciliation Board of
fourteen from each side, under an impartial chairman,
was to consider the position and make an award.

For the moment, however, the advanced labour men
were concerning themselves with " the right to work."
The directions to Poor Law authorities under the Act of
1818 were recalled, and in December Mr Keir Hardie
moved a resolution in the House expressing the new idea.
But he found only thirty-three to support him, and the
general opinion was that the efforts of Poor Law authorities
to deal with unemployment by providing work were inevitably wasteful.   A Mansion House Conference reported
at the end of the year against the notion of relief works,
saying that the employment which could be provided in
that way was only intermittent, and the knowledge that
it was being provided attracted men out of work in other
places, so producing a worse congestion of labour.   A
deputation to Mr Gladstone on the subject took place on
28th December, and received a reply on lines similar to
those of the report.

Far more directly profitable was a widely spread discussion which arose out of the debates on the Employers'
Liability Bill.   The question of what could fairly be called
ground for compensation brought up the case of trade
injuries, which were not, strictly speaking, accidents.
The most flagrant instance was that of lead poisoning,
caused by glazing processes in the manufacture of china
and earthenware, which had in the previous year been
declared by the Home Secretary a dangerous trade, under
the terms of the Act of 1891.   Mr John Burns and other
Labour members had spoken very strongly in the course of
the debates, and a committee had been appointed by the
Home Office.   It reported that it was unable to recommend
the prohibition by law of the use of white lead in such pro-

cesses ; but it endorsed to the full the terrible charges which had been made.   Certain administrative rules were proposed, and it was hoped that by insistence on better ventilation, to carry off the powdered lead in the air, and better provisions for cleanliness on the part of the workers engaged, the use of white lead might be rendered almost, if not quite, innocuous.

In truth the mind of the ordinary public was not concerned with the doings of this long-lingering session.   Its real interest in December was the Ardlamont murder trial. A baffling case had arisen out of the death at the end of August of a young man of considerable possessions in Scotland.   He had been found one day shot on his estate at Ardlamont, and his tutor, a man named Monson, was arrested.   The trial took place in Scotland, and ended in the Scottish verdict of "not proven."   It expressed probably the feelings of most of those who had followed the case ; and they were by far the greater part of the population.

Those who hardly found the murder a subject to their taste had enough to discuss in a new play, *The Second Mrs Tanqueray*, which made its appearance in the autumn of this year.   It seemed at the time to be a portentous change in native drama, which had hitherto shown no inclination towards a theatrical presentation of social or moral problems.   Such indigenous character as it had shown hitherto was rather in the vein of caricature, and, at the best, of comedy.   The burlesques of notable operas, which succeeded one another steadily at the famous Gaiety Theatre, were an imported idea ; but the Gilbert and Sullivan "comic operas" were an entirely native product, and in the early nineties a new form of entertainment, more loosely constructed, and amounting sometimes to little more than a series of "star" turns connected by a vague thread of story, had grown up out of the "comic operas."   It was so successful that people with a serious interest in the theatre began to think that the taste for the modern music halls was going to be the death of the drama in England. This feeling had coincided curiously with a largely increased interest, among people of social standing, in the theatre as such, and in artists of the theatre. It had not been an interest in drama; indeed *The Times*, in commenting on it, remarked complacently that no menace to British standards of morals and conventions was to be apprehended from the new fashion of going to see the performances of French plays by French theatrical companies in London. But comedy had undergone a revival in the works of Wilde and Barrie; and the Independent Theatre had gathered a public for the drama of social ideas. The theatres were ready for a bid in this direction, and *The Second Mrs Tanqueray* was produced. It gave us an actress of a wholly new type in Mrs Patrick Campbell; and it also gave London engrossing matter of small talk for the winter.

CHAPTER XVI

1894: LE BOURGEOIS ÉPATÉ

THE year that followed was not devoid of important political events. It witnessed the withdrawal of Mr Gladstone from Parliament, the production of the Death Duties Budget, the enunciation of the "two-Power standard" as a naval ideal, and other incidents less lasting in their effect. But the year bears quite as deeply marks of the shocks experienced in its course by the respectable strata of England, from the height of the upper ranks of the services, and the professions, down to the levels of retail trade. It was a year in which the face of a startled *bourgeoisie* looks out from every month. None of the shocks came from quite unexpected directions; but they were not the less startling.

Early in the year the rather vague horror of anarchism was focussed by an extraordinary explosion in Greenwich Park; during a fog on 15th February a Frenchman, Bourdin, was blown to pieces by a bomb which he was carrying. The incident followed closely on the execution in Paris of a man named Vaillant, who had thrown a bomb into the Chamber of Deputies. It followed also a long period of more or less reasonable uneasiness in England about the currents and cross-currents of socialism. The case of the Walsall anarchists [1] had given unnecessary prominence to a small group which had formed itself inside the Labour movement. Yet that it was not wholly a negligible group is clear from the repudiation of anarchism in the new socialist manifesto of May day 1893. There

[1] See p. 317.

had been a new tone in the meetings of men on Tower Hill ; the unemployed were still numerous, still united in a kind of loose organisation by daily meetings ; and they varied the monotony of meetings by parading the West End squares. But their actions would have had less importance if they had not succeeded in catching public attention by a disgusting phrase; their favourite threat was to send police and officials " to heaven by chemical parcel post." [1] About this time, too, a club of foreign anarchists in Soho became a familiar name to the public—the Autonomie Club. Upon these definite things respectable people vented a great deal of respectable fury. The abuse by anarchists of the asylum offered by this country to foreign refugees, the inertness of the police in the matter of the Autonomie Club (which can hardly, once it was so well known, have been the source of any anxiety to the police), the threats uttered at Tower Hill meetings, had led to many murmurings before the Greenwich explosion acted as detonator to all the stored-up anger. Writers of letters to the newspapers had their counterparts among humbler people who thought dynamite, like knives in a quarrel, a " dirty foreign trick," and the funeral procession which followed Bourdin was attacked by a mob near Fitzroy Square. Many foreigners had gathered there to see it pass, and though the police diverted the procession in order to avoid an outbreak, the anti-anarchist forces deployed on the new route in time to make a very considerable riot. Throughout the year the smallest excuse served for a little homily to Labour men or to trade unions on their neighbourhood to these deplorable anarchists.

The solid kind of Briton, who presented a less disturbed front to these anxieties, suffered from qualms of a more searching nature. The national solidity itself was, he

[1] The phrase was in existence some years earlier, but it now became common.

lamented, being sapped. The Pre-Raphaelite painters, whose work he had regarded as maundering and unhealthy, he now saw acclaimed. The death of Ford Madox Brown in 1893 had called forth the warmest appreciations of his work and his influence ; now in the very beginning of 1894 the solid Briton read that Burne-Jones had been made a baronet, and rubbed his eyes still more in amazement. He began to feel himself a stranger in his own art-dealers' rooms. If he went to the theatre he saw a procession of " women with a past " following *The Second Mrs Tanqueray* across his stage. When he read novels he found books like *Keynotes*, *The Yellow Aster*, *Dodo* and *Esther Waters*, upsetting equally his views of what women should be thinking about and his idea of what novelists should write about. *The Yellow Book* presented the work of Aubrey Beardsley to his astonished eyes. On country roads he met women not only riding bicycles, which he had not as yet admitted to be a proper occupation for them, but actually riding them without the hampering accompaniments of either a skirt or a chaperon. The " new woman " with her symbolical latch-key was a purely middle-class product ; and she shook that class profoundly. She was so mixed in her qualities. It was all very well to have a wholesome dislike of her novels and dismiss them as neurotic ; but somehow she had a way of presenting herself also in athletic shapes on the tennis-lawn or the golf-links (the latter were just now sadly depleting the former, and the " tennis girl " was dropping out of fashion) which defied the Briton to be otherwise than proud of her. Then just when he was feeling proud, the same girls would light cigarettes, and talk slang, or they would thunder round ballrooms in the *pas de quatre*. If he consoled himself with the thought that after all not every young man was too decadent, or every young woman too emancipated, to think of one another, he was reminded by the charming *Dolly Dialogues* that, even when they did think about one another, they did it in strange new ways which no old-fashioned Briton could wholly approve.

Such cross-currents made the national temper a complex thing for any Government to ride ; and now the Liberal Government had to ride it without Mr Gladstone's control. His resignation of the Premiership was inevitable, yet it could not have been more inopportune for his party. Even before the labour of the second Home Rule Bill he had been forced to recognise a failure in himself, not of intellectual but of physical powers—and among those only of his hearing and his eyesight—which he could not but admit to be the limit of his political career.[1] He had been able to give the Bill not only his constant guidance in the House, but that exacting measure of guidance which his high standard of duty demanded ; he had been able to take his very large share in the work of a long session. When therefore, with the New Year, rumours arose of his intention to retire they carried no conviction. Mr Gladstone was at Biarritz in January, and he returned to the somewhat dismal winding-up of the session. In his own mind his course of action had been settled. The immediately determining cause, sufficing to turn the scale in the final moment of decision, was disagreement with his colleagues in the matter of the Naval Estimates ; he could not accept a policy of dominant naval power in Europe without reference to any particular question of the day [2] ; and such a policy had in effect been the outcome of the naval defence agitations of the past few years. The question of the efficiency of the navy had been raised in a vague way, and efficiency cannot be determined without a standard. No current events provided one. The only thing that could provide it was an assertion of dominance in Europe ; and to that assertion Mr Gladstone declined

[1] Morley's *Life of Gladstone,* iii. 496.
[2] *Ibid.* iii. 508.

to subscribe.[1] This was enough to give him the parting
of the ways which otherwise, at a juncture of no favourable
presage for his colleagues, he would have been the last
man to see.

The whole overgrown session left the Liberals with but
one harvested sheaf—the Parish Councils Bill—and that
not perfect in their eyes ; the House of Lords had introduced alterations in it. But rather than lose this measure
also the Government accepted the alterations. They did
not affect the main structure of the Bill. The Urban
District Councils which it set up were the old urban
sanitary authorities renamed and made elective ; they
controlled matters of drainage, roads, infectious diseases
and lighting ; they had power to promote private Bills,
though the Local Government Board watched this power
jealously, and only permitted its exercise in cases in
which a Provisional Order could not be made ; and they
had the County Council's power of delegating work to
committees. The Rural District Councils were newer
authorities. The sharpest point of controversy in ·the
Bill was that providing that the Rural District councillor
should represent his parish on the Board of Guardians.
As the rural district and the union were most frequently
identical in boundary this meant a popularly elected
Board of Guardians, and the electoral qualification was
lower than any ever yet known, no property stipulations
being attached to it. Hence the strength of that attack
upon the Bill which consisted in pointing out that the
electors of the new Guardians were very largely prospective, or at least possible, candidates for relief. Parish
Councils, which were the final subdivision of the new Local
Government, were given certain powers as to sanitation
and highways, without becoming statutory authorities
for these duties ; and they were also given powers, which

[1] He went so far as to speak in private of the Naval Estimates as
" mad and drunk."

were to become more important later on, in regard to the provision of allotments.

No other Bill of importance had survived. The Home Rule Bill had been rejected by the House of Lords, the Employers' Liability Bill so fundamentally changed that the Government abandoned it. The Lords had insisted on the retention of the clause permitting " contracting out." But although meetings here and there might show signs of indignation, the feelings of the country were not strongly roused. Could Mr Gladstone have roused them ? He felt that the time had come at any rate for an attempt—that the virtual destruction of the work of an exhausting session could be made " the right moment for a searching appeal to public opinion." [1] From Biarritz he suggested dissolution to his colleagues, but received a " hopelessly adverse reply." It must have been a somewhat dreary state of mind which dictated the reply ; and it gave, no doubt, a fresh impulse to Mr Gladstone's inclinations towards retirement. Even amid all the rumour and expectation of his retirement no one recognised his farewell to Parliament. On 1st March he spoke on the acceptance of the Lords' amendments to the Parish Councils Bill, and when, "upright as ever, and walking fast, with his despatch-box dangling from his right hand," [2] he had passed behind the Speaker's chair, members dispersed talking casually about the speech. Only one or two men, as they left the precincts of the House, were struck by the sudden thought that they would probably never hear Mr Gladstone in Parliament again. In two days members were talking about that speech in new tones ; and those whose eyes had not happened to follow Mr Gladstone on that day knew that they had missed the historic sight of his final withdrawal from the House he had entered sixty-one years before.

[1] Morley's *Life of Gladstone*, iii. 505.
[2] Mr G. W. E. Russell's *One Look Back*.

On 3rd March he handed his resignation to the Queen. Generations to whom his name conveys less of love, as well as less of hatred, than it conveyed to his own time, read with astonishment the account of that final interview. It is from Mr Gladstone himself that we have it, in phrases of the greatest dignity, untouched by injured feelings.[1] At the first moment, indeed, the Queen showed apparent emotion, but she promptly recovered herself, so completely that she marked the close of over fifty years of public service by thanking her aged minister for—" a service of no great merit, in the matter of the Duke of Coburg " ! Otherwise there was " not one syllable on the past." He had slipped quietly out of the House of Commons ; Queen Victoria allowed him to slip quietly out of Windsor Castle. He himself was thinking, finely enough, less of the past than of the future. He knew how much might depend on the appointment of his successor ; already the rumours concerning him had given rise to some strong expressions among Liberals as to the need, at such a moment of conflict between the two Houses, of keeping the Premiership in the House of Commons. Mr Gladstone, curious as it may seem in view of his recent wish to dissolve on that conflict, did not agree with this feeling. He intended, if he were consulted, to advise the Queen to send for Lord Spencer ; and although there is no established custom of the Crown asking advice in such matters, Mr Gladstone might be pardoned for feeling that his unparalleled length of service and his unique position with his party would have rendered his advice in this case most valuable. It was, indeed, unbelievable to the Liberal party that Mr Gladstone was not consulted by the Queen. He had opportunity to intimate to Sir Henry Ponsonby, the Queen's private secretary, that he had " something serious to say," if the Queen commanded him. She preferred to take her own course, and on 6th March the Liberal party

[1] Morley's *Life of Gladstone*, iii. 513, 514.

found itself under the leadership not only of a peer, but of a peer who was comparatively young, and had taken no great part in recent struggles. The Queen had entrusted the formation of the new Ministry to Lord Rosebery. It must be noted that, if Mr Gladstone had been consulted, the party would none the less have found itself led by a peer. The truth was that, had a leader been sought for in the Commons, the choice must necessarily have fallen on Sir William Harcourt ; and his was a character which many of his colleagues would have found intolerably overbearing in a Prime Minister. He would beyond doubt have found great difficulty in forming a Cabinet. Lord Rosebery, on the other hand, had no trouble in securing the co-operation of his colleagues; they were loyal beyond what might have been expected. But two days after the opening of the new session, which took place on 1st March, the Government sustained a defeat on the Address. Mr Labouchere, who led the Radical feeling against the House of Lords, and scoffed at the policy of carrying on Government and allowing the Lords to " fill the cup of iniquity " by rejecting more measures, until the country should find the situation too much to bear, moved an amendment to the Address, praying the Queen to end the power of the House of Lords to deal drastically with measures passed by the House of Commons. A combination of Radicals and Irish members with some other members carried this amendment by 147 votes to 145. It was not of course thought for a moment that the new Government would resign on such a vote, but it made at least an uneasy start. Then the Home Rule odium, which Lord Rosebery had done his best to escape by all means short of actually repudiating Home Rule (if indeed they *were* short of it), was revived by a discussion of a proposal to send all Scottish Bills to a Scottish Grand Committee, which was accompanied immediately by a proposal from a young Welsh member,

Mr Lloyd George, for a similar Grand Committee for Wales.

Fortunately Sir William Harcourt was able this year to introduce the Death Duties Budget which had been postponed the year before ; and this measure was Radical enough, in its imposts on large accumulations of property, and accompanying extension of abatements of Income Tax on the lower scales of incomes, to pull the party together. The new duties were a tax on all property, real or personal, settled or not settled, passing on the death of any person dying after 1st August 1894 ; the tax varied from £1 per cent. on estates over £100 but under £500, up to £15 per cent. on estates over a million sterling. Naturally the proposal roused the sharpest opposition ; the extreme criticism was that this doctrine amounted to an assertion that the State had a right to what property a man left behind him, and that the succession to it of his heirs would be for the future only a matter of indulgence. However, Sir William Harcourt managed his Bill with patience and so much command of the House that the Bill made admirable progress without any use of severe forms of procedure, and was despatched by the House of Commons in July. It included an enhanced Beer Tax. There had been a deficit of two and a quarter millions to meet (not a single European country, as it happened, escaped a deficit this year) [1] ; and although the new death duties would in time be very profitable they were for the present somewhat counterbalanced by the extension of Income Tax abatements ; and the Naval Estimates were heavy. There was no great sympathy with the brewers' outcry against the increased taxation of beer ; but the Local Veto Bill was in existence, and the extra sixpence a barrel was therefore regarded by its victims less as a piece of taxation than as an act of political warfare.

[1] See the *Punch* cartoon, 27th January 1894.

The Local Veto Bill was dropped later in the session. It had had the disastrous effect of irritating moderate people all over the country, and this, far more than the active opposition of the licensed victualling trade, was the cause of the Bill's extreme unpopularity. There was a growing belief that the drinking habits of the country were undergoing a profound modification from changes in public opinion, which would be more effective and more lasting than any reforms by legislation could be. Lord Randolph Churchill, who had lately been devoting himself to the licensing question, had found it thorny and unfruitful.

The Naval Estimates for which the Budget had to provide showed the serious advance of three millions. That tendency to pursue a policy of dominance in European naval affairs with which Mr Gladstone had tried to contend, was given alike an impulse and a standard of effort by the visit in this year of the Russian fleet to Toulon, in demonstration of the treaty which had been negotiated between France and Russia. The meeting of the two allied fleets set comparisons going; and the general overhauling of our state of defence, which had occupied the minds of anxious members of the public for months past, was followed by discussions of whether Great Britain had or had not a navy superior to the allied fleets. From this year, therefore, we may date the appearance of the "two-Power standard" as a controlling consideration in naval policy.

Meanwhile in another kind of rivalry some attempt was being made to reform our system of secondary education; the example of Germany and her growing mastery in trading methods were perpetually being dinned into the ears of the Government. A Royal Commission on Secondary Education was appointed in March, notable, if for nothing else, for the fact that it included three women commissioners—Lady Frederick Cavendish, Mrs Henry Sidgwick and Mrs Sophie Bryant. There was, however, a strong feeling that if Germany afforded England a warning of one kind, France offered a contrary one in her immense production of men educated to the level of clerkdom and petty officialism. The National Union of Teachers was asking itself whether any real elementary education, beyond the acquisition of a cheap veneer, was in existence. On the other hand, a man of such sober stamp as the Duke of Devonshire, not at all likely to be misled by superficial appearances, was telling a Lancashire audience in November that great changes in outlook had already been wrought, and that working people had now not only the education that enabled them to earn money, but the far more valuable education that taught them how to expend it. German influence was not without its effect in higher spheres of education: in this year Oxford at last established a "research degree," to be attained by a post-graduate course of study open to those who were not members of the university. In May Professor Henry Morley died. He had taken no small share in the spreading of inexpensive culture, as distinct from mere education, by editing the most successful series current at the time of cheap reprints of the best English literature and translations of foreign classics.

In April the long and difficult work of the Royal Commission on Labour Disputes came to an end with the publication of its report. It was not a very vigorous document. Even the much-discussed solution of difficulties by the establishment of industrial tribunals received but tentative support. The report pointed out that the strength of trade unions varied so much that no general system of tribunals could be proposed. Moreover such bodies could only deal, in the opinion of the commission, with interpretation of existing conditions; voluntary arbitration boards alone could be useful where a change of conditions was in question. The more direct recommendations were, firstly, that the Board of Trade should be given more distinct powers for appointing arbitrators : " if the same persons were frequently appointed they would become arbitration experts, and might then have some kind of permanent appointment " ; and, secondly, that the Factory Acts should be more stringently applied, with a view to driving out badly managed industries dependent on cheap alien labour, which tended to lower wages. The commission also suggested that a better definition of " picketing " by trade unions was necessary. A supplement to the report appeared later in the form of some suggestions made by the Duke of Devonshire and other members of the commission, to the effect that associations both of employers and employed should be given existence as statutory corporations, so that either could be sued for breach of contract—a liability which, while it would not prevent strikes, might check hastiness in entering upon them. The question immediately raised by this notion was whether the power to enforce subscriptions from members, which a corporation possesses, would be held by the trade unions to countervail the liability to be sued as unions for the torts of members. A further supplement, being a separate report on the conditions of agricultural labour, was only interesting in that it spoke of those conditions as much improved, and the buying power of the rural labourer as much advanced. The whole report was hardly one on which action could be taken. No one was in a mood for small tinkerings of the problem. On the one hand the alarm about anarchism—a debate in January on the report of the committee of inquiry into the Featherstone riots kept alive the inclination to take panic-stricken views of labour unrest—was hardening feeling against trade unions, the congresses of which had for some years grown more and more socialistic in tone. On the other side the return from the old attitude of detachment from purely political controversy, the revulsion towards the use of

12

parliamentary power, had grown so strong that socialist
leaders were announcing their intention to abandon strikes
in favour of an organised effort by political action to obtain
control of the means of production.[1]   The same spirit was
working in the unions ; the presidential address at the
Trade Union Congress in September turned on the idea
that " Legislate " was to become more and more the
watchword of the movement.   Caught somewhat in a
tender spot by this new enthusiasm, Conservatives began
to remember uncomfortably that between the two political
parties the difference in regard to State interference was
one only of degree, not of principle ; and while this might
have mattered little so long as the interference was not at
the dictation of Labour, but was pure benevolence, Tories
felt it time to draw back when the new force proposed
to take a hand in the interference.   Consequently even
Mr Chamberlain's programme, little as it really carried of
the true labour sentiment, was more brusquely treated
by his allies when he revived it this year than it had
been on its appearance in 1893.[2]   The freedom of the
year from serious strike troubles failed to reassure the
anxious *bourgeois*.   The only strike of any note was one
of cabmen in London in the summer.   It turned partly
on the now common objection of unionists to working
with non-unionists, but chiefly on a question of the
charges made by the cab-owners for the hire of cabs.   The
strike lasted nearly a month, much to the inconvenience
of London at the height of its season ; and it ended in
the diminution of the masters' charges, balanced by the
men's abandonment of their objection to non-unionists
in the yards.   A small incidental complaint of the men is
noteworthy as a sign of changing customs ; there were now,
they said, so many large Stores that ladies, when they went

[1] See, *e.g.*, a letter by Mr Hyndman in *The Times*, 16th May
1894.

[2] *The Times*, 17th October 1894.

shopping, had less need of cabs than they had in the old days, when they were obliged to journey from shop to shop. The Coal Conciliation Board made its award, and secured peace in that industry for a time by renewing the two last 5 per cent. advances in wages until 1st January 1896; the men on their side showing less tendency to take the uncompromising position that wages should not depend upon, but govern, market prices.

The great event of the early summer, however, concerned none of these things, but was the Derby Day, when Lord Rosebery won with Ladas. He was never secure after that in his leadership of the Liberal party. His achievement was one more of the shocks of the year to an ultra-respectable public. Not a very great number, perhaps, went with the National Anti-Gambling League and its spokesman, Mr Hawke, in demanding that Lord Rosebery should choose between the Premiership and the Turf. But there were certainly many who felt that Turf interests, if not actively harmful, were not a dignified trait in the successor of Mr Gladstone; many again who felt that a party recently vocal against the gilded irresponsibilities of the peers was oddly led to triumph at Epsom. Add these mixed feelings to the prejudices and disaffection under which Lord Rosebery entered on his Premiership, and the result was enough disagreement in the party to render it somewhat ineffective. The famous Budget passed the House of Lords without a division; it enjoyed the traditional impunity of a Finance Bill in that House. But the Evicted Tenants Bill, founded on the work of the commission whose appointment had been one of the first acts of the new Government in 1893, was thrown out; and went to help in the "filling of the cup." In effect the Bill would have authorised an evicted tenant in Ireland to regain his farm over the landlord's head by decree of the Estates Commissioners, if the landlord had acted "unreasonably" in the eviction. For a time Liberal concern

for Ireland occupied itself with the Royal Commission on
Financial Relations between Ireland and Great Britain,
which was designed to remove from the path of the next
Home Rule Bill a difficulty which had greatly impeded
the two Bills of Mr Gladstone. A Registration Acceleration
Bill (which incidentally gave one more chance for the
Woman Suffragists to advance their claims) was dropped.
In spite of their apparent truculence, the House of Lords
chose this year to pass the principle of " betterment "
against which they had stood firm until now. The committee was composed of such peers as Lord Halsbury, Lord
Salisbury, Lord Egerton of Tatton, Lord Belper and Lord
Onslow ; it is evident that the principle must have made
considerable headway with the general public. This
removed the final difficulty in the completion of the Tower
Bridge, by making possible an adequate approach from
the south side ; the bridge itself was finished and was
formally opened in June.

From time to time during 1894 South African affairs
came disturbingly into view. The British South Africa
Company had been engaged in war with the Matabele, and
the dual position of Mr Cecil Rhodes, who was now Prime
Minister of Cape Colony as well as managing director of
the Chartered Company, was apt to lead to situations in
which he appeared to be using the authority of the one
office to advance the interests of the other. He had cast a
glamour over the British public ; his vigorous imagination
had made so vivid the idea of a British South Africa,
" which must ultimately mean the whole region south of
the Zambesi," [1] that it appeared as almost an established
national policy. Consequently when in the summer the
question of the status of British subjects in the
Transvaal was raised again, the Boers found themselves
addressed less as the independent nation which they were
in their own eyes than as a population which was rather

[1] *The Times*, 20th June 1894.

obstinately delaying a general federation of South Africa. A " Transvaal National Union " was set on foot, to demand the franchise for all foreigners resident in the Transvaal ; and its proceedings were strong enough to bring upon it a temperate reminder from England that the grant of the franchise must, by all international custom, deprive its members of their previous nationality, a dilemma little to their taste, since serious trouble had but just been avoided this year by the abandonment of the Boer claim to the right of " commandeering " alien residents. If they ceased to be aliens, there would be no grounds for refusing military service. The situation in the Transvaal in general had been so much upset by the numbers of immigrants in connection with the mines, and by the vast wealth which those mines enabled a section of the foreign population to wield, that President Kruger was requesting, as yet without any aggressive tone, a revision of the constitution established by the Convention of London.

In the autumn the licensing sessions of the London County Council produced more shocks for the respectable. The growth of the taste for music halls has already been noted more than once. The placing of the licensing authority for such halls in the hands of the council brought a new spirit of criticism to bear upon them. The kind of human traffic which could be left unanalysed—or at any rate *was* left unanalysed—among the various elements that made up the attractions of the old " gardens " of Vauxhall and Ranelagh and Cremorne became somewhat too obvious in the more confined spaces of a music hall. Moreover certain specific performances, especially in this year the presentations of " Living Pictures " on the stage, once they had definitely shocked some people, could hardly be passed over in silence at licensing sessions. But prudery is easily pushed into an ugly and unpopular position, and, on the whole, public opinion sided with the music halls ; the latter, too wise to be defiant, moderated their customs enough to tide over the attack of the champions of morality.

Another kind of alarm worried the middle class, in respect to its pockets. In January the Manchester Ship Canal was opened, but without any enthusiasm from those who had subscribed the millions sunk in its construction. Early hopes had been dashed by the great discrepancy between the estimated and the actual cost of the work; and the enterprise was now felt to be launched rather in faith than in hope. For the general investing public, the South African booms, first in gold mines, and secondly in chartered company projects, had produced a very speculative market in which the company promoter had gone to work. The consequence was that, in a time not otherwise bad for trade, millions were being lost every year; the report of the Inspector-General in Liquidation published this year showed that in 1892 the public had lost no less than twenty-five millions by investments in more or less fraudulent companies. The Board of Trade once more set up an inquiry into company law.

Another activity of that Board marks the practical development at last of an enterprise which we found making several false starts in the early eighties. The time had arrived for considering seriously the regulations which Government should apply to the establishment of electric traction on tramways; and the Board of Trade called various experts in consultation. Ten years earlier the propulsion of trams by transmission of current from overhead wires to motors on the car had been successfully achieved in Kansas City, U.S.A. Here was the idea which obviated all the old difficulties, alike of carrying stored power in cells and laying down "live" rails. But no example of its use occurred in England until November 1891, when the Roundhay Electric Tramway at Leeds, five and a half miles in length, was

opened. It was owned by the corporation, but leased
to a company. Its success was now established, and
immense developments of the principle were so certain
that the Government regulations of this year set free
an abundant stream of enterprise. Municipalities which
already owned tramways set to work to convert them to
the new system; and those which did not found a fresh
incentive to purchase the undertakings of private companies, since electricity now promised efficient, clean,
quiet and cheap traction. The London County Council
at once advanced its purchase schemes energetically, and
they became prominent in municipal history, because the
council based its terms of purchase on a calculation of
what it would have had to spend to construct the tramway,
a basis which was bitterly attacked as unfair to the companies. At the very last moment, so to speak, of tramway
development, one more invention of a different kind of
propulsion made its appearance. It is of less interest
as a belated tramway invention than as a sign of the
influence of the internal combustion motor. It was a
gas-driven tramcar, using engines of the Otto type,
exploding gas in the piston-cylinders by means of an
electric spark.

England was still watching helplessly the advance of
motor-car invention abroad. From her own roads such
cars were banned. The chief centre of activity was
France, where several firms were now showing what
astonishing power and force internal combustion engines
could produce. In this year a race of motor cars from
Paris to Rouen was organised, and the results gave a
great impetus to the industry.

In December, Robert Louis Stevenson died at the
height of a fame in England which, however much it may
have been intensified by the knowledge of his gallant,
even gay, struggle against fatal illness, was genuine and
not sentimental. He brought the frank adventure-book

back to the shelf from which, since the death of Mayne
Reid, it had been pushed down by the new analytical
school and reduced to the level of " books for boys," a
shelf which in January of this year suffered a loss in the
death of R. M. Ballantyne. Stevenson had the gift of
impressing romance upon the streets and the daily life of
a great modern city ; and had really prepared the ground
upon which *Sherlock Holmes* was at this time flourishing.
It was, however, rather to his known fight with mortal
disease than to intrinsic merit that his essays owed their
vogue ; they had the appeal of one who looks on at life.
At the same time, their self-conscious grace of style commended them to a middle class still a little conceited
about its newly acquired artistic appreciation. The year
witnessed also the death of the greatest, though the
obscurest, of the prophets of the new appreciation.
Walter Pater died on 30th July. He had exercised a
very great influence on many generations of Oxford
youth, and there could be no clearer symptom of the
general uneasiness of the *bourgeois* at the moment than
the guarded tone of *The Times* in its obituary notice of
him. " That his influence was always healthful," *The
Times* remarked,[1] " we do not pretend to say." A school
of thought which had but recently enunciated the proposition that a colour-sense was more important to the
development of the individual than a sense of right and
wrong, and was continually enunciating propositions of
a similar kind, had appeared a positive devastation to the
respectable mind of the country. Pater's true relation
to this school was as much misapprehended as Pusey's
relation had been to what the same kind of persons had
thought an earlier devastation emanating from Oxford.
Just as Pusey, remote, ascetic, severe, lived in pious
practices far from the extravagances of the Ritualist
movement, so Pater, equally remote, equally pious and

[1] 31st July 1894.

equally stern in personal habit, looked as from a distant
height upon the curious twists given to his devoutly
passionate theory of an existence infinitely sensitive and
responsive.   Yet, inasmuch as he was associated in the
popular mind with the extremes that were rampant at
the moment, it was a happy thing for him that he did not
live to see the year which was to follow.

CHAPTER XVII

1895: A RETURN TO SAFE GROUND

FROM the various undercurrents which were affecting the mind of the solid classes of the country, as well as from its own shortcomings, the Liberal Government now suffered. It had never been firmly seated. It possessed a Gladstonian, and not a generally Liberal, majority. It was genuinely in touch with the Home Rule movement, but very imperfectly in touch with advanced reforming feeling in Great Britain. It did real disservice by producing a throw-back in the growing readiness of the labour organisations to believe in parliamentary action. Yet at the same time it had a vague militancy which seemed to attach it to the spirit of social change and upheaval, regarded by solid minds with anxiety, and even with terror. It produced sweeping measures; its relations with the House of Lords had aspects which lent themselves to charges of promoting class hatred. Little though the Government had been able to achieve, it still aroused nervousness; and its practical powerlessness under the House of Lords was, so far from reassuring the nervous, a source of uneasiness. The launching of projects which were destined to no fulfilment seemed to threaten a dangerous exasperation of Radicals and Socialists. The Socialists and Radicals, on their side, irritated by the existence in office of a party which, concentrating its idealism in Mr Gladstone, had perforce shared his limitations, spoke louder and louder in the effort to gain a hearing for the new demands, an understanding of the new forces.

Mr Gladstone had never distinguished them from the Liberalism which he was accustomed to find at his command.

One man who could recognise these things was Lord Randolph Churchill. If his career had developed to the full, the democratic feeling which reached its triumph in 1906 might have been earlier in the field. The damage done to his career by the presence of new men on his side after the Home Rule split was not solely, or even principally, due to the fact that one of them was Mr Goschen. It was much more due to the fact that one of them was Mr Chamberlain. He brought into the alliance of Conservatives and Unionists a kind of democratic feeling which "blanketed" the much more real feeling of Lord Randolph Churchill. Mr Chamberlain's Radicalism was of that middle-class kind which, disturbing enough in 1880 to a party of landlords, had become by 1888 almost Conservative in its distinction from the newly grown popular demands. It was taken, so to speak, as a homœopathic dose against Lord Randolph Churchill. He, more true to his class than his fellows were, maintained the old spirit of dislike of the manufacturers. The changes of ten years had brought the landlord and the manufacturer together behind his back. The aristocracy was in trade. Scions of great houses acting as touts for business firms provided material for *Punch* to satirise; but the more profound truth was that the vast extension of the limited liability principle in trading, advertised as it had been by Stock Exchange booms, had brought the aristocracy as well as the professional classes, and the upper middle classes generally, into one large new division of the population—the "absentee employer" class. Savings and surplus income went no longer into Government securities; they went into industrial and trading stocks; and thus the labour question was no longer one between workmen and a distinct class of masters of industry, but

between trade unions and the whole conglomerate mass
of investors, who were in effect absentee employers.
Hence Mr Chamberlain's idea of what was democratic
had become, since it was a manufacturer's idea, the
kind of sop which the propertied public could endure to
see administered ; while Lord Randolph Churchill's sense
of a duty to the workman belonged to the old landlord
spirit. Lord Randolph Churchill might have recovered
his ground ; but in the very years in which his rival was
advancing his health gave way. A certain wildness
crept into his too unrelated appearances in public, and
no one would believe that he had outgrown the slashing
days of the Fourth Party. For some time now he had
ceased to be a force in political life, and on 24th January
in this year he died.

Parliament met dejectedly, with a taste of stale gun-
powder on its tongue. During the winter, members of
the Government had tried to rouse some feeling in the
country against the House of Lords ; but no explosion
had followed, and the result was that when the Government was accused of staying in office for the sake of
office, knowing that the country was not with it, its
followers had little choice but to accept this dispiriting
view. The Government's weakness increased the appearance of foolhardy violence in proposals that came before
Parliament. A London Valuation and Assessment Bill,
presented by the London County Council, altering the
whole law of assessment in order to provide a common
basis for imperial and local taxation, fell inevitably under
the ban of the Speaker, on the ground that such a drastic
change was not proper matter for a private Bill. It was
a belated offspring of certain ideas embodied in the
Newcastle programme [1] ; and so was the Plural Voting
Bill, introduced by the Government, providing that all
elections should take place on one day, and that no man

[1] See p. 300.

should vote in more than one constituency.   A private
member's Bill to put an end to nomination, by the Lord
Lieutenant to the Lord Chancellor, of persons for appointment as Justices of the Peace was another drastic proposal.   It arose out of a controversy which had raged
somewhat hotly in 1893, the Tories accusing the Liberal
Lord Chancellor of flagrant party spirit in such appointments (he was said in April 1893 to have appointed
four hundred and thirty-three borough magistrates, of
whom four hundred and one were Home Rulers), and the
Liberals had replied by complaining that, even so, it was
impossible to give their side a fair proportion on the
Bench.   This was, however, hardly a fit matter for a weak
Liberal party to handle by legislation.   The Local Veto
Bill still hung in the air, as did the Welsh Disestablishment
Bill.   A Factory Bill, the chief object of which was more
stringent inspection of factories employing women, and
stricter regulation of their hours, brought upon itself
criticism from two directions.   Women Suffragists attacked it as likely to diminish the employment of women ;
and the Irish party attacked it because by including
laundries [1] it necessitated inspection of convent laundries ;
this in the end caused the Bill to be dropped.   This job
lot of Bills was accompanied by a similar job lot of debates.
Unemployment had recurred with some severity, especially
in the building trade and in agriculture.   The new spread
of education was causing inquiries about the system of
appointments in the Civil Service, which still depended
upon nomination, and there was a debate on this subject.
A motion to keep out foreign prison-made goods, a
tentative scheme by the London County Council for
beginning the purchase of the Water Companies' undertakings in London, an attempt made by the Lancashire
members to have continuous High Court sittings in

[1] A disastrous fire at a laundry in January had brought out the
fact that laundries were not under the Factory Acts.

Lancashire—all these took their turn and disappeared.
The last mentioned was a project not without considerable support at this period.   In 1892 there was a weighty
body of opinion in favour of a sweeping decentralisation
of High Court administration; not only Manchester,
but Liverpool, Birmingham, Sheffield and Leeds might,
it was thought, be given permanent sittings of High
Court judges.   Another legal proposal in 1895 was for the
appointment of a Public Trustee.   There had been some
serious defalcations by solicitors, and five at once were
struck off the rolls in March.   Both the Liberal Lord
Chancellor of the time and the Conservative Lord Chancellor of the last Government were in favour of the
appointment of a Public Trustee.   Two subjects which
had a hold on the general mind took no shape in Parliament.   One was elementary education, which was
becoming a very controversial matter between Voluntary
and Board schools ; and the other was old age pensions.
The committee on the latter [1] reported in April ; the
report was a complex production, including a majority
and a minority report, and a great number of individual
memoranda.   The minority, headed by Mr Chamberlain,
wished to recommend a contributory system of old age
pensions ; the majority contented themselves with making
little more than a statement of the problem of the aged
poor, and recommending certain changes in the method
of administering out-relief.

The feebleness of the House of Commons, the public
knowledge of the Government's futility, were not the only
reasons for the complete lack of interest in parliamentary
proceedings.   Two affairs, each in its different way
serious enough, were distracting people's minds.   In
April the world of solid respectable citizenship, which
had for years suffered in baffled rage the scorn and the
airy superiority of the æsthete and the artist, came to a

[1] See p. 320.

grim, and for the time startling, revenge. Mr Oscar Wilde, at the conclusion of an action for criminal libel which he brought against Lord Queensberry, and lost, was arrested on charges which the plain man took as ample confirmation of the plain man's position—that no one can make a jest of morality and respectability without some flaw in his own morals. The case against Mr Wilde was, of course, no real indictment of æstheticism, but it was the end of the æsthete as he had been felt for fifteen years in social life. It was also lamentably the end of a very brilliant writer. At the moment of Mr Wilde's arrest two comedies by him were being played simultaneously in London, and one of them, *The Importance of Being Earnest*, had revealed in him a genius not only for clothing his comedies in unfailing wit, but for essentially comic construction. In his assertion of the function of criticism, and in his richly varied vocabulary, lay his chief artistic claim. In his social gifts of wit and swiftness lay his most lasting effects. The widespread modern capacity for " taking things with a light hand," the distaste for solemn attitudes and obvious statements, the easy carrying of personal attainments, which formerly had taken some generations of high breeding to produce, may be largely traced to Oscar Wilde's influence. The particular form of wit for which he was most famous, the paradoxical epigram, was not exclusively his ; Whistler was even more brilliant at producing it. But its combination with genuinely social gifts, which Whistler had not, makes Wilde's career the more interesting. He bore a large part in a readjustment of values in life which survived his own fall. The crash of the fall certainly affected the whole spirit of this year. There were few great houses in London where he was not known ; fewer still where there was not among the younger generation an aggressive, irresponsible intolerance which had some relation, however vague, to his brilliant figure. Even athleticism rejoiced at this date to dissociate itself from anything that might have been in danger of easy approval from an older generation, by being also æsthetic ; captains of university football teams had been seen with long hair. There was too much of real revolt in the movement to allow the fate of one man to hold it lastingly in check ; but a certain silence, almost, if not quite, shamefaced, settled for the moment on much of the social life of the country, and this had its part in the obvious impulse, when the General Election came, to return to safe " English " ground in every possible direction.

The other affair, which took much attention, especially as the year drew on, was a heavy slump in South African stocks and shares. The immense fortunes which had been made in that country had rather upset London. The diamond magnate and the gold magnate were building palaces for themselves in the West End, and setting, so to speak, a financial pace which took London's breath away. Speculation increased enormously. Society rushed to the new form of gambling ; women who had never seen " the City " went off in hansoms after breakfast to consult their brokers ; gilded youths in clubs of an afternoon turned the evening papers at once to the list of Stock Exchange quotations. Rich men with no other passport into society were asked to dinner on the chance that they might have good speculative tips to give. What had caused a more acute run on South African ventures was the shadiness at the moment of industrial stocks. The misguided energies of the company promoter were referred to in a recent chapter.[1] The report of the Committee on Company Law, which was published in August of this year, showed that the limited liability capital in Great Britain in 1894 was no less than £1,035,029,835, while in France similar capital was only about £400,000,000, and in Germany £300,000,000. This

[1] See p. 358.

comparison caused the committee to decide that it must be careful not to disturb unnecessarily the employment of wealth, and to remember that prudence and business-like use of wealth could not be inculcated by law. It therefore declined to recommend any of the drastic provisions which had been suggested as to double registration, or a compulsory reserve liability, and confined itself to recommendations as to disclosure of the vendor's name and his price, and as to statutory meetings. But indeed recent events in the industrial market, and some severe writing down of capital, were enough to produce prudence for the moment in that market. The consequent rush to the South African stocks was followed by a serious slump, and what was nearly a panic on the Stock Exchange. The situation was saved by the intervention of some of the magnates, notably Mr Barnato, who stepped in, and bought freely, just in time to prevent a finally disastrous sagging of prices. There was nothing wrong with the gold industry itself. On the contrary, everything pointed to the Rand mines being far more valuable than anyone had at first supposed. A report made in 1893 had placed the value of the reefs at £315,000,000, which meant that all difficulties from shortage of gold supply, and the prospect of a complete revaluation of the world's currency, were removed for at least a generation or two. The gold output of the Rand in 1895 was between 150,000 and 200,000 oz. a month. The slump therefore was not due to any failure or overestimation of the wealth of the gold mines. It turned out, before the year was past, to be the beginning of trouble of a more threatening kind.

Parliament pursued its uninteresting way until the third week in June. It passed with reluctance a vote of £80,000 for a new Colonial possession, Uganda, which the British East Africa Company had left, like a foundling, on the doorstep of the Government. The Government had also recovered its reputation in the matter of Jabez Balfour, the absconding head of the Liberator Society.[1] After two years of the most ingenious proceedings he had at length been extradited by the Argentine Government, and was landed in England and brought up at Bow Street early in May. From time to time since the beginning of 1893 reports had reached home that his extradition was granted; each time an appeal had followed, and all sorts of delays had spun out the proceedings. The last ingenuity had been the discovery that in the province of Argentina, where he was living, there was a law that a plaintiff with a monetary claim against any person possessed the right to prevent that person from leaving the province; after the decision of the Supreme Court at Buenos Ayres confirming the extradition order, a plaintiff had lodged such a claim against Jabez Balfour. The matter came to debate in the House of Commons in March 1895, and the Government had some uncomfortable moments attempting to defend its having allowed the man to leave the country some months after the Liberator Society suspended payment. But, after all, the last defence against extradition was a weak one; payment of the claim broke it down at once, and the fugitive was brought to justice. He was sentenced in November to fourteen years' penal servitude; but the case turned on such intricacies of financial operations, and the disaster to the poorer public, now largely repaired by the Relief Fund, was so far past, that the final stages of the case excited little interest. However, if the Government had failed to bring him to justice, there would have been interest enough to turn votes. There were not many places in England which had not some instance of the effects of the Liberator disaster.

The Government took the first possible exit from its position. The Army Estimates of the year were interest-

[1] See page 326.

ing, because at last the abolition of the post of Commander-
in-Chief, which many reformers had desired for years,
was in sight. A commission over which the Duke of
Devonshire, then still Lord Hartington, had presided in
1888, had reported in 1890 in favour of the abolition of
the post. But the difficulty in the way of carrying out
the report was that the Commander-in-Chief was the
Duke of Cambridge, and his royal blood, his venerable
but vigorous old age, and his undoubted services and
devotion to the army, made the task peculiarly delicate.
It had at last been managed, and the statement on the
Army Estimates of the year announced the fact. But no
one imagined the estimates to be so important that the
Government would go out on them. A division on
the supply of cordite in reserve was carried against the
Government by 132 to 125, and they resigned. The Welsh
Disestablishment Bill, which was in committee at the
time, expired. Lord Salisbury took office, and formed
the first Government in which Liberal Unionists and
Conservatives coalesced. There was still lack of cordiality
on the Conservative side. Mr Chamberlain had cast a
vote for Welsh Disestablishment which rankled in Tory
minds, and there was some criticism of the number of posts
which had gone in the new Government to Unionists.
A more acute criticism, which might have been recalled ten years later, was made by Sir Henry Howorth,
who pleaded for fusion and not coalition on the ground
that the existence of separate organisations would leave
open a gulf which might widen.[1]   In view of the important
part played in the Tariff Reform agitation by the existence
of separate electoral organisations for Conservatives and
Unionists, this plea appears singularly prescient. But in
1895 all that was required seemed to be provided by Mr
Chamberlain's announcement that he would not in the
new Parliament issue separate whips to his supporters.

[1] Letter to *The Times*, 27th June 1895.

The election was a disastrous one for the Liberals. At its outset the chief line of attack upon them was the revolutionary nature of their proposals ; and in spite of the fact that in no one of the most frequently quoted instances had they achieved any success, Home Rule, Welsh Disestablishment, Local Veto, and the abolition of the House of Lords made a sufficiently alarming list for platform purposes. Early in the contest Mr Morley was defeated at Newcastle and Sir William Harcourt at Derby ; Home Rule and Local Veto were the easily assigned causes in the respective cases. The Independent Labour Party sustained blow after blow ; Mr Keir Hardie was beaten, and so were Mr Hyndman and Dr Pankhurst, and in fact almost all their candidates. Mr John Burns just managed to retain his seat. By the end of July the new Parliament was complete, with 411 Conservatives and Liberal Unionists, and only 259 Liberals and Irish Nationalists—a majority of 152. The Liberal Unionist forces had risen again, and stood at 71.

The fall of the Independent Labour party was curious. Trade Unionism certainly showed no weakening. One of its most far-reaching demands—that of the eight-hours day—had been strengthened by the results of practical experiments made by two great firms, Mather & Platt in the engineering trade, and Brunner, Mond & Co. in the chemical trade. The former made a year's experiment ; the latter had just finished a six-years' experiment. The former reported a fractional increase in the wages bill, balanced by a saving in wear and tear, lighting, etc., a marked diminution in the percentage of lost time, and a healthier and keener body of workmen. The latter reported that the slight increase at first in the wage bill had disappeared, and that the effect on the sobriety, regularity and health of the men was excellent. The Trade Union Congress of this year showed no real slackening of the general Labour movement. The Seamen's

Union, damaged by violent and unsuccessful strikes, had dropped in membership from 80,000 to 6000, but the membership of the congress showed a decline of only 20,000. The congress passed resolutions in favour of the nationalisation of land, minerals and railways—by specifying these sources of wealth, it was distinctly reconsidering its general adherence to socialism—and of the placing of docks under municipal authority. This year, as it happened, had brought a curious tribute to the lasting success of the men in the London Dock strike. The secretary of the London Docks had written to the papers to say that casual labour there had now sunk to 2 per cent. of the whole ; a new system was in operation by which notices were posted every night, giving statements of the number of men that would be wanted for work the next day. Trade Unionism had no reason in the general outlook to feel weakened. At this time even the National Union of Teachers was considering joining the congress, and though no proposal came up for discussion at its annual meeting, it was remarked that the teachers showed the true Union bent in their objection to any relaxation of the rules of entrance to the profession. The explanation of the Labour downfall at the election probably was that in the general futility of the Liberal term of office the fresh tendency towards reliance upon parliamentary action had received a check ; and at the same time the erratic and unimportant tendency to violence had rendered the Labour programme liable to misrepresentation.

The organisation of women's labour was greatly forwarded in 1895 by the establishment of the National Union of Women Workers. It was not in the technical sense a trade union, and its relations to the various branches and societies affiliated to it were left very loose. But by providing a centre through which all information as to women's labour, all cases of hardship and underpayment, all local efforts of organisation and combination, could be given a voice, it promoted enormously the interests of labouring women. Those interests had recently been officially recognised by the appointment of a woman, Miss Collet, among the labour correspondents of the Board of Trade. A report by her, published in this year, showed that, contrary to the general opinion, employment of women in industry had not very largely increased. In the census of 1881, 34·05 per cent. of girls and women over ten years of age were returned as occupied ; in that of 1891 the figures were 34·42 per cent. The number of domestic servants had actually decreased ; and in clerkships the numbers of women employed had not advanced nearly so fast as the numbers of men.

The death of Professor Huxley occurred at the end of June. The controversies with which his name had become most commonly associated had ended some time before. Already people had begun to see that the evolutionary theory had its place in the intellectual world, but need not drive out other philosophies. In its early days the theory was a sort of fetish. It had been just sufficiently within the understanding of the ordinary mind to be misused. Advanced as an hypothesis, it had been taken by minds unaccustomed to the scientific uses of hypothesis as almost a statement of fact. An age still ringing with ecclesiastical and theological controversies seized the new weapons ; and men " who were trying to explain why the giraffe's neck grew long, found themselves called upon to say how heaven and earth came out of chaos." [1] What is astonishing to a later generation is not only the eagerness with which the theory was used, but the universal attention which was paid to the religious controversy. Its later manifestations—the battle between Professor Huxley and Dr Wace in the pages of *The Nineteenth Century*, for instance—had perhaps shown

[1] *The Times*, 1st July 1895.

signs of the shrinking of interest ; and by the time of
Huxley's death such engagements would only have
appealed to a very restricted public.

In the summer, rather too late to be fully lionised,
a man came to London bringing with him an even more
adventurous atmosphere than that which had surrounded
Stanley five years before. He was Slatin Pasha, an
Austrian, who had been governor of the Soudanese
province of Darfur at the time of the Mahdist rising.
Taken prisoner by the Mahdi, he had spent eight months
in chains, and after that, eleven years always in the
circle of the Khalifa's bodyguard at Omdurman, the
city which the Khalifa had established for himself on
the opposite bank of the Nile from Khartoum. Slatin
Pasha had escaped at last, and his worn figure, bearing
the signs of his captivity, was the first breaking of the
silence which since 1885 had encompassed the Soudan.
Here was a man who could tell the world the conditions
of the Khalifa's rule, who could give information as to
its extent, the provinces he yet held, and those, like
Darfur and Bahr-el-Ghazal, which he had abandoned.
To England generally Slatin was a personage of romance.
To the Government at home and the authorities in
Egypt he was much more ; and the idea of the reconquest
of the Soudan took a new vitality For the present,
however, the finances of Egypt seemed to be engaged.
The growing prosperity of the country had made practicable the idea of a large scheme of irrigation, involving
the construction of a great barrage at Assouan ; this was
given the preference over military operations, and it was
announced that there was no immediate prospect of the
British Government consenting to a Soudan expedition.

This summer witnessed a renewal of that rivalry
between the great railway lines to the North which had
been an excitement in 1888.[1] This year the goal was

[1] See p. 235.

Aberdeen, instead of Edinburgh, and by 29th July
(the racing began on 1st July) the West Coast time
for the journey was ten hours and five minutes, and
the East Coast time ten hours and twenty-three minutes.
The normal time hitherto had been on the West Coast
route eleven hours, fifty minutes, and on the East Coast
route eleven hours, thirty-five minutes. For two months
the contest went on, until by the end of August the West
Coast had actually cut its time down to eight hours,
thirty-two minutes, or little more than the best record
for the run to Edinburgh in the earlier race. This meant
an average speed over the whole 540 miles of 63 miles an
hour, and a maximum speed of 74 miles an hour was
attained at some points. The best maximum of the East
Coast was 66·7 miles an hour. The race, of course, had
little relation to ordinary railway work ; it involved
cleared lines, and a dislocation of the usual traffic which
could not long be tolerated. But it was a glorious affair
for the onlooker, and it left behind it some acceleration
of journeying in the normal time-table. The speed was
the more notable in that by this time dining cars and
corridor coaches, with all their extra weight, were in
general use on the large Northern lines.

It is no insignificant proof of the change of feeling in
1895 that *Trilby* took the country by storm. Its author,
George du Maurier, used to express his bewilderment at
the vogue of the book ; and one who had been occupied,
as he had been for thirty years, in representing week by
week for the pages of *Punch* the passing foibles of the
English, may well have been astonished. What was
there, he might ask himself, in his gentle story to charm
a world which, when not sophisticated, was still strict,
even a little prim, in its outlook, and when not rich enough
to be absorbed in money, was chiefly absorbed in athletics ?
The main part of the secret was, no doubt, that the story
was genuinely charming ; but some of its success may

also have been due to the time of its publication. On the one hand, reaction against languid cleverness made people ready to enjoy the youthful romance of du Maurier's book. On the other hand, the relaxing of conventions, the altered ideas of what was genuinely immoral, the saner judgments, the greater personal freedom which, with all its faults, the æsthetic movement had helped to bring about, had the effect of giving entrance to the book in a thousand homes where ten years earlier it would not have been accepted. In this latter respect *Trilby* is, however, only one sign (though perhaps the most striking one) of a change of thought. In the other respect, that of its reception by the sophisticated world, it falls little short of a historical event. People who had made so complete a surrender to a book entirely devoid of pose or perverseness could hardly return to the old superior attitudes. *Trilby* did, in fact, break down a kind of angularity which æstheticism had been producing, and people became less afraid of acknowledging that they liked a book or a picture or a poem for no particular reason. Both as a book and in dramatic form at the Haymarket Theatre, *Trilby* was one of the great events of the year. It was in general a time of somewhat mild flavours in literature. A year or two earlier J. M. Barrie's *Auld Licht Idylls* had set a fashion, of which other Scottish writers were quick to take advantage. The sentimental air of the "kail-yard school" blew over the libraries. That school and Miss Marie Corelli divided at this period the affections of the great middle class. Equally sentimental was the taste of the moment for coon songs. Miss May Yohe, at the summit of her fame, was singing haunting melodies in a patch of limelight on the stage of musical comedy; and "Honey, my Honey," and "Linger Longer Loo" were running in the heads of most young men, and not a few young women.

The high-water mark of the passion for cycling was

surely reached in this year, when permission was given for cyclists to ride in Hyde Park, though during the season they were confined to the hours before ten o'clock in the morning and after seven o'clock in the evening. Since the old high bicycle had disappeared, and the new type of cycle had made the pastime possible for women to indulge in, the slightly ridiculous figure cut by the cyclist had ceased to exist. The pneumatic tyre and a better knowledge of gearing made the machine easy and comfortable to ride ; and as motor cars were not yet in use it was also the most rapid means of road-travelling. Doctors took advantage of the craze in order to make people take exercise. The result was that, in this year and the next, cycling was not only the great Saturday afternoon amusement of the worker, and the new resource of people living in the country, but was also the fashion in town. Mayfair abandoned its morning canter for a few turns round the Park on a bicycle, and even went so far afield as to Battersea Park, where the restriction of hours did not exist; breakfasts in Battersea Park became the new adventure. Meanwhile cycling had equally captured the athlete, and long-distance races and twenty-four-hour races were frequent.

The new Government settled itself quietly into place. Mr Chamberlain, for whom rumour had proposed various posts, including that of Secretary for War, had taken, somewhat to the surprise of the country, the Colonial Office, not hitherto a department in which reputations were made. It was not long before he caused it to be known that appointments under the Colonial Office were no longer going to be at the easy disposal of patronage [1]; and a more compact co-operation between the different portions of the Empire was aimed at in his circular despatch to all colonial governments, asking for discussion of the possibility of increasing their trade with

[1] *The Times,* 12th November 1895.

the mother country: No tariff suggestion was made ;
the desire expressed was rather for more knowledge at
home of the needs of colonial traders and of the demands
which home manufacturers might be expected to meet.
For the rest the Government's policy, as announced to the
meeting of the National Union of Conservative Associations, was firstly to set the supremacy of the British navy
beyond question, and secondly to alter the rating system,
so as to give some relief to agricultural interests. The
third place was allotted to educational proposals ; but
it was quite clear that this subject was going to be pressed
forward from various directions with a vigour which would
be ill satisfied with a third place. Early in the year a
committee appointed by the two Archbishops to inquire
into the condition of the voluntary schools had reported
upon the increasing difficulty of meeting the demands
of the education authorities in the matter of school
accommodation, and efficiency of the teaching staff, out
of voluntarily subscribed funds. As assistance from the
rates would necessarily carry with it some form of public
control of the schools, the committee agreed that the
Church should rather ask aid from the Imperial Government, in the form of a general maintenance grant.
Incidentally the committee remarked that the pressure
on elementary schools was growing, because the curriculum was now so good that many parents, who could
afford to send their children elsewhere, were content
with an elementary school. Lord Salisbury had taken
an early opportunity of ranging himself on the side of the
Voluntary schools, expressing the belief that they would
outlast the Board schools [1] ; and the natural result was
that, when he returned to power, the Church school
authorities were ready to ply him with suggestions.
Already the situation was so acute that on the clerical
side the common way of regarding the School Board

[1] *The Times,* 22nd March 1895.

system was to speak of it as competition with Church schools, and to think of it as unfair competition.[1] The report of the Commission on Secondary Education somewhat turned attention from this particular question, because it proved to be a very sweeping document. It recommended the appointment of a Secretary of State for Education, so as to give the work the full status of a Cabinet office ; the setting-up of new local authorities, to be drawn partly from the county and borough councils, and partly by co-optation from experts outside those bodies ; and the endowing of these authorities with power to impose a twopenny rate for secondary, as well as purely technical, education, and power also to administer funds for building and equipping schools. It was the report of a commission appointed by a Liberal Government ; but the Duke of Devonshire had taken the office of Lord President of the Council in the new Government, which made him responsible for national education ; and he had long ago accepted a liberal view of what education should mean.

During the autumn the solid citizen had more than one occasion to be thankful that he had restored to power a solid Government. In October a labour dispute broke out which seemed likely to rival in severity the greatest strikes of recent years. It began with a demand among the Clyde shipbuilding hands for an advance in wages. There had been a reduction during recent bad times, and, as the yards were now busy again, the men asked for an advance of two shillings a week. The masters admitted that business was better, but maintained that, as they were still carrying out contracts at the low prices of the bad times, they could not afford the advance. The Clyde men did not immediately proceed to a strike, but the Belfast men, who had joined in the demand, did so. Thereupon the Clyde masters, no doubt convinced that the strike was bound to spread, took the aggressive,

[1] *The Times*, 21st November 1895.

and locked their men out in the third week in October.
For the remainder of the year the struggle continued, but
in the closing days of December a settlement appeared in
sight. At a conference in Glasgow the masters offered an
advance of one shilling a week to commence in February,
and stipulated that these terms should be unchallenged
by the men for six months after that date. Although
the men asked for the advance in January, and were
disinclined to bind themselves for more than four months,
the struggle seemed unlikely to continue.

A short passage of strained relations with Belgium in
October was less important for its cause than for its sequel.
An Englishman named Stokes, engaged in trading in
the Congo Free State, had been executed by a Belgian
official, Captain Lothaire. The accusation made against
Mr Stokes was of some evil-doing in his commerce with
the natives; the gravamen of the British complaint
was that, instead of allowing the accused man to exercise
his undoubted right of appeal to the tribunals of the
Congo State, Captain Lothaire had hanged him out of
hand. The British Government insisted that, besides
payment to the dead man's family of an indemnity of
150,000 francs, reparation should include the bringing
of Captain Lothaire to trial. But what the incident
really brought upon the King of the Belgians was a sudden
sharpening of suspicion as to the whole administration of
the Congo territory. Hitherto there had been only a
vague idea that the administration was not prosperous;
but the Stokes incident opened the way for those who
knew something of the actual nature of that administration. As yet the atrocities of the rubber trade seem to
have been unknown; but various articles published during
this controversy with the Belgian authorities expressed
grave distrust of the methods of the ivory trade. It was
the beginning of the long task of letting light into a very
dark place.

Next, with some suddenness, a sharp tone began to appear in reference to the Transvaal. This was the more serious effect of the slump in gold-mining shares, which had caused such nervousness in England. As long as all went well at home, little attention was paid to the complaints of the settlers in the Transvaal. But now, remarkably coincident with the accession to power of the Conservative Government, came a change of tone. The Boers were reminded that complaints of insufficient police protection, of total neglect of educational facilities, and of general disregard of the interests of the Rand, could not properly be set aside, when they proceeded from an industry which provided nine-tenths of the revenues of the State, and had, moreover, transformed that State from a bankrupt community to a prosperous and thriving one. A disposition in France to regard the agitation of the Uitlanders' grievances as a preliminary to the usual British acquisition of territory added fuel to the fire; and before the year ended, the situation was growing tense.

But even more suddenly a situation had arisen in quite another quarter which far outweighed this in gravity. A comparatively insignificant dispute with Venezuela, as to the boundary line between that country and British Guiana, was magnified into a threat of disastrous war by a wholly unexpected pronouncement from President Cleveland, to the effect that the United States claimed the right to a predominant voice in any territorial dispute on the American continent. "The Monroe Doctrine," on which the President's Message to Congress was based, was thus introduced to an astonished and angry England. The doctrine had been formulated by President Monroe in 1823 for the protection of the young South American republics against intervention, which at that time seemed probable, by Roman Catholic powers in Europe. That it should be thrust forward in the Venezuelan controversy amazed England; and it was unfortunate, if absurd in a connection of such gravity, that two sporting events of this year had caused bad blood between Englishmen and Americans. At Henley Regatta, in July, an eight from Cornell University had been drawn against an eight of the Leander Club. There was a high wind on the day of the race, and, when the starter asked the crews if they were ready, he failed to hear from the Leander boat the reply that they were not ready. He started the race, and the Cornell boat went off alone. This roused a furious discussion, and the Cornell crew were roundly accused of unsportsmanlike conduct in not waiting for their rivals, when they saw them not ready for the start. In September Lord Dunraven sent over another yacht to challenge for the America Cup. He protested strongly against having to start the race amid a crowd of excursion steamers, which made the sailing of a racing yacht not only difficult, but risky; and as no notice was taken of his protest he contented himself, when the third race came on, with formally crossing the starting line, and then turning his yacht immediately back. Of course such incidents as these were as much indications of existing bad feeling as causes of new irritation; but the danger of them, when the Venezuela difficulty arose, was that they had made popular a sense of rancour and hostility. Lord Salisbury had given himself no sinecure when he returned, in his new Government, to the control of the Foreign Office. His presence there prevented any of that inflammation of public opinion which might easily at this juncture have forced the diplomatic situation. Lord Salisbury contented himself with the knowledge that the approach of a presidential election in the United States might account for a good deal; and set himself to producing a way of escape for President Cleveland from a situation which had probably become rather more serious than he had intended it should be.

CHAPTER XVIII

1896: THE JAMESON RAID, AND MOTOR CARS

NEW YEAR'S DAY brought most astonishing news. On 29th December a body of troops of the British South Africa Company, under the command of Dr Jameson, the Administrator of Mashonaland, had crossed the frontier of the Transvaal, on the way to give armed support to the residents in Johannesburg, who had been, it now appeared, banding themselves together against the Boer rule. With but vague recollections of complaints of Boer tyranny, yet a lively sense that this was no new quarrel, and that there were old sores between the Boers and the English, England generally took the news with some satisfaction; it served the Boers right. A letter was published, which had been sent from Johannesburg to Dr Jameson, saying that the wives and children of Englishmen there were in danger, and armed help must be despatched. There was no hesitation in believing this, though it implied a state of things of which no knowledge had yet become public. But at once it appeared that something was wrong. Mr Chamberlain from the Colonial Office instantly repudiated Dr Jameson and his men, and he called on the British South Africa Company to do the same. The High Commissioner in Cape Colony ordered the instant return of the force. On 3rd January it was announced that Dr Jameson had received, and disregarded, these messages, had pursued his course into the Transvaal, but, while bivouacking at a little place named Krugersdorp, had been surrounded by Boer commandos, and forced to surrender after a brief attempt at fighting. The invasion had turned into a raid.

But how had it happened at all, men asked themselves. What had produced the explosion ? For certainly such hazy ideas as the ordinary Englishman had acquired of recent affairs in South Africa had not led him to suppose that blows were about to be dealt. There was not much satisfaction for the inquiring mind. It was clear that the Boers regarded the growing power of the Rand with dislike and suspicion, and their feelings led them into treating its residents intolerantly. Their attitude was dictated firstly by the belief that the English were determined to filch their country, in order to make a compact whole of British South African territory ; and secondly by a confidence that they could frustrate any such schemes. Their fear led them, on every agitation of the Uitlanders' grievances, to take a stiffer attitude towards franchise demands, which they met with increasing conditions as to length of residence ; and towards complaints of insufficient attention to the Rand's requirements, which they treated as so many ingenious attempts to rouse feeling in England. Their confidence led them, on any sign of British enterprise in South Africa, to strengthen every resource they possessed and to improve their armaments. Thus the progressive occupation by the British of Bechuanaland, of the coast-line of Zululand, of Mashona-land and Matabeleland, had been taken as so many threats ; and the one outlet left to the Boers—that by way of the Dutch railway to Lourenço Marques—grew the more precious. The railway became a weapon in President Kruger's hands ; and when the traders of Cape Colony, objecting to the freight prices charged in the Transvaal, took to convoying their goods by waggon into the country, the President closed the " drifts," or fords, of the Vaal River. A perpetual succession of expansions on the one side, and self-assertions on the other, had

13

produced a situation in which neither side could move without adding to the other side's preconceptions. That the situation could have arisen with so little concurrent knowledge in England was due in great part to the position occupied by Mr Cecil Rhodes. As Premier of Cape Colony he was liable to the dissemination of such knowledge of his policy as Blue Books afford. As director of the British South Africa Company he had, so to speak, an unsupervised range of action. He had a power-supply affixed to the main outside the meter.

The news of the failure of Dr Jameson's attempt was followed by an incident which embittered British feeling. On 4th January it was announced that the German Emperor had telegraphed to President Kruger, congratulating him on repelling an armed force and maintaining the independence of his country. To the most sober-minded in England this was an inflammatory encouragement to the Boers to assert a liberty of action which, however futile the provisions of the Convention of 1884 may have been, was not officially accepted by Great Britain. To less sober minds it was a provocative crow from a jealous rival in Europe. Luckily the Government was able to announce before many days had passed that President Kruger had waived his rights over Dr Jameson and his captured force, and had handed them over to Great Britain for trial. Leading members of the Uitlander community in Johannesburg were arrested, and remained in the Transvaal for trial. The British Government had not swerved an inch in its policy of repudiating the raid. Mr Rhodes was reported to have remarked lugubriously that Dr Jameson had " upset the apple-cart " ; and for the moment the whole episode settled down into an armed truce.

This incident had thrown into the background the threatened quarrel with the United States ; Lord Salisbury had made soothing proposals for arbitration respecting

the Venezuelan boundary; and the alarm died down so
rapidly that before the year was a fortnight old there was
already a suggestion that the occasion might be seized upon
to draft a general arbitration treaty between the two
countries.   The shipbuilding strike was settled before the
end of January on the terms offered by the masters at the
Glasgow conference.[1]   The national revenue was recovering itself so handsomely that there was good prospect of a
surplus for the Budget.   On the whole the new Government entered on its first session with the confidence of
men who had risen not unsuccessfully to trying occasions.
The Opposition on their side foresaw the old familiar
weaknesses to attack—the customary Tory embroilment
in complications abroad, the customary readiness to plunge
into little wars (an expedition had started for Ashanti to
bring to submission an unruly monarch); and as if to complete the case, there were again "Turkish atrocities" to
revive the Gladstonian spirit.   Massacres of Armenians
were mounting to an appalling story.   When Parliament
met there was no lack of promise of domestic legislation.
A new Irish Land Bill, an Education Bill, an Agricultural
Rating Bill, and measures dealing with light railways, with
friendly societies, with company law, and with Irish
education were in the Government's list.   But if the
Ministry had had nothing but domestic legislation to
handle they would have had a singularly comfortless time;
and to that extent the instincts of the Opposition were
just.   In affairs abroad lay the Government's main interest.
The first work of the new Parliament was one more piece
of tinkering with its own procedure.   Mr Balfour proposed
new rules for regulating Committee of Supply.   This was
the part of a Government's work which had offered the best
target in the days of organised obstruction, because it
could not be dropped, as any other piece of business might
be.   The worst effect of this was that supply had lost its

[1] See p. 381.

importance; criticism of estimates had become, not a member's duty, but a suspect proceeding. Mr Balfour set up a time-limit, with no pretence of applying it in cases of urgency or obstruction, but as a normal method. Certain days were allotted for supply, and on the nineteenth day money votes not yet passed were to be closured, and on the twentieth day the report stage was to be taken under closure.

Before the end of February the principal offenders in the Jameson Raid were in England, and were brought up at Bow Street. These were Dr Jameson, Sir John Willoughby, and eleven others. The authorities, pursuing still their policy of repudiation, took pains to prevent anything like public demonstrations on the prisoners' behalf. The steamer on which they came home was brought round to the Thames, and in the lower reaches they were transferred to a launch which landed them unnoticed at Waterloo Pier. Until they came into the police court there was no chance of cheering them, but then the chance was taken, in spite of severe strictures on the indecorousness of such a display of feeling. The charge brought against the prisoners was that of unlawfully fitting out a military expedition against a friendly State. Now that the first surprised feelings were over, and the momentary satisfaction of the transfer of the offenders to Great Britain had cooled, a vigorous discussion of the terms of their surrender arose—of the question whether the Johannesburgers had been induced to lay down their arms by the threat that the lives of Dr Jameson and the others depended on their doing so, whether Dr Jameson's surrender had been unconditional—and so on. It was not an important discussion except for the soreness it revealed. Mr Chamberlain, who had gained ground with even the extreme Tories by obtaining the transfer of the prisoners to British justice, had now to lose a little. He fell into the mistake of attempting a counter-stroke, and attempting it so publicly that its failure was bound to add to the general irritation. Instead of taking clearly the position .that the Raid had rendered impossible for some time any official representations of the Uitlanders' grievances, he wrote a despatch to President Kruger, recapitulating the grievances, and suggesting a plan of municipal government for Johannesburg. It was not likely that in their suspicious temper the Boers would take this as anything but one more covert sapping of their rule ; and an invitation, also conveyed in the despatch, to President Kruger himself to come to England for a discussion of the position, was plainly ill-timed. Mr Chamberlain published this despatch in England before it was delivered to President Kruger, an obvious breach of official good manners. There were advisers at President Kruger's elbow clever enough to see this, if the President himself did not. The reply was not only a refusal of the invitation, and a putting aside of the suggestion, but also a rebuke. Ill-feeling had one more thing to feed upon. What really forced the feeling in every possible way was the question of the complicity of British official authorities in the Raid. Coming as it did so soon after the accession of the Conservatives and Unionists to power, representing as desperate a situation in the Transvaal which the ordinary man had never regarded as acute, the Raid seemed to throw a light, by some considered sinister, on Mr Chamberlain's choice of office in the new Ministry. He was the man about whose post there had been most speculation. He had chosen one not hitherto associated with great energy or scope for ambition ; and within six months he was dealing with the matter which was practically the only subject in the public mind. Late in April it became known that certain cipher telegrams which had fallen into the Boers' hands on the capture of Dr Jameson were held by the Boers to establish the fact that Mr Rhodes and Mr Beit (a millionaire of the Rand mines) knew of the plans being made in Johannesburg for the calling in of an armed force. If Mr Rhodes was cognisant of the plot, was the Colonial Office wholly ignorant ? And if it was, why was Mr Rhodes still Prime Minister of Cape Colony ? Such doubts had their effect on both sides. The Liberal demand was plain enough ; there must be a full and drastic inquiry. The Tory attitude could not be one of opposition to such a demand. No mistakes could be afforded, and the Colonial Office must, if possible, be absolved from complicity in such a fiasco. A few weeks later Mr Rhodes resigned his Premiership, but it was not until the end of the session that the Select Committee on British South Africa was set up. Liberals could not complain of their representation on it. It consisted of the Attorney-General (Sir Richard Webster), Mr John Bigham, Mr Sydney Buxton, Sir Henry Campbell-Bannerman, Mr Chamberlain, the Chancellor of the Exchequer (Sir Michael Hicks Beach), Mr Alfred Cripps, Sir William Hart Dyke, Mr John Ellis, Sir William Harcourt, Mr W. L. Jackson, Mr Henry Labouchere, Mr Wharton and Mr George Wyndham. In moving the appointment of the committee Mr Chamberlain stated that his policy had been to allow time for the feelings of irritation both among British and among Boers to subside, before reviving in an inquiry the grounds of the irritation. He had not succeeded, for while the Boers put the worst possible construction on the delay, the British in South Africa were becoming convinced that it was the intention of the Transvaal to push home its strong position by declaring entire independence. Meanwhile the sentences on the prisoners on either side were an indication of the feelings aroused. Dr Jameson and the twelve others in England were sentenced to short terms of imprisonment. Indeed, it seemed to be likely that the jury would return a verdict of acquittal, but the Lord Chief Justice, Lord Russell of Killowen, summed up in such a way as to leave the jury virtually no alternative. Colonel Frank Rhodes (a brother of Mr Rhodes), Mr Phillips, Mr Farrer and Mr Hammond, the leaders of the Johannesburg Uitlanders who were tried in the Transvaal, were condemned to death, the sentences being commuted immediately afterwards to heavy fines and two years' imprisonment.

However, if Mr Chamberlain meant that his policy was to wait until merely popular feeling in England died down, he was justified. The newspaper sensation barely lasted into the early summer. Trade was reviving strongly, and the quantity of money seeking investment was reflected in the price of securities. Consols were up to 113, and all gilt-edged securities were high with them. This was, of course, partly due to the suspicion under which company-promoting had fallen. The " guinea-pig " director had been flagrantly in evidence for some years past. The Government introduced a Companies Bill, which went further than the recommendations of the recent Committee on Company Law; it insisted on the filing of balance-sheets for public inspection, and on a shareholding qualification for directors. This may have restored confidence to some extent ; but the search for investments would in any case have revived speculation. Speculation had also become, in the recent gold-mines boom, an amusement and a possibility of profit, which people of leisure would not easily drop. New material for it was at hand. Gas, after all the fears expressed in the early days of electric light, had held its ground as an illuminant, and was now even gaining ground by the recent invention of the incandescent mantle. Litigation in 1896 with regard to certain patents brought the invention into prominence, so that it caught the eye of the speculator. But a still more profitable field was opening. The immense craze for cycling was swamping the manufacturers with orders, and capital for developing their capacities might well be called for. The opportunity was seized, and during this year and the following year cycle companies were a safe draw for money ;

reconstructions of existing companies with very large increases of capital were of weekly occurrence ; every component part of a cycle seemed to offer a fresh opportunity for the flotation of a company to make it. Capital to the amount of something like eleven millions went into cycling in 1896 alone ; the Dunlop Pneumatic Tyre Company took five millions. It was the new boom. No one at the time thought of it as rather too late in the day to be a safe one, though a warning might have been derived from a paper read by Sir Douglas Fox before the British Association this year, in which he spoke of motor cars as offering an opening for engineering skill and invention even more important than that offered by cycle-construction. As yet these cars were only known to the general public as an invention developed chiefly in France but not to be taken very seriously. They were thought a noisy method of locomotion, uncertain in control, somewhat ridiculous in appearance, and terrifying to horses.

At the moment other scientific inventions were more in the public eye. The theory of mechanical flight was already liberating itself from the old belief that a lifting agent, such as light gas, was an essential for passage through the air. Mr Hiram Maxim was making experiments with lifting-planes actuated by a light engine ; and Lilienthal and Pilcher were in the midst of their experiments in gliding. The work of Professor Langley, who had since 1887 been investigating the behaviour of plane surfaces subjected to resistance of the air, and had published elaborate tables of mathematical calculations, was greatly assisting such experiments. But the discovery most seized upon by popular interest was that of the Röntgen rays. It needed no scientific knowledge to see that this opened a new world of possibilities, and was a fundamental disturbance of ordinary conceptions of matter.

Parliament came early to the discovery that its long and energetic programme was meeting with a rather unexpected check. It had attacked a fine variety of subjects. Some Bills have already been mentioned. Besides these there was a Light Railways Bill, setting up a body of commissioners for the consideration of local projects, and authorising the Treasury to make loans, provided that not less than half the capital required was subscribed by the public, and that not more than a half of that was found by local authorities. There had been a good deal of discussion of light railways during 1894, the chief idea being that they would assist agriculturists to supply markets beyond their immediate neighbourhood ; and the setting up of special commissioners was intended to overcome the objection that parliamentary costs were too high, and parliamentary requirements as to construction too severe, for such transport. The Bill was, with the Agricultural Rating Bill, an attempt to cure rural distresses, which not only damaged the country districts, but also added to urban problems, by causing rural labourers to invade the towns and augment the congestion and unemployment there. The rating proposal was that agricultural land should be assessed at one-half its value, the deficiency being made up by a grant from the Imperial Exchequer to the Local Taxation Account. It brought a fresh complication into the already confused system of rating, and was a piece of specialised legislation not easy to defend. The Irish Land Bill, again, had no easy progress. A large part of it was occupied with a statutory fixing of rents (rendered necessary by the passage of time since the Act of 1881, which only fixed rents for fifteen years), and this was a repetition of proposals of which the Conservatives had complained strongly, and which the House of Lords had rejected, in Mr Morley's Bill of 1895. Tories could hardly like such a position ; and they liked no better the proposals for Land Purchase, designed to facilitate and quicken the working of the Act of 1891, which had so far been largely a failure. Between the desire to have the Nationalists on the side of the Bill (as an effective answer to Home Rulers) and the pressure of Irish landlords against conciliation of the tenants, the Bill had stormy hours to weather. The House of Lords introduced some strong amendments, but ultimately surrendered to the House of Commons' refusal to accept them, and the Bill became law.

In these rather strained conditions of Irish affairs, it was inevitable that the report of the Royal Commission on Financial Relations between Great Britain and Ireland should fall flat. It was published in September, the chairman, Mr Childers, not living to see the publication. He had died in January. The commission was of Liberal appointment,[1] and though the result might rather be described as several reports than as one, there were some points on which a majority of the commissioners were agreed, as, for instance, that the two countries must be regarded for financial purposes as separate entities, that the burden of taxation imposed by the Act of Union was too great, and that in such a period as that from 1853 to 1860 an unjustifiable weight of taxation had been placed upon Ireland.[2]

But to return to the session. Neither Agricultural Rating nor Irish Land proved so difficult a subject as the Education Bill. Proceeding largely on the lines of the recent commission's recommendations, the Bill set up the county and borough councils as the education authority, to work through special committees. Under the general supervision of the Board of Education the new authorities were to have charge of the inspection of schools, and entire control of the parliamentary grant ; to develop technical schools, and take over all local duties under the Technical Instruction Act. Then came another piece of specialised legislation. The voluntary schools were to receive an

[1] See p. 356.
[2] For an interesting comment by Mr Gladstone on this point see Morley's *Life of Gladstone*, i. 646.

additional Exchequer grant of four shillings per child ;
and it was also provided that in any elementary school,
if " a reasonable number " of parents applied for separate
religious instruction for their children, the managers must
allow effect to be given to this desire. From the very
start the Bill gave trouble. All the Liberal strength went
into denunciation of the special favours to Church schools,
and the implied destruction, by the provisions for separate
religious teaching, of the Cowper-Temple agreement. The
Irish party, it is true, were not with them ; as a party
mainly Roman Catholic, they never could take the un-
sectarian line in matters of education. But Liberals
knew that, however widely he had parted from them in
some directions, Mr Chamberlain could not be pleased
with this Bill ; and they shrewdly suspected that Sir John
Gorst, though officially responsible for it, had no great
love of it as a whole. They were therefore unwearying in
the proposal of amendments ; and the fact that, although
few amendments commanded the support of more than
a hundred and fifty members, five days were spent in
committee on the first two lines of the Bill, showed the
Liberal party that the Government felt their hold on
the Bill to be weak. Conservative supporters outside the
House were not well united on the matter ; they differed
as to drawing the extra grants from taxes or from rates,
and more seriously as to the amount of the grant. In the
end the Bill was dropped. Sir John Gorst was, more or
less accidentally, prominent in another debate of this year
which deserves mention. He had presided at the meeting
of a limited liability company, of which he was chairman ;
and occasion was taken to raise the question of the propriety of Cabinet Ministers holding directorships. During
the Liberal Ministry of 1892-1895 Mr Gladstone (on the
advice, it is said, of Lord Rosebery) had made it a rule
that members of his Cabinet should not hold directorships.
But that was a rather severe ideal, since even Cabinet

Ministers could not afford wholly to abandon sources of private income ; and for the present the rule was not revived by Lord Salisbury. It remains to be added that the session was not a success, and Mr Balfour was taken to task for " airiness " and " inattention to detail " in his conduct of the business of the House of Commons. There was more than a hint that, if he could not do the work successfully, it was quite possible that Mr Chamberlain could.[1] Two minor matters helped to make the Government rather less popular in the country than it had been a year earlier : Mr Walter Long, President of the Board of Agriculture, decided to make permanent, and to enforce more strictly, the regulations for the slaughter of imported cattle at the port of entry ; and the muzzling of dogs was largely increased owing to serious outbreaks of rabies in Lancashire and Yorkshire.

A matter of much greater moment, though its full development was long delayed, was the appointment of a Royal Commission on the Licensing Laws. We have already seen a previous Conservative Government attempting, though vainly, to respond to a certain force of moderate opinion which was uneasy about the position of the licensed victualling trade in the community.[2] Under the Liberal Government the extreme party of abolitionists held the ground, with their policy of Local Veto. The complete defeat of that policy now left room once more for moderate opinion ; and the new government, committed by the earlier attempts to taking some action, appointed a Royal Commission. Its chairman was Lord Peel, who had in the previous year resigned the Speakership of the House of Commons. The Commission was constituted on a new principle, three groups being deliberately chosen to represent the licensed trade, temperance advocates, and men of open mind. Each group consisted

[1] See the *Punch* cartoon, 4th July 1896.
[2] See pages 230 and 270.

of eight men. The most prominent and capable members of the Commission were Lord Peel and Lord Windsor among the neutrals; the Archbishop of Canterbury, Mr T. P. Whittaker and Mr W. S. Caine among the temperance men ; and Mr North Buxton and Mr George Younger among the representatives of the trade.

One decision the Government had taken at a time when the excitement about the Jameson Raid obscured it from the popularity it would have enjoyed. It was the decision to permit an advance up the Nile for the reoccupation of part of the Soudan. Events which brought forward the possibility of an expedition have already been mentioned.[1] The event which now caused the Government to reverse its decision of the previous autumn was the crushing defeat of Italian forces by Abyssinian troops at Adowa. In the rearrangement of territory after the withdrawal of Egyptian forces from the Soudan, Italy had acquired the district of Massowah, on the Red Sea ; and her defeat seemed likely to bring the dervishes down in an attempt to occupy the whole province. The desire to assist Italy by causing a diversion of dervish forces was given by the Government as the second of the reasons for sanctioning an expedition. The first was merely stated as " the advice of the military authorities in Egypt." It is more than likely that a consideration of some weight in the giving of that advice was a French advance in the Soudan by way of Darfur, one of the provinces which the Khalifa had abandoned. The resentful surprise in England when Captain Marchand was found two years later at Fashoda, would have been less bitter if more attention had been paid in 1896 to this move on the part of France. Sir Charles Dilke who, after six years' withdrawal, had returned to the House of Commons at the election of 1892, as Member for the Forest of Dean, spoke in the House of the French advance, but no one else outside official circles appeared to

[1] See p. 375.

attach any importance to it. In Egypt itself France took the anticipated line of opposing and hampering the British decision. For the purposes of the expedition it was proposed to allot a sum of half-a-million from the Egyptian Treasury. But access to Treasury accumulations could only be granted by the authority of the International Commissioners of the Debt. A majority of four to two of commissioners agreed to the payment of the sum, but the two dissentients, the French and the Russian representatives, brought an action in the Mixed Tribunal of First Instance at Cairo, and obtained a verdict that the withholding of their consent was sufficient to prevent the payment of the sum ; the verdict was upheld on appeal. The British Government, desiring nothing better, repaid at once into the Egyptian Treasury the sum of £515,000, and also advanced a further sum of £800,000 at $2\frac{3}{4}$ per cent. for the expedition. But for the Franco-Russian intervention it would have been difficult for Great Britain to undertake so thoroughly the conduct of the affair. The expedition was commanded by Sir Herbert Kitchener, who knew his ground.[1] He had been continuously with the Egyptian army for fourteen years, and since 1888 had been, first as Adjutant-General and then as Sirdar, the maker of its new qualities. Early in the expedition he laid his plans to " blood " his men with a battle. The difficulty was to make sure of a downright engagement with the dervishes, but locating them at last, at Firket, he made a masterly night march in two columns, which converged with complete success upon the enemy. The dervishes were routed with heavy loss, and the Egyptian forces were put in heart to withstand a somewhat trying summer of cholera, and of heavy storms, which damaged the railway communications. Nothing occurred to hinder Kitchener's plans, and Dongola was occupied on 23rd September.

[1] See page 133.

The summer in England was abnormally hot and dry. It was full of sporting interests, beginning with the winning of the Derby by Persimmon, the Prince of Wales's horse. It was the first time that the Prince had won the Derby, and the popularity of the event was immense. The dryness of the air favoured large scores in cricket, and a reputation was made in this year which seemed likely to rival in interest that of Dr W. G. Grace, who had achieved in 1895 the feat of reaching his hundredth century in first-class cricket. Prince Ranjitsinhji, a young Indian who was in residence at Cambridge, shared with Dr Grace in 1896 the idolisation of cricket crowds. A less pleasant incident of cricket was the heated debate aroused by the action of the Cambridge eleven during the university match of this year, in bowling deliberate " no-balls " for tactical reasons. All sorts of persons rushed into the fray of deciding whether this was, or was not, sportsmanlike. The affair itself mattered less than the revelation which it produced of the place sport was occupying in the national life. Observant philosophers attributed this to the reign of commerce and machinery. The individual, they said, withered at the counting-house and the factory, but returned to his own stature at cricket or cycling. Other philosophers discerned the new force less in the active pursuit of sports than in the looking-on of crowds. Facilities of transport, easier earnings, and an easier inclination to spend them, combined with the increasing distribution of cheap newspapers to make sporting experts of even the most sluggish members of the public.

The number of cheap newspapers had increased this year by the addition of one that was soon to become by far the most prominent of them all. *The Daily Mail* was first published in the spring of 1896. It was founded by Mr Alfred Harmsworth, who had made a large fortune out of a penny weekly paper, *Answers*. He now saw that there was no reason whatever to suppose that only the Radical working man wanted to have a daily paper for a halfpenny. He therefore offered a Conservative newspaper for a halfpenny ; and, with that reliance upon the profits of enormous sales which had made the success of the penny weekly papers he promised his readers no less adequate and no less distinguished foreign correspondence than was published by the papers which cost a penny, or even by the paper which cost threepence. They could at the same time depend on no less keen a scent for the exciting and the amusing than the existing halfpenny papers had accustomed them to expect ; while a general Conservative tone would make the excitement a little more reputable. It was, as events proved, the final word in a cheap Press.

A grave result of the heat of the summer was a water famine in the East End of London. Fortunately the fears which it caused of a serious spread of disease were not realised ; but the danger was no imaginary one, and the mere inconvenience of the failure of supply was great. Naturally the incident revived the question of the purchase of the water undertakings of London by the County Council. The piecemeal system had come to a serious breakdown. But the probable cost of taking over the various companies was put by some experts at no less than thirty millions, and this was a daunting sum. The County Council did deposit this year a Bill for the purpose. The companies, however, were wise enough to profit by the year's experience ; and they created a new system of inter-communication between their various supplies, which rendered an acute water famine in any single district much less likely, and so removed a source of friction with the public. In the absence of such friction they knew that the municipalisation of their undertakings was but a remote possibility. Some uneasiness was arising about the state of local taxation all over the country. The general local debt was put at over two hundred and two millions, and only fifty-six millions of this sum were in directly remunerative undertakings, such as gas and water supply. Nor was it only the amount of debt which was being criticised. The more penetrating comment was that the incidence of local taxation had never been properly worked out, and that there had been no attempt to redistribute the pressure of the swiftly growing burden. At any rate, as the London County Council, in its short career, had already amassed a debt of thirty-eight and a half millions, the London Water Companies had no great fear of compulsory purchase. The council had enough to do in defending its existing enterprises, especially the Works Department, which was accused of spending more than contractors would have asked for its undertakings, and also of choosing the jobs which would be most likely to turn out well financially, leaving the others to the contractors.

During the summer there was a murder trial which has to be mentioned for the quality rather than the extent of the public interest in it. It was the trial of a woman named Dyer for killing children put out " to nurse " with her. It drew attention to the horrors of baby-farming ; and the general conscience was so much stirred that other problems of slum childhood received more attention than might otherwise have been given them. Poor Law schools fell under the strong condemnation of a committee appointed to inquire into them, and it was decided that the children should be placed under the new education authorities, as soon as these were set up. An experiment by the Chorlton Board of Guardians, in Lancashire—a " model village " for boarding-out workhouse children, consisting of sixteen cottages accommodating nearly three hundred children, with a swimming bath for their use, and workshops for teaching carpentry, bootmaking and plumbing—was started in September ; and other towns, such as Sheffield, made the same experiment in a less costly way by taking houses in different parts of the town, and placing pauper children in them. The Dyer case had for the moment made the boarding-out of children rather unpopular. The case had nothing to do with Poor Law children, but it created an uneasiness about placing children in any circumstances except those of direct public control. Early in the following year a new Poor Law Board, for superintending matters connected with pauper children, was set up as a sub-department of the Local Government Board.

When the autumn revived political interest, the Liberal party had to choose a new leader. Lord Rosebery had had enough in two years of leading a party which found him light, and which he found preposterously heavy. The course taken on his resignation showed how deep was the disintegration of the Liberal party since the retirement of Mr Gladstone had removed the bond of personal loyalty to him. At the time of his retirement the party had been in office, and the choice of its next leader, being the choice of a Prime Minister, had been the business of the Crown, and not of the party. Now that the party had to find a leader, the case was seen to be very different. After these two years it would have been impossible to propose a peer again, and so Lord Spencer missed finally the chance, which most people thought should have been his, beyond question, on Mr Gladstone's resignation. In the Commons it was practically impossible to pass over Sir William Harcourt ; and yet it was only too well known that he would not command even a decently unanimous allegiance. In the end the real difficulty was shirked. Sir William Harcourt was chosen leader of the party in the House of Commons ; and refuge was taken from the greater problem by the decision that the actual leader of the party as a whole need not be chosen until there was a likelihood of the Liberals coming into power. The controversy on the Government's proposals for education showed no diminution of bitterness. A new line of criticism suggested that there should be no attempt to deal with elementary and technical education together. The latter had been well handled under existing arrangements. A report of the Technical Education Board of the London County Council, published in this year, is a useful guide to the elaborate and successful scholarship system which had grown up. The first stage was provided by six hundred scholarships allotted to elementary schools, for boys and girls under thirteen years of age, whose parents had incomes not exceeding £150. These insured free education for two years at improved secondary or upper schools, and a money payment of £20 a year. None of these scholarships went to children of middle-class parents, and 1·5 children per thousand in the London area had made this first step. The next was by intermediate scholarships for boys and girls under sixteen years of age whose parents had incomes not exceeding £450 a year. They ensured free education up to the age of nineteen at public schools, and a money payment of £20 or £30 a year. There were thirty-five of these scholarships, and only five had gone to children whose parents' incomes were over £250 a year. Lastly, there were senior scholarships, carrying free education through a university course with a payment of £60 a year. There were also a hundred exhibitions tenable at evening art schools, and over three hundred exhibitions for higher training in domestic economy. This was an example of work now being done all over the country, work which in the north especially was transforming the lives and prospects of the intelligent workmen. Curiously enough, it depressed the patient philosopher whose writings had their chief influence amongst these very people. Mr Herbert Spencer finished in this year his *Synthetic Philosophy* ; and admitted himself depressed by the spread of socialist views of the functions of the State.

Yet it was his doctrine which, more than anything else, was sought after by the advanced working men ; and his philosophical speculations, never much esteemed by academic teachers, had their real public in the people whose opinions he disliked. In labour matters generally the year was a quiet one. There were one or two strikes for Trade Union principles, and at the end of the year the case of Flood v. Jackson became famous. It was one in which certain shipwrights engaged on ironwork were discharged on the complaint of the ironworkers, and brought an action against the delegate of the Ironworkers' Union. The jury held that the latter had acted maliciously ; and the case was so difficult that the House of Lords, when the appeal reached it, had to call in the aid of judges of the High Court. In the end the original verdict was reversed, and the union won the case. But there could be no mistaking the reluctance with which this decision was reached, or the growing dissatisfaction in a large part of the community with regard to the apparently privileged position of trade unions under the common law. An effort towards genuine political recognition of trade unions was made in this year by Lord James of Hereford, who introduced a Bill for the registration of conciliation boards, and to give the Board of Trade a statutory power of intervention in labour disputes. Meanwhile the cooperation movement was in some difficulty. The extension of its productive side had brought it to the problem of fluctuation of demand, and of the locking-up of capital, which was imposed by the necessity of holding goods against a recovery of the market.

The year had a heavy death-roll of notable men. It included some distinguished artists—Lord Leighton, master of graceful and delicate opulence in painting and in personality, and Sir John Millais, one of the pre-Raphaelite group, who had found his brush not incapable of command of a popular style. The

death of these two 'men left academic art in England
singularly bare and lifeless in the face of the newer
generation of painters.   Another artist who died this
year was George du Maurier ; he had brought *Punch*
into true relation with an altering social structure by
giving to satire of Society tricks and fads and changes of
view that prominence which Leech and Charles Keene had
given entirely to middle-class foibles.   In October died
William Morris.   His difficulty in associating himself
with the labour movement of the last eight or nine years
gave some colour to the criticism that his socialism was
rather a sentimental form of protest against the ascendancy
of the commercial spirit than a true political conviction.
But the profound influence he exercised was easy to
recognise ; and, though his own manufactures were too
costly to reach any but those of considerable means, his
gospel of design had already modified the taste of even
suburban furnishers.   Archbishop Benson, while on a
visit to Mr Gladstone at Hawarden, died suddenly in a
pew in church.   His one outstanding action, the trial of the
Bishop of Lincoln, was an error ; but he had otherwise
filled his throne with dignity and grace.   He was apt to be
misled by picturesque possibilities, and in this year had
been engaged in the rather unwise movement to try to
obtain from the Vatican a recognition of Anglican orders
of priesthood.   Some of the High Church leaders had
been persuaded that the attempt might meet with unexpected success.   The Papal Bull published in September
was a perfectly conclusive refusal of recognition ; and
Archbishop Benson had to content himself with giving the
English Church such consolation as might be found in the
fact that, as he put it, " Infallibility had this time ventured
on giving its reasons."   The appointment of his successor
revived for a moment ecclesiastical bitternesses.   Dr
Temple, Bishop of London, was nominated.   He had been
one of the authors of *Essays and Reviews*, and there were

many who gravely questioned his orthodoxy. He had, during his rule of the London see, shown in the matter of the reredos at St Paul's an inclination to override doctrinal controversies, and anxious Evangelicals believed that as Archbishop he would still further damp down anti-Ritualist feeling.

One of those extraordinary incidents in which London delights, as revelations of the crude romance which can lurk in a large city, occurred in October. It suddenly became known that a Chinaman named Sun Yat Sen was being imprisoned with a high hand in the house of the Chinese Legation. He had in fact been ten days in durance before he was able to communicate with friends, who took the story at once to the Foreign Office. Lord Salisbury represented to the legation that, whatever complaints it might have against the man, it was impossible to acquiesce in the bland kidnapping which had been practised. The legation, shrugging its shoulders at the strange concerns of Western civilisation, released its captive. Little was said of any charges against him ; it was only understood that it was obnoxious to the Chinese Government that he should be at liberty, and the legation had calmly taken steps, when an occasion offered itself, to end that liberty.

The 14th November of this year is an important date. On that day the legal provisions, which enacted that every mechanical locomotive on a highway must be preceded by a man walking with a red flag to warn drivers of horse vehicles, ceased to exist. They had been an absolute bar to the use of motor cars in this country. That their removal would lead to anything like the amazing developments which ensued no one suspected ; the agitation for removal had made only the feeblest appearance in the newspapers. The comparatively few people who really understood the potentialities of the new invention had against them almost the whole of the world of wealth and

influence.   The very persons, who were in a few years to
make a complete surrender to motoring, took towards it
at this time much the same attitude as they had taken
earlier towards cycling.   They abused the invasion of the
highways, they sneered at the smells and the noise and
the discomforts of the cars, they predicted death or
mutilation for the drivers of the machines.   Those who,
having no horses and no aristocratic traditions, were not
inclined to be angry, were nearly as annoying in their
sniggering disbelief in the power of cars.   Amid the
mingled chorus of abuse and jeers preparations were made
for a suitable demonstration, celebrating the end of the
red flag regulations.   It was to take the form of a procession of cars from London to Brighton.   An enormous
concourse of people watched the start from a hotel in
Northumberland Avenue, and to the crowd's immense
gratification some of the cars failed to start at all.   Others
broke down on the way.   Yet enough performed the
journey to put an end to mere cavilling, and at the same
time the confidence of the people who really understood
the new invention was so firm and assured that from
that moment the progress of motor cars in England was
unchecked and rapid.

CHAPTER XIX

THE nation came to the celebration of the second Jubilee in a different spirit from that in which it approached the first. It may be said that Queen Victoria was herself the centre of the loyal enthusiasm of 1887, and that in 1897 the toast was rather " Our Noble Selves." The display of military contingents from all over the world was far more elaborate than in 1887 ; while the crowning glory of the second celebration was the naval review at Spithead, the triumphant exhibition of the massive results of the advanced naval policy of the preceding years. The colonial representatives were also more deliberately brought into the foreground. To make a broad distinction, the Jubilee of 1887 was royal, and the affectionate participation of Europe in doing honour to a revered sovereign was the keynote; the Jubilee of 1897 was imperial, and the source of pride our vast territory and our possessions in men and money.

The year began in a singularly bad spirit with the Welsh slate quarry dispute. The quarrying system was a curious one, which had hitherto given the men no small share in the control. The quarries in question belonged to Lord Penrhyn, but the custom of working them had been to sell to contractors the right of removing the slate. Direct relations between the workmen and the owner's manager had, however, been maintained, by the existence of a men's committee ; so that, in spite of the contracting system, the men were in the last resort Lord Penrhyn's men. In September of 1896 the men had complaints to make against contractors, and had appealed for the establishment of a new system in the quarries. Lord Penrhyn did not agree to this ; and, thinking it necessary to take some forcible step to insist upon his attitude, he suspended seventy-one of the men. In effect, as these were the men who had been prominent in stating the workmen's case, he suspended the committee. Later on he locked out the whole body of quarrymen. The dispute became at once extremely bitter. Lord Penrhyn refused to have anything more to do with a committee, and the men, whose system was, after all, older than Trade Unionism, were indignant at his adoption of the ordinary attitude of a fighting employer, and his treatment of their committee as if it involved a case of recognition of Trade Union representation. The dispute had elements which made it more of a deadlock than even the most obstinate of disputes had been hitherto. Firstly, Lord Penrhyn declined flatly the offer of the Board of Trade to intervene; secondly, the quarrying was highly skilled work, and there could be no cutting of the knot by importing labour ; thirdly, the quarries suffered no injury from being left unworked (as coal-mines, for instance, suffer), and therefore one powerful inducement to settle the dispute was lacking. The struggle was made the subject of debate in the House of Commons early in the session, but no good came of the discussion. Even those whose natural instinct in any labour quarrel lay on the masters' side found it difficult to defend Lord Penrhyn, and had to content themselves with a general feeling that everyone concerned was behaving badly.[1] But the men's case was both skilfully and inspiringly presented in England, and a relief fund was organised, which enabled them to hold out far longer than was expected.

Apart from this, the year at its beginning was of good promise. British relations with France were believed to

[1] See, e.g., The Times, 5th January 1897.

be improving. A terrible disaster to a great liner, the *Drummond Castle*, off the coast of Brittany, had brought into evidence the heroism of the Bretons ; and the result had been a softening of international feeling. Even in Egypt signs were perceived of the passing away of irritation. The resentment aroused by the German Emperor's telegram to President Kruger had subsided in the prudent silence which he had since observed. Although there was anxiety enough about the Transvaal in official quarters, where Kruger's purchase of armaments and approaches to certain European Powers were seen as an assertion of independence, the public had in its easy way forgotten its wrath ; and was suggesting that the Raid prisoners might now be released, and the affair passed over. As for Parliament, no doubt the Government would have learned its lesson from the previous year, and would be wise enough not to attempt too large or too disturbing a programme. The new Education Bill certainly looked lighter than its predecessor ; it was quite a short measure, dealing only with the gift of State aid to the voluntary schools. While maintaining the principle of drawing the aid from the taxes, and not from the rates, the Government met some of the criticism of its supporters in the previous year by making the amount of the grant five shillings instead of four shillings. The Bill encountered none of the trouble inside the Cabinet and the party with which the Bill of 1896 had had to struggle, and it was passed. So was the Law of Evidence Amendment Bill, by which prisoners were allowed to give evidence on oath ; those who expressed fear of great change being wrought in the character of a trial were met with the answer, that in effect the statements which prisoners were already free to make had great weight with a jury, and it would be all to the good that they should have the sanction and the restraint of being made on oath. In other ways the criminal law was at the time being reconsidered ; the movement for a court of criminal appeal was revived—cases on the capital charge, however, were proposed to be excluded from the court's power—and a committee presided over by Mr Asquith to inquire into prison administration reported in June. It found great changes for the better, but expressed the wish for more elasticity, more variation in the treatment of prisoners, amounting even to separate prisons and systems for the habitual offender and the more incidental criminal.

The great measure of the session, the Workmen's Compensation Bill, would have appeared to the onlooker quite as full of danger as the Education Bill had been in the previous year. It embodied a fairly drastic new principle. Under the existing law a workman, in order to obtain compensation for injuries caused during his employment, had to prove that they were due to negligence on the part of his employer or a fellow-workman, and had also to be free himself of any charge of contributory negligence. By the new Bill the whole range of accidents came under an automatic system of compensation. It was only by a modification introduced in committee that the employer was allowed to set up a defence against claims. Compensation was placed, in case of death, at three years' wages or £150, whichever was the larger, with a maximum payment of £300; and in case of disablement, at a weekly payment of half the wages the worker earned, with a maximum of £1 a week. It was in many respects an astonishing Bill. Hard as it was, for instance, that possible cases of contributory negligence should be included, the Government risked the hardships in order to keep the Bill workable, and close the door against the more stultifying kinds of litigation. It was no wonder that Tories asked themselves what they were coming to, nor that the usual answer to the question was that they were being swallowed by Mr Chamberlain. For the present the Bill was confined to workmen employed in railways, factories, mines, quarries, engineering works, and docks. However, this was a wide enough range to cause masters to speak very strongly about the " charge on industry " ; and in the broadest sense this was in fact the first time that industry, and not the profits of industry, was made to bear a statutory burden of responsibility. The previous Employers' Liability Acts had all proceeded upon the basis of some tort for which employers could be sued, merely enlarging the list of torts. But the Workmen's Compensation Act made the employer liable for compensation for accidents which were inseparable from the employment, and not necessarily due to any shortcoming either in fellow-workmen or in machinery or plant. It gave a proper occasion for raising again the problem of lead-poisoning, phosphorus-poisoning in match-making, diseases of the lungs from file-cutting, etc. Mr H. J. Tennant, who had been secretary to the departmental committee on lead-poisoning, and was chairman of a similar committee on dangerous trades, which was sitting at this time, moved an instruction to include the victims of various industrial diseases in the Compensation Bill. But in view of the strong opposition which the Government had already to face on their own side, such an extension was hardly to be accepted. After all, the Bill as it stood was an immense advance.

Not the least interesting incident of the session was provided by an announcement which Mr Balfour made, almost casually, in reply to a question as to a possible inclusion of Ireland under the Agricultural Rating Act. Mr Balfour answered that, as there were no county councils in Ireland, there was no such means as the Local Taxation Exchequer Account provided in England for supplementing the remitted rates. But, he went on to say, a large payment would be made by the Exchequer, not merely to put agricultural rating in Ireland on the same footing as in England, but to allow for the landlord in Ireland not being, as such, rated at all. Thus the way would be cleared, he added, for an Irish Local Government Bill without fear of over-taxation of landlords. This was a rather sweeping instalment of the "alternatives to Home Rule," and the announcement called forth sharp criticism. Mr Balfour, the Conservatives thought, had done enough for Ireland in 1890. His Congested Districts Board had worked energetically, and the principle involved in it was more to the taste of Conservatives than was any form of local government. Indeed, the principle was being applied unofficially in Scotland to meet the crofters' grievances. Home industries were being encouraged by landlords and by committees of ladies all over Scotland, who made a market in London and elsewhere for cottage products, and so helped the crofters and cottars to earn the living which their holdings had ceased to provide, or had never provided. The year 1897 saw Harris tweeds and homespuns becoming a craze in England, and house-parties for shooting felt it a duty to be scented with a mild flavour of peat-reek.

The retrospects of domestic affairs, indulged in as the Jubilee approached, are peculiarly interesting. The previous Jubilee had produced a summing-up of the enormous advances in invention, means of communication, and all the mechanism of modern life. On the present occasion reflection was rather directed to changes in habits, and points of view regarding social responsibilities. Thus the change in the business world which was most noted was the greatly increased value attached to statistics, the advantage taken of information about the world's markets, and in general the tendency to set up a common stock of knowledge for the use of the trading intellect. In internal government the new cult of public health was singled out for comment. It is not without significance that, whereas the Prince of Wales had proposed to commemorate the earlier Jubilee by the foundation of the Imperial

Institute, he suggested as the memorial of the second Jubilee the establishment of the Hospital Fund for London which still bears his name. We have already seen the new cult at work in connection with the periodical alarms of cholera or fever, and in the attitude towards Pasteur and Koch. The feeling was strong that remedies, instead of being the main point, were rather a confession of failure ; and that the medical faculty was better occupied in producing healthy conditions than in waiting to deal with disease when it appeared. The campaign against slums, against adulteration of food, against over-pressure in factories, against sweating, now included, in alliance with those pioneers who assailed these things because they were morally wrong, the new fighters who said that they were stupid and suicidal, and gained thereby the ear of many who would have stood aside from what they considered the sentimentalities of the earlier efforts. Cleanliness and the ideal of physical fitness were vital elements in the new doctrine of efficiency ; and though the desire for fitness was producing an exaggerated passion for exercise, in some ranks of the community, it had vastly improved the standards of amusement and occupation. It was easy to see, and to deplore, the fact that the new spirit could not consort with the dignities and the ceremoniousness of other days. Rotten Row of a morning now was full of tweed jackets and bowler hats ; and the cycling clubs that streamed out of the large towns on a Saturday afternoon gave vent to their high spirits in a manner which profoundly offended the country gentleman. Authority was not what it had been ; but the collapse of some parts of its structure had let light in upon regions where at one time there had been darkness. The great advance of the serviceableness of electric tramways was promising to supply one of the solutions of slum problems, which had found a place in the Housing Commission's recommendations. Improvements in cheap locomotion might be used to break up congested areas, by enabling the workman to live farther from his work ; and the opening of the Blackwall Tunnel in this year—an undertaking by the London County Council which not even its severest critics condemned—led to the suggestion that the council's greatest service might well be to increase the traffic facilities of London.

One retrospect made at this time, though not suggested by the Jubilee, is of some historical interest. Sir Isaac Pitman, the inventor of the most successful system of shorthand, died early in the year ; and the occasion was taken for the question whether the greater facility for providing verbatim reports of speeches, which had been the result of his invention, had tended to the clarifying of politics. When the question was asked, there had not been time to see that recent developments of the Press were of a kind to nullify very largely Pitman's invention. The halfpenny newspaper, necessarily smaller than the penny paper, had not space to give to verbatim reports of speeches. Moreover, the public to which it appealed did not, as a whole, want to read entire speeches ; it wanted to be given, as briefly as possible, enough of the tenor of the speech to be able to talk about it. Therefore even if the invention of shorthand had in the past done anything to clarify politics, it was already too late to think of it as an effective force. The halfpenny Press was to be increased, before many years were over, by the lowering in price and size of two of the penny morning papers, which had suffered from the competition of the original halfpenny Press. That competition was also to act in subtler ways by making the people who still held to penny papers impatient of long reports. Shorthand had a firm foothold in commercial life, and Pitman remained a great inventor ; but for newspaper purposes his system had already seen its best days.

Although the populace made this second Jubilee much

more imperial in spirit than the first one, yet to the inner circle by the throne it was more domestic. The Queen's age now weighed heavily upon her. She hardly ever appeared in public; and those whom she received in audience noticed change creeping at last upon the venerable figure. It had come rather suddenly. It was but three years since Mr Gladstone, as Prime Minister, had seen her frequently in audience, and yet, when he was received by the Queen at Cimiez in the spring of this year he noticed a great difference. "The Queen's manner," he wrote at the time, "did not show the old and usual vitality"; and, remarking that the Queen's answers in conversation appeared to him to be very slight, he adds: "To speak frankly, it seemed to me that the Queen's peculiar faculty and habit of conversation had disappeared."[1] Queen Victoria was now not far from eighty years of age, and such ceremonies as those of 1887 were out of the question. In place of the service of that year in Westminster Abbey a less fatiguing form of thanksgiving was devised, which spared her even descent from her carriage. The procession went to St Paul's Cathedral; and the service was held on the great west steps, which were massed from top to bottom with notabilities in uniform. In the centre the rich copes of archbishops and bishops, and the white surplices of the choir, climbed the slope from the point at which the Queen's carriage was to stop. The glitter of equerries, aides-de-camp, and the escort filled the level semicircle facing the steps; and the immense, glowing picture was framed by tiers upon tiers of spectators in the houses overlooking it. The crowd in the streets was not quite what it had been in 1887. Observers noted that, while for three or four days vast numbers of people had paraded the decorated route of the procession, there was not on the morning of the procession that early rush for places which had been so remarkable ten years before.

[1] Morley's *Life of Gladstone*, iii. 524.

There was certainly much of the flatness of a repetition.
Yet London and the whole country kept holiday to the
full. The Queen gallantly bore her share in the festivities,
and gave a garden-party at Buckingham Palace, which
was chiefly remembered as drawing off so many Members
of Parliament from their duties that the Government
suffered three successive defeats in the division lobbies.
But the great event of the Jubilee celebrations was the
naval review. Assembled for it at Spithead were a
hundred and sixty-five warships, the fruit of ten years'
costly work—the navy of the new spirit. It was the Home
Fleet only, no ships having been recalled from foreign
stations. Next to the ships themselves, the presence of the
colonial representatives at the review was the centre of
interest. Mr Chamberlain had announced at the opening
of the session that the Prime Ministers of the self-governing
colonies had been invited to the Jubilee, not only to take
part in the celebrations, but also to confer with the Government on imperial questions. Their visit was made of
much greater importance than it had been in 1887. Mr
Chamberlain had struck a new note in his administration
of the Colonial Office, and the colonies were no longer
regarded as possessions making somewhat exacting demands upon the mother country's provision for defence,
but as sources of power and energy.[1] The Colonial
Conference showed the new feeling in an absence of the
somewhat barren amiability of the proceedings of 1887.
Thus the discussion of naval affairs was accompanied by
a warning to Australia to beware of her inclination to
think of her contribution to imperial naval expenditure
as necessarily entitling her to a kind of private sentry-go
on her coasts. Mr Chamberlain appealed to the Premiers
to remember that legislation in the colonies against
immigrant coloured labour could not be made a local
question in an empire which had responsibilities to

[1] Mr Chamberlain at the Colonial Institute, 31st March 1897.

14

millions of coloured subjects. A resolution was passed at
the conference in favour of federation, wherever such a
movement was geographically possible ; and an offer by
Canada of a preferential tariff in favour of British trade
led to a complicated discussion of existing fiscal treaties
and most-favoured-nation clauses. The idea of a Customs
Union within the empire was never very far from Mr
Chamberlain's thoughts.

Just as the great days of the Jubilee came to an end,
there appeared in *The Times* [1] a poem which stirred the
nation to an extraordinary degree. Afire with the pride
of the spectacle of power and majesty, it struck a chord
which prolonged as nothing else could have done the
reverberations of the vibrating national spirit. It was
Mr Rudyard Kipling's *Recessional*. In that poem,
more than in any of the pomps of the Jubilee days,
history will see represented the spirit of this year. In
a nation which for a century had not had to fight for
its life, which had in that period grown so wealthy that
huge increases in its bill for armaments were met with
little more than momentary murmurs, what was the true
range of patriotism ? In a community so accustomed to
security, so confident in its material resources of defence,
what was happening to the soul of the people ? To many
it seemed to be growing at once more assertive and less
determined, more demonstrative and less persistent, more
swiftly responsive but more easily diverted in attention.
Mr Kipling had made actual to the English populace
the daily round of far-distant wheels in the machine of
empire. He had created a consciousness of the curious
dullness, which familiarity with catch-words of rule produced in the heart of empire—the routine response to
patriotic stimulus, which was really no response at all.
He now struck this new consciousness a ringing blow.
With an insight brilliantly alert he gave to the pride of the

[1] On 17th July 1897.

moment exactly the right turn for the moment. On one side of the modern mind, the dislike of ostentatious superiority, the worship of fitness rather than superficial appearances, *Recessional* went to the very heart of the matter. To another side, the side of easy lip-patriotism, it was a warning. To the people as a whole it emphasised in the most remarkable way the feeling that the displays of naval and military power were a fresh start. A start for what end ? That, apparently, did not matter. The point was that we were not, as in 1887, to review achievements, and sun ourselves in them ; we were to set our faces forward.

On the north-west frontier of India operations had been undertaken against the warlike tribes inhabiting the mountain regions between India and Afghanistan, and were proving difficult and dangerous. The mountaineers, though not at any point in the campaign a really large force, made skilful use of the baffling nature of their country, and the heroism of British and Indian troops was severely tried. As the year advanced, temper was rising again in South African affairs. In April Sir Alfred Milner, a young man who had hitherto been known only for his work in connection with Lord Cromer's re-establishment of the finances of Egypt, and as Chairman of the Board of Inland Revenue, left England to succeed Sir Hercules Robinson as High Commissioner of Cape Colony. Such an appointment must obviously have special reasons ; they were found by the general public in a belief that Sir Alfred Milner went out as Mr Chamberlain's mouthpiece. The nature of his instructions was guessed at when Mr Chamberlain, at a dinner to Sir Alfred Milner on his departure, spoke of the hope of persuading the two white races in South Africa to live together in goodwill, but also spoke with firmness of the Convention of London, and of the British as " the paramount power in South Africa." In July the report of the South Africa Committee, ap-

pointed to inquire into the Raid, was published. Mr Cecil
Rhodes had been called as a witness ; *Punch's* cartoon that
week was of the shade of Warren Hastings meeting Mr
Rhodes at the committee-room door, and saying : " *I*
succeeded, and was impeached. *You* fail—and are called
as a witness ! " [1]   The report laid the responsibility for the
plans in South Africa, of which the Raid was the premature
revelation, on Mr Rhodes, Mr Beit and Mr Rutherfoord
Harris. It exonerated the High Commissioner and the
Colonial Office of any privity to what was going on, and in
that opinion the four principal Liberal members of the
committee, Sir William Harcourt, Sir Henry Campbell-
Bannerman, Mr John Ellis and Mr Sydney Buxton, agreed.
Mr Rhodes was by this time no longer either Premier of
Cape Colony or managing director of the British South
Africa Company. Men condoled with him ; those vast
schemes which had touched the English imagination
seemed to be driven into abeyance. The publication
of the report was followed within a few days by a
debate in the House of Commons. Certain telegrams
bearing upon Mr Rhodes's position had not been produced. They were in the possession of Mr B. F. Hawksley,
solicitor to the British South Africa Company. He, when
in the witness chair, had declined to produce them ; and
before he was called, Mr Rhodes, who might have been
asked to insist upon their production, had returned to
South Africa. It was believed that the committee had
not full information before them without those telegrams. Sir William Harcourt and Sir Henry Campbell-
Bannerman, to whom attack upon this point had been
specially addressed by Mr Philip Stanhope and Mr
Courtney, denied that there was any reason to suppose that
the telegrams would materially have altered the committee's decision. Mr Chamberlain, free of the accusations
that by the unofficial medium of Miss Flora Shaw, a

[1] *Punch*, 6th February 1897.

special correspondent of *The Times*, he was secretly in touch with Mr Rhodes, made his own vigorous defence of the committee. The feeling behind the attack was not solely concerned with the committee. It was almost as much an anxious suspicion that this clearing of reputations was really a clearing of the decks for action; and that if Mr Chamberlain and Mr Rhodes had not understood one another before, they did so now. President Kruger had sent to the British Government a claim for a large indemnity for the Raid. This "bill for intellectual and moral damage" became at once a joke in England; but it was a wry joke, and people grew more and more inclined to say that, if President Kruger was determined not to let the affair blow over, Mr Rhodes and his friends were not to be deserted.

"Africa," said Lord Salisbury at the Guildhall banquet this year, "was created to be the plague of the Foreign Office." He was not thinking of the Transvaal, which was the concern of another department. Central Africa, which a few years earlier had laid Uganda upon the Government's shoulders, was now offering a new burden in the shape of Nigeria. The Royal Niger Company, owing to the successes of Sir George Goldie in Nupé and Ilorin, was now within range of the spheres of influence of other European countries; and it was therefore becoming impossible to leave the affairs of their territory any longer in private hands, capably though the company was being administered. The massacre of an unarmed British expedition near Benin City had called forth another small war. French influence was extremely active in regions bordering on the Niger, and the Foreign Office could not regard its new tasks with complacency. At the same time the charges against the administration of the Congo State became more direct and articulate. The root of the matter was laid bare in the argument that a country like the Congo could not by legitimate means be made to produce revenue, not only for the cost of administration, but for enriching exalted persons in Belgium. The virtual closing of the country to traders of other than Belgian nationality was suspicious, and some of the missionaries were giving terrible accounts of the forcing of the rubber trade. The trial of Dr Carl Peters in Berlin this year on charges of excessive cruelty in German East Africa, for which he was sentenced to be dismissed the service and to pay fines, was disturbing the general conscience on the conditions of European rule in Africa.

A curious incident of the year in England was a fresh onslaught on betting, which threatened at one time to have astonishing results. The Anti-Gambling League had brought an extremely bold test case. Its secretary, Mr Hawke, sued a bookmaker named Dunn, and in the result three judges, including so notoriously sporting a judge as Mr Justice Hawkins, held that Tattersall's ring was a "place" within the meaning of the Act of 1853, which made illegal resort to any place for the purpose of betting. Dunn was merely walking about in the ring at Hurst Park without any mark of his calling, and therefore the case appeared to settle the whole question of the legality of betting. If betting in the ring was illegal, would not any place where a bet was made become a "place" under the Act? It must be said that a number of sporting people were not sorry to see the attack upon professional bookmaking. It had spread from horse-racing to football; and seemed likely to provide a form of excitement which might in the end destroy interest in sport and athletics, and reduce them to mere means for gambling. In a second case, Powell v. Kempton Park Racecourse Company, the Lord Chief Justice, following the previous decision, held that the plaintiff was entitled to an injunction restraining the defendants from opening Tattersall's enclosure; and the company's defence, that they did not open it for betting purposes and need not be held to know

what went on in it, was in vain. The situation promised
to become farcical, when the Court of Appeal (the case
reached that court in a month, which gives some measure
of the place of sport in English affairs) reversed the Lord
Chief Justice's decision. One Lord Justice in the Appeal
Court still held to it that every place where a bet was made
was a " place " within the Act, not shrinking from the
logical conclusion that this would render every private bet
illegal. The case was carried to the House of Lords, and
there went finally against the Anti-Gambling League, by
a majority of eight to two of the law lords. The vexed
question of the meaning of the word " place " in the Act
of 1853 was settled by the House of Lords' judgment,
which ruled that the word must be held to apply to some
" house, room or office," or place of that kind, and could
not fairly be applied to a quarter of an acre of ground on a
racecourse.

The Penrhyn quarry dispute lasted until nearly the end
of August. Helped by private collections all over the
country, and also by funds raised by Welsh choirs,
the men had held out for almost a year. In the
settlement which was reached at last they won the right
of combination in a minor degree, but Lord Penrhyn
carried his decision to allow no general quarry committee,
and to refuse to receive any complaints except from
individuals, or from a deputation of the particular class
of men professing a grievance—in a word, his refusal to
recognise the men as a body corporate. The men also
obtained the stoppage of the practice of sub-letting contracts, which had led to a sweating of wages. Meanwhile
a serious strike of engineers had broken out ; the London
men demanded an eight-hours day. The masters replied
by discharging 25 per cent. of their men ; and the masters
in the north-east of England and on the Clyde, in order to
stand by the London masters, discharged men in the same
proportion, with the intention of burdening the trade

union with out-of-work pay to a degree which would prevent the union's resources being exclusively at the service of the London men. Then the union called out all its men in the trade, and by the beginning of July the dispute, which had started in London in May, had reached very grave proportions. Seventy thousand men were on strike ; and the strike came at a time when the works were full of orders ; electric tramways were spreading with great rapidity, and there was a vast quantity of work to be done in equipping them. The strike was a determined one ; the trade union held out in a manner which caused the masters to assert that it must be using for strike pay funds accumulated for other purposes, such as superannuation pay. It was suggested also that, in order to keep the funds up, the union was winking at the return to work of some of its men. In December two proposals for a settlement, reached by conference, were put to a ballot of the men—the first that the masters' assertion of unquestioned control of their works should be accepted, and the second that there should be a provisional arrangement for a fifty-one-hours week, as approximating to the men's demand. Mr John Burns (himself an engineer) and other leaders of the strike introduced into the eight-hours-day demand an offer to take only one meal-time in the day. The proposals were rejected by an overwhelming majority of the men, and the strike continued. There were threatenings of strikes among the railwaymen and the cotton employees as well, but these were fortunately averted. Labour was concentrating its aims anew, after its defeats at the polls two years previously. The Trade Union Congress of 1897 put forward a very large programme, which included, in addition to the eight-hours day, the taxation of ground values, the limitation of shop hours, reform of the law of conspiracy, the abolition of child labour under the age of fifteen and of night labour for all persons under the age of eighteen, and a number of detailed matters of inspection and supervision of industry. The milder form of comment on this list was that it lacked legislative definiteness ; but the social legislation of the past years was producing a sharper comment to the effect that Labour was acquiring a privileged position in the community. The annual Labour report of the Board of Trade spoke of general diminution of hours of work, and general increase of wages, including even the agricultural labourer. The case of the small employer was felt to be growing hard ; but it was not perceived that the economic changes, which had drawn so much accumulated capital into manufacture, must necessarily alter the position of the small employer. He could not regard his returns in the same light as a man could, to whom they were but dividend on money invested. However, some of the conferences of Labour, such as those of the Miners, the Co-operative Societies, the Friendly Societies, suggested the comforting comment that Labour had more interests and more voices than its most advanced spokesmen represented ; in the multiplicity some safety for the employers was felt to be implied. A suggestion was made, upon the publication in July of a Home Office report on some dangerous trades— the handling of horse-hair and rags, especially—that the trade unions might do good by calling the attention of workmen to the perils of carelessness in such trades, and educating the men to attend to the precautions specified in Home Office rules. But for the moment the unions could hardly deal with more than their conflicts with capital.

The year witnessed two notable events in the history of art in England. The Tate Gallery was opened, and for the first time the work of modern English painters, who had led a genuinely indigenous movement, became an acknowledged portion of the fabric of British art. In the main the collection housed in the Gallery was, indeed, a thoroughly official collection ; the Royal Academy held sway, and at once began the policy of using the Gallery as a repository of works bought under the Chantrey Bequest. Yet even this was not altogether a disadvantage ; the accumulation in public of the fruits of a fund administered in a spirit completely at variance with the most enlightened and most informed views of the day was a demonstration of the narrowness of the Academy's range. The other event of the year was the passing of the famous Wallace Collection into the possession of the nation. It had long been known as one of the greatest collections in existence, the main portion consisting of French furniture and decorative objects, and French pictures and sculpture ; there was also a choice collection of armour of all periods and countries, Japanese, Indian and Arabian, as well as European. The whole had been collected by Sir Richard Wallace, who was supposed to be the natural son of the fourth Marquis of Hertford, and so grandson of the notorious Marquis, who was the original of Thackeray's Lord Steyne and Disraeli's Lord Monmouth. For this account of his parentage there is no known authority. Sir Richard Wallace, who had been Lord Hertford's confidential secretary and adopted son, lived all his life in Paris, modest and retiring, but known to connoisseurs as perhaps the greatest collector of the age. At the time of his death in 1890 there was some speculation as to the future of the collection, which it was believed he had destined for the British nation. But he died without making a will, and his treasures passed absolutely to Lady Wallace. In 1897 she died, and it was found that she had done what he had been expected to do. After some discussion as to the suitable housing of the collection the Government acquired Hertford House, in Manchester Square ; and were thus able to display the wonderful things in the town mansion of the family from which their collector had derived his fortune.

One of the results of the conflict of opinion on the assistance to be given to Voluntary schools was to bring out the great elasticity with which the Education Acts were now being administered. The strides made by technical education have already been mentioned. It was basing itself on the broadest view of its objects, and a report published by the Technical Education Board of the London County Council early this year lays down, as principles of the Board's work, that the early stages of scientific training must be purely educational, not technological, and that the only lasting commercial value of technical instruction was in its being given to well-educated minds. The same conclusions, though in a negative form, were really inherent in the neat criticism made by *The Times* on the proceedings of an International Conference on Technical Education, held in June. The criticism was that in this country the quality of technical education in the upper grades was not high enough, while the quantity of it in the lower grades was wasteful.[1] The hope of those interested in national education rested largely in the Higher Grade Board Schools, institutions which had grown up quietly under the Education Acts, though they had not been contemplated by the framers of the Acts. There were now sixty of them in Great Britain, fifty-five being under School Board management. The lower classes in these schools were taught on the lines of the upper standards of a public elementary school ; the higher classes were taught as an " organised science school " under the Science and Art Department of the Board of Education. Such instruction lasted for three years, and included science, mathematics, drawing, manual training, English, and at least one foreign language. All the schools were large ones, accommodating from five hundred to two thousand children each, and all had been filled as soon as they were opened, thus proving themselves the answer to a real demand. They supplied what nothing else supplied, an extension of elementary education, by which scholars of

[1] *The Times,* 17th June 1897.

any merit could pass on without a break to opportunities of mental equipment. The Science and Art Department usually bore a considerable share of the expense of the higher classes. But there was a hostile feeling among ratepayers against the schools. True, in some cases it died down after a few years' experience of the results; but this was not a general rule. Moreover, there were a very large number of small country grammar schools, depending for their prosperity upon the fees paid by the small tradesmen or the artisans, who liked their children to go to better institutions than the elementary schools. These now found the higher grade schools good enough for their purpose, and saved themselves grammar school fees. The grammar schools consequently complained of unfair competition, and found no insignificant body of ratepayers ready to join in the charge that higher education could not be given by the Board schools without misappropriation of rates.

The new spirit in the stamping out of disease by attacking its direct and contributory causes was active this year, both in matters of housing and of water-supply, owing to outbreaks of typhoid fever at Maidstone and King's Lynn; and also in drastic orders for the muzzling of dogs. The Government pursued this latter policy in the face of grumbling, which even amounted, it was thought, to a decrease of the Unionist vote at some bye-elections. Respectable people, who could see readily enough that the application of severe sanitary regulations in poor quarters was wise, refused to have severe regulations applied in another matter to themselves. Yet the medical authorities, and Pasteur himself, had asserted over and over again that in any country a universal muzzling order, combined with measures of quarantine for all imported dogs, would entirely put an end to rabies. The Government now took the bold course, and issued a universal muzzling order in April. They could point, before the year was out, to notable proof of the value of their action. In 1895 there had been over the whole country 608 cases of rabies; in 1897 there were only 141. In London alone, where the London County Council had already achieved some good results, the cases in 1896 numbered 161, and in 1897 only 29. The previous application of a muzzling order to Lancashire and Yorkshire [1] had reduced the number of cases in those counties from 461 in 1895, to 39 in 1896. Ten years later, as has been remarked earlier in this volume, England had practically forgotten that such a disease as rabies existed.

The summer of 1897 was the period of the famous rush to the Klondyke goldfields. It had long been known that gold was in those regions of the extreme North-West [2]; but the appalling difficulties of approach to the country— access by the almost Arctic rivers and passes being only possible for a few weeks during the summer—and the miseries and privations of life there, when once the mines were reached, had hitherto held back all but the stoutest pioneers. But now the gold fever broke out, and terrors could not stand against it. Men poured northward, some by boat to the Klondyke River, others madly by the land route through Western Canada. They died in hundreds, the vast majority of men starting with no knowledge whatever of the difficulties of the journey or the delays to be provided against. Death held the Chilcoot Pass, as he had never held the most arid waste of Australia in the days of the gold fever there.

Two events filled the newspapers just before Christmas. One was the death of William Terriss, an extremely popular actor of melodrama. He was stabbed as he was entering the stage-door of the Adelphi Theatre, by a man who had been disappointed in applications for charitable relief. It was a strange thing that a man who had suffered in his life so many fictitious violences, should meet his end

[1] See page 396.   [2] See page 56.

by violence. The other event, while in one sense treated as comic, was not without serious effect upon the temper of the country in international affairs. The German Emperor had decided to send a squadron of warships to China, where some German missionaries had been killed. Throughout the year there had been a somewhat undignified scramble for advantage in China on the part of the European Powers, owing to the success of Japan in forcing open Chinese markets to her trade by operations of war. On the departure of the German squadron from Kiel the Emperor charged his brother, Prince Henry of Prussia, who was in command, to remember that he went as " the mailed fist " of German authority. Prince Henry replied in a like strain, to the effect that he would inscribe his brother's augustness on his banners. England was very ready to seize upon the ludicrous side of these exchanges ; but the jesting sprang from the spirit of suspicion with which Englishmen had regarded every act of the young Emperor, since his accession to the throne.

CHAPTER XX

1898 : MOSTLY OTHER PEOPLE'S AFFAIRS

ENGLAND showed now a singular unconsciousness of what was at hand; the army establishment was increased, the navy was strengthened both in ships and in men; and never had such increases been made with less public concern, or less anxiety as to the need for them.

In truth it was a year of lively interests quite dissociated from the main preoccupation of the Government. Some of these interests were other people's business rather than our own, but that did not prevent us from expressing ourselves about them. In one instance our expression of opinion undoubtedly did harm; in another it did good.

At the beginning of the year France was torn asunder by the violent controversy which had arisen, a few months earlier, as to the conviction of Captain Alfred Dreyfus on a charge of selling French military secrets to Germany. He had been condemned by court martial, and was now a prisoner on Devil's Island, the French penal settlement. Many notable Frenchmen found the conviction lying heavy on their consciences. Captain Dreyfus was a Jew, and there was an uncomfortable fear that Anti-Semite feeling had counted far too heavily in the trial, if indeed it had not entirely dictated the proceedings. Those who believed in the accused's innocence thought that the efforts to detect the criminal had ended somewhat too readily when suspicion pointed to an officer who was a Jew. The agitation in France rose in January to a dangerous height. One newspaper, *Le Siècle*, published in full the text of the indictment against Captain Dreyfus, which it could not have done unless the agitation had some supporters in high place in the army. Another newspaper, *L'Aurore*, published a tremendous letter from M. Zola, the novelist, accusing the Government, the judiciary, the police, the heads of the army, and other national authorities of gross perversion of justice. A new trial of Captain Dreyfus was demanded. On the other side, Anti-Semite feeling allied itself with the passionate devotion of France to her army; and all who ventured to call in question a decision by an army tribunal on an army case were assailed as traitors of the lowest kind. English opinion, not at the moment disposed to take the kindliest views of French affairs, plunged in to support the champions of Dreyfus; and when Colonel Picquart, who had boldly taken the side of those demanding revision of the sentence, was placed in retirement, English criticism grew louder. Profound ignorance of the facts of the case, and of the procedure of the court martial, did not prevent people in this country from confidently expressing their views; and the objection felt by French people to any reconsideration of an army verdict found practically no sympathy here. M. Zola was put on his trial in Paris for his assault upon the various national institutions, and was sentenced to undergo one year's imprisonment, and to pay a fine of 3000 francs. At once people on this side of the Channel, who had no good word to say for M. Zola as an author, found plenty to say for him as a martyr. In French eyes the attitude of Great Britain at this time must have been very offensive, not so much because of its busybody interference, as because of its contemptuous dismissal of French susceptibilities as to the honour of the army.

But at the height of this controversy a more startling event drew off British attention. The United States warship

Maine was sunk by an explosion in Havana harbour ; and swift as the news itself was the universal conclusion that war between the United States and Spain would follow. Those two countries had for some time been on bad terms. Spain, comparatively poor, and no longer possessing the strong arm of ancient days, had been struggling against a revolution in Cuba, which, pitilessly repressed in a sporadic way, remained vigorous and persistent. The Cuban revolutionaries had enlisted the sympathy of the United States ; but Spain, finding her task difficult enough as it was, did not incline to reply amiably to intervention by the Americans. The lives of American citizens in Havana, the seat of the Spanish Government in Cuba, were considered to be in some jeopardy when rioting took place there ; the cruiser *Maine* was sent to anchor in the harbour for their protection and their refuge in case of necessity. About this time opinion in the United States was inflamed by the publication of some unofficial letters written by the Spanish Minister in Washington, in which he had commented in undiplomatic language on the relations between the States and the Cuban insurgents. When the news came of the sinking of the *Maine* on 15th February there was probably not an American in the whole of the States who did not believe it to be the act of Spaniards—a deliberate and dastardly act of hostility.

But before war actually broke out, a third shifting of British interest occurred. The reconquest of the Soudan was undertaken in good earnest. A year earlier, on 5th February 1897, Sir Michael Hicks Beach had announced in the House of Commons the intention of the Government to " give the final blow to the baleful power of the Khalifa." The year had passed without any very spectacular movement. But the railway was pushed forward from Wady Halfa towards Abu Hamed, a short cut avoiding the bend of the Nile by Dongola, and on 7th August 1897 Abu Hamed was occupied after a sharp fight in which all the dervishes engaged against the Egyptian troops were either killed or made prisoners. So complete a defeat had its effects at once. Berber was evacuated by the Khalifa's forces and occupied by the Egyptians, the advance of the railway to that point being immediately undertaken. The beginning of 1898 brought more exciting news. Kitchener reported that the dervishes were advancing upon him from Khartoum. He made ready for them, if they should choose to be the attackers, and encamped in a strong position between Berber and the junction of the river Atbara with the Nile. The Emir Mahmoud brought 12,000 dervishes up to Nakheila, on the Atbara; as he came no farther, Kitchener, not liking his immobility, sent out reconnaissances. Mahmoud was found in a strong zariba in the bush, and Kitchener laid his plans with caution. On 8th April he attacked, and in forty minutes Mahmoud himself was a prisoner, 2000 of his men were dead, and the rest scattered to the desert perils of privation and thirst. Machine guns, vastly improved since the days of the earlier Soudan warfare, accounted now, as later in the year, for the very large numbers of the slain. News of this battle made real to people at home the work of reconquest, and during the summer British reinforcements were despatched to join the forces under Kitchener's command.

A fortnight later war had formally broken out between the United States and Spain. The States Senate recognised the independence of Cuba, the respective diplomatic envoys were withdrawn, a squadron of the American fleet sailed from Key West for Havana, and the whole energy of the American nation went into pouring troops, regulars and volunteers, southward to Florida for transhipment to Cuba. At the same time another Spanish possession, Manila, was attacked by a squadron which had been at Hong-Kong. The war has a place in a history of the

English people, because every phase of it was followed with the keenest interest here. At times it was a somewhat hilarious interest. We had not then had our own experience of the uncertainties of bombardment with modern long-range weapons and modern explosives ; so that the occasional intimations from the Spanish side of ludicrously small results of an apparently terrific bombardment (the mule of Matanzas, reported to be the only casualty of a gun-fire of many hours, became quite famous) were received with jesting. Moreover, though Admiral Dewey succeeded in promptly destroying the Spanish fleet in Manila harbour, the Spaniards showed every sign of making a good fight elsewhere. Admiral Cervera succeeded in navigating a fleet right across the Atlantic and entering Santiago harbour, eluding all the American warships that were scouring the sea to intercept him. No one thought the conflict a level one, but this achievement somewhat restored the balance for the moment.

Home affairs presented very little of interest. Business was good on the whole, and the Bankers' Clearing House returns reached the highest total yet known. Gold imports had become so large that, besides satisfying the requirements of other countries, England was at last able to increase materially her own bullion reserve. It is no diminution of these evidences of prosperity to find the Stock Exchange rather less active. There were, as we shall shortly see, reasons which checked speculation by the general public. Save for a coal strike in South Wales there was no serious trade dispute. In science no new theory or new invention arose to catch the popular mind ; but for those behind the scenes the advances made in knowledge of the properties of the Hertzian waves, upon which wireless telegraphy was founded, were considerable. Mr W. H. Preece, chief of the engineering department of the Post Office, and Dr Oliver Lodge were busy with experiments; but the experiments which were already making the name of Marconi famous were meeting with more obvious success. Parliament met for a session to which very little attention was paid. The Ministerial party was again attacked by acute indigestion in assimilating Liberal Unionism. Lingering fragments of Mr Chamberlain's Radicalism were discerned in a Bill designed to meet the unwavering hostility of large numbers of people to vaccination, by permitting parents to make a declaration before a magistrate, expressing conscientious objection to the method of inoculation. His influence, again, was traced in the introduction of the Irish Local Government Bill, which Mr Balfour had promised. Both measures were attended with friction throughout their course. But it was almost entirely parliamentary friction; and there was little controversy in the country on domestic affairs. The Army Estimates showed an increase of 21,739 men in the establishment; the Navy Estimates reached almost twenty-four million pounds, and provided for fresh construction of ships and for an increase of 6300 men. Most remarkable of all, a supplementary naval vote of no less than eight millions was passed practically without discussion during July. The spirit of the Liberal party was at a deplorably low ebb. We have had occasion to see that, even before Mr Gladstone's retirement, the party had had little unity save in devotion to him. After his retirement the rifts opened rapidly. Lord Rosebery's surrender of the leadership led only to a momentary bridging of them; and they were now opening again under Sir William Harcourt. An advanced section, joining hands with the Labour members, refused to forgive the leaders for having missed the opportunity in 1894 of trying conclusions with the House of Lords. Another section, weary of the continuance of a Whig tradition in leadership, clamoured for a leader of true modern Radicalism. Yet another section, feeling the new Imperial spirit in the air, were of opinion that a narrow and nagging temper was being displayed in perpetual criticisms of Mr Chamberlain.   The utter weakness of the opposition caused by these divisions, was responsible both for languor in Parliament and for lack of public interest in politics.

On 19th May Mr Gladstone died.   That was, indeed, no occasion for the refreshment of party loyalty alone; it was by common consent a time of universal mourning and national pride.   The four years since Mr Gladstone's retirement, to him the means of a calm and dignified approach to death, had given him back to the nation from the strife of party.   The British people rose to the height of that noble appreciation of a life greatly lived which sounded from all the world outside.   From France, from Russia, from the British colonies and the United States came tributes of honour and respect; from Italy, Greece and Macedonia came expressions of a more profound sense of loss and of a more intimate gratitude for the work of a great lover of freedom.   By a decision which had no precedent in our history, and was a worthy acceptance by the nation of the lofty sentiment of the civilised world, Mr Gladstone's body was laid in state in Westminster Hall, and for two days multitudes of people of every rank filed past the bier.[1]   On 28th May the body was buried in Westminster Abbey; and, as the lying-in-state had been the token of Mr Gladstone's place in the hearts of the people, his funeral was the token of his place among the rulers of the people.   The Prince of Wales and the Duke of York walked beside the coffin as pall-bearers; and other pall-bearers were the Prime Minister and the leaders of the two parties in both Houses of Parliament, Lord Rosebery, the Duke of Rutland, and Mr Gladstone's friends, Lord Rendel and Mr Armitstead.   Representatives

---

[1] The police calculated that 250,000 people passed through the Hall during the two days.

of foreign sovereigns were present. The mighty mould of the leader who had passed away was everywhere recognised. New problems were arising for his successors, in an England that he hardly recognised. " I am thankful," he wrote after his retirement,[1] " to have borne a great part in the emancipating labours of the last sixty years, but entirely uncertain how, had I now to begin my life, I could face the very different problems of the next sixty years. Of one thing I am, and always have been, convinced—it is not by the State that man can be regenerated and the terrible woes of this darkened world effectually dealt with." That was the voice of the past ; and yet at the moment what voice had the future ? None, it would seem, in the leaders of Liberalism, who, distracted and divided among themselves, knew not what their party was, nor where it stood. To some of those by the grave in the Abbey it may well have seemed that they were burying not only a famous Liberal, but all the Liberalism they knew.

The pace of the American attack in Cuba now quickened. Transport difficulties and delays were to some extent overcome ; and the fleet under Admiral Schley blockaded Santiago harbour. Again an event occurred at home to catch the wandering interest of newspaper readers. It was announced with startling abruptness that Mr E. T. Hooley had filed his petition in bankruptcy. He was a man who had risen almost as abruptly into prominence, a promoter of companies extremely active during the boom in the cycle manufacturing trade. He had reconstituted and refloated several large firms, and had also placed upon the investment market a good many mechanical inventions connected with cycling. In the full flush of his career he had bought large estates in the country, and made some lavish public gifts. His suite of rooms in one of the big London hotels was accustomed to witness daily levees of

[1] To Mr G. W. E. Russell. See Mr Russell's *One Look Back*, p. 265.

financiers, brokers, large and small investors, journalists, traders, inventors, cranks. Company-promoting, profitable as it had been for years past, had never before reached so picturesque a point, had never been such an obvious and theatrical wielding of forces; the limited liability system in England had never presented itself in so personal a manifestation. The news of the bankruptcy was a thunderbolt. It was the end of the cycle boom, and the beginning of difficult times for companies overweighted by a capital disproportionate to any requirements save those of a boom. Fashion had already tired of its new toy, and Battersea Park no longer glittered with expensive machines. American manufacturers were sending over by thousands machines of a lighter and less expensive type than the English; the competition in the home market was cutting prices. Meanwhile France was commanding the market for motor cars; and the British cycle firms, which might have taken up the new invention, were caught in the toils of depression. The names of various public men were bandied to and fro during the bankruptcy proceedings in Mr Hooley's case; and once again company-promoting acquired a reputation which checked even the most ardent speculator.

The war between the United States and Spain ended in August. Early in July Admiral Cervera made a gallant but desperate attempt to break through the blockade of Santiago. His fleet steamed out of the harbour, and turned along the coast. Within a few hours every ship was destroyed or captured. Some were sunk, some ran ashore blazing from stem to stern. Santiago surrendered to the American land forces on 17th July, and on 12th August peace negotiations were opened, which ended in Spain's acquiescence in the independence of Cuba, and the ceding of Manila to the United States.

The beginning of September brought news far more exciting to England. On the 2nd of that month the British

and Egyptian forces had practically destroyed the Khalifa's
army at Omdurman, and on the 4th Kitchener had re-
occupied Khartoum. The flag again waved on those ruined
walls of the palace, its absence from which had been so tragically noted on that January morning in 1885. Great was
the pride in this assertion of British power and persistence;
but not less strong an element in the enthusiasm with which
the news was received was the revelation of our possession
of a new soldier of the first rank. The battle of Omdurman
had been won by more than fighting; and the interest
in the accounts of the battle was not greater than the
interest in all that could be told of the masterly organisation, the practical care for troops, the sheer business
ability with which Kitchener had brought his army to its
victory. True, it was known later that for a short time he
had been in a somewhat dangerous position; and that, if
the Khalifa had had any officer of tactical ability, or any
renegade European adviser at his elbow, Kitchener's
communications might have been cut, and he would then
have been less able to choose the moment of attack in
confidence.[1] But there was no doubt that the movements
of the past two years had been masterly, exhaustively considered, and above all made, so far as such movements
could be made, in all the security and material comfort
that forethought could provide for the troops. Lord
Kitchener of Khartoum, as he was at once made, became
a popular idol of a new kind. Men worshipped in him a
grim and relentless efficiency, a cool soldierliness. The ideal
of the dashing warrior gave place to the ideal of the "dead-
certainty warrior." There was, indeed, a severe completeness in the battle. Of 40,000 or 50,000 dervishes who had
met him before the walls of Omdurman, 11,000 were killed
and 16,000 wounded. The British and Egyptian forces
numbered only 22,000 men—less than the casualties alone
on the other side—and their losses were but three officers

---

[1] Lord Cromer's *Modern Egypt*, ii. 94, footnote.

and forty-three men killed, and twenty-one officers and three hundred and twenty men wounded. The Khalifa himself, with a band of his principal emirs and a broken force of dervishes, escaped from the slaughter and wandered for a year in the desert. Then on 24th November 1899 he too was swept into the iron completeness of the work. One of Lord Kitchener's officers, who afterwards succeeded him as Sirdar, Sir Francis Wingate, surprised the flying, harried little army by rapid and skilful marches, and brought it to bay. When that last fight was over the Khalifa was found dead on the field, with every one of his emirs dead, each on his prayer-mat, around their leader. The total cost of the two years' campaign under the man of marvellous organisation was no more than £2,354,000.

The reconquest of the Soudan had been saved, by a mistake on the part of France and Russia, from being hampered by international complications.[1] Could the future government of it equally be saved ? Before this question was asked the British and Egyptian flags were hoisted side by side at Khartoum ; and though diplomatists might find no proper formula for a joint control by Great Britain and Egypt, in which Great Britain was first, and yet Egypt not quite second, the solution took that form, and succeeded in spite of its resistance to formulation. The most critical danger arose within a week of the battle of Omdurman. The move made by the French towards the Upper Nile, to which Sir Charles Dilke with his usual command of little-known facts had tried to call attention in 1896,[2] was made public in a perilously sudden way by the news that Lord Kitchener had started from Khartoum up the Blue Nile, in consequence of information that a French force was in possession of a place called Fashoda. Temper rose sharply both in Great Britain and in France. On this side of the Channel it was felt that an attempt was being made to wrest from us, now that we had made the

Soudan a safe region again, some part of the regained territory. On the other side it was felt that the British, greedy for rule, were denying to a band of courageous explorers the just rewards of their skill and endurance. Lord Kitchener had the wisdom not to force action upon the French officer, Captain Marchand, whom he found at Fashoda. He merely established a British post there as well, and returned to Khartoum. The fact that Captain Marchand remained at Fashoda, the fact that the British flag was at Fashoda, were just sufficient to put popular opinion on either side in the right in its own view; and two months later, on 4th November, Lord Salisbury was able to announce that the French had withdrawn from the place. By that time Lord Kitchener was in England, visiting the Queen at Balmoral, receiving a sword of honour from the City of London, and showing to the enthusiastic clamour of the populace an unmoved countenance, which exactly suited the crowd's conception of him as the embodiment of " efficiency for its own sake." The French nation, on its side, had enough to think about. An officer of the army, Colonel Henry, had confessed to forging one of three letters upon which the upholders of the Dreyfus trial largely relied, and had then committed suicide. At the beginning of October the Cour de Cassation obtained the leave of the Government to undertake revision of the trial; and in this upheaval of its confidence the French people found Fashoda but a minor incident.

Towards the end of the year Lord Salisbury fluttered public interest by appointing Mr George Curzon to be Viceroy of India, with the title of Lord Curzon of Kedleston. Mr Curzon's fame rested, so far as England at large was concerned, less on his knowledge of the Far East, where he had travelled in curious countries on the north-west frontier of India and in Persia, than on his reputation as one of the most opinionated and positive young men that Oxford had sent into public life. He had been Under-

Secretary for India just before the dissolution of 1892, and was Under-Secretary for Foreign Affairs in the present Government. He was not yet forty, and even in this year of perpetual excitements his appointment to the Vice-royalty was received with a gasp of astonishment.

Of South Africa little was heard in this year. The officers concerned in the Jameson Raid, with the exception of Sir John Willoughby and Colonel Rhodes, were restored to their places in the British army; and after the battle of Omdurman, where Colonel Rhodes, who was acting as a war correspondent, was wounded, he also was restored to his rank. Mr Cecil Rhodes was re-elected a director of the British South Africa Company. These events had their meaning, but nothing at the moment pressed the meaning home.

BOOK II: 1899–1910

CHAPTER I

ENGLAND IN 1899

ENGLAND in 1899 hardly represented the ideal spectacle of a people on the eve of a relentless trial of its spirit. The national temper at the moment was a curious mixture of hilarity and moodiness, of assurance and anxious calculations, of energy and hesitation. So indeterminate were feeling and purpose that a generally warlike disposition was presently to greet the actual outbreak of war as a thunderbolt. Politics were at an unhealthy pause, social life in an equally unhealthy fever. In commerce an unparalleled volume of business was being regarded almost askance ; prosperity was felt to be founded upon ill-considered and inadequate business methods. In this matter, as in others, the country was in an introspective frame of mind. Many elements in its activities were seen to be false. Such perception, however, formed no real preparedness for the ordeal of the melting pot. The quality of the national metal was not doubted : only its shape and the keenness of its edge were in question.

The futility of current political exchanges was obvious in each of the three political parties. The Conservative Government could not feel much interest in proposing home legislation while South African affairs were assuming daily a more menacing aspect. The Conservative majority was so large that marking time involved no danger in the division lobbies. Moreover, the Government had little to fear from an Opposition more than half paralysed by internal divisions. These had now become acute. In

December 1898 Sir William Harcourt had declined to lead any longer; and in the ensuing correspondence between him and Mr John Morley (which formed the vehicle for conveying Sir William Harcourt's decision to the public) there had been exasperated revelations of the conflict of opinion, the sectional disagreements rife among Liberals. The deepest cause of division was one which in the next two or three years was to operate more and more violently —the division to be represented under the labels Liberal Imperialist and Little Englander. Ever since the Jameson Raid there had been within the Liberals a group which regarded with the utmost suspicion the Conservative policy of expansion, believing it to involve an immoral concentration of purpose on aggrandisement. The Soudan campaign and the annexation of the Soudan, so deeply altering our position in Egypt, provided food for this belief; the victory at Omdurman appeared to these men unnecessarily murderous, and the destruction of the Mahdi's tomb and the exhumation of his body (deliberately undertaken to prevent a revival of fanaticism) they criticised as barbarous acts. This group, composed of active and energetic men, watching with gravest misgivings the trend of affairs in South Africa, was able to make its current of opinion a marked one in the party. On the other hand, many Liberals thought such views were too straitened, and that moreover they were coloured by an unpraiseworthy dislike and distrust of Mr Chamberlain's personality. The rescue of the Soudan from the Khalifa was, they said, after all, an advance of civilisation in a dark spot of the earth; and, as for South Africa, it was strange for Liberalism to be in the position of defending a state of affairs in which half a population was being taxed without representation. (For, of course, the Little Englander's criticisms of Mr Chamberlain's methods in regard to the Transvaal were readily made to appear as a defence of President Kruger's.) Lord Rosebery was generally looked on as leader of the Liberal Imperialists, but here again a side current was working. A good many Liberals who had little sympathy with anti-Imperialism considered that Lord Rosebery showed a propensity towards sentimental jingoism, and was too ready to treat the acquisition of any swamp in South Africa as of greater importance than conditions in England. There was prevalent also a feeling that the Liberal party had let slip its opportunity of guiding democratic impulse. Mr Gladstone, we have seen, had frankly held his leadership from 1886 to 1894 for one purpose only—Home Rule; he had been followed by Lord Rosebery, who had shown little sympathy for democratic movements; and Lord Rosebery had been succeeded by Sir William Harcourt, who was in every sense a Whig. That the urgent need, as well as the propelling force, of Social Reform seemed to have passed the party by was the feeling of a letter published in 1899 by a group of young Oxford Liberals—unknown at the time but to be known honourably enough before long. In this year they added to the resources of Liberalism a weekly organ—*The Speaker*.

In view of the dissensions among Liberals, it was small wonder that Professor Goldwin Smith, writing one of his letters of a looker-on from Canada, should say that what was wanted in 1899 was rather a party than a leader. But it was with the choice of a leader the disagreements at the moment were most concerned. The difficulties of this choice were so ludicrously public that *The Daily Mail* rushed in with the proposal of a plebiscite as to the future policy of the party and who should be its leader. It was all very well to say, as some Liberals did,[1] that the divisions and manœuvres were confined to the House of Commons, and counted for little in the country at large.

[1] See, for instance, an article by Dr Guinness Rogers in *The Nineteenth Century*, January 1899.

Even if that were true for the moment, it necessarily ceased to be true before very long, since Members of Parliament inevitably put their own points of view before their constituents, and the latter, in approving or disapproving them, began to share in the same divergences.

The third party in the House of Commons—the Irish Party—was at this time ineffective too. In the autumn of 1898 there had been an attempt, headed by Mr John Dillon, to close the breach caused seven years earlier by the disastrous accompaniments of the fall of Parnell : the attempt was renewed early in 1899. But it had failed ; the party remained in two unequal sections, and, as a whole, was morose and powerless. Lord Rosebery's coolness towards Home Rule [1] seemed to have its sequel this year in a statement from Sir Henry Fowler that the Liberal alliance with the Irish was at an end.[2] It was true the formula employed said that the Irish party felt itself stronger in independence of English parties ; but here was another source of cleavage for Liberal opinion. There were many Liberals who could not but bitterly resent the suggestion that certain of their colleagues looked on Home Rule as a policy to be taken up or set down at convenience.

When we turn from this confusion in politics to the world of commerce we come on a state of things that might have apparently given unmitigated cause for satisfaction. At the opening of 1899 the prospects in all trades were good. Shipbuilding had risen to a record output in 1898, and it showed no tendency to slacken. The White Star ship *Oceanic* was launched in 1899 and, with her length of 705 feet and tonnage of 17,040, she opened a new era of colossal merchant vessels. So great was activity in the spinning trade that the only apprehension felt was lest too many mills were being erected. The

[1] See page 349.
[2] *The Times*, 3rd February 1899.

iron and steel works were busy, almost to their limits of capacity. The chemical trade, though its equipment was stated to be rather behindhand as compared with that of the German chemists, was making the most of its facilities. Even farming had a share in the general prosperity. Since the depression in 1879 and 1880 a new generation of farmers had been growing up, men more ready than their fathers to experiment, to take advantage of new machinery, to relinquish the unprofitable grain crops to which the earlier generation had clung as to its honour. Lowered rents, better means of communication, had achieved something ; and, though improvement in method, co-operation, the use of light railways, consideration of market requirements, advanced so slowly that at times there seemed no advance at all, the fact remained that there was unusual hopefulness even among agriculturists. Nor was this hopefulness of prospect belied : when it came to be looked back upon, 1899 could be chronicled as an *annus mirabilis* in trade—the best year for a quarter of a century. None the less a certain uneasiness among business men was making itself felt at this time in fundamental criticisms. Whence, it was asked, was the money being drawn that was pouring into the expansion of factories and engineering shops ? Part of it could, no doubt, be traced to the growth of the new banking system —the amalgamation of small banks into huge concerns.[1] For one effect of this process had been the establishment of an immense number of branch banks in places too small for the old private banks to have been able to support branches in them, and these drew in numerous small sums which in old days would have remained outside the banking system, and so could not have been utilised as they were being utilised now. But though much loan capital might be traced in this way, a feeling was prevalent that English trade was depending too largely on foreign financing and on

[1] See page 264.

borrowing from America. Of the great firms of financiers
—Rothschilds, Raphaels, Morgans, Speyers, Seligmanns,
Hambro—none were English ; and though this of course
did not imply that all the money they handled was foreign
money, it did suggest that English industry must be uncertain where its foundations were laid.[1] Another cause
for uneasiness was found in the fact that in our foreign
trade the excess of imports over exports was heavy, and
the discrepancy was taken by some persons to mean that
the national prosperity was unreal as long as hostile tariffs
prevented our exchanging an exactly equal quantity of
exports for the imports we consumed. Mr Chamberlain
was tentatively approaching this position in January 1899,
though, as *The Times* noted, he " judiciously abstained
from offering many figures to a popular audience." [2] Sir
Robert Giffen, upon the other hand, was pointing out that
our position as the Free Trade nation constituted us " the
bankers of the world," and that our " invisible exports "
under that head were a genuine item of prosperity. Yet a
third, and a grave, source of uneasiness was found in the
nature of the company promoting which in a period of such
excellent trade was naturally enough active. The crashing
downfall of the cycle boom still reverberated in the City.
The Company Laws, so often called in question of late,
were again being criticised. It was, for instance, felt to be
a mistake that, while all private traders in bankruptcy
had to undergo public examination, the director of a
company could, according to the Act of 1890, only be
compelled to submit to such examination if the Official
Receiver saw reason to suspect actual fraud. Twice at
least in the course of the year the business community
had striking support given to its uneasiness. In February
the chairman of the Millwall Docks absconded, and he

1 See an article, " Trade in 1898," in *The Nineteenth Century*,
May 1899.
2 19th January 1899.

was found to have been falsifying the company's books in order to keep up the dividends out of capital. He was arrested later and sent to prison. Then in November when, according to custom, the new Lord Mayor of London presented himself at the Law Courts, to receive from the Lord Chief Justice the Crown's acquiescence in his election, the City had to listen to a direct reproof. The incoming Lord Mayor, Mr Newton, had been a director of a concern, named the Industrial Contract Corporation, which had just been wound up and, though Mr Newton was himself exonerated from the blame which was being attached to the undertakings of the company, the opportunity was taken by the Lord Chief Justice to substitute for the usual formalities a rather sharp speech about the too easy-going acceptance of company director-ships   The feeling remained widespread that, in spite of many recent revelations of the evil wrought by " guinea-pig " directors, money worship being much in the ascend-ant, important persons continued, in consideration of directors' fees, to lend their names far too readily.   Sharp as the Lord Chief Justice's words were, and unusual as it was to travel outside formalities on such an occasion, public opinion fully approved of his action.

Finally these various misgivings were focussed and brought to a head in an alarm as to a general " lack of efficiency " in trade theories and practice.   It became known in May that a large contract for a railway bridge across the Atbara River, carrying the Nile railway up to Omdurman, had been given to an American firm.   The outcry was immediate ;   England had paid for the recon-quest of the Soudan ;   was she not to expect that openings for commercial enterprise there should put money into her pocket ?   This claim was replied to in that business-like spirit England had so much admired in Lord Kit-chener's Egyptian campaign :   American firms had guar-anteed the work's completion in a shorter time and with more certainty than English firms, and promptness was here a quality not to be dispensed with. National heart-searchings followed this plain speaking. Manufacturers, however, refused to accept the chief blame, even if it were to be proved that English methods and training were falling behindhand. Trade Unionism in England, they pleaded, formed an element of possible delay, with which other countries had not to contend in similar measure ; while strikes were frequent, delivery at a given date could not be absolutely guaranteed.

Just at this time, as it happened, there were no serious strikes. The only one of any magnitude in 1899 was a strike of operative plasterers; they demanded that all foremen should be members of the union. In some directions, indeed, the tide of labour agitation which had risen high in the late eighties and early nineties seemed to be receding. Many small unions were losing ground ; even the Dockers' Union was regarded as not very robust ; the Agricultural Labourers' Union, on which in an earlier day much energy had been expended, had weakened as much as 90 per cent. in membership since 1892. Great unions, such as those of the miners, the engineers, the cotton and woollen operatives, were flourishing ; but the net conclusion of the Board of Trade Report on Trade Unionism this year was that only 21 per cent. of working men were members of unions, and of working women only 12 per cent. Possibly a sense of the weakness of small unions, and their consequent danger to the movement, may have dictated a scheme propounded by the Trade Union Congress in January for a national federation of unions. The federated bodies were to subscribe to the federation one or two shillings per member per year, and to be entitled in return to an allowance of half-a-crown or five shillings per member per week during a strike or a lock-out. The " General Strike " began to loom in the minds of nervous persons who read of this scheme. But such an idea had not much actuality, the likelihood of complete federation even was open to a good deal of doubt. When the South Wales miners, for instance, were ready to come into the Miners' Federation the officials of the latter body thought they detected a mercenary spirit in the South Wales men, a desire mainly to dip into the funds of the larger organisation. It seemed possible at least that similar suspicions in other large unions might handicap federation. Yet if a general strike were hardly a serious danger, uneasiness in regard to sectional strikes remained active. The question as to some form of statutory obligation was continually in the air, and the provisions for compulsory labour arbitration in New Zealand were much discussed—too much, in the opinion of people who considered that Colonial experiments could have little meaning for England.[1] Many persons, too, held that compulsory arbitration was an idle phrase, for trade unions were not entities as employers were ; they could not be compelled. " Organisation of capital," it was said, " is the industrial remedy for strikes, and incorporation of the unions the legislative one." [2]

These misgivings as to methods and organisation, so soon to be felt in other departments of national life, were for the moment confined almost entirely to persons of commercial importance. As yet the man in the street felt nothing but a sense of prosperity ; the nation at large was inclined to swagger ; widespread interest taken in the lamentable condition of the Liberal party was chiefly due to a conviction that by its distrust of the growing spirit of Imperialism it had merited disaster. Mr Chamberlain was asserting that 1898 had marked the end of the epoch of the Manchester School : " We are all Imperialists now. We realise, but do not flinch from, the responsibilities and the

---

[1] See, for instance, a letter by the Bishop of Hereford in *The Times*, 4th January 1899.

[2] *The Times*, 10th January 1899.

obligations which Imperialism brings." [1] A change too
was taking place in England's relation to other European
powers, though it was attributed rather to an awakening
of national spirit than to any specific event.[2] The new
temper was such that Lord Salisbury's handling of the
Fashoda incident [3] was felt to have strengthened his hold
on popularity to a degree which minimised any chances
Liberals might have had of returning to power. The great
trade prosperity was everywhere affecting the public mind.
The standard of wealth—of acquisition and of expenditure
—had leaped up. Not everyone could be a millionaire
created by Kimberley or the Rand ; but almost anyone
might at the moment become abnormally rich, provided
he were astute enough at company promotion. The
Colossus was the popular idol, whether he took the shape
of Mr Rhodes, with his hold on De Beers, of Mr J. B.
Robinson with his deep leads paying him 100 per cent., of
Mr Carnegie with his entrenched giant of steel production
at Pittsburg, of Mr Rockefeller with his thumb on every
little oil shop, or of Mr Pierpont Morgan with his Brobding-
nagian pocket always in the place to catch a toppling
American railroad. For the new standard of possessions
the old standard of expenditure did not suffice. Already
in London " smart " entertaining was having recourse to
hotels. A dinner-party in a glittering restaurant, filled with
people, and backed by a kitchen and cellars of which the
range was naturally wider, while the quality was not poorer,
than that of great houses, was more amusing than the
best that could be done privately. Also the newly rich,
of whom there were many, felt themselves safer in the
hands of a *maitre d'hotel*.[4] The season in London was being

---

[1] Speech at Birmingham, 28th January 1899.
[2] *The Times*, leading article, 4th February 1899.
[3] See page 442.
[4] *The Times*, in an interesting comment on this change (25th
September 1899) remarked that, as the club had originally grown
out of the tavern, so now the great hotel seemed becoming a new
kind of club.

broken up by the " week-end " habit. Families no longer moved their complete establishments to town ; they kept two or three houses open. The expense of great week-end parties was made nothing of. Autumn shooting-parties had the expectation of being provided with day after day of driven pheasants and bags running into four figures. Whist was giving place to bridge ; and the much greater gambling possibilities in bridge violently accelerated changing manners and customs.[1]

It was, perhaps, in its effects upon women that the changed spirit in society became most rapidly marked. In the recklessly lavish periods of earlier times, such as the later eighteenth century, men had on the whole had the monopoly of extravagance. Theirs were the clubs and the gaming-tables ; theirs, quite as much as their women's, was costliness in apparel and jewellery. Now greater wealth sufficed for equal extravagance in women and men. In one sense, women's clubs were not a novelty. The Alexandra had been founded in 1884. It had been followed in 1887 by the Ladies' University Club, in 1892 by the Pioneers' Club (though these two, with the Sesame, opened in 1895, embraced rather women in professional life than in society), in 1894 by the Green Park Club, in 1896 by the Grosvenor, and by the Empress in 1897. By 1898 the ladies' clubs in London had reached the number of twenty-eight.[2] Bridge owed its absorbing popularity largely to the extent to which women devoted themselves to it ; stories began to be told of play which recalled the wildest days at Crockford's, when men sat at card-tables for twenty-four hours at a stretch. In another point also eighteenth-century custom was returning ; powder and

---

[1] This change was particularly noted at the time, because of the death, on 17th February, of Henry Jones, the famous "Cavendish " of whist manuals.

[2] See an article by Mrs Anstruther in *The Nineteenth Century*, April 1899.

paint were no longer only being employed to hide the marks
of age ; they were being used again by young women.   The
" advanced woman," too, who had been making her way
for years past, mustered in force in London this summer
for an International Congress of Women.   At this many
discussions took place, on political subjects, such as woman
suffrage, and women's work in local government ;   on
technical training for women ; the ethics of expenditure ;
equal wages for women doing the same work as men ; an
equal moral standard for the sexes ; women's clubs, women
in science (Mrs Ayrton had just been reading a paper on the
Electric Arc before the Institute of Electrical Engineers) ;
and on a number of questions of domestic economy.   But
the congress was not a marked success.   It was felt to
have produced a welter of papers and discussions without
much relation to one another or to central principles.[1]   A
more ephemeral phase of advanced views challenged public
opinion this year in the Harberton case.   Lady Harberton,
who had been a consistent champion of " rational dress "
for women, brought an action against the landlady at the
Hautboy Inn, at Ockham, for having refused her admission
to the inn coffee-room.   The object was to raise the
question whether a knickerbocker costume could rightly
be considered as unsuitable for women.   The law, however,
ingeniously avoided giving a judgment on this matter.
The only ground, it said, for action would have been refusal
of reasonable accommodation and refreshment.   The landlady of the Hautboy had not been guilty of such a refusal,
and her right to serve the refreshment in a comfortable
room other than the coffee-room was upheld.   The case
never commanded more than a passing interest.

The exaggerated standard of expenditure among the well-
born and the rich had its full middle-class counterpart in
the determination to " have a good time."   All kinds of

[1] See an article by Miss Frances Low in *The Nineteenth Century*,
August 1899.

sports seemed to be taking new and lively turns. Horse-racing was stirred by the arrival of Tod Sloan and the "American seat," with the saddle placed far forward, stirrups shortened to give a crouching attitude on the withers, and the reins gripped on either side of the horse's neck. Like most American inventions it was thoroughly suited to its purpose : the jockey's weight was thrown where it was most easily carried and the retardation caused by air pressure on the jockey's body was reduced to a minimum ; Sloan almost lay on the horse's neck. There was scoffing at first ; Englishmen are not prone to think they can learn about sport from other nations. But the reasonableness of the new seat, combined with Sloan's constant successes, soon caused his attitude to be copied, and within a year or two the older manner had disappeared from racecourses. The authorities had other reasons too for welcoming Sloan. He rode hard all the way ; so his success was likely to break down the growing tendency towards *finesse* in racing, nursing horses—" messing them about " was the uncompromising phrase used by a steward of the Jockey Club—in order to bring them up with a run at the finish.[1] Cycling as a sport had been unaffected by the downfall of the cycle company boom. It was still very popular, and the names of crack racing cyclists were almost as well known as the names of jockeys. A new invention had been made—the free-wheel—and people were as wishful to ride the latest types of bicycle as they became a few years later to possess the most up-to-date motor car ; a machine two or three years old was a thing no self-respecting cyclist cared to ride. Fresh ideas too were inspiring cricket. An unusually fine and dry summer had favoured batsmen, and huge scores had been made. They resulted in a discussion of the almost too great perfection of the modern cricket pitch ; either, it was contended,

[1] See a letter by Lord Durham on American jockeys in *The Times*, 24th October 1900.

bats should be smaller or wickets should be broader. Other cricketers debated the rules for "following on." Golf was by this time so widespread that the perpetual opening of new links almost ceased to be noticed—it was now hardly possible for a watering-place to survive without a golf-course. Boat-racing was enlivened by the breaking down at last of the long series of Oxford successes. In 1899 a Cambridge crew, stroked by Mr Gibbon, and including Mr Dudley Ward and Mr R. B. Etherington Smith, turned the luck, and won a most popular victory. In athletic contests the interest of the year was a meeting between a combined team from Harvard and Yale and a similarly constituted team from Oxford and Cambridge. An entirely new sport was making its appearance in England—Ju-jitsu, a Japanese form of wrestling, in which scientific knowledge of bones and muscles was used to devise "holds" and "locks" of a kind that converted an attacker's energy to his own destruction. In football professional contests were taking on almost the nature of gladiatorial displays. The methods of the northern manufacturing towns, where football teams were maintained by a limited liability company which made dividends out of the "gates" at matches were being imitated in the south. London suburbs and southern provincial towns possessed their professional teams, and rivalry was fierce enough at times to make the referee's post a dangerous one. Late in the year a new spirit invaded even yacht-racing—a sport in which the populace hitherto had had no portion. A challenge for the America Cup was made by Sir Thomas Lipton. This became instantly a popular affair ; the ordinary man was prepared by Lipton's shops and Lipton's advertisements to accept him as the purveyor of yacht-racing. The designers set to work at contriving a "skimming-dish" vessel which should allow of sufficient temporary strengthening to be enabled to cross the Atlantic. It was believed that the necessity imposed on the challenger for the cup of sailing across to the contest accounted for previous British defeats ; a racing yacht built on the spot could be made so much more lightly, and so much further from the " cruiser " form. The building of Sir Thomas Lipton's *Shamrock* was followed with keen public interest ; and when at last she had crossed to America, and the races began, newspaper enterprise bolstered the excitement. Differences in time caused the races to be sailed when it was evening this side the Atlantic. The ingenuity of *The Daily Mail* arranged that the respective positions of the yachts during the race should be signified by red and blue lamps hoisted against a tower on the south side of the Thames. Other newspaper proprietors followed with modifications of the idea ; and so while the races were taking place the Thames Embankment was blocked every evening with crowds seeing the newest galanty show. The *Shamrock* fared better than some earlier challengers had done ; but the light airs of the American seaboard in autumn—the first race was not finished within the time limit—baffled her, and ultimately she was beaten. But this was not till late in October, and by that time sterner events had distracted the popular mind.

The affair at the time appeared to many persons, not hopelessly old-fashioned, as chiefly a proof of the menace of advertisement methods. They were shocked to see even *The Times* being invaded by stridency ; its pushing of the *Encyclopædia Britannica* was one of the jokes of the year. Illuminated sky-signs blinking from street corners and shop fronts were denounced as dangerous to horses as well as offensive to humanity. Yet all such enterprise was part of a general liveliness which, though it might show want of ballast, was hardly likely to be checked by staid protestations. *The Belle of New York, Florodora,* and *San Toy* were the successes of the theatres ; they were cheerful, irresponsible musical comedies lavishly staged. *The Gay Lord Quex, The Ambassador* and *The Canary*, all of them light comedies, were the dramatic events of the year. The catchword of the streets, " Let 'em all come," expressed the vague swagger which everywhere was the mode. The public was agape for sensation; readily gullible, but quick to forgive in a burst of laughter when an imposture it had found entertaining was exposed. A man named De Rougemont had come to London with astonishing tales of adventure in the north of Australia. He had lectured to huge audiences, and then on the first touch of investigation his whole tale collapsed like a bubble. The public laughed, enjoying the idea of the impudence of the fraud as much as it had enjoyed the wonders of the lecturer. It enjoyed enormously too the situation created on the death of Earl Poulett, when a man who for years had been grinding a barrel organ in London put in his claim as heir to the Poulett estates and the gates of the family mansion in Somersetshire were barricaded against him.

In another section of the public the general extravagance and irresponsibility were producing a reactionary pose. " Back to the land " was hardly yet a catchword; but individuals were retiring to the country and writing to the Press of the joys of small holdings. Cycling had led to a rediscovery of the country, and persons who prided themselves on their sensibility were talking of the Simple Life. Similarly, the more frivolous the normal stage became, the more strenuous became the devotees of ethical drama. The Independent Theatre had come to an end; but in the autumn of 1899 some of its disciples, combining with new forces, founded the Stage Society. Its object was to produce English plays which the commercial stage would not take up, and also translations of leading foreign plays. It opened its career with Mr Bernard Shaw's *You Never Can Tell* and followed that with plays by Mr Sidney Olivier, Ibsen, Fiona Macleod, Maeterlinck, and Hauptmann. The society had its performances on Sundays in order to secure the services of actors and actresses engaged every other night of the week. The pleasure of finding an occupation for Sunday evenings in London brought many members to the society.

In literature new names were coming to the front. Mr W. B. Yeats and Mr Stephen Phillips (whose *Paolo and Francesca* was published late in the year) gave new hopes for poetry; Mr Maurice Hewlett and Miss Fowler were the new-comers to the novel reader. An extraordinary revelation of the position Mr Rudyard Kipling had made for himself occurred when news was published at the end of February that he was gravely ill of pneumonia in New York. For a week bulletins about him were the most important items in the newspapers; and when, on the announcement that he was out of danger, the German Emperor sent Mrs Kipling a telegram of congratulation and appreciation of her husband's work, there was no incongruity in the action; for the English and American nations had been awaiting the moment of relief. Mr Kipling's only publication this year, beyond the poem, *The White Man's Burden*, addressed to the United States on its responsibilities in the Philippines, and a poem later in connection with the menace of the Boer War, was his school story, *Stalky and Co.* It caused the first slackening of his popularity; exactly the men who had most admired his " plain tales " of distant parts of the Empire disliked this plain tale of a public schoolboy's life; it was so far from the convention that Waterloos are won on the playing fields of Eton.

In the region of science much new life was stirring. Wireless telegraphy, exciting glimpses of which had been obtained from time to time in the past two years, came now to a public and practical success. In March the first wireless Press message was sent by Marconi instruments across the English Channel from Wimereux to the South Foreland. In July the system was utilised for the first

time at sea ; during the naval manœuvres a cruiser
scouting ten or twenty miles ahead of the fleet was kept
in communication with the admiral in command. Attention was turned to the steady and devoted experiments
being made in flying, by the death of Mr P. S. Pilcher
on 30th September. He and Lilienthal, who had been
killed three years earlier, lost their lives in the very necessary work of applying theories about the behaviour of
plane surfaces in air which were slowly altering the whole
line of advance of aeronautical science. The belief that
flight was impracticable without a lifting agent lighter than
air was still strong ; but breaches were being made in it.
Engineers had a new subject of interest in the turbine
motor, the invention of the Hon. C. A. Parsons, which was
a completely new application of steam propulsion. Instead
of introducing the steam into cylinders, where it acted
on pistons, which in their turn transmitted the energy by
cranks to the propeller shaft, Mr Parsons set steam to act
directly upon the shaft. He was able to transfer the
triple-expansion principle from the reciprocating engine
to his turbine engine.

The most notable step in medical science was Major
Ross's announcement in August that he had definitely
established the fact of transmission of malaria by mosquitoes in tropical Africa. The enlargement of our responsibilities in Africa, made lately more urgent by the taking
over of Uganda and Nigeria from the chartered companies,
had created a new necessity for the study of tropical
disease. Major Ross's discovery, followed as it was
by the corollary that mosquitoes could be destroyed
by treating the water where they bred with kerosene,
rendered malaria no longer an inevitable accompaniment
of tropical life. At the same time in England great
interest was being taken in the open air cure for consumption. Here again a disease had been considered
incurable by the public at large, if not by the medical

profession, until the publication of Dr Koch's theories, and the heated discussion of them, made people begin to conceive of consumption as, like other diseases, due to bacteria. A great meeting was held at Marlborough House this year, with the Prince of Wales in the chair, to give new energy to research and to the discussion of methods of cure. The open air system at Nordrach, in Switzerland, was known; but it was not until this year that it began to be understood that the essentials of the system were a strict regimen and fresh air, not any particular forests or mountains.

Two important educational movements of 1898 have to be noted. One was the gift by Mr Passmore Edwards of a sum of money for building and equipping a London School of Economics. Here that new spirit we saw expressing itself first in the foundation of University Settlements [1] may be said to have reached its most fruitful form of expression. Political economy had undergone the discipline of a searching challenge from philanthropy; it now emerged as a social science—social economy—and in its new form received again that intellectual allegiance which twenty years earlier it had almost lost. The energy at the back of the London School of Economics was largely an energy of social reformers; but they could now reassert the intellectual method of attack upon social problems. The second educational movement has also a thread of connection with settlements. These had been founded partly to let the working man see the value of knowledge, and to enable him to distinguish between true and false kinds of knowledge. Now the working man began to have designs of his own upon university education. A project had been set on foot in Oxford by two Americans, Mr Beard and Mr Vrooman, to open a hall of residence there for working men. There was no proposal to give the men a full university course; few

1 See page 112.

working men could spare the necessary four years, and if they occasionally did, the result was rather to cut them off from their fellows than to fit them for other life. The idea here was that men should come into residence for a single year or so, to attend lectures chiefly in economics and modern history, and should then return to their work, not withdrawn from their class by education but taking a new feeling for education back into their class. The hope was that trade unions and their branches would pay the fees of some promising men, while some would maintain themselves by doing the household work of the hall. The hall, under the name of Ruskin Hall, was opened on 22nd February. The second movement was an even more important one for working-class education, though at the time, being less picturesque, it attracted less attention. A conference between representatives of the University Extension System and the Co-operative Societies was held in Oxford in August. This attempt to give more solidity to the work of extension lecturers, both by organising classes and discovering the kind of instruction most wanted, led a few years later to a wider interpretation of the place of university training than Ruskin Hall was able to achieve.

Towards the end of the year learned men were called upon to take part in a controversy which was raging at dinner-tables. Was 1899, or was it not, the last year of the century ? Were we, or were we not, now to surrender that which had been our mental and moral label, our epithet in respect to our ideals and our prejudices—the nineteenth century ? To half the nation it seemed obvious that if we had described all the years beginning with 18 as the nineteenth century, then when we began with the figures 19 we must be in the twentieth century. The other half of England pointed out forcibly that there had been no year 0 at the beginning of our era ; we had begun with the year 1 ; therefore the century would not

be complete till the passing of the year 100. It
was so considerable a controversy that no less a
person than the Astronomer Royal took a hand in it.
He fixed the beginning of the twentieth century at
1st January 1901.

CHAPTER II

MR BALFOUR, in a speech delivered just before the opening of the session, deplored the " unhealthy calm " in political life. He was referring mainly, of course, to the fact that the Opposition was more concerned with internal disagreements than with attacking the Government, but he implied a certain slackness on the Government side. The complaint had some reason. A Queen's Speech, in which the chief legislative proposals were a Bill for setting up local municipalities to replace the vestries in London, a small Education Bill, and a Bill to assist workmen to purchase their homes, was a poor effort. A forecast of a session too in which disorders in the Church were specified as " the rock ahead " was not impressive. The deplored calm, however, was but superficial. The session was not six weeks old before debate on the Civil Service Vote became the occasion for discussing the policy of the Colonial Office in respect to the Transvaal. In April advanced Radicals were challenging the Government to give an explanation of a great increase of barrack accommodation in South Africa. By the middle of June a Blue Book of despatches which had passed between Mr Chamberlain and Sir Alfred Milner was published, and the tone of them left little doubt of the direction in which events were moving.

For whole-hearted Liberals to feel that they confronted these events with divided counsels, and a new leader, the choice of whom seemed merely opportunist, must have

been very depressing. Sir William Harcourt, in addressing his letter of resignation to Mr John Morley, had
appeared to indicate his successor.   But Mr Morley,
knowing that his strong convictions against the policy
that had been pursued in the Soudan, and was now being
pursued in South Africa, must cut him off from many of
the most prominent men on his side of the House, and
might even divide them finally from the party, preferred
to take refuge in the arduous task that had been imposed
on him—the writing of Mr Gladstone's biography.   Failing Mr Morley, it was taken for granted that the choice
must fall on Sir Henry Campbell-Bannerman.   As early
as 5th January, Sir Charles Dilke was alluding to him as
the probable leader, expressing at the same time his own
distaste for the prospect by describing him as " in the
whole trend of his mind one of the most Conservative
members occupying a seat on the Liberal benches." [1]
Mr Asquith was mentioned also ; but he was known to
prefer for the present to devote himself to his successful
career at the Bar.   A meeting at the National Liberal
Club exposed the differences of opinion in full blast.
Sir Henry Campbell-Bannerman was ultimately chosen
as leader in the Commons ; but, as in the case of Sir
William Harcourt,[2] the election was half-hearted ; the
choice of the leader of the party as a whole being left
until there should be a prospect of the return of the
Liberals to power.   Sir Henry Campbell-Bannerman
was regarded generally as little more than a stopgap.
He had no great reputation outside the House ; and
current opinion attributed his election to the fact that
he had not been identified with either extreme among
Liberals ; that he was neither a Little Englander nor an
active Imperialist, and might be expected to " sit on the
fence, fully satisfying no section of his followers, but

[1] *The Times,* 6th January 1899.
[2] See page 402.

at least vitally offending none." [1]   In his first week of leadership, Sir Henry showed a vigour and acuteness that may well have startled the Ministerial benches.   But it was only a brief success.   It is doubtful whether even political genius could have won any continuous success in a session when the main interest of politics was one in which many of his prominent followers were more in sympathy with the Government than with their own leader.   It was inadvisable to make even such attempts as the rules of the House admitted to bring to the front a subject which, while it was engrossing all thoughts, had no official existence.   Sir Henry Campbell-Bannerman had to flesh his sword in mock battles.

The " rock ahead " which had been so curiously looming at the opening of the session proved not very formidable. But there had been a revival of ecclesiastical controversy and an Anti-Ritualist Campaign, which had contrived to attract much attention.   This was a good deal due to the tactics pursued by a small group of persons who, making themselves technically parishioners of certain London churches where High Church practices were in vogue, attended the services and interrupted them by loud protests.   Such scenes had been occurring frequently since the beginning of 1898.   It happened also that ecclesiastical law, as a highly controversial subject, interested two voluminous writers of letters to the newspapers—Lord Grimthorpe and Sir William Harcourt. Both were strong Erastians ; and they filled columns with disquisitions on the law, the supineness of bishops, the instruments of Church discipline.   The ceremonial oblation of incense, reservation of the Sacrament, and the use of the confessional were the practices most bitterly attacked ; such services as the Veneration of the Cross on Good Friday being made also occasions of protest. The English Church Union repudiated the authorities

[1] *The Times,* 17th January 1899.

to which Lord Grimthorpe and Sir William Harcourt appealed. The reply of extreme anti-ritualists was that in that case Parliament must intervene and erect new tribunals. This attitude wrecked the agitation in 1899. An anti-ritualist meeting at the Albert Hall just before the opening of the session was followed by a deputation to Mr Balfour as leader of the House of Commons, asking for legislation from the Government. Mr Balfour held out no hopes of this. A private member's Bill was therefore introduced. But it went to such lengths in proposing to pass over the authority of the bishops, and in scheduling as ecclesiastical offences practices which hitherto had not been regarded as illegal, even by men such as Sir John Kennaway and Sir William Harcourt, that it lost the support of moderate anti-ritualists, and was thrown out decisively. The bishops, meanwhile, continued the use of admonition; and in August the two archbishops, in a case brought before them, gave judgment against the ceremonial use of incense, and against the carrying of lights in processions.

This ecclesiastical controversy was believed to be adding fuel to the controversies on education which the Government's proposals aroused. The endowing of voluntary schools, it was said, became a different matter if the Church that had control of these schools might be accused of such lawlessness as to bring up English children in beliefs not essentially different from those of Roman Catholics. Mr Lloyd George was coming to the front on the Liberal benches largely by his effective presentation of these views. However, the Education Bill of this year was not highly controversial. It took the step, which had so long been advocated, of making the chief authority in education no longer a committee of council but a separate board. The Science and Art Department of South Kensington, as well as the Education

Office, was absorbed by the new board; and thus Technical and Secondary Education were united with Elementary Education in a single system. The Bill was criticised as being but a partial dealing with difficulties. The dual local authorities remained—School Boards and Voluntary School Committees—and Liberal opinion was in favour of placing the responsibility for local administration upon the county councils, working through committees. The idea prompting this suggestion was that the religious difficulty might be removed if elementary schools were administered by bodies in the main popularly elected. The Bill, however, met with no disaster and passed into law. Another measure that became law provided for the rating of the clergy of the Church of England on only half the Tithe Rent Charge of their benefices. There had been a certain unfairness in the rating of the clergy on account of the falling tithe returns due to the lowered price of corn. But this Bill, which authorised payment from the Local Taxation Account of the Exchequer of half the rates hitherto charged on the clergy, was another of those pieces of legislation by privilege to which this Ministry seemed prone. The London Government Bill, setting up local municipalities, also became law; it might be described as an application to the London County Council area of that principle of the subdivision of local government which had been effected in the counties by the Parish Councils Act. Though there was abundance of easy jesting about the petty mayors and aldermen that the Bill would create, the ending of the old vestries had been bound to follow sooner or later the ending of the old Board of Works. A Moneylenders Bill was introduced by Lord James of Hereford, but was not passed. For some time cases in the courts had brought the money-lending business into notoriety; there was strong support for a measure which should not only limit the interest on

a loan that was recoverable at law, but should do something towards preventing the network of aliases by which
usurers, whose extortions under one name had been
exposed, continued in activity under another. The case
of Gordon *v.* Street in 1899 had raised this last point
in a prominent manner.

One item contained in the Queen's Speech made but a
poor appearance in Parliament—the Bill to enable local
authorities to advance money to working men for the
purchase of their homes. This was an old scheme of Mr
Chamberlain's, an item in that middle-class conception
of democratic reform [1] which had fallen so much out of
date. The chief objections to the Bill were, firstly, that it
would be impracticable to confine the loans to a particular
class, and, secondly, that it was very doubtful wisdom
for the working man to tie himself to a particular locality :
anything making labour less mobile must tend to congestion in times of unemployment. It was a poor attempt
to provide a sop for the Tory working-class voter. Mr
Chamberlain himself was far too busy with other affairs
to concern himself with this bantling of his, or to feel
much solicitude about another idea of his which he would
have been well advised to sustain. In July a majority
of the committee presided over by Mr Henry Chaplin [2]
reported in favour of a scheme of Old Age Pensions of
five shillings a week, payable at sixty-five years of age.
There was some taunting of Mr Chamberlain as months
went by and the report drew no word from him. He
could hardly, however, have foreseen the future, or have
given a thought to the presence on the committee of a
young member, Mr Lloyd George. The workmen's
houses Bill was easier to produce. The Tory party was
feeling also that it had provided much social reform
without a corresponding adjustment of the legal position

1 See page 320.
2 *Ibid.*

of labour, which in the case of strikes was seeming to
be privileged. The past twenty years had brought many
Employers' Liability Acts ; there had been Housing Acts,
and extensions of transit facilities financed from the
rates. Quite lately there had been the Workmen's
Compensation Act ; and masters of industry were
grumbling a good deal at the addition of this to the
Employers' Liability Acts on the Statute Book.

London was indeed rather less well provided in regard
to cheap locomotion than the large provincial towns,
with their far-reaching trams. Manchester, for instance,
had dealt with its housing problem almost entirely by
facilitating and cheapening means of transit, and had
done little in the way of building. This year there was
a demand for enforcement of the powers of the Local
Government Board to insist upon the provision of workmen's trains in London. Connected with this was a
question which became of great moment. Active spirits
in the London County Council were feeling more and
more strongly that slum problems could only be solved,
and the decent housing of the artisan achieved, by building
far enough out of London for land to be bought at a
reasonable price, and then providing cheap means of
transit. Thereupon the question arose whether, under
the Housing Act, the Council could buy land outside the
area of its jurisdiction. Legal opinion held that it could
not. Meanwhile all that it seemed possible to do within
the area was being done, and not by the Council only.
Before that body came into existence, private benefaction
had erected a number of large tenement buildings ; and
within the past year or two a successful attempt had
been made to house decently the more drifting and
solitary kind of poor man who could not afford the most
meagre flat. Lord Rowton, who in earlier years had been
Lord Beaconsfield's private secretary and henchman, set
himself to discover whether common lodging-houses,

run not for extortionate profit, but for a reasonable return, could not be contrived to provide these men with a comfortable shelter. In certain respects the tenement buildings erected by private benefactors showed what could be done. For example, the capital of the Guinness Trust had been originally £200,000, given by Lord Iveagh in 1889, and £25,000 added by the Goldsmiths' Company in 1893. In 1898 the net income, after allowing for depreciation and a contribution to the contingency fund, was £8600 ; and the capital fund had been enlarged by allotments out of income to £298,000.[1] Lord Rowton erected four lodging-houses in different parts of London, with beds and cubicles let at a charge no higher than that of the ordinary common lodging-house; and provided with large rooms in which the men could cook and eat their meals. His experiment proved that a man could live wholesomely in one of these houses for as little as 8s. 2d. a week.[2]

A subject which had begun to trouble the social conscience at a rather later date than that of housing—dangerous trades and unhealthy occupations—made some stir in 1899 on account of the reports of two Home Office committees, one on phosphorus poisoning in match-making, the other on lead poisoning in the manufacture of china. The first report was uncompromising in its assertion that phosphorus poisoning could be entirely prevented by insistence on precautions, such as mechanical dipping of matches in closed chambers. The great strides the social conscience had taken in the past twenty years may be noted in the general agreement that the enforcement of such rules was a necessity, in spite of the fact that it must involve the ruin of certain ill-equipped factories.

[1] See an article on " London Buildings " in *The Fortnightly Review,* 1899.
[2] See an article by a resident in Rowton House, *The Nineteenth Century,* September 1899.

The second report was rather less conclusive. It recorded a considerable increase in use of leadless glaze since 1893 ; for much ordinary ware dangerous glazes no longer were thought necessary. At the same time it was the contention of the china manufacturers that positive prohibition of the use of lead would be disastrous ; imported china, it was said, would then compete ruinously with the home manufacture ; and they pleaded that increasing precautions were eliminating danger to the workers. Beyond these two dangerous trades, in which sufferings had been particularly horrible, other occupations, the evils of which were more insidious—glass polishing, naphtha processes, quick-drying paint, etc.—were being inquired into. Phosphorus poisoning had been brought into public notice chiefly by *The Star* newspaper in pursuance of its avowed policy of giving some of its space to social pamphleteering.[1] It was active just now in another respect. Fires caused by oil lamps were frequent, and deaths due to them, when reckoned by a newspaper devoting itself to the subject, reached a serious total. It was thought that these accidents were due largely to the lowering of the safety standard for lamp-oil. The provisions, under which oil was not allowed to be imported and sold for ordinary lighting purposes, if it turned, in an open vessel, to explosive vapour at a temperature below 100°, had been altered in 1879, when the danger point was fixed at 73° in a closed vessel. Round these two figures controversy raged, many experts holding that the new test was by far the sounder ; and that the cause of the increasing number of accidents should be looked for in the cheap glass lamps used by the poor. A private member's Bill proposing to restore the flash point to 100° was introduced this year ; but it was defeated.

Labour, accepting these ameliorations and attempts at amelioration, did not acquiesce in the view that its

[1] See page 240.

own attitude must be modified in response to them.   In Parliament it had met with a serious rebuff at the general election of 1895 [1]; it was now preparing for the next election, which could not be far off, since this was the Government's fifth year of office.   Labour men had their explanation of the parlous condition of the Liberal party. It had, they believed, had its day; it had solved the constitutional problems of the past generation, from which it had sprung, by extension of the franchise, establishment of the ballot, and such measures.   Its " cry for a leader was really a cry for the departure of its soul."   Reform now involved what the Liberal party had never been constituted to undertake.   In face of socialism the differences between Tories and Liberals became " purely artificial."   For in the view of the Independent Labour Party reform meant " such employment of the members of the state that each would have an opportunity of becoming an effective consumer " [2]; and the immediate corollaries of that belief were the taxation of ground values and ground rents, the readjustment of mining royalties towards making them public property as soon as practicable, the nationalisation of railways and canals, and, ultimately, nationalisation of all the means of production.   However, the new policy of permeation, rather than of frontal attack upon property, which socialists for the past six years had adopted, made these sweeping manifestoes appear rather academic.   At the conference of socialists and the Independent Labour Party in April the tone was not very combative.   The foremost subject was technical education ; there was also some discussion of unemployment, and of the idea of *ateliers nationaux*.   Local government was still the main objective of socialists under the Fabian influence which had succeeded the Morris and Hyndman

[1] See page 372.

[2] Articles by Mr Keir Hardie and Mr Ramsay Macdonald on " The I.L.P. Programme," *Nineteenth Century*, January 1899.

influence.[1] For instance, Fabianism was at work in a proposal made by the committee of the London School Board that the feeding of necessitous children should no longer be left to private enterprise, but should be undertaken, as part of its routine, by the board. The proposal was rejected. A growing opposition to extensions of municipal trading was due to knowledge that this was a chosen line of socialist advance. A movement for the establishment of a joint committee of the two Houses of Parliament in order to consider the limiting of municipal trading was, during the session, receiving the support of the London and other Chambers of Commerce. Municipalities at the moment had been forced into an unfortunate position. A scheme had been propounded, in a private Bill, for generation of electricity, in bulk, at the pit's mouth, thereby saving the cost of transport of coal. The Association of Municipal Corporations had opposed the scheme. It hardly could have done otherwise ; the municipalities had so lately spent vast sums on electrical equipment and had not had time as yet to show an adequate return on the ratepayers' money. None the less the opposition was easily representable as an insistence on monopoly at the cost of national progression.

Two problems of London administration were discussed during the session. One was the question of the water supply. The London County Council again promoted a Bill for obtaining water from the Welsh hills. But at this time the Royal Commission which had been appointed to consider the subject reported in favour of a system of intercommunication between areas served by the different companies, to be enforced, if necessary, by the Local Government Board. This intercommunication was already begun,[2] and the Royal Commission's report coincided with the common-sense view that there was

1 See pages 156 and 335.
2 *Ibid.* page 400.

in fact no lack of water, and no need to go to the huge expense of the County Council project, if unification of the existing supplies were obtained. Moreover, recent investigations had thoroughly re-established the healthiness and purity of the reservoir principle, and quashed the half-sentimental ideas in regard to " water from the hills." The other London question was the congestion of traffic in the streets. Busy men were grumbling loudly at their loss of time ; and the Home Secretary introduced a Bill giving the police authorities additional powers to make orders controlling the traffic, to regulate routes of omnibuses and their stopping places, and other such matters. There had been a good deal of complaint of the empty cabs moving slowly along the edges of roadways ; the police authorities now forbade cabs to " crawl " for hire in the Strand, Piccadilly or Bond Street. This was felt to be rather hard on the cabmen ; and many people considered the first attack should have been on tradesmen's vans, which obstructed traffic not only by their slow movement, but by standing against the kerb, loading and unloading, in crowded thoroughfares.

Another traffic problem so much discussed this year that it extinguished the usual " silly season " topics was the amalgamation of the South Eastern and London, Chatham & Dover railways. Both lines had long been attacked for their slowness, unpunctuality, and the dinginess of their rolling stock. The large northern railways had familiarised the public with corridor carriages, dining-cars, and comfort, even for third-class passengers. Amalgamation of the two lines, abolishing competition between them, might, it was feared, end all prospect of their improvement. Healthiness of competition formed the chief text of the discussion that ensued. Consequently a particular degree of welcome was given to a new railway venture, when the extension of the Manchester, Sheffield & Lincolnshire Railway's system to London was opened, in March, and the name of it was changed to the Great Central Railway.

An event of considerable importance was the publication, after three years' work, of the Report of the Royal Commission on the Licensing Laws.[1] Yet it was not of the importance it might have been, for two reasons. The first was that the outbreak of the Boer War pushed all home legislation into the background, and for several years there was no chance of forcing the Government to attempt legislation which was certain to be highly controversial. The second reason was that the report was far from unanimous—the chairman himself did not sign it. There were in fact two quite distinct reports. Hopes that had relied on the unusual composition of the commission had not been justified. In appointing eight members of the licensed victualling trade, eight temperance reformers, and eight neutral men, the Government had clearly hoped for some report embodying a working compromise between extremes of opinion. Conservatives had had two or three uncomfortable experiences of producing licensing questions for debate in Parliament[2]; they no doubt hoped that in this case some of the sharpness of debate might have been got over in the privacy of the sittings of the commission, and that the next attempt at legislation (some attempt inevitably lay ahead of them, under pressure of that Church opinion they could not afford to alienate) might be upon the basis of an agreed compromise. Such hopes were shattered. In April it began to be known that there was a serious division among members of the commission; then followed the announcement that Lord Peel had resigned his chairmanship, because his draft report had not been accepted; and there ensued a most unseemly amount of bickering as to whether Lord Peel had or had not tried to be high-handed, as to whether

[1] See page 396.

[2] *Ibid.* pages 230 and 270.

certain of his colleagues had pursued purely destructive tactics in discussing the draft report; and so on. What had actually taken place was of the greatest encouragement to temperance reformers, even though it had split the commission. Lord Peel, who had entered upon his task in the most neutral frame of mind, had been converted by the evidence he had heard to becoming an ardent advocate of the return, at the earliest possible moment, to the outright annual conditions of licences—to re-endowing licensing authorities, after a certain number of years' notice, with the power to refuse renewal without any question of compensation. " It has come," he said, in his report, " to be a struggle for mastery between the State and the trade. . . . Who is to be master ? " He took the view that, by a certain carelessness, the State had allowed the purely annual character of a licence to lapse ; therefore it would not be just to refuse to recognise that the State had become responsible for a reasonable expectation of renewal; but all that was necessary was to let the trade have notice that after a certain term of years the State would resume complete possession, so to speak, of all licences ; the trade in the interim would make its own arrangements with regard to the new conditions. Such was the fundamental cause of disagreement in the commission. Members might wrangle afterwards as to whether a unanimous report on certain lines would not have been possible, if Lord Peel had shown willingness to modify his draft. It was contended, for instance, that there might have been a report recommending (1) the creation of a new licensing authority, on which county councillors would serve with justices of the peace; (2) the creation of a new Appeal Court in the place of Quarter Sessions, the new court to be not open to county justices, and therefore to be above the reach of canvassing from either side; (3) a reduction of Sunday hours, and of the privileges of *bona-fide* travellers, also restrictions as to serving liquor

16

to children; (4) prohibition under penalties for serving persons known to be inebriates; (5) the placing of pre-1869 beer-houses under the ordinary licensing authority. But it was not, after all, more than speculation that these recommendations would have been adopted unanimously. Almost certainly, even to gain these so desirable reforms, temperance members of the commission would have felt that their price, in relinquishing the policy of systematic reduction of licences, was too heavy. At any rate the commission did divide irretrievably. A majority of the members—for Lord Peel failed to carry the neutral members with him—continued to meet under the vice-chairman, Sir Algernon West, and drew up their report. Lord Peel and the temperance members signed a Minority Report.

Though for the time being the subject of the Licensing Laws was thrust into the background, it became finally so vital a matter of political controversy, and did so much to invigorate Liberalism for its revival in 1906, that no apology is needed for giving space to it here. As it is, however, impracticable to set out the two Reports in full, we may consider the main points of agreement, and of difference, between them.

1. They agreed in the opinion that there were " congested areas " in licensing, and that a large reduction of licences was necessary. But whereas this was more or less of a " pious opinion " in the Majority Report, Lord Peel's Report gave it reality by expressing further the view that there was proved connection between the number of licences in a district and the number of convictions for drunkenness. From this Lord Peel deduced the opinion that a fixed proportion of licences to population was a practicable ideal; and he recommended that the licensing authorities should be compelled to reduce, within seven years, the number of licences to that proportion.

2. The reports may be said in one sense to have agreed

that compensation should be paid for licences extinguished
on grounds other than those of misconduct ; but they
differed as to whether such compensation should only be
payable for a limited term of years.   Much controversy
later will be unintelligible unless it is made clear that the
difference upon this last point went deeper than appeared.
The Majority Report regarded compensation as payment
for the State's destruction of a valuable interest.   The
Minority Report did not acknowledge the principle of
compensation in that sense at all.   It recommended that
notice should be given to the trade that in seven years'
time the State would resume its power of granting strictly
single-year licences ; but for licences extinguished before
the close of that period a sum of money would be paid *as
commutation of notice*, not as compensation for an interest.
That is, while admitting that expectation of renewal had
been allowed to grow up, it was not admitted as being
beyond the power of the State to put an end to that
expectation.

3. The Reports agreed that grocers' licences should be
brought under the licensing authorities.   Lord Peel's
report went on to demand that grocers should keep
separate premises for the sale of intoxicating liquors, and
should not sell them in the ordinary course of their trade.

4. The reports agreed upon a need for the reduction
of Sunday hours of opening.   Lord Peel's report recommended a system of local veto, whereby a district might
establish complete Sunday closing.

We saw in the last chapter that in trade the years 1898
and 1899 were prosperous beyond all precedent.   National
finance, however, was in a less rosy condition.   All the
wealth of the country did not prevent the nation's having
a deficit ; and it was natural that there should be searching
criticism of a system of taxation which did not bring to the
Exchequer the prosperity of the community.   Something
was felt to be amiss with the income-tax.   An extra penny

on this tax now brought in £2,150,000, and twenty years earlier it had brought in £1,900,000.[1] The increase was ridiculously petty in face of the immense growth in private incomes ; and the cause was found in that extension of abatements which had accompanied rises in the income-tax, and had been especially associated with the Death Duties Budget. The " black-coated " class—the clerk class—was increasing, and this was the part of the community chiefly benefiting from the exemption of small incomes, while it contributed less to the Exchequer in duties on liquor and tobacco than did the artisan. Direct taxation seemed to be falling on a smaller portion of the public. Would it not be possible to increase indirect taxation by returning to the rather wider basis of customs dues of thirty years earlier, when the free trade principle was not questioned, and yet the tariff had a more extensive range ? Meanwhile all sorts of proposals were being made to the Chancellor of the Exchequer ; he might, it was suggested, tax bicycles, steam launches, flash signs, advertisement posters, cats, silk hats, bachelors, matches, revolvers, photographic cameras. But none of these proposals found a place in the Budget. The problem was no passing one ; it was only too clear that national expenditure was increasing, and was bound to increase. The Navy Estimates for 1899 were three millions higher than in 1898, and they were not at all likely to decrease. For just at this time the German Emperor was appealing to his people in order to make heavy increases in his navy, and thus a new element was added to that rivalry which hitherto had turned chiefly on the size of the French and Russian fleets.[2] In respect to these there was no relaxation of rivalry. Our relations with France were of the worst ; the year 1899 made famous the phrase " a policy of pin-pricks." That was the policy we believed France engaged

[1] *The Times*, 27th February 1899.
[2] See page 351.

in—a policy of petty irritations of England. Thus when France was pressing the Chinese Government for concessions at Shanghai, her action was regarded as almost hostile; and, though the concessions were refused, disagreements concerning the Newfoundland fisheries and French control of Madagascar provided sources of continuous friction. Jingoism, gratified by the course of the Fashoda incident in 1898,[1] regarded every move made by France as a provocation. It was nôt slow, either, to take the opportunity for hectoring comment provided by the Dreyfus case, which still was continuing. The Cour de Cassation in June annulled the original trial, and ordered another trial to be held at Rennes. The military and Anti-Semite party was so strong that when the prisoner returned to France in July he was landed at an obscure port in Brittany; and the train in which he was conveyed was stopped some distance from Rennes, and his journey completed by road. The second trial ended early in September in a second verdict of guilty, and a sentence of ten years' imprisonment. English comment was bitterly hostile; nor was it assuaged by the release of Dreyfus a fortnight later, on pardon; or by the comical twist Anti-Semitism assumed when a prominent Anti-Semite, M. Guérin, defied arrest in his house in Paris and sustained a thirty-seven days' siege. Throughout the year the tone of English comment upon French affairs must have been highly irritating to France; and there could not but have been ironical surprise in that country when, towards the end of the year, being involved ourselves in an undertaking not at the moment flattering our susceptibilities, we gravely complained of an outbreak of "Anglophobia" in France.

Altogether there hardly could have been a more unfortunate year for the meeting of a conference the Tsar of Russia had convened to discuss an international agree-

1 See page 441.

ment for the limitation of armaments. Not only was international temper at its best uncertain, and at its worst inflamed, but commercial rivalry was increasing ; the " open door " of trade had been forced by Japan in China, and seemed to require forcing elsewhere.[1] Every nation too had its pet invention in warlike machinery : France was experimenting busily with submarine boats; Germany with war balloons; England with new explosives. Would any nation consent to stay its hand ? But unfavourable as the time was, the conference met, and not entirely in vain. True, the main proposal, that for the limitation of armaments, disappeared. But certain conventions of war were established by Declarations, and some proposals in the imperfect state of *Vœux*—which may be translated humane aspirations—formally endorsed by the conference. The three Declarations prohibited (*a*) the throwing of projectiles or explosives from balloons, for a period of five years ; (*b*) the use of projectiles which had for sole object diffusion of asphyxiating gases ; (*c*) the use of bullets which expanded or flattened on impact. Great Britain, it must be mentioned, declined to sign the last declaration, on the ground that in her dealings with savages she could not afford to restrict herself to bullets which did not stop the onrush of an enemy ; but she undertook not to employ expanding bullets against civilised opponents. The conference achieved also the formal setting up of an International Arbitration Tribunal with a rota of judges.

The conference broke up at the end of July. A lurid light on the horizon confronted its members even as they were leaving the scene of their labours.

[1] The Cobden Club this year issued a letter to its members urging that the Club should take more active interest in questions of foreign policy, as a legitimate extension of its work.

CHAPTER III

TO the eyes of the general public in England the rupture with the Transvaal had three stages. The first was the arrival of the Uitlanders' petition setting forth the grievances of their position on the Rand, in April. The second was the conference between Sir Alfred Milner and President Kruger at Bloemfontein, in May. The third was the exchange of increasingly frigid despatches, in September. The process of gradual concentration of public interest may be traced in another way. Until June Transvaal affairs made but an occasional appearance in the leading columns of *The Times*; through June and July four or five leading articles a week, not dependent on any particular item of news, were devoted to the subject; on 7th July appeared the first announcement of military preparations; from the opening of August onwards the leading articles may be said to have appeared daily. The three stages may be noted in still another direction. The Uitlanders' petition was received in England with rather an uncertain voice; it could be spoken of as an open question whether Mr Chamberlain would, by presenting it to the Queen, identify himself with the grievances it expressed.[1] Moreover foreign opinion had not yet stiffened; leading French newspapers such as *Le Temps*, *Les Débats* and *Le Siècle*, though maintaining the suspicion, roused in 1896, that Mr Rhodes and Mr Chamberlain understood each other only too well, spoke of President Kruger as obstinate. The Bloemfontein

---

[1] *The Times*, 9th May 1899.

negotiations were regarded in a changed spirit ; it would appear however that the greater part of the British nation regarded the negotiations as a defining of the issue in view of contingencies more or less remote. During the third stage, the exchange of despatches in September, no one had much doubt of what the next step would be—those who deeply deplored it, as well as those who welcomed or acquiesced in it, thought of it as beyond question then.

To what extent may the issue be said to have hung in the balance at all ? On the one side was President Kruger, who had passed his long life in the irritated belief that it was England's ambition to rule the whole of South Africa, who had, because of England's error, been able to give a sinister aspect to the reversal of the Transvaal annexation,[1] and who of late years had been much under the influence of an adviser, in the person of Dr Leyds, Secretary of State, condemned by even the strongest English opponents of the war as " the evil genius of Transvaal politics."[2] On the other side, as British Colonial Secretary, was a business man, the best of whose life had been lived in a time when middle-class " progress " was a worshipped ideal, who believed the bonds of trade prosperity to be the real bonds of empire; a man whose energy always attached itself to action, an apostle of change, no less, though somewhat differently, as a Tory than he had been as a Liberal ; and lastly, one whose feeling was Radical without being ethical.[3] The contest was not in reality between Tory Imperialist pride and a small State which within twenty years had waxed to a rival ; that was only an element imported into the dispute. It was really between the older materialist Radical-

[1] See page 69.

[2] J. A. Hobson, *The War in South Africa*, page 33.

[3] It was once remarked by a prominent Liberal that no ethical argument is to be found from first to last in Mr Chamberlain's speeches.

ism, now by certain economic changes [1] placed within the
Tory fold, and Boer obscurantism. A confirmation of
this may be found in the prominence given to the franchise
question—the old battle-cry of the individualist Radicals.
Mr Chamberlain was following his deepest instincts, and
not the spirit of the party with which since 1886 he had
been allied, when he made that question a catchword for
the English populace.

When we have thus established the protagonists, we find
ourselves, in discussing the progress of the negotiations,
traversing ground the interest of which is hardly more
than dialectical. President Kruger was convinced that
England's mind had long been made up ; consequently
events could not be stayed by appeal to a Transvaal
tribunal he dominated. Neither could they be checked in
an English public exasperated by his attitude and temperament. None the less the course of events must be quickly
gone over.

The Uitlanders' petition, which was handed to Mr
Conyngham Green, British Resident at Pretoria, on 26th
March 1899, set forth a considerable list of grievances.
It began by pointing out that the Rand provided about
seven-eighths of the revenue of the Transvaal, and that
taxation of the gold industry had raised that revenue
from £154,000 in 1886 to a sum approaching £4,000,000
in 1898 ; but that meanwhile the foreign residents, whose
businesses provided this overwhelming proportion of
the revenue, being without votes, had no voice in its
expenditure. They were without part, therefore, in the
appointment, payment or control of the officials in charge
of affairs on the Rand. The second point was that the
foreign population was badly treated in the matter of
education, and, without votes, had no prospect of better
facilities ; the Uitlander schools—according to the petition
—received only £650 out of the £63,000 allotted by the

[1] See page 363.

Boer Government to education, and the average amount spent per child was stated to be 1s. 10d. on Uitlander children and £8, 6s. on Boer children. The next item was a demand for municipal government for Johannesburg; this was supported by charges of corruption and violence in the police force, and by instances of the backwardness of the authorities, as that no drainage system, and no water-supply except from perambulating carts, existed. After this came complaints of despotic laws controlling the Press and the rights of public meeting. Finally, there were accusations of the Boer Government's more or less corrupt oppression of the mining interests; the supply of dynamite, which was a necessity in the mines, was in the hands of a monopolist syndicate, and it was calculated that the mineowners paid £600,000 a year more than the market price for an inferior quality of dynamite; the liquor laws were said to be so ill administered that Kaffirs could obtain what was nominally forbidden to them; the State railways were complained of as extortionate and incompetently managed; concessions for the monopoly supply of ordinary articles of consumption could, it was said, be secured by bribery, the result being to keep the cost of living at an abnormal height.

The indictment was a formidable one. It acquired a force which practically swept away argument from the fact that, considered without relation to other circumstances, all the statements of the petition were true. In attempting to supply these statements with a background, it will be convenient to deal with them in reverse order.

Complaint of corrupt oppression of the mining industry may be narrowed down at once to the matter of the dynamite monopoly. The cost of the necessaries of life was already falling, the Netherlands Railway had reduced its charges by some £200,000 during 1898. Any ground of complaint that may still have existed, under these heads, was comparatively insignificant. As to the dynamite, English Liberals replied that it was rather fallacious to talk of conditions of a free market when practically only one firm manufactured it in quantity. But that the retailing monopoly of it was a bad thing, founded in corruption, and casting more than a shadow of corruption on President Kruger himself, no one denied.

The complaint of despotic laws against the Press and against the right of public meeting was less genuine. The petitioners neglected to mention that neither law was unknown to the United Kingdom (the law concerning public meetings was practically identical with that enforced in Ireland), nor did they remember to mention that no action under either law had been taken till feeling was expressing itself in terms no government would have tolerated. Even then only one street meeting was suppressed, and although the editors of certain Johannesburg newspapers were arrested in September 1899, the publication of their papers was not suspended by the Boers.

The demand for municipal government for the Rand had had Mr Chamberlain's support in 1896 ; he had put it forward then as a means of settling the Uitlander question without the grant of the franchise.[1] The proposal need not be dwelt upon, because President Kruger would not have agreed to see a part of the Transvaal territory separately administered ; he would have perceived even in municipal government the beginning of the same kind of severance which had already detached diamond-yielding Kimberley from the Orange Free State.

The franchise question wore, to the President's mind, a similar menace. If he gave a franchise on equal terms to the Rand, he gave a large share in the control of his country to foreigners who were of a kind likely by their activity, their greater familiarity with methods of

1 See page 389.

political agitation, and their greater facilities (owing to the density of their population) for combined action, practically to outweigh the Boer voice, even if, as yet, their numbers were smaller. In 1880 the qualification for the franchise had been singularly easy : it consisted merely of a year's residence. In 1885, after the Boers had obtained the Convention of London, the qualification was raised to five years' residence. This was the same as in Great Britain and the United States. Probably President Kruger was at this time taking alarm ; for, though in 1885 the Rand goldfields showed to the world at large few indications of their immense wealth, the Transvaal itself may well have suspected it. By 1890 the inrush of foreigners had become enormous, and the franchise qualification had been stiffened to fourteen years' residence. President Kruger, however misguidedly, felt then that his back was to the wall. Concessions he made in the Bloemfontein conference he was unable to make without severe and baffling restrictions. And, the moment these restrictions were objected to, his fear of the Rand's dominion of his country made him detect a baleful purpose for which such objections were but a cloak. He said that, if he granted the franchise demanded, he might as well haul down the Boer flag.

His fears may have been partly personal ; his obstinate desire to keep the Transvaal an agricultural state may have been obscurantist. But that the grant of the franchise to the Rand population must have completely altered Boer rule cannot be denied. The mass of the Uitlanders could not have made the kind of burgher President Kruger understood—the hardened campaigner ready at twelve hours' notice to be in the saddle with rifle and rations. The new electorate might have become burghers in name, but they would have remained at heart foreigners with little, if any, intention of making the Transvaal their home. But, it may be

asked, was Kruger's conception of burghership keeping
pace with even the development of the Boers themselves ?
Dangers of earlier days no longer threatened from the
Zulus, Matabeles or Mashonas. Did not Kruger's political philosophy rely a good deal on the ignorance and
lack of concern for administration in his ideal burgher,
by which a corrupt oligarchy kept itself in power ?
The question has considerable force. Kruger's objections
to the transitory nature of the Rand population, which
came into the country to make money, and went out
when it had made it, might have been applied to many
members of his own administration. The Boers had
been too small and too scattered a population to equip
fully an administrative system. Dutch officials in
large numbers had been introduced ; and many of these
had come as definitely to make money, and to go home
again, as the Uitlander had. The Boer Government,
however, had by this time largely been purged of
imported officials ; once there had been nearly 2000
Dutchmen in administrative posts ; now there were
only 306. Kruger clearly believed that, if he gave
the Uitlanders the franchise they demanded, the State
he had built up would not survive. There had been
men of weight and influence in his Government who
had not shared his fears. Once or twice, as in the case
of the Uitlanders' petition to the Raad in 1894, Liberal
opinion among the Boers had made itself apparent ;
General Joubert was known to share in it. But the
Jameson Raid had ruined the influence of this party.
It had immensely strengthened President Kruger's
prejudices and crippled the influence of those who had
worked to free his mind of its direst suspicions. From
the date of the Raid, Kruger's views were dominant,
and the most open-minded Boers dropped out of office.[1]

One possible way of peace had remained : the English

[1] J. A. Hobson, *The War in South Africa,* page 20.

might have remembered that Kruger was old, and waited for his death. It was more than likely that, when that occurred, the Liberal Boers would have returned to the Raad, and they would have been aided by the leading Afrikanders of the Cape, who recognised the necessity of reforms, and did not dread them. " One and all held that, in the more distant future, England would, and must, in the natural course of events, control the Transvaal politically as well as economically." [1] To them, all seemed to hinge on the Uitlanders' exercise of some patience. General Butler, the British Commander-in-Chief at Capetown, had said : " What South Africa wants is rest, and not a surgical operation."

Yet from the moment when Mr Chamberlain accepted the Uitlanders' petition to the Queen it was clear that the policy was not to be one of delay. What was the reason of this decision ? It cannot genuinely be found in the material conditions of the Uitlanders. They complained of taxation, but the Transvaal took only five per cent. of their profits, and most of their companies were paying colossal dividends. They complained of the cost of living, but that, as we saw, was falling. They complained of backwardness, and a certain amount of corruption in civil administration ; but that could hardly have been regarded as occasion for an outpouring of blood. Taking together the tone of Mr Chamberlain's and the tone of Sir Alfred Milner's despatches, it seems possible to trace two main lines of impulse. In South Africa there were wounded pride, incessant irritation, and a knowledge that Mr Rhodes entertained huge territorial projects. In England there were impatience with a slow-going people and a general restlessness and business enthusiasm which could be swept into any outcry for expansion. A more specific factor, but one which could only operate after the more general impulses were at

[1] J. A. Hobson, *The War in South Africa.*

work, was England's knowledge of extensive purchases
of armaments on the part of the Boers, since 1896.
It is true that Captain Younghusband,[1] from the point
of view of a traveller, and Lord Rosmead, from the
official point of view, both expressed the opinion that
these armaments were for defensive purposes. But
could such a distinction at this time be drawn ? It could
not. Temper on the Rand had risen to such a height that
no one could say what the alarm of the Boers would regard
as an implicit ultimatum. England's massing of troops
on the Colonial frontiers in September, too, was a movement of alarm, and not of offence. At any time during
1899 the Boers might have decided that, for their own
safety, they must push Great Britain back.

At the time of the Jameson Raid, England had been
startled by the revelation of a state of feeling of which
she had had no warning.[2] Now again feeling on the spot
had settled the question. But this time the formal case
had been prepared alongside the events ; and it was a
case that fitted exactly with Mr Chamberlain's mind.
He adopted with real enthusiasm demands for constitutional progress, administrative reform, and the
well-being of industry. At the time when the Uitlanders'
petition was sinking into English minds, and preparations
for a meeting between Sir Alfred Milner and President
Kruger were taking place, Mr Rhodes was in England.
He had come for more capital for his railway projects in
new British South African territories, and he had been
to Berlin for an interview with the German Emperor.
This visit, carefully chronicled, could but stimulate the
public imagination of his great schemes at the very
moment when British enterprise in South Africa was
represented as being checked by the Boers. Mr Rhodes
raised his capital without much difficulty (though it was

[1] *South Africa of To-Day*, page 101.
[2] See page 384.

believed that he had vainly tried to interest the Treasury first), and announcement of the fact was accompanied by the comment, "we must firmly uphold the flag." [1]

The meeting between Sir Alfred Milner and Mr Kruger took place at Bloemfontein on 30th May. Sir Alfred Milner proposed that Mr Kruger should grant a five years' retro-active qualification for the franchise, with adequate (not proportionate) representation in the Raad of the Uitlander population. Kruger's reply was an offer of a seven years' qualification, and five members out of a total of thirty-one, in the Raad. For the moment it seemed to casual onlookers in England that Kruger was softening. They did not realise that in Kruger's stipulation that his proposed grant should be accompanied by England's agreement to refer to arbitration any difficulties arising in future between England and the Transvaal lay all the old battered question of " suzerainty " ; and that to have granted this clause would have been to grant that England held no peculiar relation to the Transvaal. On the whole the general English feeling in June and July was that President Kruger was showing he could be squeezed, and to our advantage. That was the sense in which Milner's notorious despatch was interpreted. The despatch, though dated 5th May, was not published until 13th June, when a Transvaal Blue Book was issued. Milner wrote : " The spectacle of thousands of British subjects kept permanently in the position of Helots, constantly chafing under undoubted grievances, and calling vainly to her Majesty's Government for redress, does steadily undermine the influence and reputation of Great Britain, and the respect for the British Government within the Queen's dominions " ; he further expressed his belief that the time had arrived for " some striking proof of the intention of her Majesty's Government not to be ousted from its position in South

[1] *The Times*, 27th April 1899.

Africa." That despatch appeared to many level-headed persons in England, in no way predisposed to the Boers, to be exaggerated and rhetorical; "Helot" was a ridiculous word to employ. But still the hope prevailed that strong language was being used as a preventive. In June and July a Franchise Bill was under discussion in the Raad, and the Afrikanders of the Cape were active in persuasion in support of it. During its discussion it received practically the form of Kruger's offer at Bloemfontein. Comments of newspapers and English public men upon it were for a while non-committal. July was not far advanced, however, before English comment was clear. Two conditions were attached to the proposed franchise : one, that applicants must produce a certificate of continuous registration of residence in the Transvaal; and the other that the new burghership would not be made permanent until the first Raad elected under the new conditions had pronounced upon it. It was instantly pointed out, with regard to the first condition, that registration had been allowed by the Transvaal authorities to fall practically into disuse ; few Uitlanders, if any, could produce such certificates. With regard to the second, the members for the Rand would be so far in a minority that no one could take seriously a franchise dependent on reconsideration by the Raad. These misgivings were fatal ; the Uitlanders were afraid of divesting themselves of their existing nationality, in order to become burghers, without the assurance of being in their new state a considerable and forcible body.

From this time on the negotiations with the Transvaal in effect ceased to hang on the franchise. Mr Chamberlain sent, towards the end of July, a despatch proposing the setting up of a joint commission to examine the Transvaal's new measure ; and the controversy thenceforward turned on whether or no Great Britain still could claim suzerainty over the Transvaal. For that was the sense in which the

Boers interpreted this proposal. Little could be hoped from such a discussion. It had been raised during 1898 between Mr Chamberlain and Dr Leyds, with small profit. The Transvaal then maintained that the claim to suzerainty had been dropped in the London Convention of 1884 : Great Britain maintained that it had never been intentionally dropped, and that the mere absence of the term from the opening passage of that convention proved nothing, since that passage was not technically a preamble.

The controversy had now ceased to be one of reasoning and representation of grievances. It had bared the old root of dislike and suspicion, and had entered upon a course, the issue of which could only be the Transvaal's surrender of its claim to be an independent sovereign State, or war. It is most important to note this changed aspect. Suzerainty was not a necessary condition for obtaining redress of the Uitlanders' grievances. The fact that, after the futile discussion of 1898, it now reappeared as in the last resort the vital question, showed that each of the negotiating parties had come to the conclusion that the aim of the other party was hostile. The despatches [1]

---

[1] The character and dates of the exchanges may be briefly set out as follows :—

   (a) British despatch proposing a joint com-
      mission .   .   .   .   .   2nd Aug.

   (b) Transvaal reply, declining this, and pro-
      posing instead a five years' retro-active
      franchise, and an increase of seats in the
      Raad, on conditions amounting to recog-
      nition of the Transvaal as a sovereign state   12th Aug.

   (c) British reply, insisting on suzerainty   .   28th Aug.

   (d) Transvaal reply denying suzerainty, with-
      drawing the last offer, proposing to revert
      to the joint commission, and asking for
      explanation of movements of troops on
      the Natal frontier   .   .   .   2nd Sept.

   (e) British reply, refusing to revert, and stating

exchanged during September were a mere gaining of time. On the Boer side this time was occupied in such preparations as the burning of the veldt, to hasten the growth of new grass for the horses during a campaign ; the driving off behind the Drakensberg of the cattle and sheep of the Free State, which were accustomed to wander on the Natal boundary at pasture ; and in accumulation of stores at Volksrust, Vryheid, and Standerton. On the British side there was an increase, gravely inadequate to the event, but in itself considerable, of the forces in the South African colonies. The first move was made on 6th July, when two companies of Royal Engineers and departmental corps, and a group of officers, including Colonel R. S. S. Baden-Powell and Colonel Plumer, were ordered to South Africa, " to organise the residents, as well as the police and local forces, at various points on the frontier." On 9th August two battalions of infantry were ordered to Natal ; and the announcement was made that 11,000 men were being held ready in India. After the Cabinet Council of 8th September (the summoning of which was so eagerly discussed that it was obviously treated by popular opinion as practically a Council of War) the Indian drafts were ordered to embark.

Whether a stronger or more united Liberal Opposition in the British Parliament could have checked the course of these events must remain uncertain. Mr John Morley

that H.M. Government proposed now to formulate proposals *de novo*	.	8th Sept.
(*f*) Transvaal reply, expressing surprise at this communication, and again proposing to revert to a joint commission	.	16th Sept.
(*g*) British reiteration of the despatch of 8th September	.	22nd Sept.
(*h*) Boer despatch, requesting to know what decision H. M. Government had taken as to new proposals	.	30th Sept.
(*i*) Boer ultimatum	.	9th Oct.

was regarded as almost the only real Liberal of commanding power in a perfectly clear frame of mind ; and he, with
a small band of comrades, among whom must be mentioned
Mr Courtney, Mr Philip Stanhope, Mr G. W. E. Russell,
Sir Wilfrid Lawson and Mr Labouchere, had the courage,
at the moment when the Jingo spirit was rising in England,
to hold meetings of protest. By the middle of September
the police were warning the conveners of such gatherings
that organised interruption might at any moment amount
to breaking-up the meeting. That this band of Liberals
was comparatively small need not be attributed to a mere
inclination on the part of the rest to surrender to a violent
current. There was, as has already been said, much in
the Liberal party that necessarily responded to a skilful
statement of such grievances as taxation without representation, monopolist control of trade, mismanagement
of administration, and corruption in high places. The
questions whether or no these grievances were so urgent
as to demand instant redress, whether a few years would
not have seen profound changes in the dominant personalities of the Transvaal, may indeed have been important
—may have been even the root of the matter—but were
certainly difficult to present, and uninspiring in a time of
tense feeling. The actual balance of opinion in the Liberal
camp was not quite fairly shown by the division taken
at the meeting of the National Liberal Federation on
13th December, when a resolution that "the war was
one which a wise statesmanship could and would have
avoided " was carried by only 114 votes to 94. We had
by then been at war for two months, and were at that
moment sustaining serious reverses. The more apposite
fact is that a large body of Liberal opinion inclined
to the view that, if the Uitlanders' grievances could be
shown to be exaggerated, Kruger's attitude was equally
exaggerated.

One other point remains to be noted. In an article

in *The Nineteenth Century* [1] (valuable as appearing in a
review not given to opposing public opinion) a contributor
writing of the tone of the British Press during the month
of October remarked ; " Surely we never before went to
war when there was so much uncertainty as to the *casus
belli.*" It might have been supposed that continuous
comment on the relations between Great Britain and the
Transvaal for six months before the war might have instructed the public.   The truth perhaps was that England
had never acquired a real relation with her colonies.
A long period of indifference to them, in which self-
government was readily granted, and responsibilities were
dormant, had been succeeded by a period of sentiment
due largely to Mr Chamberlain.   When war broke out,·and
offers of assistance arrived from one colony after another
the music halls rang with songs about " the lion's cubs "
and " sons across the seas " which could not but have been
ludicrously offensive to any Colonial confronted with the
audiences that sang them.   Those who opposed the war
spirit in England were moved, not only by their view of
the policy that preceded it, but by a conviction that, in
the minds of the great mass of the people, the undertaking
was regarded with no proper sense of responsibility or
seriousness of purpose.

[1] November 1899.

CHAPTER IV

1899 : THE WAR AND THE NATION

IT is no part of the object of this book to relate in detail the progress of the war in South Africa; that has been done by works already in existence. The course of feeling in England, however, may provide some commentary on the war.

Certainly, if we never entered on a war with less knowledge of the root of it, we never entered on one in more complete ignorance of the quality of our opponents. Here, again, the absence of a genuine relation between England and the colonies was largely to blame. Had we had an honest respect for them, or they for us, such ignorance would have been impossible. But merely sentimental Imperialism was invoked; and it became apparent that the nation had but a sentimental view of its capacity for war, or of the task before it. Comic prints in England on the very eve of the outbreak presented the Boer forces as shambling regiments of bearded oafs, who grinned vacuously, and fell over their own rifles.[1] It was part of the prevailing ignorance that they were nearly always represented on foot. Again, although, in view of the many alarmist statements that had been made about the Boer armaments, there could hardly be ignorance of their possession of big and modern guns, yet the power of these guns was unknown; and the personnel of the Boer artillery arm was believed to be poor, and far below a proper standard of training in such matters, for instance, as the use

[1] See, e.g., *Punch*, 4th October 1890.

of time-fuses.[1] The party capital made by the Conservatives out of the course taken by the Liberal Government
after Majuba was now recoiling on them ; their cry had
always been that England had made an egregious surrender,
that the Boers had only won a few chance engagements,
in which we had been caught ill prepared, and that they
could never have endured a campaign. The natural
effect of this upon the public was to make it forget anything it had ever heard about the Boer's fighting qualities
in the early days of the Transvaal, and imagine that he had
no power of acting as an army against an army. True,
a general feeling existed, when the Boer ultimatum was
issued on 9th October, that we had been caught before we
had completed our arrangements : there were still contingents from India on the sea. But deficiencies, it was
thought, could swiftly be supplied. General Buller was
despatched as Commander-in-Chief, and the transport
service, which turned out before many weeks were over
to be one of the few matters on which we could pride
ourselves, began to make up as speedily as possible the
numbers of our arms in South Africa. The common
popular opinion was that the war would be over by
Christmas. Even the numbers of the enemy in the field
against us were vague to the last degree in the public mind.
To the end of the war accurate information on that point
was hardly obtained. The most usual estimates in the
Press put the Boer forces at something between 25,000
and 35,000. The British Intelligence Department, it
appeared later, estimated the Transvaal men alone at
32,000, and the Orange Free Staters at 22,000.

Before General Buller reached the Cape, England was
facing the fact that her forces everywhere in South Africa
were on the defensive, and even desperately on the defensive. Early exchanges in the north of Natal, the surrender
of British forces at Nicholson's Nek, the courageous, dogged

[1] *The Times*, 11th October 1899.

victory of Talana Hill, the dashing charges of Elandslaagte, had conveyed no particular message to the public, whatever they may have conveyed to the War Office, of revised opinions on the Boer marksmanship and the Boer artillery. But the succeeding stage, when it became clear that, even with the arrival of all the forces available, the war would have to begin at every point with recovery of our own territory, caused a great intensification of bellicose feeling in England. It grew with such rapidity that, when Parliament met, as it was bound to do, to vote supplies, and an Appropriation Bill was introduced, only twenty-eight members of the Opposition were found to vote against it. The attack on the Government for their policy had not, indeed, been a weak one. The amendment moved by Mr Philip Stanhope on the introduction of the Bill had produced one of the memorable nights in the history of the House of Commons ; the galleries and the floor were alike crowded ; and Mr Chamberlain had spoken for three hours in the Government's defence. But the division lobbies gave the first sign of that prevailing line of argument which left the Radical stalwarts so few in number—the argument that, whatever its merits, the war had now begun, and to maintain protest against it could only add to the difficulties.

Throughout November there was no event to cause any profound change in popular feeling. The general view remained that the Boer ultimatum had caught us with our dispositions incomplete ; but the adequacy of the dispositions themselves was not generally questioned. People settled down to take in how our forces lay ; early in the month the newspapers began to publish daily small articles by " military experts," with the object of making comprehensible to the ordinary reader a campaign which had, by the swiftness of the Boer attack, taken an unexpected form. The enemy's forces were in two main bodies, one on the east, besieging Ladysmith, and another on the west, which, leaving Kimberley and Mafeking beleaguered, had penetrated southward as far as Belmont, in Cape Colony. The British attack, when the main body from England with General Buller and General Methuen had settled into place, would be delivered at these two points. Between these two points, though no equally considerable force of Boers had crossed the southern frontier of the Orange Free State, was a British division under General Gatacre. For the moment even the alarm caused by the revelation of the size and strength of the Boer guns was relieved ; on 30th October, just before Ladysmith was completely invested, one of the last trains to run into the town brought a naval brigade, supplied by the cruiser *Powerful* ; and one of the happiest popular moments of the war was that in which it was known that the sailors had, by their own handiness, invented and made field carriages for some of their big guns. For this stroke of inventiveness, Captain Percy Scott, of the *Powerful*, became a popular hero. The besieging of Ladysmith was less galling to people at home (as it was now known to be less menacing to the besieged themselves) when the place had guns not incapable of replying to the enormous Creusot pieces which the Boers had dragged to the surrounding hill-tops. The naval brigade had brought with them several 12-pounder quick-firers. and even some of the big 4.7-inch guns. We had been caught at an extraordinary disadvantage in artillery. This small republic had moved into battle guns of a size which had never hitherto been regarded as mobile pieces. But at last, when we had made our bitter discovery, we had corrected our mistake in a way that might legitimately give us pride. Not only in Ladysmith, but also with General Buller at Chievely, and with General Methuen on the Orange River, there were by the beginning of November naval brigades with their big and efficient guns.

Far less criticism of the Government was taking place

than might have been expected. It was really saved from such consequences of its own apparent ignorance of the Boer resources by the fact that the Boers had attacked after a curt ultimatum. The result was that excuses were found for the Government, and the engagements at the end of October and during November did not daunt the public at home. The battles of Talana Hill, Elandslaagte, and Rietfontein in Natal, and those of Belmont and Enslin in Cape Colony, where General Methuen began his advance on 22nd November, had lost us on an average 40 to 50 killed and 150 to 200 wounded. They had shown the disastrous efficacy of Boer marksmanship, and the power of the Mauser magazine rifle. But they had been battles which had not shaken traditional opinion of the British army's methods. True, it was already obvious that use of cover was the enemy's strength, and it was also obvious that our methods were strangely ill adapted to meet an army entirely mounted ; victory on our side was inconclusive when the desperate winning of a hill revealed only bodies of the enemy scudding away on ponies out of range of pursuit. But as yet England appeared to find no heartshaking quality in the war ; the casualty lists were not yet ghastly ; subscriptions to the relief funds and a patriotic enthusiasm seemed all that was specially called for. A jest could still be made of the subaltern starting for the war and packing his polo-sticks, because his idea was that one would fight in the morning and have time for a little polo in the afternoon.

Then, late in November, on the 28th, occurred a battle which gave pause even to the newspaper reader—Methuen's battle at the Modder River. This was not so much because it was more costly in life than others had been—the casualty list amounted to about 450—as that it showed the Boers to be under leadership and discipline of a wholly unexpected kind. They had waited in unperceived entrenchments for the advancing force, and had reserved their fire till the British were within 700 yards. They had dug their trenches, not on the slopes, to which artillery fire would naturally be directed, but on the low plain. After the first outbreak of the Boer fire the British had dropped to the ground, and, save for a force which managed to work round the Boer flank, had spent the whole long day lying flat on the spot where they had been checked, firing at the rare and elusive marks the Boers gave them, while the artillery on both sides kept up a more obvious battle. This engagement was the first to startle England with certain facts which very soon became painfully evident. One was that the Boers were able to carry out secretly entrenching operations on a very large scale, so that an army could move unsuspectingly on to ground completely dominated by rifle-fire with accurately known ranges. A second was that in such cases the force immediately under fire was reduced to something like immobility; it could not retire, any more than it could advance, and was confined to maintaining a day-long rifle duel, with the disadvantage that it lay itself in the open, while its enemy was under cover. A third was that magazine rifles combined with marksmanship as good as that of the Boers rendered it impossible to carry such trenches save by more or less prolonged turning movements.

However, the main army under Buller had yet to move, and such lessons as there may have been in the Modder River battle were not pressed home. The name of Cronje, the Boer commander at this point, had not yet achieved its grimmest hold upon the public mind. A general sense that modern war produced ordeals of which the most acute military authorities could have no previous conception remained the leading idea. This caused an outbreak of resentment against the critical and even jeering tone current in the Continental Press. There might, indeed, be little excuse for our ignorance in the matter of artillery;

but no one, it was maintained, could possibly have been prepared by theory for the lessons we were learning in the power of the modern rifle well used. Consequently it were better for nations not undergoing the fiery ordeal to be thankful that the lesson was laid before them at no cost to themselves, and to preserve some show of respectful observation. The German Emperor and Empress were just at this time in England, visiting the Queen at Windsor. It was acknowledged that the visit was well meant ; but a people on the verge of exasperation felt that at such a time sympathy was rather too ostentatious to be met with real gratitude. The Queen herself was remaining away from her beloved Balmoral, in order that the people might feel her as little withdrawn as might be in a time of trial. Aged and infirm as she now was, she had inspected the composite regiment of Household Cavalry which left for South Africa in November. The country thought of her with sorrow ; that at this far period of her long reign her people should be at war seemed to most of her subjects likely to be an anxiety too great for her failing strength.

Acceptance of the Kaiser's sympathetic interest was rather hindered than helped by a speech delivered by Mr Chamberlain in November, in which he spoke of the possibility of a triple understanding between England, the United States, and Germany. He showed in this a curious failure of his usual capacity for gauging public opinion ; and he probably never in his life made a less popular suggestion. To begin with, it sounded like a half-admission, at a most inopportune moment, that we were nervous about our general position. Then it also appeared to be a rather adulatory acknowledgment of the fact that England was relieved by the Kaiser's careful abstention from anything which might be taken as an encouragement to the Boers. There were a good many who felt that Mr Chamberlain had presumed on the undoubted pre-eminence he had gained by recent events, and imagined that he had shown himself capable of directing a *Welt-politik*, or at least that his countrymen would now believe him capable of it. He was immediately undeceived. The speech had, even from the organs of his own party, the chilliest treatment ; and, although criticism of the Government was for the most part held in check on the Ministerial side, Mr Chamberlain very nearly did it the disservice of precipitating such criticism by propounding large ill-digested ideas at a moment when the Government was displayed as managing none too competently the business already on its hands.

But all such feeling was swamped, before December was half over, in a shock of bewilderment, and furious determination to underestimate no more a demand which had suddenly grown appalling. The " Black Week " of 11th–16th December made the war the frightful reality which it had not yet been, in spite of patriotic songs and enthusiastic leave-takings of regiments and endless talk of war. On the Monday in that week the news was published that General Gatacre, moving in the midway region between the two main armies, which had hitherto produced no encounters of great importance, had marched his men by night, almost certainly under treacherous guidance, into a fatal ambuscade. His troops, not having yet experienced, as Methuen's army had, the completely impenetrable character of the rifle-fire of entrenched Boers, had attempted to rush the hills from which they were being shot down. The result was that a mere remnant of the force could be extricated from the trap, and though only twenty-six were killed, and about seventy wounded, six hundred had been taken prisoners, and two guns lost. By itself this disaster at Stormberg would have been serious, but not terrible ; it was blackened by what followed. On the Thursday came news of a disaster which was wholly dreadful. Methuen had advanced from the Modder River, where, after the ultimate success of his turning movement had caused the abandonment of the Boer trenches during the night, he had rested his men (who had fought three battles in a week during November) and received some reinforcement. Cronje was known to have occupied the time in entrenching a new position at Magersfontein ; and against this Methuen now moved. What England heard was that, marching in the darkness into wire entanglements before the trenches, which had given the alarm, a column nearly 4000 strong had been absolutely cut to pieces by concentrated rifle and machine-gun fire, before it had taken open order. The Highland Brigade, led by General Wauchope, which had come up fresh and eager among the latest of Methuen's reinforcements, had been the main body of this column, and upon them had fallen the worst and most murderous slaughter of the war. No less than 600 had gone down, including the General, in the first few minutes. Again, as at the Modder River, the dreadful opening of battle was followed by a long day of fighting at a cruel disadvantage. More troops were moved up rapidly, some flanking attacks by the Boers were held off, artillery fell to work against the trenched hills, and regiment after regiment took up the rifle duel. But no turning movement could be attempted after such a disastrous beginning to the battle. The lines of Magersfontein remained victorious, and Methuen withdrew again to the Modder River. England faced for the first time a casualty list which numbered all but 1000, of which over 700 were in the Highland Brigade. Then, all too soon on this defeat, came the news that Buller himself had failed as completely in his first movement in force. Here again the Boers had amply entrenched themselves on hills north of the Tugela River. The attack upon them had been repulsed, again with a casualty list of almost 1000 men, but the centre of disaster here had been, not a sudden overwhelming slaughter of men, but the loss of no less

than ten guns. Two batteries of field artillery had
advanced to an exposed spot within 1000 yards of the
enemy's position, and the Boers shot down horses and
men with such deadly accuracy and rapidity that only a
tiny group was at last left to take refuge in a hollow,
leaving the guns bare on the plain. A gallant effort to
save them was led by three of Buller's aides-de-camp,
and two guns were actually rescued. But the remaining
ten fell into the Boers' hands. The troops were withdrawn to camp, leaving 970 on the field, and 250 prisoners.

So the week ended. There had been often enough in
English history battles far more bloody, and campaigns
in most ways more terrible. But they had not occurred
in days of cheap newspapers and instantaneous transmission of news. Casualty lists then were lump sums,
impersonal round figures ; certainty came but long afterwards to homes which through the months had lost their
men without knowing it ; and although the slow dissemination of news meant a perpetual watchfulness and
anxiety it must have been of a duller kind than the
sensation of sharing almost at the moment in defeat.
The Black Week indeed brought war home. The lists of
names occupying column after column of the newspapers,
the sombre crowds waiting round the door of that room
in the War Office where the lists were issued, the knowledge that the whole of our boasted arms were reduced
to the pause of defeat, bit as with acid. For the moment
life ran more dumbly in England than it had run since the
early days of the Indian Mutiny—dumbly, and yet intensely. It was one of the grim signs of that week that
women then first began to buy newspapers, as men do,
from the sellers in the streets.

The Government acted now promptly, and acted well,
both from the point of view of the conduct of the war and
from the point of view of restoring confidence at home.
It was announced on the Monday morning of the following

week—18th December—that Lord Roberts had been
appointed to the chief command in South Africa, and
that Lord Kitchener of Khartoum would accompany him
as his Chief of Staff. Nothing could have administered a
more immediate or more vivifying tonic. An adored old
soldier, whom men would follow anywhere and anyhow,
whose reputation rang with tales of tight places brilliantly
faced, and a young soldier who seemed to have a cold
unastonished genius for victory—the thought of these
two put fresh heart into England. It was intimated that
no formal supersession of General Buller was intended—
and indeed it had been clear that he too had a most
valuable gift of making men follow him and believe in
him, even in defeat—but that the development of events
had shown that what was intended to be the main attack
on the Boers, and as such had been undertaken by him as
Commander-in-Chief, had become a more or less partial
attack. As both our main armies at present in the field
were deeply engaged, it was necessary now to make fresh
dispositions, and to have a Commander-in-Chief apart
from both of the armies in check. The announcement of
these appointments was followed by a great outburst of
enthusiasm for extending the scope of our forces. Large
contingents from the colonies, offered while the negotiations
were running their last stage, had been accepted ; and
some had been operating with the British forces for weeks
past. Others were being raised, and now with quickened
pace. In England a great call was made for yeomanry.
If the Boers could raise a force entirely mounted, and show
us the result in an astonishing mobility, could not a fox-
hunting nation do the same ? In every shire men answered the call. At the same time infantry volunteers were
asked for, and the City of London in especial set itself to
raise a regiment and equip the men entirely at its own
expense. The end of the year was buzzing with enrollings,
drillings, equippings ; London was full of men in new

khaki uniforms, who were made free of every music hall. Crofters and gillies and miners and hard-muscled shipyard men from Scotland, farmers' sons, squires' sons, and solid labourers from the English counties, clerks and artisans from the towns, all poured into the new forces. Great lairds like Lord Lovat, rich men like Lord Strathcona, raised their own bodies of horsemen, the former in Scotland, the latter in Canada.

Both in equipment and in such hurried drill as could be given, the learning of lessons began to be evident. Already people were saying that, just as flying colours and beating drums had disappeared from modern warfare, so scarlet and brass, badges and pipeclayed belts were going now. Nothing that could give the least hold to the eye of one of those terrible marksmen in the trenches must be allowed. Our losses in officers had been especially severe. Gold lace, a buckle here and there, a sash, had made them fatally distinct marks. Henceforth a tab more or less on the collar would have to suffice. Brown leather belts, leather-masked sword-hilts, khaki-covered buttons, distinguished the new equipments that paraded London. The less there was to tell an officer by, the better officer he ; the less a mounted man looked like a cavalryman, the better for his work. Command had begun to mean a new thing—not the picturesque, gallant figure standing up and keeping the ranks calm by parade of coolness, but hitting a man between the eyes for coming out unnecessarily from behind a stone. Courage in the ranks meant less the reckless, daring charge up a slope than the infinitely patient, infinitely painful crawl through a long day.

What would come out of the melting-pot could not yet be seen. That much, very much, had gone in was perhaps the one clear truth of the close of the year. That respect for the army's heads, and for the army's officers, had not gone in too is the greatest tribute that will ever be paid to the qualities of the classes those men were drawn from.

17

CHAPTER V

THE opening of the year 1900 found the British public in a state of raw nerves. The first shock of the December disasters had been too intense for any petty expression at the moment ; and the new commands and the enthusiasm of enlistment had carried the nation through Christmas. Presents for the troops in the field, headed by the Queen's gift of a box of chocolate to each private soldier, occupied the minds and the organising capacities of a great many persons ; plum puddings, tobacco, cigarettes, and all kinds of creature comforts were sent out by tons. Public subscriptions supplemented the private efforts of all who had friends or relations at the front ; and though this kind of effort might be regarded as rather trifling, it was a far from useless distraction of thought, both at home and in the camps where the vast miscellaneous distributions were made.

But such a distraction could not be lasting. Even if anxiety had not returned in other ways, the news on 6th January would have aroused it sharply. Throughout that day the telegrams in the evening newspapers produced the most disturbing uncertainty about Ladysmith that had yet been experienced. The Boers had attacked in force, and the battle was still raging on Cæsar's Camp and Waggon Hill, two of the garrison's outposts. Of course the failure of Buller's relieving force had previously caused apprehensions. Under the bombardment Ladysmith was known to be enduring, it had hardly been regarded as likely to bear a long siege, and that it had not surrendered before Buller could move was a matter for satisfaction. But with his defeat it became obvious that relief might be indefinitely delayed. Sir George White, the commanding officer in Ladysmith, had been magnificently reassuring. To a depressed message from Buller immediately after the battle of Colenso (they were in communication by heliograph and searchlight) he had answered that he could make his supplies last out, and had no thought of surrender. But strong assault by the Boers had hardly been anticipated in England (which had been consoling itself by saying that its enemy might be a deadly shot in trenches, but would not risk charging), so that the news of 6th January brought the real dread, whether, after more than two months' siege, the holding-out of the garrison could include the repulsing of a vigorous attack.

It did. Next day England knew that, after the sharpest hand-to-hand fighting, in which the Devons and the Imperial Light Horse—a body of South African volunteers —had for all time inscribed their names on the history of the siege, the Boers had been beaten off. But, at last, the nervousness had bitten too deeply to be lessened, even by such news, and such heroism. From now onwards the references to Ladysmith always betrayed a gloomy undercurrent of belief that the town must fall, and that we had better make up our minds to the fact.[1] The two other places, the beleaguering of which had not appeared so very important while our armies still seemed to be on the move, shared now in the strained national attention. Ladysmith, Kimberley and Mafeking came to stand for all the hopes and the confidence that had formerly been given to the armies. Kimberley, whither Mr Rhodes had gone just as the war broke out, was a place of some importance—especially, to the Boers, when he was in it —and its siege was a normal piece of warfare. It was the

[1] See *The Times*, 16th January 1900.

gate on that side of the Free State for invasion. The case of Mafeking, however, was different. Situated far in the north, and not occupied by any body of troops considerable enough to require isolation, the town might apparently have been let alone. The story of Mafeking appears to be a story of unadulterated combativeness. The Boers decided to fight there, and in the town was a man delighted to oblige them, Colonel Baden-Powell. Neither side had anything strategic to gain.

But all three places became equally important now to English feeling; worn nerves needed focussing points of some kind to work at. Early in January there were signs that dissatisfaction with the Government was gathering to a head; and the news of another costly action fought by Buller, without a step gained towards Ladysmith, produced an explosion of bitterness. Starting from his base on 10th January Buller had crossed the Tugela at two points a considerable distance west of Colenso, taking a week for the operations, and on the 23rd part of his force had captured, by the severest fighting, a hill called Spion Kop, from which it appeared that the Boer trenches could be completely commanded. But owing to the disposition of the ground our artillery were unable to master the Boer artillery turned upon the hill-top; and after a murderous day in which men, forced by the small compass of the hill-top to lie in close formation, had been cruelly battered by Boer guns, the ground so expensively won was abandoned, and by the 27th Buller was back again on the south side of the river. The deliberate strategy of this battle, the splendid gallantry of the assault, the great news that at last we held a position actually commanding the terrible Boer lines, had been so cheering that the announcement of the withdrawal strained the tension in England beyond breaking point. The Government were roundly told that they had muddled from beginning to end; Mr Balfour was warned that his attitude under criticism was far too jaunty and frivolous; the war had been a series of calamitous mistakes, relieved only by the courage and endurance of officers and men ; and the result was that we stood without a plan of campaign.[1] Parliament met on 30th January, and although there may not have been much sympathy with extreme Liberal opinion against the war, the announcement that a vote of censure would be moved by the Opposition leaders was certainly not regarded as a mere hampering of the Government. Ugly things were being said already of the War Office contracts, and stories were coming to England of the miserable quality of many of the contract supplies, of dangerous rations, of wretched forage; even the ammunition was not above criticism. By the beginning of March it was becoming clear that in this matter too the grossest incompetence had been revealed ; and such serious instances were brought forward in the House of Commons that a Select Committee was appointed. The Government had certain consolations to fall back upon. The unexampled trade prosperity of the past year [2] was a great asset ; the revenue returns were very good, customs being up by £660,000 and excise by over £1,000,000, with one quarter of the financial year yet to run ; and the Chancellor of the Exchequer was evidently going to have a larger surplus than he had expected. Little legislation was proposed in the Speech from the Throne ; a measure for reforming company law and a Moneylenders Bill were the only items of any importance.

Meanwhile Lord Roberts and Lord Kitchener had been assembling a considerable force at the Modder River, combining new arrivals with the existing army under Methuen. But their preparations were being made with new secrecy, and no word of them came through to soothe English irritation. A third movement by Buller, developing into the capture, under cover of a bombardment,

---

[1] *The Times*, 27th January 1900.
[2] See page 451.

startling even in this war, of Vaalkranz Hill, and ending once again in withdrawal, was received with exasperation. The losses this time had been lighter—a casualty list of 250, as against the lamentable 1500 of Spion Kop; but the popular nicknaming of Buller as " the Bull-dog " began to assume a rueful twist under this series of exhibitions of doggedness. A good many generals in South Africa paid heavily, less for mistakes of their own than for the all-pervading original mistake as to the task set us by this war. The battle of Vaalkranz took popular attention at the moment of Lord Roberts's first movement, and little heed was paid to the advance of the Highland Brigade towards the extreme right of the Boer position at Magersfontein. So the excitement a few days later was all the more keen, when England suddenly became aware that, the watchfulness of the Boers having thus been drawn towards their right, a large body of cavalry, some 5000 in number, had ridden hard round their left, crossed the Modder twenty-five miles east of Magersfontein, and practically galloped past the only attempt made to stop it. Almost before England had had time to take in what had happened—the mustering of this flying force in the rear of Methuen's army, and its launching under the man who was henceforth to be a popular idol as a dashing cavalryman, General French—the news came that, covering 100 miles in four days, this swift march had raised the siege of Kimberley. Lord Roberts had got to work. Indeed his great name seemed to act like a charm. On the very day when Kimberley was relieved, his infantry appeared in force on the extreme left of the Boer lines, capturing as they went Jacobsdal (where the City Imperial Volunteers were for the first time in action); and the grim Cronje, alarmed for his communications with his base at Bloemfontein, had hurriedly abandoned his position; the awful trenches of Magersfontein no longer loomed over us. Now ensued the most

tense period of the war. Cronje managed to pass the outer
horn of Roberts's force; but if he were to reach Bloemfontein he must cross the Modder River, and there were
but three drifts available to him. Roberts held Klip
Drift already. French, hastening across from Kimberley,
seized Wolveskraal Drift. Cronje turned to Paardeberg
Drift, between the two—and the vice closed on him. He
lay in laager, and on 18th February Kitchener attacked
him. It was a heavy battle, with 1100 casualties; but
it pinned Cronje into a narrow space of two miles, clinging
to his waggons. So great was the change of spirit caused
at home that, when Buller now started again from camp,
it almost seemed as if the renewed confidence reaching out
to his men from England had infected them. He completely changed his line of attack, going this time to the
extreme eastward of the Colenso position, captured
Hlangwane Hill, and, planting his guns there, sent his Irish
Brigade, under General Fitzroy Hart, against the left-hand
hills of the Boer line. The furious assault of the brigade
was checked, but it lay obstinately on the sides of the hill,
while Buller behind it moved the rest of his army still
further east, lapping round the lines of Pieter's Hill. At the
critical moment of his operations, England woke one day
to the news that, after another attack on Cronje's laager,
in which the Canadians, leading the van with the Gordons,
had pushed a handful of men into a position enfilading the
Boer trenches, Cronje had surrendered unconditionally,
and between 4000 and 5000 prisoners had been taken
at a blow. On the top of the exultation came the
complete success of Buller. It had been another hard
fight; the Colenso trenches had not been hurriedly
deserted at the last, as the Magersfontein trenches had
been; the casualty list reached 1600. But no more
remained to do here, though at the moment this could
hardly be believed by the army. Lord Dundonald,
venturing greatly, took a couple of squadrons of South

African light horsemen cautiously forward. Hardly a shot was fired upon them, and in the evening of 28th February the Ladysmith siege was over, and the garrison saved.

A couple of days had changed the whole aspect of the war. A note from the Presidents of the two Boer republics to the Prime Minister, suggesting that, now British prestige was restored, peace terms might be discussed, was brushed aside as beneath consideration, save as a sign of consciousness of defeat. For the note still spoke of the republics as "sovereign international states." Bellicose temper rose again hotly, and the war spirit, which had been purged of some of its more vulgar elements during the weeks of depression, became again pervaded with boastfulness. Yet on the whole the nation had cause for pride in the story of the Ladysmith siege. It had been a cruel one. Incessant bombardment and enteric fever had literally decimated the men, without breaking their courage. Officers who could ill be spared had fallen ; a month before the end of the siege one of the best known of the war correspondents, G. W. Steevens, who had made more than a passing reputation for himself in literature, had died. Now that the whole story was coming out, it was gratifying to find that here, at least, organisation had been good, the commissariat as well managed as it could possibly have been, and the defences flawless. Of the Kimberley siege much also was reported of the most gallant kind ; lack of guns had been remedied by the ingenuity of the diamond-mine engineers, who constructed a piece of artillery ; but here again bombardment had been terrific, and as no naval gun had opportunely arrived in Kimberley, the largest Boer artillery had been out of our range. But unfortunately the Kimberley story had less gratifying chapters. Mr Rhodes, who came to England in April, published opinions bitterly criticising Colonel Kekewich, who had been in command ; and there were evidences of quarrels in the town during the siege. Meanwhile the third siege upon which English eyes had turned early in the year, that of Mafeking, was providing extraordinary and even hilarious news. Colonel Baden-Powell was holding out, not only with courage, but with inextinguishable high spirits.

Early in March Queen Victoria drove through London, facing the fatigue in order that her people's new sense of relief and hope might be provided with an outlet. On 17th March, St Patrick's Day, there was a general wearing of the shamrock, in recognition of the gallantry of Irish regiments; and it was announced later on that royal recognition was to be accorded in the raising of a regiment of Irish Guards, to be added to the Household Brigade. The wearing of the shamrock was a curious sign of a tendency now at work to express, not merely the feeling of patriotism, but patriotic demonstrations *en masse*. The Irish regiments had certainly been gallant; but not more so, when all was said, than the Highlanders, the Lancashire men who fought Spion Kop, the west-country men in Ladysmith. The mere chance that Ireland happened to have a special day of festival at the moment, however, served the purpose of this new spirit of acting in crowds. The habit continued to distort values during the war: for often the prominence of this or that event depended on its hitting or missing some popular impulse.

A few days after the Paardeberg surrender, every detail of which was eagerly welcomed in London, with the central picture of the overweening Cronje himself at last made visible—a sullen, bearded, thick-set man in a slouch hat, riding in to his submission—Lord Roberts moved towards Bloemfontein. Two battles were fought on the way, at Poplar Grove and Driefontein; but victory was in the air, and Bloemfontein was occupied on 13th March. Everyone rejoiced in the prospect of rest for men and horses after the hard and glorious work of the past fortnight.

What yet remained to do was looked at in a new spirit.
The Free State Government had gone north to Kronstadt,
and the east of the Free State was still alive with the
enemy ; but doubt of our powers had ceased to gnaw us.
Confidence was indeed so extraordinarily restored that it
became positively volatile ; a few weeks after this Lord
Milner had to telegraph from Cape Town to urge the authorities at home to stop a constantly increasing stream of
tourists. A war loan of thirty-five millions was readily
taken up in March. Bearing interest at $2\frac{3}{4}$ per cent.,
the loan had been issued at $98\frac{1}{2}$, and was subscribed eleven
times over. The Budget which followed was, of course,
largely a nullity, owing to the borrowings for the war.
But it provided a good basis, the revenue being eight and
a half millions above the estimate, and eleven and a half
millions above the previous year's revenue. True, some
of this was a fictitious increase. Customs and excise each
accounted for an increase of nearly three millions ; and
much of this was undoubtedly due to premature clearances,
since it was evident that new taxation was bound to be
imposed. Consequently the present fattening of the
revenue only meant a shrinkage in the next year, and
a partial defeat of the war taxation. But next year was
a long way off ; no one, whatever his position, imagined
for a moment in the existing circumstances that we should
have any considerable force in the field twelve months
hence ; and so the next Budget, though it would have
to carry some burden of the past, would not have to be a
War Budget. In one respect the present revenue returns
were a real windfall ; estate duty had come out at three
millions over the estimate, largely owing to the death of
" Chicago Smith," a millionaire who had lived obscurely
in a London club, and was but little known to the public,
until the death duties on his property brought £900,000
into the Exchequer. For the coming year the Chancellor
of the Exchequer put fivepence on to the income-tax,

and by this and by enhanced duties on beer, spirits, tobacco and tea promised himself twelve millions.

At the end of March and the beginning of April two occurrences in the Orange Free State chastened the over-sanguine. A force which had been operating east of Bloemfontein was ambuscaded in falling back on the town, the Boers lining a sunken watercourse in what appeared to be a harmless level plain. Cavalry and artillery rode unsuspectingly into the trap, and although the force was largely extricated, and conveyed across the river at another point, over 500 men and some thirty officers were on the casualty list, 300 prisoners had been taken, and no less than seven of the Horse Artillery guns. But the worst of this action at Sanna's Post was that it lost us the Bloemfontein water-works, and the army had to make use of the wells, which resulted in a great increase of enteric fever. Another disaster followed, a force of General Gatacre's troops being surrounded and overborne by heat, thirst and lack of ammunition. The Boers took another 900 prisoners. Criticism was more on the alert now than in the early days. From this time onwards there was a constant tendency to draw contrasts between English troops and Colonial troops, with a rather hysterical admiration of the latter and a peevish depreciation of the former. The popular picture of the British officer represented him as enslaved to drill and method, unable to see beyond his nose ; that of the Australian, the New Zealander, the South African, the Canadian, represented them as applying instinctively to war the methods of the tracker and the huntsman, scratching their rations out of nothing, and beating the Boer at his own game. There was some truth in the contrasts, though they were overdrawn ; it was forgotten, for instance, that Roberts's Horse, a body of South African colonials, had been in the Sanna's Post trap. Besides, it was obvious that British troops, not living in a land where they could learn the methods of the tracker and the huntsman, had had to buy their learning. Those numerous writers, headed by Mr Kipling, who found delight in pungent descriptions of British stupidity set off by Colonial craftiness, have perhaps never realised one lasting effect of their indulgence in these descriptions. The British public had instilled into it a sense that its lords and masters, as represented by its military officers, were neither brilliant nor men of common-sense, but dull courageous creatures of routine. It is not possible to say one thing violently at one moment, when your eye is on a single consideration, and prevent readers from gradually, even unconsciously, extending the application of what you say. The great reaction against the Conservatives in the general election of 1906, and the undermining of the landlord class, can certainly be traced in some measure to the views Mr Kipling and his followers expressed about " regrettable incidents " of the South African War.

By the month of May the Government was under a storm of criticism. The publication of the despatches on the Spion Kop engagement had drawn the attack. For one thing, it appeared that General Buller had been asked by the Secretary for War to rewrite his despatches before publication, and had declined. He had blamed Sir Charles Warren, and the despatches throughout gave evidence of a certain lack of harmony. But the Government's request suggested that, on its part, it had a bad conscience, and wished to avoid " revelations." As a consequence, every item of the management of the war was now called in question, and lack of common foresight was charged against ministers in every department concerned. On one point they had at the moment a fair answer to give ; Sir William MacCormac and Mr Treves had just returned from an inspection of the hospitals in South Africa, and had said that, whatever else might be wrong, the hospital and medical service was excellent. Mr

Treves complained only, in a phrase that became famous, of " a plague of flies and a plague of women," the latter being half-trained, or even untrained, women who had managed to be sent out as nurses with various volunteer hospital corps, enrolled with more enthusiasm than judgment. But even this bright spot did not serve the Government long. These two surgeons might be great men ; but the newspapers had had to replace the appallingly long casualty lists, happily things of the past, with extremely disturbing lists of cases of disease. This was evidence which rather undermined the rosy report ; and in June the Government was being attacked for want of foresight and provision in this department no less than in the others. Mr Burdett-Coutts, who had spent some time in South Africa investigating the subject as special correspondent of *The Times*, wrote letters to that paper indicting the Government for insufficient staffing and equipment of the medical service ; the field hospitals were all overworked, and there was no staff to spare for safeguarding the army by even the most elementary sanitary supervision. With considerable courage in the face of the anger and contemptuous speeches of his leaders in the House of Commons, where he sat as a Conservative member, Mr Burdett-Coutts continued his attack in that House, bringing out especially the fact that by the very nature of the service the men of the Army Medical Corps grew steadily out of touch with modern hospital practice and modern theories of health and sanitation. In the end he succeeded in securing the appointment of a Select Committee.

Yet all this criticism was not to be interpreted as a general change of mind on the subject of the war. A South Africa Conciliation Committee, which was founded with the object of securing at the earliest possible moment a cessation of hostilities, had much unpopularity to face. It was urging now that, as the Boers had been beaten heavily at last, and driven not only from our colonies, but from some of their own territory, England might offer peace on condition that the Boer States disarmed, and surrendered all claim to control of their own foreign relations ; at the same time the Rand might be separated from the Transvaal, as the Diamond Fields had been separated from the Orange Free State. It was doubtful, to begin with, whether the Boers in the field would agree to such terms. Recent events had shown that they were still full of fight, and by no means overawed. At any rate, the war spirit in England would not hear of such suggestions. The less firmly established Liberal papers found salvation in them. Under the pressure of competition two Liberal penny papers, *The Daily News* and *The Daily Chronicle*, had first of all reduced their price to a halfpenny, and then, finding themselves still hard pressed, had largely waived their opposition to the war. It required deep conviction and a rich and courageous proprietorship to maintain, in the face of popular opinion, that the war need never have taken place. " Pro-Boer " was an ugly label, very readily attached. In Great Britain only three prominent newspapers stood unflinchingly by opposition to war, *The Manchester Guardian*, *The Morning Leader* and *The Star*. *The Daily Chronicle* practically went with the popular tide ; *The Daily News* clutched at the programme of the Conciliation Committee, and so just saved its Liberalism. The newspapers which held out unyielding against the war clamour owed their survival to the fact that each had made itself more or less indispensable to a particular public. *The Manchester Guardian* had built up a service of commercial news which the cotton trade could not dispense with. The morning trains and trams in Lancashire were full of men who expressed their attitude by crumpling the paper into a ball and throwing it away ostentatiously, when they had read the telegrams from New York, Galveston and New Orleans.

The Morning Leader and *The Star* had made for themselves
a position as the workman's newspapers ; and it was some
time before the workman got out of his habit of so regarding them. They had nothing to gain by their policy, for
the workmen as a whole did not in the matter of the war
adhere to Radicalism. Denunciations of the war as a
capitalist war, as a spending of the common soldiers' blood
and a diversion of the country's resources for the object
of securing the gold companies on the Rand, had not succeeded in keeping organised Labour aloof from the rest of
the community. At the Trade Union Congress later in
the year there were bitter comments on the easy jingoism
of the workman, and his readiness to share in breaking up
peace meetings. At the same time it must be said that,
on the death of a Liberal member of Parliament for Portsmouth in April, the seat was held successfully by the
Liberal candidate. Liberalism had not yet passed into
its most unpopular period. It was neither attacking,
nor being attacked, with the sharpness that developed
later on, as the result of changed conditions in the
war.

The kind of feeling which might, in clever hands, be
turned heavily against any sort of criticism of the war
became manifest one night in May. In that month there
were two great popular demonstrations. The first, which
revealed no special cause for comment, was on the return
of the naval brigade which had served in Ladysmith
through the siege. Sir George White had just come home,
and had been the honoured guest of the Queen at Windsor ;
but he had avoided hero-worship ; and it all fell upon the
sailors when they appeared in London, dragging some of
the famous guns of the siege, and marched to lunch at the
Admiralty and on through the City to tea at Lloyd's.
Immense crowds gathered, but the day left no afterthoughts as to their behaviour. It was otherwise with the
second demonstration, which added to the language a word

not of wholly satisfactory content. On 18th May the news of the relief of Mafeking reached London, and though it arrived late in the evening it spread everywhere. The result was amazing ; an uninformed stranger might have thought that the whole war had depended on this news. Although the announcement was not made until nine o'clock at night an enormous crowd was soon parading the principal streets of the City and the West End. There had, indeed, been some expectation of the news, and for several nights many people had lingered near the War Office, the Mansion House, and the newspaper offices in Fleet Street, on the chance of an announcement. But when it was made the crowd swelled as if by magic. The extraordinary thing was that here was no celebration of a day arranged in advance, so that people might be expected to come in from the suburbs. The masses of people appeared to spring from the pavements. Within half-an-hour the great space before the Mansion House was packed solid, Fleet Street, the Strand and Pall Mall, Regent Street, Piccadilly and Oxford Circus were black with torrents of humanity, in which the wheeled traffic gave up any attempt to move. At every theatre and music hall the news was announced from the stage ; at the Lyceum even Madame Duse's spell was broken to allow the reading of the telegram, and the singing of " God Save the Queen." Out in the suburbs early sleepers were awakened by outbursts of cheers ; men came down by train from the seething centre of London, and rode off in cabs, shouting the news along the quiet roads of villas. Liverpool was alive with parading crowds ; Newcastle was startled by the explosion and flare of rockets ; Birmingham spread the news like wildfire from its theatres ; the brass band of the volunteers roused the streets of York ; Glasgow illuminated its municipal buildings ; Leicester and Brighton swarmed with madly cheering people, the Yorkshire dales reverberated with the sound of strangely blown mill and factory sirens. The next day was a Saturday, and no one pretended to do even the customary half-day's work.

The spontaneity of the demonstrations could hardly be denied ; they took every reflective person by surprise. But it was not altogether satisfactory surprise. People began to ask themselves, and continued to ask for some time, whether the British character was revealing in such demonstrations signs of profound change, whether we were growing unbalanced, whether, now that there had been symptoms of hysteria in rejoicing, we ought not to confess that there had been some hysteria in our depression at the end of the past year. In short, if we showed lack of self-control, were we ceasing to be capable of rule ? Were we pursuing this war in the real determination of a conquering race, or were we deceiving ourselves with a merely spasmodic imitation of it, derived from alternations of wounded and gratified pride ? The real change was probably less in the popular manifestations of feeling than in the Imperial self-consciousness thus opposed to them. The nation revealed in Gillray's cartoons of the Napoleonic period, the nation which wrapped itself in the splendour of Alma and Balaclava while it left to a single woman the care of its wounded and to a single newspaper correspondent decent foresight for the strength and health of men in the trenches, was after all much the same impressionable, stupid, successful nation which was now under diagnosis. The habit of quick and easy communication made its qualities appear more intensely ; but that was all. On the other hand it had never dawned upon Gillray that we were a nation of masters. The Imperial spirit, which the commentators on Mafeking night perceived as dimly threatened by such unbridled enthusiasm, was a modern invention. In so far as it had any real existence as a corporate emotion, it was probably more unhealthy than the " mafficking " spirit, which, so far as there is any genuine Psychology of Crowds, presented perfectly normal aspects.

" Mafficking " went on for some days. The street hawkers, by the alertness of the Jews who supply their stock-in-trade, helped to maintain it by providing the drifting groups in the streets of an evening with peacocks' feathers, " squeakers," little flags, and other such trophies. Why the relief of Mafeking, more than that of Ladysmith, more than the success at Paardeberg or the occupation of Bloemfontein, should have let loose all this hilarity, it would be difficult to say. For one thing, it was a neat rounding-off of the picture which the ordinary public had drawn for itself of the task before us ; it appeared to complete the happier turn of the tide. Secondly, it coincided with what already looked like a triumphant close to the whole second chapter of the war ; Lord Roberts had started north from Bloemfontein on 10th May, had driven the Boers from Kronstadt on 12th May, and we knew that the advance to Pretoria had begun. Methuen was moving up from the west, after a neat little engagement in which some of his volunteer mounted infantry had captured near Boshof a small Boer commando under a French colonel, de Villebois Mareuil, who was killed ; Buller was moving up the narrow northern neck of Natal, driving Boers from one position after another by out-flanking movements. Third, and by no means least, the defence of Mafeking was exactly of the kind to stir the ordinary man's blood ; and it may have been obscurely felt that we owed some singular meed of appreciation to a defence which our main military dispositions had appeared rather to leave to look after itself. There was gallantry in all that England heard of the story. Colonel Baden-Powell had not only managed with wonderful economy and resourcefulness the fighting force of the town (here, more wonderfully than at Kimberley, since the materials were far poorer, a large gun had been constructed, and

shells made for it) ; but he had organised dances and
cricket matches, sung at concerts, and descended at other
intervals from his watch-tower to go scouting by night
towards the Boer lines with a craft learned in earlier years
from the Zulus and the Matabele.   Lastly, the defence of
Mafeking had this special appeal to the imagination—
that it was, so to speak, almost an impromptu civilian
defence, and therefore might be taken to prove that
muddling or inefficiency in high places was not symptom-
atic of a general decay.   There was penetration in the
comments of *The Times*, which offered, as one explanation
of the amazing expression of popular emotion, that " it
was instinctively felt that at Mafeking we have the
common man of the Empire, the fundamental stuff of
which it is built, with his back to the wall . . . and at the
long last coming out, proud, tenacious, unconquered,
and unconquerable," a glimpse of " the fundamental grit
of the breed." [1]   At the very last the defence had covered
itself with glory.   An attack delivered by the Boers penetrated well into the town, but was so neatly and swiftly
answered that the attackers, cut off from their supports
and pinned for a whole day to the dangerous ground
they had gained, surrendered in the end, a batch of 120
prisoners.   If, as has been said, neither side had anything strategic to gain at Mafeking, the stout defence
had for seven months kept 2000 of the enemy and one
of their big Creusot guns from reinforcing the Boers
elsewhere.

The Mafeking celebrations should probably have caused
less concern to the acute observer inclined to be critical
than the subsequent slackening of interest in the war.
Lord Roberts, rendering various Boer positions untenable
by means of wide turning movements, crossed the Vaal
River on 27th May and, hardly delayed by the action of
Doornkop, was at Johannesburg on 30th May.   On the

[1] *The Times,* 20th May 1900.

previous day he had issued the proclamation annexing the Orange Free State. Yet it is on record that the newspaper placards in London on the 30th were devoted to Epsom and not to Johannesburg.[1] This slackening of interest was surely a more serious sign of superficiality in the popular mind than the recent jubilations had been. The Boers were unable to stand at any point, it was known on 31st May that Kruger had fled from Pretoria, the mines of the Rand were safe ; and even writers usually judicious were saying that " threats of an obstinate guerilla war need not be regarded seriously." [2]   Pretoria was occupied on 5th June, a mere fringe of Boer riflemen having to be swept away from before it, and a day later over 3000 British prisoners had been released. But the effect of the sudden decline of interest (although of course the actual occupation of Pretoria had been acclaimed) was seen in the irritation and resentment aroused by news of continued fighting in what was now the Orange River Colony. Lord Roberts, deciding to move on Pretoria, had been quite conscious of the Boer forces left in the eastward portion of the colony. The public at home, tiring in its easy way of details, had not taken into account the true state of affairs ; and when it found that guerilla war after all had to be taken seriously it began to call for strong measures. Throughout the month of June, England learned by painful experience the name of another Boer leader, De Wet. Flying raids upon the railway, with constant cuttings of the line and blowing up of trains, sudden descents upon isolated bodies of troops and convoys on the march, had a double seriousness. They not only provided the elusive commandos with stores, ammunition and rifles ; but they encouraged resistance elsewhere, and prevented the feeling that any district was really subdued. It began to be

[1] Sir Wemyss Reid, in *The Nineteenth Century*, July 1900.
[2] *The Times*, 31st May 1900.

more than suspected that Boers who had given in their submission were swept again into the fighting ranks by the passing of De Wet's force ; and that farms ostensibly peaceful had their ways of working with De Wet, by giving him supplies and information, if not acting as real bases. For the moment Lord Roberts had work of his own on hand. The main Boer forces under Louis Botha were too near Pretoria, lying about fifteen miles out at Pienaar's Poort. The British force was not the large one with which Roberts had first turned the tide of the war ; he had had to leave a brigade at Johannesburg, and another on his line of communications, besides the troops he had left in the Orange River Colony operating under Methuen. But he succeeded in driving the Boers westward. Moving out from Pretoria on 11th June, he sent French against the right and Hamilton against the left of the Boer position. The fighting was sharp, and the City Imperial Volunteers, who were part of Hamilton's force, had their mettle tested as severely as any troops during the war in the grim task of hanging on to the ridge of Diamond Hill. But in the end the Boers found their position untenable, and moved eastwards down the line, relieving the pressure on Pretoria. Then attention was turned more steadily to De Wet. He had fairly startled people in England by almost capturing Lord Kitchener in one of his raids. Driven back from the railway, he was operating in the Bethlehem region, north-east of Bloemfontein, when a combined sweeping movement against him was organised between the forces of Ian Hamilton, Hunter, Macdonald and Clements. As the cordon drew tight towards the Basutoland border, De Wet, leaving the main body of Boers, made a dash with some 1500 men, and got through the English lines. Troops were detached in hot pursuit, but failed to catch him. The sweeping movement, however, went on until, at the end of July, Commandant Prinsloo surrendered with about 4000 men. Although De Wet had escaped, these operations removed all possibility of danger to the Durban railway; and this was important, since it gave Lord Roberts in Pretoria a secure base for supplies twenty-four hours nearer to him than Cape Town. General Buller had before this passed, by a series of successful little engagements, the mountain barriers in the extreme north of Natal, and was in possession of Standerton, in the Transvaal, at the head of 20,000 men.

Record of the national attitude towards the war has now to take a new direction. To the public mind the occupation of Bloemfontein and Pretoria and the formal annexation of the Orange Free State and the Transvaal meant a far stage in the last chapter of the war. When, in August, Lord Roberts, having at length rehorsed his mounted troops, began a large movement eastwards, the end seemed close at hand. Buller moved up from Standerton, pushing Boer forces before him; Pole-Carew moved out along the Lourenço Marques line, and French moved parallel with him north of the line. Kruger, who had been living in a railway saloon carriage, ready to move instantly, at Machadodorp, fled across the frontier, after a few days' fighting around Machadodorp and Bergendal, at the beginning of September, had driven the Boers out of the strong positions there. Buller continued to push the disintegrated bands northward to Lydenburg, where he fought another battle on 8th September, still further disintegrating them. Hamilton and Pole-Carew drove other bands eastward, till, late in September, they had forced the fugitives across the frontier, had occupied Komatipoort, and had found there and at Hector Spruit, close by, the shattered remains of many of the treasured Boer guns, including three of the four big Creusots. The guns had been kept on the rail, to be hurried ever eastward as the pressure increased. That they had now been abandoned and destroyed was a notable sign.

It was assumed in England that, by all the rules of such affairs, the war should now end. The Boer commanders, separated and driven from all important bases of operations, should have seen, it was supposed, that no hope remained to them of regaining their country, and should therefore have surrendered. That they did not do so had the result of exasperating party spirit in England to a degree far beyond anything yet reached. On the one hand, the Conciliation Committee was urgent that, now the Boer republics were irrevocably annexed, we should not lay on ourselves the burden, and on the Boer people the humiliation, of driving the war to the point of absolute forcible submission to our arms ; but should endeavour to offer them some kind of future position in their old lands which might induce them to accept our supremacy. The idea of bargaining with them was inherent in this advice. On the other hand, the greater part of the nation, irritated that all was not over when the conditions were formally those of conquest, refused to offer a bargain at all. If the Boers thought, by holding out in their difficult mountainous regions, and carrying on guerilla war, to weary us into waiving any part of the formal situation, they should learn that they were wrong. If they would not surrender by the rules, they should be not only vanquished, but thrashed. Hence proceeded a state of feeling which led to still further exasperation. Lord Roberts was urged to enter upon a course of much greater severity towards those suspected of helping the Boer forces after taking oaths of allegiance. It was held to be clear that men operating without bases of supplies or lines of communication must be drawing maintenance from farms nominally at peace with us. It was also held to be clear, from the comparative impunity with which the guerillas managed their raids, that they had sources of intelligence which could only be found in those same farms. Instances began to be known of rifles and ammunition found secreted in homes which had in their possession the passes given by British generals to Boers taking the oath. It was agreed that leniency to the farms was from every point of view a mistake, and would only prolong the war. During the autumn greater severity was in fact at work. Farms proved to be in co-operation with Boer forces in the field were burned. But this on the other hand roused the Conciliation Committee to a more strenuous activity. This kind of punishment must always, they argued, be difficult to administer justly; it must be watched jealously. And, on the broader lines, did not England see now on what a course the determination to beat the Boers to their knees had embarked her ? When the end came, we should have in South Africa not merely people whom we had beaten in war, but people rendered sullen by the destruction of homes and the desolation of their families. Controversy in England began to take an embittered tone. Those who were for the maintenance and the increase of strong measures chafed also under the obviously growing expense caused by the prolongation of war. Those who lamented the resolution to come to no terms with an enemy feared lest the exasperation of the other side might grow into a spirit almost savage. The struggle began, as the autumn drew on, to gather to itself all the normal opposition between political parties. Throughout the session Liberal opinion had shown no decided front. Even in late July, in a division following a debate on South Africa, only thirty-one Liberals had voted against the Government. Forty had voted with the Government, and the leader, Sir Henry Campbell-Bannerman, with thirty-five more, had avoided voting at all. Radical views had their champion, not in the party leader, but in Mr Lloyd George, who, when the session was over, had made for himself the beginning of a new reputation as the most persistent and prominent in attacks upon Mr Chamberlain for his whole South African policy. But another effect of the close of the session was that speculation turned vigorously to the possibility of a dissolution of Parliament. It had for some time been thought that Mr Chamberlain, true to his constant skill with electoral machinery, felt the moment ripe for a general election. If the war were to be prolonged, public opinion might revert too strongly to the recollection of the Government's original failures of foresight, and might revenge itself upon ministers by turning them out of office. But that would be most likely to happen if the dissolution were delayed until even a prolonged war must be over, or nearly over. At the moment the Government could urge that it required strength for the final effort, could appeal to the country to give it a firm basis from which to conclude a nearly concluded task. But a year hence affairs might well be in a condition in which no such appeal could be made. It was believed that these views did not commend themselves to the rest of the Cabinet [1]; but a certain tendency on Mr Chamberlain's part to overcolour his case had a campaigning appearance. This became more obvious after the House rose. The development of the farm-burning controversy was exactly what a Conservative party agent might have hoped for. Being, as it were, not a direct indictment of the whole origin of the war, but a distinct question of its continuance, it attracted those Liberals who had not been able to take the most outspoken view in the early days. Many more, who might still have hesitated, were driven into a defence of the Liberal position by Mr Chamberlain's round accusation of the Liberals as traitors. In rebutting that rather sweeping classification, Liberals were obliged to define their own position ; and as that

[1] Sir Wemyss Reid, in *The Nineteenth Century*, July 1900.

involved criticism of what was going on, and to some extent of what had led to it, the whole affair became more and more a party question. The last stroke was the notorious " crystallising " of the position by a candidate named Wanklyn, in the phrase " a vote given to the Liberals is a vote given to the Boers." The Boer leaders still in the field were believed to be holding out mainly in the hope of intervention which would secure them some conciliatory terms ; a delegation was in the United States in May, and Kruger was expected to come to Europe to appeal to the Continental powers.

Parliament was dissolved on 25th September. A paucity of candidates on the Liberal side showed how deep exasperation had already gone. Within a fortnight the great boroughs had made it plain that the election was to be an abnormal one ; by 6th October the returns stood at 300 Unionists to 80 Liberals. The counties proved no safer ground for the Liberals, and by the end of the month, even Orkney turning Unionist, the new Parliament was complete, consisting of 402 Unionists, 186 Liberals, and 82 Nationalists, a Unionist majority of 134. Scotland for the first time had returned more Unionists than Liberals (though the difference was only two) ; Wales remained stauncher to her traditions, and returned 22 more Liberals than Unionists ; for this Mr Lloyd George was largely responsible, and his reputation was now made.

To the " Khaki Election," as it came to be called, neither side would look back a few years later with much pride. There were many Conservatives who disliked an appeal to the country in the midst of a war,—felt it to be on the one hand an almost sentimental appeal for support, and on the other hand a not very sporting advantage taken of the Opposition. Moreover, it inevitably tended to a personal glorification of Mr Chamberlain ; and his methods, his wholesale branding of people honestly opposed to him, his crude excursions into international politics,[1] the somewhat dictatorial tone that crept even into his relations with the colonies were still too much the methods of his old Radical days to commend themselves to his new party. An election focussed on a war resulting from a policy he had directed must bring him within appreciable distance of the premiership ; and Conservatives shrank from that prospect. On the Liberal side the election meant a hopeless blurring of their position. Whatever they might wish to say in regard to milder counsels, and hastening the end of the war by conciliatory proposals, was swamped in the general charge against them of abetting the enemy. Liberal argument weakened into personal attacks on Mr Chamberlain, however little many individuals wished to take this line. Nor had there been among Liberals that unity of feeling and purpose which might have given them the consolation of a party, even if sadly diminished, at any rate more united than it had been for six years past. Some still attacked the war, root and branch ; some attacked only the recent developments ; others declined to criticise it at all. Although analysis of the polls after the election showed that, in spite of the large Conservative majority in the House, the country itself was not nearly so un-evenly divided, little could be deduced from this, because of the varying standpoints occupied by Liberal candidates.

Hopes of conciliation seemed at the end of the year to be at low-water mark. All the efforts in that direction had apparently only strengthened the determination to reduce the Boers to absolute surrender. They had certainly roused against them a spirit which even the most convinced supporters of the war could not welcome. A roughness and violence crept into popular demonstrations, and was at its height when the return of the City Imperial Volunteers in October gave it an opportunity to reveal

1 See page 508.

itself. So enormous was the crowd in the streets, and
so impatient of control, that it was four hours after the
arrival of the regiment at Paddington before the last man
had entered St Paul's for the thanksgiving service. The
crowd in Ludgate Circus was so undisciplined that two
people were crushed to death. Subsequent comments on
" hooliganism " (then a new word) showed that there
could be no shutting the eyes to extremely undesirable
elements in the freshened war spirit. True, this could be
in part attributed to lack of wisdom in the advocacy of
conciliation. This same form of recrimination was not
lacking in the House of Commons. Any criticism of the
conduct of events in South Africa was denounced as
" shameless accusation " of the troops in the field.[1] The
Government may well have had no patience to spare. It
was faced with another prospect of active war expenditure,
and the revenue, as was inevitable in war time, was
shrinking ; the returns for the first quarter of the new
financial year showed a diminution (chiefly in customs and
excise, owing to the large advance clearances [2]) of one and
a quarter millions. Industries were checked by the
draining off of men, and by a rise in the price of coal. In
the circumstances the necessity for more money was met
by voting a comparatively small loan, one of sixteen
millions, and endowing the Chancellor of the Exchequer
with further borrowing powers not immediately put in
force.

A certain uneasiness in the Government, a desire to
present the best aspect of their case, may be seen in the
attempt at this time to make light of the remainder of the
war. To help in producing the impression that for all
practical purposes the war was over, they appointed Lord
Roberts Commander-in-Chief at home, published a glowing
tribute from him to his troops in South Africa, which had

[1] *The Times*, 20th December 1900.
2 See page 522.

all the effect of winding up the serious business, and
allowed him to hand over the command in the field to
Lord Kitchener. Round Lord Roberts had gathered all
the hope and confidence in the war ; his return could not
but be taken to mean that little was left to do. General
Buller had already come home, and was in England by
the middle of November. Lord Roberts left Johannesburg
for the homeward journey on 1st December. In their
anxiety to keep criticism at bay, ministers rather overreached themselves. A great thanksgiving service at St
Paul's on the day of Lord Roberts's return had been
arranged. But just before he reached England the War
Office was compelled to cancel the arrangements. It
was too obvious that the war was not ended.

Certain incidents elsewhere probably fostered the hope
that the scattered commandos would not hold out for
long. If they were looking for intervention, it had become
abundantly clear that they were looking in vain. On
22nd November Kruger landed, a fugitive, at Marseilles.
Rumour credited him with having come not unprovided
with money to plead his cause. Yet his position was
hardly for a week in doubt. He was known to base his
hopes on Germany, from which country at the time of
the Jameson Raid he had received a famous telegram
expressing interest in the independence of his territory.[1]
For a day or two opinion in England wavered as to his
chances in that direction. The Kaiser's visit to the Queen
a year earlier could not be held to be altogether definitive
as to his attitude, since the German Press had shown a
steady bias against the war, expressed at times in strong
language ; it was possible that the Kaiser might feel
himself overborne by the public opinion of his country.
On 4th December all doubts were at an end, and it was
known that he had refused to give Kruger an audience.
The popular sympathy in France and Holland, with which

1 See page 386.

the exile had to be content, might be vexatious to England; but the reflection that, as it carried no faintest possibility of a diversion of the course of events, it might, in a different way, be quite as vexatious to Kruger himself tended to square the account.

CHAPTER VI

1900 : THE CRY FOR EFFICIENCY

IF, as seems to be certain, the dissolution of 1900 was largely forced upon his colleagues by Mr Chamberlain, it must in fairness be allowed that the promise of victory in an election during the war was probably only one of the considerations in his mind. In the end, no doubt, it became the paramount one. But to a man of his energy, his ideas, and his capacity for work, the condition of the House of Commons in the session of 1900 must have offered a great temptation to sweep away this Parliament, and put another in its place. Inertia enveloped it; and when the war obliterated all other concerns it grew even more inert. It took no interest in the small programme of work set before it; the House was constantly counted out at an early hour of the evening. Parliamentary government seemed to have reached a state of collapse. There were some who discerned in this fact deeper and more lasting influences than that of the war. They recalled a warning from Disraeli that extension of the franchise must diminish the real power of Parliament, since the executive would come to rely less upon Parliament than upon the electorate; the true centre of Government would shift to the Cabinet and the permanent departments.[1] But as in war the executive must always be more independent than in peace, any subtle or far-reaching explanations of the slackness of the Commons might be left on one side. Yet the fact remained that here was a House in a thoroughly

[1] See an article, by Mrs J. R. Green, in *The Nineteenth Century*, June 1900.

unsatisfactory condition. It was true that there was no immediate danger to the Ministry. The complete change of fortune in the war meant that even strong criticism of the Government would not seriously shake its stability. The Opposition was fundamentally disorganised; and although at the beginning of the year the long-standing breach in the Irish party was healed, and Parnellites and Anti-Parnellites united once more as Irish Nationalists under the leadership of Mr John Redmond, they could not be formidable to the Government except in conjunction with a vigorous Liberal party. Moreover the Liberal leaders had in some cases so far recanted their alliance with the Irish that the likelihood of united action between the two parties hardly needed to be taken into account.[1]

But though for the present year the Government had no cause to be fearful, Mr Chamberlain was too far-sighted to be content. He could not but be aware that the ensuing year would present grave difficulties. A long-drawn, dragging tail to the war would strain the Exchequer and weary the national temper. At the same time blunders and shortcomings in the management of it, a hundred flaws in our administrative system revealed by the violent pressure of the war, would be charged upon a Government then no longer able to plead that it must be left unhampered on account of the peril of the moment. The existing Ministerial party could not be trusted, even in the face of a weak Opposition, to pull the Government through such a year as must lie ahead. Party dissensions of the kind that existed among the Liberals have a way of healing for some immediately profitable purpose. The obvious policy, therefore, was to dissolve, and provide against the difficulties by creating a new majority full of the enthusiasm of a fresh victory. Nor was this all. To pull through the

1 See pages 349 and 450 ; and *The Times,* 7th February 1900.

rest of the war, and the period of criticism and investigation, would still leave the party rather meagrely provisioned for a future appeal to the country. There must be an energetic House ready to enter upon social legislation when the war and its accompaniments were past. Had not the opportunity arrived to make Liberal Unionism the equal colleague, and no longer the mere ally, of Conservatism ? Hitherto, as we have seen, social legislation undertaken on that side had been, since 1886, liable to be regarded rather askance by Conservatives.[1] Was not the time, with Mr Chamberlain's personal predominance, ripe for putting an end to the comments that this or that social measure was part of the price paid by Lord Salisbury to Mr Chamberlain, and to make Liberal Unionism, with its programme of social change, an integral portion of a practically new party, and not a mere section of a coalition ?

Such motives as these may at any rate be taken into account in considering the dissolution. Slack and ineffective as the session was, two measures mentioned in the Queen's Speech were carried. The Moneylenders Act obliged the registration of names in which such businesses were carried on, and empowered judges to deal drastically with claims brought before them in which exorbitant interest was exacted. The Companies Act dealt with bogus qualification of directors, especially by the gift of paid-up shares (thus striking a blow at the " guinea-pig " director, who, on insufficient examination, lent a well-known name and so helped to decoy the public), and also prescribed the minimum amount of subscription of shares on which a board might proceed to allotment. A Housing of the Working Classes Act should also be mentioned ; it enabled local authorities to erect dwellings outside the area of their own jurisdiction, thus giving them the opportunity to build at less cost, and to avoid congestion.[2]

1 See pages 229, 411.
2 See page 474.

18

Another piece of work during the session was the setting up of a Joint Committee on Municipal Trading. In this matter the House was acting slightly ahead of public opinion. There had been as yet no very widespread discussion of the subject ; only two hundred members voted on the motion to set up the committee.[1] But feeling, if not widespread, was strong on both sides. The immense field of capital placed at the disposal of municipalities by the invention of the funded municipal debt had led to all sorts of enterprise on the part of the authorities of large and progressive towns. In consequence rates had risen, and thus there was an interested public backing for the arguments, whether of academic individualists, or of private traders in such undertakings as electric light supply, tram companies, omnibus companies, etc., against the socialistic tendency inherent in the provision of such services by public authorities. At this moment, indeed, the socialists themselves were criticising municipal trading ; a socialist conference in Glasgow in April gave expression to the view that considerations of public health were falling into the background, and too much attention being paid to services of convenience and remunerative undertakings ; the city in which they were meeting had an enormous debt, and some of its public provisions, such as its cheap dwellings, were a magnet to a rather worthless population.[2] Later in the year a Local Government Board report had something of the same kind to say : it called attention to cases of incompetence on the part of local authorities in matters of insanitary housing and polluted water-supplies, which had recently, for instance, caused the gravest outbreaks of disease at Camborne and Carnarvon. It happened also that in London the County Council had sustained a rebuff in the report of the London Water Commission, which,

[1] The figures were 141 for the motion, 67 against.
[2] *The Times*, 21st April 1900.

recommending the purchase of the undertakings of the various companies, and their union under a public authority, advised that this authority should not be the County Council, but a separate body, permanent and independent. If, however, the opposition to municipal trading had become more fundamental during the last fifteen years,[1] such trading did not lack defenders ; and, though the House which discussed the matter was small, the debate was keen.

Public interest was yet to be aroused. But a discussion at the Church Congress of this year reveals to what an extent municipal activity had stirred the conscience. Some of the clergy frankly confessed themselves in a dilemma ; if they told the truth about all the housing scandals that came to their notice, their poorest people, in fear of being turned out of their dwellings by compulsory closing orders, would shut doors in their faces. Nor would local authorities, being dependent on popular election, dare to put in force all the powers they had.[2] There was naturally at this congress some discussion of the attitude of the Church towards the war. It must be said that no definite attitude was to be discerned. Religious views, like extreme democratic views, proved to have no peculiar power of keeping those who professed them recognisable by any marked classification. The truism that war was sometimes necessary as the price of peace, which provided the main shelter for the clergy, cannot be said to have done the Church much honour. The Free Churches endeavoured to maintain that Christianity was a gospel of peace rather more courageously than the Church of England ; but in them also the war appeared to obscure general principles. It is more satisfactory, in the case of the Church of England, to turn to indications of a greater readiness to heal her own vexations. Three ritual prosecutions were pending

1 See page 140.
2 *The Times,* 2nd October 1900.

in the latter part of the year.   But there was a growing
desire to avoid such proceedings, and to leave extremists
to consider their ways.   The Bishop of London displayed
his own belief in the possibilities of toleration by gathering
at Fulham a Round Table Conference on the Doctrine of
the Holy Communion and its expression in ritual.   Men
of such widely differing views as Lord Halifax and Dr
Wace met thus at the same conference ;   and, if no new
formulas appeared, yet a sense emerged that men might
differ peaceably ;   and the practical effect was seen in the
quiet stopping of the three prosecutions by the bishop's
veto.

There occurred early in the year an event which called
attention in England to the fact that the Anglican Church
was not the only one to suffer from the pressure of modern
thought towards expansion of its formularies.   The death
of Dr St George Mivart in April followed painfully soon
upon the announcement that he had been forbidden the
sacraments of the Roman Catholic Church.   He was a
great scientist, great enough to cross swords with Darwin
on the subject of natural selection ;   Dr Mivart maintained
the opinion that human intelligence differed not merely
in degree, but in kind, from the intelligence of other
vertebrates.   In certain articles published in *The Nineteenth
Century* and *The Fortnightly Review* on " The Continuity
of Catholicism," he was held by the Vatican to have pitted
human reason against the authority of the Church, and he
was therefore excommunicated.   This may be said to have
been the first occasion on which public opinion in this
country was at all moved about those tendencies in the
Roman Church which presently came to be classed as
" modernist."   The general view that it was rather
shocking to see a man of notably good and earnest life
debarred from the consolations of his Church had, no doubt,
something sentimental in it.   A good deal of that quality
was rife in a year in which an American religious novel

called *In His Steps* had a great vogue. It may be added here that the religious community furthest removed from any such tendency, the Unitarians, lost in January of this year a notable leader by the death of Dr Martineau. His intellectual power and clarity of ideals had won for him a following as passionately attached as an unbendingly logical body could permit.

In the same month John Ruskin died. Burial in Westminster Abbey was offered, but his representatives declined it, and he was buried in his beloved Lake Country. At the moment it seemed that much for which he had contended so hotly, even so pugnaciously, was lost. Industrialism had created hideous towns all over England ; railways had scored the face of the country. The time had hardly yet come for perceiving that views of his which went deeper than the mere external aspects of commercialism were not lost. A few years later Liberalism, revived and strengthened, was putting into practice economic theories which, when Ruskin propounded them, were dismissed as even more impracticably idealist than his desire to stop destruction of scenery. He had pleaded so mightily for hills and valleys, for gardens and houses, over which the torrent of industrialism was pouring, that men had forgotten his pleadings for the people caught in the same torrent. He himself, aged and disappointed, could not detect the indications that the spirit of his protests was already at work in the new conditions. But there was a growing demand for some respect on the part of public authorities for canons of beauty in building. It could be discerned in this year, for instance, in the newspaper correspondence about the new road which was being driven from the Strand to Holborn. Holywell Street, Wych Street and the rookeries of Clare Market had been cleared in the course of the great street improvement undertaken by the London County Council. Here, said the critics, was a noble opportunity for street designing ;

and the council was besought to lay down a general design, and stipulate that lessees of sites should adhere to it in their buildings. A favourite plan was that of Sir Frederick Bramwell, for building on the model of the Rows, at Chester, with covered arcades on the street level and on the first-floor level. In the same spirit the plans for a new Central Criminal Court were scrutinised ; nay, even the determination to demolish Newgate was called in question. Taste had swung so far from the mere appreciation of prettiness in architecture, current twenty years earlier,[1] that the grim solidity, the blank dignity, of the old prison were felt to be a possession. An opportunity for a more obvious prodding of official callousness to considerations of art was provided by the very narrow escape of the National Gallery in June. A fire broke out on premises at the western end of the gallery, and people suddenly awoke to the fact that, not only was the gallery not isolated from buildings in ordinary use, with all the dangers of artificial light and heating, but that no supervision whatever was exercised over those buildings ; a flimsy structure with a tarred-felt roof had actually been put upon the top of the house next to the gallery. Fortunately the stupidity was so flagrant that steps were at once taken to destroy adjoining buildings, and isolate the gallery. In two specific matters the year 1900 marked itself as belonging to a new time in art. Firstly, the era of enormous prices for old masters was opening ; at the sale of the Peel heirlooms in May (the sequel to an interesting case which had tested the power of the law to permit the dispersal of heirlooms), two Vandyck portraits fetched £24,250. Secondly, at the exhibition of the New English Art Club, in April, the work of a new-comer, William Orpen, was the first-fruits of a group at the Slade School bringing a fresh combativeness to bear upon the slow-moving British taste. Between these two movements,—the incursion into the market

1 See page 63.

of certain wealthy Americans, who frankly, not pretend-
ing to knowledge of art, aimed at the safety of old masters,
and the strong backing of the young painters in England
by a young generation of art critics—the day of high
prices for Royal Academicians was over.

In other arts there was also a stirring of dry bones.
Theatrical managers, long accustomed to the public's
meek acceptance of their rather stale fare, were perturbed
by signs of impatience in gallery and pit.   The newspapers
late in the year contained long discussions on the propriety
or impropriety of " booing " plays.   Certainly there must
have been a new kind of theatrical public when Mr Bernard
Shaw could have a play staged in the ordinary course of
commercial speculation ; *You Never Can Tell* was produced
in May.   The dancing of Miss Isadora Duncan, on the other
hand, though very favourably noticed, was rather ahead
of its time.   She appeared in London in March ; but
there was no real interest in dancing as an art, and she
did not aim at the sensational.

It is interesting that a year in which so much of the
nation's energy and attention was concentrated on South
Africa should show fewer dull moments than many years
in which there was no such distraction.   Thus the failure
of interest in Lord Roberts's position at Pretoria during
the month of June was partly due to the sudden development of an alarming situation in China.   Some kind of
popular rising, very imperfectly understood, but clearly involving danger to foreign residents, had spread with such
rapidity that Pekin itself was threatened.   The rebels were
known by a name translated into English as " the Boxers,"
and their hostility to the Government in China seemed
to be a popular expression of resentment of the recent
acquisitions of Chinese territory by European powers after
the war between China and Japan.[1]   It was suspected
of being less distressing to the Chinese authorities than a

1 See page 485.

popular rising should have been. By the beginning of
July the alarm was in full blast. The German minister
to China had been killed ; and the European population
in Pekin was concentrated in the houses and grounds of
three legations, which were under siege. It was hardly
hoped that against a horde of Chinese the legations,
walled enclosures though they were, could long be defended.
News was extremely difficult to obtain, and such rumours
as came through were of the gloomiest. It was persistently
reported that all Europeans in Pekin had been massacred ;
and at last, on 16th July, *The Daily Mail* published a
telegram giving in some detail an account of the fall of
the legations, and the slaughter of the defenders. Luckily
the prevalence of rumours before this caused some suspension of judgment about the telegram. Its details had a
certain precision, but after all it did not come from any
source closer to Pekin than that of the other rumours.
Hope, therefore, revived again. Meanwhile from the
European fleets in the China Seas an allied force had
been hastily put together, and marched upon Pekin. It
met with little actual resistance, and on 19th August it
formally occupied Pekin, the Chinese Court fleeing inland
to the mountains. The Europeans who had found refuge
in the besieged legations were alive, though they had
passed days of the severest trial of their fortitude. Thus
European eyes looked at last on the famous Imperial City,
its palaces and immense walled domains ; and a complete
era seemed to close at the tramp of European feet
upon that long-forbidden ground. In the days of alarm
a great deal of agitated opinion had foreseen the whole
Chinese race descending upon Europe, and the thought
that it numbered four hundred millions of human beings
became a nightmare. The German Emperor, who had
already expressed himself somewhat picturesquely on the
exaction of retribution for murder of his subjects in China,[1]

1 See page 430.

now lent himself to the agitation about "The Yellow Peril" by painting a picture, reproduced far and wide, in which allegorical figures of the European powers, headed by Germany, cross in hand, confronted a heavy cloud advancing from the East, in the murky folds of which was a savage Chinese visage of colossal size.

The Londoner this year was provided with a novelty to which he took readily, perceiving it to be the forerunner of great changes in his methods of locomotion. It was a new underground railway, worked by electricity, clean, free of all steam and smoke, and swift. But it had other aspects which endeared it to a people fond of being managed and saved trouble. The old ticket system was to be replaced by a system of paying the same fare, two-pence, however far you wanted to ride. Thus there was no need to keep a ticket to be given up at the journey's end. As soon as you bought it, you passed a barrier where you gave it up; and then you were dropped in a lift, shot through a tunnel in long pleasant carriages not divided into compartments, and carried up again in a lift wherever you wished to be disgorged. The rapidity with which "the twopenny tube" received its nickname demonstrated its popularity. Meanwhile the motor car which was in the end to revolutionise omnibus traffic, and so save Londoners from becoming a race as devoted to burrows as rabbits, was still making headway against prejudice. It was less obviously a subject for jesting, but cars were made in queer, blunt shapes, due to the dominance of old ideas of a carriage, and the failure to arrive at lines which should express the new vehicle's power and ease. The extraordinary survival of prejudice had been seen in the previous year, when Mr Scott Montagu,[1] one of the staunch pioneers of motoring, was forbidden by the police on duty in New Palace Yard to enter the precincts of the House in a car. Motor cycles were a novelty at the

---

[1] Now Lord Montagu of Beaulieu.

cycle show in 1899, and in 1900 a thousand miles' trial of the new machines advertised their soundness and practicability.

Another striking advertisement was that of the astonishing power of turbine marine engines.[1] A torpedo-boat destroyer, the *Viper*, had been equipped with them ; and on a three hours' steaming trial she had made the unheard-of mean speed of $33\frac{1}{3}$ knots an hour.[2]

Even archæology entered into the moving current of the year. Mr Arthur Evans and Mr D. G. Hogarth had been excavating in Crete ; and what they had discovered already was enough to cause them to issue a special appeal for funds, and to rouse unusual interest. They found themselves on the tracks of a very early civilisation, which seemed likely to prove the link between that of Greece and those of Asia and Egypt. But as yet learned opinion concluded that discovery of the palace of King Minos[3] himself could not be hoped for. The excavators probably had a more shrewd idea of the marvels that were to come, and the near touch they were to establish not only with Minos, but even with the Minotaur.

Towards the end of the year all the dissatisfaction with the conduct of the war, all the exposures of incompetence in this or that branch of the War Office, all the display of lack of cohesion and co-operation between the great departments of state, and all the discussion of the education and fitness for command of English officers, produced a sweeping outcry for efficiency in administration. There had long been scattered attempts, even before the war, to stir public opinion in this direction. Now far greater force had been given to the charge that we were being inefficiently governed ; and a platform was provided by the pages of *The Nineteenth Century*. The editor printed

[1] See page 464.
[2] *The Times*, 26th October 1900.
[3] *Ibid.*, 5th November 1900.

in very large type a proposal to found an Administrative Reform Association ; and was able to back his proposal with list after list of names of important people who lent their support to it. That the country's business should be conducted on ordinary business principles sounded a straightforward suggestion; a merchant whose enterprises were as scramblingly undertaken as this war had been would land himself in the Bankruptcy Court in a month. The outcry cannot be said to have had any immediate effect. The new Cabinet after the general election showed no particular sense of a need for new methods. Its critics called it " a Cabinet of Commonplace." [1] Lord Lansdowne, who had been Secretary for War, and so the target of incessant complaint, went to the Foreign Office in place of Lord Salisbury, and was pilloried in cartoons dressed in clothes much too big for him. Mr St John Brodrick went to the War Office in his place ; and there was irritated comment on this appointment of a man who had made no distinct reputation to a department upon which the interest of the country was focussed. Lord Selborne at the Admiralty, like Lord Lansdowne at the Foreign Office, was destined to achieve good work ; but at the moment it did not seem to be an inspiring appointment. Worst of all, in the midst of a demand for business men, was the appointment of Mr Gerald Balfour to the Board of Trade ; a scholarly, cultured man, he can have had little sympathy, and less contact, with the trading community.

The bitter astonishment at this last appointment is probably traceable in some measure to that uneasiness in the business world which had been so marked in 1899.[2] With increasing competition in every market of the world, with engineering tenders from America cutting out our

---

[1] See *The Fortnightly Review*, December 1900.
[2] See page 451.

own contractors,[1] the business community was asking vehemently for help from more alert methods in the Government departments, for more information, more statistics.   But, besides this general demand, there had been a special need this year for efficiency in the Board of Trade.   In April the principal railway companies had announced that, owing to falling dividends, they intended to raise the rates for goods traffic, especially for coal ; and that the directors of the various boards had come to an agreement in the matter.   Indignation at the announce-ment was enhanced by this glimpse of a sort of monopolist trust.   Although the Railway Commissioners, whose sanction was necessary, disallowed most of the proposed increases the indignation did not altogether subside; and when, in August, a serious strike occurred on the Taff Vale Railway—the more serious because on the working of that line largely depended the supply of coal for the navy—there was more than a little inclination to warn other railway directors that responsibility for strikes was to be found partly in the bad management of the lines.   As it happened, this particular strike was not a good case, because the men made a bad mistake.   The merits of the cause of the strike, which was dissatisfaction with the conditions of labour, and especially the dismissal of a signalman concerned in a previous dispute, were unfortunately obliterated by the fact that the men came out before the expiry of their notices.   The strike lasted only some ten days, and ended on terms not unsatisfactory to the men ;   the strikers were to be taken back within a month, and not to have the lost days counted against their pension service.   Moreover a Conciliation Board was set up ;   and altogether the intervention of Sir W. T. Lewis had been most successful.   But the comparative mildness of the directors may have been partly due to the knowledge that they had a case against the men for damages, and

[1] *The Times*, 19th April 1900.

intended to try it. They proceeded first against the union for damages for unlawful picketing. Mr Justice Farwell gave judgment against the trade union, believing that the law did not intend to set up bodies of men capable of holding property and acting as agents, but not responsible in damages. The Court of Appeal reversed this judgment. But the House of Lords finally pronounced for Justice Farwell's view; and trade unionists awoke to the disturbing fact that their funds, which they had thought to be secure, were at the mercy of legal actions against the unions.

But more perturbing, alike to the business world and the community at large, was the serious damage done this year to public confidence in the solicitor's profession. A case that occurred in April was grave enough : a firm of solicitors failing for the enormous sum of £364,000. One of the principals of the firm had absconded, and the Official Receiver had felt himself obliged to say that the case was " pervaded with fraud." [1] That suspicion was not confined to this particular case was clear from the comments it called forth [2]; and also from the fact that the Incorporated Law Society undertook an inquiry, with the object of reassuring the public. The inquiry covered a wide field of professional conduct, from the demand for separate banking accounts for trust funds to the suspicion that some solicitors in a small way of business frequently bolstered up inadequate claims at law for the sake of the costs, and even undertook cases in a purely speculative spirit. But reassurance of the public failed most grievously when, late in the year, Mr B. G. Lake, the very man who had, as chairman of the Disciplinary Committee of the Law Society, been conducting the inquiry, was himself charged with misappropriation of funds. The absconding solicitor in the earlier case had been extradited from America by this time,

[1] *The Times*, 13th April 1900.
[2] Ditto, 27th April 1900.

and the spectacle of two prominent solicitors charged in the police court was disturbing.

It has to be remembered in this connection that the system of credit operations was now so highly organised, and bankers' cheques so universally used, that not only rich people but all who had a certain income had ceased to think of money except as a banking credit. As long as their drafts were honoured to the extent they had reason to expect, people concerned themselves no more about their property. This threw an unfair amount of responsibility upon solicitors, who were left in unsupervised control of the principal sums or the securities of their clients, no questions being asked, or even dreamed of, so long as the client's bank account gave him no reason to make investigations. By this time the absorption of private banks into large joint-stock concerns had grown to an enormous system.[1] Whereas in 1800 there had been forty-six private banks in London, there were in 1900 only three; and not much more than a dozen were left in the rest of England. But the big concerns rather extended than contracted the number of local banks, opening branches in places where smaller firms in the old days would not have found business worth their while. Thus it came about that, though the actual number of banking firms in England was now 303, as against 458 in 1800, there was a branch to every 6900 persons, as against a bank to every 19,200 in 1800.[2]

The large public which had no securities or trust funds to cause them to take an interest in trials of solicitors had an interest more to its mind in a murder discovered at Yarmouth in September. A woman was found strangled on the beach, and eventually her husband, a man named Bennett, was put under arrest. The case has its interest,

1 See page 264.

2 See a paper read by Lord Hillingdon to the Institute of Bankers, 9th November 1900.

because it revealed how elaborately and unrestrainedly the newspaper Press could set itself to work in a matter of circumstantial evidence. Clues and correlation of facts were no longer left to the police and the prosecuting counsel, nor even to the defending counsel. They were saleable goods; and most of the newspapers were by now concerned less with the guidance of public opinion than with selling a marketable thing. So much feeling was roused in this case, and so much had been published about it, that when it was sent to the assizes the trial was transferred from the local assize court to the Central Criminal Court, on the ground that a fair trial could not be expected in the local court.

Popular interest was suddenly diverted again by an alarm about the presence of arsenic in beer. There had been some mysterious cases of illness, especially in Salford; and, in the course of investigating them, suspicion had fallen upon beer. Scientists admitted that sulphuric acid, which was used in the preparation of glucose for brewers, might, if even slightly contaminated, produce arsenic. Uneasiness about beer was enough to trouble the whole country, and the last days of December were passed in a dismay so national as to be rather comic.

Dismay on a very different plane was spread in the same month by the famous Cockerton judgment. This brought to a point all the long-standing hostility to the work of school boards in the domain of higher education—hostility compounded of the feelings of secondary schools suffering from subsidised competition, ratepayers who provided the subsidy amid groans at rising rates, and reactionary malcontents who saw no good in advanced education for the children of weekly wage-earners.[1] It had for some time been known that the legal position of Higher Grade Board Schools was, to say the least of it, doubtful; the " block grant " system had been busily discussed earlier in this year. Now a London School Board auditor, Mr

1 See page 428.

Cockerton, disallowed the payment of certain sums out of the rates for science and art teaching in elementary schools, and surcharged the boards with the payments. Mr Justice Wills, before whom the case brought by the London School Board came, upheld the auditor. The legal position ceased to be doubtful ; boards all over the country made up their minds that, until Parliament altered the position, higher education must cease. Meanwhile technical education had been magnificently advanced by the opening in May of fine buildings in connection with the Textile Industries Department of the Yorkshire College at Leeds. General ideas on technical education also were becoming clarified ; and it was being urged that in country districts such education should be more exclusively on rural subjects, and not on subjects scheduled alike for town and country.

The sittings of Parliament at the end of the year— chiefly for financing the war—must be noted for the first emergence of the subject that was destined to play a large part in pulling the Liberal party together on a common policy. Not that it was so perceived at the moment. To all observers the party appeared to be without anything to weld it. A change of leadership was the remedy usually prescribed ; yet only Lord Rosebery could be suggested.[1] But in these brief sittings there appeared in debate the question of labour in the Johannesburg mines, and the Opposition showed some alertness.

[1] See *The Times*, 19th November 1900.

CHAPTER VII

1901 : THINGS NEW AND OLD

WITH the passing of the old century passed also the sovereign whose name signified an historical era in life and thought, art and letters. The coincidence of the nineteenth century and the Victorian period was complete.

The anxiety about Queen Victoria was first made public on 19th January, in an announcement that " the Queen had not been in her usual health," and had been instructed by her physicians to stay indoors, and abstain from business. The announcement was at once taken seriously. The general character of its terms was alarming ; because, if it was thought advisable without specific information to warn the public, obviously the intention was to prepare for more serious news. It had needed no special knowledge to be aware that the war must inflict upon the Queen at her age a grievous strain. She had seen her country through the worst of its effort, and days terrible to her subjects must have been terrible to her. Now, though hostilities were not over, suspense was past ; and it fell out that her last public act was to be the honouring of the great soldier under whom the fortunes of war had turned. She received Lord Roberts at Osborne, and bestowed upon him an earldom, together with the greatest distinction at her command, the Order of the Garter.

The nation had been taken into confidence not a moment too soon. The first announcement was published on a Saturday. On the Monday morning the

newspapers had to announce that the Queen's condition
was one of "increasing weakness, with diminished power
of taking nourishment." On the Tuesday morning the
bulletins told of a slight rally ; the Queen had been able
both to take nourishment and to secure some sleep. But
it was a brief flicker. On that same day she died, at
6.30 in the evening.

The Privy Council was summoned immediately to
proclaim the new sovereign. Parliament was summoned
to take the oath of allegiance. For the moment the
reality of what had happened was partially obscured in
the general excitement about long unwitnessed ceremonies.
Nearly sixty-four years. had elapsed since the last death
of a British sovereign. No man alive had ever taken part
in the formalities attendant on a demise of the Crown.
Comparatively few even were the living people who
remembered the last occasion of the kind, and fewer still
who, in those days of no railways and rare newspapers,
had had any first-hand knowledge of the ceremonies.
The strangeness of the occasion affected everybody, from
the great ones of the Privy Council, assembling at the
palace in some nervousness at finding themselves more
than a mere name, down to the populace, excited by the
prospect of seeing real live heralds in tabards making a
proclamation. The council heard from the lips of the
new sovereign that it was his pleasure to take his place
in the line of British kings by that one of his names which
was in the regular succession. He had, as Prince of Wales,
used always the two names, Albert Edward ; he determined, he said, to leave the name Albert to be associated
solely with his honoured father, and to ascend the throne
as Edward the Seventh. So he was proclaimed. In the
mellow old Friary Court of St James's Palace a grey
January morning saw the low balcony blaze with strange
splendours—heralds, trumpeters and great court officials
stepping from the high windows to announce the accession

of King Edward the Seventh ; and as the King-of-Arms
cried, at the end of the proclamation : " God Save the
King," the words unheard for so long were followed by
the rolling of drums and the solid beat of the National
Anthem from the Guards' band in the courtyard below.
Hence the heralds proceeded to Charing Cross, Temple
Bar and the Royal Exchange, reading the proclamation
at each point.

The King—words so strange in the mouths of Englishmen seemed to revive associations of majesty and state
which had long been in abeyance.   There had been a time
when people resented the withdrawal of Queen Victoria
in her personal grief on the death of the Prince Consort.
But for a long while now the nation had acquiesced in
her distaste for ceremonies ; the Court had had but a
shadowy existence, the Queen had been an august but
remote presence, honouring the nation that honoured her.
But national pride in her had not for thirty years been
able to see itself, so to speak, pictorially expressed in the
sovereign.   The name of king roused extraordinary expectation.   It was as if the days were returning when the
monarch of this realm could be addressed in his own
person as " England."   Yet they returned with a difference.   The new reign was but three days old when there
began to be discussion of possible amendment of the royal
style and title.   It was suggested that the time had come
for the inclusion of the colonies.   Twenty-five years earlier
this idea had been mooted ; but then rather as a criticism
of the decision to take the empire of India into the title
than as a deliberate proposal.[1]   Now the intention was
different ; and in the ensuing session of Parliament the
change was made, and the King became " King of Great

[1] Mr Robert Lowe, in the debate on the Royal Titles Bill in
April 1876, asked if it were logical to include India, while not
recognising the colonies ; and Mr Gladstone associated himself
with this criticism.   See Hansard, Third Series, vol. 227, c. 1740.

Britain and Ireland and of all British Dominions beyond the Seas." The idea must have been already well matured, either in the King's own mind or the mind of his advisers, before the suggestion was made public ; because the very form of the new phrase was foreseen in the ascription of one of the messages promulgated by the King directly his immediate obligations were at an end. The messages were addressed, one "To my People," one "To my People beyond the Seas," and one "To the Princes and People of India."

Those immediate obligations recalled the nation from its distractions about the new to undertake its tribute to the old. For ten days the body of Queen Victoria lay in state at Osborne, soldiers of the Guards leaning with bent heads on rifles reversed at the four corners of the draped coffin. But this was the private state in which so much of her life had been passed. Her family gathered there ; and the German Emperor had gone far to winning affection in this country by the great promptness with which he had come to take his place among the mourners. On 1st February came the preliminary stage of a funeral expressing all the might and majesty that were Queen Victoria's right, however little of late years she had seemed to care for the parade of them. The fact that she had died at Osborne brought it about that the first grandeur of ceremonial remarkably expressed her rule over an island dominion bulwarked by sea power. The first thunder of the minute guns of her passing came from her warships. At the opening of her last journey through the midst of her people her way was in the sea and her path in the great waters. The leviathans of her fleet lay marking her passage ; and from battleships among them floated the ensigns of foreign nations—France, Germany, Japan and others—adding their guns to the salute of a Queen of the High and the Narrow Seas. Yet not even in the immensity of that spectacle was sight lost of the long-familiar pathos of the small, solitary figure of her people's remembrance. The little *Alberta*, with the canopy aft sheltering the coffin under its dead-white pall, with the gold emblems of sovereignty dimly to be descried upon it, floated very small and lonely between the towering warships from which the sharp flashes leaped into a sombre air. Eight destroyers escorted the *Alberta*, and so solemn was the speed of the procession that men on the warships noticed that the propellers which could drive at so tearing a pace made now no sign of their revolution in the water. Behind the *Alberta* came the larger royal yacht, *Victoria and Albert*, bearing the King and the Duke of Connaught; and behind that the high white sides of the German Emperor's yacht, the *Hohenzollern*. As the procession reached Portsmouth Harbour the sun at its setting broke through the clouds, drawing a low line of red light across the horizon.

Next day the funeral procession passed through London on its way to Windsor. It was a grey winter's day, but long before daybreak the route of the procession was heavily crowded. Now on land, as on the sea the day before, the power of the Sovereign of England surrounded the dead, with all the pomp of a military funeral. Long lines of troops were mustered, the head of them being in St James's Street before the procession started. Volunteers, militia, yeomanry and the regular troops all sent detachments; and band after band took up the Dead Marches. Behind the last of the troops came riding in more spaced array the foreign military attachés, the Headquarters Staff, officers of the Royal Household and aides-de-camp. Then came the gun carriage with its burden, as nearly magnificent as anything could be in the greyness. Upon the bright silken pall rested the Crown, the Orb and the Sceptre. She whom in life London hardly remembered except in the mourning of her widowhood went this time in shining array. The company that followed her was splendidly royal. In honour of a Mother among rulers, crowned heads for the first time attended a crowned head to the grave. In the front rank rode the King, the Duke of Connaught on his left hand and the German Emperor on his right ; three kings, of the Belgians, of Portugal and of the Hellenes, rode next ; and in the other ranks, conspicuous with fluttering plumes, bright unusual uniforms and ribbons of foreign orders, were the Grand Duke Michael of Russia, the Archduke Franz Ferdinand of Austria, the Duke of Aosta, the German Crown Prince, and the Crown Princes of Denmark, Norway and Sweden, and Siam.

For once some unity of conception and some dignity were apparent in the adornment of the streets. It was so obviously not an occasion for the usual inane paper roses and flags that invention had to be set to work. The houses were draped with purple and white, and along the pavements heavy festoons of laurel swung from pillar to pillar, with wreaths of laurel at the fastenings. Thousands of the people, when the procession had passed, took away leaves from the festoons in memory of the day.

At Windsor an awkward moment gave the navy its opportunity to come to the front again. The artillery horses waiting there with another gun carriage grew restive in the delay, and became unmanageable. With a fortunate readiness, bluejackets, accustomed to drawing their own guns, took charge, and drew the gun carriage up the hill to the castle. Over the open vault in St George's Chapel sounded again the strangeness of long-unused ceremonial when the herald stepped forward and read that stately recognition of the old and the new : " Forasmuch as it hath pleased Almighty God to take out of this transitory life to His divine mercy the most high, most mighty, and most excellent Monarch . . ." Then the pageantry was closed. On the following day the body of Queen Victoria was laid in the mausoleum at Frogmore, beside the body of the Prince Consort.

It was soon made clear that the new order was to be imbued with new ideas. The King allowed it to be known that the tendency, which had naturally increased under Queen Victoria's force of habit and advancing years, to interpret court and personal mourning as withdrawal from public appearances, was not to continue. A man so exact in feeling for state etiquette as King Edward could see as well where etiquette ended as where it began. His conception of a court was that it should be careful not to allow its own necessarily wide obligations in such matters as mourning to become an oppression. As Queen Victoria grew old and saw, as the old must see, a greater number among the dead than among the living of those she had known and been attached to, the Court Circular had become more and more often an announcement of elaborate memorial services. King Edward, while careful not to relax established formalities of mourning, was equally careful that they should not encroach upon the sovereign's public life. He returned with the Queen to London a few days after the funeral ; and proceeded on 14th February to open Parliament in full state. Here again was a ceremony disused for more than fifteen years. It appeared incidentally that, while the King's clear conception of etiquette was in some respects to be a relief, it was in others to exact stricter recognition of forms. Since the Queen had given up opening Parliament in person, the Speech from the Throne had become almost avowedly a mere Cabinet announcement ; and its terms were usually divulged in advance. From this time a change took place, and nothing was disclosed beforehand. The people, pardonably eager for pomps of which they had long been deprived, gathered again in immense crowds on the short route of the procession. It was known that the revival of court ceremonial was to be supported by the appearance of all the handsome old dress coaches that the peers could produce ; and the heavy painted vehicles, with their tasselled

hammer-cloths and footmen in state liveries standing on
the board behind, enlivened the period of waiting for the
amazing gilded glass coach in which the King and Queen
rode down to Westminster. Excitement even unduly
affected the honourable members of the House of Commons.
When Black Rod summoned the Speaker to attend upon
his Majesty, the solemn stillness of the waiting House
of Lords was invaded by an unseemly mob; the rows
of peers in their voluminous scarlet and ermine, and of
peeresses glittering with diamonds, the orderly ranks of
officers of state around the steps of the throne, even the
King and Queen in their magnificence, turned eyes of
pained surprise towards the trampling irruption of the
Commons. Certainly there was little in the speech itself
to cause excitement. But this being the first occasion
of the new sovereign meeting Parliament, it was his duty
to make the Accession Declaration, expressing his adherence to the Protestant faith; and out of this grew at once
a controversy. One of its effects was to show an extraordinary laggardness in some regions of thought. The
Roman Catholics raised vigorous objection to the survival
in this declaration of phrases which they deemed offensive
to their consciences, and which appeared to the greater
number of their Protestant fellow-subjects to be at least
couched in terms discordant with taste and proper feeling.
The Roman Catholics pointed out that they had long been
admitted to full civil liberty in this country, and could hold
offices, sit in Parliament, exercise the franchise, and be in
the most complete sense the King's loyal subjects; was it
right, therefore, that the King should be compelled still
to affront the susceptibilities of such subjects? Yet no
sooner was the question raised than a body of opposition
began to appear which showed no sign of change from
the days before Emancipation. It would hardly have
been surprising to wake up in London some morning and
find " No Popery " chalked again upon doors. A change

which might well have seemed certain beforehand to proceed by common consent was checked.

After the opening of Parliament there was no further great ceremonial this year. The King did not, as has been said, neglect the formalities of court mourning. But in spite of the proper quiet that was observed the changed spirit of the new regime was present. It was felt in several subtle ways. London, for instance, it might be said, had become again a genuine capital of the kingdom. Queen Victoria had grown less and less inclined to live there ; Balmoral and Osborne had her heart, and Windsor was as near as she cared to be to the seat of government, even in times of important events. The King was a Londoner. Balmoral had in his mind only the place that a Scottish castle naturally has in the mind of a great gentleman, a place for deer stalking and grouse shooting at the proper time of year. Osborne had no meaning at all for him. He had long owned a considerable estate at Sandringham, where he preserved on a large scale ; and this place represented to him another of the usual requirements of a great gentleman ; there was no shooting at Osborne. The result was that the Court became again the natural head of society ; its ways were the ways of society, and London was its centre. Government, again, had no longer a divided habitation. Life returned, on less important planes, to many empty shells of duty : levees and courts, meetings of the Privy Council, and even such affairs as the daily changing of the guard at the palaces. The interests, the talk, the cheerful expectations of the people pivoted upon London again.

It was just as well that the public mind should be mildly distracted, for the year did not open prosperously. Trade had been declining for the past six months ; the drain of men for the war had at last made itself seriously felt, and as coal had risen in price the iron and steel trades and shipbuilding were in a depressed condition. The declaration of railway dividends in February provided another blow. Naturally the attempt to raise freights in the previous year [1] had been a warning to railway shareholders not to expect too much; but the dividends were lower even than had been anticipated, and the explanation offered, which was to the effect that for some time past directors had been dividing too much and spending too little upon improvements, was not of a kind to raise hopes for the immediate future.[2] On top of all came a very serious failure in the City. The London & Globe Finance Corporation announced that it was unable to meet its engagements, and soon afterwards the Standard Exploration Company, an allied concern, went into liquidation. These companies were chiefly the creation of a financier of the modern comet-like kind, Mr Whittaker Wright. He had drawn an immense amount of money into operations of a kind very difficult for anyone but a Stock Exchange expert to follow. The companies, of which there were three principal ones in alliance, owned certain mining properties and land concessions, but the profits largely depended on complicated dealing among the companies, and upon the results of a sort of stock and share trust which they comprised. Their failure not only involved monetary loss to thousands of comparatively small investors attracted by large dividends, but also brought back again all the old mistrust of " show " boards of directors. Lord Dufferin had been chairman of the London & Globe Finance Corporation; and it was melancholy to see a man of his most distinguished record and his high public service confessing that he had found it impossible to master the intricacies of the operations of a company over which he nominally presided. This was exactly the kind of incident to check investment; and a year starting in trade

1 See page 556.

2 See *The Times*, 17th February 1901.

depression could ill afford coyness in the money market.

Meanwhile there was the financial drain of the war, still going on, and hardly on a less expensive scale. In February Lord Kitchener asked for 30,000 mounted men. The war had early become a lesson in the value of extreme mobility; and the guerilla fighting was driving home the conviction that until we worked almost entirely with mounted men we should never wear down the resistance of fighters who could always move quickly enough to break cordons and make off for a rest—quickly enough also to be perpetually refitting by swift raids on our less mobile convoys. A third War Budget had to be faced, and a fresh war loan. The latter had to be issued at a price considerably lower than the earlier ones. Thirty millions of Consols, ranking with " Goschens " (that is, bearing $2\frac{3}{4}$ per cent., to sink to $2\frac{1}{2}$ in 1903) were put on the market at $94\frac{1}{2}$, and at this price were subscribed about five times over. Another thirty millions were placed privately with the big financial houses.[1] These two sums raised the total of the war loans to a hundred and thirty-five millions. For the Budget extra millions had to be found. The revenue returns had, indeed, exceeded the estimate by nearly three millions; but once again the figures were deceptive, because of advance clearances. It had been plain that new taxation would be imposed, and bonded goods had been cleared to escape it. Sugar was pretty well known to be in for a large part of the burden, and there were shrewd guesses at an intention to tax corn.[2] " Broadening the basis of taxation," which had for years been a Conservative ideal, seemed now to be the only method in the mind of the Chancellor of the Exchequer. A duty of 4s. 2d. a cwt. was imposed on sugar, to raise five millions; and an export duty of 1s. a ton was placed

[1] *The Times*, 27th April 1901.
[2] *Ibid.*, 5th March 1901.

on coal, to raise two millions. A further 2d. on the income-tax, raising it to 1s. 2d., was to provide the balance. The coal-duty made trouble at once; and the Chancellor of the Exchequer found that " broadening the basis " was apt to lead to unexpected complications. He spent much of his time with deputations of coalowners, who brought before him strange results of his new tax.

This kind of finance, bringing neither courage nor originality to bear upon circumstances demanding both,[1] was of a piece with the rest of the year's work in the Commons. The new Parliament was not answering to any hopes Mr Chamberlain may have entertained. The enthusiasm of victory soon waned; Ministerialists returned to their slack ways in face of the weakness of the Opposition; ministers were described by their own organs as careless and shiftless, and Mr Balfour's leadership was not admired; lapses of memory and frequent absence from the Treasury Bench were charged against him.[2] The Cabinet held hardly any meetings; this fact was so patent that political philosophers even began to ask whether the theory of the Cabinet was undergoing a change—whether Government was really carried on by a small inner Cabinet, meeting informally, and obtaining the formal consent of other members by letters and telegrams.[3] The ineffectual mood of the Government was shown by the feebleness of its attempt to deal with the situation produced by the Cockerton judgment.[4] The Appeal Court upheld the divisional court, and so hastened the complete stoppage of all higher-grade education. It was impossible to acquiesce in this; Conservatives and Unionists showed quite as strongly as Liberals their feeling that the cutting short of such activities on a point of law called for instant

[1] See *The Progress of the Nation*, edited by F. W. Hirst, p. 690.

[2] See *The Nineteenth Century* for June and September 1901.

[3] *The Times*, 15th October 1901.

[4] See page 559.

remedy. But the Bill which the Government introduced in response to the general demand was obviously a half-measure, hastily framed. It proposed to set up local committees over the school boards, with control of the spending of the rate, but no power to impose rates ; and in the making of this new authority to get behind the legal stumbling-block of the existing Acts. Within a month the Bill was abandoned ; and a one-clause Bill was introduced, by which local authorities were permitted to empower school boards to carry on secondary education for a year. There was considerable debate on this, the Opposition asking why this empowering of school boards could not be done directly, without the intervention of local authorities. The Government was really enunciating the principle of a new educational authority. But the situation was thus patched up for the moment ; and Sir John Gorst, President of the Board of Education, made reassuring statements to the effect that after all the Cockerton judgment had only affected some fifty higher-grade schools, and 900 out of the 7000 science and art pupils.

The only other matter of importance in Parliament was the production of a new scheme of army organisation. Its keynotes were decentralisation of commands, and the maintenance in peace time of commands under the generals who would command in war. The army was to be organised into six army corps, three of them in efficient existence, and three skeletons for training purposes, to be filled at need from the reserves. The scheme was not received with great enthusiasm. It was criticised as aiming too high and missing the immediate necessities ; for before making an ideal organisation it was necessary to obtain the men to put into it. Recruiting had fallen off, and this scheme did nothing to provide fresh inducements to recruits, either in improved pay or better conditions of service. The " skeletons " were really nothing but phantoms. The most cynical critics alleged that Mr Brodrick had been induced by the military authorities to give a final proof of the impossibility of maintaining an adequate army on the principle of voluntary enlistment, and so to pave the way for compulsory military service. Ultimately Mr Brodrick weakened one of his chief arguments by his appointments to the three main commands. The 1st Army Corps was given to General Buller ; the 2nd to Sir Evelyn Wood, and the 3rd to the Duke of Connaught. People very naturally asked what had become of the principle that the corps should be commanded by the men who would command them in war.

This was efficiency on paper—with Lord Kitchener complaining of the poor quality of the mounted men sent out to him, men so largely untrained that they had to be drilled on arrival. The outcry for real efficiency was growing in strength, with the eloquent voice of Lord Rosebery added to it. Sometimes it took the line of the widest philosophical criticism, reviving Matthew Arnold's reproach of England as " out of the centre of thought," and " pecking at the outside " of her problems. From that it passed most easily to discussion of our methods in secondary schools, and public schools, to which the Board of Education was beginning to pay particular attention. A report was published this year on the preparatory school system, which had been practically a growth of the last thirty years, and was excellent from the standpoint of the individual attention given to pupils, but not wide enough in curriculum, being limited by the requirements of public schools. The most advanced areas of education were equally stirred. The London School of Economics put forward a claim to support on the ground that its training would turn out men able " to get the affairs of the nation on a business footing." The university of Birmingham set to work to create a Faculty of Commerce. Mr Carnegie gave an immense sum of money, the income of which was calculated at £100,000, to be held on trust, half of the income being applied to the endowment of fellowships and the forwarding of research, and the other half to pay class fees and provide maintenance grants for poor students. At the lowest end of the educational scale a new effort was set on foot, largely by the advocacy of Mrs Humphry Ward, to bring in to the educational system those who had hitherto been kept outside it by physical deficiencies. The scheme, financed by private funds, but approved by the London School Board, was to provide ambulances to take crippled children to the schools, and couches for their use in the schoolrooms.

Then the cry for efficiency turned in other directions. It deplored the difficulties of reform in a nation so easily diverted from its intentions by any new scent of amusement or passing interest.[1] And having thus approached the ordinary member of the community, it fell upon the workman. Did he work keenly enough ? Did not trade union rules tend to limit output, to make men adhere to some particular standard of work, not pitched very high ? Was there not even now a resentment of new machinery and speeding-up of production ?

In December the restless distrust of ourselves was quickened by a speech made by the Prince of Wales. He had just returned from a tour of the colonies, his return being marked first by the King's assumption of the new royal title embracing the colonies, and secondly by the elevation of the Duke of Cornwall (as the Duke of York had been termed since the King's accession) to the dignity of Prince of Wales. Speaking at the Guildhall, he gave, as one of the lessons of his tour, the warning that England should take to heart not only the example of the progressive communities she had founded, but the competition produced in their growing markets, and should " wake up." So the year ended with the demand

[1] *The Times*, 16th October 1901.

for efficiency undiminished; and even roused to more activity.

Yet, though so many people talked about it, the proneness to easy distraction showed little sign of disappearing. The great beer alarm occupied as much of the beginning of the year as was not given to greater events. So national a subject was it that a Royal Commission was appointed. A Local Government Board report, by one of the board's medical inspectors, showed that the cases of poisoning had been very numerous, about 2000 in Manchester alone, nearly 800 in Salford, and over 500 in Lichfield. The area thus known to be affected was comparatively small; but, since the origin of the contamination appeared to be a process employed in most breweries, the alarm spread to every part of the country. But people remained high-spirited enough to invent a cheerfully idiotic form of riddle; the "What gave Barry Pain?" type of question flourished, and produced a competition in equally idiotic answers. Then an unusually hot summer exaggerated the growing habit of taking week ends out of town, and inclined men to longer holidays—facts sure to be noted by the apostles of efficiency. The " back to the land " pose was also remarked this year in a sudden outburst of gardening books; the craze spread upwards from the people with week-end cottages to great ladies, who suddenly began to take a violent interest in the beautiful old gardens of their country houses, and frequented flower shows with pencils and catalogues. As for the holiday habit, it may be said now to have lain in the direction, not only of lengthened holidays at the normal time, but of new holidays at unheard-of times. Winter sports were beginning to be known in England. As yet they were pursued mostly in Sweden and Norway [1]; but descriptions of them sowed the seed which a few years later was to take business

[1] *The Times*, 28th February 1901.

men by the hundred and the thousand to Switzerland at Christmas time. Moreover, the conducted tour was reaching up to social strata which had hitherto despised it ; the inventor of Cook's travels must have smiled when he saw deans and parish priests, dons and school-masters launching out for the Isles of Greece in large steam-vessels chartered to carry a select company.

In the autumn Sir Thomas Lipton, with a new yacht, *Shamrock II.*, had everybody out on the Embankment again of an evening, watching coloured lights—even huge outlines of yachts moving as the telegrams came in from America to show the fortunes of another challenge for the America Cup. The British yacht was beaten again, but by such narrow margins of time that people began to think this must surely represent the best we could possibly do under the exacting conditions. Flying leapt into the place of a popular excitement with the performances of M. Santos-Dumont, a rich young Brazilian resident in Paris, who had built a cigar-shaped dirigible balloon, and had actually steered it on a circular course round the Eiffel Tower, before the wind pressure caused the nose of the gas-bag to collapse, and foul the screw. The aeronaut was saved by the balloon catching on the corner of a high building. The success of the venture was more emphasised than its failure ; and as yet the " heavier than air " principle entered into no competition with such displays. In another sphere of mechanical invention, the Marconi system of wireless telegraphy made one more great stride. A station had been erected at Poldhu in Cornwall, and thence signals were exchanged across the Atlantic to a station in Newfoundland.

Motor cars were distinctly under a cloud. Many power-ful people had refused so far to surrender to their utility, and still swelled the ranks of those who complained of the noise, the dangerous speed, the raising of dust, the destruction of the road surface, and all the other counts in the indictment.   Demand grew loud for the numbering of all cars, and the licensing of drivers ; though it was hardly believed, since such restrictions had not been imposed as a condition of the liberty of the road in 1896, that motorists could now be subjected to them.[1]

In one connection, however, the internal combustion engine had made a change of which there was no criticism. Submarine boats had become practicable.   In 1901 the British Government made its first provision for adding some of those boats to our navy, experiments by foreign countries, notably by France, having been watched with profit.   The other new glories of the navy had come to a sad end.   Both the turbine-equipped destroyers, with their marvellous turn of speed, the *Viper* and the *Cobra*, had been lost, the former being wrecked during manœuvres, and the latter, more mysteriously, during a voyage in the North Sea.   From the first the truth was guessed at ; the question asked was, not what had she collided with, but had she broken her back by hitting something or by a mere wave-shock.   In other words, had the frightful speed been too much for her ?   The court martial on the loss of her decided, in effect, in the latter sense : the ship's structure had not been strong enough for a speed so far beyond any of the ordinary calculations of strain.   It must be remarked here that the navy, like everything else, came into the range of the critics.   The education of our military officers had been shown by the war to be somewhat in default ; was the education of our naval officers as good as it could be ?   And in ships, as well as in personnel, were we answering the requirements of an age of standardisation ?   This last word was rapidly becoming the catchword which " progress " had been twenty years earlier.

The Church was not without response to the probings which were being everywhere applied.   Its voice was not

[1] *The Times,* 12th April 1901.

very helpful, perhaps, on such matters as workmen's wages, or the erection of model dwellings. But it continued to try hard to drop unprofitable disputes about ritual. Certain changes of this year in the episcopate tended in one sense in that direction, though in another they exasperated extreme Evangelicals. Dr Creighton, Bishop of London, died, a man who had merged great historical learning, and a student's love of the quiet paths of knowledge, in the demands of a high administrative office; and had had the consolation of applying the balm of scholarly wit and intellectual detachment to the sore places of a bishop's work. He was succeeded by Dr Winnington Ingram, who as head of Oxford House and afterwards Bishop of Stepney brought to the episcopal throne such intimate knowledge of the poor working London as had never yet found a place there. His appointment was a most striking case of preferment turning rather to faithful and, one might say, inspired Church work than to scholastic reputation. But he was known to be a High Churchman; and a later appointment during the year, that of Dr Charles Gore to be Bishop of Worcester, was even more markedly of a kind to cause a return of strife. The High Church party had just lost a notable member by the death of Canon Carter, of Clewer, who had been one of the most active in reviving the work of Sisterhoods in the service of the Church. The new Bishop of London set himself to apply to his rather vexed diocese (though certainly less vexed than it was once, thanks to Dr Creighton's judicious control) that method of " godly monitions " which at the beginning of the year the archbishops and bishops had appealed to the clergy to heed. The strong desire now was to show that ritual prosecutions were harmful in every direction, and that both extremes should avoid them for the sake of the Church's influence.

There was not so much " taking stock " of advances and

changes in thought and taste as might have been expected at the opening of a new century. In art the work of Rodin was beginning to be known and discussed in England. But rich people were still some distance from speculating in the work of modern artists ; and a craze just now for the collection of mezzotints and old coloured prints was the excitement of the salerooms. However, a certain sense that design and craftsmanship had genuinely revived in the applied arts expressed itself rather deplorably in the market for objects of L'Art Nouveau ; they were, even at this early period, tortured in outline and affectedly barbaric in material. Lumps of turquoise matrix did duty for jewellery ; and articles of silver or pewter were given shapes and surfaces which suggested that the metal had somehow guttered in a draught. The opening of the Whitechapel Art Gallery, given by Mr Passmore Edwards, must be recorded, as a sign of the now established position of an excellently managed system of interesting East London in pictures. The drama hung very much between old and new. On the one hand, Mr Beerbohm Tree drew upon modern ingenuity to stage *Twelfth Night*, with an elaboration of detail and a degree of artifice never before attempted. On the other hand, *The Times* had taken for its dramatic critic Mr Walkley, whose articles in *The Star* had shown no particular reverence for established tradition ; and Mr Henry Arthur Jones was hinting at a possible future for a repertoire theatre in London, and perhaps also in Manchester or Birmingham.[1]

One of the most startling publications of the year was a series of articles by Dr Robert Anderson on prison management. The subject was not a new one. From time to time there had been an inclination to plume ourselves upon the growing wisdom of our prison administration ; and recently the separate treatment of first offenders, and

[1] In *The Nineteenth Century*, March 1901.

the provision of special places of detention for lads (the
best known being at Borstal in Kent), where the time of
detention was used for educational purposes, had been
a source of gratification. The hooligan was becoming
a cause of much public anxiety—a Twentieth-Century
League was inaugurated for dealing with him—and it was
believed that the Borstal system offered new hopes for his
case. Public attention of a different kind was, as it happened, called to Borstal at the end of 1900 by the escape
of two prisoners, who managed, in spite of the spirited
hunting by newspaper reporters, to remain at large until
well into 1901. Dr Anderson, who had been Assistant-
Commissioner of Metropolitan Police, and was now on the
verge of retirement, disturbed complacency by something
very like scornfulness. His view was that all the modern
classification and separation did not touch the root of the
matter ; and he affirmed that what was wanted was a
classification apart of habitual criminals, and the imprisonment of them for life. But the amazing point in his
articles was his assertion that if only seventy men, upon
whom the police could lay their hands without much
trouble, were thus put out of the way, the organisation
of crime against property would be dislocated to such a
degree that in ten years the community would be free of
it.[1] The difficulty felt by those who read his articles was
that juries would be slow to convict a man in such a way
as to shut him up for life for offences against property ; and
the tone of Dr Anderson's articles was not altogether of a
kind to win assent.

Casual distractions of the year were not the only
hindrance to the cry for efficiency. The nation could
hardly be expected to pay heed, when it was in a state
of division which increased rapidly in bitterness. At
the beginning of the year the Conciliation Committee
was so far unpopular that it was labelled " the stop-

[1] *The Nineteenth Century,* March 1901.

the-war party." Two prominent Afrikanders of the
Cape Ministry, Mr Merriman and Mr Sauer, were in
England in the summer; and addressed meetings which
in some cases were noisy, and in others were besieged
by crowds outside the building. A new subject of
controversy had arisen. The pursuit of the war by
methods of cordoning districts and clearing them
up by mobile columns, together with the burning of
farms, had necessitated the removal of Boer women and
children to large concentration camps. By the month of
June there were some 25,000 Boer people in such camps,
living mostly in tents, but sometimes in temporary structures of wood and iron. They were supplied daily with
rations, and dairies were attached to the camps. There
would in any case have been a feeling among Radicals
that this was one more of the lamentable lengths to which
we were being driven by determination to stop at nothing
short of absolute subjection—one more of the seed-beds
of lasting hatred. But Miss Emily Hobhouse, who had
visited the camps, brought back news of distress and illness
and terrible death rates, which made the Conciliation
Committee fasten sharply upon the concentration camps
in their attacks upon the Government. For the latter
half of the year one side answered another with ever-
growing animosity. A meeting was actually called at
the Guildhall to protest against criticism of the war and
the camps. Cheers were given at a meeting in the Queen's
Hall for De Wet. Any tendency there may have been (and
there was certainly some tendency) to admit the justice
and truth of Miss Hobhouse's reports was swamped in
anger at the activity of the conciliatory propaganda.
The average death rate in the camps in May was about
117 per thousand, but the highest rate, at the Bloemfontein
camp, was shocking, amounting to 383·16 per thousand.
Yet when once this matter had become connected in the
public mind with " Pro-Boerism," it could not be regarded

wisely or patiently. A Blue Book was published late in
the year, admitting that there had been much sickness
and death in the camps, but pointing out that the Boers
in them could not be induced either to submit properly
to medical treatment or to obey sanitary regulations.
This was not likely to satisfy people who maintained
that the camps ought never to have been brought into
existence.

The very serious animosity prevalent throughout the
autumn and winter in England was partly due also to
a wave of depression about the war which had swept over
the country in the summer. We were spending a million and
a half a week in the attempt to gather into nets scattered
commandos, which not only continually cut off detached
bodies of troops and convoys, stripped them of clothes,
arms, ammunition and provisions, and retired to mountainous country to refit, but even brought about a second
invasion of Cape Colony. Lord Kitchener's determined
and deliberate methods, the cutting up of the country
into sections by lines of block-houses, and the perpetual
sweeping movements in these sections, were eminently
sound, but were not of a kind to stimulate martial excitement at home. Every week he reported to the War Office
his bag of prisoners, often balanced by losses and failures
on our side ; and the dragging length of the tale exasperated and depressed a public which throughout had not
shown much either of patience or of intellectual grasp of
the operations. Hasty expectations meant disappointment ; and bad temper turned naturally to vent itself
upon fellow-countrymen who said that we had better
acknowledge that we were aiming at a wrong object, and
make terms. To criticise the concentration camps was to
criticise the whole of the work that Lord Kitchener was
doing ; the camps could, from the war party's point of
view, be regarded as a piece of almost quixotic humaneness.
Then the foundation of a League of Liberals against

Aggression and Militarism, with a programme of meetings throughout the autumn, was interpreted as a general accusation of bloodthirstiness. Feeling rose hotly and rapidly. Conciliation meetings were broken up, and ended often in free fights. Miss Hobhouse, starting on a second visit to the concentration camps, with a relief fund to administer, was prevented from landing at Cape Town, and sent back to England. Finally in December came the worst riot of all. Mr Lloyd George had undertaken to speak in Birmingham; and this was regarded as an unwarrantable intrusion into a city devoted to Mr Chamberlain. The town hall, where Mr Lloyd George was to speak, was besieged by an extremely angry crowd. Stones and bricks were hurled through the windows, one of the doors was broken down in a rush, and pistols were fired. The police did their best; no less than ninety-seven of them were injured. But at last relief came with the descent of a snowstorm at about 10.30 P.M. The crowd slowly dispersed, and Mr Lloyd George was removed in disguise from the town hall. One man lost his life during the evening.

Again the party of opposition to the war was involuntarily sheltering the Government. The chagrin of the nation vented itself on the " Pro-Boers," and the slackness on the part of the Government, which had been matter of complaint at the end of the session, was again forgotten. The Ministry could even blunder with comparative impunity in efforts to put a good face upon the situation. For instance, a proclamation fixing 15th September as the close of " legitimate hostilities " was a complete fiasco. It had no effect whatever on the course of hostilities, and was merely a threat delivered to empty air. Then Lord Halsbury, the Lord Chancellor, speaking at Sheffield in October, tried his hand at minimising the long drag of the campaign by saying that " a sort of a war " only was now going on. If national irritation had not had other victims,

these Ministerial stupidities could hardly have escaped
as lightly as they did. Comparatively few discontented
people were heard asking what the Cabinet was doing.
Nor was there any real Liberal strength to be thrown into
attack on normal party lines.   Active and vigorous as the
" Pro-Boers " were, the Liberal party in general presented
no formidable sight. Wrangles in its high places were constant ; and, though a meeting of the party at the Reform
Club in July produced a formal resolution of loyalty to
Sir Henry Campbell-Bannerman, it was not taken very
seriously. He had had his part in criticising the conduct
of the war ; and, in the mood of too-ready labelling with
opprobrious phrases, a comment of his upon certain
specific proposals as " methods of barbarism " had been
spread abroad sedulously as expressing his view of the war
in general.   Hence Liberals of less determined views on
the subject, like Mr Asquith, publicly denied the right of
Sir Henry Campbell-Bannerman to regard his declarations
as representing the true Liberal faith.   All that observers
could foresee was an eclipse of the present leader, which
should involve also Sir William Harcourt and Mr Morley,
and the return to power of Lord Rosebery, with such lieutenants as Mr Asquith, Sir Edward Grey and Mr Haldane.
The resolution at the Reform Club meeting was wittily
described as a resolution of " loyalty with a latchkey " [1] ;
and it was supposed that Lord Rosebery would have
no difficulty in making a following.   When he " came out
into the open " in July with a public speech, speculation
grew keener.   True, he spoke of himself as " ploughing
a lonely furrow," but he added : " before I get to the end
of the furrow I may find myself not alone."   Still stronger
grew the interest when it was announced that he was to
address a great meeting in Derbyshire in December.
The scene of the meeting—the small town of Chesterfield, where there was so little accommodation for a gather-

[1] Article by Dr Joseph Parker in *The Times,* 1st October 1901.

ing of this kind that a large railway shed had to be employed
for the occasion—gave a singularly detached and " free-
lancing " air to the proceedings. But it was significant
that Liberals of all shades of thought assembled to hear
Lord Rosebery, even to the point of calling forth satirical
remarks about the contending factions sitting down
together. Most of them must have ended by asking
themselves what they came into the wilderness to see.
The essence of the speech again was easy to bandy about,
Lord Rosebery being a master of phrases. He besought
the Liberal party to " wipe its slate clean " in certain
respects, and consider very carefully what it was going
to write upon it in future. The " clean slate " was a chilly
metaphor for a December gathering ; and provoked the
reflection that Lord Rosebery's own slate had never been
remarkable for any bold inscriptions. The Chesterfield
speech rapidly fell back into a mere bid for a Centre Party.

CHAPTER VIII

1902 : CORONATION YEAR

IN 1902 the national life, after the distortions of the last few years, began to shape itself again. In one sense, with all the excitement of the coronation, and the King's serious illness on the very eve of the ceremony, this could not be called a normal year. Yet below these incidents the currents of national affairs began to return to habitual channels. The uneasy search for new methods of efficiency largely subsided ; the Ministry and the Ministerial party were not always being nagged at for slackness ; the Liberals, though still deeply divided, found more common ground than for years past, and grew less assiduous in duelling with one another. Finally, the war at last came to an end ; and people found themselves free to confess weariness of penny trumpets and peacocks' feathers without being labelled " Pro-Boers."

The man whose life had been spent in the making of a united South Africa did not live to see the close of the war. Cecil Rhodes died on 26th March. He was not yet fifty years old, but he had deeply impressed himself on his generation. The earlier conception of the quiet mysterious financier in Disraeli's novels, pulling the strings of courts and cabinets, had given place before Rhodes's stubborn figure to the financier creating continents in the light of day. It was remarked as one of his prominent characteristics that he " cordially disliked the purely parliamentary type of man " [1]; and he preferred to have as his fulcrum the business community, and the general public's con-

[1] *The Times,* 27th March 1902.

fidence. He had small charm, but an extraordinary power
of impressing people. So wide was this faculty that men
as different as the German Emperor, Lord Rosebery
and General Gordon all believed in him profoundly.
The greater part of his enormous fortune he placed by his
will in the hands of trustees, a sum amounting to nearly
two millions, for the income to be applied to a system of
scholarships designed to bring England and the colonies,
America, and Germany into a better understanding of one
another. Sixty scholarships at Oxford of £300 a year
each were to go to young men in the colonies, twenty-four
of them to be from South Africa. Two scholarships were
allotted to each of the United States ; and fifteen to
Germany of £250 a year each. The total endowment was
£51,750 a year, for 170 scholarships. The scholars were
to be chosen, not merely for intellectual attainments, but
also with regard to general good-fellowship and bodily
activity. At the same time £100,000 were bequeathed
to Rhodes's own college of Oriel, with the stipulation that
his trustees were to be consulted about the spending
of it, since dons lived remote from the world, and were
" children in commercial matters." It was a will that
struck resoundingly upon the impulse towards efficiency ;
and resoundingly too upon the new admiration for the
colonies and the men they turned out.

Parliament went unusually early to work, meeting in
the middle of January. The Government seemed to
have reformed its ideas of a session's business, and the
programme was energetic ; it included an Education Bill,
aiming at no less than a reconstruction of the system of
control ; a Licensing Bill ; an Irish Land Purchase Bill ;
and a London Water Bill. At moments in the early
months of the year the Liberal party appeared to be
hardly in better condition than before. Lord Rosebery's
Chesterfield speech was still reverberating ; and the
expectation that he intended to remain in the open, and

active in politics, seemed to promise a conclusive struggle
for leadership, and some definition of official Liberalism.
Even the prospect of conclusive struggle was more healthy
and natural than the uncertain swayings of the past two or
three years. The conflict was at any rate fairly openly
declared when, in February, the National Liberal
Federation professed its loyalty to Sir Henry Campbell-
Bannerman, applauding his determination not to clean
the slate; and Lord Rosebery immediately announced his
"definite separation" from Sir Henry. He followed this
by founding the Liberal League, an organisation rather
adroitly described by its nickname of "the Liberal
Imps"; Lord Rosebery's purpose was better served by
using only the adjective "Liberal," but the league consisted of those who had classed themselves during the war
as Liberal Imperialists. Mr Asquith, in a communication
to his constituents, stated that the members of the league
did not regard themselves as a body outside the party,
but meant to stay inside; he also made it clear that
Home Rule was one of the items to be cleaned off the
slate. The league started with some notable men in it,
men who could not be conceived of as absent from the
next Liberal Ministry. It was no wonder, therefore, that
the common belief should be that the Liberal Imperialists
would gradually, but finally, take charge of the party,
forcing Sir Henry Campbell-Bannerman either into their
attitude, or out of leadership. He, however, showed no
sign of being easily disposed of. He whipped up his
own supporters, took his line firmly against Lord Rosebery, and surprised everybody by the imperturbability
with which he confronted alike the slashing attacks of
Mr Chamberlain and the open disagreement of his neighbours on the Front Opposition Bench. In truth, he had
no need to make way for another leader. The Liberal
League might gather to itself notable names; but what
would Lord Rosebery, Mr Asquith, Sir Edward Grey, Sir

Henry Fowler and Mr Haldane represent to the Radical working men when the emotions of the war died out ? Even as things stood, 123 members went into the Opposition lobby on a war amendment to the Address. The session was not three months old before the Liberal fortunes had taken a turn which showed that those who proposed to label themselves by an attitude arising out of the war alone had forgotten a very old-established line of division between parties outside the House. The Education Bill was introduced in March. It set up one form of local authority for elementary, secondary and technical education, the authority to be a committee of the town or county council together with co-opted members. It was to be the rating authority for educational purposes, and in the allocation of funds the voluntary schools were to rank with board schools. This abolition of school boards was not received without regret ; the boards had done good work, had acquired experience and wisdom, and had been wholly free from corruption. At the same time, however, the unification of the whole system was a gain ; the " educational ladder " was made more practicable of ascent ; vexed questions of what school boards could or could not do would be at an end ; and education would be associated with the general activities of local life. But the case of the voluntary schools instantly aroused controversy. The argument that, if they received public funds, they must surrender private management, returned in force. How great the struggle was to be no one fully foresaw.[1] In a month it had developed on a large scale. The Government had indeed challenged fundamentally the Nonconformists' objection to the use of local rates for the support of denominational schools. The provision that representation was to be given to the local authority among the managers of such

[1] For instance *The Manchester Guardian* at first welcomed the Bill without any hint of sectarian controversy.

schools did not conciliate the Nonconformists. The
Government admitted that a dual system of management
was not ideal; but it existed, and it was not going to be
allowed to interfere with the general unification. Secular
education—the only method that could give complete
uniformity, since churchmen objected as much to colourless religious instruction under the Cowper-Temple compromise, as Nonconformists objected to definite Church
instruction—was not agreeable to the majority of the
country; and Mr Chamberlain was the mouthpiece of this
conviction, the more effectively because he had himself
once been an advocate of secular education. The power
of the local authority to appoint as many as one-third
of the managers of a voluntary school would, it was
agreed, be enough to ensure that the school buildings
were adequate and in proper repair, and that other
than religious education was not unduly narrowed.
But a meeting of the Council of the Evangelical Free
Churches in April made nothing of such arguments.
Dr Clifford called for another Cromwell; Mr Hugh Price
Hughes fulminated against " this infamous new Church
rate "; and the realities of the Bill were obscured by a
violent sectarian storm. The Order paper became
choked with amendments; clauses were fought word by
word. It might have seemed that the House of Commons
really needed some such obstinate fighting, for both sides
grew rapidly the better for it. Ministerialists had to be
more diligent in attendance; the Opposition found itself
reunited in the division lobbies; and, though the debating was sharp, there were fewer of the contemptuous
recriminations that had become common.

The Ministry's programme of legislation was not,
however, the first point of interest in the session. That
was found rather in Mr Balfour's new rules of procedure.
The main object of them was to reserve more of the time
of the House for Government business. This was in

future to occupy all sittings except the evening sittings
on Tuesday and Wednesday after the dinner-hour, and
the short day of the week on which the House met at
noon ; after Easter, Government business was also to
occupy Tuesday evening, and after Whitsuntide the
Wednesday evening as well. The growth of the habit
of week-ending was shown in another rule providing that
the early sitting should be on Friday, instead of on
Wednesday. Debates on the first reading of Bills were
abolished ; and it was ordered that first readings should
be a mere formality, unless, in the case of a Government
Bill, the minister in charge wished to make a short
explanatory speech, in which case he was to be allowed
ten minutes, but no debate was to arise. Naturally
there were lamentations over the vanishing prerogatives
of the private member ; but on the whole the new rules
made an easier passage than had been expected. If the
private member lost much on the one hand, he had gained
a little by the earlier hours of meeting which had been
established of recent years. In the long sitting from
2.30 P.M. to 7.30 P.M. there was more time for the
lesser lights of the House to make speeches ; and it was
thought that young members advanced more quickly to a
reputation.[1]

There were wry faces when the time came for the
Budget. The revenue had not done badly. The last
quarter of 1901 showed a return of three and a half
millions more than the last quarter of 1900 ; and the
financial year ended with the receipts a little over the
estimate. Sir Michael Hicks-Beach had budgeted for
one hundred and forty-two and a half millions,
and he received one hundred and forty-three millions.
But the Budget must be another War Budget, with
another war deficit ; and the worst of the problem was
that indirect taxation had been by now strained rather

[1] See *Punch*, " Essence of Parliament," 18th June 1902.

hard. The Chancellor of the Exchequer believed that the limit of profitable taxation had been reached on spirits ; the consumption of both spirits and beer was falling ; and indeed in every direction consumption appeared to be rather at a standstill. The Budget anticipated an income of one hundred and forty-seven and three quarter millions, and a deficit of forty-five and a half millions. Another loan of thirty-five millions was issued ; and to raise the balance a penny more was put on the income-tax, the tea and sugar duties were raised, and a shilling duty was placed on imported corn and flour. Much more would probably have been heard about the last-named tax if the Chancellor of the Exchequer had not also proposed to raise the duty on cheques to twopence. This roused so much opposition that in the end, after several proposals for mitigation and rebates, the impost was withdrawn. The corn-tax was also helped by the protestations of the Government that it was only a "registration duty," and strictly a war-tax, not intended to be permanent. Even so, it became one more bond of possible union on the Liberal side. The Cobden Club woke to the old cry of the Corn Laws ; and there was plenty to do in warning the country that taxes were not so easily taken off as put on. Mr Chamberlain was already speaking again about an Imperial Zollverein, and the corn-tax would be a useful item to bargain with. The Opposition recorded their hostility to the tax, and the Finance Bill had some stormy moments before it became law. Its last days in the Commons were ingeniously designed to coincide with the approach of the coronation, when a little matter like a shilling corn-duty was not likely to take public attention, least of all since the approach of the coronation itself coincided with the long looked-for declaration of peace, and therefore the end of war budgets.

Lord Kitchener had been firmly pursuing his method

of sweeping operations between lines of block-houses. A constant trickle, both of prisoners of war and burghers who came in to surrender, resulted. Some sixty different columns were operating in the Transvaal and the Orange River Colony, varying in number from 200 men to 2000 ; and the columns worked generally in groups. The Boer commandos were under three principal leaders : Louis Botha, De Wet and Delarey. Small garrisons here and there were constantly attacked, convoys were struck at, the railways cut and trains blown up. Occasionally the Boers united suddenly into considerable forces, and captured guns and set the British newspapers to printing casualty lists of fifty and sixty killed. But the British had learned much by this time. Even the regiments of yeomanry, of which Lord Kitchener had had to complain, were acquiring skill and craft ; and no Boer successes had any effects upon the final course of the operations. For many months past the war despatches had contained almost as many names of new troops as of the familiar old ones. Canadians, Australians, New Zealanders and South Africans were in nearly all the columns. Vigorously though hostilities were proceeding, strong as the Boers could yet show themselves to be at times, a sense of nearing the end was given by the commencement of civil reorganisation in South Africa in January. Depression at home had passed away ; for whatever our occasional reverses might be, the main current of the war set steadily in an unmistakable direction. Commando after commando was broken up, and turned into mere batches of prisoners, seventy, a hundred or a hundred and fifty at a time. When in February Mr Chamberlain went to the Guildhall to receive the freedom of the City of London, he seemed to be very near his zenith. Popular at home, better known in other parts of the empire than any British statesman before him, he had gained greatly and lost nothing by the war. Whatever blunders there had been, none were attributed to him. He gained even by these. Popular feeling had to have its idol; it could not find one in Lord Salisbury, remote and dignified; in Mr Balfour, a shade too cool and impenitent even in the eyes of his followers; in Lord Lansdowne or Mr Brodrick, who had to bear on their shoulders all the War Office failures. So idolisation turned to Mr Chamberlain. It did not, of course, turn merely by exclusion of others. Mr Chamberlain had all along been the prominent figure; and his ever-ready and ever-vigorous defences of his policy, his slashing ways of dealing with critics, cither of himself or of his colleagues, the irrepressible energy with which he flung himself into every debate on the war, into public meetings on the war, above all into the election on the war, had naturally attached to his person all the "patriotic" enthusiasm. That the state of the War Office might have been a consideration to him before he pressed his policy quite so far—that he might have been a little more sure of the machinery before he put it in motion—this was no blot upon his position. Nor was the fact that slashing oratory is a dangerous intruder into foreign politics. He had arrived at the happy situation in which the negative side is only put into words by political opponents.

Now, as he drove to the Guildhall amid cheering crowds, he was on the crest of a wave which was not allowed to break ineffectually. Before the end of March it was known that the Boers who were still acting as a Transvaal Government, Schalk Burger, Reitz and others, had appeared at Middleburg, and asked to be forwarded to Pretoria to interview Lord Kitchener. From this time on there were constant rumours of peace, which became really excited when it was known that the redoubtable De Wet and Delarey, with Steyn, had also appeared at British outposts, in this case at Klerksdorp, and had been in conference with the Transvaalers. When the whole party moved to Pretoria, on 11th April, hopes ran high ; and there was a readiness to be patient when it was announced a week later that the Boer leaders had gone back to the commandos to take counsel with them. A month passed, but the fighting now was very desultory. Two delegates had been chosen by each commando in the field, and the whole lot, numbering sixty-four, met at Vereeniging on 15th May, with the leaders and so many of the people of political importance in the late republics as were still in the two territories. There was another fortnight's delay, broken in England by occasional intimations which seemed to point in the right direction. On 22nd May it was announced that Lord Milner had gone to Pretoria to be ready to meet the Boer leaders. On 23rd May there was a Cabinet Council, and the hope was that it had been called to consider a settlement of terms. Practical certainty seemed to have arrived with Mr Balfour's statement in the House of Commons on 30th May, a Friday, that he " hoped to be able to make an announcement on Monday." Before Monday came England had the most welcome news : peace had been signed at Pretoria on the Saturday night, and the fact had been made public on the Sunday evening. The announcement was posted at the War Office at five o'clcok, and at six o'clock a huge streamer bearing the words " Peace is Proclaimed " was hung across the pillars of the Mansion House façade. On the Colonial Office the flag was hoisted ; but, as it was Sunday, no other public building showed this signal. The fact that it was Sunday did not, however, prevent the rejoicings of a crowd larger than any that had gathered since Mafeking night. This time there had been general expectation of the news, and many people had mustered in the centre of London on the chance ; again, as the news spread, thousands came in from the suburbs. The scenes were the more unusual because, there being no shops and no theatres open, the light was more subdued than on a weekday, and the crowds surged more blackly over the roadways. Instead of the familiar Sunday hush of the City, there was a perpetual diffused clamour, the sound of songs, the squeak of toy trumpets and the rolling mutter of innumerable voices. Yet even those who came upon the commotion unexpectedly knew instantly its meaning.

For that night the simple fact was enough. Next morning the newspapers gave the terms of peace. The principal were : that the Boers acknowledged themselves subjects of the King, and laid down their arms ; that the prisoners taking the oath of allegiance should be returned to their homes as soon as possible ; that military government should speedily be succeeded by civil government, and ultimately by self-government ; that, while English was to be the official language, Dutch should be taught in the schools, and allowed in the courts ; that Boers should be permitted to own rifles on taking out licences ; that no special tax should be imposed on the territories ; and that assistance should be given for repatriating the exiled Boers, the British Government making a gift of three millions to hasten resettlement on the farms. The terms were conclusive ; British territory now stretched without question from Cape Town to the Zambesi—a single South Africa. It had been won at the cost, on our side, of two and a half years of fighting, 20,000 lives, and over two hundred millions of money. On the Boer side the cost was never so definitely known ; but Botha at Vereeniging had spoken of 3800 Boers killed, and over 31,000 taken prisoner. Some 20,000 now surrendered on the signature of peace. This came as a rather startling surprise to Englishmen who had spoken of the war as a mere trifle nine months earlier, and gave a new sense of what Lord Kitchener's task had been.

Nothing now remained to cloud the coming coronation. Indeed, it must be admitted that the war, even if prolonged, could hardly have clouded it, so keen were the interest and the anticipation. This was to be such a coronation as no monarch ever had. The British Empire, as it stood, had practically come into existence since the last coronation. The colonies then had been distant, thinly populated for the most part, comparatively poor ; now they were great countries, with premiers and ministers to represent them in Westminster Abbey, and troops to take their place among the forces of the Crown. India had then been a trading territory administered by a company. Communication had now grown so quick and easy that there was not a single small Crown colony which could not take its part in the coronation. So there mustered in London during May and June such an assemblage of dominion and power as had never in the world's history been witnessed. Camps sprang up in the parks, and alien regiments dwelt in the tents. Thus at Hampton Court were gathered soldiers of the Indian Empire—Sikhs, Goorkhas, Rajputs, with sentries on duty over cooking places lest the shadow of an infidel should defile the meat of the faithful. At Alexandra Park Colonial troops camped in their expert fashion, covering the slopes with their khaki and slouch hats. In Kensington Gardens and Hyde Park the turf was scored with the lines of the British regulars and volunteers ; and Londoners never wearied of gazing at the streets of tents, the long rows of picketed horses, the parked waggons and guns. Elsewhere gathered the strangest regiments of all, Hausas from West Africa; Chinese from Singapore; Malays; and Fiji police, their bushes of hair coloured with yellow earth.

In June too began to arrive the great personages who were to represent the Empire. Premiers came from the self-governing colonies, to be greeted with all the popular enthusiasm for the work of Colonial troops in the war ; and governors from the Crown colonies. Maharajahs and princes from India, some of them already well known in London, others here for the first time, dazzled drawing-rooms with the clicking glitter of their ropes and tassels and gorgets of jewels. One great maharajah, whose caste was so precious that none of his line had ever yet left India, landed at Tilbury Docks with row upon row of huge brass pots filled with soil of India and water of the Ganges. Lastly, two overwhelming days brought to Victoria Station the representatives of foreign powers, and special trains disgorged a royal personage at every six feet of the platform. King Edward had taken a holiday in the spring, yachting on the south-west coast, and visiting Cornwall and the Scilly Islands. He had since been keeping fairly quiet; but in June he had begun his own part in the celebrations by attending a great review at Aldershot. There was some concern when it was seen that on the next day, Sunday, he was not present at church parade, and it was announced that he was confined to his room, suffering from lumbago caused by a chill. Rumours as to his health, which followed, were roundly denied; but when, on 23rd June, he arrived in London with the Queen, none who saw him make the brief passage from the railway saloon to the carriage in which he was conveyed to the palace could be quite content with the official denials. The King obviously leaned heavily on his stick, and he looked pale and unlike his kindly, gracious self. London as a whole only saw him seated in the carriage. Yet even those who had seen some cause for anxiety had seen none for alarm. The news published on the morning of 24th June came like a bomb. Not only was the King ill, but he was so seriously ill that the surgeons had had to perform immediately an operation for perityphlitis. The coronation was postponed. The operation had been successful, but for the present the surgeons could say no more. With his courage and his dislike of disappointing his people, the King had struggled on in the hope of being

able to bear the fatigue of the coronation. Now the
decorations and the mustered troops and the splendid
strangers were left unnoticed behind the backs of the
crowds that grew and melted and grew again all day long
in front of the palace railings, whereon hung the small red
boards with the white bulletins upon them. For five days
the gravest uncertainty lasted. Then on 29th June it was
announced that the King's life was no longer in danger.

The royal guests from abroad had gone back. But
there was now the prospect of a coronation once more,
and the troops of the empire were to wait in London for it.
It became an amusement again to walk the decorated
streets. Not that these showed much of originality or
fineness in design ; the most original thing, the Canadian
Arch in Whitehall, with its masses of wheat and apples
and its tinselly cupolas, strung with electric lights of an
evening, was not beautiful, and soon became tiresome.
By the King's wish all the celebrations that could go
forward were carried out : the festivities in the towns and
villages, and the King's dinner to the poor, and the
Queen's tea to general servants. In July the King was
well enough to go to Cowes for final recuperation.

By that time there had been some shifting of the figures
that would play a prominent part in the coronation. For
one thing, Lord Kitchener would now be at home in time
for it. He reached London on 12th July, with his new
honours of a viscounty, the rank of General, and a grant
of £50,000 ; and was met at Paddington by the Prince of
Wales, with whom he drove to luncheon at St James's
Palace. General French and General Ian Hamilton came
to London in his company. But it was Lord Kitchener
that the crowds came out to see ; and more than ever they
cheered the grave man, his blue eyes so light in the deep
bronze of his face that they looked like the eyeballs of a
statue.

A greater change was caused by the fact that, on 13th

July, Lord Salisbury resigned the premiership. " The
last great statesman of the Victorian era " [1] was not, after
all, to stand as Prime Minister at the coronation of King
Edward. Mr Balfour succeeded him. It was a natural
and inevitable succession ; yet it can hardly have taken
place in this quiet, simple fashion without affording Mr
Chamberlain food for thought. No man stood so much
in the public eye as he did. He had just come to the
success of the greatest venture on which the country had
ever been embarked by one man. The Conservative
party at the crisis had really hung upon his power with
the populace. There must have seemed to him to be something impenetrable and almost uncanny in the inability
to make the final step to power. Mr Balfour had to carry
out some reconstruction of the Ministry. Sir Michael
Hicks-Beach resigned the Exchequer, and was succeeded by
Mr Ritchie ; Mr Austen Chamberlain became Postmaster-
General ; and Lord Dudley Lord Lieutenant of Ireland ;
Sir John Gorst gave up the Board of Education (an act
which in the middle of the Education Bill's career could
only be interpreted as a confession of failure), and was
succeeded by Sir William Anson.

On 6th August the King returned to London, strong and
debonair, the King that everyone knew so well by sight,
and not the worn figure of two months earlier. On the
9th he was crowned in Westminster Abbey. No detail of
the day, from the troops in the procession to the symbolism of the garments he wore for the solemnity, from the
night-long vigil of the crowd to the preparations in the
Abbey, was too small for record in the newspapers. And
when the King and Queen returned from the Abbey, even
a crowd that already loved to label itself " Twentieth
Century " in its advancement and sophistication, thrilled
at the spectacle of a King and Queen actually wearing
great crowns.

[1] *The Times,* 14th July 1902.

One more occasion remained for excitement. The
reviews and parades of the Indian and Colonial contingents
took place in Buckingham Palace Gardens, and so were
witnessed only by the privileged. But the Naval Review,
though it suffered in some respects from the postponement,
was for all to see. It happened to coincide with the arrival
in England of the three most prominent leaders of the
Boers in the field during the past two years : Botha, De
Wet and Delarey. As they came up the Solent in the
early morning of 16th August they passed the ends of the
long lines of warships, a whole world of the power of
England that they had hardly come in contact with at all.
Lord Kitchener went on board their ship to meet them,
and conveyed them to another ship on which Mr Chamberlain and Lord Roberts had embarked for the review. They
were introduced to Mr Chamberlain and Lord Roberts,
and were then invited to remain and see the review. They
declined, and went on to London. There they must have
been as puzzled by the spirit that met them as perhaps
they had been by the invitation on the moment of landing
to stay and witness alongside Mr Chamberlain a display
of the power and wealth of their conquerors. Even
without bearing grudges or malice, these three grave burly
men must have felt London remote from seriousness,
when staring easy-minded crowds ran to cheer them in the
streets, and shout after them words of patronising admiration. What, they may have asked themselves, was the
nature of a country which could sit so lightly to five and
fifty months of war that the men who had strained her to
the utmost were no more to her than new toys ? When the
three failed to respond with equally facile smiles and bows,
the public, chilled in its gratified sense of openhanded
cancelling of bygones, began to ask contemptuously if the
three fighting men were going to throw in a sullen and
resentful lot with Mr Kruger and Dr Leyds. It was the
old habit of swinging from mood to mood. The generals

went over to Rotterdam almost immediately, returning to London later on for consultations with Mr Chamberlain and Lord Kitchener at the Colonial Office on the resettlement of the conquered territories.

A great many people in England resented the sentimentalism of the London crowd, and would have sympathised with the Boer generals' feelings. Though the cry for efficiency was thrust into the background by the excitements of the year, the movement went on. Mr Kipling flung his reputation into it, in a way that almost lost him his popularity, He published in January a poem called *The Islanders*, full of scorn for a people that preferred games and sport to equipping itself for war, that boasted of empire, but made no personal effort to preserve it. One line in the poem, " flannelled fools at the wicket, or muddied oafs at the goals," was all that it was necessary to remember ; it contained the heart of his reproach, and also the deeply resented scornfulness of tone. Englishmen were by this time a little wearied of the admirable example of the colonies and of Colonial troops. Yet it was no wonder if a man with a gift for picturesque expression found himself impelled to make use of it. The war seemed now to have made so little difference ; and those who had expected a national regeneration looked round in despair. They saw the rich overwhelmed by a positive mania for bridge ; the guardsman or cavalryman, when he came home from campaigning, seemed to make a point of picking life up casually just where he had left off, sitting down to take a hand of an afternoon, or a morning, or an evening, just as if there was no Empire. More infuriating still to the strenuous was the mania for ping-pong, a sort of table tennis, which, beginning with the middle class, had spread upwards with astonishing rapidity, and devastated evening parties. Even in its patriotic manifestations the crowd exasperated the searchers for efficiency. On the one hand it could not even produce a passable comic song for pavement use (we are hardly now able to recall the feeble idiocy of " We'll all be merry on Coronation Day ") ; and on the other hand it could not rejoice without bringing to the surface a lot of wastrel youths, who in other countries would have been undergoing their period of military service.

The attack on the trade unions continued no less vigorously. They were charged with limiting output (on the " Ca' canny " principle), and articles appeared contrasting the number of bricks a man could lay in a day with the number of bricks a trade unionist actually would lay.[1] Employers complained that they were hampered in tendering for contracts by the stipulations which public bodies made for the employment of union labour, or the payment of union wages. Public bodies replied that they were justified in taking every precaution against the delaying of contracts by strikes. Again, employers fell under criticism for inefficiency in their relations with their men ; they did not encourage new ideas, or do anything to make the workmen take a living interest in the business. They aimed at altering trade union law, instead of defending themselves by combination and a system of profit-sharing with their workmen. But no one offered any suggestion based on the truth of the new situation which the last fifteen years had brought about in industry. Each master had practically, under the Limited Liability Acts, become in his own person a combination of capital ; and if these combinations were to combine, trade unions naturally aimed at a General Federation in response. Incidental criticisms cut at various angles into the main controversy. Mr John Burns defended workmen from the charge of limiting output, but told them at the same time that there was a good deal in the complaints of their inefficiency, while they spent so much health and money in drink and

[1] *The Times*, 10th March 1902.

gambling. Others complained of the Board of Trade
Labour Department as a sham, politically one-sided, and
not trusted by employers as a conciliatory medium.
Even such a matter as the closing down of the steamer
service on the Thames was regarded as another piece of
inefficiency : London had not the sense to make use of
her river as other capitals did.

A certain response to criticism of the mind of labour
was made by the foundation of the Workers' Educational
Association. This was an attempt to grapple in a new
way with the difficulty of bringing university education
within the outlook of the artisan. Ruskin Hall had
become by this time something more than an experiment.
But it had not solved the difficulty. For one thing, its
students showed some tendency to quarrel with the whole
tone of Oxford education, as a middle-class tone, and to
wish rather to inform the university than be informed
by it. Besides, the hall could not accommodate many
men ; and the time seemed to have come for a new effort.
The Workers' Educational Association aimed at bringing
the universities to working people, instead of sending
working people to the universities. Its purpose was to
organise extension classes in a more systematic way than
had hitherto been attempted ; to create a co-operation
between pupils and lecturers, which should lead to more
profitable selection of courses of instruction ; to give
a more deliberate continuity to those courses ; and to
create between the lecturer and his class in a manufacturing town a relation more akin to that between tutors and
pupils in a university. The association received the
support of trade union leaders, and no less warm support
from university authorities. For a few years its progress
was rather slow ; the *Intransigeants* of Ruskin Hall had
not ineffectually decried the " orthodox " history and
economics of university teachers. But the association
had patient and enthusiastic service behind it ; and

before the end of our period it numbered over one
hundred branches and over 3000 students.

In learning and science we were not doing so badly. The
founding of the British Academy early in the year was
an easy subject for jests ; but a roll which included Lord
Acton, Mr Lecky, Mr Bryce, Mr Balfour, Mr Morley, such
professors as S. R. Gardiner, Pelham, J. B. Bury, Jebb,
Robinson Ellis, Bywater, Munro, S. G. Butcher, Dicey,
Holland and Maitland, and antiquarians like Lord Dillon
and Mr Arthur Evans, was one worth drawing up, even if
the British genius might be held not to favour academies.
Unfortunately one great name was too soon to drop out
of the roll ; Lord Acton died in July. He had as an
historian done much to reinstate the infinitely patient
collection and sifting of evidence ; and his lectures at
Cambridge were mines generously laid open for the digging
of others. His own work had a dignity and detachment
which set as fine an example as his laborious habits of
research. He had during his life amassed a library of
the rarest value for such research. He was, however, not
a rich man, and had been obliged to make preparations
to sell it. Mr Carnegie stepped in, and bought the whole
70,000 volumes, leaving them in Lord Acton's hands for
his life. Now at his death Mr Carnegie requested Mr
Morley to take the responsibility for it ; and Mr Morley
found a happy end to the trust by offering the library to
the university of Cambridge, where it remains as the one
memorial to Lord Acton which he himself would most
have wished for. Another member of the Academy, Mr
Arthur Evans, was just now discovering that very Minoan
palace at Cnossus which no one had expected him to find.[1]
Professor Dewar and others were making most important
experiments with gases at extremely low temperatures.
Nor could there be any complaint about the use of scientific methods in medical practice. Systematic investiga-

1 See page 554.

tion of cancer had progressed so far that a scheme was started for raising a fund of £100,000 for the purpose. The treatment of tuberculosis was greatly forwarded by King Edward's application of a gift of £200,000 (at first anonymous, but soon known to be Sir Edward Cassel's) to be spent on a sanatorium.

The demand for efficiency had begun, simply enough, from the contemplation of our scrambling entry upon what proved to be a long and complicated war. From that, and from the anxiety about hooliganism, grew the foundation this year of the National Service League, for the advocacy of compulsory military training. But another element was now creeping in, and that which had begun in our own consciences was kept alive by a spectre of more or less hostile rivalry. National feeling between England and Germany had taken a disagreeable turn. In the previous year it had seemed probable that of all the Continental comment on the war, which had been hard to bear and bitterly resented, that from Germany would be the soonest forgotten. The promptness with which the German Emperor acknowledged family claims at Queen Victoria's death has been mentioned.[1] The action of King Edward in making him a Field-Marshal in the British army, and in investing the German Crown Prince with the Order of the Garter, had been well received ; and more intimate relations between the two countries seemed about to be set up. Yet even then comparisons were at work between the British and the German navies, of a tone sufficiently indicated by the conclusion that the question was not one of comparative tons of commerce, or pounds sterling of naval expenditure, but one simply of Great Britain's security at sea.[2] While the ultimate trend of our relations with Germany was still in question, Mr Chamberlain made, in November 1901, a speech in which,

[1] See page 564.
[2] *The Times,* 8th February 1901:

discussing the possibility of our having been too lenient in the later stages of hostilities, and too little inclined to act on the principle that guerillas were not entitled to the honourable provisions of war, he had referred to the Franco-German campaign, and the treatment of the *francs-tireurs*. Mr Chamberlain never appeared at his best in his references to other nations, and his words provoked an outburst of violent replies from Germany. The German Chancellor took up Mr Chamberlain's remarks sharply in the Reichstag, and other hot speeches followed. This was in January 1902—so vigorously had the German newspapers kept up their comments. Great projects for the extension of the German navy were in the circumstances likely to be used here to raise still more the spectre of rivalry. Anything in Mr Brodrick's army schemes that had an air of being borrowed from Germany came in for sarcastic notice ; and he himself became a butt when he went to attend the German manœuvres with Lord Roberts, wearing a yeomanry uniform of khaki. The German Emperor was again in England in the autumn, staying with Lord Lonsdale, and going to shoot at Sandringham. He certainly showed, both by his visit and his invitation to Mr Brodrick and Lord Roberts, every indication of a desire to override the heated newspaper exchanges.

Mr Brodrick and the War Office generally were given uncomfortable moments whenever the public had attention to spare. The Commission on the War Hospitals had reported in 1901, finding that, while the Royal Army Medical Corps had done what it could, it was deficient in strength, organisation and training, and was imperfectly equipped ; it was undermanned and overworked ; and it ought to have been provided long ago with a special sanitary branch. The Commission on Army Contracts was still sitting. Then a fresh storm broke about the Remount Department. It had, of course, been known

to the public in a general way that, even when we had
learned in South Africa the immense value of mounted
men, our generals had been unable to put the lesson into
practice, because they could not get horses quickly, or
get good ones at all, from the department responsible for
remounts. Stories had been current, too, of the pedantic
requirements of remount officers ; and of horses refused
for some red-tape reason. Early in the session of 1902 the
matter suddenly took a more serious turn. In an apparently innocent debate on some supplementary estimates,
it was charged against the War Office that a most extensive " deal " in horses from Hungary had been ludicrously
mismanaged ; we had paid hundreds of thousands away
for horses at £35 apiece, which turned out to be next to
useless, and were known later to have been acquired by
the dealers for £10 apiece or less. In September a Royal
Commission was appointed, with sweeping terms of reference. It was " to inquire into the military preparations
for the war in South Africa, and into the supply of men,
ammunition and equipment, and transport by sea and
land in connection with the campaign ; and into the
military operations up to the occupation of Pretoria."
The commissioners were Lord Elgin, Lord Esher,
Field-Marshal Sir Henry Norman, Sir George Taubman
Goldie, Admiral Sir John Hopkins, and two prominent
men of business, Sir John Edge and Sir John Jackson.
The public would have preferred a commission with
rather more men of business on it. But it was
satisfied with the terms of reference, and the decision
of the commissioners to sit in private promised a less
delicate procedure than would have been likely in
public.

Meanwhile efficiency was at work in the navy. Under
Lord Selborne a new scheme was set on foot for training
officers, with due regard to the importance of the machinery
in a modern ship ; it was intended to procure more inter-

change and interaction between the executive and the engineering branches.

Uneasiness about our business supremacy received a double shock in the autumn, from two great operations of American capitalists. One threatened to sweep the whole retail tobacco trade into an American trust. There had arisen during the year a violent competition between American and British tobacco manufacturers for the custom of the retailers. The immense spread of cigarette-smoking had filled the shops with packets of cheap cigarettes ; and it now came out that American firms were pushing their goods by offering the retailers bonuses in addition to the regular profits. There ensued a period of frantic counter-bidding, the bonuses finally reaching a figure at which even the biggest manufacturers began to quail. But the Americans were combined in a trust ; and unless the British combined they must ultimately be forced into surrender, and join the trust. The Imperial Tobacco Company was formed, taking in large businesses like Players', Ogden's and Wills's ; and it was just in time to save a few other British firms from coming under the American trust. Several had already joined it. The two trusts came to an agreement, and the bonus war ended. The affair would have attracted much less attention had it not coincided with a far more colossal American stroke. As early as May a debate had arisen in the House of Commons in regard to a combination in the North American shipping trade. A " pool " had been in process of formation, so enormous that it threatened to transfer the control of our Atlantic lines—by far the greater portion of our shipping, and the newest and fastest —to American hands. What made the case worse was that the German Atlantic lines, which the " pool " had attempted to draw in, had apparently shown more independence in making their terms than our own. Ultimately the Board of Trade was able to announce that the

British ships in the combination were to remain under British control, and the British flag, and were to carry a proportion of British officers and men, as the Government might require ; at least half of the new shipping of the combination was always to be British ; and the British ships were to remain, as before, subject to the British Government, and to rights of temporary acquisition by the Government. The Cunard Line, which remained outside the combination, was to receive a special subsidy of £150,000 a year, and a loan for building two new fast ships. Thus the American deal became a purely trading agreement, and the worst of public alarm was soothed. But it remained a little humiliating ; and the immense amount of the combination's capital, said to be twenty-four millions, all found by persons interested, was hardly consoling.

The House met for an autumn session on the Education Bill, to find that the restoration of affairs to the old party shapes had proceeded swiftly in the recess. There had been a tremendous campaign against the Education Bill on the Liberal side, and the Nonconformist support of the Liberal party had been drastically pulled together. Already refusal to pay rates was in the air. On the Tory side there was some anxiety, and a disposition to make concessions, the chief outcome of which was the Kenyon-Slaney amendment, strengthening outside control in the management of voluntary schools. But no concessions could meet the complete objection of Nonconformists to the support of definite Church instruction. So strong was the Opposition to the Bill that it was pushed forward by severe forms of closure. It became law before the end of the year. Thereupon the refusal to pay rates was launched as a definite campaign ; and the Act promised to continue that process of reuniting Liberals which it had already begun. The bond provided by attacks upon it had made itself evident in the summer, when Lord Rosebery had displayed less inclination to criticise publicly the Liberal Front Bench; and Sir Edward Grey had intimated that the " clean slate " had not been intended to be *quite* clean. Lord Rosebery had even gone so far towards extreme Radicalism as to tell a meeting of Nonconformists in December that, if they submitted to the Act, they would have ceased to exist politically. They happened to lose in this year two very prominent leaders, Dr Joseph Parker and Mr Hugh Price Hughes. The former had been a notable preacher, able to gather to the City Temple crowds of busy City men on a weekday, as well as his congregations of Sunday. The latter had been an earnest social worker, but at the same time more active in political questions than Dr Parker. He had been the most notable Nonconformist to take the side of the war party in the recent controversies. Liberal polls at by-elections in the late autumn in the Cleveland and East Toxteth divisions had been most encouraging. Lastly, the debates on the Bill had shown that the Opposition, if numerically weak, had fighting power; Mr Lloyd George had greatly consolidated his reputation.

Besides the Education Bill, the Government passed the London Water Bill, setting up a separate body to which the water companies' undertakings were to pass. It introduced an Irish Land Purchase Bill, enabling land-lords to sell their estates whole to the Land Commission, if not less than three-quarters of the tenantry wished to purchase; payment was to be by cash, and not in Land Stock. The Bill was dropped; but its appearance tended to keep down agitation in Ireland, and after it had disappeared the air was full of talk of conferences and compromises, one scheme, propounded by Captain Shawe-Taylor, even suggesting a conference between Irish landlords and Irish tenants. The mere suggestion was a far cry from the ideas of twenty years back.

Another measure of the session was a Licensing Bill.

It was not a striking measure; but Lord Salisbury's refusal in 1900 to take any action on the Licensing Commission's report had given so much offence to leaders of Church opinion that, for fear of losing the support of the clergy, the Government no doubt decided that it must delay no longer. The Bill contained provisions for putting clubs under registration; and for giving the justices control of grocers' licences; and some further proposals as to habitual drunkards. The previous year had seen the publication of the first report on Certified Retreats under the Inebriates Act of 1898; and it had on the whole been encouraging. But it had spoken of a good many relapses; and an attempt was now made to "black list" habitual drunkards, who had been committed to retreats, and to forbid publicans to serve them with liquor. In truth this year's Bill was hopelessly out of date. Licensing reform, proceeding on another route, had left such proposals a long way in the rear. The famous Farnham licensing cases, and the Birmingham agreements, had become by the autumn of 1902 the centre of interest. Lord Salisbury, in refusing to act on the commission's report, had certainly underestimated the feeling in favour of a reduction of licences. This was proved by the movement that now took place among the justices. At Farnham there had been the extraordinary proportion of one licensed house to every 124 persons. The licensing justices attempted to reduce the number by negotiation; and when that failed they took their stand on the Sharp v. Wakefield decision,[1] and refused to renew eight licences. The licence-holders appealed to Quarter Sessions. In two cases renewal was ordered, on certain conditions; in the other six the justices' decision was upheld. In Birmingham, chiefly owing to the activity of Mr Arthur Chamberlain, a strong reduction movement had also been going on; but here

1 See page 271.

negotiation was more successful. Ninety-nine licences were the subject of negotiation, and the brewers agreed to surrender fifty-one. In Liverpool also there had been reductions, assisted by insurance of licences having been in practice here ; and at Nottingham. As so often happens in England, local procedure seemed likely to be caught up and generalised into a system. The failure of the Bill of 1902 to propose anything in the way of reduction of licences had strengthened the feeling that the justices must act for themselves ; and in the Farnham cases their action was pretty generally approved.[1] But brewing firms were not unnaturally alarmed. They had only succeeded, by the Farnham appeal, in strengthening the justices again. They had raised the question whether licensing justices sat as a court of law or as an administrative body. The point was important, because, if they sat as a court of law, they could only hear evidence on cases brought before them ; whereas, sitting as an administrative body, they could act entirely on their own initiative. The appeal led to the decision that they sat purely as an administrative body.

Another movement which, if less immediately alarming to licence-holders, yet showed the wide area of inclination towards temperance, was the starting in 1901 of the Public House Trust, the object of which was to secure licences on a principle of disinterested management. No profit was looked for beyond a sum sufficient to pay five per cent. on the capital invested ; so that there need be no encouragement to drinking. More money would go to improving the amenities of the houses, and tea and other such drinks were to be kept as much in the foreground as intoxicating liquors. The trust, which was headed by Lord Grey, was organised by counties, and was already drawing to itself much of the moderate opinion on licensing questions.

[1] See *The Times*, 4th October 1902.

The end of the year was overcast by a depression of trade
and a grave lack of employment. Wages had been falling
generally ; and the metal, shipbuilding and engineering
trades especially were on a down-grade for the first time
since 1894.[1] The return of reservists from the war added
to the distress ; and the winter opened badly. Nor was
peace much less costly for the moment than war. In
November Parliament had voted eight millions of money
for South Africa, three as a free gift to repatriated Boers,
two in aid of distressed loyalists in the old colonies, and
three for loans to be used in the organisation of the new
colonies. Before the end of the year 21,000 prisoners of
war had been returned, and the numbers in the concentration camps had fallen from 103,000 to 34,000. But
the disastrous disturbance caused by the war was only
slowly revealing its extent ; and it seemed likely that
more money would be called for. Everything possible
was done to hasten the transport of machinery to reopen
the Rand mines after their three years of idleness ; but
here the difficulty which had made its appearance two
years earlier grew formidable. In August the proposal
to meet the shortage of labour for the mines by importing
Chinese began to be discussed. It was at first coldly
received. The mine-owners were told that the Kaffir
problem was serious enough, without being complicated
by a Chinese problem. The other colonies, which had
done so much to make the Rand British territory, were
angrily amazed at a proposal to import the very kind
of coolie labour which they had all made up their minds
to shut out. White labourers out of work complained
bitterly of the refusal to employ them, although Mr
Cresswell, the manager of the Village Main Reef mine,
asserted that 250 white men would do the work of 900
Kaffirs ; the suspicion was that the objection to white
men was their proneness to join trade unions. As for the

[1] Board of Trade Report on Wages, published 29th August 1902.

Kaffirs, the mine-owners declared that labour-recruiting among them was tiresome and unsatisfactory. For the time being, however, the question fell into abeyance, because it was announced in October that Mr Chamberlain was proposing to visit South Africa, and study on the spot all the problems rising out of the war. The King gave his approval; the *Good Hope*, a new armoured cruiser just in commission, was placed at Mr Chamberlain's service; and he started off almost in state. He may well have been glad to leave the Education Bill behind him; but events were to show that he dropped out of more than the Education Bill.

CHAPTER IX

1903 : MR CHAMBERLAIN'S HIGH BID

THE next year opened in a rather sober mind. Trade was giving signs of slight recovery, especially in iron and steel and textiles; but it was too slight to be exhilarating as yet. The revenue showed lowered consuming power. The stock markets remained under a cloud; for the failure of the Whittaker Wright companies, occurring, as it did, just when the war would in any case have caused a shortage of money for speculation, had proved to be even more disastrous than was anticipated. It was now two years since the first announcement of failure. Nearly twelve months had been spent on investigating the affairs of the London & Globe Finance Corporation alone, before the Official Receiver could issue even his first report. There were two other principal companies and some minor ones to be investigated; and as another twelve months passed it became increasingly clear that the position of the shareholders was extremely bad. The financial operations between the various companies were far too complicated for the ordinary person to follow; but there were City men fully convinced that these operations had been of a kind that should bring Mr Whittaker Wright to the dock. Shareholders were ready enough to accept this view; and during 1902 there had been constant expressions of indignation at the inaction of the Public Prosecutor. Finally, a private committee of City men was formed, and a prosecution fund of £5000 was raised. When Parliament met, one more attempt was made to move the law authorities of the Crown ; but both the Attorney-General and the Solicitor-General remained of the opinion that the materials for a prosecution were inadequate. The difficulty of tracking out exactly what had happened was so extreme that a prosecution might break down on some technical point ; and in that case more harm than good would have been done, since the suggestion would have been conveyed that financial juggling, if only sufficiently complicated, and on large enough scale, could be practised with immunity. However, the prosecution committee had seven good legal opinions on their side. They made application in the regular way to the High Court, and early in March Mr Justice Buckley ordered the Official Receiver to prosecute Mr Whittaker Wright. These were not events calculated to assist the speculative spirit in the city ; and the Stock Exchange felt no breath of better times.

The nation fingered ruefully its already lean pocket when telegrams came from South Africa reporting promises made by Mr Chamberlain out there. Speaking at Johannesburg, on 18th January, he informed his audience that the British Government would undertake a loan of thirty-five millions, floated with the Government's guarantee, and secured on the assets of the Transvaal and the Orange River Colony. It would be spent in paying off the debts of the late republics, in expropriating the existing railways, and building new ones, and in forwarding land settlement. True, Mr Chamberlain announced at the same time that the Transvaal would pay thirty millions towards the cost of the war, ten of them being subscribed by leading financiers, and the remaining twenty placed on the market. But this was regarded as a rather illusory contribution. The net upshot of the whole transaction was that fifty-five millions more would be dumped upon a market longing to be free of those masses of national stock, and to return to flutters

of its own. Meanwhile daily processions of the unemployed, carrying collecting-boxes,. in the London
streets did not look like any immediate return of trade
elasticity.

Parliament reassembled without much expectation
of renewal of the great contests of the previous year.
The Education Act was to be extended by a separate Bill
to London. That admiration for the school boards which
had been quick to express itself on the introduction of
the Bill of 1902 was even stronger in this particular case ;
the London Board had been in old days the one really
efficient form of local government that London could
boast, and of recent years it had been in the forefront of
education. But it could not be left an exception to a
universal scheme ; and the Opposition could not fight
a subordinate measure as keenly as they had fought the
general principle. Moreover, the battle was now raging
outside Parliament, and the real progress of the cause of the
Opposition was in the country. Refusal of rates, " passive
resistance " to the Bill [1] was in full cry; and the
Government would clearly have to face the odium of
prosecutions which could be represented as persecutions
of conscience. Besides the London Education Bill the
measures expected during the session were a Port of
London Bill and, as the great item, an Irish Land Purchase
Bill. A Royal Commission had reported on the Port of
London in 1902, recommending the establishment of a
public authority ; but no proposal was made in this year,
and in fact the subject was to wait for five years before
it was undertaken. The Irish Land Purchase Bill promised a good passage. There had actually been a conference in Dublin, though not quite of the kind projected

---

[1] This phrase did not appear now for the first time. Disraeli,
in *Sybil*, writes of the possibility of a " passive resistance
Jacquerie," among the starved and ill-housed peasantry of
England.

by Captain Shawe-Taylor.[1] Lord Dunraven and Lord Mayo had met Mr John Redmond, Mr William O'Brien, Mr T. W. Russell, and Mr Harrington ; and the principle of the buying-out of owners seemed likely to offer no serious difficulties. The only obstacle would be the cost. The Bill proposed purchase on a much greater scale than had hitherto been attempted, and the question was whether, after all the large Government loans of the war time, millions could profitably be raised for Ireland. Mr Wyndham, the Chief Secretary, put the figure at twelve millions ; but it became very clear in the course of the debates that this would not be the limit. However, the floating of the Transvaal loan was such an unexpected success that there was less anxiety as to putting the Irish stock on the market when the time should come.

There seemed to be little opportunity for the Liberals to exercise their growing strength. Irish land purchase they could hardly oppose ; and it suited them better to look on while some of the Irish landlords expressed their far from friendly feelings for a Unionist Government producing such a Bill. It was simpler to make capital out of attacking Mr Brodrick's army schemes. The " phantom army corps " had become a public jest ; the real army corps were obviously going to cost a great deal of money, and increase permanently the Army Estimates. Recruiting was being bolstered up by methods not at all satisfactory ; the requirements as to height and chest measurements had been relaxed, and weedy recruits were nicknamed " Brodricks." Reform of details, such as changes in the pattern of soldiers' caps, was peculiarly open to ridicule, while more important reforms seemed to be in suspension. Mr Winston Churchill, who was entering on his third session, having been returned as Conservative member for Oldham at the 1900 election, made himself prominent in these attacks. The question

[1] See page 612.

of labour in the Transvaal mines offered as yet no particular foothold to Liberals.   It was raised on an amendment moved by Sir Charles Dilke to the Consolidated Fund Bill at the end of March.   By that time Mr Chamberlain was at home again, having landed in England on 14th March, and he was in his place in the House to deal with the question.   He had taken a perfectly clear line in a speech at Johannesburg in January.   He had told the mine-owners that there was a strong current of opinion against the importation of Chinese labour, both at home and in the colonies ; he expressed the belief that the mine-owners had not sufficiently worked out the problem, and would be well advised to see what could be done, by means of improved machinery and the employment of white labour, to bridge over the present shortage of black labour. Now in the House of Commons he was equally clear about the objection of the colonists to Chinese labour.   But he gave less weight to the objection of the mother country ; and implied that, if the colonists most concerned, those in South Africa, should change their mind, the Government neither could nor would interfere.   However, this drew no particular attention.   A mass meeting at Johannesburg protested vigorously against any introduction of Asiatics ; and the matter was not seriously regarded.

The Budget was awaited with flat dreariness.   The war was over, but its burdens were not.   The income-tax payer hoped for a little relief, but did not expect much ; and, if he got any, what new experiments in broadening the basis of taxation might be looked for ?   Sir Michael Hicks-Beach had been speaking, in his retirement, as if the national revenue was rather at a standstill, and yet national expenditure of the normal kind could not but rise.   Where was the necessary resiliency to be found ? The revenue returns stood at £633,000 below the estimate ; but for the falling-in during the year of the duties on a great millionaire's estate, that of Colonel McCalmont, the figures would have been much worse. After all, the Budget was better than the forecasts. No less than fourpence was taken off the income-tax. Yet Mr Ritchie's arrangements for the Sinking Fund were sound enough to please the City, and to prevent any appearance of bidding for popularity at the cost of prudence. The shilling corn-tax was also taken off. There were murmurs from some quarters. A Protectionist party was still represented in the House by Mr James Lowther and Mr Chaplin ; and their complaints about this disregard for continuity in financial policy were prompt. Mr Balfour, however, receiving later on a deputation representing these views, was quite firm in maintaining the official attitude of the moment when the tax was imposed—that it had been put on for war purposes, and had instantly become so much a bone of contention that it could not be regarded as a permanent item of the country's fiscal policy. He went a good deal further when he added that Protection could not possibly be introduced into that policy silently, without a distinct vote from the country. The corn-tax had been a registration duty ; and it was now represented, by certain agricultural interests, as of value to them. The truth behind the disappointment was that Sir Michael Hicks-Beach's gloomy views of the limit of elasticity in indirect taxation had produced a good deal of discussion of a broadening which should even extend to moderate all-round duties. This was very largely not a Protectionist but a genuine financial theory. It was at least open to argument that markets in England were becoming too cheap. In one respect, while there were so many unemployed and ill-paid workers, living could not be too cheap, But the increase of money in circulation had combined with business enterprise, advertisement and competitive transport, to enlarge extraordinarily the workman's range of purchase. Tinned foods and chilled meat were added to our already cheap loaf ; and the great trading stores which had arisen in the eighties for the middle classes had been copied in immense grocery concerns which by sticking to the stores system of cash purchases and by acting through a very large number of branch shops—most of all, perhaps, by being their own manufacturers and wholesale dealers—were able to cut profits very small. Clothes and boots, by the gradual perfection of machinery, had become worth selling cheaply in the modern rapid circulation of money. Oil had been cheapened by the standardising tendency of a great American trust looking for unchecked sales. Vegetables and fruit had come within the reach of town dwellers of a class that twenty years before would never have indulged in such things. Here again the use of cold chambers for transport had brought about a change ; it was now worth while to send to England, in quantities large enough to make a cheap market, perishable stuff that had formerly been limited to the home-grown. Apples had for many years now poured in at all seasons ; the imports had first become astonishing in 1891, when the quantity from Tasmania alone rose suddenly from 8798 bushels to 64,034 bushels, and other colonies saw the opening for their produce. Since then it had dawned upon the big merchants that money only had to be looked for—that if they chose to stock a market they could be sure of a return. Thus grapes, even pineapples, tomatoes, and other fruits which were once hothouse delicacies, appeared on the costers' barrows ; and so firm had this kind of market become that a regular mail service to the island of Jamaica, a boon long desired by the inhabitants, had been inaugurated largely in the assurance that bananas could be sold in such quantities, once they were fairly on the streets, as to become an unfailingly profitable cargo. The middle class, gaining equally by the cheapness of food supplies, showed in other ways that mere housekeeping had become a small item of its expenditure. The craze just now for what was generically described as "Arts and Crafts" furni-

ture—partly a translation into dealers' terms of William
Morris's designs, partly an importation of modern German
and Austrian designing—meant that middle-class families
were replacing their fathers' and grandfathers' furniture
by new roomfuls from top to bottom of their houses.
Even expensive toys like mechanical piano-players, which
were first advertised heavily in this year, found their most
numerous purchasers among the middle class, since the
hire system played so large a part in the sales.   Again, a
matter like that of " capping " at hunts, which became an
established custom in 1903, points in the same direction ;
it meant that numbers of people were able to afford hunting who did not belong to the old hunting sets, and so
did not attach themselves to a single hunt, and become
subscribers.

It seems quite probable that, if no one had generalised
about the process, the pressure of growing expenditure
upon Chancellors of the Exchequer with no gift for fundamental reconsideration of taxing would have brought
about a definite enlargement of the tariff list.   Each
Chancellor was confronted with a community steadily
spending on a wider range of both necessaries and luxuries ;
but not capable of more than a certain elasticity in the
narrow range of dutiable goods.   Moreover, there were
a good many Liberals who felt that the readiness of the
workman to applaud a war was partly due to his escape
from direct taxation, such as the income-tax, and the comparatively small impost laid on him by the existing area
of indirect taxes.   But now a generalisation was made,
and in such a way, and by such a man, that the whole
matter ceased to be one of making ends meet at the
Exchequer, and became a struggle on root-principles.

Mr Chamberlain had spoken more than once, since he
took the Colonial Office and began to make colonial
subjects of importance to political audiences, of the reality
which might be given to our relations with the colonies by

a tariff agreement, such as existed between the various
states of the United States, or between the countries of
the German Empire. His first speech to his constituents
after his return from South Africa was made on 15th May.
He put forward at more length than he had yet done a
plea for the establishment of preferential tariffs within
the empire. At present we left the colonies to fight the
battle of our markets without any favour ; we were
obliged to submit to their tariffs, because, if they lowered
them in our favour, foreign countries threatened reprisals
(this had just happened between Canada and Germany),
and we, having no tariffs to lower to our colonies, could not
indemnify them against such reprisals. This, he thought,
was a situation Cobden and Bright had not foreseen. He
expressed his desire that a discussion on the subject should
be opened. Within three days it had dawned upon Great
Britain that this was not a mere passage in a speech. It
looked like Mr Chamberlain's greatest bid for fame. He
had made Colonial administration a vital piece of Cabinet
work and parliamentary government ; he wanted to
make it the central pivot. He had made the Colonial
Secretaryship a most important office in the Ministry ;
he wanted to make it *the* most important office. In an
Imperial nation the Colonial Secretary should hold threads
that ran through every other office ; an Imperial Customs
Union would be the first step, and a long one, towards that
end. Nay, in an Imperial nation, the Colonial Secretary
should be Prime Minister. So Mr Chamberlain made his
high bid.

He had a great popularity, and a great following. He
might in any case have made people actually consider an
ideal. No one else could have done it. The agitation for
efficiency was already drooping under the bland inattention of England. It was all very well for a restless
inquirer like Mr H. G. Wells to talk about the future as
lying with the middle class ; and for middle-class men

to lift their eyebrows at reports of "ragging" in the Grenadiers,[1] or outbreaks at Sandhurst, and feel themselves at any rate not brought up to that kind of behaviour. But the middle class showed no sign whatever of getting over its proneness to easy distractions. The Stock Exchange, always falling back on sporting interests in times of slack business, organised a walking race to Brighton on May Day. For the rest of the summer, so acutely was the public fancy tickled, all kinds of walking races were arranged, until the summit of hilarity was reached with a race for tea-shop waitresses. A great swimmer decided to attempt swimming the Channel; that turned into a craze also, and the daily doings of half-a-dozen swimmers were chronicled in the newspapers. Girls took to playing hockey, and not a suburb or a small provincial town but must have its hockey club. Music by Richard Strauss appeared in London concert programmes, and the world might stand still while people argued whether he had, or had not, rendered all other music obsolete. The ordinary halfpenny newspaper had ceased to be facile enough ; a halfpenny picture paper must be launched, and *The Daily Mirror* made its appearance, shrewdly aimed at opening a new market among women, whom it must have been galling for the newspaper proprietors to see not spending their halfpennies at a bookstall as they caught trains to the City. The elaboration with which interest was enlisted in criminal cases had an unusually busy field this year. First, there was the Moat House Farm case, a peculiarly exciting one, because it opened with a man being charged with forging cheques in the name of a woman, mistress of the farm, who had disappeared, and ended in the discovery of her body, and the alteration of the charge to one of murder. Newspaper enterprise was so active that the search for the body was conducted behind temporary hoardings. Two other

[1] In February 1903.

murder cases, and a piece of wild shooting down a suburban road, in which three Armenians were killed by a
compatriot, while the neighbourhood went into something
like a panic, provided other excitements on the street
placards. As if these cases were not enough, the cheaper
newspapers spent a breathless fortnight, in September,
hunting for a lady who had mysteriously disappeared,
and was ultimately found dead in a coppice in a park near
London. The irresponsible fervour of this public hunt
had an offensive element. Odd moments spared by the
populace from these affairs were given to expressing resentment against one of the strange prophets that occasionally
appear from America. This was Dr Dowie, who flourished
in a sectarian settlement on the shores of Lake Michigan,
with a creed that made him personally little lower than the
angels. In the strong belief that charlatanry was turned
to Dr Dowie's own material comfort, with a good deal of
blasphemous nonsense in the process, crowds broke up
meetings held by himself and by his wife and son. Another American doctrine was more quickly obtaining a
following. Christian Science had gathered by now a
body of English adherents.

It was part of Mr Chamberlain's genius that he could
pitch politics in the key of a public excitement ; he could
make his ideas " good newspaper stuff." His first speech
would, however, not have fallen into that category. The
despair of ardent Imperialists is that colonies, simply as
colonies, never are good newspaper stuff. But though
the direct reference of Mr Chamberlain's speech was to the
colonies, it was equally clear that he had in mind a revival
of a general customs tariff in England ; and within a week
the Free Trade counterblast had begun. The Birmingham speech was elevated into a regular political programme ; party war was declared over it, and it was very
quickly apparent that the unifying influence of an educational question upon the Liberal party was nothing to

the unifying influence of a call to the defence of Free Trade.
A debate was raised in the House of Commons on 29th
May : was Mr Chamberlain to be taken as speaking for
himself or for the Government ? Mr Balfour merely
replied that he and Mr Chamberlain were in complete
agreement, but did not intend to produce details at this
early stage for the Opposition to tear to pieces. This was
all very well ; but as Mr Chamberlain had not shrunk
from facing the dilemma presented—that he must either
tax food-stuffs or else have no tariff advantage to offer to
the colonies—and had boldly admitted that taxation of
food-stuffs was in his mind, a great many of the Ministerial
party began to be apprehensive about presenting such
a programme to their constituents. The first comments
sent home from the colonies, especially from Australia,
were not very friendly. Fiscal independence was too
precious to be easily given up, and a Customs Union must
mean surrender of purely local power of taxation.

Practically no other subject counted for anything in
Parliament during the remainder of the session. To
earnest Liberals Mr Chamberlain's proposal was an
attempt at pure reaction. At its best, it would be
Imperialism as a yoke. But the mere suggestion of a
tariff brought out all the Protectionist feeling that was
in the country. The scheme, launched for an ideal of
co-operation with the colonies, found itself suddenly in
alliance with arguments for forcing open foreign markets
and keeping our own markets for our own manufacturers.
Earnest Liberals fell upon this, in turn, as an attempt to
secure more profits for manufacturers and shareholders
at the cost of higher prices to the poor, and at the cost
of perpetual embroilments with foreign countries. The
reply was that, if we had a large population too poor to
stand a small tariff, then Free Trade had not achieved
much for the working man. So the controversy waxed
within a month to the broadest possible basis on either

side. It was sharpened by the immediate party difficulties it raised. A debate on the new lines during the discussion of the Finance Bill had drawn from Mr Ritchie professions of the stiffest adherence to Free Trade. How then were he and Mr Chamberlain going to continue sitting in the same Cabinet ? In the House of Lords it appeared that the Duke of Devonshire and Lord Goschen were Free Traders. The opportunity for splitting up the Government was obvious, and was pursued relentlessly. The chief split, that between Mr Balfour and Mr Chamberlain, could not be brought about ; they appeared together at a luncheon at the Constitutional Club, deliberately arranged for party purposes ; and were still—without details—in agreement. But besides the Cabinet there was the Ministerial party ; and by the beginning of July Unionist Free Traders were holding meetings as a separate group in the House. The Opposition naturally made every possible opportunity for raising a question of such obvious profit to themselves ; the Government as naturally declined, whenever it could, to allow the question to appear. The only further item of importance elicited during the session was the admission drawn from the Duke of Devonshire by Lord Rosebery that the Cabinet was holding some sort of inquiry. This hint that the Unionist party might, as a party, be committed to a tariff was emphasised by the appearance of a flood of leaflets from the Liberal Unionist headquarters. Mr Chamberlain had been as prompt as ever to set party machinery in motion. At the same time a league designed to act for the new policy alone, the Tariff Reform League, came into being ; and on the other side the Cobden Club, which had for years led little more than a formal existence, awoke to activity, and the Free Trade Union was founded to counterbalance the flood of Mr Chamberlain's leaflets and speakers. When the House rose, there was little expectation that this Parliament would meet again. So profoundly had the political currents been stirred that a dissolution early in 1904 was anticipated. The Government had had some very uncomfortable experiences at by-elections. In the Rye division of Sussex a Unionist majority of 2500 had been turned into a Liberal majority of 500. At Woolwich a turnover of no less than 6000 votes had given the seat to a Labour member, Mr Will Crooks ; and another Labour candidate, Mr Arthur Henderson, had won the Barnard Castle division of Yorkshire, though the vote against the Unionists had been split between him and a Liberal candidate. The Government had also lost North Fermanagh to a Nationalist. These losses were for the most part put down to the mismanagement of the war, and to a general irritation with the failure to show energy in reform. No one could yet tell how Mr Chamberlain's policy would affect the country. But his personal popularity was an enormous asset ; the impression of vigorous proposals would be another ; and the enthusiasm for the colonies during the war, however sentimental, would be a third. When once the new question had become so pressing, it was supposed that the Government would not long carry on without an election.

Besides the Irish Land Bill and the London Education Bill little had been done in Parliament. One or two other matters had, however, made an appearance. The brewing trade had expressed its perturbation at the new movement of licensing justices. Lord Burton put certain questions in the House of Lords, to which the Lord Chancellor had replied that licensing justices must not act on grounds of general policy, but on equity and expediency in the particular case. Mr Balfour, replying to a deputation, had taken the line that licence-holders were right to ask for some security, since, if licences were to be absolutely insecure, no decent man would engage in the trade. It was rather cynically noted that the Rye

election result had been cheered at a meeting of the
Beer and Wine Trade Defence League, a sad sign of
discontent from those upon whom the Unionists had
been accustomed to rely for support. Yet the general
approval of the policy of reducing licences was not to be
denied ; a strong appeal to the Government, signed by
prominent people in every rank and walk of life, was based
on the feeling that, if the justices' movement was to be
checked, as Mr Balfour's remarks implied, it must only
be by the establishment of some other system of reduction. The principle of compensation, which an earlier
Tory Ministry had endeavoured to incorporate in local
government schemes, made its reappearance now in
discussion. Temperance principles had been much
assisted by the cry for efficiency ; they made a new, if
mildly grotesque, appearance this year in a gospel of
taking no drinks between meals ; there were those who
complained of the amount of overeating that this called
for.

Motor car legislation also appeared during the session.
For some years there had been a growing public demand
for licensing both cars and drivers. Great rates of speed
and frequent accidents had irritated people ; and it was
urged that cars ought to be numbered, since identification
of the car against the will of the owners in case of an
accident was impossible without numbering ; and that
drivers should be required to pass some test of efficiency.
A Bill was introduced by the Government to achieve
both of these objects. By way of sugaring the pill of
the registration fees, the measure handed the money
over to the local authorities, for improving the roads.
Local authorities were also empowered to make a speed
limit in their districts. But on this latter point public
opinion forced the Government to amend their Bill,
and introduce a universal speed limit of twenty miles
an hour. After that the Bill made a quick passage.

Motor cars had by this time been greatly improved. Breakdowns were infrequent; speed and power had immensely increased, and the appearance of cars had changed; they no longer looked like carriages accidentally detached from horses. Motor racing over long courses, with its deadly accidents, still flourished; but manufacturers in England were beginning to pay more attention to long " reliability trials " than to mere speed tests. Cars were still very expensive ; and it was believed that " not this generation nor the next will see the disappearance of the horse from London. Can anyone record the smallest diminution in the number of hansom cabs, or any shortening of the long line of horse omnibuses ? " [1] But motor omnibuses were already on trial.

The year is notable in the history of science for the discovery of radium. A French scientist, Professor Curie, and his wife had succeeded in extracting from pitchblende, a curious substance found hitherto only in certain mines in Austria, an element with amazing properties. It had activities similar to the X-rays, but the astonishing thing was that its output of energy seemed not to diminish its volume. It had destructive effects upon the human skin and cell-structure ; but it was believed that these effects might be turned to useful medical purposes. Professor Curie was lecturing at the Royal Institution in June.

The fiscal controversy overwhelmed almost all the interest that might have been taken in two reports published this year. One was the report of the Joint Committee on Municipal Trading. It was not a very remarkable document, amounting to little more than a proposal for a uniform system of auditing municipal accounts, the auditors to be professional accountants, appointed for five years, and subject to the approval of the Local Government Board. But it was believed that

[1] *The Times*, 13th November 1903.

really drastic and disinterested auditing would be a check on much of the modern municipal activity. Since the joint committee was appointed, there had been more deliberate attempts to make "municipal socialism" a vital question. Some of the attempts were wasted, being directed against extremist proposals, emanating from sources of no authority, for municipal supplies of such things as bread and tobacco. A shrewder attack was that delivered against the system by which the landlord compounded for rates on his property, and the tenant paid an inclusive rent ; this, it was argued, blinded the working man—and in London or Glasgow with their blocks of flats blinded many of the middle class also—to the cost at which municipal enterprises were undertaken : the heaviness of rates was not really felt. Then there was the question of the large number of municipal employees, and their natural influence at an election on the side of the enterprises which gave them employment. Birmingham, for instance, had 7000 of such men, and would have 1500 more when the tramways were taken over. The housing work of municipalities was criticised as costly, slow, and aiming at ideals which placed the tenements, when built, beyond the means of the workman. Insanitary areas had better be dealt with by drastic action against the owners. Some feeling was aroused, but on the whole municipal trading was successful in giving the communities, in which it was active, efficient and unstinted services ; the mere label of socialism could not prevail against this practical usefulness. It happened that municipal housing had enlisted the interest of King Edward, ever since his work on the Housing Commission. He visited in this year the new blocks of dwellings erected by the London County Council on the Millbank site, and showed himself very expert in such details as cupboards. It may be mentioned here that the council most successfully solved in this year the problem of naming the new streets of its Strand Improvement Scheme. All sorts of people had rushed into print with suggestions; but the council—thanks, it was believed, to its distinguished clerk, Mr Gomme—bettered all the advice by naming the broad straight road through to Holborn, Kingsway, and the crescent uniting it with the Strand, Aldwych—a name which preserved the ancient associations both of Wych Street and of the Danish settlement commemorated in the name of St Clement Danes Church. A less happy movement of local government, which provided the critics of municipal trading with a most useful text, was the acquisition by the Marylebone Borough Council of the electric light undertaking in their district; the cost, one million and a quarter, was actually in excess of the rateable value of the area.

The other report which failed to obtain due public attention was a much more serious one. It was the Report of the Royal Commission on the War, and it was a document little short of appalling. It told of hundreds of thousands of Lee-Enfield rifles wrongly sighted; of sixty-six million rounds of ammunition of which the bullet stripped in the rifle, to the ultimate danger of the shooter; of cavalry swords thoroughly bad in material. Reserves of supplies at the beginning of the war had been disgracefully low: of cavalry swords there were only eighty in reserve. There were no reserves of proper khaki uniforms, but some 400,000 drill suits too thin for use in South Africa. Two of the army corps had neither transport materials nor transport animals. The Remount Department had no system of obtaining in time of peace information as to available supplies of horses. Such things, and many more, were exposed in detail. In general, the recommendations were that the office of Commander-in-Chief should be abolished, and War Office control reorganised on the lines of the Board of Admiralty. Specific changes in War Office administration had already been recommended, and proposals for reorganisation drawn up, by a Departmental Committee.

The truth was thus as bad as the worst accusations against the Government had asserted it to be. But Mr Chamberlain was still, as he had been before, the " lightning conductor." [1] The whole political energy of the country was switched on in his direction, and there followed an autumn and a winter of such indefatigable speech-making as had never been known; it beat the most strenuous periods of the war time. The Liberal party showed a wholly united front. Here and there were prominent individual cases of independence. Liberals, for instance, were gravely astonished when Mr Charles Booth, whose work, *Life and Labour in London*, had reformed sociological methods, declared himself a supporter of Mr Chamberlain. But no uncertainty existed as to the co-operation between leaders who had recently been so openly at variance. Lord Rosebery, Mr Asquith and Mr Haldane were as stout defenders of Free Trade as Sir Henry Campbell-Bannerman and Mr Lloyd George. A moment's hesitation on the other side had attended a statement by Mr Chamberlain, to the effect that he would not even press for inquiry into his proposals if he found the people unwilling to bear a slight burden for an Imperial ideal. But now that business men anxious for a tariff had enlisted under him these exalted attitudes were rapidly modified by clever organisers, and the " slight burden " was soon made to appear no burden by intimations that a system of Colonial preference, putting duties upon corn, mutton, etc., would bring in money enough to allow the duties on tea, sugar and other articles of food to be lightened, so that a balance would be struck.

Liberals, while maintaining the broadest principles of Free Trade—the absence of perpetual opportunities

[1] See *Punch*, 22nd July 1903.

for friction with foreign countries, the freedom from acrimonious bargaining with colonists, the immense subtleties of the industrial structure which we had reared upon free imports—unwearyingly attacked Mr Chamberlain in every detail of statistics and every specific instance he produced. A relentlessly wet summer and autumn, accompanied by depressing floods, disposed people to welcome a new thing to think about. By its disastrous destruction of crops, the weather also assisted the Protectionist element in Mr Chamberlain's forces. The trade depression and the lack of employment produced a vague inclination to try a new way with industry. As the arguments for Retaliation in hostile tariffs and Protection for our own industries slowly made headway in the propaganda against Mr Chamberlain's original idealistic proposal, his standing as a business man, whose reputation had been made before the world knew him, in an enterprising city, was remembered more than his capture of the public imagination as Colonial Secretary.

But before the remarkable autumn campaign began, there were extremely exciting passages in the inner circles of politics. The Cabinet was summoned in September, and everyone was on the alert. Did it mean dissolution ? And, if not, what rearrangement was going to take place ? Would Mr Chamberlain resign, and so leave the Free Traders to pull the party together, or would the Free Trade Ministers resign, and so leave the party committed to Mr Chamberlain ? For, according as these events fell out, Mr Balfour's position, it was thought, would be determined. He had all along asserted the absence of any disagreement between himself and Mr Chamberlain ; but the conviction was strong that, if the Free Traders in the Cabinet won, Mr Balfour would, to say the least, welcome a situation in which he need not commit himself further, and would hold the party aloof. One influence, powerful still, though in retirement, had just

been removed. Lord Salisbury died on 23rd August.
In view of the recent turns of political events, both the
war and the fiscal campaign, it was natural to sum up
his contribution to English life by saying that, while
he could not create ideals by force of imagination, or set
popular feelings in motion, he could lay a hand on public
opinion, and could, in the widest sense, govern.[1] An
aristocrat, a true Conservative, he never quite adjusted
himself to a world in which newspapers spread over all the
country speeches meant only for a particular assembly ;
he was given to saying things which looked cynical and
provocative in print. Hence arose the view that in
much of his social legislation he was impelled forward by
Mr Chamberlain. The truth was rather that he was never
reluctant to meet the given case, nor blind to the political
impulses of his day. But he disliked the wrapping of
a given case in large phrases and democratic generalisations ; he disliked the pretence of doing from emotion what
was done from a purely intellectual acquiescence in a
certain presentation of facts. The appearance of cynicism
was usually due to this obstinate clearing of his own
conscience.[2]

Now that he was dead, there was no one in the party
of more administrative or parliamentary weight and
experience than Mr Chamberlain. He fought against
no odds. This added sharpness to the country's expectation of a decisive struggle in the Cabinet. But when the
announcement came, on 18th September, it left the public
bewildered. Mr Ritchie, the Free Trade Chancellor of
the Exchequer, had resigned, and Lord George Hamilton,
who had also been a strong Free Trader—but Mr Chamberlain had resigned as well. Then two more Free Traders
resigned, Lord Balfour of Burleigh and Mr Arthur Elliot.
It was a tariff "purge," but why had Mr Chamberlain

[1] *The Times*, 24th August 1903.
[2] *Cf.* page 315.

gone ? The reason given was that he wished in any case to have a perfectly free hand to urge his proposals, to take any steps he liked for laying them before the country, to be unhampered by obligations to colleagues. Then men turned their eyes back to the Cabinet, and saw that the Duke of Devonshire remained in it. Hence arose an embittered discussion of whether the Free Trade members of the Cabinet had known of Mr Chamberlain's intention to resign before they intimated their own resignations—whether, in fact, they had been jockeyed out of the Cabinet. When, on 6th October, the Duke of Devonshire's resignation was announced, it was accompanied, most unusually, by the publication of the letters on his decision exchanged between himself and Mr Balfour. They were not comfortable reading, and Mr Balfour's showed querulousness. They seemed to make it clear that Mr Balfour had not regretted the loss of the other Free Traders, though his silence as to Mr Chamberlain's purpose had been dictated solely by the ordinary rules governing correspondence between gentlemen ; but he had distinctly hoped to keep the Duke. The Cabinet was committed to no more than inquiry, and the Duke might, he thought, have remained within it at least until he knew the result of inquiry.[1] Mr Balfour's tone suggested that he felt the weakness of the material to his hand for a reconstruction of the Ministry, and indeed, if the Cabinets of 1900 and 1902 had made a poor show to a nation demanding business energy in government, this reconstructed Cabinet of 1903 made a still poorer one. Mr Austen Chamberlain went to the

---

[1] It may be remarked that Mr Balfour should have known better. The Duke was the most clear-headed man of his day. Mr Gladstone had tried exactly the same method of securing him for the Cabinet of 1886. The Duke had replied that inquiry raised such hopes that a Cabinet which undertook it was in fact committed to more than inquiry. See Holland's *Life of the Duke of Devonshire*,

Exchequer, an appointment which, if it hinted at more than mere " absence of disagreement " between Mr Balfour and Mr Chamberlain on a question wholly concerned with the Exchequer, was otherwise insignificant. Mr Alfred Lyttelton went to the Colonial Office. Mr Brodrick took the opportunity of a " general post " to leave the War Office, deserting his army corps, and removed himself to the India Office, to succeed Lord George Hamilton. Mr Arnold Forster, a young man of vigorous ideas, but regarded as a light-weight for the job, undertook the War Office. Popular opinion summed up the whole transaction as the making of a warming-pan ministry, to await Mr Chamberlain's triumphant conversion of the country. Everything now, even the premiership, was cleared for his high bid.

There could be little doubt of this. At the very moment when Mr Chamberlain accepted the Tariff Reform League's full position, that the object of the campaign was " to consolidate and develop the resources of the empire and to defend the industries of the United Kingdom "—a frank Protectionist position—Mr Balfour was saying that public opinion did not seem ripe for a change in our basis of taxation if preference involved, as it almost certainly did, taxes, however light, upon food-stuffs. If Mr Chamberlain won, therefore, he won for his own hand. He went resolutely to the campaign. At his first great meeting of the autumn, in Glasgow, he produced what the Free Traders had all along challenged him to produce—a preliminary sketch of a tariff. He proposed a two-shilling duty on corn, and the same on flour ; a 5-per-cent. duty on foreign meat and consumable produce, except bacon ; the reduction of the tea-duty by three-quarters and the sugar-duty by a half, and corresponding reductions on coffee and cocoa. He still cherished his Colonial ideal himself, warning his audience that the colonies would not wait for ever, and the chance of a fiscally consolidated empire might pass. Before the end of the year he had made speeches also at Greenock, Newcastle, Tynemouth, Liverpool, Birmingham, Cardiff and Newport. As the plan of his campaign developed it was seen that he was taking in each case the local industry as an example of the need for Protection—sugar-refining at Greenock, iron and steel at Newcastle and Tynemouth, metal manufacture at Birmingham, tin plates at Newport. Liberals joined battle with him unceasingly. They produced statistics to prove that Mr Chamberlain selected certain years, in order to make out that trade was declining. They defied him to unify his doctrine—to explain the remedies he produced for the sugar-refiner to the soda-water and jam manufacturers, who depended on cheap sugar; or his remedies for the iron and steel trades to the ship-builders who worked on cheap imported plates. They defied him to reconcile the statement that a tariff would keep out foreign goods with the statement that foreigners would pay such duties that other taxes could be taken off. They defied him to show how, if trade was to be protected, prices would fail to rise all round. Mr Chamberlain, his eye firmly fixed on his ideal, boldly declared that his figures were employed merely as illustrations; and harped perpetually on the facts that there was unemployment, that we admitted foreign goods which gave our own work-men no employment, and were shut by tariff walls out of markets abroad.

Liberals kept as firmly to other broad assertions—the "big-loaf" of Free Trade, the "starvation line" among the poor. An extraordinary revival of political economy began to occur. Fourteen professors of the subject (no one had ever thought there were so many in the country) signed a manifesto against Mr Chamberlain; a smaller, but equally eminent, number produced a counterblast. Statistics on either side were so riddled that wholly new theories of statistics emerged. Whatever the end of the immediate affair might be, there was the consoling thought that business must be the better for the destruction of weaknesses in economic theory; and politics must be the better for it too, since all big political questions nowadays were in the last resort economic questions.[1]

One or two foreign affairs had received rather more than just the dregs of interest left over from the main political struggle. The King, on his way abroad in the autumn, had broken his journey at Paris, and the fact that Paris was fond of him was beginning to obliterate antagonistic feelings, and pave the way for friendship. The assassination of the King and Queen of Servia in the summer was reported in such terrible detail that public opinion went so far as to demand the recall of our minister from the blood-stained scene. It was decided, however, that so pronounced a step had better not be taken; and the minister remained, but only to watch events, and not to maintain diplomatic relations.

The great alarm about poisoned beer had largely died down before the appearance in December of the report of the Royal Commission on Arsenical Poisoning. The commission was inclined to suspect the presence of arsenic in a good many foods and drinks; but its recommendations were practically confined to stricter inspection. Beer itself was already made under more careful supervision by brewing firms, and had quite recovered its reputation.

In December were issued also new Home Office rules governing the use of lead in the manufacture of china and earthenware. Since the evils of lead-poisoning had first become matter of common knowledge,[2] the attempts to minimise them had been frequent. The special rules of 1894 had been supplemented by new rules in 1898, enjoining monthly medical examination of women and young persons, the use of overalls and head-coverings, etc. Meanwhile the enforcement of notification of cases of

---

[1] *The Times*, 4th June 1903.
[2] See page 339.

lead-poisoning, under the Factory Act of 1895, had
provided statistics showing that the number of cases
annually had been still well over 300, up to 1898. There
now arose a movement against the use of lead at all, since
even constantly improved rules appeared to leave so
large a margin of danger. Inventors had set themselves
to produce a satisfactory leadless glaze; and the agitation
was so successful that in 1900 draft rules had been
issued by the Home Office, proposing to limit the presence
of lead in glazes to 2 per cent. of soluble lead. The
manufacturers objected to this; it would interfere less
with expensive wares than with the cheap wares, in which
foreign manufacturers, not subject to so drastic a rule,
might disastrously drive them from the market. Some
of the best of them argued also that in well-equipped
factories, properly ventilated and supervised, lead could
be used safely; the majority of the cases of poisoning
came, they said, from the small factories which could
not by any ingenuity be healthily ventilated or adequately
inspected. Lord James of Hereford was appointed to
arbitrate on the draft rules, and in 1903 he issued his
award, on which the new rules were founded. They
abandoned the attempt to limit the percentage of lead.
But they added stringency to the rules of 1898, particularly in respect of exhaust ventilation; they provided
for monthly medical examination of all workers, including adult males; and they established a scheme of
compensation for workers certified to be suffering from
lead-poisoning.

A literary event of the autumn fully able to hold its own
even in the turmoil was the publication of Morley's *Life
of Gladstone*. Literature and art sustained a curiously
large number of losses during the year: Henley, Lecky,
Shorthouse, Seton Merriman, George Gissing and Whistler
all died in 1903. Two men, both concerned with the
bettering of life in towns, in very different ways, had passed

away—Lord Rowton, whose quiet fame as Disraeli's private secretary had been overshadowed by his later fame as builder of model lodging-houses, and Mr Quintin Hogg, who founded at the Polytechnic Institute a system of technical education in days before London had stirred itself to the need for such education. Herbert Spencer died in December. His erudite *Synthetic Philosophy* had been completed some years earlier. It appeared likely that he would survive rather as a great organiser of philosophical investigation than as a great philosopher. His actual structure already showed signs of disintegration; it had its foundations in the Darwin period of scientific hypothesis, and some of his premisses had by now been modified, or even superseded. The tendency in philosophy at this time was towards a different use of science. Speculations in moral philosophy were based less on the deductive method of the origin of species, and more on what might be called pathological psychology. In one respect the mark of its period so distinct in the *Synthetic Philosophy* kept it in the peculiarly English type; its end was ethical. But it failed of its full effect largely because of its essential scheme. Philosophers now tended to distrust schemes, to dislike the logical whole, to make for compromise, to accept the irrational elements in human composition and translate them, rather than endeavour to expel them. It was, for instance, highly characteristic of the philosophy of these years that Professor William James, almost its acknowledged leader, should have investigated the psychology of religious experience. Scepticism of a militant kind was disappearing, and the moral philosopher reached out for every support of the moral instincts in man. A new pragmatism was the guiding star of the universities, and the eschatology of Herbert Spencer's best days made but little appeal.

CHAPTER X

1904 : THE TURN OF THE TIDE

THE face of political life was now completely changed. Liberals were united, energetic, impelled by a cause. The doubt and hesitation had shifted to the Unionist party. Some of its members were in open rupture ; the Duke of Devonshire had gone so far in December as to advise Free Trade Unionists among the electorate not to vote for a Unionist, if he were a Tariff Reformer. Many others, less decided in their attitude, asked with growing impatience what leadership they were under. They found a suspended judgment, which was Mr Balfour's official state of mind, impossible to present to their constituents as a policy. Were they to follow Mr Chamberlain ? But in that case their duty in the division lobbies would often be most obscure. Some even came to asking themselves, if they did not ask publicly, whether Mr Chamberlain's genius was of the egoistic kind that must inevitably cut sooner or later across his party. He had borne a prominent share in the shattering division of one side ; he had now divided the other. There was an echo of many thoughts in *Punch's* quotation of the text : "Had Zimri peace, who slew his master ? " [1]

A little less idealistic, but not a whit less resolute, Mr Chamberlain continued to urge on the fray. Early in the new year was published a list of persons who had consented to act as a commission to investigate depressed industries, and to draw up a suggested tariff. It contained several well-known names—Sir Alfred Jones, the ship-

[1] *Punch*, 17th June 1903.

owner; Sir Alexander Henderson, a railway chairman; Sir Vincent Caillard, banker and financier; Sir W. T. Lewis, the coalowner; Mr Charles Parsons, inventor of the turbine engine; Sir Robert Herbert, formerly Under-Secretary for the Colonies; Mr W. H. Grenfell, athlete and squire. The rest were mostly business men of some eminence in their business, but not known to the world. On 19th January Mr Chamberlain spoke in the City of London on the theme that our supremacy in banking, which the Free Traders attributed to our being the great open market of the world, and therefore the centre of bills of exchange and all the apparatus of commercial credit, must fall away, if our industrial supremacy fell.

If he had miscalculated the task he had undertaken, these opening days of the new year must have given him his lesson. At a by-election in the Ashburton division of Devonshire the Liberal majority was doubled; at Norwich, in spite of a split vote, the Liberal candidate won the seat from the Conservatives by a majority of 1800. Nor could there be much doubt as to the cause of these events; nothing but the tariff question counted in politics for the moment. Another question was ripening which, within a few months, was also to be a weapon in the hands of Liberal candidates. The Transvaal made its choice in the labour question. Its mind was changed. In November 1903 intimations had reached England that "South Africa had gradually reconciled itself to the Chinaman"; but American experience showed that he could not come in as a simple immigrant; he must be under rigid contract.[1] In December the Legislative Council of the Transvaal had adopted Sir George's Farrar's motion for the importation under indenture of unskilled Asiatic labourers. In January 1904 the Draft Ordinance was out. The imported labour was to be confined to the Rand; the labourers were to carry passports, renewed annually; were not to be allowed

[1] *The Times*, 13th November 1903.

to settle permanently in the country, or to mix with the rest of the population ; and were not to move outside the ground allotted to them except by permit lasting only for forty-eight hours.   The means by which public opinion in South Africa, which only a year before was holding mass meetings of protest against the Chinaman, had been converted were not difficult to perceive.   Prosperity in the last resort depended on the Rand.   Agriculture could only get under way very slowly after the dislocation of the war ; and even when restored to activity could absorb but a limited amount of labour, and produce but a limited revenue.   The mines, now that their machinery was re-newed, could open almost at a word the stream of wealth. It rested with the mine-owners to dictate the word ; and they dictated " Chinamen."   Once they had carried their point in South Africa, they had a short way with the home Government.   Mr Chamberlain had said that he neither could nor would interfere with local opinion ; and Mr Lyttleton held himself bound by this promise.   The mine-owners used it as a virtual settlement of the question ; and before the home Government had had the Draft Ordinance a month in its hands they were demanding of Lord Milner that he should press for its instant ratification. There were certainly dangers ahead.   Mr Seddon, Premier of New Zealand, had proposed to the other colonies a formal united protest against this flouting of their experi-ence and their determined policy towards Chinese labour. If the protest took shape, it would be an odd commentary on Mr Chamberlain's imperialistic ideals to have the home Government vacillating between the opinion of one colony and the opinion of all the others.   Moreover the Liberals were arousing feeling at home.   Had we endured the war, with all its cost in British lives and British money, to see the Rand mines full of labour that was not British in the remotest sense of the word, and a peculiarly depraved form of labour ?   Meetings of protest were taking place all over England.   Even the House of Lords had witnessed the expression of some uneasiness about the moral aspects of the strict indenturing.   But by taking their stand on Mr Chamberlain's words the mine-owners put themselves ahead of dangers ; and on 12th March it was announced that the Ordinance had been allowed.   Another by-election was going on at the moment in East Dorset.   This question was made by the Liberal candidate as prominent as Free Trade, and another Unionist seat was lost.   Men began to look at the Opposition, and speculate on the quality of material in it for forming a ministry.

In January the long trial of Mr Whittaker Wright reached its end ; but the end was more terrible than the law could make it.   The preliminary hearings had occupied many sittings before a King's Bench judge during the autumn.   No ordinary person, as has been said, could pretend to follow the intricacies of the methods by which Mr Whittaker Wright had arranged the balance sheets of his various companies for the annual meeting of each ; but transfer of shares among them was the root of the methods. The trial ended on 26th January, in a sentence of seven years' penal servitude.   But the evening papers announcing this were still on the printing press when the information came that, while waiting in a room at the Law Courts, after the sentence, for removal to prison, Mr Wright had apparently had a seizure of some kind, and was dead.   The inquest proved that he had killed himself.   It was a story of extraordinary calmness and determination.   A loaded and cocked revolver was discovered on the body ; but the death was due to poison.   He had been able to find an occasion for giving himself cyanide of potassium, and had then gone on talking for a few minutes, perfectly quietly, to his solicitor and a friend.   He had been smoking a cigar, and as he asked for another he fell from his chair, and was dead before a doctor could be brought to him.   He had had ten years of wealth and of power in the City ; and he had been even more dazzling in his period of success than other company promoters.   He had set about building a colossal house on a Surrey hill, and his billiard-room, with a glass ceiling under a lake, so that the roof seemed to be of water, became a standing example of fantastic extravagance and the craziness of sudden riches.   A footnote to the trial is that Mr Rufus Isaacs finally established his reputation at the Bar ; he moved through the intricate mass of figures with unfaltering skill.   It was asserted that, if the Judge put to him a question about some item in a balance sheet which had been mentioned weeks before, Mr Rufus Isaacs could answer at once, without reference to his papers.

Before the House met, a new line of army reform had been entered upon.   A small committee, consisting of Lord Esher, Admiral Sir John Fisher and General Sir George Sydenham Clarke, had drawn up a scheme for reconstituting the War Office on the model of the Board of Admiralty, according to the Royal Commission's recommendation.[1] The Commander-in-Chief was to be abolished, and an Army Council of four military members, with the parliamentary heads of the department, was to take his place. Commands were to be decentralised, and unity was to be given by the creation of an Inspector-General. A Board of Selection was to control promotions.   Finally, the Committee of Defence, which Mr Balfour had constructed in 1903 on a basis of permanence to replace the Committee of the Cabinet, which had been the first experiment in this direction, was given a staff of a secretary and some ten officers of either service.   The new Army Council was composed of Mr Arnold Forster, Secretary of State, Lord Donoughmore, Parliamentary Under-Secretary, and Mr Bromley Davenport, Financial Secretary ; General Lyttelton, General Douglas, General Plumer and General Wolfe Murray.   Sir Edward Ward was appointed Secretary to the Council, and to the Committee of Defence.   The

1 See page 634.

Duke of Connaught became Inspector-General and President of the Board of Selection. The new broom had in four months swept Mr Brodrick and his army corps clean out of the office. It was on the whole a good start. The council represented both the older generation among army commanders and the new generation, which had come home in such a bewildering batch of very young generals from South Africa. Sir Edward Ward, the one man who had acquired a thoroughly business reputation in the war, was hailed as eminently in his right place. The Duke of Connaught was known as a plain, keen soldier ; and his presidency of the Board of Selection promised an end to private influences in promotion. The looser organisation of local commands, in place of the tight machinery of army corps, would provide a better means of employing the young generals. With no little relief, the country decided that it had at last a reform worth leaving to itself for trial, and removed the subject from everlasting discussion. The old Duke of Cambridge just lived to hear of the new ideas. He died on 17th March. He had never been a friend to the remodelling of our military notions, and had stood actively in the way of some earlier attempts. But that could be passed over now ; and there was much on the positive side to remember. He had been devoted to the army ; and, after all, no scientific methods and no reorganisation would be of much use if his example in that respect were forgotten.

There was so much on the parliamentary *tapis* that the army could well be allowed a little peace. The debate on the Address gave an early opportunity for harrying the Government on the fiscal question ; and in division on an amendment moved by Mr Morley the Ministerial majority dropped to fifty-one—half its normal size. Mr Lloyd George showed in this debate that his reputation was not going to rest solely on his attacks upon Mr Chamberlain during the war, or his skill in the Education Bill debates. He could be slashing enough on the Free Trade side at public meetings (he had just denounced the Tariff Reform campaign as " the inauguration of an era of universal loot "), but he could also make a Unionist minister refer to his speech on this amendment as the only speech really dealing with the question.[1] Mr Chamberlain was at the moment abroad. He had had an exhausting winter, and had just lost, by the death of Mr Powell Williams, a friend of many years. The Opposition were in high feather, Lord Rosebery making gay speeches to the Liberal League, and Sir Henry Campbell-Bannerman and the Radical stalwarts sharing the enjoyment. The by-elections greatly inspirited them. Besides those already mentioned, there had been one in Scotland, for the Ayr Burghs ; and although Mr George Younger, the Unionist candidate, entirely repudiated Tariff Reform, the Liberals captured the seat. The signs of a turn of the tide could not be mistaken.

The session promised increased ground for fighting. The Government had decided to introduce a Licensing Bill, and Mr Balfour advised magistrates to await amendment of the law before proceeding with reduction of licences. The Bill introduced a system of compensation for licences refused on other grounds than those of misconduct. A fund was to be raised in each quarter sessions area, by a graduated levy on licences. The quarter sessions area was selected, rather than the brewster sessions area, in order to make the fund large enough to meet considerable cases. From this fund compensation was to be paid calculated on the basis of the death duties that would have been chargeable on the property as licensed premises, deducting the value of them if unlicensed. The principle of the Bill was that, whatever may have been the original theory of licensing, the practice of the justices had led to the establishment of a reasonable expectation

[1] *The Times,* 16th February 1904.

of renewal, except in cases of misconduct. Licences had
thereby acquired a recognised value ; they paid death
duties, and, while the State assessed a value for this
purpose, it could not deny it by reverting to a purely
annual basis for licences. But once the question had
been raised, new licences might be prevented from acquiring that value (the phrase " monopoly value " was coined
at this time), by imposing such duties that the value
reverted instantly to the public purse. Compensation
would not therefore be recoverable for new licences.
Liberals opened a broadside attack. The Bill destroyed
the unfettered discretion of the justices under the Sharp
v. Wakefield decision, substituting a system of reduction
limited by the amount of the compensation fund. It
placed the fund on such a wide area that the justices'
dealings with their own district were controlled by conditions in other districts. It abolished the power to
affix conditions to the renewal of licences—a kind of
reform in which the Liverpool justices had been notably
active, securing the abolition of back-door entrances to
public-houses, and of the serving of drink to children.
But the main attack went to the root of the Bill. Compensation on these terms was not only a recognition of the
growth of a vested interest, but the permanent establishment in law of such an interest. Liberals and the mass
of temperance reformers did not attempt to deny that the
general practice of renewal had led to the growth of an
interest ; but they maintained that justice could be met
by giving notice that, at the end of a certain period, the
annual nature of the licence would be reasserted ; during
that period the trade should readjust itself by mutual
insurance to meet the new conditions, and, if a licence
was taken away before that time had elapsed, a sum of
money should be paid, as it were, in lieu of warning.
Compensation in the Government's Bill had not this
meaning. As Sir Robert Reid put it in one of the debates

on the Bill : " Compensation had been offered as a compromise, and accepted as a principle." The Liberal attack on the Bill therefore concentrated itself on proposals to limit the payment of compensation to a certain period ; seven, fourteen or twenty-one years were offered in different amendments. When lost in the House of Commons, these amendments reappeared in the House of Lords, where they had strong support from the Bench of Bishops ; but they met with no better fate.

The truth was that the interest in licences was not merely the interest of " the trade " in its narrower sense. The great brewery flotations of the eighties [1] had spread the interest over the whole community. Licensed premises had become, by the policy of buying houses, the largest asset in the balance sheets of brewing firms. Prices for them had risen enormously in the competition, and the defeat of Local Veto in 1895 had sent them still higher. Anything that put these values in doubt would have shaken the stability of every brewing company in the kingdom. The Liberal position was that deflation of the over-capitalised could not be allowed to weigh as an argument ; and that the sound firms could, within a time limit, achieve the necessary readjustments. The strength of the Government's case lay really in a general feeling that the justices' movement for the reduction of licences, successful though it had been in various districts, was bound before long to meet with checks. It rested on legal decisions which, technically indeed quite sound, did not wholly satisfy popular ideas of fairness. When refusal of renewals had passed beyond operations in such places as Farnham, with its obvious disproportion of licences to population,[2] and came to deal with districts in which the ideas of temperance reformers would less easily coincide with ordinary views of what might be

1 See page 230.

2 See page 613.

permitted, reduction of licences would either be stopped,
or only carried out at the cost of irritation and an appearance of grandmotherliness.　The licensing situation after
the decision in Sharp *v.* Wakefield may not unreasonably
be compared with the case of higher education after the
Cockerton judgment.[1]　In both cases the law, when set
in motion, trapped customary practice ; and the average
man did not approve of such uses of the law.　His inclination in both cases was to stand by custom, and correct
the letter of the law.　The justices' movement, if left to
proceed by itself, would inevitably have become in time
as impossible to pursue as a policy of continual Cockerton
audits would have been.　If the Government had accepted
even the longest time limit for payment of compensation
the Licensing Bill would have had little real opposition
from any quarter except the Prohibitionist core of the
temperance party.　As it was, the closure had to be
drastically applied before the Bill passed into law.

For the rest, the session was tame.　The Budget was
not one to restore the failing hold of the Government.
Trade was much better, and the Stock Exchange, in spite
of the welter of war stock, and a steady fall in Consols
in place of the expected rise after the war, was hopeful.
But the revenue was no less than two and three-quarters
millions below the estimate, a melancholy state of things
for a young and untried Chancellor of the Exchequer.
There was no novelty in the Budget proposals.　Mr Austen
Chamberlain just re-imposed one of the pence on the
income-tax of which the taxpayer had rejoiced to be rid
in the previous year, and put twopence on the tea-tax.

A Penal Servitude Bill was introduced, in which there
were traces of the influence of Sir Robert Anderson's
theories.[2]　It recognised the argument for long periods
of detention in the case of habitual criminals, and

1 See page 559.
2 See page 580.

recognised also that judges reasonably shrank from long
sentences of absolute penal servitude on other than the
most serious charges. The Bill proposed, therefore, to
empower judges to order that part of a long sentence
should be served in a place of detention for habitual
offenders, where penal servitude was not exacted. This
was a compromise quite ineffective from Sir Robert
Anderson's point of view; to him the detention of an
habitual offender was useless unless it was for life. The
Bill in the end was dropped. It could not have been very
fortunately pressed forward at a time when the police
administration was gravely called in question by the
case of Adolf Beck. This man had been arrested in 1895
on suspicion of having defrauded various women; and
having been "identified" by the usual processes as a
man named Smith, previously convicted for similar
offences, was sentenced to seven years' penal servitude.
He protested his innocence, and while in prison was able
by certain physical facts to prove that he was not Smith;
but it was nevertheless believed that the women who
charged him with fraud had at any rate recognised him
as the defrauder in the present cases. He was therefore
made to serve out his sentence. In April 1904 he was
again arrested on similar charges, and convicted, again
protesting his innocence. The judge, remembering that
identification in the earlier case had been shown to have
overreached its object, postponed sentence. Before the
case was brought up again, a man came under arrest who
was proved to be the original Smith; and the "identification" of Beck in both the trials he had undergone was
revealed as completely fallacious. The Home Office
offered Beck a sum of £2000 as compensation, and a
formal free pardon. He refused the offer, and demanded
a full investigation. A committee was appointed which
entirely established his innocence. It did not recommend, as many hoped that it would, the establishment

of a Court of Criminal Appeal ; but naturally the whole
affair revived the movement in favour of such a court.
Until it was established, public opinion was bound to be
shy of supporting the idea of prolonged detention for
habitual offenders when it had been shown that a man
who had committed no offence at all might be in imminent
danger of being classed as a habitual offender. The
finger-print system of identification had only been introduced into British police administration since 1900 ; and
most of that branch of the police work depended as yet
on more rough and ready methods.

Two other items of the session's work may be mentioned,
since they were the beginnings of new movements. One
was the statement made in April by the Colonial Secretary
as to experiments under official auspices with a view to
growing cotton in West Africa. For some time there had
been discontent among the Lancashire spinners at their
dependence upon the American market, and the subjection
of their requirements to purely speculative operations.
This year operations of that kind had been peculiarly
marked, Mr Sully having attempted a huge/ gamble.
He failed, but the affair gave a great impulse to the
movement for British cotton-growing ; and experiments
were now made in Southern Nigeria, Lagos and Sierra
Leone. The other matter was the Aliens Bill. Springing
from various causes—from the investigations into sweated
labour, from the processions of the unemployed, from
fear of anarchistic socialism, and now from the movement
for protecting industries—an outcry had arisen against
unchecked immigration. No other country in the world
permitted it ; and the question was asked why we alone
should admit foreigners without any stipulation as to
their past record or their present ability to maintain
themselves decently. Appalling pictures were given
of quarters of the East End from which native-born
inhabitants had entirely withdrawn before an invasion

of foreigners with a low standard of living, who swarmed in the poor houses, produced unhealthy conditions, and undercut the wages market. For the present, the controversy remained rather vague.

The Tariff Reform campaign seemed to have produced something of the effect aimed at by the apostles of efficiency. The subject was serious, yet the nation took to it ardently, and did not tire of it. True, it is necessary to record in this year one of the most childlike crazes of our period. Some weekly papers, ever inventing new attractions for readers, hit upon the boyishness of grown-up people by announcing that metal discs had been concealed in certain spots, the neighbourhood being more or less obscurely indicated, which would entitle the finders to a sum of money. This " treasure-hunting " developed into an astonishing nuisance. In vain the papers concerned kept on stating that the discs were not on private property, and were not buried. Men with a regular *Treasure Island* fever upon them invaded the front gardens of inoffensive citizens, and grubbed up the flower beds ; dodged the park-keepers in order to tear up the turf of public parks ; quarrelled violently with other treasure hunters who had worked out the given indications in the same way and pitched upon the same point. The moment a man began to probe a spot a crowd instantly collected, on the chance that he might have guessed the spot rightly, but might not be the first to discover the disc. After all, except for the injured owners of suburban gardens, it was an engaging manifestation of ingenuousness in the sophisticated Londoner. Unfortunately London lost this year the man who was beginning to reveal the suburbs, Dan Leno. He had invented a new music hall convention ; he relieved his audiences of the everlasting bar loafer, and gave them instead the man behind the counter of a suburban shop, the landlady of the suburbs, the museum attendant—

a host of lower middle-class figures rendered in all their bland unconsciousness. He made genuine low comedy.

In the summer Colonel Younghusband's advance into Thibet caught the popular imagination. The Indian Government had decided to obtain a definite footing in Thibet, and an expedition was sent of no threatening size. The Dalai Lama, the ruling authority in Lhassa, refused a passage to the mission; but patient methods were pursued, and, though there was some opposition on the road, there was no very serious fighting. The Dalai Lama fled, and the Tashi Lama, who was known to be more friendly, was left in authority. The British expedition reached Lhassa on 3rd August, and another of the great secrets of the world was unveiled. The Imperial City of Pekin had four years earlier been entered by Europeans; and now the greater mystery was opened. The expedition had to wait some time for a satisfactory end to its work. Thibet professed itself under the suzerainty of China, and awaited China's sanction to a treaty of commerce permitting the establishment of British trading posts. The treaty was signed about a month later.

Russia, the still-dreaded influence on the northern frontiers of India, was too busily engaged elsewhere to take any hand in this matter. At the end of 1903 her relations with Japan had been growing very strained. Japan, regarding Russia's advance in Manchuria, had reason to suspect the establishment of Russian influence over Korea. This would have been too threatening an approach. She demanded from Russia reassurances as to Korea, the acknowledgement of the territorial integrity of Korea and the Chinese Empire, and equal rights of trade. Failing to get them, she declared war. The comparative size of the countries made it appear the struggle of a man against a giant; but the Japanese had for years been perfecting their warlike resources on a European basis, and were believed to be a model of efficiency. They soon began to prove it. In February they sank several Russian battleships of the Port Arthur squadron. In April their forces carried the Ya-lu River against a vast Russian army ; and were making dispositions for attacking Port Arthur itself. In their turn they lost some warships by the action of floating mines. British sympathy was throughout with the Japanese. An extraordinary incident of the autumn produced the further element of active resentment against Russia. The Russian fleet in the Far East had been reduced to uselessness ; the ships that had not been sunk were blockaded in the harbour of Port Arthur. The Russian fleet in the Baltic was therefore ordered to the East, and left Kronstadt, under the command of Admiral Rozhdestvensky, at the end of August. It lingered about the Baltic for some time, and was not really on its way until October. Suddenly, on 23rd October, England was astounded to hear that the Hull fishing fleet had put into that port, with a tale of having been heavily fired upon by the Russian ships. A night or two earlier, while they were at their fishing in the North Sea, they had perceived the approach of a fleet. All at once searchlights were turned upon them, the warships opened fire, one trawler had been sunk, two others riddled with shot, and—most serious of all—two men had been killed, and sixteen wounded. The dead bodies, both of them headless, were brought back to England.

A storm of fury swept over the nation. The affair looked like a gratuitous piece of dastardly bullying. Men from the fleet were brought up to London on the day following their return, a Sunday, and crowds thronged about them. They were taken to the Foreign Office on the Monday, to give their evidence. The King, telegraphing his sympathy with the widows and the injured men, used the phrase, exceedingly strong for one in his position,

" unwarrantable action." Public opinion demanded that
a British fleet should instantly be despatched after the
Russian ships, which had by this time gone down the Bay
of Biscay, and should arrest them, by force, if necessary,
in the Mediterranean. Nor is there any doubt that some
such course would have been pursued, had not the Russian
Government made immediately the amends dictated to it.
It apologised in set terms, detained at Vigo that part of the
fleet which had been responsible for the firing, paid liberal
compensation, and agreed to an inquiry by an International
Commission under The Hague Convention. It appeared
that the Russians' defence of their action was that they
had reason to suspect that Japan had sent torpedo boats
to waylay their fleet, and they believed they saw torpedo
boats lurking among the trawlers. This dispelled the
appearance of mere wantonness in the firing ; but left a
rather scornful opinion of the Intelligence Department
that was directing the Russian fleet. By the end of the
year the Japanese were closing on Port Arthur, having
captured one of the most important hills among its out-
works ; and firing from that hill over the town they sank
the Port Arthur squadron at its moorings.

In the quick settlement of the North Sea incident
England certainly owed something to the support she had
from Russia's ally, France. So rapidly had events moved
since the Boer War, when we were on acrid terms with the
whole Continent, that in 1904 France and Great Britain
were in a position only just short of formal alliance. In the
popular estimation, this was largely due to King Edward.
He liked the French, and they liked him. He had a
wonderful gift of being able to keep on terms not only with
the aristocracy in Paris, but with the Republic as well.
It was believed that his genial presence, and his conversations with the President of the Republic, had paved the
way quickly, so that in April of this year a formal agreement was signed. It was on lines of definite recognition of

policy. We agreed to recognise French interests in Morocco, and they to recognise ours in Egypt ; we undertook not to alter the political status of Egypt, and they undertook to cease to ask for a fixed time for our withdrawal, and to leave us freer in dealing with Egyptian revenue surpluses.[1] There were other items of mutual recognition, but these were the chief. The completion of the great irrigation dam at Assouan, which had been formally inaugurated by the Khedive in December 1902, promised new wealth to Egypt ; and English people felt that they had earned the acknowledgment of their rights in the guidance of that country. With Germany, meanwhile, our relations remained very guarded. King Edward visited the German Emperor at Kiel in June, and the German fleet visited Plymouth a week or two later ; but it was not likely that on the morrow of the agreement with France there would be much cordiality in these meetings. The French Foreign Minister, M. Delcassé, gave signs of rather assertive views of French expansion. Besides, definite naval rivalry on our part with Germany was growing more marked ; " No phantom as to German aggression haunts us, but it is our duty to watch the progress of German naval power." [2] The British Admiralty was in energetic hands. Sir John Fisher became First Sea Lord, and the fleets were being reorganised on a basis of commissioned squadrons with reserve ships manned by nucleus crews ; four powerful cruiser squadrons were formed to be attached to the fleets ; and homogeneity of ships in each battle or cruiser squadron was the object in view. The year gave a grim intimation that submarines had brought into the navy a service which would never have the safety of peace time : Submarine A1 was sunk with all hands off the Nab lightship in March.

The army manœuvres of the year must be mentioned, because they showed the new spirit of reform in the un-

1 See page 398.

2 *The Times*, 1st July 1904.

usually practical shape they took. Troops were conveyed
in transports to the Essex coast, and the manœuvres were
designed on the scheme of an invasion. They proved rather
more costly than instructive. In December began the
rearming of the artillery which the Boer War had shown
to be very necessary ; the new quick-firing guns—a 12½-
pounder for the Horse Artillery, and an 18½-pounder for
the Field Artillery—were believed to be really efficient.

Church affairs for once provided something almost like
a popular interest. The case of the Free Church of Scotland
was, indeed, in its reality as far as possible removed from
the popular mind of England. Only in Scotland could
a public be found hard-headed enough and sufficiently
grounded in ecclesiastical controversy to follow the terrific
metaphysical arguments before the House of Lords. The
majority of the Free Church had in 1900 come to terms of
union with the United Presbyterians, healing the famous
breach of an earlier day. A minority of the Free Church
—a small minority, the " Wee Frees " their countrymen
called them—denied the right of the majority to consider
this the end of the Free Church as a separate body, and
claimed all the material goods of the Church. The Edinburgh Court of Session decided against them, on the broad
ground that to refuse to acknowledge the majority must
hamper religious growth. The House of Lords, however,
pinning itself strictly and heroically to the pure metaphysics
of faith, upheld the Wee Frees, and put them in possession
of something like four millions of property. This at least
was real to the English public, and it took a kind of sporting
interest in the decision. The Church of England remained
successful in avoiding the deep ritual controversy ; Dr
Wace, who had become Dean of Canterbury in succession
to Dr Farrar in 1903, followed up the Round Table Conference by proposing that the basis of ritual practice should
be the established uses of the Christian Church in the first
six centuries of its existence. Compromise lay in too

delicate a balance to be capable of accurate adjustments like this. Militant Church energy was for the moment engrossed chiefly in the region of education. Radical county councils in Wales, not content with passive resistance, were so applying their powers as to render it unlikely that Church schools under their control would obtain any funds from the rates. On the other hand, the Government was wounded in the house of its friends when the Church Schools Emergency League publicly resented a circular of the Board of Education which intimated that school time-tables allotting time for the children's attendance at church would not be sanctioned. The insistence of the league in such a matter was exactly the kind of sectarian spirit which Unionists did not want in the foreground; it went no small distance towards justifying Nonconformist refusal to pay rates for Church schools. The Board of Education was vigorously directed now, having been largely reconstituted under the Act of 1902, and placed under a secretary brought in from outside the regular Civil Service—Mr Robert Morant.

The growing strength of new movements in art and new standards of appreciation was revealed by the inquiry this year into the administration of the Chantrey Trust. The money, left by Sir Francis Chantrey to the Royal Academy, for the purchase of the best current work year by year in England, was never expended outside the walls of the Academy, although that had long ago ceased to be the only great public exhibition of pictures and sculpture. Moreover its disposal inside the Academy was bitterly criticised. A House of Lords committee was set up and art critics girded their loins for a joyous fray. It was a little more joyous than they had bargained for; they met in Lord Carlisle, himself an artist of no mean reputation, a very doughty defender of the management of the trust, and, as he was also a wit, the crossing of swords was remarkably brisk.

The interest in the Tariff controversy was, as has been said, extraordinarily maintained. Mr Chamberlain spoke in August at Welbeck, coming to closer quarters now with the agricultural interest, which had been postponed at first to industrial interests. They were not very close quarters. He tended in the main to plead that agriculture and manufacture should not be regarded as in " water-tight compartments " ; what was good for the one would help the other. He did not put forward his two-shilling corn-duty as a protection to agriculture, because it was of the essence of the Tariff Reform League's recommendation of the scheme in towns that the tax would be insufficient to raise the price of bread. But a population more generally in employment must, he said, mean better prices for the agriculturist, and more stimulus to organisation by co-operative marketing, land banks, etc. The speech rather added to, than diminished, the openings for attack by the Free Traders. The tide still set in their direction. They had won a seat at Devonport in June by a majority of over 1000, and in the same month increased their former majority in the Market Harborough division ; at a by-election in the Chertsey division of Surrey, a thoroughly Unionist neighbourhood, though they failed to capture the seat, they halved the Unionist majority. At a by-election in the Thanet division of Kent, several leading Unionists had signed the Liberal candidate's nomination papers. It was no wonder that a speech by Mr Balfour at Edinburgh in October was looked upon as a distinct sign of " hedging." He repudiated any Protectionist intentions—his proposals were not Protectionist. You could protect industries against the attack of foreign governments, delivered by such means as the bounty and drawback systems, without protecting them against honest manufacturing competition. But what caused most stir was his statement that, if the Unionists were again returned to power, they would consider it their duty to call a Colonial conference before

P

proposing a tariff; and he implied that that tariff would be referred to another general election before it was enforced. This looked very much like a shelving of Colonial preference indefinitely, Liberals asserting roundly that, when it came to details at a conference, no tariff would ever be drawn up to command adhesion.   Moreover, Mr Chamberlain had been involved so deeply in the Protectionist accretions on his original scheme that Mr Balfour's remarks might mean a parting of the ways.   But Mr Chamberlain, speaking soon afterwards at Luton, the centre of the straw-hat industry, in pursuit of his campaign on particular manufactures, welcomed Mr Balfour's declaration.   The suggestion may be offered that the difficulty which many people felt in understanding Mr Balfour's position arose largely from the modern habit of keeping a very short memory for public affairs.   This was due to the enormous increase of newspaper-reading.   With the whole world brought freshly to their breakfast-tables each day by the incessant activities of the telegraph, men lost much of their sense of continuity; editors could hardly publish a paragraph on some affair of a month or a fortnight previously without a footnote to explain the references.   One of the most curious features of Mr Chamberlain's campaign was the fact that it presented itself to the great majority of the people as a wholly new idea.   It would not, perhaps, have been surprising that a younger generation should forget the " Fair Trade " movement of the early eighties.[1] But it might reasonably surprise Mr Balfour that the country should so soon have forgotten the financial discussions which immediately preceded Mr Chamberlain's famous speech in May 1903.[2]   From several points of view, as we have seen, Unionists were then approaching a determination to reconsider the customs tariff.   Moreover, for years past the Budget had always been accom-

[1] See pages 57, 171.
[2] See page 622.

panied by comments on the obvious discrepancy between an increasing national turnover in trade and a perpetual liability to deficits in the public revenue.[1] Mr Balfour continued, in fact, to maintain the attitude occupied by most of his party, and by not a few of the opposite party, before Mr Chamberlain's formulation of these tentative reconsiderations into a set fiscal policy.   It is true that the launching of this policy would have cast suspicion upon any attempt to return even to the wider, yet historically " Free Trade " tariff of thirty or forty years earlier ; and to that extent Mr Balfour's continuity of opinion had been falsified.   But it was not fair to him that people should think of his position as one taken up scramblingly in response to Mr Chamberlain's movement. It was naturally capable of approximation to that move-ment ; if the tariff was to be widened, the possibilities of retaliation against foreign duties, and of Colonial preference, might easily be taken into account.   There was, however, nothing either incomprehensible or insincere in Mr Balfour's assertions that his was not a Protectionist policy; or in his refusal to sever himself from Mr Chamberlain.   He represented exactly the development of Exchequer policy that would in all probability have taken place if Tariff Reform had not created a distrust of any extension of the list of dutiable articles.   That the course of development was considerably modified by the new campaign was not any reason for allowing a wedge to be driven by opponents between himself and Mr Chamberlain.

Even on the Unionist side there would have been some relief if a wedge could have been driven.   The party, as a parliamentary entity, did not know where it stood. Mr Balfour professed adherence to a policy of inquiry, followed, in the event of victory at the next election, by a Colonial conference, but without intention of deliberately

1 See pages 483, 593.

protecting industry. But then Mr Chamberlain, who was dealing with industry after industry, lamenting its accomplished or approximate downfall, and implying that his scheme would arrest the process, was publicly welcoming Mr Balfour's words. Many would have rested content with a policy of inquiry, little inspiriting though it was as a programme of leadership. But they could not escape the feeling that they were really being hustled to something much more definite, and would awake to find that, pursuing Mr Balfour, they had somehow come up with Mr Chamberlain. Was either of them really in command? Had not the Tariff Reform League taken charge ? They saw one of their soberest newspapers, *The Standard*, pass into the hands of Mr Pearson, an avowed Protectionist, and a prominent member of the Tariff Commission ; they heard rumours (promptly denied, it must be added) that even *The Times* might change hands. The ground seemed uncertain beneath their feet. The Unionist party organisation had definitely taken the step of allegiance to Mr Chamberlain, as against the Duke of Devonshire, who had attempted to maintain its original character as a body concerned with Irish legislation. As it happened, events in that connection towards the end of the year still further shook the Ministerialists. Lord Dunraven put forward, rather suddenly, a suggestion for "Legislative Devolution," which involved setting up a local legislature in Dublin to deal with Irish business, while avoiding matters of Imperial concern. It could hardly be regarded as anything but Home Rule under another name. Yet it came from a Unionist peer ; and what made it more serious was that Sir Antony Macdonnell, who at the end of a distinguished career in India had been appointed Under-Secretary for Ireland by Mr George Wyndham, was known to be concerned in the scheme, at least to the extent of advocating a financial "devolution." Mr Wyndham hastened to declare that the party was still " against any multiplication of legislative bodies." But there remained an uncomfortable feeling that some sort of coquetting with Home Rule was going on ; and it added gravely to the party's embarrassment and uneasiness. If Mr Chamberlain, as appeared by his action in the matter of the Liberal Unionist Association, put his present campaign in a position which overruled the old meaning of the association, could that meaning be said to have any vitality at all ?

For the most part the Unionist Free Traders refused to be excommunicated, and fought for their own hand. One of them, who had now come definitely into the front rank, Mr Winston Churchill, declined an equivocal standing, and joined the Liberals. He had previously shown himself almost too democratic for the other side ; and had been warned of his tendency to pursue " the somewhat devious paths by which his father climbed to power." [1] Before the notable new recruit joined them, Liberals lost a veteran from among their leaders. Sir William Harcourt, who had just inherited the family property at Nuneham, and, hoping for repose in that peaceful place, had intimated that he would not stand another election, died rather suddenly before he could attain his hope. His career had at the moment the melancholy aspect of frustration. His last years were belittled by the perpetual appearance of jealousy between him and Lord Rosebery, from the time when Lord Rosebery, and not he, had been sent for by the Queen in succession to Mr Gladstone. He was loyal to the true Gladstonianism in his attitude throughout the war ; but he was also Gladstonian in regard to modern social movements, and never understood the position of labour. Still, he might have led the party, but for a certain overbearing habit of mind ; it came out even in the long lectures which he read the Church of England on ritual subjects. Colleagues often found it difficult to work with him, and shrank from the prospect of working under him.

[1] *The Times,* 14th August 1903.

It remained his greatest glory to have achieved the one strikingly original conception of his time in national finance. The Death Duties of his Budget of 1894 had established themselves firmly in our fiscal system, and never failed in their productiveness.

CHAPTER XI

1905 : ACADEMIC DISCUSSION

THE winter was a bad one for workmen. A grave lack of employment set in, and so much distress had been anticipated that a conference was held at the Local Government Board in the autumn of 1904. Relief works, as such, were not favoured ; the conference devoted itself rather to devising schemes of intercommunication between local authorities, whereby any openings elsewhere might be made known in congested districts. The suggestion was made that any work projected by a local authority should be hurried forward, so as to absorb some labour during the distressed period. This constituted an attempt at least to arrive at a new formulation of the problem of the unemployed. Labour had little mobility ; and once it became congested in certain areas it was helpless. At the same time the ordinary processes of trade, using labour as raw material was used, were apt to set loose floating masses of it. A few firms made deliberate efforts to hold their workers together. Some years previously Messrs Cadbury had built a model village at Bourneville, near Birmingham, for the employees in their cocoa-works ; and in 1904 Messrs Rowntree had done the same thing at New Earswick, near York. These were regarded as rather philanthropic than business methods ; but when Messrs Lever, the soap manufacturers, built a model village at Port Sunlight, near Liverpool, it looked as if the decasualisation of labour might have a real business value in enhancing the energy, steadiness and intelligence of employees. The promoters of the Garden City Movement now put forward the possibility of transferring large works to the country, and thereby relieving town congestions. The garden city idea had gained its first strength from the middle-class reaction towards a country life.[1] But inherent in it was the belief that healthier conditions, and the decentralisation made possible by railway services, would help the efficiency of industry. These, however, were long-range attacks upon the problem. For the present, the bulk of the difficulty fell back upon the Central Unemployed Committee in London, which managed to find employment for 6000 men. An attempt was made this year to deal with the matter by legislation ; a Bill was passed proposing to set up bodies, half-way between the Poor Law Guardians and private charity, which should provide work on farm colonies (an acknowledgment of Mr Joseph Fels's ideas) without the disqualification attaching to poor relief.

The unemployed were a standing argument for the Tariff Reform movement. True, it was one of the wide arguments which on either side irritated opponents by their facility. The Free Traders' contrast between the big loaf and the little loaf was resented by the Tariff Reformers ; the latter's argument that retaliatory duties would provide " work for all " was equally resented by the Free Traders. Yet a political subject could hardly be rampant on every platform in the kingdom without producing these sweeping generalisations. Behind them acute brains were at work ; no question has ever been argued better in England. The most fundamental aspects of commerce were unearthed. Did Protection actually create trade, or only affect distribution ? Did Free Trade tend to the abolition of elementary forms of manufacture in favour of the more advanced and skilled forms ? Was not the phrase " invisible exports " merely another way of saying that we paid for the surplus of our imports in cash, instead of in exports that had given

1 See page 576.

employment ?   Was it, on the other hand, possible in the
last resort to pay (whatever the material of payment) in
anything but work ?   If we cut down our imports from
a foreign nation, did we, or did we not, thereby destroy
work that would have paid for those imports ?   Of equal
value with this seriousness of argument was the wholly
new importance given to the interpretation of returns and
statistics.   The monthly returns of the Board of Trade
appeared beyond all cavilling prosperous.   But the
figures of our trade were given in pounds sterling, and a
rise in market prices might conceal a decline in volume of
output and therefore in labour.   The relations between
wages and cost of living, the proportion of re-exports to
the gross imports, the comparative figures of unemployment in this country and elsewhere, comparative prices
of means of life, comparative hours of work—all these,
and many other such points, were hotly debated.   From
the intricate transactions of a bill broker's office to the
making of pearl buttons no single stone in our commercial
structure was left unexamined.   On neither side were the
sweeping generalisations an outcome of laziness.

Yet, if no question had ever been so handsomely discussed in this country; none had ever placed party voters in
such a predicament as that now experienced by Unionists.
In the Home Rule split the two wings of Liberalism had
been led with determination in two clearly opposite directions.   In the later difficulties of Liberalism the Imperialists had frankly repudiated the party leader at the polls.
Unionists were now confronted with a situation in which
their leader was not repudiated, yet the policy which
Liberals were attacking was not the official policy of that
leader.   Mr Balfour had begun the year by refusing to
refer to the fiscal controversy in his speeches, leaving the
propaganda to Mr Chamberlain.   This attitude, since his
constituency was East Manchester, in the cradle of Free
Trade, made his meetings there so full of interruptions

that it was hard indeed to remember, in reading the reports, that they were meetings addressed by a Prime Minister. He abandoned his attitude so far as to produce in January, at one of his meetings, in response to a challenge by Mr Morley, the famous statement of his policy " on a half-sheet of notepaper." These were the contents of the half-sheet : " First, I desire such an alteration of our fiscal system as will give us a freedom of action impossible while we hold ourselves bound by the maxim that no taxation should be imposed except for revenue. It will strengthen our hands in any negotiations by which we may hope to lower foreign hostile tariffs. It may enable us to protect the fiscal independence of those colonies which desire to give us preferential treatment. It may be useful where we wish to check the importation of those foreign goods which, because they are bounty-fed or tariff-protected abroad, are sold below cost price here. Such importations are ultimately as injurious to the consumer as they are immediately ruinous to the producer. Secondly, I desire closer commercial union with the colonies, and I do so because I desire closer union in all its best modes, and because this particular mode is intrinsically of great importance, and has received much Colonial support. I also think it might procure great and growing advantages both to the colonies and to the Mother Country by promoting freer trade between them. No doubt such commercial union is beset with many difficulties. These can best be dealt with by a Colonial conference, provided its objects are permitted to be discussed unhampered by limiting instructions. Thirdly, I recommend, therefore, that the subject shall be referred to a conference on those terms. Fourth, and last, I do not desire to raise home prices for the purpose of aiding home production."

Mr Balfour could fairly assert that this document embodied all the prominent aspects of the question ; it included Colonial preference, retaliation against hostile

tariffs, and the prevention of " dumping " (as the importation of goods " below cost price " was called). Was it
not, then, a definite piece of leadership ? But nearly two
months elapsed before Mr Chamberlain and a conference
of Tariff Reformers decided on hearty acceptance of the
" half-sheet." This delay stimulated the feeling of
uncertainty, and made unreal the announcement of loyal
adhesion to Mr Balfour, when at last it was made. The
agitation against which the Liberals were working did not
desire the enunciation of our freedom from the maxim of
taxation for revenue ; it desired the imposition of a tariff.
It did not wish that tariff to be dependent on the decisions
of a Colonial conference. Unionists felt, rightly or
wrongly, that behind Mr Balfour's promises of consideration and inquiry they were being " rushed," and rushed
not so much by Mr Chamberlain as by an organisation
suspiciously packed with manufacturers. The questions
their constituents put to them were aimed at this organisation ; they had to reply from the wholly different plane
of Mr Balfour. He had manœuvred them into " dead
ground," where they could not respond to the enemy's
fire, but were peppered by their own shrapnel. It was
a wholly false relief when Mr Balfour, adopting the
attitude that debates on the subject in the House were
purely " academic," since the Government did not propose to take any steps, advised his party to abstain
from the division, and himself walked out. Certainly
divisions were not to be desired by the Government ;
on a motion by Mr Churchill against preferential duties
the Ministerial majority had fallen to forty-two.
Yet abstention from the lobbies, besides having the
absurd effect of placing on the Journals of the House
an unopposed decision against the programme which Mr
Balfour said he " desired," and which Mr Chamberlain
was preaching as the whole duty of Unionists, had also an
appearance of callousness to feeling outside the House.

22

It was, no doubt, true that Liberals thirsted to pursue in the House the advantage they were gaining outside. Mr Balfour's difficulty arose from his continuance in office in almost unparalleled circumstances.

The general assumption was that he wished by every possible means to avoid making an appeal to the country from a hopelessly divided party. Mr Chamberlain had asked at first for inquiry. Mr Balfour had not found himself so wedded to Free Trade principles as to be unable to go so far as this. But the inquiry had arisen spontaneously. It was no longer a question of returning a government to investigate, but one of returning either a government which should alter our fiscal relations, or one which should not. The only hope then was to prolong the period of discussion, in order that the more exact arguments might have time to emerge from the generalities, in order even that Unionists should have time to learn the arguments ; in order lastly, perhaps, that the actual proposals might shake themselves clear of the obscuring cloud of Protectionist schemes which had with such violent energy swarmed upon Mr Chamberlain's idealism. This last hope is clear from a pronouncement by Mr Chamberlain at Birmingham quite late in the year, when there was no longer much doubt of an approaching election ; he said that there would be no possibility of a reversion to Protection ; all that was wanted was a modification of the Free Trade system.[1] It seemed that Mr Balfour remained in office to try to take to the polls a party enunciating a policy of its own, and not forced merely to defend against Liberals the policy of the Tariff Reform League. He wanted to occupy a kopje of his own choosing, and to bring the Liberal attack upon this ; the kopje against which that attack was being directed had been so bombarded that its trenches, to an army being forced back upon it, appeared little but pitfalls.

[1] *The Times*, 4th November 1905;

But, in avoiding one danger, Mr Balfour was caught
by another. He gave his opponents what amounted to a
year's start in an election campaign. The party in office
must as a rule be more on the defensive than on the offensive. Moreover a session with an insignificant legislative
programme made administration peculiarly liable to attack.
The uneasiness caused by Lord Dunraven's devolution
proposals was busily kept alive. It was seen that Sir
Antony Macdonnell's position offered the best point of
concentration. The Government was not allowed to ride
off on the line that he was a subordinate official. Could
that description, it was asked, properly be applied to one
who had been lieutenant-governor of an Indian province ?
A man did not return from the crest of one service to take
a merely subordinate post in another. It was, in any case,
curious that a distinguished Indian civilian should join
the executive in Ireland. The next step in conjecture
was boldly taken : Mr Wyndham must have promised
Sir Antony Macdonnell somewhat the position of a colleague, and in that case there had been more than coquetting with Home Rule. The conjecture proved to be not
far astray, as regarded the terms on which Sir Antony
took office. Now arose an outcry from Unionists ; Mr
Wyndham might make all manner of explanations, but,
while Sir Antony remained in his post, the explanations
were futile. The correspondence between the two on the
subject of the under-secretaryship was published ; the
Government majority on an Irish question fell to forty-two.
This state of affairs could not last ; Mr Wyndham had to
resign, which he did on 6th March. He had by general consent done brilliantly with the Irish Land Bill ; he was well
liked in the House, and his term of office in Ireland had
been calm and hopeful. To Irish Unionists this hopefulness had now a suspicious tinge. No trafficking with
Nationalist ideals could be allowed, and Mr Wyndham
was thrown over. The whole affair damaged Mr Balfour's

position ; either he had not kept an eye on his Chief Secretary, or he had made a Strafford of him. It was not thought at all improbable that, with the warning of the by-elections before his eyes, Mr Balfour had conceived the possibility of withdrawing Irish support from the Liberals in the next House of Commons. What was described as " the severest electoral blow that the Government has had to suffer " occurred in April.[1] At Brighton, with all its naturally Conservative traditions and feelings, a Unionist majority of 2000 was swept away, and a Liberal returned, in spite of the Unionist candidate being a well-known resident. There were undoubtedly special elements in the contest, the local Unionists disliking the arrangements proposed by the central organisation for the next general election ; Sir Edward Clarke, who had opposed the war, being a prospective Unionist candidate. But while this accounted for part of the turnover, the fear of a rise in prices under a tariff alarmed lodging-house keepers, as it had done in the Thanet election, where Margate and Ramsgate were concerned. Moreover, the dislike of Chinese labour on the Rand was as active here as it had been in other constituencies. In vain the use made of this cry by the Opposition was denounced by Ministerialists ; in vain were their attacks described as " clouds of sentimental error." [2] In vain was it pointed out that, if the actual labourers were Chinese, the opening and working of the mines (which would not have occurred, it was remarked, without them) gave employment to white overseers and white employees of other kinds. The stubborn fact remained that, after all the cost of the war, the mine-owners had been allowed to import cheap labour on ignominious terms. Hence the strength of the double attack of the Radicals—that the war had been fought on behalf of, if not actually at the bidding of, a number of

[1] *The Times*, 6th April 1905.
[2] *Ibid.*, 18th March 1904.

more or less alien financiers, and that the Government
had consented to the establishment of a form of slavery.
Both were sweeping generalisations, of the kind that
produced so much irritation in the tariff controversy.
But both had a substratum of truth. The mine-owners
had certainly been allowed to force their case ; and the
indentured Chinese were in no sense members of the
community. Such heat of feeling was engendered that
Mr Lyttelton was howled down in the House by the
Opposition when the subject came up in debate, and
the sitting had to be adjourned. Mr Balfour himself was
similarly howled down on another occasion. These were
undignified incidents in an undignified session.

It ran its course for the regulation period. But little
reality was in it. When the Government began to talk of
some redistribution resolutions—a hint of dissolution—
it came out that Mr Balfour had taken so perfunctory
an interest in them that he had not even consulted the
Speaker as to the procedure. The resolutions, it was ruled,
could not be submitted *en bloc*, but must go into Committee
under eight or nine heads. They had to be dropped.
Mr Balfour was uncertain about his followers, who were
becoming increasingly slack in attendance ; and on 20th
July, upon a motion by the Irish leader, Mr Redmond,
for reducing the salary of the Chief Secretary, the Ministry
was defeated by 199 votes to 196. This was not a small
House ; and only two days earlier Mr Balfour, at a party
meeting, had been urgent with his supporters to attend
more faithfully. It was not an impossible opportunity
for resignation ; and the mass of Unionists in the country
were really more annoyed than the Liberals when Mr
Balfour refused to resign. They could not understand
what he was waiting for, with the building, so to speak,
crumbling about his ears. There was in the constituencies
much less hope of the emergence of a party policy than Mr
Balfour himself would appear to have been led by.

Every incident seemed to occur with some grudge against the Government. With trade not yet on its feet again, and a disturbed feeling, due to the invasions of American capital,[1] that big combinations were in the air, of which the first profits went to the promoters,[2] the revenue remained stagnant. It was, indeed, only £24,000 under the estimate; but that result had been achieved by a greater stringency in the collection of income-tax, which had thereby produced an unexpected million and a quarter. Useful as the greater stringency might be, it was not quite the way for an expiring government to recommend itself to the country. Then an extraordinary religious revival in South Wales, due to the preaching of Evan Roberts, gave backing to the Nonconformist resentment of the Education Act, and to the Liberal attacks on the Licensing Act; it flung at the Ministry the unpleasant cry of "Beer and the Bible." The revival half-emptied—in some places more than half emptied—the public-houses and the football grounds. It made the light of the Torrey-Alexander mission in London, taking place at this date, show rather pale.

The promise of a payment of thirty millions from the Transvaal towards the war proved double-edged. It had sounded well at first; but as time went on, and nothing more was heard of it, it opened another point of attack. The Boers were declining to take any part in public life until responsible government should be granted; and Lord Milner, coming home in March and closing his term of control in South Africa, came back to no striking reception. The appointment of a Royal Commission on War Stores revived the least happy passages in the Ministry's career; and the satisfaction with the progress of army reform was checked by the sudden announcement that a new rifle, shorter in the barrel than the existing one, was to be

---

[1] See page 610.

[2] *The Times*, 1st January 1905.

introduced. This " arbitrary rearmament " [1] looked like a return from large matters to tinkerings.

When it began to be known that Lord Curzon and Lord Kitchener were in acute disagreement, it seemed that even the ends of the earth were having their kick at the Ministry. Here was their own Viceroy, honoured by appointment to a second term of office—a thing which had never happened before—quarrelling publicly with the great soldier whom the Government had sent proudly to command in India three years ago. Lord Kitchener was at work reorganising the distribution and commands of the Indian army. The point of conflict was that Lord Kitchener wanted to abolish the Military Member of the Viceroy's council, holding that this post practically amounted to a dual control with the Commander-in-Chief ; while Lord Curzon maintained that the Viceroy must have the independent advice of the Military Member, and introduced a note of personal recrimination in remarking that Lord Kitchener had, after all, had the full support of the Council in his reforms. Lord Curzon in the end resigned ; but, though the Government was thus saved from the public blow that Lord Kitchener's resignation would have dealt it, it had given one more impression of muddling.

The failing heart of politics seemed to weaken the circulation all through the national system. It was a year without excitements or interests. The rather hazy popularity of Japan waxed with her deliberate, amazingly patient, amazingly gallant victories. Port Arthur fell in January, after eight months of isolation and five of actual siege, counting from the attack on the outlying defences. The story of every battle brought to England the same account of the Japanese coolness and disregard of death. In March the battle of Mukden, fought for several days, turned the Russians back practically into their old territory. In April the fleet of Admiral Rozh-

[1] *The Times*, 3rd February 1905.

Q

destvensky, which had made a hesitating passage, appeared in the Pacific; but displayed a tendency to hang about the coasts of French colonies, while Japan protested at this apparent affording of shelter, and France denied having any such intention. In August the fleet made its desperate effort to reach Vladivostok, fell into the grip of the Japanese fleet in the straits of Tsu-Shima, and was, at long range, pounded to extinction with hardly any casualties on the Japanese side. The apostles of efficiency took the opportunity offered by the popular enthusiasm for Japan; she had shown how an efficient nation could carry through a war. It should be noted here that in February the international commission on the North Sea incident [1] gave its finding, practically granting all the British case; the judgment was that there had been no torpedo boats among the fishing fleet, that the fishing fleet committed no hostile act, that the firing by the Russian fleet was not justified, and was continued too long.

The opening of the breach between Norway and Sweden —the ostensible bone of contention being Norway's demand for a separate consular service, which was merely a formula for her assertion of completely different interests in trade, manufacture and customs tariff—had more intimate associations for Great Britain than at first seemed likely. When the separation had been peaceably accomplished, Norway, looking round for a sovereign, offered her throne to Prince Charles of Denmark; and, as he had married King Edward's youngest daughter, our King became related to one more European sovereign.

The quality of our agreement with France had been expressed in a phrase new to the British public. It hardly savours too much of cynicism to say that this fact greatly assisted the establishment of friendly feelings. The " entente cordiale " became a street catchword; and so an idea that might have taken years to bear fruit

1 See page 658.

found its way at once to the populace.   If it had remained
entirely, or even almost entirely, on the diplomatic plane,
it would have been seriously shaken this year.   For, as far
as the principal bargain was concerned, France appeared
to have made a miscalculation.   She had bargained a
certainty in Egypt against a speculation in Morocco.
The situation in Egypt had lasted long enough to make
our position assured.   But it soon appeared that there were
others besides ourselves with a word to say about Morocco.
The German Emperor visited Tangier in the spring of
1905 ; and in a speech there remarked that he could not
allow any power to step between him and the free sovereign
of a free country.   Incidentally, this event gave a new text
for the Free Traders.   A nation that set up tariffs and
protected markets, like the French, could not move a step
towards new expansion without alarming a great trading
nation like Germany.   Expansion to France meant a new
closed market : expansion to us meant a new open market
for everybody.   But this was a minor aspect of the affair.
The more important aspect was that friction arose between
France and Germany, and arose from an agreement of
which we seemed to be getting the only profit.   As it
turned out, the storm fell solely upon M. Delcassé.   King
Edward went yachting in the Mediterranean in the spring,
and, both on his way south and on his return, he stopped
at Paris to visit President Loubet.   M. Delcassé could not
be saved.   A logical people, like the French, could see the
mistake he had made, and in June he resigned the Foreign
Ministry.   It was thought, perhaps with some truth,
that Russia's grievous preoccupation in the Far East,
paralysing her for the moment in Europe, had deprived
M. Delcassé of power upon which he had relied.   A meeting
between the Tsar of Russia and the German Emperor on
their yachts in the Baltic added to French uneasiness.
But the friendliness with England stood the strain.   The
French fleet visited Spithead in July, and was fêted ;

the Municipal Council of Paris visited the London County Council in September, and were received by the King.

But those who looked below the surface found more cause for anxiety than for ease. Superficially, it appeared we had advanced beyond our position of a few years back, when the whole Continent had been stirred against us by the Boer War. In the summing up of the career of Mr Balfour's Government after his resignation, the most prominent piece of enduring achievement was found in Lord Lansdowne's policy of ceasing " to treat foreign problems as isolated affairs." [1] This referred to his success in welding together in the Anglo-French agreement a variety of large and small questions which had for years been opened at any moment of strained relations. But he seemed to be little alive to the danger of the Anglo-French agreement becoming in a different sense an isolation of foreign problems, if it developed into an understanding exclusive of other nations. With an eye upon this danger a committee was formed in November of persons anxious to prevent this kind of impression arising in the mind of Germany.

It was a merit in Lord Lansdowne, less remarked at the time, but warmly appreciated by many who kept alive the Gladstonian belief in international righteousness, that he took a courageous and liberal attitude upon such subjects as Macedonia and the Congo. A rising in Macedonia had been severely repressed by Turkey in 1903. Those who set on foot relief funds for the oppressed had reason to be grateful to Lord Lansdowne for the support he gave them in enabling them to administer the fund in Macedonia. In the matter of the Congo, it was to Lord Lansdowne that the famous report of Consul Casement was due. The agitation for reform in the Congo had been gaining strength, slowly but surely. Suspicion arising from the testimony of missionaries, backed by the practical closing

[1] *The Times*, 5th December 1905.

of the trading districts to all but Belgian officials, and strengthened by the revelations of the vast revenue which the region was producing, had led to more deliberate inquiry.   But while several people were vaguely concerned about the matter, one man made it his deepest concern. Mr E. D. Morel laboured unceasingly at collating all the evidence that could be gathered—the positive evidence, of witnessed cases of cruelty to natives, and the indirect evidence, implied in the concealment practised, and the enormous quantities of rubber which were produced— quantities which alone amounted almost to proof of the gravest extremes of forced labour.   The Aborigines' Protection Society had prevailed upon Lord Lansdowne to authorise an investigation ; the Congo State had been founded by international agreement, and it could not be denied that any country concerned in that agreement had a right to be reassured as to the condition of the natives handed over by it.   Consul Casement's report was the most serious justification of the charges of savage cruelty, murder, and conditions of slavery, prevailing under the administration of the King of the Belgians.   It was an awful commentary on the enthusiasm with which this region had been handed over to the blessings of " civilisa- tion."   A public meeting in 1904 demanded an extension of the British consular service on the Congo, and the summon- ing of an international Conference of the Powers that had joined in founding the Congo State.   Lord Lansdowne stood by the demand, and a conference, with Mr Casement's report before it, met in Brussels in January 1905.   It was confronted with difficulties. The terms on which the territory was held, while they threw no responsibility on Belgium as a nation, yet allowed the King of the Belgians to play upon national susceptibilities.   But by this time a force of opinion had been roused in Great Britain which, united into the Congo Reform Association, could not easily be destroyed.

In September Dr Barnardo died suddenly. His work for destitute children had become such a recognised and admirable part of the life of the nation that people realised almost with a shock the greatness of it as an individual achievement. He had set on foot forty years earlier, by his own unaided effort, an organisation which now possessed homes in London and the country capable of housing, educating and training for a useful life thousands of the waifs and strays of city streets. In the forty years he had rescued from the gutter no less than 60,000 children. They had been kept until they were fitted by training for artisan's work, for domestic service or for emigration ; 17,000 had been sent to occupations in Canada. Helpers had gathered about him, and his work was now on a plane of established success. But at his grave his own great personal devotion was recognised.

Another by-election in the autumn, again a striking Liberal victory, the seat for the Barkston Ash division of Yorkshire being won against a Unionist candidate belonging to a great local family, Mr Lane-Fox, revived the weary wonder as to how many more blows Mr Balfour was going to await. Mr Chamberlain was openly pressing for a dissolution. The party, as he said at Birmingham, might lose the battle, but on what other issue than Tariff Reform would it be more likely to win ? One incident occurred to demonstrate what it was that Mr Balfour had waited for. Speaking in November he appealed to the party to fight for his idea of a kind of educational campaign on the subject, which should end in empowering a Unionist Government to frame some suggestions. Mr Chamberlain promptly responded with an appeal to fight for the more drastic end of empowering a Unionist Government to set up a tariff, and then make its offers from a definite stand-point to the colonies. The issue was thus after all cleared only for the Liberals, and not at all for the Unionists. It hardly mattered to Liberals that Lord Rosebery,

speaking at Bodmin about this time, should repudiate
Home Rule, and refuse emphatically to fight under that
banner, to which Sir Henry Campbell-Bannerman had just
been reasserting his allegiance. Differences of this kind
were as nothing in the shadow of the more violently agitated
question.

One card remained for Mr Balfour to play, and he
played it. By resigning, rather than dissolving, he might
so force into the open the old disagreements between the
Radicals and the Liberal Imperialists that the Opposition,
instead of carrying on triumphantly their Free Trade
campaign, would be suddenly disunited and discounten-
anced by a public and ludicrous failure to form a ministry.
The feeling for some time had been that, even if Mr Balfour's
Government was weak, Liberals could hardly produce anything better. If Sir Henry Campbell-Bannerman were sent
for, would the Liberal Imperialists think of taking office
under a man who had but lately been so unpopular ? If
Lord Rosebery were sent for, Radical extremists would be
infuriated. By all the indications it was at least an open
chance that there might be, if not actual failure to form a
ministry, at any rate failure to form anything but a makeshift cabinet. By compelling the Liberals to present to
a general election their actual cabinet, Mr Balfour might
produce a spectacle which, even for the sake of Free Trade,
the country might be unable to tolerate.

On 4th December, Mr Balfour therefore resigned ;
and on the 5th Sir Henry Campbell-Bannerman became
Prime Minister. Ten and a half years had passed since the
last Liberal Government expired, and of that Government
Sir William Harcourt, Lord Kimberley and Lord Hers-
chell were dead; Lord Rosebery was ostentatiously standing
aside ; Lord Spencer was at the moment seriously ill; Lord
Ripon was seventy-four, Sir Henry Fowler seventy-five; Sir
George Trevelyan, Mr Shaw Lefevre, Mr Arnold Morley and
Mr Arthur Acland were no longer in political life. Of men

of cabinet rank there remained only Sir Henry Campbell-Bannerman, Mr Morley, Mr Asquith, Mr Bryce and Lord Tweedmouth. Men who had earned cabinet rank since those days were easily discerned in Sir Edward Grey, Mr Haldane, Lord Elgin, Sir Robert Reid, Mr Herbert Gladstone and Mr Lloyd George. Out of these two groups three of the most important men, Mr Asquith, Sir Edward Grey and Mr Haldane, were avowed Liberal Imperialists ; Mr Asquith and Sir Edward Grey had both repudiated Home Rule. One curious element in the speculation of the moment must be mentioned. It was assumed at once that Labour would have a representative in the Cabinet.[1] Nothing could have shown more clearly the great advance which Labour politics had made. The last glimpse of an older fashion remained in the doubt whether this representative would be Sir Charles Dilke—who, though admirably informed on Labour questions and deeply understanding them, was of the cabinet tradition in rank—or whether it would be Mr John Burns. Speculation took another turn in the suggestion that Sir Henry Campbell-Bannerman might go to the House of Lords, partly because it was thought that he might not be a match for Mr Balfour and Mr Chamberlain in the Commons, and partly because, if the Liberal Imperialists had the chief places in the Commons, that might provide a bridge to bring them into the Cabinet ; indeed, it was rumoured on 8th December that Sir Edward Grey had declined office because Sir Henry Campbell-Bannerman refused to translate himself thus.

Rumour had but a few days in which to exercise itself. On 11th December the list of the new Government was published, and it was seen that there were no notable absentees. The list was almost dull, after the days of gossip about it. Nearly everything had fallen out in the most obvious way. Mr Asquith was at the Exchequer ;

[1] See, *e.g.*, *The Times*, 5th December 1905.

Sir Edward Grey at the Foreign Office; Mr Haldane at the
War Office.   Sir Robert Reid was Lord Chancellor; Lord
Elgin took the Colonial Office; Mr Lloyd George the Board
of Trade; Lord Aberdeen the Viceroyalty of Ireland.
One or two of the appointments were mildly surprising.
Mr Morley went to the India Office ; it was, perhaps,
only his friends who fully understood to what degree the
presence of this deeply philosophical, courageous and lofty
mind in control of India would liberate the Ministry's
energies for its home work.   There were traps enough
ready for any man in that post whose zeal was greater than
his intellect.   Mr Herbert Gladstone at the Home Office
was a surprise of rather a different kind ; but he might
prove an able administrator.   Mr Churchill, as Under-
Secretary for the Colonies, was considered to be a rash
experiment ; he had a vigorous tongue, and the colonies
were prone to stand on their dignity.   Mr Birrell as
President of the Board of Education was hailed as a
distinctly happy thought ; a man of letters with a turn
for office could not be more neatly placed.   The Labour
member of the Cabinet had the office most naturally
congenial to him : Mr John Burns was at the Local
Government Board.
᠄ Not the smallest of small change for electoral purposes
was, after all, to be got by the Tories out of Liberal disagreements ; there was, indeed, some attempt to suggest
that, if the Liberal Imperialists had joined the Government,
a bargain must have been made which would hold back
any legislation vigorously democratic.   But there was a
shrewd suspicion that there had been no bargaining ; it
was said that Sir Henry Campbell-Bannerman had made
his offers, had held no parleys, and had asked after a
reasonable interval for a definite reply.   There was a
momentary recurrence of gossip in view of the forthcom-
ing meeting of the Liberal League, which Lord Rosebery
was to address ; would there be any revelations ?   Lord

Rosebery, quietly congratulating the league on the presence in the Cabinet of three of its prominent members, remarked only that, for reasons unknown to him, but which obviously seemed to them good, they had taken office. It was hardly conceivable that, if there had been bargaining, he should not have known of it, nor been consulted.

Sir Henry Campbell-Bannerman had the incidental honour of being the first Prime Minister with an official status as Prime Minister. Hitherto the chief adviser of the Crown had always held some office, even if only formally ; the premiership had been a practice, not a constitutional position. The Premier, in matters of court precedence, took rank according to the Cabinet office he held, usually that of First Lord of the Treasury. King Edward had been desirous of regulating the position, and making the post of Prime Minister an office by itself. Mr Balfour preferred that the change should be made for his successor, and it waited therefore till Sir Henry Campbell-Bannerman's appointment. Then a Royal Warrant was issued, giving the Prime Minister precedence next after the Archbishop of York; and establishing his position as an office of State.

CHAPTER XII

1906 : LIBERALISM TAKES CHARGE

THE general election of January 1906 produced the most sweeping reversal of party balance ever experienced in the House of Commons. Parliament was dissolved on 8th January; and so keen was the eagerness to open the fray that one borough, Ipswich, went to the poll on 12th January—twenty-four hours ahead of what was generally regarded as the first possible polling day. This unprecedented effort gave the Liberals their first victory, the borough returning two Liberals, instead of one Liberal and one Conservative. The uncontested elections were extraordinarily few—no more than four or five in Great Britain. The first considerable polling day, 13th January, brought results so astounding that it appeared incredible that they could be real indications. In Manchester alone five seats had been won by the Liberals, and they included Mr Balfour's seat. When the excited crowds went to bed on that Saturday night the returns stood at 52 Liberal, Labour and Nationalist members, and 14 Unionists. There was at that moment one consideration with which Unionists could solace themselves. Lancashire had, as usual, been foremost in the polling, and in that county above all the Free Traders would be most sure of their ground. But the polls of Monday, spread over the whole country, were no less menacing. That day's results gave a return of 132 Liberals, Labour members and Nationalists, and only 30 Unionists. Mr Gerald Balfour and Mr Long had followed their leader into exile. On the Tuesday night the Liberal gains already amounted to 84, and the Unionists had won but a single seat, that at Hastings ; two more members of the late ministry, Mr Lyttelton and Mr Arthur Elliot, had been defeated. With only 247 members of the new House returned, the majority of 68, with which the Unionists had gone to the country, had been converted to a minority of 98. A week after polling had begun, the Liberals had a majority which was independent of the Irish vote. With fading hopes, Unionists turned their eyes to the rural constituencies ; but these went as heavily against them as the towns. When the last returns were in, the total net gains of the Liberals stood at 212 ; and the astonishing new House was composed of 397 Liberals, 51 Labour members, 83 Nationalists and 157 Unionists. There was a possible maximum majority for the Government of 356 ; without the Nationalists it had a majority of 273 ; and, in the improbable event of the Nationalists and Labour members going into the division lobby with the Opposition, the Liberals singlehanded could defeat that combination by the handsome majority of 88.

The result baffled all attempts to explain it. Many of those who made attempts had been watching the course of the election from London, where it might well appear as almost a nightmare. The modern competition of newspapers for the public fancy turned the political contest into a kind of sporting race. They recorded its progress exactly as they had recorded contests for the America Cup, by coloured lights. At various points, such as the National Liberal Club on the Embankment and the corner buildings in Trafalgar Square, magic lanterns displayed the results on huge sheets. But the newspaper organisations fixed rather on the large space of waste ground at Aldwych, cleared by the County Council's improvement scheme, as the ideal spot for the show. Here night by night immense crowds blocked the roadways under a glare of coloured lights and magic lantern beams from half-a-dozen buildings. The magic lanterns projected names and figures ; the coloured rays, too impatient for the process of writing upon the lantern slides, darted blue or red into the air. From one roof blue and red rockets exploded, to carry news to inhabitants of the heights of the Crystal Palace or Hampstead. Blue and red Bengal fires would be burning in another place. The crowd, garishly illuminated, seemed in the mass to have no thought more stable than if it were still being informed about the America Cup. The cheering of a Liberal victory might be answered by a heavy roar of hooting ; but in the next minute the defeat of Mr Balfour himself would be greeted with excited laughter. In the great genial easiness of the London crowd it was impossible to discern what was going on. Yet even London was stirred by the impulse at work, to the point of returning a remarkable proportion of Liberal members.

In their effort to understand the disaster which had overtaken them, Unionists agreed upon one point—that their organisation had been slack and imperfect. The inertia of the party had not been confined to the House of Commons ; the constituencies had been neglected. They agreed also in attributing much to the swing of the pendulum. Unionism had had ten years of office ; the country desired a change, and the events of the past two years—the disagreements about Tariff Reform, the maintenance in office of a weak cabinet, the uncertain leadership—had added impatience and irritation to the desire. The fate of the Unionist Front Bench certainly gave some reality to the traditional opinion of a defeated party that, however well governments did, the country always tired of them. The defeats of ministers and under-secretaries were as much a marked feature of this election as the extraordinary number of seats gained by the Liberals. Mr Balfour, Mr Lyttelton, Mr Walter Long, Mr Gerald Balfour, Mr Pretyman, Mr Arthur Elliot, Mr Brodrick,

Lord Stanley, Mr Ailwyn Fellowes, Mr Bonar Law ; and
among members who had formerly been in office, Mr
Chaplin and Sir William Hart Dyke—these made a total
of twelve occupants of the Unionist Front Bench rejected
by the electorate.   Nor was the case less striking from the
point of view of the offices they had held ; that the Prime
Minister, the Colonial Secretary, the Secretary for War,
the President of the Board of Trade, the President of the
Local Government Board and the Postmaster-General
of the late Unionist Government should all be defeated
gave to the election results a flavour of something very
much like deliberate punishment on the part of the
nation.

To those who merely sought for the immediate explanations, the use made by the Liberals of their two main
platform cries accounted for much.   Unionists bitterly
resented the employment by Liberals of certain cartoons
and posters.   One especially, representing Chinese in
chained gangs being driven to the mines, was denounced
as absolute misrepresentation.   A Blue Book had been
published, on the eve of the election, reporting on the comfortable conditions provided for the indentured labourers
in the compounds ; and it was angrily urged that these
conditions could not possibly be fairly spoken of as slavery,
much less represented by chains.   Yet the poster would
have had little real effect had there not been, among
ordinary Englishmen, a dislike both of the introduction of
coolie labour and of the idea of the " compound " system.
The fact that indentured coolie labour had gone on for
years in other parts of the empire was of no avail against
the unhappy prominence which it had attained in the case
of the Rand.   Nor could there be, in the last resort, much
sympathy for the Unionists.   That very Colonial ideal
which they had done so much to foster played its part
against them, in the resentment of the other colonies at
the employment of Chinese.   Moreover the plea, genuine

as it was, that the Rand mines would not be opened unless the Chinese Labour Ordinance were sanctioned, was an undignified position to have to take. It lent itself too easily to the view that we had fought for the mine-owners after all.

Unionist complaints about misrepresentation of the Tariff Reform ideal were also frequent, but are to be more easily dismissed. Wholesale catch-phrases about " the food of the people " were no more common than equally wholesale catch-phrases about " Work for All," or " The Foreigner will Pay," or " Tariff Reform means Social Reform." Argument both conscientious and acute was not lacking on either side. But the complicated movement which had sprung into being around Mr Chamberlain's central idea had this grave defect—it made visible the danger that, if once considerations other than those of revenue directed the framing of budgets, no one could arbitrarily limit those considerations. If a proposal for Colonial preference could so rapidly shift into proposals for retaliation on hostile tariffs, and for protection of home industries, if the ideal of a commercially united empire so naturally absorbed in its progress ideals of generally regulated imports, would not similar shiftings, similar absorptions, be likely to attend the framing of a tariff ? It may have been an obscure feeling against Tariff Reform that turned the main current of the election ; but a feeling is not necessarily the less genuine for being obscure. At any rate, so strong a national conviction, after two and a half years of incessant argument by either side, was a great and incontrovertible fact.

Beneath all the recriminations and all the analysing of party cries, both sides displayed a consciousness that there was profound and serious meaning in what had taken place. Both sides were startled. To account for the results by saying that the working men were having their day—that the franchise extensions of 1867 and 1885 had now been given their first full expression by the generation that had come to electoral age since the Elementary Education Acts and the circulation of cheap newspapers— was too superficial to be satisfying.[1] The working man's politics were no longer the united Radical force of the Chartist days, and the most exclusively industrial towns could show a Unionist poll too considerable to be made up entirely of small tradesmen and out-voters. Yet it was plain that the Labour vote had become a new thing. In the constituencies accustomed to return Labour members —such as Newcastle, Northumberland, and some of the mining towns—the Labour majority had become overwhelming; in other industrial places—such as Barrow-in-Furness, Middlesborough, Stockport, St Helen's—Labour candidates had swept out of the field the Unionists who had held those seats. The Labour party for the first time became more than a group in the House ; fifty-one members made it genuinely a fourth party. Here again there were immediate causes upon which the observer could put his finger. On the whole the past ten years had been fairly free from strikes ; the forces of the trade unions had had time to take in the circumstances of their position, and to fix their eyes on far-reaching aims. Over-logical socialism had given place to a watchfulness for any promising opening for advancing Labour interests. The election of 1895 had turned the energies of Labour leaders into steady organising work.[2] The Taff Vale case came at exactly the right moment to fuse that work into a vital whole, to concentrate it upon a clear purpose.[3] Ever since that case the Labour leaders had had at their back an army answering to a purely Labour watchword. The combined workmen felt that, as long as the law held trade unions liable to be sued in damages for tortious

[1] See, *e.g., The Times,* 16th January 1906.
[2] See page 372.
[3] See page 557.

acts of members, and picketing and peaceful persuasion were held to be tortious acts, trade unions were paralysed. The central argument was that Parliament, when it sanctioned the trade unions, had never intended this; it was a mere flaw in the position, discovered by the ingenuity of lawyers, and it must be mended. The defeat of Sir William Hart-Dyke in a division of Kent which was almost a family possession was the most striking example of the influence of the Taff Vale case. By the railway vote in this constituency he was ousted for a Labour member.

But while the Taff Vale case served well enough as the obvious factor in the Labour party's success, it did not provide that deep meaning which both sides felt to be inherent in the election. Even when account had been taken of the lack of cohesion among Unionists on the Tariff Reform programme, the sum did not seem to be complete. The truth began, however, to emerge in a comment made before the election was over. " Speaking broadly, we should say that the result of the elections is a protest against dilettantism in politics, a vice common to both parties." [1] The phrasing was coloured by the now frequent misgivings as to Mr Balfour's leadership, the distrust of his " airiness " and elegant trifling. But that the comment itself was sound could be clearly proved by the new House when it met. It was largely a House of youngish men, still more a House of " new " men in politics. Just as the Reform Bill of 1832 had added the manufacturer and the man of business to the aristocrat and the man of affairs, so the election of 1906 added to those classes in the House the man of ideas and the sociologist. For the first time the Commons contained a large number of men who had entered it, not on the strength of their hereditary position, their local importance, their forensic skill, or their intellectual reputation ; but solely on the basis of their sociological enthusiasm and their political idealism.

[1] *The Times*, 24th January 1906.

R

Never had there been a House so full of men whom a
member in the late eighteenth century would have found
it impossible to place in any category known to him.
The type was, of course, more common on the Liberal side
than among the Unionists ; but even in the Opposition
ranks could be found the man who had gone from his
university, or even his school, into some activity of social
reform, or some propaganda of the new political economy,
and passed thence into Parliament. It is largely to that
new political economy that we must look for the explanation of the general election of 1906. We have seen in
the former volume of this history how the philanthropic
spirit, by which the old individualist economy had been
undermined, had given way, partly by the advance of
Fabianism and Trade Unionism, partly by the philosophical thought associated with the name of T. H. Green,
to a reformed political economy, a kind of economic
sociology.[1] We have seen how this change was helped
forward firstly by the inclusion of hygiene in the ideal of
material progress ; and secondly by the movement for
efficiency in public administration.[2] We now add the
important fact that the reaction against the purely
philanthropic spirit was a return to belief in the efficacy
of legislation.[3] The ineffectual career of the Liberal
Government of 1892-1895 inflicted a set-back upon that
belief. But it had recovered strength ; it had become
an enormous reservoir of power, waiting to be tapped.
Mr Chamberlain had perceived its readiness, and had
done it the honour of proposing to employ a new tap.
The old served better.

As the Liberals had had less apparent prevision of the
new forces, so now their acquaintance with them, gratifying as it was for the moment, brought some apprehen-

[1] See pages 111, 223, 465.
[2] See pages 115, 574.
[3] See page 246.

sion to the thoughtful. This was perhaps best expressed in a letter from "A Liberal Voter," published in *The Times*,[1] suggesting that "the Labour vote had introduced into middle-class Liberalism, now perhaps for the last time triumphant, the seeds of disintegration." That was one more meaning discovered in the election results. But it was only a partial truth. Its flaw lay in the phrase "middle-class Liberalism": in the sense in which the writer employed the phrase, that Liberalism was already past its last triumph—the poor triumph of 1892. As the new Government pursued its course it became abundantly clear that it represented a new Liberalism. Throughout the election the reliance of Liberals was placed, even if sometimes unconsciously, upon a wider basis than its old middle-class support. Symptoms of this reliance can be found in items of the programme put forward at the National Liberal Federation's meeting in 1905—such items as legislation on trade disputes, the taxation of site values, small holdings, the payment of members, and especially, perhaps, in the introduction for the first time of a resolution that "the disabilities of sex in the Parliamentary and local suffrage should be removed." The most deliberately democratic appeal of all did not appear in any programme, but it played a large part in the election. It was to be found at its clearest and best in Sir Charles Dilke's speeches. He frequently directed the working man's hopes towards a great Budget which should not only be aimed at bringing into the State coffers a larger proportion of the wealth of individuals, but should "entail legislation outside its own sphere"—a Budget, that is, which should be a kind of nursing mother of social reforms. This was to be the real answer to Tariff Reform. A customs tariff was, after all, a middle-class idea, a middle-class conception for meeting the cost of social reform. The new Liberalism would find one that was not middle-class

[1] 31st January 1906.

in conception. As for unconscious regard paid by Liberals during the election to the new forces, it can be seen in the broad play upon instinctive dislike of the Chinese labour expedient, and instinctive mistrust of Tariff Reform. It can even be seen in the comparatively slight place taken in the election by Home Rule. Heated controversy on that subject had always been more characteristic of the middle-classes than of the working man, who was not deeply interested, either for it or against it.

Apart from other considerations, there was no need for the Liberals to make much of Home Rule in this election. Before the polls began, Mr Redmond had taken up a position which prevented any possibility of co-operation with the Unionists ; he had repeated the full Nationalist demand, which would not be satisfied with " devolution," but only with an Irish Parliament, and an executive responsible to that parliament. The most that Unionist candidates could hope for was to make capital out of the difference between Sir Henry Campbell-Bannerman's frank declaration of adherence to Home Rule and Sir Edward Grey's statement that progress in that direction must be gradual—that no thorough-going Bill would be passed without an appeal to the country. The fact was that the events ending in the resignation of Mr George Wyndham had relieved the Liberal party of any need to bid for Irish support ; it had become again the party to which the Nationalists were compelled to look. Nor was it difficult for them to look hopefully towards a cabinet which, if it contained Sir Edward Grey and Mr Asquith, contained also Mr Morley, to maintain the Gladstonian tradition, and a strong contingent of democratic Radicalism.

Home Rule occupied, in fact, a prominent place in the King's Speech at the opening of Parliament on 20th February, though the terms of the reference to it were vague, and without promise of immediate action. The

two most important items of the speech concerned matters
to which the Liberals had professed their paramount duty
—a new Education Bill and a Trade Disputes Bill.   But
far more interesting at the moment than either of these was
that passage in the speech which dealt with South African
affairs.   It was stated definitely that no more licences
would be issued for importing Chinese labourers ; and that,
as soon as the details of the constitution could be worked
out and drafted, self-government would be bestowed upon
the Transvaal and the Orange River Colony.   The Chinese
labour decision was drastic.   It was, and had been throughout the election, open to the Opposition to score the point
that, if Chinese labour was indeed the slavery which
Liberals alleged it to be, then they could not do less than
repatriate the Chinese out of hand.   If they did not do so,
manifestly the cry of " slavery " was insincere.   This was
a neat " score," but the Government could afford to leave
it as a score.   An attempt had indeed been made to interfere at once with the indentured immigration.   A few days
before the Unionists surrendered office, licences had been
issued for the importation of 14,000 Chinese.   It was a
much larger number than usual, and this suggested that
the mine-owners, aware of, or suspecting, the imminence of
a change of government, had hurried to secure a big draft,
in case it should be the last.   The Liberal Cabinet wished
to prevent the landing of these 14,000 ; but found that,
once the licences were issued, there was no way of interfering.   For some time afterwards it continued to be a
Unionist taunt that the " slaves " were still left, in spite
of the hot Liberal indignation ; those already indentured
were allowed to serve out their term.   But the concession
did no real harm to the Government, which showed at any
rate some courage in flatly overriding the power of the
Transvaal authorities to issue the licences ; Mr Lyttelton
had been explaining carefully during the election that,
once the Ordinance was allowed, the issue of licences was

not in his hands. Moreover the Cabinet maintained its attitude when self-government was granted to the colony ; the letters patent, reciting specifically " Whereas it is Our will and pleasure that all persons within Our dominions shall be free from any conditions of employment or residence of a servile character," placed questions of imported labour among the subjects of legislation which the Governor had not power to assent to, but must reserve for the Home Government's decision.

The session was not an easy one. The Trade Disputes Bill, as introduced by the Government, did not wholly satisfy the Labour party, and a Bill was also introduced by Mr Hudson, one of the Labour members. In the end an important clause from this latter Bill was incorporated in the Government measure, which in its final form virtually abolished the last application of the law of conspiracy to trade unions, and enacted that what was legal for an individual should be legal for a combination of individuals, thus permitting peaceful persuasion, picketing, and other such methods during a strike ; it also enacted that the funds of trade unions should not be liable to actions for damages. Much more serious difficulty attended the Education Bill. This was largely due to the Government's attempt to make, not a mere reversal of the Act of 1902, as was alleged to be their object, but a measure which would leave no section of the community as seriously aggrieved as the Nonconformists had been by that Act. The chief proposal of the new Bill was that, in order to make all public elementary schools " provided " schools, the local authorities should arrange with the managers of voluntary schools for the use of the buildings on five days of the week, leaving them to the managers on Saturday and Sunday, the local authorities in return becoming responsible for the upkeep and repair of the school buildings. The local authority was to have the sole power of appointing teachers ; no religious tests were to be applied in the appointments, and teachers under the local authority were not to be allowed to give instruction on Saturday and Sunday. This fully met the Nonconformist position. But it was also proposed that in towns, facilities for denominational teaching should be given in schools taken over by the local authority, if four-fifths of the parents of children attending the school expressed a wish for it, and if, further, there were schools available for children whose parents preferred the undenominational teaching. The Bill never had a united force of opinion behind it. Nonconformists disliked the concession of denominational teaching in any schools at all. The Labour members disliked the perpetuation of undenominational teaching as much as they disliked this particular concession ; they wished for a wholly secular system. The Irish members, while admitting that the concession would meet for the most part the Roman Catholic demand (since the strength of Roman Catholicism was chiefly in towns), disliked the stipulation for a four-fifths vote from the parents. English Churchmen joined in this dislike. But the question of the proportion of parents that should settle the matter was but a small, though persistent, part of the Opposition's antagonism to the Bill. The confining of denominational teaching in voluntary schools to two days of the week ; the power of the local authority to appoint all teachers ; the absolute forbidding of the teachers to give instruction on Saturday and Sunday—these proposals were enough to destroy the Government's hope of allaying the Nonconformist grievance without aggrieving others. Churchmen denounced the Bill at large for endowing undenominationalism, while refusing to support denominationalism—that is, for deciding arbitrarily that one form of religious teaching was good and another bad. The Bill had some uncomfortable moments even in the House of Commons ; on one amendment in July, when the Ministerial whips were taken off, and the question left to the unfettered

judgment of the House, the Government majority was
only sixteen.   When the Bill reached the House of Lords
in October, that assembly made no pretence of accepting
it.   Drastic amendments were introduced into practically
every clause.   The action taken by the Government, when
the amended Bill was returned to the House of Commons,
was extremely important. It proposed that the amendments
introduced by the Lords should be considered, not in detail,
but " as a whole," the House agreed to this course, and
proceeded to reject the amendments " as a whole " by
a majority of 416 to 107.   This meant that the work of
the Lords was regarded, not as a fair attempt to meet
Nonconformist grievances from the Church point of view,
but as a determination to maintain the position under
Mr Balfour's Act.   In other words, the Lords were treated
as holding the fort on behalf of the enfeebled Opposition
against the Liberal majority, in a particularly flagrant
manner, since the Liberals had everywhere announced to
their supporters that an Education Bill would be their first
care.   On the second appearance of the Bill in the House
of Lords, Lord Lansdowne expressed strong objection
to the course taken by the Government, and the House
insisted on its amendments.   Thereupon the Government announced on 20th December that it would proceed
no further with the Bill.

Thus opened another fundamental contest raised by the
astonishing general election.   Could this new House of
Commons—new in so many traits of outlook, of reliance
upon the electorate, of political philosophy—coexist with
a Second Chamber unaffected by the vote of constituencies?
The answer of Conservatives was, broadly, that with our
electoral system it was possible for the House of Commons
to be a complete misrepresentation of the state of feeling
in the country.   A bare majority sufficed to put a member
into the House ; and it was therefore not unfair that some
automatic check in the constitution should represent the

many Tory votes which had just failed to keep Liberals
out. The weakness of this answer was that the Lords had
hitherto never represented the many similar Liberal
minorities when Unionists were in office. They had not,
for instance, on this very matter of education, paid heed
to Nonconformist dislike of the Act of 1902, as they now
paid heed to Church dislike of the Bill of 1906. Extreme
democratic opinion also chafed at the conception of an
automatic check. It is quite possible that in their dealings
with the Education Bill the Lords intended no more than
a strong reminder to the Government that it must regard
its majority rather as a great asset for bargaining purposes
than as a supreme authority. The rejection of their
amendments as a whole, with the consequent repudiation
of any suggestion of bargaining, practically set for trial
the question whether the 1906 election revealed a passing
wave of feeling, or a genuine fresh start in the country's
political development—whether it was only an extreme
case of the old " in and out " politics, or an indication of
entirely new ideas of control in national affairs. The safe
passage of the Trade Disputes Bill through the House
of Lords added force to the discussion. Here was a Bill
denounced by a considerable portion of the community
as a very grave innovation, setting certain people above
the law by Act of Parliament ; yet the guardians of an
established order had passed it. The argument used on
behalf of the Lords was that this measure had been so
specifically before the country at the election that the
electors had only themselves to blame for returning a large
majority pledged to the innovation. The Plural Voting
Bill, designed to abolish the casting of votes by owners
of property in more than one constituency, was thrown out
by the Lords, on the ground that reform of the franchise
should not be undertaken piecemeal. The net result by
the end of the year, in the Liberal belief, was that the
House of Lords intended to pursue a policy of rejecting

all the measures it dared to, or so amending them as to
destroy their purpose, while passing a few popular or
ultra-democratic measures as a set-off.

Heavily though the Tariff Reform party had suffered
at the polls, it was far from abandoning its propaganda.
Mr Chamberlain had held his city impregnable; Birmingham returned a solid block of Unionists. His general
popularity was not what it had been; in some of his
campaigning speeches outside his own region—notably
at a meeting in Derby—he had been subjected to constant
interruption, and had had to curtail his speech. Moreover,
when a Unionist party meeting was held at Lansdowne
House in February, to profess loyalty to Mr Balfour, who
had returned to the House of Commons, as member for the
City of London, the official programme on Tariff Reform
had become rather colourless. The meeting only pledged
itself " by some means or other to procure the lowering
of hostile tariffs, and by conference with the Colonies to
reach some arrangement for attaining closer commercial
union with the Colonies." It was added that "the methods
are left open, until the principle is accepted, and the party
are asked to abstain from discussing them until that time
comes." However much one party might wish to abstain,
the other party was not likely to; nor were the carefully
non-committal terms of the pledge secure from attack.
Free Traders argued stoutly that " some means or other "
must in the end imply a preferential or protectionist tariff;
and Unionist Free Traders were not placated. They came
to the conclusion, after the publication of correspondence
between Mr Balfour and Mr Chamberlain, that the two
were in substantial agreement, and therefore the formal
programme, however worded, must involve the Tariff
Reform proposals. One of the first activities of the Liberal
Government was to pay attention to the official production
of statistics. New distinctions and subdivisions were
made in the Board of Trade Returns. Investigations were

set on foot into the relations between wages, hours of work, and cost of living in the United Kingdom and other countries. Most important of all, Mr Lloyd George proposed to hold a census of production at stated intervals ; and, as it seemed that manufacturers might reasonably be chary of their business secrets, a Bill was introduced to make the census compulsory, and to secure that business returns should be as confidential as income-tax returns. The Bill was welcomed by both sides. Liberals were fully alive to the energy that still directed the Tariff Reform propaganda. They did their best to meet the new and exacting requirements of economic discussion by trying to arrive at the real condition of wages, the real meaning of imports and exports, the real balance of British trade. For the ordinary person the year only showed one exciting passage in the Tariff Reform controversy. It became known that, in spite of recent denials, *The Times* was likely to undergo a change of proprietorship, and rumour attributed to Mr C. A. Pearson, who had taken *The Standard* and made it a thorough-going Protectionist organ, a scheme for now acquiring *The Times*, and putting it to the same service. However, when in December the High Court, in an action brought by some of the proprietors of *The Times*, sanctioned the conversion of the proprietor-ship into a limited liability company, with Mr Walter as governing director, it was known that the new force was to be, not Mr Pearson, nor a syndicate of Free Traders who had also made a bid, but Lord Northcliffe, the chief proprietor of *The Daily Mail*.[1] This was, on the whole, a relief ; for although *The Daily Mail* had, after a slight hesitation, embraced Mr Chamberlain's proposals, it had never shown the " whole hogger " Protectionist bias of Mr Pearson's newspapers. There were, it is true, some other serious considerations. One more step (and a great one,

[1] Sir Alfred Harmsworth's peerage had been one of the honours granted on the resignation of the late Ministry.

in view of the unrivalled position of *The Times*) had been taken in that concentration of newspapers in comparatively few hands which had been proceeding quietly for some time. Both Lord Northcliffe and Mr Pearson controlled or owned outright provincial newspapers in all parts of the country, as well as their London newspapers. The result complained of was that, when any great subject arose in politics, the country had, not a discussion from a number of points of view, largely local and individual, but a parrot-like repetition of dictated opinion. There was, however, less ground for the complaint than the political opponents of those two newspaper-owners imagined. For one thing, provincial newspapers, with the exception of the few great ones which remained independent, *The Manchester Guardian*, *The Yorkshire Post*, *The Scotsman*, *The Glasgow Herald*, and so on, had little or no individual opinion to express on great political subjects ; the mass of them followed the London papers so closely that the simultaneous dictation of opinion to them made little difference. For another thing, the idea of newspapers as guides of public opinion had in reality long ceased to be true to facts ; they were symbols rather than guides, and men read them to find grounds for their established convictions, or even prejudices, not to find means of arriving at convictions. When Lord Northcliffe entered the field of cheap newspapers he frankly aimed at selling "a good thing," not at supporting causes, which only took their place as part of "a good thing" or otherwise. The one real danger nowadays was the possibility that the dictation of a single opinion to a large number of newspapers in different parts of the country might produce a false impression of the bent of the public mind—might, for instance, produce the same sort of effect as that by which *The Pall Mall Gazette* in 1884 had made itself largely instrumental in the sending of Gordon to Khartoum.[1]   But, in point of fact. the con-

1 See page 124.

centration of newspapers in the hands of certain individuals diminished, rather than increased, the danger of such misapprehension. The process had been now too well observed to leave any uncertainty as to what might be behind those periodical choruses.

Nevertheless, anxiety about the effects of this process was largely responsible for the foundation of a new Liberal newspaper, *The Tribune*, which appeared on the morrow of the general election. It restored Liberalism for a time to a place among the penny newspapers of London,[1] and it began its career with a brilliant staff. It survived only for two years. Its fall was treated by many people as a deplorable proof of the lowering standard of the modern newspaper reader ; he had, they said, become accustomed to so little seriousness of purpose in his newspapers that a reasoned presentation of Liberalism failed entirely to impress him. The professional journalist was rather inclined to attribute the fall to other reasons. An even briefer career was the lot of another newspaper founded in this year, with the title of *The Majority* ; it was published at a halfpenny, and proposed to be " the organ of all who work for wage or salary." Unfortunately, such people were less a public than a number of publics, each of which responded to a more precise appeal from existing newspapers, and *The Majority* only lived for a week or two.

The one thing which could compete for public attention at the beginning of the year with the Liberal triumph was the launching of the *Dreadnought* in February. There had already been some stimulation of interest, because of the secrecy attending the construction of the ship, and still more because of the amazing fact that she had been laid down in October with the intention of launching her in February and completing her for sea within eighteen months—a feat unprecedented in naval construction. Now that she was launched, it was obvious that she repre-

[1] See page 526.

sented a startlingly new theory of design, the result of the deliberations of a special committee, whose report had been kept secret. Two main characteristics of the *Dreadnought* marked her off at once from all other battleships. Her immense sides were unbroken by any casemates—any of the recessed or projecting semicircles that had hitherto diversified the outlines of warships ; hers were as clean and simple as the sides of an ocean liner. Secondly she was designed to carry only one type of gun, and that a large one—ten 12-inch guns mounted in barbettes ; the absence of secondary armament freed her from any necessity for openings in her watertight compartments. Moreover the clearness of her lines would help to give her speed. She was to steam twenty-one knots, against the eighteen and a half which had hitherto been the swiftest pace of a battleship. She marked at the same time an advance in size, displacing 17,900 tons against the 16,500 of the *King Edward the Seventh.* It was well known that consideration of the naval engagements in the Russo-Japanese War—the first time that modern warships had been in action—had largely dictated the new design. Tsu-Shima had been a " heavy-gun " battle ; and the purpose in view was to create a battleship capable of inflicting the maximum injury at the maximum distance, while herself offering the least holding ground for the enemy's shells. It was remarked, with gratification, that a line of ten *Dreadnoughts* would be equal in fighting power to twenty *Dominions* or twenty *Agamemnons* (the two latest previous types), and at the same time would be much easier for an admiral to handle. A suitable footnote to the launching of this great ship was provided later in the year by the wonderfully efficient gunnery scores made by the various fleets at gun practice ; the percentage of hits to shots had approached eighty ; and the presence of Captain Percy Scott at the Admiralty was a guarantee of continued efficiency.

The navy made a less happy appearance in November, when a mutiny occurred at the naval barracks at Devonport among the stokers. Their version of the affair was that an officer, in drilling them, had hectored them in an abusive way, and one phrase he was said to have used, " On the knee, you dogs," had a brief notoriety. The officer was court-martialled, and acquitted of the charge of using abusive language ; but he suffered a reprimand for having behaved in such a way as to lead to the rioting. The ringleader of the stokers was sentenced to five years' penal servitude.

It was natural that a good deal of interest should attach itself to the first Labour member of an English Cabinet ; and there was much speculation as to how Mr John Burns would bear himself. Some of it was mere gossiping speculation : would he retain his democratic bowler hat, and would he expect to go to Court in a " reefer " suit ? He sensibly settled all such talk by adopting Court dress for the occasions when it was necessary, and remaining faithful to the bowler hat on all other occasions. As for more serious speculations about him, he did not leave the country long in doubt that the Local Government Board was to be a watchful and vigorous department, and not one masking administrative slackness by showy legislative schemes. He frankly postponed Poor Law reforms, with which the air was thick, to tightening up local administration. A ruthless hand was needed. In this year two of the London boards of guardians were attacked for corruption and maladministration, the Poplar Board in July, and the West Ham Board in November ; and various guardians and officials were brought to trial, chiefly for corrupt practices in connection with the boards' contracts. Mr Burns was indefatigable in personally visiting all sorts of institutions within the Local Government Board's sphere.

The bringing to light of corruption among London

guardians was turned to use by the Moderates of the London
County Council in their preparation for the election in the
coming spring. This party now called itself the Municipal
Reform Party, having found that its old name of " Moderates " conveyed little to the voter, except that the party had
the same ideals as the Progressives, but in a less advanced
degree. That was in some measure true of the Moderates
in the first Council. Since that day of high hopes, the
Progressives had moved far and fast ; under the attack
upon municipal trading they had come to stand for an
extreme type of socialism in local government. "Municipal Reform " meant a determination to arrest this kind
of socialism ; and the criticism of municipal trading had
grown strong enough to give the newly named party hopes
of a victory next year, and the first expulsion of the
Progressives from the helm of London government.
Meanwhile, the latter succeeded, after several attempts,
in securing parliamentary powers to run trams along
the Embankment, and the new service was opened in
December, on the same day as the latest " tube " railway,
the Great Northern, Piccadilly and Brompton. London
traffic problems were changing with extraordinary
rapidity ; already motor omnibuses were on the main
routes, and these and the tubes had solved some of
the old difficulties, even if they created new ones.

Business was in a condition to encourage a Free Trade
Government to invite the most searching examination
of trade statistics. A steady recovery from the lowering
effects of the war was providing hopeful figures ; the Stock
Exchange was cheerful, in spite of the advent of Liberals
to power, and the City looked forward to the Budget
serenely. When it came, the revenue was a million and
a half above the estimate ; and Mr Asquith was able to add
half-a-million to the provision for meeting National Debt
charges, besides restoring the full operation of the Sinking
Fund. That he took this line, rather than the line of large

remissions of taxation (the coal-duty was removed, and a penny was taken off the tea-tax), showed intentions sound enough to please the financiers. The most anxious period of the year for the business world was in October, when the failure of the Knickerbocker Trust Company in New York brought about a run on the banks there. A panic followed in Wall Street; one bank after another suspended payment, and for a few days the whole credit system of the United States was in danger. In London, besides the inevitable disturbance of the stock markets by the failures and the uncertainty, there was the " pinching " effect of the heavy call for gold from the United States. The treasury of that country ordered an immediate coinage of three millions sterling in gold, but fifteen millions had also to be drawn from London. The Bank Rate rose at once, and went as high as 7 per cent. ; at that figure the influx of gold was sufficient to meet the strain, and, though the depressing effects of the panic lasted for some time, the English markets came very well out of the trouble. The most interesting operation in England at the moment was an amalgamation of some of the largest soap manufacturing companies. It attained more than a stock market notoriety, because it was violently attacked by certain newspapers as the beginning of a monopolist trust which would capture the retail trade, and prevent honest competition in either price or quality of soap. These newspapers worked up their indignation on behalf of the poor washerwoman, and other such members of the community not often within the purview of the editors concerned. When the indignation reached the point of accusing Messrs Lever Brothers of selling short weight, the latter entered a libel action, which ended in the following year in an agreed verdict of £50,000 damages and costs. Another important trade matter of the year was the meeting in England of the International Federation of Master Cotton Spinners' and Manufacturers'

Associations. It marked the foundation of a system of collecting and publishing cotton trade statistics from all over the world, which added one more improvement to the already high organisation of the trade. The establishment of the new system was largely due to the energy and patience of Mr Charles Macara.

The new Government naturally had to receive a great many deputations from people anxious to enlarge or to accelerate, or sometimes to retard, its programme of legislation. Liberal and Labour members were urgent for the production of a scheme of Old Age Pensions ; women suffragists for extension of the franchise to women ; licensed victuallers for some information as to the Ministry's intentions on the licensing question. An important deputation waited on Sir Edward Grey from the Congo Reform Association. The sitting of the commission in Brussels had resulted in a scheme of reform which was regarded as wholly inadequate ; the King of the Belgians was apparently impenitent to the last degree in the matter of the Crown Domain of the Congo, as to which he refused to acknowledge any right of interference by the Powers, although it was said to be "the worst of the Chartered Company excrescences" on the original purpose of the Powers. Mr Morel, indefatigable as ever, was roundly attacking one of these companies, the Kasai Company ; and the appalling evidence he produced, and upheld undauntedly against the most persistent vilification of his objects and his methods, was at last beginning to receive serious attention in England.

The Woman Suffrage deputation to the Prime Minister, which took place in May, gave small indication of the extraordinary complexity which this question was shortly to assume. The Prime Minister in his reply, while assuring the deputation of his personal sympathy with their cause, declined to promise a Bill, remarking that no party was as yet united on the question. This, no doubt, was true ;

and it was also true that, as compared with other business
on the Government's crowded—and overcrowded—
programme, woman suffrage could not be said as yet to
have much interested the country and the electors at large.
The Woman Suffrage Bills that had appeared fairly regularly in the House of Commons had provided light-hearted
debates on private members' days ; and although the
subject had come up in the official programme at the election, and as many as 420 members of the new House were
said to have professed allegiance to the ideal, no one expected it to become a burning subject immediately. That
it did so was due to an organisation called the Women's
Social and Political Union, hitherto a comparatively
small body of women suffragists recruited chiefly from
the manufacturing towns of Lancashire and Yorkshire.
Dissatisfied with the small progress made by the older
Woman Suffrage societies, with their appeal chiefly to the
highly educated from highly educated women, the new
body based itself rather on the working woman's necessity
for a vote, to improve her industrial position and her
domestic rights. The union had been active in Manchester during the election, and it now entered upon a
sensational career in London. It organised a procession
of women and a demonstration in Trafalgar Square, in
connection with the deputation to the Prime Minister ;
it made itself conspicuous in the Ladies' Gallery at the
House of Commons during a debate on a Woman Suffrage
resolution brought forward by Mr Keir Hardie ; and some
of its leading members paid organised calls on ministers.
Finally, in October, the union began the policy of sending large bodies of women to the central lobby of the
Houses of Parliament to interview ministers ; in October,
November and December several women were arrested
for riotous behaviour, and, refusing to pay fines, were
sent to prison.

The general public took as yet but a casual interest in

these proceedings. Recovering from its absorption in the sporting excitements of the election, it went its ways. Skating on artificial ice at Prince's Club was the new amusement of the rich, who now diversified their habits of speech by tacking a meaningless " What ? " on to the end of remarks which called for no answer. Less exalted people were provided with a new craze in the watching of wrestling bouts, with immense champions struggling on exiguous mats ; and the emancipation of the middle classes began to display itself in a revolt against the wearing of top hats in city businesses, and against the wearing of any hats in hours of holiday or relaxation. Indeed, in every direction men were affronting traditions of dress. The frock coat had ceased to be the smartest thing to wear ; the well-dressed young man affected elegant forms of what the tailors call a " morning coat." The curious point for the social observer was that this new fashion was actually a revolt against Court etiquette. King Edward held to it that the frock coat was the garment for formal occasions ; the exquisites of White's and the Bachelors' " regretted " that they could no longer recognise Court dignitaries in the street, since the latter had to continue wearing frock coats. Nay, more ; it was no longer impossible to be seen in Pall Mall or St James's Street of an afternoon in a jacket and bowler hat, or straw hat. Partly this subversive change could be traced to a good cause. The young men of the Guards and other smart regiments were said nowadays to be so keen on their profession that they were constantly at Aldershot or Pirbright, and, running up thence to town, naturally came West in " out of town " clothes. The more general cause, however, was a happy inclination to reconsider most traditional habits, and, if any were found exacting, to drop them.

In December the Transvaal received its Constitution, and entered upon self-government and the full status of a responsible colony. There had been no little anxiety in some quarters with regard to this step, which was looked upon as a piece of Liberal quixotism. Only four years had passed since the two races in the Transvaal had been at war ; was it possible that already the country could safely be left to their joint direction ? As far at least as immediately appeared, the bold experiment was not ill-advised ; the mining market showed, not only absence of uneasiness, but a slight improvement.

In the last days of the year Lady Burdett-Coutts died. She had controlled an immense fortune with dignity and thoughtfulness ; and her burial in the Abbey was a testimony, not merely to her generous philanthropy, but to the honourable simplicity with which she had maintained a difficult position. Miss Dorothea Beale, who died in November, had also done much to exalt her sex. Founder and headmistress of the Cheltenham Ladies' College, it was her special achievement to have broken down the convention of the private governess in the education of upper-class girls, and, by so doing, to have opened wide realms of knowledge to a class that before this time had been inefficiently taught.

CHAPTER XIII

1907 : PAGEANTRY, SUFFRAGETTES AND THE DRUCE CASE

THE year 1907 was marked by a certain, and rather strange, lull in politics. A new Government pledged up to the eyes to legislative activities had hardly been expected to make its second year of office a quiet one. Various influences were at work. The Prime Minister was not in good health. His wife, to whom he was devoted, had been stricken with a long illness in the previous year, and he had constantly gone from a night's work at the House of Commons to her sick-bed. This strain, ending in the grief of her death, had gravely affected his strength. Again, ministers were nearly all over-pressed in their departments. The work of Government offices was said to have fallen grievously into arrear during the declining years of the late Government. It happened also that the principal measure of the session was Mr Haldane's Army Bill, and this excited only a very small section of the public outside the service and the Houses of Parliament.

Roving attention on the look-out for interests was caught before the year was many days old. A most destructive earthquake in Jamaica, whereby the town of Kingston was practically thrown into ruins, happened to strike home to the Englishman. Sir Alfred Jones, the head of the steamship line trading to Jamaica, had just conveyed thither in one of his ships a distinguished party of persons whose interest he wished to enlist. Consequently there were a good many anxious families in England when news of the earthquake arrived. One of the travellers, Sir James Fergusson, a former member of Parliament for Manchester, and at one time an under-secretary in a Unionist Government, had been killed. An incident of the succeeding days of relief work was curious. Some ships of the United States navy were ordered to Kingston to render assistance. Friction arose from a difference of ideas as to how the work should be effected, and from what the English people felt to be a too great inclination on the part of the Americans to show off their efficiency, and to accuse the Englishmen of having none. England had, as we have seen, wearied of the doctrine of efficiency in the persons of her own colonists ; in the case of Americans she roundly dubbed it fussiness, and the American ships were withdrawn in some dudgeon.

Hardly had the excitement of these events passed off, when a murder case with some unusual elements provided matter for discussion. Mr Whiteley, the head of the great stores that bore his name, and the first man to introduce English people to such stores, was shot dead in his office by a young man who claimed to be his natural son. This allegation, while it was of less account in England than it might have been in France, where extenuating causes were more easily made to include moral questions, nevertheless was widely debated by the public. The young man was sentenced to death, but the sentence was commuted to one of penal servitude for life.

He had the distinction of facing the first murder trial in the new Central Criminal Court which the King opened on 27th February. Newgate Prison had disappeared. Its grim yards and corridors and cells—peculiarly grim because for many years the prison had been only a place of execution—had been opened to trampling crowds at the heels of an auctioneer ; and doors and window bars and gates had been bought as curiosities by showmen. On the old site had arisen a very different building ; the heavy grey walls, which could never have been mistaken for anything but a gaol, had given place to façades that might appertain to any sort of public service. Inside the building, court-rooms cheerful with green leather and light unpolished oak panelling and frescoed staircases now replaced the dusty Old Bailey courts, in which the huge size of the dock had been eloquent of days when batches of men were hanged for petty felonies, and where the reek of a poisonous past seemed to exude from the walls.

Early in the year it became evident that the leaders of the new agitation for woman suffrage had discovered how to attract the notice of crowds. On the evening of the day after the session opened, and again a month later, when a Woman Suffrage Bill introduced by Mr W. H. Dickinson had been talked out, the Women's Social and Political Union organised large processions to the House of Commons. These were developments from the smaller affairs of the previous year, the object now being to force the police to arrest women in considerable numbers, with the view of producing an embarrassment for the authorities. Sixty-five women were arrested on the first occasion, and seventy-six on the second ; and all of them refused to pay fines, and had to be committed to prison. The crowds that watched the scenes in Parliament Square were for the most part of a rough or careless type, only there as spectators of struggles of women and policemen. But certainly one result of the notoriety attained by these methods was that suffragist speakers at meetings up and down the country were able to gather audiences which even a year before they could never have mustered. The Women's Social and Political Union prided itself on bringing as much new life into the propagandist side of the work as it had brought into the direct demand upon the Government. None the less, the union was associated in the minds of ordinary persons less with meetings than with public agitation. The older bodies of suffragists, not at all convinced that their object was really furthered by notoriety, were inclined to distinguish themselves from the new body ;

1907] PAGEANTRY, SUFFRAGETTES

and the attachment of a popular label, "The Suffragettes,"
to the latter helped the distinction. What chiefly marked
the suffragettes' position was persistence in countering or
over-riding all the stock political objections to the urgency
of their case. They maintained unflinchingly the attitude
that woman suffrage was not a question which ought to be
subject to the normal course of political questions ; it
ought not to depend on the state of opinion in the Cabinet,
on the state of business in the House, or on the pledges of
members to their constituents. They presented it simply
as a demand ; and treated lack of response to the demand
as hostility to it. The subject had not been mentioned in
the King's Speech. No one imagined it would be, but the
suffragettes took the fact as a form of refusal. Mr Dickinson's Bill did not satisfy all in the House who supported
woman suffrage, and in any case a private member's Bill
could not, by any normal political canons, bring about a
change so vast. Yet the talking out of the Bill was again
treated as a refusal. The suffragettes decided to work
in the constituencies against every Liberal candidate,
whether he were personally a suffragist or not, so long as the
Liberal Government did not produce a Woman Suffrage
Bill. They had clever and energetic speakers, who entered
with zest into street-corner meetings, faithful to the
union's original reliance upon the working woman, and
they added immensely to the vigour and interest of by-
election campaigns. During the year it became plain
that an extraordinarily baffling situation could be brought
about by the uncompromising position the suffragettes
had adopted.

A vacancy occurred during the spring in the representation of Wimbledon. Mr Chaplin became the Unionist
candidate, and the Liberal candidate, Mr Bertrand
Russell, put Woman Suffrage in the forefront of his programme. This may in itself have been the step forward
which suffragists considered it to be ; but the result

showed that as an appeal to the electorate it was not very effective. Mr Russell was beaten by nearly 7000. Mr Chaplin was an avowed anti-suffragist. Parliament passed in this year the Bill qualifying women to serve on county and borough councils. Many people had been disappointed when the test case brought after the first London County Council election in 1889 exposed the fact that women could not legally be elected ; and the Bill now establishing their right to sit was generally welcomed.

At the beginning of the session there was not much sign of the comparative lack of legislative work which has been mentioned. The King's Speech referred to the differences which had arisen between the two Houses, but did no more than record the fact. The programme laid before Parliament included Licensing Reform, an Army Bill, and a Criminal Appeal Bill, besides the Women's Bill just mentioned. To this list were added a Bill to set up councils in Ireland with some power of legislation —an attempt at a new form of Home Rule, based largely on the " devolution " ideas, and owing, in fact, much to Sir Antony Macdonnell ; an Education Bill, being a fresh effort to settle the vexed question by agreement ; a Land Valuation Bill ; and certain Small Holdings Bills. But the licensing question was postponed. The terms of educational settlement proposed by Mr McKenna, who had succeeded Mr Birrell at the Board of Education, did not commend themselves to the Archbishop of Canterbury, and the Government dropped that Bill. The Irish Councils Bill was also dropped. It was in charge of Mr Birrell, who, on the appointment in the previous December of Mr Bryce to be ambassador in Washington, had left the Education Office, in some disappointment at the loss of the Bill which had cost him so much labour, and had undertaken the Irish Chief Secretaryship. He was not now more fortunate, except that he wasted less labour.

The new proposal ·for Ireland was far removed from Home Rule. It made no difference to Irish representation at Westminster; it stipulated what the new bodies should be competent to deal with, instead of merely what they should not; it set up no new Irish executive. It was, in fact, a measure which might almost have been within the contemplation of Mr Wyndham two years previously. At the same time, it was the nearest to Home Rule that the present Cabinet and Parliament could venture after the statements at the election of Sir Edward Grey and Mr Asquith. At first the measure seemed to be a success; it was not refused point-blank by the Irish Nationalists. But a convention in Dublin in the spring settled its fate; the party returned to the full Home Rule demand, and the Bill was dropped.

The Army Bill was chiefly remarkable to the general public for its reorganisation of the auxiliary forces. It proposed to throw the militia, the yeomanry, and the volunteers into a single arm, to be called the Territorial Force. This was to take a definite place in national defence, with more effective training and a closer relation to the regular army. Recruiting was to be assisted, and the drain of camps and equipment on the private purses of officers and men to be lightened, by placing the Territorial Forces under county associations, presided over by the lords lieutenant, who were thus restored to a long-lost position of military authority. Strong objections were raised to the inclusion of the militia in the new force; and in the end Mr Haldane gave way on that proposal. The assigning to the volunteers of a definite place in our lines of defence, the assurance thereby given of more generous consideration of their needs and more serious attention to their training on the part of the War Office, gave real encouragement to the men. Those who had ceased to believe in the efficacy of voluntary service, and were agitating for compulsory service, were not converted ; they laughed to scorn Mr Haldane's contention that, with the new training, the Territorial Force could at any time, with six months' hard continuous work, fit itself to take the place of the regular army, in the event of a war drawing off the whole of the latter. Critics remarked that in such a war we could hardly arrange for a peaceful six months to practise our territorials. It was also said that the force could never be worked up to the establishment projected for it. But the immediate effect was undoubtedly to give the volunteers fresh vitality, and in spite of the grumbles the new scheme started well. Later in the year the King summoned the lords lieutenant to Buckingham Palace, and commended the scheme to their patriotic energies.

On the whole the year's work was not very Radical ; and indeed the Opposition began to pluck up heart. Mr Balfour was leading them again with some spirit. He had been curiously ineffective in the first session of the new Parliament ; and nothing could have shown more clearly the truth of the belief that the Parliament stood for a great change. His skill in debate was for a time completely lost upon a House that regarded his airiness and his light-handed dexterity with an amazed impatience. It had slowly learned the power that lay behind the lightness ; and although Liberals felt, with a growing resentment, that the true opposition to their purposes was not in the House of Commons at all, they came to regard Mr Balfour's leadership as a reality. The apparent failure of the Government to keep up the pace of its programme, the postponing or dropping of various measures, gave the Opposition some opening; and they took full advantage of it. The most Radical work of the session was to be found in the Budget, when Mr Asquith introduced into the system of taxation a distinction between earned and unearned incomes, and laid a supertax, in addition to increased death-duties, on estates of over a million pounds. On earned incomes the income-tax was reduced to ninepence, while on unearned incomes it remained at a shilling. In conjunction with the concession, income-tax surveyors were empowered to examine the salary-books of firms, a check upon evasions of the tax which were believed to be becoming serious and habitual. Out of his surplus, Mr Asquith allotted a million and a half to reducing the National Debt. By his energetic restoration of the sinking fund, and by allocations of his surpluses, he had in these two years taken some twenty-six millions off the debt.

Lapse of time since the general election inevitably tended to weaken the impression of that event as a national awakening. There was a disinclination on the part of the public to face in any large way the problem of the House of Lords, or to formulate a struggle between the electorate and the hereditary legislators. London, as if to balance its unusual return of Liberals to Parliament, turned the Progressives out of office at the County Council election, and gave a large majority to the Municipal Reformers. The International Horse Show in the summer, with the ring turned at vast expense into a bowery garden, and millionaires' horses stabled in luxury like that of the famous horse of Caligula, was a thoroughly popular affair, and roused no democratic ire. Opportunities occurred for disgruntled Tories to maintain the view that the result of the general election had its root, not in deep political conviction, but in mere caprice, and a disregard of tradition and authority, which was in many ways deplorable, and in some dangerous. The outbreak of " living statuary " exhibitions at music halls ; the turning of country-house parties into reckless " rags," with young men and women pillow-fighting in corridors, or squirting soda-water siphons at one another ; a cheerful irresponsible interest in crime, which laughed at the impudence of the theft of the Gold Cup from Ascot racecourse, and enjoyed the wildest gossip about the far more mysterious and unpleasant loss of the regalia of the Order of St Patrick from Dublin Castle in July ; even such a break with tradition as the fact that the notable recipients of degrees at the Oxford Encænia were popular idols like Mark Twain, Rudyard Kipling, and General Booth—these were regarded as instances of the deplorable side of the change. The dangerous side was discerned in the introduction of Radical feeling into our control of Egypt and India. There was a fear lest expectations aroused among the Nationalists of those countries by the overwhelming return of a Liberal Government should be precipitated into open revolt. India, indeed, was already disturbed ; rioting took place in Calcutta in September, and a visit paid by Mr Keir Hardie about that time was deeply resented by the authorities. Lord Cromer, resigning in April the post in Egypt which he had held for nearly twenty-five difficult years, and returning to England in May, spoke with bitterness of the delivery of speeches by " irresponsible politicians " rousing unrest among Eastern peoples under our control. There was certainly on the Ministerial side a group of members who did not hesitate to affirm that both in India and in Egypt a Liberal Ministry ought to be taking steps towards establishing self-government, and with-drawing from a control which was " of little profit " to " the democracy " either in those countries or in England. Lord Cromer himself had fallen under special attack in 1906. A riot had occurred in a village in Egypt to which some English officers had gone for pigeon-shooting ; one of the officers had died of injuries inflicted by the natives. For this four villagers were hanged, and eighteen others sentenced to various periods of penal servitude (two for life) and to flogging. It was argued that British officers had no right to go shooting in places where their presence was likely to cause such outbreaks, and that in any case the vengeance exacted had been outrageously severe. If such measures were necessary for upholding British prestige, then our presence in the country was unjustifiable. It was inevitable that the new Parliament should display a good deal of hostility to the traditional structure of our position both in India and in Egypt. It was a structure with which the aristocracy and the upper middle class chiefly had been concerned ; and members who felt their support to lie in other ranks of the community were not disposed to pass over in silence the activities of administrations based on conditions of an earlier day. The mistake of such members was to suppose that the British voter had any real knowledge of, or concern for, the affairs of our dependencies. The interest in them still remained an aristocratic and upper middle-class interest ; and spasmodic newspaper intelligence concerning India and Egypt, or even concerning the colonies, did nothing to create real opinion.

In the sphere of foreign politics there did appear to be some change of the national habit. Since the *entente cordiale* had caught popular fancy, there had been an impulse to make our foreign relations depend less upon the exchanges of diplomacy than upon mutual acquaintance. The municipalities of capital and provincial towns visited one another, and these visits were interchanged not only between France and England, but also between Germany and England. A party of British journalists went to Germany in May, were received by the Emperor at Potsdam, and were fêted in all the principal towns. The Lord Mayor and Corporation of London were the guests of the Municipality of Berlin in June. This new faith in the efficacy of a spirit less formal than that of diplomacy was largely due, of course, to the conviction that we owed our friendliness with France to the personal popularity of King Edward in Paris, and his own liking for the French. It was, in its way, a more striking

example of the working of new ideas in national life than
the general election had been, and even more hopeful
from the Radical point of view. If the ordinary Englishman could feel that our relations with foreign countries
depended on himself, a new era of peace and common-
sense might be dawning. Yet the movement became
in this very year unexpectedly complex. Russia began
to be drawn into our range of agreements. When the
King was at Marienbad in the summer, for his accustomed
" cure," he entertained the Russian Foreign Minister at
lunch ; and a few weeks later an Anglo-Russian agreement, embodying terms of settled policy in regard to the
relations between the two countries at certain long-vexed
points of contact in Asia, was published. Now Radicals,
if they were to encourage a popular interest in international
affairs, were not going to let it be blindfolded, and they
considered it to be a mockery of the democratic spirit
to invoke its friendly inclinations on behalf of a tyrannical
government. In the previous year a violent repression of
revolution in Moscow had been succeeded by the summoning of the first attempt in Russia at a popularly elected
assembly. The Duma, as this assembly was called, had
shown considerable spirit ; it had demanded an amnesty
for all political prisoners, the establishment of constitutional monarchy and the concession to itself of the
right to initiate legislation. The Russian executive, not
at all inclined to move at this speed, thwarted all these
proposals, and the Duma was dissolved by the Tsar after
ten weeks' existence. It happened at that moment that
the Inter-Parliamentary Union was meeting in England,
and representatives from this youngest parliament had
been welcomed enthusiastically. When the news came
of the abrupt end of its career, Sir Henry Campbell-
Bannerman, speaking at a luncheon in honour of the
Inter-Parliamentary Union, used the words: "La Douma
est morte; vive la Douma!" Radicals could not embrace

the prospect of a closer relation with the government
which had treated so summarily the hopes of a new
regime; and they began to wonder if the appearance of
fresh influences in international affairs had not been a
little illusory.

The summer of 1907 was the great Pageant summer.
In 1905 the ancient little town of Sherborne in Dorset had
felt impelled, largely by the fortunate fact of its having
a claim upon the interest of a popular playwright—Mr
Louis Parker—to celebrate its antiquity by an open-air
dramatic representation of notable events in its history.
These performances were a great success, and the town had
found so much amusement in mustering its performers,
dressing them, and beholding Saxons and Danes,
Plantagenets, Tudors, Cavaliers and Puritans walking
its streets, that other towns were filled with emulation.
Writers were not wanting to construct episodes; persons
with some experience of the stage were ready to drill the
performers; few towns of importance were without a
Saxon battle, or a charter from some Plantagenet king,
a visit from Queen Elizabeth, or an association with the
Civil War; and few towns, too, lacked inhabitants with
leisure enough to enjoy the mild fuss of committee work
and organisation. Oxford, St Alban's, the Isle of Wight,
Warwick, Coventry, Bury St Edmunds, Liverpool set
up wooden structures in fields or parks, and inhabitants
going about their daily affairs would be confronted with
knights in armour; ladies in gay colours, farthingales
and ruffs; rude bowmen and long-haired Saxons. The
fashion lasted into the two following summers, but with
declining energy. It produced no really new or vital
form of art; the books of pageants were mere skeletons;
the episodes were monotonously similar in different towns,
consisting almost always of battles, royal visits and other
occurrences, which were local merely in the sense of
having happened on the spot, and not at all in representing

local character or atmosphere. At Oxford a Masque of Learning, interposed into the succession of episodes, afforded a glimpse of better things ; it depended for its effect upon ideas, as the old morality plays did. But it was the only attempt of the kind, and the Pageant movement died away without having called into being either a local art or a feeling for local history. It had been a mere excursion into amateur open-air performances of conventional stage notions.

On the stage itself, however, new ideas seemed to be gathering strength. At the Royal Court Theatre Mr Granville Barker, in conjunction with Mr Vedrenne, had for some time been boldly producing plays which four or five years earlier would have appeared only at the Stage Society. There now existed a public for the drama of ideas, of social problems, of class foibles, and even of national foibles ; and in 1907 the Vedrenne-Barker management moved to a larger and more central theatre, the Savoy. New methods of acting were as characteristic of the management as a new standard of plays ; unfortunately the larger size of the Savoy seemed to militate against the subtlety of the acting, and the venture lost some of its earlier success. One of the interesting results of the Vedrenne-Barker management was that it provided a rallying-point for dramatists who were trying to break new ground. Mr Bernard Shaw had by this time attained a popular success ; and he had been the main support of the Court Theatre. Mr John Galsworthy, Mr St John Hankin, Mr John Masefield and Mr Granville Barker were the other notable figures of the group. An immediate consequence of the attempt to produce plays challenging the conventional judgments of society was increased resentment against the autocratic operation of the Lord Chamberlain's power of censorship over the London stage. An agitation was now set on foot which led to the appointment in 1909 of a select committee.

Outside London, the most interesting theatrical developments were the great success of the Abbey Theatre,
Dublin, where the work of a group of Irish dramatists—
among whom Lady Gregory, Mr W. B. Yeats and Mr
J. M. Synge were prominent—was played by a company
of actors more homogeneous than London, under the
sway of the " star " actor or actress, ever produced ; and
the establishment about this time of a Repertory Theatre
in Manchester, which soon made its name for courage in
the production of plays, and success in acting them.
But interest in the drama still remained the mark of a
rather limited section of the public.

In literature change and development were far more
free. Of the older novelists two, who had had for long
to be content with the devotion of the few, began to find
their way to a wider recognition. The appointment of
Mr George Meredith to the Order of Merit in 1905 made
his admirers rejoice that there was, in this order, a
personal distinction which he could accept with dignity ;
as people had previously rejoiced in its bestowal upon
Mr John Morley.[1] Mr Henry James saw his art by now
more widely appreciated and understood. Fame had
been reached at a bound by Mr William De Morgan,
more slowly by Mr Arnold Bennett, both of them writers
in the true succession of the romantic English novel. Mr
De Morgan, bringing the experience of a long life and an
extraordinary human sympathy to bear upon the way-
wardness of his fellow-men, touched the feelings of a
generation which (if sometimes only from slackness) was
on the whole more genial and kindly than its predecessors.
Mr Arnold Bennett, keenly alive to the swiftness with
which traditions were being undermined, gave preserva-
tion to lower middle-class types of a period incredibly

---

[1] The Order of Merit had been established by King Edward in 1902,
largely with the intention of honouring those to whom the traditional
honours could not be acceptable.

close at hand in mere date.   A mind as keenly, and more
nervously, aware of change was that of Mr H. G. Wells.
Having first found his public, in the days of the worship
of science and invention, with novels that prolonged
to most entertaining distances the avenues of possibility
opened by the scientist, he had reacted immediately to
the cry for efficiency.   An early member of the Fabian
Society, and imbued with the methods of the laboratory,
he had thus two lines of intellectual response to that cry ;
and he began to throw into the form of fiction, more and
more characterised by wide sweeps of social analysis, his
vision of the wastefulness and inefficiency of domestic,
civic and political life.   Curiously enough, as the novelists
grew more searching, taste in literature became wider in
its scope.   Novels had to compete in the higher social
ranks with volumes of memoirs and letters, which were
often more entertaining in a society which had known
the personalities appearing in such books, or knew their
descendants.   Less exalted people turned again to the
essay, which had had little vogue since the death of
Stevenson ; Mr Belloc, Mr E. V. Lucas, and Mr Max
Beerbohm brought light hands to the practice of this art ;
and Mr A. C. Benson occupied something like a popular
pulpit.   With the taste for memoirs went a taste also for
history within reach of our own day ; Lord Rosebery's
Napoleon, The Last Phase, and Mr George Trevelyan's
works on the campaigns of Garibaldi largely formed this
taste.

For some time past, women had taken an increasingly
high position among English writers of novels ; more
than one of the most prominent, such as Miss Robbins
and Miss May Sinclair, were by now also responding to
political developments in virtually restricting themselves
to Feminist topics.

In the autumn various stout efforts were made to
convince the world that navigable balloons were to be

our means of commanding the air. The achievements of M. Santos-Dumont have already been referred to.[1] The French Government had an airship, *La Patrie* ; the German Government was supporting Count Zeppelin's experiments with enormous dirigibles, of which the gas-chambers were constructed from rigid materials, instead of from silk reinforced by rigid frames ; and the British army had an airship, the *Nulli Secundus*, on which great hopes were centred. When it sailed up from Aldershot to the Crystal Palace there was much excitement. But it was unable to make its way back against the wind, and was anchored in the Crystal Palace grounds. There it justified those who maintained that the vast unwieldiness of the " lighter-than-air " structure must always prevent it from becoming really effective. A storm came on, and the *Nulli Secundus* was ignominiously wrecked at its moorings.

A labour movement which arose in the late summer concentrated sharply all the alarm which the Government's great majority had provoked among persons of property. For some weeks a prospect of a general strike threatened the railway system of the country. Railway employees were dissatisfied with their position, and the Amalgamated Society of Railway Servants was making representations to the directors of various companies. The directors now took the line of refusing to recognise the right of the society to general representation of railway men, and said that complaints would only be heard by each company from its own men. In minor ways this question of the " recognition " of trade unions had often been raised before. In some important cases, such as the cotton trade, it had never been fought as a principle ; in others, such as the mining industry, it had been settled years ago. It was, perhaps, unfortunate that in the case of railways the question should have been left open until

1 See page 577.

a time when it appeared to many people to be an ostentatious exploiting by labour of a Government placed in power largely by a working-class vote. The railway directors pointed out that the Amalgamated Society only included one-fifth or one-sixth of the railway employees of the country, and therefore could not properly even raise the question of corporate representation. This implied almost as profound a disturbance of the practice of trade combination as the Taff Vale decision had made. If a union was to measure its responsibility solely by the proportion of its membership to the number of persons in the industry the work of a good many years would be largely lost. The society threatened a general railway strike, and for some weeks the position was full of anxiety. Mr Lloyd George intervened on behalf of the Board of Trade ; and when, after long negotiations, he succeeded in the peaceful establishment of a system of conciliation and arbitration, there was so great a relief that a certain tendency to regard him as a hot-headed demagogue underwent modification. He was credited with possessing more genuine gifts of administration than his opponents had supposed. The settlement to which the two sides agreed under his guidance consisted in the division of railway employees into groups; the creation on each railway system of a conciliation board for each group, composed of representatives of the masters and of the men ; and the appointment for each railway of a central board, with an independent chairman, on the principle of the Coal Conciliation Board. The chairman would have the power of making awards.

The opening in June of one more tube railway—from Charing Cross to Hampstead and Highgate—completed this new network of London communications. The circle of the old Underground Railway had been cut, first lengthwise by the Central London Railway, and now from north to south by the City & South London Tube on the east, the Highgate & Hampstead line in the middle, and the

Bakerloo & Piccadilly tubes on the west. Some curious results followed. Brompton, for instance, had become a more convenient place of residence than parts of Westminster ; Chelsea Embankment was practically farther away than Hampstead. New suburbs began to arise in Hampstead, and the Garden City Movement could profitably set itself to work there. The more distant suburbs reached from Waterloo and Charing Cross had fresh means of pouring inhabitants into all parts of working London ; and the problem of the dreariness of Clapham or Stockwell lodgings for clerks, which at one time had begun to lead in the direction of hostels for young men, ceased to be important. Clerks could now lodge within reach of tennis and cricket and football. The capacity for " having a good time " had taken one more turn, and opened itself to more people.

The end of the year saw also the end of a fantastic case, in which the public had from time to time found amusement. The fifth Duke of Portland, who died in 1879, had been notoriously eccentric. He had been given to disappearing for weeks ; he had avoided the sight of his fellows, and built himself strange underground rooms and passages in his great park at Welbeck. Hence, when a story arose that a certain Thomas Charles Druce, the head of a furniture business in London, had really been this duke—that the Duke, when he disappeared, was really carrying on a second existence as Mr Druce—the wild romance obtained no little credulity. It became after a time a more serious affair, since the representatives of Mr Druce based upon it a claim to the Portland estates. They alleged that the coffin supposed to contain the remains of Mr Druce contained nobody at all, but that the Duke, in order to put an end to a double life which at last embarrassed him, had caused a mock funeral to take place. For some years this story was no more than a pastime to the public, and Mrs Druce's various applications to the law were regarded as

the fruits of delusion. But in 1907 she brought forward
evidence of a more definite kind; her witnesses were a
man who alleged that he had attended the Duke, and had
known him also in his Druce impersonation, and a woman
who professed to tell the story of the empty coffin.
Mrs Druce's case had become a joint-stock affair; people
invested money in it as a speculation, to be repaid with
interest in the event of her success. The production of these
witnesses brought matters to a head. There had always
been assertions that the individuals in possession of the
Portland estates had contrived to burke inquiry; but there
was no difficulty of that kind now. The only hesitation
of the authorities arose from the fact that the whole story
was so notoriously fantastic that to make any concession
to it might seem undignified. On 27th December the
chancellor of the diocese of London issued a faculty for
opening the grave of T. C. Druce in Highgate Cemetery.
Early one winter's day the work was done in the presence
of accredited witnesses; the coffin was found to contain
the body of an aged and bearded man, " unmistakably "
the Thomas Druce who was said to have been a fiction.
Except for some necessary perjury proceedings against
the two sensational witnesses, this closed the romance.

CHAPTER XIV

1908 : THE LICENSING BILL AND FLYING MACHINES

THE year 1908 was the year in which the world first saw men flying. For some time it had been well known by those who had more than common knowledge of aeronautical invention that the "heavier than air" principle had been making great strides. The gliding experiments of Lilienthal and Pilcher had given such assurance to mathematical calculations of the behaviour of plane surfaces in air that the advent of very light motors had almost immediately turned gliding into flying. Vague reports arrived at intervals from the United States of experiments which were being conducted in secrecy at Dayton, Ohio, by two brothers named Wright. The general public was rather sceptical, and inclined to scoff at these rumours of flying men. Having no idea of the behaviour of plane surfaces in air, it imagined that tremendous lifting apparatus—heavy lifting propellers —would be absolutely necessary. So far as the public had seen any aeroplane inventions, it had acquired little respect for them ; it had witnessed small models at the Alexandra Palace flying about as well as superior paper darts. Mr S. F. Cody, with his large apparatus rather like a vast combination of box-kites, had no engine powerful enough to produce by traction the pressure required to lift the affair. The best brains of motor engineers were not in England, but in France ; and the engine-makers naturally preferred to conduct their experiments in that country. It was France that now first witnessed a man flying in public. On 13th January M. Farman, a Frenchman, but the son of an English newspaper correspondent in Paris, leapt into fame by winning the Deutsch-Archdeacon prize of £2000 for a circular flight in a machine heavier than air. Broadly speaking, there had as yet been no other type of machine than the one he used ; therefore to speak of it as a biplane is an anachronism ; but for purposes of description the name may be allowed.

Frequently after his prize flight M. Farman was seen in the air ; and when it was announced in September that Mr Wilbur Wright also had flown, covering a distance of thirty miles in forty minutes, it was a natural conclusion that mechanical flight would now develop very rapidly. If the Wrights had been brought out of their long seclusion by M. Farman's sudden success, and had triumphantly flown, then the problem was solved, and the world had only to await swift developments. Nevertheless unbelievers were not at once converted. Flights as yet had only taken place in calm weather ; the Farman and Wright biplanes, though much less cumbrous than Mr Cody's evolution of the box-kite, were still very large things, and considered as lifting agents for a single human being were unwieldy and disproportionate. Moreover they rose but slowly from the ground, and required an apparatus of running rails, with weights and pulleys on uprights, to give them the initial impulse.[1] It was still easy, even if rash, for sceptics to express the conviction that flying could not be more than a cumbrous performance of short distances by single individuals. But enough had

[1] A curious example of the slowness of even brilliantly quick imaginations to distinguish between the essential and unessential elements in these first experiments may be seen in Mr Kipling's *With the Night Mail*, published this year. Professing to forecast the state of mechanical flight in A.D. 2008, it includes among advertisements of " crack " aeroplane makers, sets of running rails for starting. Such things had passed entirely out of use within twelve months of these first flights:

been done already to cause the experiments at Farnborough, first made notable by the patience and admirable self-confidence of Mr Cody, to be infused with new life. A biplane of the Farman type was secured. Men with real knowledge of engineering refused to see limits to possibilities now that engines of the kind used on these machines had been put together, and driven with success. The navigable balloon was not abandoned ; its power of lifting a number of persons remained a strong advantage over the aeroplane, and *Zeppelin No.* 4 in June made a flight with fifteen passengers on board, behaving well against the wind. But she was wrecked in August, and her achievements did not for a moment turn men's minds from the aeroplane. The latter was far less costly than an airship, could be much more easily housed, and even at this early stage was more to be trusted against a wind. Experiments with airships continued for some years ; but the enormous bulk of their gas-envelopes, combined with the fact that, being lighter than air, they were extremely difficult to control at anchor, rendered them possessions beset with anxiety.

The assassination of the King and the Crown Prince of Portugal in the streets of Lisbon on 1st February was received with sorrow in England. King Edward was known to have a particular liking for King Carlos. One sequel to the event has importance for the observer of English manners and customs. King Edward and Queen Alexandra attended not only a memorial service at St Paul's, but a Requiem Mass at the Roman Catholic Church of St James's, Spanish Place. There was still, as we have seen in the matter of the Accession Declaration, a body of opinion in this country which regarded Rome as the Scarlet Woman ; but that King Edward should be able to attend a Requiem Mass showed a considerable advance in national common-sense and national respect for the sovereign. He was extraordinarily careful of public

24

opinion, and not at all the man to affront it in such a connection, however strong his own wishes might be. There were some who managed to regard the incident as one more sign of the general loosening of ties of authority ; the bulk of the people, they said, sat so loosely to religious observances that it had ceased to matter what kind of service the King attended. It was at least equally true that a great part of the nation had infused a new life into their religion. If going to church had ceased among people of education to be a sign of respectability, if men of all classes used Sunday openly as a day of physical recreation and stayed away from church without any sense of being outcasts, the converse of this state of things was that the people who did go to church did not go for conventional reasons, but for spiritual reasons. Hence there had arisen a new respect for all religious observances—a respect which ceased to regard them as mutually exclusive. King Edward could attend a Requiem Mass without being misunderstood. The Pan-Anglican Conference, which assembled this year, stimulated reflections on the Englishman's religion. When such a conference had first been called, some thirty years earlier, there had been scoffing at the idea of the Church of England proposing to issue encyclicals or to command the lives of men by conclaves of bishops ; that might be done by the Church of Rome, but was not, it was said, the genius of the Church of England, which would only make itself ridiculous. In 1908 the Pan-Anglican Conference met without any such assumptions, but in very good heart. Those who listened in Canterbury Cathedral to the Archbishop's address to the concourse of dignitaries from the ends of the earth may well have been startled, as their eyes fell on some recumbent archbishop of the Middle Ages, to think how puzzled he must have been if he had returned to life at that moment. Here were the leaders of a Church whose boundaries reached far, and very far, beyond anything he had dreamed, bishops whose presence would have been to him the token of an incredible authority over the life and wealth of many nations. Yet they were listening to no discourse on control or the enriching of the Church; they were being addressed as having assembled to face humbly and patiently the advances of science and secular thought, and to consider how best in modern life the spirit of the Church might be upheld. How slowly, perhaps how scornfully, would that mediæval prince of the Church have come to the knowledge that this ecclesiastical host had gathered, not as the relentless engine he would have aspired to wield for the purging of heresy, but as a contemplative assembly! Yet if the conference met without conclusive power, it met without defiance or misgivings. Congregations in churches might be smaller than they had been; but the work of the Church in general had returned to work of faith; ethical impulses and intellectual activity were falling into line now as companions of, not the substitutes for, that central appeal.

The political year began much more briskly than it had done in 1907. A Licensing Bill was known to be in readiness, as the chief work of the session, and a scheme of Old Age Pensions was to make its appearance in connection with the Budget. A by-election in the Ashburton division of Devonshire early in January was fought with a good deal of fury. The militant suffragists had now attained a financial position which enabled them to take a prominent part in elections, and their policy of working against the Liberal caused some violent and unpleasant scenes. In the end a Liberal majority of 1283 was turned into a Conservative majority of 559. This was an unexpected shock to Ministerialists; it had the effect of concentrating the party more keenly upon its work, with a desire to achieve more social legislation than the comparatively thin harvest of the previous year.

But the session had hardly opened before it became

apparent that the Prime Minister was seriously ill. He
contracted influenza, and the strain of the past two years
ill disposed him to meet it. The time approached at which
it was King Edward's custom to go to Biarritz, to avoid the
east winds of an English spring. There was some speculation as to whether he would hold to his plans, or would
feel obliged to remain at home in case of a transference of
the premiership. When it was announced that he was
going abroad, as usual, the general supposition was that
there would be no need for changes in the Government
until his return. He went to call upon Sir Henry Campbell-
Bannerman before leaving England, and spent an hour
with him. King Edward was, as events proved, bidding
farewell to a minister whose career had been in some ways
as astonishing as any that ever brought a man to the right
hand of the Crown. Left to bear the brunt of criticising
the inception and conduct of the Boer War, he had come
through the ordeal with only one phrase quoted against
him, and that not an ill-tempered one. An uninspiring
holder of office in earlier days, he was not a brilliant
leader ; but, at the time he came into office, fight was itself
the inspiration of the party under him, and all that his
followers demanded was that the fire they could provide
should be in hands in which it would burn clearly. He
was clear and honest. He spoke plainly, and he could
be silent. He knew better than to talk of one thing only,
or on one level. He was kindly, and socially was never a
bore ; he was not, like Mr Gladstone, an infliction to the
sovereign. He had managed a difficult cabinet without
leakage of secrets, and he had restored to Government
a dignity of closed mouths, which it had recently come
near to losing. It might be said by some that he trod
on foes, rather than flourished banners, but the exclama-
tions of the trodden-on sufficed to show his party where he
was. It found him always where it expected to, and that
was mainly the secret of his achievement. He died on

22nd April, and was buried at his home in Scotland. Many men found that their loss in his death was greater than they would have thought possible three or four years earlier.

He did not die as Prime Minister. He had resigned office on 5th April, having felt, no doubt, that affairs in Parliament demanded that the presence of a Prime Minister should be not lacking. Mr Asquith had been summoned to Biarritz. Again the observers of manners and customs had a theme for comment. The realm of England was left for some days without a Sovereign, a Prime Minister, or a Prince of Wales (for the Prince happened to be visiting the German Emperor in Berlin). This again was a matter of common-sense ; with the rapidity of modern travel, and the constant communication by telegraph, there was no need to put the sovereign to inconvenience. Mr Asquith returned as Prime Minister, and some other changes befell. It was no surprise that Mr Lloyd George became Chancellor of the Exchequer. He had gained, before the Liberals came into office, a reputation that made him secure of a high position. The courage and debating power he had shown during the war and during the progress of the Education Bill of 1902 had been followed by a display of extraordinary platform adroitness during the fiscal controversy; he and Mr Winston Churchill had been the most persistently prominent champions on the Free Trade side. Now Mr Lloyd George had been able to add administrative reputation to his former achievements. His two chief Bills—that establishing the Census of Production, and a Bill in 1907 compelling the working in this country of patents taken out in Great Britain, under penalty of the withdrawal of the patent—had both been generally welcomed; and his settlement of the railway difficulty, followed in the early part of 1908 by the settlement of a strike of shipyard engineers on the north-east coast, in which 30,000 men had come out against a reduction of wages, had displayed a capacity for sober and patient negotiation little expected from a man supposed by his opponents to be a courtier of the populace. None the less, his appointment to the Exchequer, though it had been anticipated, did not pass without shaking of heads. He was still, to a great part of the nation, essentially a demagogue. Mr Winston Churchill succeeded him at the Board of Trade. Lord Elgin left the Colonial Office, not unaccompanied by rumours that his more Radical colleagues had found him wanting in enterprise. He was succeeded by Lord Crewe. Mr Runciman took over the harassing post of President of the Board of Education. Mr McKenna left that office for the Admiralty.

This last change was associated with a curious story. Early in March a letter published in *The Times*—headed " Under Which King ? "—disclosed the fact that Lord Tweedmouth, then first Lord of the Admiralty, had been carrying on a correspondence with the German Emperor about British and German naval policy. This was felt to be extending, to a strange degree, the doctrine of personal acquaintance in foreign relations. Such an interchange might be good, or it might be bad ; but it was at any rate disturbing at a moment when our naval policy was being based more openly than ever on rivalry with Germany. The building of the *Dreadnought*, which had been so gratifying to national pride, was now perceived to be attended by most serious consequences. If battleship design was to be wholly altered, then that advantage over other nations which we had possessed in the numbers of our fleet had been in effect thrown away. If the battle fleet of the future was to be a *Dreadnought* fleet, then we started almost at scratch with other nations—at least, with only the smallest start. When the Naval Estimates of this year came up for discussion, both the Prime

Minister and Mr McKenna had to take quite openly, as the basis of debate, comparison of our position with that of Germany. Germany had passed a new Navy Law, involving the replacement of her first fighting fleet by ships of the *Dreadnought* type; Mr Asquith and Mr McKenna had to give the House their calculations of the comparative strength of the two new navies in the years when the German law would have produced its full effects, principally in regard to 1911 and 1912. This was an awkward moment for the disclosure of correspondence, however admirably intended, between Lord Tweedmouth and the dictator of the German navy. Lord Tweedmouth's resignation of the Admiralty was inevitable. He was at the time falling into bad health, and he only held for a few months the office of Lord President of the Council, to which he was transferred.

During the year the public became as keenly interested in the new cruisers of the navy as it had been in the *Dreadnought*. Turbine engines had been introduced into a class of cruisers so big and well armed that they were hardly inferior to battleships. One of these vessels, the *Indomitable*, 17,250 tons, with eight 12-inch guns, was detailed to take the Prince of Wales to Quebec in the summer. On the return she was given a speed and endurance trial right across the Atlantic. The Prince, true to his profession as a sailor, took the greatest interest in the cruiser's performance, and stood his turn at helping the stokers. The average speed made throughout the run was 24·8 knots.

The new Government required all its energy. The Licensing Bill had been introduced on 27th February, and a storm had broken about it immediately. In brief, it proposed to establish the Peel system of reduction of licences till they reached a statutory proportion to population, with payment during a definite period of compensation, in lieu of notice, for licences suppressed

before the end of that period. The statutory proportion
was to be : in areas where the population averaged two
to the acre, one licence to 400 persons ; where the population averaged from two to twenty-five to the acre, one
licence to 500 persons ; and so on, up to a proportion of
one licence to 1000 persons where the population averaged
over two hundred to the acre. The time-limit was
fourteen years. Over new licences the Bill established
a system of local option ; and a certain form of option
was to apply to old licences after the fourteen years. It
was calculated that the number of licences which would
be suppressed by the operation of these proposals was
about 30,000. It was certainly a drastic Bill, and,
as has already been remarked, in the wide field of the
brewery share market the Bill became of immediate
financial concern to a very large portion of the community.[1] Those opposed to it were able to assert that,
in its hostility to a specific trade, the Government was
attempting to ride roughshod over the legitimate expectations of innocent persons ; it was proposing to destroy
assets upon the credit of which brewing firms had invited
the investments of the public. Moreover, as debenture
shares were open to trustee investments, a peculiarly
unguarded class of the community—those who as widows
or orphans or otherwise were subject to trustees in the
control of their means of livelihood—would suffer. All
the elements of opposition were organised skilfully. A
mass meeting was held at the Queen's Hall early in March
to protest against the Bill; a loftier sphere of influence
was stirred at the meeting of brewery debenture-holders
under Lord Rothschild. By a coincidence unfortunate
for the Government, a Liberal member for a London
constituency, Peckham, died just at this date. A by-
election in any part of the country would have been
a serious affair, but happening in London it became

1 See page 652.

the most amazing battlefield of contending interests.
Never before had such a crop of minor political organisations sprung up to obscure the regular party battalions.
Some, which were nominally independent, like the militant
suffragists, were in practice anti-Liberal. Some, like
the Tariff Reform League and the Free Trade Union, had
become familiar at all elections for the past four years.
Others, mysterious in origin, such as a body calling itself
the Coal Consumers' League, were transient crystallisa-
tions of floating mistrust of the most democratic Government of modern days. Finally, the various avowed
leagues of brewers and licensed victuallers naturally
occupied all the space they could. The contest developed
so extraordinary a character that within a few days it
had became a kind of show. People from all parts of
London joined the crowds in Peckham High Street, and
through the packed masses round the various temporary
platforms rolled waggons conveying " object-lessons "—
men dressed as miners protesting against a statutory
eight-hour day; imported manufactured goods with staring
labels of their country of origin; woman suffragists in
prison dress. The misfortune of the election, from the
Liberal point of view, was not only that it occurred in a
spot to which all sorts of organisations could without
effort despatch their speakers, but that Peckham was a
Unionist seat, only won in the general triumph of 1906,
and almost sure to revert now, even without such various
appeals. It did revert; the seat was won by the Unionist
candidate, by nearly 2500 votes; and the opponents
of the Licensing Bill scored a useful point.

It was doubtless an aftermath of this uproarious election
which caused the mobbing of a meeting held by the United
Kingdom Alliance in support of the Bill. But these
scenes were associated with a particular kind of hostility
to the Bill which the brewing firms and their supporters
soon found it necessary to repudiate. They would have

preferred rather less enthusiasm on the part of the licensed victualler, who as a class was not discreet in his methods or his expressions. Anything that could be called " the public-house element " had better have been out of the way. As it was, the supporters of the Bill outside the Liberal party ranks found new texts for their advocacy in the posters displayed at the bars and the working up of bar opinion. The Archbishop of Canterbury frankly spoke in the Bill's favour, and the Bishop of London presided at a demonstration on the same side. The Bill was taken as far as the end of the first clause in Committee, and was then carried over to an autumn sitting.

There was some deploring of this postponement, on the ground of the opportunity it would give to rouse further feeling against the Bill. But a corresponding opportunity was open to advocates of the Bill, and their campaign was vigorous, and not ineffective. At any rate it was wise for the Government to give itself now to the popularity of introducing Old Age Pensions. The Budget statement (made by Mr Asquith, since the new Chancellor of the Exchequer had so lately assumed office) was cheerful. There had been a realised surplus of four and three-quarter millions, which was applied to the reduction of the National Debt. The estimated revenue for the coming year was £157,770,000 and the estimated expenditure £152,869,000. This allowed a remission of the sugar-duty, costing £3,400,000 ; and left enough for the cost of the first quarter's Old Age Pensions, £1,200,000, which was all that would fall on the present Finance Bill. Thus announced, the Pensions Scheme was introduced in a separate Bill. Pensions were to begin at the age of seventy years, and were to be five shillings a week. It was calculated that half-a-million people would come into the scheme, and that the cost would amount to about six millions a year. The hope was held out that in time the pensionable age would be reduced to sixty-five years.

There was criticism of the scheme from the Opposition. The Unionist theory of Old Age Pensions had always been that the scheme should carry with it some form of contribution during early life—should be, in fact, rather an insurance than a gift. But the theory had never been worked out in detail. The complaint about the free gift of the pensions was largely met by the answer that very many of the beneficiaries would, without the pension, be costing the community money as inmates of workhouses and infirmaries. Criticism of the Bill was, of course, dangerous ground; few men wished to be notable in their constituencies as opponents of Old Age Pensions; and the measure had therefore no real difficulties in the Commons. In the House of Lords, where there was no fear of constituents, opposition was rather more open. Lord Cromer went so far as to carry an amendment limiting the operation of the Bill to seven years. But this was an infringement of the privileges of the Commons, as touching finance, and the Speaker disallowed the amendment.

Mr Burns appeared in the legislative programme this year with a Housing and Town Planning Bill. Arising out of the helplessness of town councils to prevent the haphazard growth of ugly and crowded suburbs, which ate up land that might have afforded open spaces and natural amenities, the Bill empowered local authorities to acquire land for other than immediate building purposes, and to lay it out on considerations other than those of strict commercial value; and gave them some rights of control over the development of private estates. In his administrative work Mr Burns was as busy as ever. There were more prosecutions of local authorities in London—some Mile End Guardians, and some members of the Poplar and Stepney Sick Asylums Board.

It should be mentioned that in this year the Court of Criminal Appeal at last came into being. It had been

set up by an Act of 1907, and held its first sitting on
15th May 1908. Its work proved to be more expeditious
and less heavy than some people had expected. Lord
Halsbury had secured the introduction into the Bill of
an amendment requiring that no appeal should be allowed
except upon a certificate from the judge who tried the
case. This was a guarantee against merely frivolous
appeals, and also went some way to secure that juries
should not be influenced by the chance of an appeal, a
point about which a number of lawyers had been anxious.

The summer brought a new amusement, the great
exhibition ground at Shepherd's Bush. It was a much
more magnificent affair than Earl's Court, where the
Londoner had first learned to stroll about and listen to
bands. The new ground was more spacious, and modern
methods of building, with iron frames and reinforced
concrete walls, had conjured up, on what had been almost
a swamp, a small city of structures of most entertaining
flamboyance. They were occupied this year by a Franco-
British Exhibition ; and the *entente cordiale* was still
fresh enough to render the show very popular. The
President of the French Republic paid a state visit to
King Edward in May, and they visited the exhibition
together. With its gardens, its waterways, its electric
lights, its loggia restaurants, the White City sprang into
a well-advertised popularity ; its amusements, such as
the flip-flap and the scenic railway, suggested that the
last traces of British self-consciousness had disappeared.
The Olympic Games were held in England this year, and
a large stadium had been built for them on the exhibition
grounds. The public wearied rather quickly of watching
the contests, and only the Marathon race stirred much
excitement. It was run on a very hot day in July. An
Italian, named Dorando, was first at the tape ; but he had
fallen from exhaustion fifty yards from the finish, and
some officials, with unfortunate zeal, had helped him to

his feet. This was enough to disqualify him, and the race was awarded to the second man, an American, named Hayes. The results of the excitement lasted for some time, in the way that was by now growing familiar. Cheap newspapers caught at the word "Marathon," and any long race received the name; there were even in due time four-in-hand Marathons. The United States kept the affair up more specifically. The respective merits of Hayes and Dorando were fought out in three or four later races in New York. There was, on a review of the results of the Olympic Games, some chagrin that Great Britain had not fared better; the remarkable thing was that the chagrin should not have been greater. The croakers wagged their heads, and said that British youth was turning into a mere population of spectators at cricket and football matches, and had no longer any care for athletic reputation. It would have been sounder to take the view that the great spread of athletics, rather than a decline of interest in them, caused the philosophic temper with which the Olympic results were received. In the old days, when cricket and football were sports of the comparatively few, lawn tennis and swimming still more limited, and golf unknown in England, the less privileged part of the nation had to cling to the belief that its favoured members were the best athletes in the world. But now that hundreds of thousands were discovering by playing games themselves that prowess in games was difficult to attain, they had a more reasoned view, and were able to take defeat sportingly. It was because they played games now, that they could enjoy the game for its own sake. The only thoroughly satisfactory section of the Olympic Meeting, from the British point of view, was the regatta at Henley, where Great Britain swept the card.

Soon after the autumn session began, the authorities took more severe action against the militant suffragists than they had hitherto cared to take. On several occasions throughout the year there had been scenes of disorder. In January women attempted to force an entrance to the Prime Minister's residence, while the Cabinet was sitting; and the arrest of some of the women and their conveyance to the police station took place amid riotous scenes. A few days later the houses of various ministers were visited, and windows were broken. On 11th February there was another attempt to march a large procession to the House of Commons, and some fifty women were arrested; and two days later about ten of another deputation were arrested. At the end of June, after a further fight with the police in Parliament Square, there were twenty-nine arrests. The Women's Social and Political Union had grown enormously in numbers and influence; an offshoot from it, the Women's Freedom League, was pursuing much the same methods of propaganda. The union had considerable funds; and women of wealth and education, attracted by the focussing power of a single objective, threw in their lot with the new societies. Thousands of women also who had never seriously considered the political or legal position of their sex embraced with fervour a fiery presentation of the wrongs and slights to which it was subject. The Government was confronted with large numbers of women who, considering themselves outlaws under the existing system, determined to defy every convention or statute which had hitherto bound political action, whether it were an old law against assemblages within a certain distance of the Houses of Parliament, the customs governing behaviour at public meetings, or the conventions surrounding private life. Moreover, they exacted the infliction of the penalties most likely to offend public taste. They refused to pay fines, and went to prison, adding thus not only an appearance of harshness in the attitude of the authorities, but a new form of attack on masculine government by agitation as to the conditions of prison life. Their answer to every protest against their behaviour was that the Government could put an end to it in a moment, by carrying a Woman Suffrage measure. To any objections on the ground of party disagreement on the subject, or the comparative indifference of the electorate, their answer was that the women's demand for a vote was a fundamental demand.

Undoubtedly the agitation had completely altered the status of Woman Suffrage as a political question. In earlier years the efforts of suffrage societies had but slowly gathered adherents, and the mass of people never gave a thought to the matter. Now it was argued at street-corner meetings in every by-election ; campaigns were conducted up and down the country ; clever women speakers caught in the open-air people who would never have entered an ordinary meeting. Opposition and criticism of the methods pursued were persistent ; but that fact was in itself a great proof of the advance. Formerly the subject had hardly been vital enough to stir opposition. The older societies were themselves invigorated. Their dislike of violent methods became tempered by their admiration for the devotion and courage displayed, and by gratitude that the demand had been made real to the public. So the older societies joined with the new in great processions and demonstrations, such as those of the summer of 1908 in London. The processions were not only great in numbers, but were at times artistically impressive.

Another riot in Parliament Square on 13th October was attended by circumstances that led the authorities to take fresh steps. On 11th October a meeting had been held in Trafalgar Square, and handbills were distributed inviting the public to " help the suffragettes to rush the House of Commons." On this, summonses were issued against three of the most prominent leaders of the Women's

Social and Political Union for inciting to an illegal act, and as the summonses were disregarded the three were arrested. Parliament Square was held by police on the evening of the 13th, and women again marched up in detachments to struggle with the cordons. The handbill did not seem to have had any effect upon the public ; the crowd retained its usual attitude of curiosity and amusement ; but twenty-one women were arrested. The three leaders endeavoured to give importance to their case at Bow Street by issuing subpœnas to Mr Gladstone, as Home Secretary, and Mr Lloyd George, who had been present at the meeting in Trafalgar Square. But as a great many of the questions put for the defence were of a kind easy for the magistrate to disallow, the move was not effective. Nor was the attempt to prove that the word " rush " was not intended to be an incitement to violence. In default of being bound over in sureties to keep the peace, the three defendants went to prison. By this time the question was arising whether women suffragists in prison should be treated as political offenders and placed in the first division. Other uncomfortable questions were raised when, at a large suffrage meeting in the Albert Hall, at the end of November, militant suffragists interrupting Mr Lloyd George's speech were ejected with some violence from the audience. The policy of interrupting public meetings had long been pursued ; and the irritation of audiences at the hampering of well-known speakers had already led to unpleasant scenes ; but this occasion at the Albert Hall was the most important that had yet occurred. Briefly, the situation at the end of 1908 was that the whole subject of woman suffrage was on a new plane of reality ; support which had hitherto been given from considerations of expediency, or with the idea that the movement would not have any immediate importance, had fallen away ; on the other hand genuinely convinced politicians were formulating distinct schemes, some for partial

woman suffrage, giving the vote to women occupiers
and to married women whose husbands were qualified,
or to women occupiers alone, others for complete adult
suffrage.   Finally the presence of a large body of women
refusing to recognise anything but a Government measure,
brought in at once, had united all women suffragists in
a demand that the present Government should attend
to the matter ; and the general public, fairly sure that
nothing of the kind would be done at present, looked on,
partly with indifference, partly with a vague feeling that
the women had a good case, partly with resentment at
the way they were pressing it.   The elections in this year
of two women as mayors, Mrs Garrett Anderson at
Aldeburgh, and Miss Dove at High Wycombe, were useful
to the feminist cause.

Just before Parliament met for the autumn sitting
there was a great demonstration in Hyde Park against the
Licensing Bill.   Special trains from all parts of the country
brought up contingents.   The Commons pursued their
work on the Bill unmoved by the spectacle.   Surmises
were rife as to the treatment the Bill would receive in
the House of Lords.   It was to be expected that drastic
amendments would be introduced.   But the support which
prominent members of the Bench of Bishops had given to
the Bill, together with a feeling that important Unionist
peers would not wish to identify themselves too strongly
with the licensed victualling trade, led to the hope that
the amendments would not be beyond negotiation.
There was great amazement when the fate of the Bill was
actually settled by the Peers without the formality of
waiting for a debate upon it.   A meeting was held at
Lansdowne House on 24th November, at which a resolution was taken to reject the Bill, as not advancing genuine
temperance reform, while causing inconvenience to many
of his Majesty's subjects, and violating the principles
of equity.   This meeting soon came to be regarded as a

tactical error. It had not been easy hitherto to make the question of the powers of the House of Lords appeal stirringly to Liberals. Even after the failure of the Education Bill, though a stout Radical core of the party was for a campaign against the House of Lords, the mass of Liberal electors felt only a grievance for which abolition or curtailment of the powers of the Lords seemed to be a remedy rather out of proportion. But the complete rejection of a measure, which was the outcome of much Liberal campaigning and of long-established tendencies, by a private meeting of peers, called forth a very different feeling, and was, indeed, a very different assertion of power. Besides, it affected the Liberal party in the Commons differently from the loss of the Education Bill. It produced a more profound sense of struggling against unfair odds, and a more angry resentment. There was no longer any doubt that the results of the election of 1906 had implied something which could not continue to exist without challenging the House of Lords. Before the year ended there had been more than one hint of the form of that challenge. The financial powers of the Commons had hitherto been regarded as supreme. If the recovery of the monopoly value of licences by the State after a limited period of years was refused by the Lords, steps could be taken to obtain a greater share of that monopoly value at once in the Finance Bill. At the same time, with the establishment of Old Age Pensions and a certainty of heavy Naval Estimates, the time was ripe for giving taxation a wider grip upon private wealth. That Radical Budget which had been foretold during the election was now in the making; and there was little concealment of the fact that it was to be the ultimate challenge to the Lords.

CHAPTER XV

1909-1910 : THE PEOPLE'S BUDGET

EVERYTHING in the following year seemed to conspire to keep the country at a pitch of excitement in which it would, so to speak, take a general election in its stride—a state of affairs always fortunate for the party in office.

First of all wireless telegraphy stirred the public. A large Atlantic liner, the *Republic*, was rammed at sea by an Italian emigrant steamer, the *Florida*. Urgent distress signals were sent abroad by wireless, the *Baltic* (of the same line of steamers as the *Republic*) hurried to the rescue, and was in time to arrest disastrous loss of life. The marvellous summoning of ships from far beyond sight or sound vastly struck the popular imagination. It seemed to diminish almost unbelievably the perils of the sea.

Dramatically following this achievement of civilisation came an incident which seemed to show that, the more civilisation advanced, the more easily could its machinery be jarred by any who did not shrink from extremes of force. Two foreigners robbed a clerk in a Tottenham street of eighty pounds, which he was carrying from the bank to pay wages. They sprang upon a tram, forced the driver with a pistol at his head to drive on, and fired vigorously upon their pursuers. They shot dead a policeman and a boy. Leaving the tram, they made a final dash on foot, still using their weapons. Fourteen more people were wounded, and then, as the chase closed on them, both men shot themselves. One was found dead beside a ditch ; the

other, who had taken refuge in a cottage, terrifying all
its inhabitants, was found so badly wounded that he died
soon after in hospital. Civilisation, it might be said, had
after all reasserted itself, not in the mere finish of the
chase, but in the extraordinary unconsciousness of peril
with which the crowd kept up the pursuit. Miscreants
might, it appeared, reckon on a modern citizen having
forgotten that pistols existed. He had indeed so far
forgotten as to have little fear.

Events of a different kind stirred other sections of the
community. The long-expected report of the Royal
Commission on the Poor Law was issued in January, and
proved to be two reports. Both groups of the commissioners agreed in recommending the extinction of boards
of guardians ; but while the majority desired the appointment of new specific authorities, controlling large areas,
working on a wider and less penal theory, and exterminat-
ing the old ignominious associations of poor relief, the
minority wished to see the various branches of Poor Law
work separated from one another and placed under existing local authorities, so that in fact no Poor Law should
continue to be. Mr John Burns, in whose department
this matter fell, held out no hopes of legislation on either
report. He believed that he had power, by orders of the
Local Government Board, to go very far towards breaking
up the rigidities of the Poor Law, and its combination
of processes better attended to separately. He preferred
proceeding by administrative detail to introducing a Bill,
which must inevitably suffer by criticisms aimed upon it
from all angles of detail at once. Mr Burns had by this
time fallen far out of favour with Labour representatives,
largely because of his apparent indifference to their eagerness for Labour legislation.

In Labour circles, the interest of the moment was the
resignation of Mr Ramsay Macdonald, Mr Keir Hardie,
Mr Philip Snowden and Mr Bruce Glasier from the

National Council of the Labour party, "owing to the movement of irresponsibility which has grown up inside the party." In the previous year a resolution had been carried by a rather narrow majority at the Labour Party's annual conference, identifying the party with socialism. Previously there had been no such identification. The carrying of the resolution followed upon the appearance among Labour members of Parliament of Mr Victor Grayson. He had made it clear that he was hostile to the Labour party's general method of co-operation with the Liberals. He was an advanced socialist, and parliamentary methods were to him a middle-class sham. For defying the rules of the House, in pursuance of this conviction, he had been suspended in October 1908. This was the most public sign of the "irresponsible spirit" against which the leaders of the party now protested. The party was in an uneasy position. One of the effects of the general election had been to put capital on its guard. Labour was to be shown that, if it had advanced far, it had not a secure base to rely upon. The refusal of recognition to trade unions by masters was a step in this direction. Another, and a more serious one, was the discovery, by a judgment of the Court of Appeal delivered late in November 1908, that a compulsory levy by the unions on their members for purposes of parliamentary representation was not sound in law. Unable really to affect the Government's position in the division lobbies, yet losing ground with its own supporters because it failed to press for more Labour legislation ; suspecting that masters of labour in many industries were not indisposed to let the unions try their power, on the chance that the public would weary of strikes, and the unions would find out weaknesses in themselves—the Labour party seemed in 1909 to retain little of the triumphant glow of 1906. Yet two of the measures of this year were directly for the amelioration of labour. One was the Trade Boards Bill, setting up boards with power to appoint a legal wage in certain industries peculiarly subject to sweating. The other was the Labour Exchanges Bill, dividing England into ten divisions, each with a clearing-house for labour co-ordinated with a central clearing-house in London; 30 or 40 exchanges were set up in large towns, 45 in smaller towns, and 150 minor offices. A joint advisory committee was to be formed from representatives of employers and employed in every large centre, under the chairmanship of a permanent official. Any person out of work could apply for registration at one of the exchanges; and if openings were found in other places applicants were to be given cards which would provide lodging at Poor Law Institutions on the way, without incurring the disabilities attaching to poor relief. Unemployment had been given a new voice by the strange and almost fantastic organisation of the "hunger marchers." These men were not appealing quite vaguely for aid; they were banded together on a theory that work could be found, and even a modest competence, for the unemployed, by putting them to cultivate waste lands. But the majority of them hardly had the determination required to sustain life on cabbages and potatoes; that freedom of soul was confined chiefly to their extremely idealist leader.

The great battle in Parliament was not long in coming to a head. The King's Speech called attention to the fact that, owing to the necessary provision of money for Old Age Pensions and the increased Naval Estimates, the Budget would require both long and serious discussion, and would be the principal business of the year. On 29th April it was introduced. The cost of Old Age Pensions had, it appeared, been under-estimated; it would be a good deal more than six millions, and indeed the Opposition was not far out when it put the cost at something like twelve millions. The charge for this service, and the demands of the navy, meant a prospective deficit, as taxation stood, of fifteen and three-quarter millions. The first step towards meeting this would be to diminish the provision for repayment of the National Debt by three millions. Then came the unfolding of new methods of taxation. The distinction between earned and unearned incomes was to be carried further. On all earned incomes under £3000 the income-tax was to remain at 9d.; on earned incomes over that figure and on all unearned incomes the tax was to be 1s. 2d.; on incomes over £5000 a super tax of 6d. was to be paid on the amount by which they exceeded £3000. Lower middle-class incomes were relieved by an abatement, on those below £500, of £10 of the income for every child under sixteen years of age. Next came landed property. A tax of 20 per cent. was levied on " unearned increment " in land values, payable on the sale of land, on leases for more than fourteen years, and on the passing of land or landed interest at death, the increase in the value to be reckoned from 30th April 1909, or from the last payment of the tax. Agricultural land, small residences, and small holdings were exempted. A duty of a halfpenny in the pound was levied on undeveloped land, where the site value was over £50 an acre. In the original proposal the same duty was levied on ungotten minerals; but this was altered in committee to a tax of one shilling in the pound on mineral royalties. Next came the turn of the licensed victualling trade. A tax of 50 per cent. was laid on the annual value of all licences, hotels and restaurants to have the alternative of paying either 25 per cent. of the annual value or a duty according to the proportion borne by sales of intoxicating liquor to total sales. A proposed duty of threepence in the pound on the sales of liquor in clubs was altered in committee to a duty of sixpence in the pound on the club's purchase of liquor. The spirit-duty was increased by 3s. 9d. a gallon; the tobacco-duty by 8d. a pound. A graduated tax was placed on motor vehicles used for other than business purposes, and a tax was also placed upon petrol.

The outcry against such a Finance Bill was immediate. Super-taxation was denounced as a deliberate piece of class legislation ; taxation of land values even more so. The Government was warned that the cost of the enormous labour of land valuation, which must be undertaken in order to provide a starting point for assessment of increment, would so far swallow up the proceeds of the tax that its unprofitableness would expose it as a mere vindictive attack. Licence-holders equally asserted that the new duties falling upon them were a piece of revenge for the failure of the Licensing Bill. On the Liberal side there was satisfaction at the determination to prove that under a Free Trade system taxation still had its elasticity, and that Tariff Reform could not be advanced as the only method of meeting steadily growing expenditure. A Budget that could deal immediately with a deficit of fifteen and three-quarter millions could afford to include proposals for land taxes, which must, when once the valuation was accomplished, bring in an ever-increasing revenue. Moreover, such a valuation, with the accompanying tax on undeveloped land, would tend to bring land into the market, and so meet a bitter Radical grievance. The Conservative answer was that it would bring so much land into the market that prices would fall disastrously, the countryside meanwhile being everywhere robbed of the old relation between great landowners and their people.

It was not, in spite of Lord Rosebery and others who applied this epithet to it, a " revolutionary " Budget. People who spoke of it in that way had presumably little acquaintance with the doctrines of the land-taxers, the single-taxers, and others who wished to see new principles of taxation rather than even the most drastic readjustment of existing principles. The Budget was, indeed, a social

rather than an economic achievement. For twenty years
past the rich had been growing richer ; very large incomes
were much more numerous than they used to be ; and it
was equally true that high middle-class incomes, running
well into the thousands, were much more numerous.
The super tax was, in a sense, the State's claim for a return
on the amazing field it had opened by the Limited Liability
Acts, and on all the indirect services by which it rendered
possible a world-wide trade. But to many reformers it
appeared that the time was ripe for fundamental reconsideration of taxing. Strong as the present Budget was,
it was of the old family of Budgets in its combination of
direct and indirect taxation, its gathering of a handful
here and a handful there. Pitt would have understood
what it was all about.

However, opposition to the Finance Bill was not likely
to enter into considerations such as these. The proposals
aimed high and far. Mr Lloyd George supported them in
a speech at Limehouse, which was seized upon as a frank,
if not shameless, confession of legislating against one class
for the sake of another. " Class " by this time had come
to mean almost entirely a distinction of wealth. In the
heat of the controversy men threatened to sell their
estates, and invest the money abroad ; women threatened
to dismiss servants ; financiers to transfer their business
to foreign capitals. Yet it remained a most striking fact
that not all the loudly proclaimed uneasiness about a
Radical Government, not all the fear of democratic upheaval and the power of trade unions, hampered the growth
of trade. The monthly returns advanced almost without
a check. Consols were falling ; but the rate of interest
on them was so low that in the great modern field of investment they could not possibly find a strong market. At
any rate, trade in general remained so buoyant as almost
to suggest that a democratic government which kept
the peace abroad was less disturbing to business, when all

was said and done, than a Conservative government which broke that peace.

It must be said that below the surface the atmosphere was not altogether calm. The year 1909 witnessed a very acute stage of naval rivalry between Great Britain and Germany. Public opinion was agitated by a violent outburst of criticism of the Admiralty's policy, in which Lord Charles Beresford was prominent. Nor was it quieted when, on the production of the Naval Estimates, the Prime Minister and Mr McKenna stated that the comparisons they had made in the previous year had been based upon an erroneous assumption as to the rate of construction of ships in German yards. The crucial moment was now put at March 1912, when it appeared that on existing arrangements Great Britain would have twenty Dreadnoughts and Germany seventeen. The Government's policy showed some consciousness of uncertainty by including in the programme of new construction four " contingent " ships, to be laid down if the German naval programme appeared to threaten the margin of superiority. These ships were in addition to four definitely on the year's programme. Sir Edward Grey announced that, if the Government found information as to the progress of German building difficult to obtain, it would give Great Britain the benefit of the doubt; and, in fact, on 26th July, Mr McKenna announced that the " contingent " ships would be laid down at once.

These proceedings brought vigorous criticism on the Ministry from a large section of its supporters. England appeared to these critics to be pursuing not a line of international understanding and plain dealing; but a policy of combinations of Powers from which she had for many years now been fortunately free. The agreement with France, which had been so generally welcomed at first, seemed now to be rather more like an alliance, though not one in technical terms. The agreement with Russia was too much like the old sort of diplomatic sequel to be

popular with Liberals ; and the meetings between King
Edward and the Tsar at Reval in 1908 and at Cowes in
1909 had been attended by a less general sympathy than
had attached to the King's relations with the French.

Even the Budget and the Naval Estimates had other
excitements and interests to compete with. Indeed,
discussion on the latter point was entirely swept out of the
public mind for a few days by the fact that, just after
the estimates had been introduced, telegrams arrived from
Lieutenant Shackleton, the leader of an Antarctic expedition, conveying the news of a journey which had so nearly
reached the South Pole that for all practical purposes the
feat had been accomplished. By a curious coincidence,
the North Pole took also in this year its share of popular
excitement. On 1st September it was announced that
an American, Dr Cook, had returned to the habitable
confines of the Arctic circle, having been successful in
reaching the North Pole in April 1908. This thrilling
news was amazingly followed by an announcement, five
days later, that Peary had reached the Pole in April 1909.
Peary's name was well known ; he had done already
much Arctic exploration. Dr Cook's name was not known
at all. By itself the first announcement had not been
regarded with any deep suspicion ; the world was prepared to await Dr Cook's account of his performance, and
the production of his observations. But when Peary's
announcement was made, the liveliest controversy was
seen to be looming ahead ; he would not like to have been
beaten. Both men returned to civilisation. On the face
of it, Dr Cook's story was less convincing than Peary's,
and his statement that he had left his scientific records
behind in Greenland was a particularly weak point. Peary
pursued his rival with determination ; he went and interviewed the Esquimaux whom Dr Cook had designated
as his companions for the greater part of his journey,
and their evidence was sufficient in the public mind

to destroy, finally, the claims of Dr Cook. Peary's achievement was real. His observations passed the scrutiny of scientists and Polar explorers ; and the discovery of the North Pole was acknowledged to have been made.

In the summer mechanical flight was seen to have advanced with a rapidity which took people's breath away, when they reflected that it was little more than twelve months since the first public flight. Not only was the thing being done almost daily in France, but already daring pioneers had discovered that single planes would keep them in the air, instead of the double planes which made a rather cumbrous machine. In July a machine of the new type crossed the Channel and came safely to earth in a field behind Dover Castle. It was piloted by M. Blériot. An attempt to cross on a monoplane had been made on 12th July by M. Latham, but his motor failed and he fell into the sea. After M. Blériot's success, on 25th July, M. Latham tried again on the 26th, but again his motor failed, this time when he had almost reached the English coast. The aeronauts had waited some time on the French side for favourable weather. But, before the year was out, the conception of what was possible weather for flying had undergone a great change. Nothing was more extraordinary about the progress of flying than the rapidity with which it made its advances. Machines as clear and simple in their lines as a great dragon-fly had been evolved within twelve months from the double-plane machines. Now in the autumn of 1909 men affronted in the air winds which even in the summer of that same year would have been considered prohibitive of flight. Several aviation meetings had taken place in France before England saw one. On 15th October a flying week began at Blackpool. There M. Farman first surprised the people by flying for half-an-hour in gusty and uncertain weather ; but the final sensation was provided by M. Latham's flight twice round the course in a wind that seemed to the spectators not far from a gale.   Some persons put the strength of the wind at forty miles an hour.   After this, aeroplanes may be said to have shaken off the last disbelief in their future. They were not any longer toys for a still day.

Besides being the flying year in England, 1909 was also the motor-cab year.   Although these cabs were principally a London affair, and were only introduced in other large towns slowly and in comparatively small numbers, they had a significance not confined to London.   The first great epoch of the motor car had closed.   The period of the enthusiasm of pioneers and the period of large, kingly, powerful machines for the fortunate few had expanded into a period of moderate, admirably efficient cars for people of merely comfortable incomes.   But other grades of income and social position had to be tapped, if the motor manufacturers were to create the market required by establishments set up at the highest point of the boom.   Could cars be made cheaply enough for use as cabs, and at the same time well enough to stand the inevitably severe wear and tear ?   For a year or two experiments in this direction had been discouraging. But with perseverance success was attained ; and once the new cabs, fitted with taximeters, had become numerous enough to avoid disappointing a public ready to look out for them, their advance was unchecked.   The speed of the new conveyances, the ease of their motion, combined with the positiveness of the taximeter in place of the weary old uncertainty of cab fares, delighted the public. Moreover, Londoners possessed for the first time a closed cab which was clean and pleasant.   Motor omnibuses had for months past been ousting the horsed omnibuses.   In spite of their noisiness they offered advantages of speed which made their future assured.   When motor cabs came with a rush, in 1909, the streets of London underwent suddenly that change which had not been expected to

occur for a generation at least.[1] A typical photograph of
such a spot as Broadway, Westminster, in the coronation
year showed not a single motor vehicle; motors then were
the private conveyances of the rich. A photograph of the
same spot in 1909 showed hardly any horsed vehicles,
and such as there were, were tradesmen's vans. The
change had several points of subsidiary interest. Humani-
tarians rejoiced to see the disappearance of horses from
the inevitably cruel work of drawing omnibuses on hard,
and too often slippery, streets. The controllers of traffic
saw the advantage of vehicles taking up far less room than
those drawn by horses. Sanitary authorities and officers
of health began to look forward to a day when the detritus
of town roadways would cease to be offensive and dangerous to human life. In a more general respect, this
familiarising of the public with the use of motors practically put an end to the old outcries against them.
Wealthy owners of big powerful cars, it is true, no longer
wanted so much to show them off; but the hirer of a
taxicab had his share in the change, by ceasing to regard
cars as privileged possessions. The success of the motor
cabs was also one more proof of a widely spread increase
in the means of middle-class people, and an equally wide
inclination to spend money. The cabs were more expensive to maintain than the old horsed cabs; and could
not have become so numerous without a considerable
increase in the habit of hiring cabs. Such general considerations as these make the appearance of the taxicab a matter of national, and not merely London, interest.

In the campaign which, during the summer, Liberal
members fought for the Finance Bill, its value as a triumphant assertion of Free Trade played a great part. The
Tariff Reform movement had hardly been checked at all
by the general election; its advocates confessed that the
country needed more education on the subject than they

1 See page 632.

perhaps had foreseen ; and they laid themselves out to
provide it. But the leader of the movement, the source
of the power which it had attained over the public mind,
the man who had been able to give such new life to the
idea of a tariff that men forgot all the Fair Trade movement of the eighties and all the more recent talk about a
broader basis of taxation, and thought of Tariff Reform
as a new thing, sprung up in a single conception—this
leader had fallen out of the fight. Mr Chamberlain had
had a paralytic stroke ; and, although hopes were entertained of his recovering from the worst effects of it, he
was not expected to be active in politics again. Few men
had lived as hard in political life as he had. If he had
missed the supreme prize of political power, he had attained
a personal influence in the nation such as a great many
Prime Ministers had missed ; and his was one of the names
that could not drop out of the political history of his
country. Even apart from the details of his career, he
would stand for some of the most remarkable developments
of middle-class politics that had ever taken place. His
most ardent followers were not the young men, but the
men of ripe years and experience. This was the truth of
the admiration for him as a " business man " in politics.
He was not really that, so much as an idealist. But he
caught the imagination of the business man as no one
else had ever done. Without bringing it to such a pitch
of formulation as Disraeli achieved with Young England,
he stood for England in the Prime of Life, and that was the
robust core of his Imperialism. He saw Great Britain as
the father with grown sons—the situation in which old
home instinct must be replaced by some new bond of
interest and understanding, if the family is to hold
together.

England lost in this year two mighty voices—Swinburne and George Meredith. Widely different as their
work was, a like fire had inflamed their genius. Both

had been gloriously kindled by the uprising of Italy;
the manhood of both found its brightest hopes, the object
of its most ardent admiration, in the triumph of the French
Republic. Some of the noblest passages that either of
them wrote resound with the feet of marching nations.
But Swinburne, flooded with passionate exaltation, fixed
his rapt eyes upon the flutter of banners; Meredith
scrutinised the faces of the men that marched. Consequently Meredith's spirit, less carried away by the rushing
wings of the *Mater Triumphalis*, was saved from the savage
depression of *The Halt before Rome*. In truth, the likeness
of their youthful inspiration falls into insignificance before
the unlikeness of their maturity. One was a visionary,
the other a seer. Swinburne, early acclaimed by eager
youth, had for some time before his death passed his
zenith. Impatient, overbearing, he lost sight of humanity
when the flags no longer waved. Life ebbed from his
palaces of poetry; and too often the later structures he
raised seemed designed to put artifice in the place of life.
He came to dwell increasingly upon the past of England,
rather than on the present or the future; the poems he
published during the Boer War had only this mechanical
inspiration. Meredith, on the other hand, had turned
early, not only from the flamboyances of poetry, but from
ordinary conceptions of that art, to " strike earth," and
in his poetry, as in his fiction, to probe the facts under-
lying existence. His noble work was strengthened, not
sapped, by the passing years; life ran ever more strongly
into the moulds of his thought. It does not fall within the
scope of this book to appraise his position in literature.
But the immense influence he exerted upon the minds
of intelligent English men and women, and his Liberal
creed triumphantly upheld during a long life, are historical
facts. Men felt at his death both how giant-like was the
personality that had fallen, and how his unswerving
insight had broadened the realm of the spiritual.

The Liberal stake on the Finance Bill was high. Lord Lansdowne intimated early in August that the House of Lords was ready to try conclusions on that issue. This meant that the long-established immunity of financial measures from the power of the House of Lords was to be set aside, and the conflict between the two Houses raised in a form which must bring about a general election. If Liberals were beaten, they would not only be put back in a position in which their next return to power must be under the same ultimate control of their proposals; they would also have given Tariff Reformers the right to say that the electors did not support the kind of finance which a Free Trade Government must pursue, in its need for money. The conclusion would be that the country was prepared to see a Tariff Reform Budget. The game was played through. The House of Lords, taking its stand chiefly on the argument that this was not, in the old sense, a financial measure, but a bundle of legislation tied round with the Budget string, and arguing also that tradition forbade the Lords to amend the Commons' proposals for finance, but did not forbid them to reject, threw out the Finance Bill. The Liberals, winning the election, won not only their Budget, but also a long step in the conflict between their party and the House of Lords. It was now clear that as heavy a stake had been laid down by the other side as the Liberals had put on the table. Electors had decided outright on a question between the two Houses; and not even Mr Gladstone had been able to bring the country to that point before.

Nor was this all. The Liberal party returned to office on this second occasion diminished to some degree in numbers, but vastly more sure of its ground. The results in 1906 had had some of the unsatisfactory character of a "freak." Liberals, not having expected any such overwhelming triumph, were rather at a loss to gauge the feeling behind it. In so far as that feeling had been one

25

of irritated impatience with the late Unionist Ministry, it would be likely to turn into equal irritation with advanced Radical legislation. Moreover the very general belief that the results were due more to Labour than to Liberalism had caused some uneasiness in the Ministerial party, and some mistrust of the Government's being driven further than it was wise at the moment to go. That uncertainty, too, was swept away by this second election, following on the course of events in the Parliament of 1906. The Labour party had achieved the principal items of its programme—the Trade Disputes Act, Old Age Pensions, measures aimed at dealing with unemployment and sweating. The passing of these Acts had revealed the Labour party as devoid of any systematic new principle of politics—as advanced Radicals rather than revolutionaries; and advanced radicalism, though enough to keep Conservatives anxious, was not enough to make Liberals afraid, as many had been in 1906, of a remaking of their party creed. Finally, the effect of this second election was to suggest that, if in 1906 the country had embarked upon an experiment, it had not been appalled by the results. Free Trade had, of course, again played a considerable part. But the Liberals stood now to be judged on accomplishment, not merely on expectations; and their return to power was free from much of the ambiguity that had attended their position before.

From this time Unionists began to face at last the fact that the mind of the country was deeply altered. This does not mean that it had become necessarily more Radical. But the Unionist party had not perceived that it was itself as much a party of change as the Liberal party was. Tariff Reform was not, as some Liberals were apt to say, pure reaction. It was not the traditional Protectionist policy of Mr Chaplin. It was a transmutation of previous movements into a new spirit of change, of national self-consciousness alike in foreign and

colonial affairs, of industrial efficiency and economic
sociology as the governing factors in domestic affairs.
Unionists now at length awoke to the fact that unconsciously they had swum as much with the altered social
current as the Liberals had done consciously. The Social
Reform group that was shortly to appear on the Unionist
side was really an acknowledgment that that party
depended no less than Liberals upon the interest it could
arouse in a nation which, rendered lively by the high-
pitched notes of its newspapers, by the universal spread of
the means for having a good time, by a spirited liberty
in its tastes, and an incessant opening of new vistas in
scientific invention, rallied no longer to old party cries.

The Government, assured now of the passing of its
Finance Bill, could not rest here. A Bill for regulating
the relations between the two Houses of Parliament must
follow, if the Ministry was to hold its supporters together.
But an event intervened which caused this measure to
belong to a new era rather than to the one with which
these volumes deal.

When King Edward went abroad, for his usual spring visit
to Biarritz, it was known that he was not in good health.
Indeed, he had not been as well as usual when he paid that
visit in 1909 ; and the year had been an anxious one for
him. During the later stages of the Finance Bill, when the
intentions of the House of Lords had been made clear, he
had taken the unusual step of receiving in audience Lord
Lansdowne and Mr Balfour; and the nation had thus known
that the King was giving more than a formal attention
to the course of politics. On his return from Biarritz, in
1910, it was at first announced that he was the better for
the change. But early in May his condition again gave
rise to anxiety. The end came quickly. On the morning
of 6th May a most serious bulletin brought back to the
gates of Buckingham Palace the same sort of quiet,
troubled crowd that had kept watch there in June 1902.

In the evening the physicians had to state that the King's condition was critical, and after that the people prolonged the vigil into the night. At about ten o'clock, on the announcement that no further bulletin would be issued, the waiting groups dispersed. Only a few remained when, shortly after midnight, it became known that the King had passed away. He had spent the day sitting up, fully dressed, conscious, and quite fearless. But his fits of coughing grievously exhausted him; and during the evening his heart ceased to respond to the oxygen which had been administered to him since the previous evening.

King Edward was genuinely mourned. He was a popular figure; he had a deep instinct for the popular occasion, while avoiding anything approaching a democratic pose. Often as it was possible to see the King on his way in and out of town, London did not, as a matter of fact, see him in the casual way in which some capitals see their sovereigns. He was not to be met riding out simply with an equerry, as the German Emperor might be met in Berlin, or walking, as King Leopold used to walk in Brussels, and King Christian in Copenhagen. No doubt, with his keen sense of fitness, King Edward saw that the long retirement of Queen Victoria made such ways unsuitable. Englishmen would have felt no real ease in seeing him thus. But on the other hand, when his colt Minoru won the Derby in 1909, he went down with the frankest simplicity into the crowd to lead in the winner; and his concern for housing and for hospital work showed in surprise visits paid without any formalities to workmen's dwellings and hospitals. Moreover, after the remoteness of the sovereign at the end of Queen Victoria's reign, King Edward's appearances at the theatre of an evening, a glimpse of his face through the window of a quiet brougham bringing him back from a dinner-party at some friend's house, made men feel he was living among them in a way they understood.

That comprehensibility was largely the secret of his influence. He was felt to be a man of the world. At the time of his accession there were some people who considered that aspect of his character as a drawback. They were people who did not comprehend the tradition to which King Edward belonged. He himself, belonging to the old " high life "—perhaps, indeed, the last survivor of it— fully perceived the changes that had occurred. Up to the seventies of the nineteenth century there had existed a class of rich, well-born people whose amusements and wildnesses took place on a kind of stage, at which the rest of the London world gazed. Stories ran current, tales of doings at race meetings, card-tables and theatres. Yet the gossip was never sniggering or familiar, because the difference in the means and the habits of life between those who were on that stage and those who were not was clearly defined, and was never questioned. But during the eighties, with the rise of new wealth and the breaking-down of distinctions of birth, that old spectacular world had disappeared. Most of its members had fallen into the manners of the new sets, and lost their tradition. King Edward preserved his. He liked card-playing ; he loved horse racing ; he enjoyed the theatre ; he paid visits to Paris ; he understood a good dinner. Yet he could draw his lines very sharply. His style of betting, his objection to high card-play in drawing-rooms, his careful regard for Sunday, were not quite comprehensible to the younger generations of men about town. These were all natural to the men of the sixties, who, if they went far themselves, were perfectly clear as to the necessity of maintaining observances which should prevent less exalted people from upsetting society. Consequently gossip about the King, flavoured with the publicity of the old spectacular " high life," and therefore genial and almost loyal, came to be perceived as different from the gossip, generally vulgar and often contemptuous or resentful, which grew up round the modern rich sets, extravagant and idle without being exclusive or picturesque.

King Edward's revival of frequent state appearances, royal processions in London and royal visits to other parts of his kingdom, did much to strengthen the prestige of the Crown. The populace liked the cheerful shows, and the Londoner became amusingly keen on recognising the familiar figures of the Court. The trading community profited by the brisker flow of money in London life. Republicanism, of which the England of 1880 had some real fear, had first begun to decline when advanced Labour leaders were absorbed in the vigorous Trade Union movement of the later eighties. King Edward's pleasant activities made the sovereign a more human and less sentimental figure to the popular imagination than Queen Victoria had ever been ; and republicanism in consequence appeared not so much an objectionable political doctrine as a form of rather gratuitous rudeness to an English gentleman.

King Edward's reign was not long ; yet his personality may prove to be sufficient to attach his name to a period. With his varied interests and pleasures (he was not a great reader, and had no need to be, since he could be sure of personal touch with the men who knew things and did things) he may stand as representing the inclination of his time to call in question hard and fast judgments. The inclination was not confined to moral distinctions ; it dissolved also many conventions of class. It proceeded, too, from various motives. The breaking-down of the old barriers of society in London originated largely in the aristocrat's becoming aware how good a time was to be had in houses commanding new resources of wealth ; and in the consequent challenging of the tradition that it was right to go to certain houses, and visit people who fulfilled certain conditions, but wrong to go to others, however inviting. Again, the spread of sports and games may be traced to the same spirit.   While it was right only for a class of more or less favoured persons to spend their money or their time on out-of-door pursuits, it had been snobbery on the part of middle-class folk to amuse themselves in the same way.   But when the traditional distinction had been called in question, the ordinary man was free to get all the pleasure in exercise he could, without being accused of aping his betters.

It is curiously characteristic of this period that the word "respectable" practically ceased to have any weight in upper and middle-class life, where of old it had borne a moral significance.   There still were most excellent reasons for doing or not doing various things, but that it would or would not be "respectable" to do them ceased entirely to be a guidance in conduct.   It would have been difficult to imagine King Edward governing his opinions or actions by such a word, though quite possible to imagine Queen Victoria's employing it.   King Edward had his conventions ; as has been remarked, they appeared stringent at times to younger men about town.   He drew lines too at points where he believed harm to others came in.   It is open to moralists to argue that such lines afford small defence when once rigid distinction between good and bad has been abandoned.   But if not so easy of definition, the newer standards appealed to a public in love with common-sense as an ideal, and in love, too, with science, hygiene, experimental politics, and other such matters in which right and wrong were inapplicable epithets.

King Edward, genial, experienced, but never disillusioned, may well stand at the head of a period of English life enfranchised from strict upbringing, making mistakes, spending rather wildly, inclined to be noisy, but on the whole demanding reality, and seeking more delicate estimations of character than were to be achieved by hard and fast rules.

BOOK III: 1910–1922

CHAPTER I

THE death of King Edward cannot, of course, be represented as a turning-point in the national life of his country. It neither opened the way to fresh currents nor diverted the course of those that were already in motion. A new world, both socially and politically unrecognisable by the great Victorians, had been coming into being before his accession, and had shown its characteristics strongly enough while he yet reigned. Moreover, in the last four years of his life domestic politics, culminating in the People's Budget, and foreign politics, restless and uneasy since the Boer War, had already disturbed men's minds with the sense that the foundations, as well as the surface, of a long-familiar world were moving. The Liberal-Labour triumph of 1906 had lived up to a good deal of what had been expected of it. On the other hand there can be no reason to suppose that, if King Edward had lived longer, the course of events would have been other than it was. His death made no serious difference to the arrayed political forces.

Yet, though no turning-point, the date of his death does seem to associate itself with an uncomfortable change in the country's state of mind. From such beginnings as serious strikes unauthorised by the Trade Union leaders, the early demonstrations of the new movement for Women's Suffrage, and the platform extravagances of the 1909 Budget campaign, it grew until a temper of sheer fighting seemed to invade every aspect of affairs, working up to the verge of actual civil war in the summer of 1914. It would not be fanciful to see this in more than politics. In art (though here the attack upon old conventions always has some intolerance) the new methods of painting, the new conceptions of music, the new exploitations of the stage, were all more or less lurid ; violence of expression was an essential part of them. In social life the old steady penetration of the world of fashion by a world of wealth, glad to maintain the old barriers once it was inside them, gave way to a feverish, contemptuous construction of a new world of fashionable idleness, only too well attuned to a world of lurid art. Industry took on more and more the aspect of two massed opposing forces, between which compromise became ever more precarious. The four years between King Edward's death and the outbreak of war may well be labelled with a word that a single movement of the period appropriated to itself : they were militant years.

The immediate sequel to his death, however, was a brief lull in the fight for which, this year, the political stage had been set—the fight between the Government majority and the House of Lords. The struggle was, of course, an old one ; almost it might be called hallowed in Liberal annals as a Gladstonian tradition. Gladstone had discharged the first shots in 1861, and come to much closer range with his Home Rule Bills. The years of revived Liberalism since 1906 preserved the tradition of those encounters. The general feeling in the party that its career could not but be punctuated by trials of strength between the two Houses was worked upon by the determination of a considerable section not to stop short of a trial of conclusions ; they would be betraying their opportunity if they now failed to clear the way for Liberalism of the future. The most had therefore been made of every rejection of a Bill by

the Lords ; and as these had naturally been the Bills of
most controversial Liberal complexion—a Plural Voting
Bill, a Scottish Land Bill, an Education Bill, a Licensing
Bill—the temper of the party in the House had needed
no other sharpening.   But their leaders were far too
clever to think that the mood of the party in the House
was enough for such a battle.   They did not fail to
observe those factors in the country at large which
must encourage Conservatism and the Lords.   There
was, first, the " chilling off " of the electorate from its
mood of 1905, its distinctly nervous reconsideration of
what its enthusiastic backing of Free Trade might have
committed it to ; it had been discovering, rather naïvely,
that the alternative to Conservative Governments with
which it had grown impatient could only be a Liberalism
which had moved a long way forward since 1895, and
fully intended to register its advance in drastic social
legislation.   Secondly, the Free Trade issue having
largely died away (for no one, after the election of
December 1905, could imagine that the country would
stand a Protection campaign), an electoral struggle
would go back to the confused *mêlée* of ordinary party
strife, and it would be impossible to present clearly and
conclusively the case against the Lords.   A third point
was that in such an ordinary party struggle the Conservatives would have some distinct strategical advantages ; not only could they point to a large mass of
Liberal legislation which had not been interfered with
(some two hundred Acts had gone on to the Statute
Book since 1906),[1] but they had especially refrained from
hampering the legislation which would peculiarly appeal
to Labour, such as the Trade Disputes Act, and Old
Age Pensions.   In the face of such facts as these, could
Liberals pin much hope to a struggle on a constitutional

[1] See a speech by Lord Lansdowne in the House of Lords, 25th
November 1910.

question too dry to rouse enthusiasm except among the stalwarts, based mainly upon a rejection of traditional Liberal principles of no sharp social interest, and very apt to degenerate into rambling calculations and counter-calculations of the actual loss and gain of Bills ?

Hence the remarkable skill—not fully perceived at the time by the Conservative leaders—of the Budget of 1909 as a party manœuvre. The fight with the House of Lords must be pegged to a single issue, of strong appeal to Labour, and startling. If that House could be lured, by rejecting a Budget, into an assertion of their ultimate power, not merely in ordinary matters of legislation, but in a sphere in which for two hundred years they had admitted a tradition of non-interference, the flagrantly obstinate nature of their party spirit would be displayed. If the Budget could be given a markedly social colour, that obstinacy could be made to appear an entrenched class obstinacy of a kind to rouse even the least politically minded voter to some feeling on a constitutional matter. The taxation of what seemed a peculiarly idle form of capitalistic profit-taking—the increment on land values—for the purpose of establishing new social services, without draining the means for national defence, was a perfect electoral formula.

So the struggle for the Budget of 1909 had been entered upon as in itself the final struggle with the House of Lords.[1] In that spirit the new Commons, after the Budget election of January 1910, had met, and in that spirit the passing of the delayed Budget had been followed by Mr Asquith's introduction in April 1910 of Resolutions preliminary to a Bill, the Parliament Bill, regulating the relations between the two Houses. If there had remained any doubt as to

[1] See pages 758, 762 and 769.

the reality of the constitutional issue, or any feeling
that, with their Budget secure, Liberals, relying on
the socialistic glory of that achievement, might think
the final stages of the great issue not worth while, Mr
Asquith's speech swept it away. For he used phrases
which could only mean that, in the event of the House
of Lords refusing to accept the result of the recent
election as authorising a curtailment of their power, the
Government contemplated overbearing opposition by
a creation of peers sufficient for the purpose. That, at
any rate, was the amplification which was immediately
given to his words. What he had actually said was that,
in the event of the issue being further forced, Ministers
would not advise a Dissolution except on such conditions
as would enable them, if successful at the polls, to place
the Parliament Bill upon the Statute Book, despite the
resistance of the House of Lords. But the use of such
words inevitably sent minds back to the last occasion
on which a vital constitutional battle had had to be
carried through more than one election and the overbearing of opposition had been similarly threatened—
the Reform Bill of 1832. As the " conditions " then
for securing the passage of the Bill had been the Royal
authority for a sufficient creation of peers, it could only
be assumed that this was in Mr Asquith's mind.

The speech let loose floods of speculation. It revealed
the fact that, whatever the rank and file might think
of the results of the election, the leaders knew that
the House of Lords was far from accepting it as final.
The gigantic Liberal majority had gone ; there was no
more than a good working majority of Liberals and
Labour combined, not impossibly beyond the reach of
the revived Conservative Opposition. Of more general
interest was the incredulous questioning whether it
could seriously be proposed to overbear opposition in a
House of Lords so much larger than it had been in

1832, and so much more unevenly divided ; Lord Grey could then have achieved his purpose with a score or two of new creations, but a Liberal Premier now would require several hundreds. Supporters of the Government asked themselves whether so sweeping an action were possible ; its opponents asked whether such an unseemliness were conceivable. Promptly, too, unseemliness was charged upon Mr Asquith from another angle—the impropriety of introducing into the controversy, at the first production of his proposals, so broad a hint of the Royal Prerogative. But Mr Asquith was to show how skilful and resolute he could be. Amid all the clamour of speculation and of dignified surprise and rebuke, concealing a secret hope of trapping him into some more specific and vulnerable statement, he maintained his cautious formula unimpaired until the right moment came for plain words, sure that his supporters would deduce enough to give them confidence, and determined that his opponents should have nothing more definite to exploit.

It was immediately obvious that his words had not been a piece of uncalled-for emphasis. The Parliament Bill was going to be fought. But before the forces had deployed, King Edward's death made an interruption which, though brief, was enough to lead to a suspension of hostilities. There was a large body of sober opinion on both sides which felt that a fight to a finish would be, at the least, a pity ; and throughout the preliminary skirmishes Conservative voices enough had been heard admitting that the existing House of Lords needed reform. Was there not then possibility of compromise ? Men gossiped of what might well have happened if the King had lived, and again called the leaders to conference. There was at any rate this ground for such speculation, that King Edward was fairly well known to have used what influence he could, within his marked

discretion, to prevent the precipitation, by the rejection
of the Budget, of a struggle which he deplored as bad
politics.[1] There was no great surprise, then, but a
considerable sense of relief, when, upon the resumption
of political life, it was announced that a conference
was to meet, composed of Mr Asquith, Lord Crewe,
Mr Lloyd George and Mr Birrell on the one side, and
Mr Balfour, Lord Lansdowne, Lord Cawdor and Mr
Austen Chamberlain on the other. It entered upon its
meetings in June.

Deprived for the time being of the spectacular in
politics, of which it had lately had a good deal, the
public mind was ready for a return to what was becoming a principal interest of summer months—the progress
of aviation. It had not yet reached beyond the stage of
a fair-weather enterprise. The event of the year was
an aviation meeting at Bournemouth, on the lines of
the successful one held at Blackpool in the previous
year ; flying was still in the main a performance round
and round a course. The meeting was marred by the
death of the Honourable C. S. Rolls, of the famous Rolls
Royce car firm, who had taken to flying ; he crashed in
the sea. Oversea flying was considered a daring feat ;
a fourth crossing of the Channel, this time by a Mr
Moisant, an American, and a flight by Robert Loraine
to Ireland in September were admiringly chronicled,
as were also the facts that Loraine had flown on one
occasion in a storm, and that another aviator had
attained a speed in the air of some 75-95 miles an hour.
Airships too were still considered to be in competition,
as it were, with aeroplanes for the future of flying ;
Mr Willows flew a small dirigible from Cardiff to London,
and later flew it round St Paul's, by way of demon-
strating its possibilities as a " one-man " rival to the
plane.

[1] See page 771.

But even the new thrill of flying had to give place, in July, to a wildly excited absorption in a murder case, in which the usual gruesome " mystery " of the discovery of a woman's body buried in a London house, shortly after the unexplained absence from his usual business of her husband, was heightened to an extra-ordinary pitch by a first, and very theatrical, intrusion of " wireless " into such affairs. This was the notorious Crippen case. For ten days the story had pursued an ordinary course in the newspapers, with the details of the finding of the body, of the missing man's life and ways (he was an American who had been running a patent-medicine business), and of his disappearance from London in the company, it was said, of a young woman. Clues which pointed to her having gone with him in boy's clothes, and other clues which led detectives over to foreign ports, had kept public interest at the too familiar level, when suddenly, on 25th July, *The Daily Telegraph* published the amazing news that the captain of a steamer on the way to Canada had sent a wireless message stating that he believed himself to have the missing couple on board. This, then, was the explanation of the hurried departure, for Canada, on 22nd July, of the Scotland Yard inspector in charge of the case. Not one savour of this incredibly dramatic turn of events was lost. Instead of the meagre fare of carefully doled-out clues, and the more or less blind interest in the case, here was the whole nation behind the scenes, watching (this was the thrill of the piece) those two fugitives in mid-ocean, and they, to whom alone it was life and death, alone unaware that they were already discovered. It seems almost impossible that they should not have felt the glare of the thousand million eyes following their tiny figures all unconscious of the racing detective who, on a faster steamer, would land ahead of them. Never had the public so watched

the closing-in of doom. That stage of the case ended a
week later, when Inspector Dew, boarding the fugitives'
ship on its arrival, confirmed the captain's identification,
and made his arrests. But this fantastic keying-up of
the excitements of a murder case prolonged itself into
whole-page reports of the trial, when it came on in
October; Crippen was condemned to death, and his
companion acquitted.[1]   Another crime of the year
should have passing mention, because it was remarked
upon as the first " scientific burglary "; in September
a strong-room door in some business premises in Birmingham had been cut through with an oxy-acetylene
blow-lamp, and the burglars, interrupted at their work,
had escaped to London in a motor-car.

Of more importance in this connection are the prison
reforms initiated by Mr Winston Churchill, at this time
Home Secretary. Not the least interesting point about
them is that they are an authentic instance of the moral
influence often claimed for stage plays, but seldom so
acknowledged; Mr Churchill, giving honour where
honour was due, acknowledged the help which had
been rendered by Mr Galsworthy's play *Justice* in
bringing the public mind, always rather callous about
convicted offenders, to the point of accepting new and
kinder ideas. Indeed, the theme of the play was clearly
traceable in some of the reforms—the reduction of
solitary confinement, the abolition of the " ticket of
leave," and the provision, tentative as yet, of lectures
and concerts in prisons. There were other reforms
affecting young offenders, and the Borstal system
received an extension by the opening of a new institution
on those lines at Feltham.

Justice was one theatrical event of the year. Another,
Sir Herbert Tree's production of *Henry VIII.*, may be

[1] She was defended by a young barrister already becoming famous,
Mr F. E. Smith, now Lord Birkenhead.

allowed to emerge for this reason, that, with an amusing truculence, he was countering what he called "the affected simplicity of art nouveau," which had been clamouring for less scene-painting and more of the art of acting, with a more showy and expensive production than ever. He had his success, too; for the play-going world was not in serious mood. Pelissier's "Follies," with their "potted plays," were at the height of their fame; and dancing drew larger audiences than any plays, whether the appeal was that of the sensuous "self-expression" and rhythm-interpretation of Maud Allan's *Salome* (many were copying her in drawing-rooms, and Lady Constance Stewart-Richardson even took to the stage in the autumn), or that of the perfect mass movement and strong colour and sound of the Russian ballet, which had become so popular that this year Mordkin and Pavlova left the ballet, on its departure for Russia, and stayed in London. Perhaps the powerful exhilaration of the Russian dance-rhythms had something to do with a tendency to what older generations regarded as almost riotous dancing in the season's ballrooms; though modern generations must wonder how any dancing at all, let alone vigorous dancing, was possible in the long tight "hobble skirts," which, with enormous hats, made just then the fashionable outline. They were such close sheaths that even walking was barely possible.

People drifted back from holidays spoiled by a soaking August to their normal occupations. The House of Lords question had disappeared behind the closed doors of the Conference; and those of the general public who still thought of it were not apprehensive. There might, after all, be no grave break with tradition. Strangely, the deaths of some notable people at an advanced age in the late summer and autumn turned the mind backward, in an unusual degree, to traditions. Lord Spencer, "the Red Earl," who died in August,

had been Mr Gladstone's staunch man in the now
threatened House. Florence Nightingale, who died
in the same month, and Holman Hunt, who died in
September, stood for traditions that seemed even
dimmer. On the other hand, Mr Frank Podmore, the
spiritualist, who had been found drowned in a pool
on the Malvern Hills, and Professor William James,
the American philosopher, had in their different ways a
considerable hold upon modern minds uneasily seeking
for their comfort new spiritual assurances and new
formulæ for the religious instinct. And it was pre-
eminently its own baffling contradictions which the
modern world saw reflected in the news, in November,
of the last tragic stage of Tolstoy's mortal journey.
The chafing of long years against the inconsistencies
of the life he had to live as a Russian landowner with
the creed of simplicity he preached so passionately in
his books had torn him at last from his family ties,
and driven him, with what should have been something
of the dreadfulness of Lear, into the world alone and
penniless. But the feebleness of his great age dwarfed,
in the publicity of newspaper columns, a noble gesture
to a pitiful petulance. Too weak of body to shake off
the family attentions he longed to repudiate, he died in
the waiting-room of a railway station not far from his
home.

With the constitutional truce in being, politicians
had at least two other questions to occupy them:
Women's Suffrage, and the position that had been
created in the trade union world by the Osborne
judgment. The suffrage movement also had been in
something like a state of truce since the introduction
in May of what was called a " Conciliation Bill "; the
name sufficiently indicates the hopes that were entertained of it. But the suffragists, who had managed to
maintain a rather mistrustful patience, had now to see

politicians again deciding that another question had prior claim upon them. This was no time to chill Labour supporters by leaving " in the air " the situation created by the Osborne case. Hardly had trade union funds been protected by the legislation evoked by the Taff Vale case [1] when this fresh difficulty had arisen. Mr W. V. Osborne, a railway employee, had brought an action against the Amalgamated Society of Railway Servants seeking to restrain, as *ultra vires*, the expenditure of union subscriptions for political purposes. Now the considerable growth of Labour representation in the House of Commons had been made possible only by the levy on trade union funds; and when this case, fought up to the House of Lords, was finally decided, in December 1909, in Mr Osborne's favour, Labour felt that, as in the Taff Vale case, vagueness of earlier legislation, due to the equivocal position of the unions, was being most unfairly clarified. Trade unionists might well be impatient with a world which professed to urge upon them political activity as better than the strike, and then forbade them to use their funds for political purposes. Nor is it any wonder that Mr Osborne's motives were misrepresented. But his own explanation for his action had dignity. He was a Liberal, with a strong family tradition of Liberalism; and his dislike of the assumption, inherent in the political levy, that trade unionists could have no independence in politics, was honest, if unfortunately fanatical. [2]

The case produced no such clear reaction as had followed the Taff Vale case. On the whole there had, in the latter, been little doubt, except among extremists, that the new interpretation of the law had been contrary to the intentions of the legislators; and an amending Act had been the one remedy envisaged. The Osborne

1 See pages 546, 547 and 700.
2 See an interview with him in *The Daily News,* 7th October 1910

case was in several respects less simple. The final
decision had been based on the view that, as the Act
of 1876, intending to recognise trade union activities
(and for that reason always regarded as a great step forward for the unions), had included specific statements
of those activities, nothing outside those statements
could be a legitimate object of expenditure. However
hard it might be to be tied down to the definitions
of an Act passed long before their modern political
activities had developed, even trade union leaders
could hardly maintain that this judgment was, like the
other, a manifest distortion of the original intention of
the law. Moreover it was obvious that the use of the
fund for the support of a single political party involved
denying individual liberty of view ; and no progressive
party could easily commit itself to overriding the
courts of law, the traditional refuge of that liberty, by
an Act simply, in effect, reversing their decision. Labour,
then, no less than public opinion in general, looked
at first in other directions for a solution. Naturally
there were those who maintained that political funds
should be voluntary contributions ; but this, while
manageable in the classes which could give in pounds
and hundreds of pounds, would lay an impossible burden
of toil upon a party which could collect only by pennies
and shillings. Quite a different line of adjustment
took prominence in the summer. Long before modern
trade unions had built themselves up, Labour's own
idea of its way into Parliament had been the payment
of members—one of the points, in fact, of the People's
Charter. Would it not now meet the difficulty ?
It hardly could, satisfactorily ; there would remain
election expenses and, still more, the constant running
expense of political work in the constituencies. But
it had its place in Labour speeches, as well as in
those of Liberals and of Conservatives of such different

generations as Sir John Gorst and Mr F. E. Smith ; and
the new prominence thus given to the subject helped
to bring about the institution of payment of members
in the following year. However, as 1910 drew on, there
was less and less prospect of avoiding direct legislation
in the matter. The trade unions hardened at their
Congress in September, though still only after much
debate, to a demand for " reversal " of the judgment ;
various Ministers began to announce in speeches that
the matter was under consideration by the Cabinet ; and
in November Mr Asquith definitely committed the
Government to the production of a Bill.

At the same time Labour had to listen to a good deal
of lecturing from Liberals. There was an uneasy strike
spirit in the air ; and it was unfortunate that, just
when the leaders of Labour had a case to state, so much
should happen to discredit their hold upon the unions.
A shipbuilding lock-out in September, a much more
extensive cotton lock-out in October—both arising out
of dismissals of individual workmen—and a strike in the
South Wales coal-field which provoked serious rioting
at Tonypandy in November, had all displayed impatience
with union leadership, and had an " anarchic " look.

Revolution was in the news in October. On the 5th
came accounts of a *coup d'état* in Lisbon and the proclamation of a Republic. For some days the information
was chaotic ; no one knew what had happened to the
young king, though he was believed to have escaped,
and the full extent of the disaffection was not known.
But in a few days, as the situation cleared in Lisbon
itself, the newspaper correspondents were allowed to
send off their messages ; and it became evident that
the assassination in 1908 of King Carlos and the Crown
Prince, regarded at the time as an isolated act of
violence, had set light to much smouldering disloyalty
to the dynasty—so much that by the time King Manoel

arrived in England (he had been got to safety on a British warship) there was but little idea that he would ever regain his throne.

As the time approached for the reassembling of Parliament, eyes were turned again in the direction of the Conference. The Government majority was none too easy in its mind, for the very aspects of the business which tended to keep the ordinary man from too much apprehension spelled misgiving for the convinced party men in the House. It had been openly said during the summer that the Ministry had been less determined, at the beginning of the session, than the rank and file; and the Liberal Press seemed to be betraying a little anxiety in its insistence from time to time that "the nation intended to be master in its own house." There was no disguise of its anxiety when, in the autumn, articles in the Press of the other side, notably a series signed "Pacificus" in *The Times*, opened up, under the guise of conciliatory suggestions, a vista of compromise on all sorts of subjects which was positively alarming. Nor did the Conference find many more friends among the Unionists, who were on the whole inclined to feel that any reform schemes or any invention of systematic machinery of co-operation between the Houses would come too near surrendering a battle which was by no means lost. On both sides, therefore, there was more relief than disappointment when the announcement was made on 11th November that the Conference had broken up without reaching any agreement. Nothing was said of the causes of its failure; but rumour justified the mistrust of Liberals and Labour. Just before the break-up it had been said that a deadlock had been reached over the question whether on "constitutional measures" the House of Lords should retain its full powers; the ominous aspect of this was that "constitutional measures" must include much of

what was vital to a Liberal programme. And a few
days after the break-up *The Daily Mail* stated that a
" secret caucus " of peers had forced Mr Balfour to bring
the Conference to an end and to " let the constituencies
decide "; which meant that only a disastrous degree of
compromise would have kept the peers from gambling
on the Government's either shrinking from the drastic
proposals of Mr Asquith's Resolutions or failing to carry
the constituencies at another election. It was, then, with
a sense that the air was clearing that on 15th November
Parliament met.

There had been some changes in the Ministry. Sir
Rufus Isaacs had become Attorney-General, and this
left room to strengthen the debating power of the
Treasury Bench by making Sir John Simon Solicitor-
General. Lord Morley, feeling the work of a Department
too much for him now, became Lord President of the
Council, Lord Crewe took the India Office, Mr Lewis
Harcourt the Colonial Office, and Lord Beauchamp
the First Commissionership of Works.

Battle was joined at once. Lord Lansdowne asked
for the Government Bill, and Lord Crewe introduced
it with the plain intimation that " there could be no
settlement by agreement now." The terms of the Bill
were that, pending a reform of the composition of the
House of Lords, any measure which passed the Commons
in three successive sessions unchanged might be presented for the Royal Assent without the consent of the
Lords; and that any finance measure might receive
the Assent in the same way if, at the end of a month,
the Lords' consent was withheld. It was an uncompromising demand for surrender, and there was really no
need to await formal refusal by the Lords. This did
not come until 21st November, when Lord Lansdowne
carried the adjournment of the Second Reading, in
favour of a debate on his own Resolutions for the reform

of the House. But already, on the 18th, the announcement of the dissolution of Parliament had been made. Mr Asquith had repeated, in making it, the formula he had used in April about the conditions upon which the Ministry would take this course; and the significance which had all along been attached to his words now clothed them to the full, for just before Parliament met he had been to see the King at Sandringham, and just after it met the King had come to London and received Lord Crewe, Mr Asquith and Sir Edward Grey, leaving London immediately afterwards, almost as if to heighten, by its isolation, the meaning of his action.

As it happened, the announcement of the dissolution and of a second General Election within twelve months occupied the next day's papers less than what had happened in and around the precincts of the House at the very moment when the announcement was being made inside it. This was another of the big and deliberately violent Women's Suffrage demonstrations at Westminster; and it was followed a few days later by a yet bigger one, in the course of which 153 women were arrested. Nothing, after all, had occurred to diminish the exasperation of the new movement. The old impasse remained between politicians unable to see how anything could be allowed to interfere with a programme of Liberal legislation which had already had to wait so long, and women who would only see how long their own cause had waited; between a Government unable to see why a point-blank division of opinion in the Cabinet should not produce in this matter the suspension of action which it would produce in any other, and women asserting a plain right beyond the rules of normal political behaviour. The Conciliation Bill had, as it turned out, hindered rather than helped peace. Carefully framed to avoid too large a feminine intrusion into the electorate, it laid itself open to the

charge of being undemocratic and, as such, a Bill for
which even convinced suffragists in the Government
could not press for facilities ; Mr Lloyd George had
been taking this line, and was specially singled out for
the accusations of quibbling and dishonesty which it
not unnaturally aroused among the suffragists. Faced
now by another General Election, in which, so far as
Liberals and Labour could help it, no other subject
than the "Lords' veto" was to be raised—their Press
had openly deplored the danger of the suffrage question distracting the electorate—it was no wonder that
the suffrage movement expressed itself once more in
calculated disorder.

Parliament was dissolved on 28th November ; by
5th December the first election returns were coming
in. No one had wanted a long campaign ; the shorter
and sharper it was, the better. The new House, complete by 21st December, consisted of 272 Liberals,
42 Labour members, 76 Irish Nationalists, and 8 Irish
Independents on the Government side ; on the Opposition side 253 Unionists and 19 Irish Unionists. The
Opposition Press might analyse the figures, and prove
that, without the Irish and Labour, whose vote on the
House of Lords could not be called disinterested, the
Government had only a majority of 18.[1] But even so
the constituencies had decided ; and the plain fact
was that the Government could rely upon its whole
majority of 126.

At the very end of the year there came a reminder
that uneasiness in our foreign relations was lurking
all the time behind these months of absorption in a
domestic struggle. Articles that had been published
in France by M. Deschanel on the "Triple Entente" of
Great Britain, France and Russia had provoked comment
in Germany. For the time being a minimising in the

[1] One Liberal member had been returned from Ireland.

British Press of M. Deschanel's rather too candid interpretation of the obligations of the Entente smoothed the surface of affairs, even to the extent of suggesting that there really existed no obligations that need prevent an Anglo-German Entente. But in fact, in so far as our relations with Germany had been in the public mind at all, there was little sign of real friendliness. Newspapers which one day were deploring jealous rivalries would on another congratulate the nation on the skill with which the secret of our new 13·5 naval gun had been kept; and the publication of Mr Norman Angell's *The Great Illusion*, with its thesis that war among great modern communities was financially unthinkable, seemed only another indication of how near they were coming to thinking about it. If for the moment party exchanges in the Commons on the subject of our naval rivalry with Germany had become less acute (though Mr Balfour had been accused of " scare-mongering "), there was matter for concern outside Parliament in the unfriendly irritability which was beginning to express itself in spy-scares. Two Englishmen had been condemned in Germany on a charge of espionage; and *Punch* was giving rein to contemptuous pleasantries about the surreptitious activities of the German waiters in British hotels and restaurants.

CHAPTER II

THE new year was ushered in by an occurrence which gave startling emphasis to the feeling that the general amiability, on the whole, of the social structure, to which the later generations of Victorians had grown thoroughly accustomed, was disintegrating. Throughout the morning of 3rd January bullets were whistling up and down a street in the East End of London, grimly empty save for a few policemen at posts of vantage in sheltered entries, and a line of Scots Guards, prone in the roadway, sniping at the windows of one of the houses. It was the notorious " battle of Sidney Street," and it even reached a point at which Horse Artillery, though in the end they never came into action, were bringing up guns. A fortnight earlier a gang of men, interrupted in a burglary in Houndsditch, had fired on the police, killing three of them. Two men believed to be of the gang, whose names, " Fritz " and " Peter the Painter," were now to be on everyone's tongue, had been traced to a house in Sidney Street. The police quietly cleared other people out of the house in the small hours of 3rd January, occupied a brewery building overlooking it, and at 7 A.M. attempted to make their arrests. But they had failed to catch their men napping. Shooting began, and rather than waste lives, which would certainly have been lost by tackling the two at close quarters, the police withdrew from the house, and besieged it in form, sending for a half-company of Scots Guards

from the Tower of London. About midday the Home
Secretary, Mr Winston Churchill, arrived on the scene,
and soon afterwards the guns were sent for. But just
before half-past one the house was seen to be on fire,
and that was the end. When an entry could be made,
two bodies were found, and, though the inquest failed
to establish anything clearly, it appeared most likely
that the men had at the last shot themselves; but
whether they, or the firing from outside, had set light
to the house was never known.

Coming, as it did, while the Tottenham affair, in
which also foreigners had used firearms murderously,[1]
was still fresh in the memory, the battle of Sidney
Street was instantly followed by an outcry against
undesirable aliens, swelled by disgust at a coincident
affair. A Frenchman had been found murdered on
Clapham Common, with the letter S slashed into both
his cheeks, and another foreigner, Stinie Morrison, was
soon under arrest. For the next three months the two
cases ran a curious course in the newspapers. Morrison,
protesting his innocence, and able in fact to produce
some evidence of an alibi, was condemned to death.
But meanwhile the case against certain persons arrested
in connection with the Sidney Street affair had been
slowly petering out in a maze of unsatisfactory evidence,
and dwindled to the sentencing of a woman to two
years' imprisonment for conspiracy. Both cases had
proceeded through a confusing cloud—clamour about
seedy foreigners, irritation with the police for letting
London in for a kind of Parisian apache affair, and
an uneasy sense that all this was not the atmosphere
of fair trial. Morrison, after failing in an appeal against
his sentence, was reprieved. The hostility to undesirable aliens remained, and was given a new turn
by the articles called forth just at this juncture by

[1] See page 755.

the death of Sir Francis Galton, one of the pioneers of
eugenics; why should the nation submit to having
foreign degenerates added to its own? The Government introduced during the session a Bill meeting the
complaint that magistrates were using inadequately
their powers of expulsion of aliens, by giving the Home
Office power to issue expulsion orders.

There were some less justifiable political reverberations. Mr Churchill's presence in Sidney Street was
sharply criticized; and, though he could afford to
ignore taunts suggesting that his motives had been
merely theatrical, and could disprove more serious
accusations of interfering with the police and giving
orders over their heads, the attacks on him had significance as indicating the pitch of party temper. They
had a kind of parallel later in a campaign of virulent
sneers which pursued him and Mr Lloyd George in the
matter of "the Dartmoor shepherd." This individual
was an elderly man who, convicted of a small theft and
known to have served a number of terms of imprisonment, had been sentenced under the new Prevention
of Crimes Act to three years' penal servitude and ten
years' police supervision. Mr Churchill, interested in
a case which seemed typical of the results of the old
rather thoughtless penal administration, and Mr Lloyd
George, interested because the man was Welsh, had
visited him in prison, and he had been liberated. He
proved later to have been too much affected by the
old methods to be a very shining example of the new.
Attacks on Mr Lloyd George, in connection with the
embarrassed circumstances of the Birkbeck Bank, for
creating an atmosphere of financial mistrust were
perhaps less perverse; though as a matter of fact the
Bank's difficulties had begun with a "run" probably
traceable to the failure early in the year of the Charing
Cross Bank, when depositors had lost £1,750,000. The

taking over of the Yorkshire Penny Bank by a London banking group on the ground that it had "outgrown its constitution" may be mentioned here. Sharpness of party feeling was also to be seen in the extraordinary number of political libel actions which arose out of the two General Elections of 1910 ; there were no less than thirty before the Courts. The "raging and tearing propaganda" of the Tariff Reform controversy, the growing incursion into by-elections of mushroom "ad hoc" organisations of licensed victuallers and coal-owners,[1] and the uncompromising methods of the new suffragist movement had all helped to exasperate political tempers rasped by the "landslide" of 1906 ; and electioneering was growing so abusive that Mr Masterman, who had to stand for re-election in July of this year, could be described as having "emerged from a mud-bath."

Yet over the immediate Liberal measure of the moment a distinct difference was observed between the temper in Parliament and general feeling outside. For good or ill the final stages of the controversy with the House of Lords aroused but little interest away from Westminster.

Two of the notable men of the party who had had the longest share in it were not to see its end, Sir Charles Dilke and Sir Henry Fowler. The latter, making his way into politics from municipal affairs, had risen quietly to office in Mr Gladstone's later administrations by gifts of clear thinking and moderate, sensible presentation of a case. Sir Charles Dilke's career, on the other hand, had been one of strong lights and shadows. He had entered the 1868 Parliament as a young man of twenty-five, already with a reputation ; a tour round the world had led him to the writing of a book, *Greater Britain*, of which the theme and title, both original, gave

1 See page 745.

him, in a period just becoming consciously Imperialist,
a brilliant start, to which a strange, arresting element
was added by his open and extreme republicanism.
A young man of birth and fortune, deeply impressed
with the extent of British sway, yet roundly attacking
the Crown as a useless and expensive encumbrance,
was not a figure that could be missed. Though he soon
dropped republicanism of this kind, he remained to the
end a mixture, baffling to younger politicians, of equally
convinced Radicalism and Imperialism. Just when his
high talents were overriding Mr Gladstone's dislike of
his Radicalism the shadow fell. Made co-respondent in
a divorce case, in which he asserted his innocence, and
the verdict in which did not in fact condemn him, he was
tragically unable to clear his name in the public mind.
Though he returned soon, undaunted, to Parliament,
he was never now to be more than a private member,
but a private member of a weight and wisdom almost
absurdly out of place away from the Front Benches.
Speaking with authority on foreign affairs (no one else,
save King Edward, who had early sought his friendship,
was so much at home in Paris alike with Royalists and
with the statesmen of the Third Republic), and on affairs
of the Empire, he had also an unrivalled grasp of the
relations of industry and the State, and was a peculiarly
trusted ally and adviser of the Labour group. Such a
career, with its high-lighted opening, its shattering
check, and the dogged picking-up of what was left, made
him a curiously enigmatic figure ; seldom, in British
politics, can such great powers have been so generously
used—even, perhaps, so happily—in such comparative
obscurity.

The general lack of interest in the Parliament Bill was,
no doubt, largely due to the feeling that after the two
elections all was really over, bar the shouting. This was
not quite true. The Bill, introduced in the Commons

on 21st February, and passed by them in May, was given
a second reading in the Lords only under the threat of
" grave amendments." Earlier in the month Lord
Lansdowne had produced again his scheme for reform
of the House, having preceded this by a proposal to pray
the Crown for leave to bring in a Bill limiting the Royal
Prerogative—a necessary preliminary if peers of Parliament were in future not to be the same body as the whole
peerage, though at the moment it sounded like a truculent
counter-move to a possible wholesale creation of peers.
For his prospectively reformed House he now attempted
to retain power by amendments to the Parliament Bill
providing for a Joint Committee of both Houses in
matters of disagreement, and reserving for a Referendum
Bills " establishing national Parliaments " or " raising
issues of great gravity."

But the country did not take all this very seriously.
Besides, the Government, anxious both to keep the fight
from becoming a bore, and to display the positive ameliorations for which it was to clear the road, were switching
attention on to the next stage, after Old Age Pensions,
of dealing with the grim insecurities of the worker, the
Health and Unemployment Insurance Bill. They had
also to meet their undertakings by introducing the Bill
to deal with the Osborne Judgment. The latter Bill
was not, in the end, carried this year. Labour, meeting
the concern for individual liberty by abandoning the
signed party pledge, and abolishing, on the inclusion
of payment of members in the year's Budget, the
Parliamentary party's salaries from trade union funds,
disliked the other provisions for individual liberty which
the Government had included in their Bill ; and rather
than risk, on a Committee stage, a parting of forces
which might react upon the fortunes of the Insurance
Bill, the Trade Union Bill was taken no further than
the second reading.

And then in later spring there were yet other distractions. For this was Coronation year; and in May, as a kind of preliminary spectacle, came the ceremony of the formal opening of the Queen Victoria Memorial with the new Mall and the Admiralty Arch. This has its peculiar interest now as the last occasion on which the German Emperor was to show himself to a London crowd. He and the Empress came over; already his wearing of a British Field-Marshal's uniform had an odd look; and what geniality there was for him in the streets was fairly deeply coloured with the comforting assurance of such facts as the commissioning a few months earlier of the first "all-big-gun" battleship in the world, H.M.S. *Neptune*, the laying-down of two improved Dreadnoughts, and the increase of the Naval Estimates for the year by nearly £4,000,000; the crowd might feel that it could afford to be pleasant. Not that there was any lack of a less confident point of view. We might keep ahead in a naval race, but would that avail a nation disunited by heated politics and more and more industrial unrest? The epidemic of strikes was continuing. One had broken out on the North Eastern Railway in February, against the instructions of the union leaders; and there had been more rioting in South Wales. Those who liked to exaggerate the subversiveness of Labour had their opportunity when, early in the year, a paper called *The Liberator* published an article giving currency to rumours that King George, before his marriage to the Queen, had contracted a marriage at Malta, during his service in the navy, with an admiral's daughter. The putting of the author on his trial caused more sensation than the article. Confronted in the conduct of his defence with the constitutional impossibility of calling the King in evidence, the accused man gave up his case and was sentenced to twelve months' imprisonment. After the sentence,

when no constitutional point could be involved, the
Attorney-General read in court, by the King's direction,
an explicit denial of the rumours, signed by His Majesty,
an incident which sufficiently showed a sense of the
prevalence of the rumours, and a determination that
no one should be able to say that, though the offence
of publication had been dealt with, the point of fact
remained obscure behind a constitutional formality.

Summer, coming in early with promise of far better
weather than that of 1910, brought the preparations
for the Coronation. It had not the excitement of King
Edward's coronation as a spectacle which, owing to
Queen Victoria's long reign, few living people had seen.
The newspapers could still, in mid-May, give the best
of their space to the death, in a fire on the stage of an
Edinburgh music-hall, of " The Great Lafayette," an
" illusionist " who had curiously caught the popular imagination by the elaborate splendours of the stage *décor*
with which he travelled and amid which he perished.
But as the great days approached in London, the mere
preparations for crowds drew crowds to look at them.
Not only were there the vast wooden stands along the
route of the procession, but the streets along the route
and giving access to it were equipped with gates and
rails to help the police in controlling the streams of
humanity. For if the Coronation had not the novelty
of the last one, modern transport developments would
give some novelty in the far larger crowds poured in to
see it. For several days before it they drifted about,
looking at illuminations of an evening, and at London's
attempt to overcome the reproach that it had poorer
ideas of decorating itself than any other great city in
the world. Pageantry had broken out in the theatres,
for the taste for barbaric Orientalism had brought
Reinhardt's Arabian Night *Sumurun* to London, and
Mr Oscar Asche had followed with the spectacular

displays of *Kismet.* Military camps to house the contingents of show troops sprang up in the parks, as in
1902. The bounding trade returns, constantly trumpeted
by the Free Trade Government, were reflected in the
ready and luxurious spending which filled hotels and
restaurants and theatres. Finally the weather was at its
most gracious when on 22nd June the King and Queen
were crowned, and on the following day drove through
miles of London streets. Nor was this Coronation year
to be a mere repetition ; it had its own distinctions.
The Investiture at Carnarvon in July of the Prince of
Wales, whose robed and coroneted boyishness had made
such an attractive little figure at the ceremony in the
Abbey, was a picturesque invention, and the Imperial air
which had blown round the Coronation of King Edward
—the first British Sovereign to ascend the throne since
the Colonies had become great dominions and India
had been added to the titles of the Crown—was to blow
more strongly round King George in a visit to India for
the Indians to see the King-Emperor taking his power
upon him in their own presence in durbar.

The occasion of the Coronation, bringing, as it did,
the Colonial Premiers to England, had been used for
another Imperial Conference, which was opened in May.
It was more important than the public at the time
quite understood. Sir Joseph Ward, of New Zealand,
produced a motion in favour of an " Imperial Council of
State "; its withdrawal two days later did not mask
the fact that every other Dominion had repudiated with
energy any supreme machine of Empire policy. Here
then perished finally all the hazy conceptions, from
Disraeli and Tennyson onwards, of some kind of
Parliament and Cabinet of Empire, sitting in London
and ruling as a political unity the British communities of
the world. They perished not only in the failure of Sir
Joseph Ward's motion, but also in the strength already

attained by very different conceptions. In March a
debate in the Commons on the reciprocity treaty between
Canada and the United States—raised by the Opposition
in order to charge the Government with driving Canada
towards annexation by the States for lack of any
preferential tariff with Great Britain—had elicited from
Sir Edward Grey the information that, in the course of
the negotiations for the treaty, the idea of a Canadian
Minister in Washington had emerged. Now at the
Conference Sir Edward Grey, criticised for not consulting
the Colonies in the negotiations for the Declaration of
London, promised consultation about international
agreements in future; Mr Fisher, of Australia, was
demanding that the Dominions should no longer be
represented in the British Government by the Colonial
Secretary, but should, as equal Powers, deal with the
Foreign Secretary direct; and the Colonial Secretary
announced that the Government at any rate proposed,
by making two Secretaryships, one for the Dominions
and one for the Crown Colonies, to recognise that the
old position of subordination no longer applied to the
greater colonies. Both this change and the change
envisaged by Mr Fisher's proposal had to wait for
some years; and when they came they rested on a new
conception, tried in the most fiery of furnaces, of what
empire might mean. At the moment they were little
regarded by a British public which had not been taught
even by the Boer War to think about Imperial questions; it was still content with sentiment. But to the
interested observer it was clear that a process of evolution, marked at the previous Coronation by the phrase
on the new coinage, " all the Britains," had at this
Coronation advanced very much further.

For a moment in July interest in the Parliament Bill
did flicker up again, when the Royal guarantee to the
Prime Minister, so much discussed and discounted that

no one knew now any better than twelve months earlier whether to believe in its existence or not, actually took shape. It was, indeed, by this time something of a damp squib. In the mysterious way in which such impressions get about, the public had put its own value upon the manœuvres and resistances of the extreme Conservatives in both Houses, who at this time added the phrase " diehards " to political nomenclature. Led by the aged Lord Halsbury, they presented the spectacle of a forlorn hope to an age with singularly little use for such things. So side by side with the solemn passing of Lord Lansdowne's amendments there ran the conviction that in the end the Lords must give way. If it was barely credible that there could be a wholesale creation of peers, it was no more credible that the " diehards " would venture to repeat the performance of 1909, when, to throw out the Budget, noble lords had appeared who actually had to ask the policeman at the door the way to their hereditary Chamber ; incidents of that farce of the " backwoodsmen " had been only too well exploited on Liberal and Labour platforms. To those behind the scenes the real consideration undermining the " diehard " position was the general indifference of the country. For that meant a conviction that the Budget election had decided that the House of Lords, however it might " pin-prick " Liberal Governments, could not stand out on a real issue of the national life against the vast modern electorate. It was, then, essentially unimportant, as all recent generations had believed it to be, and as the placid absence from it throughout their lives of two-thirds of its members indicated.

Still, there remained a point of crisis. The Bill, amended in a way which would have left the Lords free to block precisely the measures now vitally in the Government's mind, must come back to the Commons. Would it travel to and fro in a maze of disagreement, or was this the

moment for unmasking the guns ? Were there guns
to unmask, after all ? There were. On 21st July, the
day after the final stage in the Lords, a letter from
Mr Asquith to Mr Balfour was published, stating that
the Commons would be asked to disagree with the Lords'
amendments, and proceeding thus : " In the circumstances, should the necessity arise, the Government will
advise the King to exercise his Prerogative to secure
the passing into law of the Bill in substantially the
same form in which it left the House of Commons, and
His Majesty has been pleased to signify that he will
consider it his duty to accept and act on that advice."
There, then, was the guarantee, full and unequivocal.

The publication of it in that way may, perhaps, be
considered the one tactical mistake Mr Asquith made.
So far his discretion, as he could make plain when, some
weeks later, Mr Balfour moved a vote of censure on him
for " abusing his right as the adviser of the Crown " and
keeping the guarantee in his pocket for eight months,
had been unassailable. He had given no advice to create
peers until the House of Lords had actually wrecked
the Bill. Till then, he had himself said nothing about the
use of the Royal Prerogative, whatever interpretation
others had put upon his words. The letter to Mr Balfour
had been written—a final effort of discretion—to keep
the matter of the Prerogative, if possible, out of public
view to the last ; it was intended for communication to
Lord Lansdowne and his friends, before the final vote
in the Lords. But as it failed to affect that vote it
turned out to be an unfortunate step. For when Mr
Asquith rose in the House on 24th July to move the
rejection of the Lords' amendments, and to make his
statement, the Opposition, the facts being now known,
simply refused him a hearing. He was howled down,
and the Speaker adjourned the House without question
put. The whole affair was made even more foolish and

undignified by the publication next day of a letter from
Mr Balfour to Lord Newton advising the House of Lords
to accept the original Bill and drop their amendments.
For a few days some tension remained ; it was not quite
certain that Mr Balfour or Lord Newton or anyone else
could persuade enough of the extremists to abstain from
voting to leave the victory to the small Liberal numbers
in that House. A narrow margin of obstinacy would
defeat them ; and there was a proposal that it might be
as well to create a kind of preliminary batch of fifty
peers to allow for the margin and to show that business
was meant. However, the risk was taken with success ;
and on 11th August, by a majority in the Lords of 131
to 114, the Parliament Bill was secured.

Strict thinking may regard the whole Act as hasty
and muddled-headed. For years past Liberals had been
decrying the composition and disputing the powers of
the House of Lords ; they had taken office convinced
that the struggle would have to come to a head. The
controversy had been carried on to an accompaniment
of the largest and most fundamental discussion of what
a Second Chamber should be in a modern community,
what it should represent, what functions of legislation
and control it should exercise ; with a strong undercurrent of opinion that a modern community needed no
Second Chamber at all. Yet the Parliament Act decided
none of these things. It assumed that for the present a
Second Chamber should continue to exist ; it relegated
to the future the question of its reconstruction ; and,
pending that, it assigned to the Chamber powers which
might, on the analogy of some Second Chambers, be
regarded as its due functions in that ultimate future
or might be taken as a mere temporary bridle. After all
the years of premonition, Liberals had no clear and
definite Second Chamber to produce ; not one of their
clever lawyers, apparently, could come down off plat-

forms to do a piece of respectable machine-work. They scrambled out of their great " veto campaign " with this shoddy makeshift.

There is more than one answer to the strict thinker. The obvious one is that real Second Chamber reform was not practical politics. Even if proposals based on a real theory of the place of a Second Chamber in representative government had been ready to hand, they would have embroiled the Ministry with those of its supporters, numerous among Liberals and almost the entire force of Labour, who saw no useful place for a Second Chamber ; and would have involved it in weariful campaigning amid a mass of detailed schemes. For that it had no time, believing (and one need not attribute this to the motive of piling up electioneering capital) that there was social work more urgently needing to be done. But the better answer is that here again, as in the Budget fight, the Liberal leaders were shrewd. Broadly speaking, the Parliament Act, imperfect and tentative as it is, represents ordinary British common-sense. In the rather vague mind of the public two ideas were recognisably at work. On the one hand there was a distinct feeling that, after all, the House of Lords was a not quite " sporting " element in the Constitution ; it did let through any Bills one side might send it, and only threw out Bills of the other side. There might be all sorts of sound reasons for this—the inevitable conservatism of any senate, the fact that it was precisely the more openly advanced side which must naturally undergo the checking, and so on ; all that the plain man noticed was the obvious one-sidedness. But on the other hand he did not want the House of Lords " messed about with." He did not think that an irruption of " backwoodsmen " was very likely to be seen again, and he felt that the normal working House of Lords was probably about as representative of what a senate should represent as any new-fangled Chamber could be, with the merit of a prestige which a new Chamber might never acquire. Nor, finally, was he sure what powers he would wish even a reformed Chamber to have ; roughly speaking, he did think already of the functions of the Lords as pretty nearly what the Parliament Act laid down—impotence in finance, and a power in other legislation to make the country think a bit longer. Therefore on the whole the Parliament Act was not merely the work of politicians ; it can claim statesmanship. On purely party lines, or on doctrinaire lines, a more complete and impeccable measure might have been forced through ; on lines that should compose the national mind by meeting its vague sense of what was fair all round nothing better could have been devised. Even the very element in it which has been most ridiculed, its temporary and provisional character, may be the most statesmanlike part of it. For it is equally true that the nation was in the main content to have something done about the House of Lords, and that it was not then, has never since been, and perhaps never will be, content to have anything permanent done with it. All this is not to say that the Parliament Act was consciously a building upon that " general sense " which is so difficult to find. It was, no doubt, for men absorbed in other purposes, the quickest way to free their hands. But that does not necessarily exclude some streak of genius in the affair as later reflection envisages it.

Certainly no such ideas were current at the time, for the measure was taken as genuinely temporary. That is partly why the country was so little interested at the end. The great struggle had led, not to condemnation and sentence, but to a remand—in custody. It is reminiscent of the long wrangle over the suspension of unruly members of the Commons, which never reached a conclusion, and has left one of the Standing Orders of the House ending to this day in an undignified dash. It was, too, a piece of political history made for the humour of one who died just at this time, Sir W. S. Gilbert. He was drowned at the end of May bathing in the grounds of his house at Harrow. He had deserved his fame, for he and Sir Arthur Sullivan had beyond question given the English stage a new and native art-form ; and he had a rare kind of immortality, in that his name had given to the English language an adjective for just such unintentional whimsicalities of politics as this invincible old reprobate of a House of Lords.

Early in the summer that heavy curtain of apprehension which, through all these years, hung behind the restlessness of home politics was violently shaken again. On 2nd July news arrived of the appearance of a German gunboat, the *Panther*, at the port of Agadir in Morocco. This focussed sharply all the recent suspicions of mutual international obligations ; was Germany determined to test them by a renewed intimation that she did not accept one of the cardinal points of our relations with France ? Hot-headed tendencies to regard the gunboat's mission instantly as an act of hostility were certainly not checked by Mr Asquith's statement in the Commons, with its references to British interests and our treaty obligations to France ; and drew something like definite authority from a speech by Mr Lloyd George at the Mansion House a fortnight later, which had a startling tone of warning to Germany. Three days later rumours—inevitable after such a speech—of orders to the British fleet marked the peak of the excitement ; it subsided rapidly after a prompt denial of the rumours, and even more after another statement by Mr Asquith which, though not very clear, implied that intervention at Agadir had never been in question, and hinted at prospects of territorial arrangements elsewhere in Africa, compensating Germany for French predominance in Morocco. The air, then, must be clearing.

And none too soon, was the feeling of those who lived in expectation of every kind of disaster under a Liberal Government. For, in a summer of extreme heat, industrial tempers were going from bad to worse. Not only was there, as it seemed, a kind of running fire of strikes —seamen had come out at various ports in June, carters and vanmen (a partly sympathetic strike refusing to handle goods for the shipping lines with which the seamen were in dispute) in July, the London dockers at the beginning of August—but every strike was attended by violence. At Hull and Cardiff, at Manchester, which had had to call for a strong force of London police and for Scots Greys from the York garrison, there had been fighting in the streets. Strikes were, indeed, settled ; Mr Askwith, of the Board of Trade, constantly negotiating, became one of the best-known public figures of the time. Seamen and dockers gained at least some of the most pressing of their points. But hardly had these settlements been announced when the railwaymen began to move, and after violent scenes in Liverpool, where two men were shot dead and two hundred people injured, and at Llanelly, where again two were shot and four more killed by the explosion of a petrol tank, the whole railway system was suddenly threatened. On 15th August twenty-four hours' notice was given of a general railway strike. It was a serious climax in more ways than one—serious in its causes, for the men were coming out to break up the conciliation boards they had accepted so recently as in 1907, in which they had entirely lost faith ; and serious in its character, because for the first time the two great skilled unions, the Amalgamated Society of Railway Servants and the Locomotive Engineers and Firemen, were acting together in conjunction with a newer body, the General

Railway Workers, which included all the unskilled. Here were more signs of the times which were not passing unobserved, the massing of the unions and the sympathetic strike ; it had been remarked that the seamen had won their case largely by the coincident strikes of carmen and dockers ; and, lest they might in some way be used to mitigate the effects of the railway strike, the London lightermen, whose case had just been settled, were coming out again. " Continental," the newspapers cried ; our strikes, like our crimes, were becoming disturbingly un-English.

The railway strike did not last long. After a vain truce for possible conciliation it began on all railways on 17th August. On 19th August it was over. The men's case had nominally been met by the promise of an immediate Special Commission, all strikers being meanwhile reinstated. But the truth was that the strike had been too big an attempt. Work never did quite cease on all lines, and motor traffic was already at a stage of development which, though far from adequate to meet very grave difficulties, was enough to bring some discouragement to the strikers.

Moreover they had not timed their effort well ; the beginning or the end of the holiday season would have given them more chance of producing disorganisation. Striking in the middle of it, they did little more than give a mild shock to a not very interesting summer. Flying made no notable advances, save for the first non-stop flight from London to Paris, and was still so experimental that Army Estimates providing five aeroplanes met with no criticism ; and the first naval airship, launched in May, broke her back in her first voyage after only two minutes' flight. The popular craze of the moment, roller-skating, which for a few months invaded all social ranks, as cycling had done in an earlier year, and was seen at Prince's as well as in cheap rinks hastily run up in the suburbs, was not an occupation for a hot summer. " Standard bread " and " paper-bag cookery " were little more than newspaper rivalries, one paper offering facilities for getting a guaranteed bread, another providing its readers with paper bags ; but both ideas had the quality so essential for newspaper purposes of being endlessly discussable in the morning train to the City : was it true that a too-white bread meant the elimination from flour of elements vital for our teeth and our digestion, and that we must go back to sound old rural stone-milling ? Did paper bags, which in any case added an amusing kind of conjuring element to the dull round of saucepan and oven, really retain indispensable juices in the food, and had they qualities peculiarly commendable in small kitchens ? So the respective " stunts " tacked themselves on to the growing movement for fitness and week-end cottages and garden suburbs and daylight-saving (was not this the first year of whole-page advertising of penny packets of garden seeds ?), and on to a kitchen economy that the lady of the house could manage herself, for bungalow towns were also beginning to grow along the coast. As for sport, we were not as yet hardened enough to foreign competition to take quite easily French victories in lawn tennis ; there was hardly consolation in the laugh against them when their famous *La Gioconda* was calmly stolen from the Louvre under the noses of the guardians. But Burgess's success in swimming the Channel on 6th September—the first since Captain Webb's feat in the seventies—had a comforting John Bull quality about it ; he had set himself to the task through so many defeats.

The railway settlement, it soon appeared, satisfied nobody. The companies, thinking they had taken the measure of the unions, regarded the Special Commission as a futility ; and the men were merely exasperated

when, at its meetings in September, they heard railway managers proposing that all railway employees
should be put permanently under military law. In this,
as in the other cases, peace was the very flimsiest
papering over of cracks. Nor were the cracks only between masters and men. Labour was inclined to quarrel
with the Liberals, resenting, however unreasonably, the
sharp measures taken to keep order, and even more
the signs of a counter-organisation in reserve which
had been revealed by the announcement that the
country had been mapped into " military areas " for
emergencies. It was taken as a piece of gratuitous
emphasis when, a month after the strike was over, the
War Office published a provisional scheme for subsidising motor-lorries in return for the right to mobilise
them in case of " national danger." Labour was unnecessarily sensitive about this : it was not a scheme
for industrial emergencies in its origin. Civilian motor
equipment had advanced so rapidly (the London General
Omnibus Company, for instance, ran its last horse-bus
on 25th October of this year), while military replacement
of the old horse - transport was cramped inside the
Estimates, that some scheme for a claim on civilian
motors was to be expected.

Pat on the speculations this aroused as to what the
next war might be like, a war broke out. But it was
one which promised little novelty ; it was of only too
familiar a type. Italy, cutting abruptly into the bigger
Powers' allocations of African spheres, descended upon
Tripoli, after a sketchy ultimatum alleging the condition
of government in that region to be a menace to her
interests. An easy landing of troops was soon followed
by a most awkwardly determined and fanatical resistance ; and for the rest of the year subjugation went on
in ways which revolted the war-correspondents of other
nations. Anxiety was reawakened ; but France and

Germany, after a brief flare-up of alarmist rumours in September, were coming to terms on the basis which had been indicated in the early days of the Agadir affair : Germany was to have compensations in the Congo territory in return for recognition of predominant French interests in Morocco.

But that affair had left its mark upon the supporters of the Government in a mistrust of their leaders, which came into the open in a debate on foreign policy in November. This was the first systematic expression of the protest against " secret diplomacy " which, in the years to come, was to be the line of democratic effort for peace. It had, of course, its specific point to fasten on ; it was easy enough, behind all the crises of this year, to perceive the " blind spot " which was making international relations so unsteady—the unknown factors in our understanding with France. Sir Edward Grey's assurances in this debate that, beyond the arrangements about Morocco, which had now been made fully public, there were no secret treaty engagements, was not so conciliatory as it was meant to be ; the use of the word " treaty " was noticed, for it left the door uncomfortably open to engagements not necessarily in treaty form. More generally the rank and file had observed much in the pronouncements of Ministers which seemed to them deplorably far from what Liberal language should be in a time of such mutual suspicion. An exchange of offices by which Mr McKenna went to the Home Office and Mr Winston Churchill to the Admiralty was not reassuring, and had in fact all the meaning which the party put upon it. Nor had the echoes of Mr Lloyd George's Mansion House speech died away. Sir Edward Grey's statement in the debate, that no Ministerial explanation had followed it because the German Ambassador's request for one had been in terms which precluded explanation, showed that Germany had taken such a speech from the most democratic member of the Cabinet as the clearest possible indication that the Cabinet was united in a rather hostile attitude about Agadir. That had, indeed, been the only conclusion that most Liberals could draw ; how could they believe what a few knew and a few more suspected—that Mr Lloyd George, for the sake of an effective appearance before City bankers with no love for his finance, had dangerously committed a divided Cabinet, and done so with a sudden reversal of the very line he had himself been taking in the division ? But even without this knowledge the incident was sinister enough ; Conservatives saw in it a weakness of foreign policy liable to issue in erratic demagogic plunges, and Liberals a rather ignoble surrender to cheap national pride.

However, as was to happen more than once in Mr Lloyd George's career, his immediate importance to the party threw mistrust into the background. He was the main power-unit of their social reform, and they needed now all his energy. For this year's great instalment of reform, launched, it had appeared, smoothly enough in the spring, was running into stormy waters. This was the Invalidity and Unemployment Insurance Bill. The Bill was in two parts : Part II., the insurance against unemployment, applied only to certain trades ; Part I., the health insurance, applied to practically all employed persons, and was, for all interest of the moment, the Bill. The scheme, in brief, was that every employed person should be obliged to keep a card upon which every week the employer was legally bound to place an Inland Revenue stamp. The cost of this stamp, 4d., was to be provided, half by the employer, and half by deduction from the wage ; the State's addition of a contribution, and its provision of the cost of management of the fund, would so raise the value of the weekly payment as to make it, in effect, a weekly premium of 9d. " Ninepence for

Fourpence " became the catchword of Liberal speeches
on the Bill. The benefits of the insurance were to be free
medical attendance—practitioners grouping themselves
upon panels for the purpose—and necessary drugs and
appliances.

On the whole, the Bill had had a friendly reception.
It was criticised, of course, especially in regard to the
actuarial basis. Here the Government had laid themselves open by their original miscalculations on the
previous great social reform, Old Age Pensions.[1] In both
cases estimates were, inevitably, difficult ; really adequate statistics were not to be obtained. It was strongly
felt that the figure of ninepence was a far too rosy guess,
and had been too easily concocted for platform use.
But these were details ; amid the distractions of the
Coronation, and the last rumblings of the House of
Lords controversy, the Bill had made a good start. All
the talk for years past about national efficiency, a sense
that in this matter at any rate Germany was ahead of
us, combined with all the inclination — earnest at its
best, vaguely pacificatory at its lowest—to do something
for the industrial unrest, produced acquiescence ; some
such measure was bound to come.

A different spirit now appeared, and worked itself up
to strange heat. It might almost seem that Parliament
was falling into a habit of bringing back from its holidays
a sharp change of temper ; just as in 1910 it had reassembled in a mood of suspicion of the Conference, so
now its mood on the Insurance Bill had sharpened. The
truth was that the Opposition were beginning to see
chances. They did not exaggerate the effect of Liberal
disaffection in the matter of foreign affairs ; still, it
was a weak spot on which to play. Far more to their
purpose was Labour disaffection in the matter of the
strikes, because it was evident that differing ranks

1 See page 758.

of Labour had criticisms of the Bill to make, which
in that mood of disaffection might drive some wedges
into the Government's majority. The first criticism had
come from the great friendly societies. To begin with,
it had been little more than a kind of jealous guarded-
ness ; the Foresters, for instance, had protested against
any " taking away of the right of the Order to continue
its own arrangements for medical benefit." But this
opened out into a jealousy which struck at the roots of
the scheme. The Bill had had to envisage two methods
of insurance — one through the friendly societies and
trade unions, and one worked, like the Savings Bank,
through the Post Office; it would have been wasteful and stupid not to make use of the system which
already insured vast numbers of wage-earners just
because another system had to be devised for those
outside such insurance. But here a serious danger
emerged. The whole point of the Bill was to bring
every employed person under insurance ; that must
necessarily mean bringing in, as the direct Post Office
contributors for whom the State must be responsible, a
very large number of cases which the friendly societies
would think too bad to insure ; the result of the Bill,
then, would be to force the friendly societies to pool
their own wealth, securely based on experience of their
business, with all the risks of the Post Office insurance
which had to proceed at present upon a good deal of
actuarial guesswork. Thus the aristocracy of employment was up in arms. Its humbler ranks were also
ready to be restive. For the mere instinctive dislike of
having their wages docked every week, whether they
liked it or not, was made far more serious when it was
led by such prominent Labour men as Mr Lansbury,
Mr Snowden, Mr Jowett and Mr Will Thorne into a
protest against any contributory element in the scheme
at all. This protest was a perfectly sound corollary of

the claim to "a right to work"; the nation must be
responsible for the labour it needed for its prosperity; it
had no business in existing economic conditions to make
that labour even partially responsible for itself.

There was matter enough here, it might seem, with
the barely expressed but real Liberal resentment of such
ungrateful attitudes, to imperil the Bill. But it was all,
so far, within the normal range of political controversy.
There was now to appear hostility which was the first
movement of a kind of opposition to an elected majority
new in British politics. One section of it was almost
ludicrous. Conservative newspapers, making the discovery that under the Bill housewives would actually
have to stamp the cards of domestic servants, worked
up a wild campaign against the indignity of "stamp-
licking," and filled the Albert Hall with a befurred
meeting of Society ladies and comfortably circumstanced women who, fired by some rhetoric from Mr
Hilaire Belloc about "the infernal impudence" of
asking "the better classes" to collect a tax for nothing,
registered their determination to refuse obedience to the
law and put the Government in the impossible position
of having to punish them by the thousand. This was
rebellion *pour rire*. There was something much more
serious in the hostility of a large part of the medical
profession. Here, as in the case of the friendly societies,
at first only a rather guarded attitude had been taken
towards the Bill, with some criticism of the scale of payment, and of the arrangements for the provision of drugs.
But feeling grew stronger and stronger, until late in the
year the British Medical Association definitely demanded
a revision of the scale to their satisfaction, the fixing
of a limit of income for panel patients, and more medical
representation on the local committees under the Bill.
These were all points which might quite properly be
raised for discussion. Unfortunately the profession,

kindest and most generous to the poor of all professions, was stampeded by the same Conservative newspapers into the same kind of undignified protestations about its dignity, and into an Albert Hall meeting of refusal to work the Bill when passed.

Militancy, it can be seen, was spreading. The new suffrage movement had laid down the proposition that a cause which had no adequate political weapons was justified in refusing obedience ; they had earlier in the year even found a way to break so mild an affair as the Census legislation, by sleeping out on commons so as not to be included in the returns. Now opponents of the Government were going to take the line that, swamped by a mass electorate led by mercenary promises, and deprived by the Parliament Act of any check upon the caprices of a General Election, they also might use the weapons of lawlessness to make the Government's path impossibly difficult. It was, however, insincere to contemplate using them against the Insurance Act. For when it became clear that internal party feelings on the Government side were not, after all, going to hinder its passage, the Opposition, walking out in a body when the closure was put, evaded actually voting against it ; and the Lords did not exercise upon it even the suspensive powers that were left to them. Not that this meant merely an unworthy fear of the working people in the constituencies. Social reform was far from being a monopoly of one side ; and Unionists would be stulti-fying themselves if opposition to the Liberal way of doing things was always to go to the length of trying to prevent the things being done. They would only try to make distinctions between the recognised need for social reform and a dictation of the terms of reform at the polls. They found a kind of ally in the new Dean of St Paul's, Dr Inge, who in this October earned at one blow the title of " the gloomy dean " by a jeremiad

on " the fetish of democracy," the " dehumanised
industrialism " which was dragging England to a fall,
and on modern tendencies towards an " unnatural and
flabby horror of taking life."

The Opposition had had some party dissensions themselves. The Conference on the House of Lords had
produced a rank-and-file mistrust of leaders among
Unionists as well as among Liberals, and its break-up,
it will be noticed, had been said to be " forced " upon
Mr Balfour. It was felt now that he was too steeped in
the traditions of older parliamentary days and older
habits of debate to be the leader the party required for
the new and less scrupulous fighting which each side was
now attributing to the other ; if the Government's opponents were refusing to obey the law, the Government,
they could say, was refusing to be bound by the constitution. Moreover, Mr Balfour had never really recovered
his ground with the nation after the long and precarious
balancing act of the days of the Tariff Reform campaign ;
an appearance of indecision, never far from him throughout a career made a little misty to the ordinary man by
his reputation as a philosopher, had become then securely
fastened upon him, and the result was that now " Balfour
must go." He " went " in that sense by resigning the
leadership of the party on 8th November. The clamour
against him had concerned itself little about considerations which had kept the party in Parliament a good
deal less emphatic than the popular Press—the problem
of his successor. For that raised the question whether
the party was still Conservative with a Unionist wing,
in which case Mr Walter Long, a member of the traditional country gentleman type, was the heir to the
leadership, or was in all its effective fighting capacity
Unionist, in which case Mr Austen Chamberlain, the
son of the great fighter, had his claim. In the end a
decision which should have been historic was burked

by both of these standing aside, and the party, to its
astonishment, found itself being led by Mr Bonar Law,
a Glasgow member, of a certain shrewd strength in
debate, but with no Cabinet experience (his only office
so far had been that of Parliamentary Secretary to the
Board of Trade) and unknown to the general public.   It
was a flattish ending to so much swashbuckling about
leadership.

Before it awoke to the enormities of " stamp-licking "
London society had been besieging at one moment the
philosophical lectures of M. Bergson, in one of its
periodical highbrow crazes, and at another the ticket-
offices for a projected prize-fight between Jack Johnson,
the American negro, and Bombardier Wells. These affairs,
under the influence of American mass-methods, were
issuing from the plush-and-gilt privacies of the National
Sporting Club into premises that would hold enough
money to bring such champions into the ring.   This
particular affair did not come off.   Protests against it,
as not legitimate boxing on points, but " a thinly veiled
reversion to the prize-ring," induced the London County
Council to threaten the licence of Earl's Court, where
it was to have taken place, and the Home Secretary to
intimate that he would consider it illegal.   In the end
there was no direct clash with the authorities ;   the
Earl's Court freeholders, concerned for their licence, got
an injunction in the High Court, and on that the promoters of the fight abandoned it.   But the interest of
the whole incident is that the real inhibition of the fight
lay in a public opinion still capable of revulsion from
American exploitations of " bruising," and still more
from the invasion of such spectacles by women, who—
curious as it may sound in those days of excessively
feminine skirts and uncropped hair—were being accused,
with their sports and their cigarette-smoking and slang
and " ragging," of aping men to a deplorable extent.

The publication of the first analysis of the Census statistics, revealing the fact that there were over a million more of them than of men was, of course, seized upon by the opponents of Women's Suffrage, who were holding their ground. Once more a Bill had been passed in May and delayed and quibbled over, till once more in the dark days of November, with the end of the session bringing the Bill's extinction, the exasperation of the militants broke out. On the 22nd a force of them, with hammers and other implements concealed, burst upon the West End streets, smashing club and shop windows indiscriminately; 223 were arrested. Hitherto all their violence had been confined to the regions of Government and Parliament; this meant that they were going to make war, so far as they could, on society, till society moved its legislators to action. A hint of the extent to which various modes of the warfare had been planned was given a month later, when a woman was charged with attempting to set fire to the contents of a post-box, though that kind of destruction did not become serious till the following year. The destruction of property by the window-raid was alarming enough; it had followed the reception of a deputation by Mr Asquith, to which he had been more uncompromising than ever: "Get rid of me," he had said, "if you can. But I am head of the Government, and I am not convinced." The situation grew steadily uglier. Suffragist interrupters of meetings (they entirely prevented Mr Asquith from speaking at the City Temple by fastening themselves to pillars) were being thrown out with increasing violence, especially when, as at a speech by Mr Lloyd George in Bath, the interrupters were male sympathisers with the movement — women were finding it increasingly difficult to get into meetings, whether they were suffragists or not. Meetings of their own were being forcibly broken up. But it was at least better to be thought dangerous than regarded as a show, or damned as an exasperating irrelevance.

The King and Queen had sailed for India in November, and the Great Durbar was held at Delhi, the old capital of the emperors, on 12th December, in a vast new city of temporary but marvellously elaborate camps, which suddenly took on a new meaning when the Royal Proclamation revealed the well-kept secret that a new Delhi was to arise, and the seat of government to be transferred thither from Calcutta. Whatever nervousness there may have been about the occasion, in view of the growing acuteness of Indian national feeling, there was nothing publicly to mar its *éclat*, save that one Indian prince had to explain away an act of apparent discourtesy. National feeling was recognised by an announcement in the proclamation that the partition of Bengal, a source of recent irritation, was to be reversed ; and it was hoped, too, that the placing of government at Delhi, with its new House of an Indian Parliament, and the sense of a return to the traditional scenes of such unity as India had ever known, would give fresh and more conciliatory meaning to British rule than had attached to it in Calcutta, where it had simply dropped aforetime into the seat of John Company, with all its associations of exploitation and subjugation, and " carried on."

Fresh life was stirring in the Far East in more exciting ways. In October, rebellion had broken out in China. It happened that the public mind had been turned in that direction only a few weeks earlier by the obituary notices of Sir Robert Hart, who, in a remarkably long career as Inspector-General of the Chinese Customs (he virtually created their maritime customs system), had come nearer to the rulers and high officials of China than any European before him. But anyhow the newspapers could reckon on popular interest in the rebellion, for it was headed by Sun Yat Sen, and the incidents in which he had figured at the Chinese Legation in London in 1898 were too much like a sensational novel to fade easily from the memory. London had quite believed then that, as an undesirable agitator, he had been decoyed into the Legation for the purpose of being beheaded with Oriental imperturbability in a London back garden. His election as the first President of the Chinese Republic, and a colossal substitute for the now weakening pantomime, Reinhardt's production of *The Miracle* at Olympia, provided the big headlines for the end of the year.

CHAPTER III

UPON politics just now the curtain was never
rung down. After the delayed Budget of 1909
and the crisis with the Lords in 1910 the country
had grown accustomed to a rise, rather than the old-
fashioned decline, of political activity in the winter
months. So the great London stage which he had enjoyed and scarified through a long life was full when
the news came of the death of Henry Labouchere. He
reached very far back into the life of the Liberal party,
for as a young diplomat he had unpardonably "cheeked"
Lord John Russell at the Foreign Office, and he had
first entered Parliament as Bradlaugh's colleague in the
representation of Northampton. The whole odd make-
up of his character had been entertaining. A very
wealthy man, with the cynical detached air of one
without a serious interest of any kind, he was a convinced and passionate Radical. Known to the world
for his relentless pursuit in *Truth,* the weekly paper he
founded, of every kind of knave and sharper, he always
used to say that it was mainly his own association with
such people in a reckless and extravagant youth which
had given him the " nose " for them. His " black list "
was the dread of shady characters who kept just inside
the law, for he had not the slightest hesitation in carrying exposure of them beyond the edge of the libel laws.
He would pillory a rogue, even if the rogue were clever
enough to get damages out of him; and thus did work
for society that no one had done before him.

Politics could not in any case have declined much at the moment, for the Insurance Act was still very much a battle-ground. It was on the Statute Book, but it was not to come into force until 1st July 1912, and that left space for animosities to survive. One serious danger was over; the great friendly societies, as well as the trade unions, finally agreed in January to become " Approved Societies " under the Act—that is, to combine the new insurance cards with their own systems. But the stamp-licking opposition was still in violent action, and the medical profession had not been conciliated. Mr Lloyd George, whose efforts in a series of conferences had brought in the friendly societies, now assailed in a characteristic way the formidable difficulties which remained. He was still negotiating with the doctors; he set to work to mobilise popular support if necessary against them (he was talking of the possibilities of a State medical service), and certainly against the stamp-licking campaign. Absurd as its shrill cries were from one point of view, Mr Lloyd George was too clever to under-estimate their effect. He knew that, however safe his scheme might be in the great industries and in the publicity of factories and workshops, yet over a vast field of more traditional and intimate employment steady influences were active against him—mistresses with their maids, masters with their butlers and gardeners and chauffeurs, farmers with their men. Had they not always, it was asked, been sure of kindliness and help in sickness and unemployment? And could they now wish to chill the old association into the hard business-like relations of a stamped card, losing incidentally twopence a week from their wages? If the bland conviction with which the questions were put showed a sad lack of humour, the people to whom they were put were hardly in a position to reply; personal contacts were too close. Mr Lloyd George

was not blind to the possible creation in this way of a
dead-weight upon the working of his Act, by the alienation
from it of this mass of employed persons always rather
inert politically, strangers to far-reaching industrial
ideas, and even ready to resent being classed with
" industry." So under his ægis a " Liberal Insurance
Committee " was formed, whose business was to go up
and down the country combating these influences. This
was a new portent in politics, and was hotly attacked.
Was this official evangelising to be expected always
now in Mr Lloyd George's train, and were the funds for
it drawn from public sources ? The latter implication
was easily rebuffed.

Alongside this battle not yet closed were the preliminary flashes of the one not yet opened in form—
Home Rule. For that and for Welsh Disestablishment
the Government could afford to wait no longer, since it
was certain that both would have to be driven through
the three years' suspensive process which the Lords
could still impose. Through how much else Home Rule
might have to be driven was still a matter of opinion.
As it had become plainer and plainer, in the previous
year, that nothing could save the absolute veto of the
Lords, Irish Unionists had entered upon speech and
action too uncompromising to sound at that early stage
otherwise than exaggerated and unreal. Even Unionist
papers had denied the stories of arming for rebellion in
Ulster which other Unionist papers had been printing ;
and talk at the Ulster Unionist Council in September
about a " provisional Government " had sounded more
petulant than ominous. So now, in January 1912, when
Mr Churchill was being warned about a meeting that had
been arranged for him in Belfast, and was being told
that Ulstermen would prevent by force the delivery of
a Home Rule speech by the son of the man who had
told them once that they would fight and they would be

right, there was no great alarm; most people took it
as a police matter of a kind quite familiar in Belfast.
Naturally there was still more discounting of high talk
when the news came that Mr Churchill, giving up the
provocation of a Home Rule demonstration in Ulster
Hall itself, and speaking instead in a huge marquee,
had had a most successful meeting; yet the fact that
4000 troops had been under arms in the city at the
time did not entirely escape notice.

But the Insurance Act and Ulster were not really
the two preoccupations of the country. These were
much more the industrial situation and the militant
suffragist campaign. The latter, because it was becoming clear that every one of the various attitudes which
the nation was taking (and it was a tribute to militant
methods that no one now was without one attitude or
another) was so beautifully conclusive that all avenues
of understanding were closing. The Government's
position was unanswerable when it said that, in view of
the existence not merely of shades of opinion but of
definite opposition from some of the most important
members of the Cabinet, it was impossible to produce a
Government measure. The rank and file of the Liberals
were on quite sensible ground when they maintained
that the party had definite previous engagements to
much social legislation, and that to risk disintegrating
their majority by setting all this aside for a highly
controversial measure would ruin suicidally the best
chance that, with a bit more patience, the suffragists
might have. Equally defensible was the line of many
good Liberals that so great a change in the electorate
could not be patched on to an already patchwork
franchise, but must come as part of a fundamental
new enfranchisement. Almost as strongly held, if less
defensible, was the other Liberal line that, as the
only measure which could possibly pass in existing

circumstances would be very limited, they could not be
expected to make special efforts for a Bill which would
create mainly a propertied vote for the Unionists.
Outright opponents of the movement could fairly say
that a proposal which so cut across all party lines must
not be allowed to force a vital change upon the country
in a fog of heat and confusion. But the suffragists as a
body were unanswerable when they said that the very
fact of absorption in social reform made the claim of
women in the modern world to a vote more and not
less urgent ; and that the repeated passage now of their
Bills, no longer an empty gesture in a desultory House,
but the result of real debate, did give them a right to
demand that so great a cause should cut across party
lines to the end. There lay the insoluble difficulty ;
one side certain that you could not, the other that you
not only could but should, leave politics out of it. The
militants, reasonable in unreason, were at any rate
unanswerable when they said that, difficult or not, the
thing could be done, and that they would make the
Government's life impossible till it was done. And
finally the general public was unanswerable when it
replied that that merely put its back up, and just
showed why women had no votes. All these conflicting
attitudes were far too defensible, and the consciousness
of this was what was worrying everybody. The question
was being shut into a space handsomely provided with
any number of doors quite well constructed save for
the simple purpose of opening.

The other anxiety of the moment, the industrial situation, continued to do the very thing which so angered
the militants—put their claims on to a secondary plane.
The depicting of Labour and Capital at a tug-of-war
on the title-page of *Punch* for the year was not a piece
of casual generalisation. More and more that was
how the country came to see the situation—as one big

encounter heaving obscurely under the various particular
struggles. Strikes of which the obstinacy bore apparently
no relation to their origin in insignificant points of
punctilio; settlements which one side or the other
almost openly refused to work on the very morrow of
their acceptance; a strike in one occupation exploding
a kind of Chinese cracker of strikes in trades more or
less associated with it; a harder tone in employers
summoned by the Board of Trade to negotiations; a
growing familiarity with violence in the struggles—all
suggested even to the least attentive mind that something more was afoot than an epidemic of striking.
This was true; Labour was moving, and Capital knew it.
The easy party thing to say was that, with Liberals in
office, relying largely upon Labour support, and in any
case somewhat hand-tied by humanitarian sentiment,
Labour was out to make the most of its opportunities,
regardless of all considerations. But the matter was
more serious than that. The unrest was due to causes
which, whatever party had been in office, would have
had their way. The broad simple one moving in the
mass was, no doubt, plain discontent feeling the strength
it could now wield. Generations which had had an
increasingly efficient education had also had now for
twenty years a cheap Press to make them more actively
conscious, and also more aware of all that — in no
derogatory use of the phrase—money could buy. And
those same twenty years or so, creating with swift
developments of markets and transport wholly new
standards of wealth among the wealthy, had displayed
to a Labour world, widened in its ideas and singularly
well able to watch what was going on, a really tremendous profusion of spending. Meanwhile the strong
revival of Trade Unionism in the late eighties and
nineties of the last century had come to its growth, and
the unions were vigorous. Here was the raw material of

trouble ; and to recognise it as discontent did not, to any thoughtful people, put it out of court.

Then there were political causes. It was true (though here we are rather in a circle of cause and effect) that the change of Government in 1906 had emphasised the unrest. Partly that was the Conservatives' own fault. In the Tariff Reform campaign they had raised something which was bound to confront Capital and Labour ; there was no phase of the discussion of industrial prosperity which did not provoke the question of what voice Labour had in the disposal of it. It would hardly be too much to say that in its later, rougher stages the issue of Protection had been mainly a class issue. The sweeping victory of December 1905 had excited Labour ; since then Liberal finance, with its steeply graduated taxation and heavy death duties, and the Budget of 1909, with all its platform accompaniments, had hardened the heart of capital.

And finally there was another element at work upon all this raw material of the deep disagreement which was felt to be reducing strike settlements to mere temporary smoothings of the surface. The impulse of the mass might be little more than plain impatience with its conditions ; the leaders on both sides knew that this was the force to be used for more than adjustments of wages and hours. Trade Unionism had looked abroad, both to the Syndicalists of France and to the Industrial Workers of the World in the United States. The ideas of the two were different—the one that of great corporations of labour controlling distinct industries (an idea translated just now in England by some of the movement's intellectuals into the form of Guild Socialism), the other that of universal and not local action—but they both had one object, the complete change of the existing economic system, and one policy, that of "direct action." Of course the knowledge

of these tendencies was not confined to industrial
leaders; they were hinted at in all the newspaper
comments on the "un-English" aspects of recent
strikes, and broadly enough too in Mr Gosling's remark,
at the Trade Union Congress of 1911, that there would
be no more sectional strikes. But not everyone perceived that these were the real reasons why, in almost
every case just now, the strikers sooner or later raised
questions of union recognition and resented local or
sectional negotiations; and why the employers on their
side stiffened themselves against recognition and against
agreements of a national scope. And it was for these
reasons that the Government's efforts to find some
general machinery for the adjustment of disputes, the
appointment at the end of 1910 of Mr D. J. Shackleton
as permanent Labour Adviser to the Home Office,
and the appointment of thirteen representatives of
employers and thirteen Labour leaders to act as an
Industrial Council, had had but disappointing results;
the Council soon fell into inanition.

The question of union recognition was still keeping
the railway world at thinly disguised war. The Government had not been able to persuade the managers to
accord open recognition to the unions; they continued
to insist that the men's representatives on the Conciliation Boards must be sectionally elected. The men had
been just enabled to accept the settlement by a provision
that they might elect their own secretaries on the
boards, which opened the door to the admission in fact,
though not ostensibly, of union officials. It was only
one of those truces that both sides use for rehabilitating
their forces. The process on the men's side revealed
ominously what the fight about recognition was coming
to; the beginning of 1912 saw the combination of all
grades of railway workers (with the important exception,
however, of the Locomotive Engineers and Firemen)

into one big National Union of Railwaymen ; the strike
of 1911 bore at least that fruit.

The other question, that of national scope of agreements, was at the root of trouble which now rose with a
swiftness that drove everything else into the background
when Parliament met. The indurated struggle in South
Wales, over the case of men whose work at a peculiarly
difficult part of the coal-face made piece-work rates
most unfair to them, had turned from the insoluble
complexities of all attempts to arrive at abnormal piece-
rates to a demand for a minimum wage, as the only fair
basis, which spread with alarming rapidity to the other
great coal-fields. By the beginning of March more than
1,000,000 men were out for a national minimum wage,
and that was a figure no strike had ever yet attained.
The Government had already intervened, its formula for
meeting the contending views being, for the miners, the
recognition of the claim to a minimum wage, and for the
coal-owners, the negotiation of the exact figure not on
a national but on a local basis. The miners might have
accepted the formula, but as some of the coal-owners
refused, and as these included the South Wales owners
with whom the dispute had grown so bitter, the miners
swung back to a demand for a national element in the
shape of a stipulation that, whatever the locally agreed
figure, it must not anywhere be less than five shillings
per shift. Negotiations broke down ; the prospect of the
disorganisation which a long coal stoppage would produce (the railways, though they had now learned their
lesson and were never to be caught again with such
short stocks, were already reducing services) compelled
the Government to take other action. Mr Asquith
introduced on 19th March a Bill embodying his formula ;
the swiftness of its passage—it became law within a
fortnight—and the abstention of the Opposition from
voting showed such a force of public opinion for the

ending of the dispute that neither owners nor miners
could afford to wreck it. The latter, indeed, balloted
for continuing the strike, but the smallness of the
majority allowed the Miners' Federation to order a
return to work. They had, after all, achieved the
principle of a minimum wage, and the Act, passed at
first for a period of three years, remains by annual
renewal in operation. The importance of such a step
forward in industrial legislation almost escaped the
notice of the country at large in the pressure of its
anxiety. Its mind was so set upon the formula as terms
of peace that it hardly noticed the vital change in the
conception of the relations of the State to industry ;
the enactment of a minimum wage, not for a poor and
unorganised class of workers, but for a very large and
powerful body of labour, surrendered all the old ideas
of competition. What did not, however, pass unnoticed
was the ominous portent of " direct action." The
miners' strike gave it a new meaning. Any kind of
strike might cause loss of wealth : what had now
come home to the least observant was that in a highly
organised modern community there were some strikes
which could cause paralysis.

There had not been much freedom of mind to attend
to the news on 7th March that Amundsen had reached
the South Pole ; he had just returned to Hobart. It
was twelve months since the ship of Captain Scott's
expedition, back there from landing him and his party,
had awakened the world to the fact that Amundsen was
then making his dash, and added all the excitement of a
contest to the dangerous enterprise. Now there could be
little doubt that Amundsen must have the glory of being
the first to reach the Pole. However, until news actually
came from Captain Scott, the laurels need not quite pass
from the country which had been the pioneer of polar
exploration. But the coal strike was over, and attention

only too free to take the shock when, on 15th April, came the appalling news of the loss of the White Star liner *Titanic*. At her launch in the previous June there had been much in the eulogies of her, as by far the biggest liner in the world, which now reminded men of that old Greek shrinking from the over-confidence which provokes high heaven. For she had been described as so huge that the sea, so far from endangering her, could scarcely even disturb the comfort of life aboard her ; passengers need not know, if they did not want to, that they were at sea at all. And now the sea, calling up its terrors, had drifted an iceberg across her track in the night, and engulfed her in a few minutes. Nor did the news come as a single shock. The earliest curt telegrams had indicated that no lives had been lost ; this could be better believed in the light of all that had been written about her than the frightful fact, which followed immediately, that 1635 persons had been drowned. Long official inquiries into the disaster came to little in the end. It certainly appeared that regulations about boat accommodation had not kept pace with the rapid growth in the size of these great liners ; they had not actually been revised, though of course in practice much extended, since 1894, when only ships of some 10,000 tons had been contemplated, whereas the *Titanic* was a ship of 46,800 tons. It was made clear, too, that whatever dangers these huge vessels might diminish or eliminate, they actually created a new one in the difficulty of launching boats from such heights ; it might even be impossible in some conditions to launch boats at all on one side. What suspicions emerged at the inquiries of human failure in the crisis of the disaster may be left now unexplored ; there was more than enough of human fineness. Many distinguished people, both British and American, attracted by the experience of making the first voyage in the vaunted liner, perished

with her. Of all of them the individual most vivid
to the public mind was probably Mr W. T. Stead. His
earliest fame, when articles of his in *The Pall Mall
Gazette* trying to rouse the social conscience on the
subject of prostitution had been pushed to a point that
landed him in gaol, was by this time rather forgotten.
Later activities of his busy mind—the success of his
ingenious periodical, *The Review of Reviews,* his eager
absorption in spiritualism and the problems of the life
after death, and his published " conversations " with a
disembodied spirit whom he named " Julia "—had built
up for him another kind of fame.

One curious incident of the wreck may be mentioned.
The Hope diamond was on board the *Titanic* on its
way to a new owner in the United States. This was
one of the notorious jewels of the world to which superstition had always been attached, and there were many
who believed that it had now accomplished its final
stroke of maleficence.

Long before anything was published of the results
of the official inquiries, the shock had passed. But an
almost angry tone in the investigations on both sides
of the Atlantic (on some points Great Britain and the
United States were not far off recriminations) was one
sign of how severe it had been. That is not difficult to
understand ; there was more in the shock than the
heavy loss of life. Such a disaster had the aspect of a
terrible reminder to a human race growing more and
more confident of its command over nature and the
material world. Scientific knowledge covered now more
ground with any single step it took than a whole
century's movement of human progress a short time
ago. Chemical discovery and mechanical invention
were wholly remaking the range of men's lives, and not
by slow separate stages ; each fresh leap opened up one
longer and more startling. An invention, for instance,

had but just begun to revolutionise ideas of transport
on land when it launched mankind at last into the air.
Old fears became ridiculous; possibilities of exhaustion
of coal supplies only turned invention towards less
reckless and extravagant production of heat and power.
Panic about a world populated beyond the means of
supporting life gave way to a comfortable assurance
that long before that time science would have provided
undreamt-of methods of sustenance. "Synthetic" was
the blessed word of the age. In this very year it was
soothing, perhaps a little prematurely, the alarms of
the new industrial giant, the motor-car industry, about
the world's supply of rubber; it was announced at the
meeting of the Chemical Industries Association that
synthetic rubber could be produced on a commercial
scale. Medicine and surgery were as tirelessly inventive
in their own spheres. People were really in the mood
to think that some day (and it might be even in their
own day, so swift and sudden now were the final steps
of any advance) human life would give itself almost indefinite prolongation. It was its impact upon this kind
of mood that made the *Titanic* disaster so overwhelming.
Titanic — the very name became sinister, with its
suggestion of the fate of the colossally defiant.

Rubber and oil were the wild excitements of the
Stock Markets in these years. Rubber more especially,
because, terrific as was the pace at which modern
manufacturing methods consumed any raw material, it
became even more serious when an industry expanding
so insatiably, and almost explosively, as the motor-car
industry had done, depended upon a raw material which
up to then had had so narrow a range of use that its
supply had never needed to be developed beyond the
unaided provision of nature. Now that such development became urgent it met with the awkward fact that
the rubber-producing tree matures very slowly. The

market in rubber plantation shares was one of wildly
fluctuating hopes and fears. Oil, upon which the industry equally depended, was a matter of less anxiety ;
there was little mistrust of the supply, and knowledge
enough for the finding of new fields. That share market
lay much more in the hands of big capital. The
Weetman Pearson firm was this year upon great enterprises in Mexico and Central America, of which the
public knew mainly because the chief Liberal Whip, the
Master of Elibank, relinquished his political career to
join them.

Wireless, which had already performed its new
miracles of life-saving at sea, and was to perform them
again in the *Volturno* disaster of 1913, had failed to help
the *Titanic* ; the time had been too short. The word as
yet carried none of its later significance ; it meant only
wireless telegraphy, and so far its only use as entertainment was for a few scientific people with a knowledge
of Morse and other telegraphic systems, who amused
themselves by picking up on private installations
messages telegraphed from the wireless stations. Two
forms of more sheer amusement which science was
providing for mankind were making a curious way
upwards through the strata of the great British public.
The cinematograph, as a means of passing the afternoon
or evening, was regarded as a cheap form of amusement,
in every sense ; educated people would watch for a
few minutes, during some other entertainment, pictures
of actual current events, and would discuss the educational possibilities of the invention ; but there were no
great cinematograph theatres as yet, and no elaborate
programmes of tragedy and comedy. The action film
was in the crude melodrama and knock-about period,
and the photography, though less jerkily dazzling by
now, dim and coarsely lighted. The business had not
yet reached, so to speak, the legitimate theatre ; it

was still barn-storming, housed in roller-skating rinks (that craze had passed) and obscure little halls, under the name of Electric Theatres, and regarded as an amusement for the poor. The gramophone had got a little further. One reason for this lies in the advertisement picture which just now became so familar, the fox-terrier with his ear cocked to a gramophone trumpet listening to his master's voice. More recent generations would find it hard to believe that the tonal quality of a 1912 gramophone record was good enough to deceive even a fox-terrier. Yet in its day the picture was certainly justified ; in comparison with the harsh metallic noises of the early gramophone these new H.M.V. records had a sweet and almost natural tone, which was bringing the gramophone for the first time into houses where it had hitherto been regarded as a tasteless amusement of the somewhat lower classes. But it was still considered rather eccentric to possess one otherwise than, so to speak, apologetically. More recent generations, again, would find it hard to believe that the motor-car industry in 1912 need have caused much anxiety about the supply of its raw materials. In fact, in this country the anxiety arose less from our own demand than from the effect upon it of the far more rapidly expanding American demand. We had as yet practically no cheap cars, save for one or two productions which were really motor-cycles on three or four wheels instead of two, but with little less noise and vibration. Familiar as motor-cars had become, they were still the vehicles of the rich or of professional people, like doctors, who could not now do without them. Anyone who wanted a cheap car had to run the gauntlet of the jests which pursued a Ford. The rest used the new vehicle only in the shape of motor-cabs and motor - buses. These latter, too, were mainly confined to London, and even there it had not dawned upon the companies that the new mechanical propulsion could be used to extend enormously the range of the old horse‑buses. The outer residential regions, to which, as the new Census figures showed, people were moving more and more, depended on the railways and tubes, which had just introduced an innovation for dealing with their traffic in the shape of the " escalator," the first moving staircase, at Earl's Court : a small one had been one of the amusements at the White City shortly before.

It can be seen that this was a world far too much interested in many things at once to have much patience with the desperate concentration of the suffragists upon one idea. The first effects of the militants' campaign against the community at large, instead of against politicians only, were beginning to show themselves. There had been two more days of window-smashing at the beginning of March, following a vigorous Anti-Suffrage meeting at the Albert Hall, at which several Cabinet Ministers were present, and the Prime Minister expressed his conviction that the grant of the vote to women would be " a grave political mistake." Open threats of the kind of deliberate damage which might now be expected led to the closing of the Old Masters Exhibition at Burlington House, and the closing also of the British Museum for several weeks ; such depriva-tions, and the suspicions under which any woman now fell who carried a muff or a handbag, if not very serious, were irritants. An article by an eminent specialist, Sir Almroth Wright, treating the militant extremists as " sexually embittered " or " epicene," drove them to fury. Foolishly flattered in their self-importance as they were by a police raid on the offices of the Women's Social and Political Union, they could scarcely profess to have advanced the cause when, on 28th March, their Bill, for the first time since the question had had political reality, was defeated, and not in a small House, by 222 votes to 208. The best they could say was that they were clearing the issue, by forcing the half-hearted cumberers of their cause to come into the open as opponents ; but this was unconvincing. The division was serious as a mark of a general drawing-back of public opinion. In *Punch* the older suffragist—who had figured there in the seventies and eighties of last century as an unattractive stalwart female—was now depicted reproaching with gracious good looks the militant on whom her ancient forbidding dowdiness had descended. That kind of presentation was, of course, absurd ; the militant ranks were young in the main, well dressed, and by no means fierce to look at ; plenty of them were ready to " dine and dance " at night. It was beginning to be one of the peculiar trials of a Member of Parliament that he never knew when or where he might meet a militant in the most deceitful clothing.

Indeed it was the common complaint of an older generation which had not yet given in to new pressures that one never knew who or what one might be called upon to meet anywhere. Socially there were such shocks as trafficking in badges of admission to the Royal Enclosure at Ascot ; Lord Churchill this year had to apply for an injunction in Chancery against a lady for that offence. Most of the diversions of life also provided shocks. The theatre this year, as it happened, was no offender. It was mainly distinguished by Mr Granville Barker's Shakespeare productions, a brilliant compromise between the flamboyant old style of production and the drabness of the Elizabethan Stage Society ; the entirely golden fairies of his *Midsummer's Night's Dream* were a vivid invention. All that the older generation had to deplore in this sphere was the passing of some of its own favourites—Florence St John, a sparkling memory to men about town, and George Grossmith, following thus soon W. S. Gilbert, of whose comic operas he had been almost as essential a part in his day as the author and composer themselves. There was, however, a conflict of ideas in this sphere, though not necessarily between older and younger generations; it was the question of the censorship of plays. This had been for some time in agitation, and was one more of the many things which the advent of a Liberal Government had been expected to amend. Persistent raising of the point in the House by Mr Robert Harcourt, himself a writer of plays, had indeed led to the appointment of an experienced playwright to assist the official of the Household who decided these matters. But as the new assistant was principally known for his skill in the adaptation of risky French farces, the appointment had a certain air of cynicism. For the whole conflict had revolved upon the absurdity of banning from the stage any intellectual presentation of certain aspects of human conduct which romped there freely in farce and musical comedy.

Literature had more successfully liberated itself from old ideas of what should and should not be put into words. Violence of language, as in Mr Masefield's *The Widow in the Bye Street*, one of the long narrative poems which were the form of his work just now, or the subversive tendencies of Mr H. G. Wells's *Marriage*, also published this year, could now disturb only a rapidly decreasing number of people. But vague alarms about the general impact of modern literature upon the structure of society were strong enough to stand in the way of the Report of the Royal Commission on Divorce, which was published late in the year, recommending the admission of fresh grounds for divorce, such as incurable insanity or drunkenness, or desertion for three years.

All that could be called an outcry in literary matters

of the year—and it was but mild—concerned manners
rather than morals on the publication in the supplementary volume of the *Dictionary of National Biography*
of Sir Sidney Lee's *Life of King Edward*. This contained
passages about the relations between him and Queen
Victoria which elderly repositories of the gossip of the
Court seemed to think had better have been left to die
with them. In general, however, the *Life* was welcomed
as a justly admiring presentation of a King whose
qualities had had later recognition than they deserved.
Meanwhile, King George and Queen Mary, back from
India early in February, were very graciously, if a trifle
domestically, as some might feel, at the disposal of their
subjects. One of their first public acts was the laying
of the foundation stone of the new London County Hall
on the south bank of the river opposite Westminster. It
was no mere formal gesture, for the King and Queen
had a real interest in the work of great town authorities,
and especially, like King Edward before them,[1] in the
efforts to improve housing — a matter in which the
London County Council were just now very busy. Mr
John Burns, turning his back on spectacular politics
in a way which surprised those who could think only
of his old Trafalgar Square days, and absorbing himself
in the good dull work of local government, was putting
his driving energy into the working of his Housing and
Town Planning Act; in 1910 there had been an international conference on the subject in London, and the
great name of Lord Kitchener had come in to help
because of his interest at the moment in the making of
the new Khartoum. The London authority was making
a start upon the rebuilding of an area in Southwark
possessed of a notoriety going back to the days of

---

[1] He had served in 1884, when Prince of Wales, as a member of the
Royal Commission on the Housing of the Working Classes ; and he
began that personal interest in the Duchy of Cornwall estates in London
which his successors as Princes of Wales have steadily maintained.

Dickens, the Tabard Street area ; and the King and
Queen had taken an immense. interest in the minutest
details of the modern working man's flat. Two of the
great pioneers of the crusade against the miseries and
moral degradations of slum dwellings died this year—
Miss Octavia Hill and General Booth. Miss Hill's whole
life had been given to housing problems, and her fame
cannot be better seen than in the fact that Berlin, the
city in all Europe which attended most to such subjects,
had established an "Octavia-Hill Verein." General
Booth, by his book *In Darkest London* (the title itself
was a challenge to people who had been eagerly reading
Stanley's *In Darkest Africa*, and forgetting the horrors
under their eyes), had, as his biographer puts it,
"unroofed the slum to Victorian respectability." One
impulse which most people had at his death was to be
glad that he had lived so long. Fifteen or twenty years
earlier he would have died without seeing his Salvation
Army emerge from the obloquy which its frank loudness
and emotionalism brought upon it, into the recognition
that it was doing work which no other methods could
achieve. He had that reward for thirty-four years of a
"Generalship" narrow and harsh, no doubt, in mentality, but broad, intense and genuine in feeling. It
was not altogether a small matter that a touch of Jewish
blood had made him exactly what people would expect
a devouring Old Testament prophet to look like.

After a visit to Henley Regatta—which gave an unexpected day of life to the old Royal barge and displayed
the professionals of the water-side in the unfamiliar
glories of the Royal bargemen's costume—and a vast
garden-party at Windsor—the guests for which filled no
less than eleven special trains—the King and Queen
carried their interest in housing to other parts of the
country. In South Wales they took tea with a miner's
wife. And during a visit to Yorkshire they saw much of

mining and manufacturing home-life : it befell them to
see it at its greyest, for while they were there an explosion at the Cadeby colliery killed thirty men, followed
by a second, which killed fifty of a rescue-party. It
looked as if the new Sovereigns meant to mark their
reign by a new knowledge of the lives of their people ;
and the entry of the Prince of Wales at Magdalen College,
Oxford, in the autumn, not in the isolation which had
hedged about his grandfather at Christ Church, but as
an ordinary undergraduate, was thoroughly " in the
picture "— a picture markedly different from that of
the German Emperor's odd semi-paternal visit this year
to the great Krupp munition works.

There was policy in all this too, for who could tell
what kindliness of purpose might not be called upon
to play its part very soon ? The political year was
thoroughly turbulent. The Home Rule Bill and the
Welsh Disestablishment Bill were both in being. The
former, introduced on 11th April, gave Ireland a Senate
and a House of Commons, reserving certain subjects of
legislation and taxation to the Imperial Parliament, but
making provision for a possible larger transference of
powers later on. However, later events have removed
all importance from the details of this Bill. The Welsh
Bill, introduced on 23rd April, based the disendowment
provisions largely on a distinction between ancient
revenues and the Church's acquisitions in more controversial centuries ; it provided revenue of £180,000
a year for the Disestablished Church, allotting the remainder of the endowments to educational and other
purposes. Both of the Bills went into acrimonious and
often noisy debate ; the Welsh Bill rather unexpectedly
produced more personal recriminations than the other,
Mr Lloyd George reminding the Cecils that their own
origins as a powerful family made them poor opponents
of a diversion of Church property, and much play being

made with the spectacle of Mr F. E. Smith, who moved
the rejection of the Bill, as the champion of " the soul
of the Christian peoples of the world."

There were again some changes in the Ministry.
Lord Loreburn resigned on grounds of health, and Lord
Haldane became Lord Chancellor, Colonel Seely succeeding him at the War Office, where the Haldane reorganisa-
tions—the Expeditionary Force, the Territorial Army
and the Officers Training Corps—were by now well established. Lord Loreburn had, for the past year or two,
been the object of some of the disaffection in the party.
Among the many results of the long exclusion of the
Liberals from power had been the overwhelmingly Tory
colour of the benches of magistrates ; and, as in so
many other directions since 1906, there had been a far
too facile impatience for remedy. Lord Loreburn had
consistently held out against pressure : he set up, after
a Report from a Select Committee, advisory committees
to act with the Lords Lieutenant of counties in bringing
forward names for appointment to the benches ; he
refused to override their work by direct appointment of
known Liberals, since this would have fastened upon the
benches of magistrates that very habit of party feeling
which Liberals were holding up to reprobation.

Before the Second Reading debates on the two big
Bills were finished the thin crust of peace over the
seethings of industry was broken again with a transport
workers' strike. Like their allied industry, the railwaymen, they were out for the full recognition of the union's
power. Hours and rates of pay, and the hampering by
some employers of the settlement of the previous year,
were the specific grievances ; but the real struggle was
over the demand that the possession of the Transport
Workers' Federation " ticket " should be invariably a
condition of employment. Though the men professed
themselves willing to waive this point when arbitration

was offered by the Government on the other points, the
employers were so sure that the " ticket " battle was
the real one that they were very slow to meet the
arbitration offer themselves. The result was the development of the most openly angry conviction which had
yet shown itself that the masters were determined to
" smash " the men. That feeling was lurking now in all
strikes, but in the London strike (the hope that it would
spread to other ports had not been fulfilled) it stood out
sharply, because it was concentrated on one man :
Lord Devonport's powerful personality virtually *was*
the Port of London Authority. He was taking an
exceedingly stiff line against all efforts at conciliation ;
and he drew the lightning to such an extent that Ben
Tillett got a big meeting of strikers on Tower Hill to
repeat after him : " Oh, God, strike Lord Devonport
dead." After scenes of the violence now usual, in fights
with blacklegs and with the police, the strike ended
inconclusively early in August, just when the Bill dealing with the Osborne judgment was in its final stages.
The political use of union funds was allowed ; but the
liberty of the individual was guarded by provisions that
a ballot of members must first approve such use, that the
political fund must be kept separate, and that any
member could claim exemption from contribution to the
fund without losing the other benefits of the union. The
Opposition gave the Bill little trouble, but on the other
hand Labour gave it little support. One reason was
that the hardening of employers against the unions had
made Labour leaders far less willing than they had been
immediately after the judgment to yield any inch of
their position. Also at the time they expected far more
trouble from these provisions than actually resulted ;
in fact it was to be held some twelve years later that
for various reasons of complexity of procedure and the
invidiousness of this " contracting out " the individual

had received no adequate protection. But the apprehensions of difficulty were enough to stimulate a little further the uneasiness of relations between Liberalism and Labour.

The truth was that, although Unionists were fond of representing the Government as helplessly driven along by their two supporting groups, the Irish and the Labour members, the latter knew very well that they had little real effectiveness. For if the Ministry was in some sense dependent on them, they were much more dependent on it, since to defeat it, or allow it to be defeated, would be to destroy what chance they had of influencing the course of events. Consciousness of this was partly the strength of the growing movement for " direct action " among the extremists, which had got Tom Mann sentenced to imprisonment at the Manchester Assizes in March for an article in *The Syndicalist* inciting the armed forces to mutiny. That kind of thing in its turn was alienating Liberals : there was a debate in the Commons about *The Syndicalist* and its provocations; and the by-election at Hanley in July, when a seat vacated by the death of so prominent a Labour leader as Mr Enoch Edwards went to a Liberal, with the Labour candidate badly at the bottom of a three-cornered poll, was an uncomfortable indication of what was happening. The new life in the Labour movement was wearing very thin the association with Liberalism; and it had now a newspaper, *The Daily Herald*, first published as a daily on 16th April of this year, of which the entire policy was to make Labour a self-sufficient independent force.

Mr Tillett's leading of the London strike meeting in a " prayer " probably had been suggested to him by Sir Edward Carson's action at a great Unionist demonstration in Belfast when, after a march past of eighty thousand men, he bade the meeting repeat after him :

" We will never in any circumstances submit to Home
Rule." His example was being used, too, by the militant
suffragists as defence for their actions; if Front Bench
politicians were publicly making arrangements to defy
the law without being prosecuted, why should women
go to prison for defying it ? Mr and Mrs Pethick
Lawrence and Mrs Pankhurst had taken this line in
their trial at the Old Bailey in May, when they were
sentenced to nine months in the second division for
conspiracy. That trial had arisen out of more window-
breaking raids and firing of the contents of pillar-boxes.
There were threats of other forms of property destruction : two women found in the grounds of Nuneham,
the country seat of Mr Lewis Harcourt, one of the
Cabinet opponents of Women's Suffrage, were suspected
of intentions of arson; and on the night before Mr
Asquith was to speak in a theatre in Dublin there had
been an attempt to burn down the place. While the
Home Secretary was being attacked for failure to keep
order, the militants were sharpening a weapon that was
to add enormously to the complications of his position.
A big hunger-strike had been started by the women
undergoing sentence at Aylesbury, and the forcible
feeding to which the prison authorities resorted was
making unpleasant reading, and almost driving into
sympathy a great many women who had no liking at
all for these doings. Yet the stiffening, on the whole,
of opinion against the suffrage movement because of the
excesses had another proof towards the end of the year.
Mr George Lansbury, a Labour member, resigned his
seat for Bow and Bromley deliberately in order to
provide a test case for Women's Suffrage ; he was
handsomely defeated in his own citadel, his Unionist
and anti-suffrage opponent winning the seat by 4042
votes to 3291.

All the while tempers heated over the Insurance Act

kept open another wide area of threats to break the
law. Domestic servants were organised to demonstrate,
like their mistresses, at the Albert Hall ; the doctors
were still pledged to complete refusal of their services.
Mr Lloyd George, freer this year from the House of
Commons than he had been for some time past (he was,
of course, prominent in the Welsh Church debates,
but was not in charge of the Bill), held confidently on
his way. He kept on asserting that the Act would come
into operation with far less trouble than its opponents
chose to think, that the actual disobedience would be
out of all proportion to the oceans of turgid talk, and
that the magistrates were not really going to be very
busy with delinquent mistresses. In that he proved to
be right ; the Act came fairly quietly into force in July,
without many prosecutions. But his satisfaction was
not as complete as it sounded ; he knew that he was not
over the worst of his fences, and that when he came
to it, it might be, after all, to find the one he was
apparently over rebuilt in a new place. The process
of insurance began on 1st July ; the title to medical
benefits would begin only at the New Year of 1913, the
intervening six months establishing the fund. This
meant that the crisis with the doctors had yet to come ;
and the comparative collapse of all the opposition of
domestic employers to the Act was largely traceable to
their belief that, when that crisis came, the Act would
break down far more hopelessly than by any disobedience
of theirs. Not only would it be reduced to a dead
letter ; but all the discontent about deduction from
wages would rise to a formidable height, if it appeared
that the contributors had endured it for six months, to
find none of the promises fulfilled. Even Mr Lloyd
George could hardly keep the mass of workers behind
the Act in face of such a failure to " deliver the goods."

So the militancy in that affair had not really faded ;

it had only shifted its ground, and was waiting. Militancy in the Irish question grew more open. "Ulster Day," 28th September, saw the immense signing of the Ulster Covenant, to obey no laws and to pay no taxes imposed by a Parliament at Dublin ; it was followed by inspections and reviews of forces. They were armed as yet in the open only with dummy rifles ; but it was known that these were not the only weapons in the country, and the satirical comments on "General Carson" and "Galloper Smith" (the two were constantly together) masked but imperfectly a very real anxiety.

The anxiety was not only on the Liberal side. There were many Conservatives who disliked the open threat of rebellion, and would rather, in any case, not have seen Mr F. E. Smith in it. The last thing the party wanted was any new possibility of division of opinion. It had strengthened its organisation in the summer by amalgamating the two wings of party machinery, Conservative and Unionist, which had all this time been kept separate ; this piece of work first made Mr Steel-Maitland's reputation. But better machinery was not going to help a party disagreed as to one of its most important uses ; the long dispute was still in progress between the "whole hog" protectionists and those who were convinced that taxes on food must be dropped before they could ever hope for a majority again. Sparks of the dispute flew round the fiasco of an attempt in the autumn to raise funds for Tariff Reform propaganda as a celebration of Mr Chamberlain's birthday ; this dissolved in a ridicule it did not deserve when it was announced, without a gleam of humour, that donors of £1000 would have the privilege of an invitation to dinner with the Duke of Westminster at Grosvenor House.

It was in any case poor tactics to suggest that that

side had its eye on Park Lane when the other side was
so successfully keeping its eye on the workshop and
kitchen, and even on the seats upon the Embankment.
Mr John Burns announced at the end of the year his
scheme for dealing with the homeless people there.
He knew London well, and used often to be seen on the
Embankment late at night. His scheme was thoroughly
practical. There was a great deal of shelter available
for the homeless, but no easily working channel between
the two. By instituting a system of distribution of
tickets for shelter Mr Burns was able to state, perhaps
a little optimistically, that the Embankment had been
cleared.

The Opposition was in no way out of fighting form
when, on the resumption of the session, they returned
to the Irish and Welsh Bills. They managed to make
a stir by catching the Government majority napping
one afternoon; Sir Frederick Banbury moved an un-
announced amendment to the financial resolution on the
Home Rule Bill, and by suddenly refraining from further
speeches on it at an early stage in the afternoon, before
the Government benches had awakened to the need for
carrying on the debate, they got a snap division which
defeated the Government by 228 to 206. Mr Asquith,
imperturbable, was not of course going to resign ; but
the necessary sequel, a rescission of the amendment,
was so unusual a step, and in the case of that important
part of a Bill so complicated, that when it took place,
two days later, the Opposition once more by disturbance
forced the Speaker to adjourn the House. One of their
leading newspapers was urging them to a prolonged
campaign of disorder, and there was much noisy and
abusive debating of the guillotine time-table for the two
Bills ; but behind it all was the consciousness that in
the country at large " the burning question of Home
Rule," as another of their papers observed, " would not

burn." The very thing which, constitutionally speaking, ought to have made it burn—the fact that it was practically bound to become law under the Parliament Act—was the very thing that made the whole business too mechanical to interest the ordinary man. He went on singing *Yip-I-Addy-I-Ay* (though this performance of the young George Grossmith was a poorish echo of *Ta-ra-ra-boom-de-ay*) with a general sense that life was anyhow rather exciting.

CHAPTER IV

1913—JULY 1914 : THE SLIPPERY SLOPE

EARLY in the next year, on 10th February, came news which, like the loss of the *Titanic*, had power to hush all else—the news, so long awaited, of Captain Scott's South Pole expedition. The ship which should have re-embarked his party on its return from the dash for the Pole had brought back only the vision which now burned itself into the mind of the whole world—the little tent in the appalling loneliness of snow where eyes and lips frozen in death waited to send their message to England. Caught by frightful weather on the return journey the party had, by a bitterly small margin of space, just failed to struggle on to the provision base which would have saved them, the last before they would have reached the coast again. In full consciousness of this they had faced death in " one noble temper of heroic minds." Two of the party had died earlier, and the account of their deaths, told in the diary found in the tent, added to the greatness of it all. One man, Bowers, a seaman, had literally worn himself out rather than surrender ; the other, Captain Oates, reaching a point where he could have gone on only by taxing the strength of the others, had gone deliberately out of the shelter tent one night, to die in the pitiless storm. Not even their triumph in reaching the Pole had been unalloyed. They found there evidence that Amundsen had been before them, and that they had not won for their country the untouched glory they had hoped for. Captain Scott's diaries were ample enough to

give an almost terribly intimate knowledge of the grim
struggle south and north again, of the gallantry and
gaiety that were now heart-rending. The cinematograph
added a poignancy of its own ; no written words could
have had upon the mind the effect of the actual picture
of the polar party as they left the rest for the final
dash—the dogged trudging figures with their sledges
moving so confidently away across the blank interminable snows into the dimness which slowly blotted them
from view. To see them live again with their fate
upon them was almost more than could be borne. The
story was not, and it never can be, a story of failure ;
it remains one of the perfectly flawless flamings of the
human spirit.

That had need to burn bright and high somewhere.
In most directions it showed but a smoky and turbid
flame. No mere description of events can give a true
account of English history during the next eighteen
months. The events were serious enough, the problems
they presented were inextricably baffling. But far more
serious was the country's state of mind. In one way
after another all the old loyalties, the old values, even
such standards of behaviour as still survived, gave way.
The more difficulties there were to meet the more it
appeared that habits of conduct to which appeal could
once have been made were no longer there to appeal to.
At the moment when the wage-earner was most restless
and discontented, the wealthy were most careless and
ostentatious. At the moment when government by an
elected majority was being most challenged, politicians
were floundering perilously near a morass of disingenu-
ousness and disrepute. And all the while so many
problems of government and administration were being
hustled along in a despairingly empirical fashion that
public affairs became rather like a herd of nervous
animals jostling one another down a lane of which the

walls were remorselessly closing in. People began to
think fatalistically that only an open smash somewhere
could clear the road. This was not only because three
specific questions—the Irish problem, Women's Suffrage,
and aggressive Trade Unionism — were heading for
deadlock ; they were but the detonators.

The deep sense of conflict had its roots in the two
elections of 1910, not in the sweeping electoral change
of December 1905, in spite of its more obviously disturbing appearance. For, as has been said, that could be
regarded as in some degree a freak, and not beyond
explanation. The voter had been stampeded. But the
elections of 1910 bore a much more sinister complexion
for the Conservative interests. Twice, in none of the
wild heat of 1905, they had been defeated, and no one
could feel sure that this did not indicate that the mass
electorate, which had not hitherto greatly upset party
calculations, was definitely taking shape as, by whatever
fluctuating margin, a majority against Conservatism.
Earlier generations had perhaps flattered themselves
too soon that the famous " leap in the dark " had
landed them after all in no very strange regions. It
now began to appear that those generations had never
landed at all ; the leap had begun, but not ended. They
had been in the air all the time, and only now were
parties really landing upon a fully wakened and conscious
wage-earning vote. Was this to mean the end of the
old alternating hold of two parties ?

So it came about that at the very moment when the
structure of representative government was being undermined both by Labour movements, which found it too
deeply bonded in to the economic structure they were
attacking, and by the Women's Suffrage movement,
which was discovering how elusive an opponent, just by
reason of its very openness, a representative system can
be, one of the great political parties was questioning

Parliamentary authority. There grew up among those
to whom the forms of government and order should
have been of most concern a feeling that the country
needed a lesson, and was asking for it. The more
intolerant and obstinate part of the world of vested
interests meant to give it a lesson in the resources of
the capitalist system. The Opposition in Parliament
meant to give it a lesson on the futility of supposing
that there was no limit to the power of the polling
booth. In each case militant Labour and militant
suffragists had exactly parallel lessons in view. In
every case the lesson was to be that force, in the last
resort, remained.

Not the least of the perils was that Parliamentary
government itself should slip into this atmosphere of
force, and so fail of its service to civilisation. For in
this way even those who were averse to physical force
were falling unwisely into the temper of it. The danger
lay not only in the recurrence of violent scenes in the
House, but in the justification alleged for them—the
plea that the Government's recent work and its use of
its majority were reducing legislative methods to a farce,
so that, with a muzzled House of Lords and limitation
of debate in the Commons, no activity was left to an
Opposition other than outbursts of disorder, alternating
with marked and studied indifference to Bills under a
" bullying " time-table. To display the elected majority
as governing by force was now the line of the Opposition,
together with seizing upon anything that could be
attacked as a sign of the muddle and haste produced
by such overbearing law-making. The affectation of
indifference was to the fore mainly in the debates on the
Irish and Welsh Bills, still in full swing in the beginning
of the year ; for the session could not be prorogued by
a Government intending to work the Parliament Act
until these Bills had, for the first of the three necessary

times, passed the House of Commons, and the heavy
programme of the past year had driven the passing of
them late. The Home Rule Bill got its third reading
by 367 to 257 on 16th January. What efforts there
were to amend the Welsh Disestablishment Bill, still in
Committee, came mainly from Liberals. There were
good churchmen on those benches—Mr Gladstone's own
grandson among them by now—who without contesting
the principle of disestablishment found much to criticise
in detail. The Bill was, as the Home Rule Bill had been,
slightly amended; but, in the main, party divisions had
their way, and on the evening of 5th February a most
unusual sound of melody in the lobbies announced that
it too had achieved its third reading: Welsh members
were singing "Land of my Fathers." Both Bills underwent immediate rejection by the Lords.

Meanwhile the Insurance Act had been steered past
its last dangers of open wreck. The Opposition made
play with some charges of muddle and haste. There had
been cases of delay in treatment, mistaken diagnosis,
errors of prescription or dispensing, some of which
had proved fatal. Such things were inevitable at the
start of so large a scheme (14,000,000 persons were
now insured, and only 5,000,000 had had claims to such
treatment before) and in the overpressure of routine
work which it entailed. The great thing was that the
Act was working. In the last few months the hostility
of the doctors had weakened. Mr Lloyd George had
met their demands by some concessions; and though the
British Medical Association officially held out to the end
of 1912 for its full requirements there were signs of
disunion. Whereas 27,400 of the profession had signed
the original pledge of 1911 to refuse to work the Act,
only some 13,000 voted in a ballot in December 1912 on
the questions still in negotiation with Mr Lloyd George.
The fact was that general practitioners, concerned for

their " club practices," were beginning to see themselves
as dragged along by the heads of the profession, who
were far above such humble considerations, in a warfare
which was as much political as professional, and were
beginning to doubt if they could afford the luxury. All
through the controversy the leaders had shown a good
deal of ignorance of their less famous brethren's habits.
They had fulminated about the indignity of contract
terms for their services, when all the time practitioners
in poor quarters and manufacturing districts had drawn a
great part of their income, and much the steadiest part,
from contracts with the friendly societies and trade
unions. Thus again Mr Lloyd George's confidence in
his Act triumphed. Just as the cards had for months
now been quietly stamped, so the panels of doctors were
quietly filling ; in January 1913 the British Medical
Association released from their undertakings all who had
signed the original pledge. Mr Lloyd George was entitled
to his pæans. He had added to Old Age Pensions and
his Budget of 1909 an immense piece of social reform, of
which many had talked, but which owed quite as much
now to his tireless energy, his quick mind, and his
buoyant countering of opposition, as to the patient
advocacy of others before him. It could, indeed, be said
that he was the member of the Cabinet who aroused
the bitterest hostility, the most open maker of " class "
appeals, so that in other hands the Insurance Scheme
might have had to confront less difficulty. But the
share of his personality in the feeling against the measure
can easily be exaggerated ; and it is certain that no
Minister could have brought it through so successfully,
except Mr Asquith, and perhaps Mr Winston Churchill.

Mr Churchill was occupied with matters which, if they
lent themselves not at all to pæans, were worth the
reach of high ambition. For the work of his Department,
the Admiralty, was at the very core of our relations with

Germany. Here again the public mind, when it looked in the direction of foreign affairs at all, was drifting into a kind of fatalism. It had complicated with spasmodic outbursts of interest, as it always does in foreign affairs, the efforts of statesmen. The attempt of Lord Tweedmouth in 1908, taken up again by Mr Churchill, to find some basis for a truce in naval armaments, had been interrupted by the periodical exaggeration into newspaper " stunts " of normal party exchanges on the Estimates, as well as by really critical events like the Agadir affair. When that died down, the public had been ready in 1912 to listen again to talk of a " naval holiday " ; but only because it thought that the peaceful issue of the crisis might mean that Germany, after all, " knew her place " in naval affairs, and that therefore we could afford to talk of a truce. Not, however, except upon that condition ; and the public was growing less sure that the condition was being observed. It had become more mistrustful when the news that Lord Haldane, who knew more of Germany than any other member of the Cabinet, was visiting Berlin, and the less widely spread knowledge that Sir Ernest Cassel too had gone there, were followed by no further information, either good or bad. No mood could have done better for Mr Churchill in the difficult path he had now to tread. He needed a public opinion not alarmed but on its guard. For he had the authentic German naval programme in his pocket, and he had to act upon convictions which could not be avoided, and yet could not be made public. He could not openly say that the enormous increase in personnel which the German Navy Law was providing, and which would commission fully a number of ships ostensibly inactive, made quite hollow the unaggressive professions with which Germany kept inside her published shipbuilding programme. But he had to act on that knowledge, and the public mood was what he wanted. His task was no less essential to these years than the more lime-lighted work of Mr Lloyd George. It was not his fault if, following superficially the Estimates of 1912, 1913 and 1914, for which he had to hold out so strenuously in the Cabinet, with their increasing impression of strength, speed and efficiency— hulls with power in every line, bigger guns, oil fuel and the rest—the country drifted into fatalistic acceptance of a struggle for sheer superior force after all.

This was the main subject now in the Cabinet, for after the overfull programmes of the last four or five years the Government set forth a very light one for the House, when it returned from a brief prorogation in March to the new session. The light programme, however, landed the Ministry in another difficulty : it cleared the way for recurring discussion of the suffrage *impasse*, which grew worse and worse. As if by a perverse fate every year now provided a fresh exasperation of temper ; and before the prorogation something had happened which seemed more perverse than ever, in that an attempted solution, which looked like a way out of the extraordinary maze, was "torpedoed" at the start. There had been in these years, as has already been said, a three-fold difficulty : first, the terms of any Bill alienated some supporters, yet to invite free amendment was to render its passage most unlikely ; secondly, a divided Cabinet could not take up a Suffrage Bill ; and thirdly, there was a genuine feeling in the House, however insincere the suffragists might choose to think it, that the franchise system needed more than a simple extension to women ; based on definitions of a past day, it was disfranchising a great many men. There was, therefore, every appearance of an ingenious piece of tactics at last, when the announcement was made that the whole suffrage question was to come up on a Franchise and Registration Bill. For this, besides

28

opening the door to the passage of amendments enfranchising women coincidently with the clearing away
of various disqualifications of men, also saved the face
of the Government in the matter of securing its passage.
They could not take up a Women's Suffrage Bill; but
they need not drop a Registration Bill of their own
because it had absorbed women's suffrage on the way.
They were not, however, to be allowed to " get away
with it." Anti-suffragists raised, not without justification, the point that a Bill so profoundly amended would
become in fact a different Bill, and must in the procedure
of the House be reintroduced in its proper form. After
a day or two's consideration the Speaker announced
that, in the event of such amendment taking place, he
would certainly rule in the sense of the point raised.

There is no need to jump, as the militants did, to the
conclusion that the whole plan had been nothing but an
elaborate trick. The Government stood to gain nothing
by tricking suffragists : it was already deep enough
in their disfavour. Private members were much more
likely to have intended a genuine, if blundering, way out
of their dilemma than a piece of chicanery. But the
militants cannot be wholly blamed for their attitude.
They had become convinced that much of the acquiescence in their demands of candidates at elections was
mere lip-service to escape their hostility at public meetings ; they deeply mistrusted the divisions on their Bills
of late years, for one-third of the House was generally
absent. They took this latest incident as an indication
that talk of support for their claims as part of a general
franchise reform was another shuffle, like the criticism
of their direct Bills as either too democratic or not
democratic enough. And since direct Bills were now
thrown out, the end of the attempt at an indirect
method undoubtedly looked like final refusal. Before
Parliament was prorogued their war upon society at

large had opened out. Another burst of window-breaking was followed rapidly by serious pillar-box outrages (they had discovered what phosphorus compounds could do), the partial destruction by a bomb of a house in building for Mr Lloyd George at Walton Heath, the burning of two or three railway stations near London, systematic ruining of golf greens, and the cutting of telegraph and telephone wires.

The last straw in the complication of the question during the new session was the hunger-strike. The Home Secretary had to stand a baffling cross-fire of criticism. On the one side were the insistent demands that he should keep order ; on the other a rising protest, by no means confined to supporters of the suffragists, against the revolting brutalities (and it could not, with the best will in the world, be other than brutal) of forcible feeding. Yet the only alternative to forcible feeding was release from prison ; and that meant impotence of punishment. The law was being broken, and then broke in the hands of its guardians. Mr McKenna, unable to get out of this cleft stick, tried to make it at least nip the militants as well. He introduced a Bill giving him powers to liberate prisoners on licence while of good conduct ; he was thus enabled to put released militants back in gaol on further offence without the bother of trial, and yet to escape forcibly feeding them by turning them outside again when that step would have become necessary. A few more outrages of bombing and arson hastened its passage ; it was put through all its stages in the House of Lords on one day, and became law on 25th April. But the famous " Cat and Mouse " Act might almost as well have been called the " Squirrel in the Cage " Act, for it left the Home Secretary pattering round and round in an alternation of imprisonment and release which hardly seemed to check the movement. Burning of houses and stations and race-course grand

stands went on, and no one knew how long only empty
buildings would be fired. It might be charitably
thought that the bad clockwork of a bomb found under
the Bishop's throne in St Paul's and of one sent to
the Bow Street magistrate indicated intention that the
things should not explode, but that again might be a
restraint which would soon break down. In the shattering of nerves and health which hunger-striking and
" cat and mouse " imprisonment must be producing, the
brink of assassination might any day be passed. How
near that desperation might be was only too forcibly
suggested by the miserable incident of this year's Derby
Day, when a militant who had been more than once
in prison dashed out on to the course in front of the
horses as they poured round Tattenham Corner, and
was so crushed that she died within a few hours.

Through all this the Government had at least some
sympathy ; people, even if they were impatient, could
be fair enough at times to see what the difficulties were.
It was now to find itself exposed in a far less excusable
muddle. Towards the end of 1912 two awkward
questions had arisen. One concerned a heavy purchase
of silver by the Indian Government in operations
for the exchange value of the rupee. The purchase
had been conducted entirely through a single firm,
Samuel Montagu & Sons ; a member of the Montagu
family was Under-Secretary for India, and an active
partner of the firm was Liberal member for a London
constituency. However, in this affair explanations were
not difficult to accept. Both the extent of the Indian
Government's purchase—six million pounds sterling—
and its urgent character had dictated quiet operations
through a single firm rather than open-market operations
which would inevitably have forced up the price of
silver. Mr E. S. Montagu, the Under-Secretary, had no
business connection with the firm at all ; and neither

his official position nor Sir Stuart Samuel's membership
of the House could be said to have brought any " inside
knowledge " into the transaction, since the Indian
Government itself was giving all the inside knowledge.
The suggestion dwindled, then, to one of favouritism in
the choice of the firm for the operation, and even that
could not be seriously sustained in view of this firm's
long association with the Indian Government.

But this reminder that political integrity cannot be
too sensitive was seen against a background of other
disturbing rumours which early in 1913 became more
widely current. The Government had concluded with
the Marconi Company an agreement for the erection of
an Imperial chain of wireless stations. There had been
some jealous rivalry between competing wireless systems,
and this gave sinister point to vague hints that members
of the Government had been speculating in Marconi
shares. At last a French newspaper, *Le Matin*, used
names ; and Sir Rufus Isaacs, the Attorney-General
(whose brother was a member of the Stock Exchange),
and the Postmaster-General, Mr Herbert Samuel,
brought a libel action. It came on in the end only as
an application for costs, the newspaper having already
withdrawn its charges and apologised, on proof that the
shares dealt in were shares in the American Marconi
Company and that the dealings, therefore, had not had
the impropriety of being a speculation on inside information before the agreement with the Government was
generally known. If that agreement had at all affected
the American shares it had done so openly, in a manner
of which any individual could take advantage. But the
affair could not rest there. For one thing, other names
were involved in rumour ; for another, the rumours and
the rivalries together were casting shadows on the
honesty of the agreement ; and altogether it was a case
for investigation by a Select Committee. The Committee

soon found that it had to divide its work. One part of
its reference, that concerning the agreement, was highly
technical; it involved questions of the comparative
efficiency of various wireless inventions and systems,
and the validity of patents which the Marconi firm was
undertaking to operate; there had for some time been
dispute on this point between Mr Marconi and other
inventors, especially M. Poulsen. This investigation was
delegated to a sub-committee presided over by a judge
of the High Court expert in patent litigation; all that
need be said of its work is that, after the Marconi
Company had vented, so to speak, a tiff with the British
public by talking of repudiating the agreement, the
report pronounced for the Company and established the
honesty of the primary transaction.

The inquiry into the conduct of Ministers, thus left
isolated, was followed by the public with far more
interest, especially as it gradually came out that not
only Sir Rufus Isaacs and the Postmaster-General, but
the late Chief Whip of the party, the Master of Elibank,
and the democratic anti-capitalist Chancellor of the
Exchequer himself were implicated. The Government
unpardonably aggravated a situation in any case
awkward enough. Having received from the Ministers
concerned, quite early in the stage of rumours, their
explanations, and accepting the excuse that the shares
in question were in the American Company, the Prime
Minister had agreed to the plea that no serious charge
could lie against their integrity. With the pressure
of the Home Rule and Welsh Bills upon them, and
Mr Lloyd George still deep in securing the free course
of the Insurance Act, the Ministry had far too easily
decided that the trouble would die down. They had not
seen that the wise course would have been to challenge
the rumours at once with a Select Committee. Now,
with the truth apparently dragged out of a Ministry

which had apparently hoped to conceal it, they frankly
admitted their mistake. Their excuses were good enough,
no doubt ; but they were landed in a very unpleasant
muddle.

They were lucky that it was no more than that.
The Committee was divided, a minority report going so
far as to speak of " grave impropriety." But fortunately
for Ministers it *was* a majority which reported in terms
of exoneration. There followed a debate in the House ;
the Postmaster-General had been cleared, and the
Master of Elibank was abroad, but Sir Rufus Isaacs
and Mr Lloyd George made their statements and withdrew. They were sensible enough to speak in complete
humility, and the Prime Minister made no effort to
minimise the lack of wisdom only too visible throughout
the affair. The debate finally turned on the question
whether the House should express its regret at the
conduct of Ministers, the form of the Opposition motion,
(in which case Sir Rufus Isaacs and Mr Lloyd George
would have resigned), or should accept the Ministers'
expressions of regret, the form of a Liberal amendment.
The latter won by 346 to 268, and technically the situation was saved. The Chancellor of the Exchequer
remained in his post ; the Attorney-General only left
his to become in the following October Lord Chief
Justice. But Liberals and Labour could be more
forgiving with their votes than with their thoughts.

The historian may well ask whether the most serious
aspect of the whole affair was not that it was so little
serious. In the House itself perhaps Mr Balfour's
question—" What would Mr Gladstone have thought
of a Chancellor of the Exchequer engaging in private
operations on the Stock Exchange ? "—may have had
some reality ; outside it was hardly more than rhetorical.
Thirty years earlier, no matter how satisfactorily the
strict letter of the rules of integrity had been kept,

no matter what saving distinctions might be drawn between English and American shares, Ministers who had so involved themselves might well have had to leave public life altogether ; now they need not even leave a Government. A world sitting loose to most things except its amusements and the means of commanding them could not expect that. Nor could a world which opened its drawing-rooms and gave dinner-parties mainly to throw a wide net for financiers with Stock Exchange " tips " really profess to be shocked. The trouble was not that of voices crying in the wilderness, but of voices crying in the very heart of Jerusalem ; there a whip of small cords is required. Lord Roberts was, indeed, doing his best to use one at the moment in an energetic campaign for some form of national service.

This movement rather entangled for a short time the progress of another movement which had had an amazing success, Sir Robert Baden Powell's Boy Scouts. They were an extraordinarily happy idea. Sir Robert, by his picturesque defence of Mafeking in 1899, and by his reputation for craft in game-tracking, and all the lore of jungle and wild, had captured the imagination of boyhood all over the country ; he had become a kind of hero of open-air cunning and wise dodges. By a stroke of real genius he turned all this into a channel which was to give to thousands of boys in dreary towns and dull industrial quarters and mean streets a vivid interest in their lives, a pride in handy usefulness, and hours—days and weeks, with luck—of fresh air, the countryside, and camping. He knew exactly how to hit the imagination of boys with his organisation of patrols and totems, the uniform of loose shirt and shorts, with just the right romantic touches of broad-brimmed hat and jack-knife slung at the belt, and with badges for proficiency in all the arts of camp-life. Not

the least part of it was that in classes and practice so
much scout-life could go on in winter, and keep boys
keen. The movement spread very rapidly, and managed
to keep its influence for self-respect and cleanliness and
health from becoming boring. In time girls grew so
envious of it that they had to have their own form of
it, Girl Guides. Because Sir Robert had been a soldier,
and because patrol organisation carried with it some
necessary drill, there were over-scrupulous people who
suspected it of being a surreptitious means of edging
the nation towards compulsory national service. But
that prejudice never did the movement much harm. It
was soon spreading to other nations.

What now hampered Lord Roberts was less the
counter-movement for peaceful gestures in our foreign
relations than the bland existence of young men with
their hair long and smoothly plastered back, their feet
devoted to the new and thrilling intricacies of the tango
or the gaieties of the turkey trot (there was a new dance
every year; it had been the bunny hug in 1912) and
their heads buzzing with rag-time music, which was the
latest discovery. Money, for those who had it at all,
was only too plentiful; and in these years old families
which had been a little left behind in the race for it
were tapping a new source. These were the years in
which prices for famous pictures first began to touch
figures that seemed fantastic. There had been much
talk in 1911 of offers of £100,000 to Lord Lansdowne
for a Rembrandt; in 1912 Lord Feversham had sold
one to a New York purchaser for £50,000; now in 1913
a Romney fetched £41,570, a Gainsborough £19,200,
and a single day's sale at Christie's reached a total—a
record at that time—of £120,000. For those who were
inclined to be depressed this was merely one more
ground for depression. We were doing badly at the
Olympic Games; we could not play polo as well as the

Americans, or at least could not afford so many ponies ; their boys could beat our hardened professionals at golf (Ouimet had been defeating Vardon and Ray) ; and now they were opening purses with which we could not compete to remove our art treasures. Lord Curzon had saved the Tattershall fireplaces, but then he had married American millions. It was all very sad, and all more than likely the Liberals' fault.

Even St Paul's Cathedral began to fail us. In June a report was published by Sir Francis Fox, conveying alarming intimations about the cracking of pillars and insecurity of the dome ; the inclination at the time was to attribute the damage to the making of tubes and underground railways, which, by draining off water, had disturbed the strata upon which the foundations rested. People began to wonder whether the £90,000 which had just been subscribed to secure the Crystal Palace for the nation had not better have waited for this purpose. Much money had also just been spent on the recon- struction of the façade of Buckingham Palace, which was completed this year, when the King entertained at a restaurant the five hundred workmen engaged on the job. The exasperating element in this business was that the old dingy front of the Palace, which was now felt to be a quite impossible background for the new Mall and the Victoria Memorial, need never have become so dingy if the Prince Consort, in his enthusiasm for modern invention, had not had the front treated with a patent substance for preserving the stone, which also proved to have a dismal capacity for preserving London dirt.

The King and Queen had again been making friendly visits to their people. In April they had been at the great railway works at Crewe, and had gone on to see the towns of the Potteries ; in July they spent a week in Lancashire, where their visit coincided with a curious industrial portent, a strike of agricultural labourers, who had been regarded as helplessly outside militant unionism. The ceremonial occasion of the year in London was the reopening of the Chapel of the Order of the Bath in its ancient but long-disused surroundings, Henry VII.'s chapel in Westminster Abbey. Little could be made of a visit the King and Queen paid in May to Berlin. Formally the occasion was one of reconciliation. A probable abandonment of the long feud between the House of Cumberland, reigning in Hanover, and the Hohenzollern dynasty had been rumoured in 1910 ; and now was to be made actual by the marriage of the German Emperor's only daughter to Prince Ernest Augustus of Cumberland. This might be styled rather pompously a reconciliation of Hohenzollern and Guelph ; but its message to the Guelph House of Great Britain seemed to be, if anything, an intimation of German solidarity.

International nervousness had been taking a new turn. There were still espionage cases on both sides ; this year the new uneasiness in England was about mysterious sounds of aircraft over the land at night. The earliest reports of this kind of thing had been in October 1912, when during a heavy fog people at Sheerness had been convinced that they had heard an airship moving above them ; a regular crop of such rumours followed in 1913, and Germany even thought it expedient to announce publicly that none of her airships had been over England. What the rumours really indicated was, of course, the discomfort of the knowledge that the Germans had in the Zeppelin an airship of proved practical use, while we had only doubtful and precarious experiments. So for the first time the Army Estimates opened up a considerable debate on air defence. Much that Colonel Seely said then, in his anxiety about these mysterious noises, makes strange

.reading on this side of the war ; he virtually ridiculed
the idea of any direct danger to life or property from
the air, and, though he may have been concealing much
that he knew of such possibilities, his reassurances were
effective, because the very general view at that time
of the value of aircraft in war was confined to their
use in scouting and intelligence work—as new eyes of
miraculous power for army commanders ; aircraft were
certainly not regarded by the public as fighting instruments.   Colonel Seely had much to say of our advance in
aviation.   A military flying school had been established.
There were now three squadrons, a total of 120 officers
and 598 men, and this year was to see the number of
squadrons raised to five.   One obstacle in the way of
development was the difficulty of procuring British
machines and engines ; the corps possessed 101 planes,
to be raised this year to 125.   He was also able to say
that as yet no fatal accident had occurred at the school.
The year 1912 had been rather alarming ; 95 people had
been killed in accidents in various countries, and Great
Britain had lost 7 officers.   The loss was not a heavy
one, as later years learned to reckon losses ; but it was
heavy in so small a corps, and in September the use
of monoplanes had been suspended as being " too
dangerous."   The ban did not last long, for in the
summer of 1913 M. Pégoud was revolutionising ideas of
what stability in the air could mean.   He had flown
upside down, and had come over to England to give
us at Brooklands the first thrill of watching a man
" loop the loop " ; there lay, though few can have
known it at the time, the germs of all the incredible
developments of flying in the war, which were to use
the old " accidents " of early aviation—nose-diving,
side-slipping, spinning, and the rest—as deliberate
methods of air-fighting.

One of the most patient of early experimenters was

killed this summer, Colonel Cody. He had for years
been working, more or less in conjunction with the
army authorities at Aldershot, on man-lifting box-kites.
Of late years he had been building biplanes of a sort,
but his box-kite predilections made them by a queer
combination both too light and too clumsy. He crashed
in one of them in August.

The Opposition's policy of exhibiting legislation under
the Parliament Act as a mere farce had at least relieved
the Government of much trouble with their Bills.
There was little debating of Home Rule and Welsh
Disestablishment when they came up for the second
time. " Cabinet tyranny " was the catchword, and it
was used for criticism of one interesting Bill of the
session—the Provisional Collection of Taxes Bill. A
curious constitutional point had been raised in the
previous year by Mr Gibson Bowles, a Conservative
member long known for his ability in financial matters,
and for his skill in technical procedure. He had used
both for years in a jealous defence of the private
member's rights in the House. He used them now in a
wider affair. He had brought an action in the High
Court, in 1912, which raised the question whether the
financial resolutions always passed on Budget day were
a proper legal authority for the collection of taxes—
could the subject be taxed constitutionally except by
Act of Parliament ? He brought his action against the
Bank of England, for deducting from some dividends
due to him income tax at the new rate imposed by the
resolutions of that year before the Finance Act had been
passed ; and the Court of Chancery upheld him. The
serious aspect of the judgment was this—that if the
Budget resolutions were not valid authority, and no
collection of a new or increased tax could take place till
the Finance Act of the year was duly passed, there
would be an interval of months, or at least weeks, after

the announcement in the Budget speech of the new duty, during which traders could clear stocks from the bonded warehouses and import fresh stocks at the old rate of duty, thus completely upsetting the Exchequer's calculations of the yield of a new tax. There was, of course, a simple way out of the difficulty : Parliament, being sovereign, had no more to do than pass an Act giving to the Budget resolutions the force of law until the passing of the Finance Act each year. But there remained the interest of the extraordinary fact, which the case had revealed, that for a century and more people had paid taxes without a murmur before the authorities had the right to collect them.

No Government could have existed without taking some such step ; and the Opposition was therefore straining a point rather far when they attacked the Bill as one more instrument of Cabinet tyranny, the line being that the Government, having altered the constitution to free their hands in legislation, had now done it again to ease their way in taxation. But the Opposition had to keep attention fixed on any point of attack they could make, and as far as possible off their own programme, because the only positive plank in it was Tariff Reform, and it was not even yet clear what as a party they meant by that. True, they arrived this year at a kind of formula for holding them together. In January correspondence and conference among the party leaders had ended in a pronouncement by Mr Bonar Law that a Unionist Government would impose no food taxes unless and until a General Election distinctly authorised them. But that gave no one much satisfaction. It did indeed allow Tariff Reformers who were not food taxers to act for all electoral purposes with those who were ; but it left them both open to what had proved so fatal in December 1905—the assertion that sooner or later Tariff Reform meant taxation of

food. Hamstrung like that, how could the party bring
into the open the reality of the large economic question
which, with a sound instinct for the vital concerns of a
modern industrial community, they had made the line
of party division ? Everything else could turn upon it,
for the social life as well as the national existence of
such a community must come in the last resort to its
command of wealth, private and public. Liberal finance,
therefore, had been steadily aimed at proving that there
was no need to be taken in by the blandishing offers of
money from a tariff ; Unionists were as steadily replying
that old methods of taxation could foot the bill only
by impositions which were driving capital out of the
country, and therefore could not last long ; that familiar
jeremiad of the moment at shareholders' meetings,
and in country-house parties up and down the kingdom, had had in 1912 the sanction of the Governor
of the Bank of England himself, in a speech at the
annual City dinner of the bankers. With the controversy
still so much alive, and a dropping fire of propaganda
carried on around the old questions of the effect of a
tariff on volume of trade, on wages, on steadiness
of employment, on credit, Liberals were not likely to
give any rest to the Unionist difficulty about food taxes ;
and Mr Bonar Law's pronouncement made very porous
shelter.

It was a strange fate which carried off together this
summer two Unionists so similar in type as Mr
George Wyndham and Mr Alfred Lyttelton. Both of
them belonged to the charmed inner circle of the party,
both had peculiar personal attractiveness, both in
different ways had embittering ends to happy careers.
Mr Wyndham, singularly handsome with his silver-grey
hair and young face (he was not quite fifty when he
died), had a delicate culture which, with his love of the
English country, may have softened for him the sudden

failure of his work as Irish Secretary.[1] Mr Lyttelton, a first-rate cricketer and for years amateur champion of tennis, had had to face the ruthless storm aroused by the Chinese labour ordinance on the Rand after the Boer War, and to see all his other achievements borne down by it.[2] Lord Avebury, who also died this summer, was another Unionist who had many interests besides politics. A naturalist of repute, and a successful banker, he had in 1871 brought into being almost unwittingly something which was to develop into one of *the* characteristic institutions of English life—the Bank Holiday. The name has, like so many others, acquired a familiarity which has obscured its original meaning. Sir John Lubbock, as he then was, had no conception of what his plan for securing a little leisure for the ranks of his own profession was going to effect. It is a pity that he did not live a little longer to see his modest holiday rise to its amazing importance in 1914, when the closing of banks on the first Monday in August was used to tide the City and the nation over the first financial shock of war. In its turn the expansion of his original idea reacted upon him; it must have been his association in this way with the leisure time of the people which set him upon his ethical writing, and the famous listing of the Hundred Best Books.

The fact that from a session comparatively quiet in legislation Mr Lloyd George should have gone out to speak to great Liberal meetings of " a deliberate conspiracy to overthrow democratic government " may well serve to point the remark that no mere narrative of events can give the history of this time. He could use these phrases without appearing to his audiences to exaggerate. Conditions in Ulster were such that the Government was being seriously asked whether it was not its duty to put Sir Edward Carson under arrest. Two

1 See page 675.   2 See pages 676 and 692.

seizures of arms had been made in Ireland ; large forces
were drilling steadily in Ulster, and the whole organisation of an army—Signal Corps, Army Service Corps, and
so on—was in being. The reply of the Government
was that they preferred to regard Sir Edward Carson as
a safety-valve ; his activities blew off much of the
steam and relieved the pressure. They could point
to the result of a by-election in Londonderry, where
a Liberal won the seat, as a proof that Ulster had
no right to pretend to dictate with one voice to the
British Parliament. It had been a remarkable election,
even for Ireland ; so thoroughly had every possible
voter been polled that dying men went to record their
votes with doctors at their side ; and it cheered a
Ministry which had been suffering some nasty losses,
including that of Sir Rufus Isaacs's seat at Reading
when he became Lord Chief Justice. Still, no one
imagined that their ostensible calm about. affairs in
Ireland represented their real feelings.

There was other trouble there too. In August a
reverberating industrial struggle had broken out in
Dublin. For some years two men had been busily
organising labour in Ireland. James Larkin, breaking
away in 1908 from English Trade Unionism, on the
fringe of which Irish labour had existed as a rather
neglected dependent, had founded the Irish Transport
Workers' Union, with all the more ease in making a
militant body of it because labour conditions in Ireland
were so far worse than in Great Britain. In 1910 he was
joined by James Connolly, who had spent the previous
seven years in the United States, and been deeply imbued with the fighting spirit of the Industrial Workers
of the World. The two began a regular campaign of the
most " direct action " kind of strike, launched upon
employers in an industry without any notice, and
extended, if necessary, by sympathetic strikes. They

had had no little success in improving conditions, so much, in fact, that by the summer of 1913 employers in Dublin decided that the time had come to smash this sectional striking by one fight on a scale too large for the unions to stand up against. They began dismissing members of the Transport Workers' Union from their employment ; Larkin retaliated by calling a general strike, and the employers capped it with something like a general lock-out.

This was far franker warfare than England had yet seen, for the new Irish unions were socialist and " direct action " from top to bottom, and that was not the case in England. Larkin was now to discover this. Naturally he looked to British Trade Unionism to help him by refusing to handle any goods for Irish trade, carried on as it was by blackleg labour. British leaders would not go so far. They dreaded the effect of the strike upon the " direct action " influence in their own ranks ; they were very uncertain about their power to manage successfully sympathetic strikes ; and under Connolly's influence there was a large element of open Republicanism in the Irish movement with which they did not want to associate their resources. Larkin got very little by his visit to England. But this did not mean that the effect there of Larkinism was small. It set the militant sections of the British unions seething ; and the leaders, though they might refuse to act in alliance, could not miss the warning conveyed by the attack of the Dublin employers. There in full operation was the lesson hanging over their own heads—the first undisguised union-breaking.

One result was that, cool as they had been to Larkin's own approaches, they were prompt to take a very strong line when, in October, he was sentenced to seven months' imprisonment for using seditious language. The Ministry were hotly attacked in the

House, and Labour members had plenty of support
from Liberals in vigorous resentment of what they
called the introduction into British courts of the idea
of *lèse-majesté*. The implied reference was, of course,
to Germany, where one of the worst obstacles in the
way of labour leaders was the constant possibility of
their being handily locked up on some almost mediæval
charge concerning the Emperor's dignity ; the vague
word " sedition " might easily apply as mediæval a
muzzle in England. Besides, it was more than a little
absurd for a Government which had for months been
listening quietly to the things said in Ulster to clap a
man into prison for using seditious language in Dublin.
Ministers surrendered with amazing swiftness. Larkin
had hardly served a fortnight of his sentence when he
was released. Here again the prevailing new spirit had
shown itself : a big meeting at the Albert Hall had
decided to use militant suffrage methods of heckling
Ministers every time they appeared in public until
Larkin was released.

For the moment, militancy in the suffrage movement
was rather less violent. Suffragists were interrupting
church services by interpolating chanted petitions of
their own into the Litany, in the form of prayers for their
hunger-strikers. But there was a lull in destructiveness.
One reason was that an action brought by a firm in
Regent Street for damage to their windows had ended
in a judgment which might render any individual
member of the Women's Social and Political Union
liable to be cast in damages, whether she had or had
not been directly concerned in the destruction in question. But a reason which probably had more influence
was that the whole tide of the movement was changing
curiously. Vast numbers of women who had never
thought about the vote at all had been made to think
of it, numbers more who had been lukewarm were

gathering heat. Those even who definitely objected to violent methods were being moved by the devotion of the militants. The most casual sporting and dancing young woman began to be attracted by the putting up of such a good fight. The most uninterested of business men's wives began to be aware of sympathy ; after all, the "Cat and Mouse" prisoners were women too. On the surface there might still be all sorts of differences ; a large meeting of women in Hyde Park might adorn themselves, as they did in July, with badges inscribed "Law-abiding Suffragists "; and active militancy might be small in extent. Yet there was a feeling in the air that underneath all this women were drawing together. It was even slightly mysterious ; no one could quite tell how it was happening, or when it had begun ; but certainly during 1913 one sex was subtly consolidating against the other.   Unwelcome though the conclusion might be, it was beyond doubt that militancy had produced an enormous change ; and that is probably why in this winter it somewhat relaxed its energies.

Not even the Established Church was to escape the atmosphere of conflict. At the end of 1913 the Kikuyu controversy penetrated to England.   Its origin lay as far back as July, when a missionary conference at Kikuyu, in Uganda, called for the purpose of finding a basis of united action among missionaries of the various Protestant persuasions, and ending in a joint Communion service, had led the Bishop of Zanzibar, a "high" Anglican, to accuse the Bishops of Uganda and Mombasa of heretical inclinations in matters of the episcopacy, the rite of confirmation and so on.   By references to *Foundations*, a recently published volume of theological essays, he swept into the controversy the whole school of modernist religious thought which was rising in Oxford, and was providing the young Mr Ronald Knox with admirable material for transcendental squibs.[1] But it was thunder and not squibs that filled columns of *The Times* in this December and the following January. As ecclesiastical thunder is apt tô do, it receded placidly to a horizon of postponement when the Archbishop of Canterbury, to whom the Bishop of Zanzibar was making " bell, book and candle " appeals, intimated that he was waiting for a " precise question " to be submitted to him.

To this may be appended a remarkable instance, a few months later, of religious concord—the unveiling of a statue of Bishop Gore in Birmingham. The event had less attention at the time than it deserved, for it occurred in the midst of acute alarm about Ireland. Dr Gore had been translated from Birmingham to Oxford in 1911 ; it was a most striking testimony to the quality of his strong personality that a great business city, where the prevailing religious influences were not, perhaps, those of the Established Church, should have paid him the rare tribute of a statue in his lifetime. But it might be said with some truth that the incident was no less striking a testimony to the character of Birmingham.

That city suffered two losses just now in the family which the general public could not think of apart from Birmingham. In October Mr Arthur Chamberlain had died. Less famous than his brother, and never a man for huge political meetings, he was said to be in fact the more able of the two ; but he had been content to devote his capacities mainly to his city and his business. He had, however, made one great contribution to politics ; for it was a scheme that he had devised for reduction of the number of licensed houses in Birmingham

---

[1] Just before, in November, there had died, at the age of ninety, one of the great Victorians whose work had called modernism into existence, Alfred Russel Wallace. He had been intimately associated with Darwin in theories of the origin of species, the hypothesis of natural selection having flashed upon their minds almost simultaneously.

by means of a compensation fund which provided
the model for the Unionist Licensing Act of 1904.
In the Tariff Reform controversy he had been on the
Free Trade side, but as he avoided public platforms
the brothers had been in no sensational opposition.
The other loss was the intimation in January 1914 by
the more famous brother that he would not stand
again for election. He had hardly appeared in the
new Liberal Parliament at all. The violent strain of
the Tariff Reform campaign had suddenly revealed its
effects upon him, and he had had to live very quietly.
Yet, even if he never went to the House, it seemed
impossible to think of the representation of Birmingham
without him. His lifelong companion, Mr Jesse Collings,
faithful to the last, certainly could not think of it, and
retired with him.

The space that Kikuyu had been able to occupy in
the newspapers may have indicated a readiness to find
refuge during the holiday time from the lowering sky
of politics. But few subjects seemed to provide gratifying refuge just now. Early in December a big glove-
fight had at last been staged for Bombardier Wells with
a young Frenchman, Georges Carpentier. The crowds
of rank and fashion that paid their large prices to see a
couple of very good-looking young men stripped for the
ring were able to look at them for precisely seventy-
seven seconds, the time that it took the Frenchman
to knock the Englishman out. The appointment of an
American railway man, the General Superintendent of
the Long Island Railway, to be General Manager of the
Great Eastern Railway, excellent as it may have been
for a line with the heavy suburban " rush " traffic in
which he was peculiarly experienced, rather rubbed in
a sense of our incompetence. Meanwhile the athletic
authorities of Oxford were considering whether the
merely English talent of Cambridge could fairly be

expected to stand up to the lavish supply of Americans and Colonials which the Rhodes Scholarships brought to Oxford, and whether they must not put themselves under some self-denying ordinance in sport. The year had also seen our consciousness of failure in the Olympic Games issue in a proposal to raise a fund for training competitors; the proposal came to nothing, mainly owing to the dislike of the veiled professionalism which it would involve. Literature entertained itself by entertaining M. Anatole France to dinner during a brief visit he paid to London in December; and then by organising a mock trial of John Jasper for the murder of Edwin Drood, with Mr G. K. Chesterton as judge and Mr Bernard Shaw as foreman of the jury.

New Year's Day set the Tadpoles and Tapers of party headquarters all agog again with an interview which Mr Lloyd George gave to *The Daily Chronicle*. For his remarks about naval expenditure, the un-aggressive temper of Germany, and the danger of Liberalism "betraying its trust," were plain enough advertisement of Cabinet dissensions on the Estimates, which its opponents might exploit. Mr Winston Churchill was at the moment in Paris; Mr F. E. Smith, however, could gratify both his political feelings and the impulse of his friendship with Mr Churchill by informing Mr Lloyd George at the earliest opportunity that he was " a bungling amateur."

Then for a few days the industrial world and Ulster divided interest fairly equally. In the former a strange situation was developing out of the Dublin struggle. While this had apparently shown that English Trade Unionism was still rather slow and steady, there was in fact grave anxiety. The extremists both among employers and labour were, of course, more than ever convinced that they were right; the full-sized struggle had opened. But more grave was the state of mind of

the moderate men. Trade union leaders, by the very fact
of holding back from direct action, had the more need
to press on in their own chosen direction—federation
into big powerful unions; and masters could not watch
this without apprehension, for it must mean that
the amicable employer would suffer even more than
before with the stiff-necked in a dispute. Sheet anchors
were dragging, too, on both sides; if the Amalgamated
Society of Engineers had repudiated the agreement of
1907, the Cotton Spinners' Amalgamation had repudiated
the famous Brooklands Agreement, which had kept the
peace in Lancashire, to the envy of all other industries,
for twenty years. If cotton was losing its common
sense, what hope was left ? Now in January 1914, when
the struggle in Dublin was dying down to a drawn
battle, a relic of it loomed over England with the announcement of the " Triple Alliance "—the agreement
between the unions of the three great industries of
railway workers, miners and transport workers. This
nominally was not for the purposes of sympathetic
striking. The idea was to enter upon working agreements of equal duration, so that if one of the industries
decided at the expiration of its agreement to refuse work
without a reconsideration of terms, the two others
would be free at the same time to hold off from renewal
of theirs. It was a subtle distinction without much
meaning. The public was less concerned with this hair-
splitting than with the obvious fact that, whether the
General Strike was the deliberate policy of the leaders
or no, a simultaneous strike of the Triple Alliance must
paralyse the whole of industry. So here also a kind of
fatalism crept in. Just as in the case of our relations
with Germany, though there might be comparatively
few men with clear purposes in mind, the bulk found
themselves sliding forward in a bewildered way, doing
things which they might think it foolish to do, but

which in the circumstances they would be fools not to
do. It was, however, only for a short time that public
interest was divided. Ulster soon took it all. Few
perhaps could have quite accounted for the access of
hopelessness that ensued upon Mr Bonar Law's speech
at Bristol on 15th January, when he warned the country
that it was "rapidly drifting to civil war." That was
not much more than had been said by many people for
a twelvemonth past. Yet it had an extraordinary effect,
and almost as much significance hung round a sermon
by the Archbishop of York, ingeminating peace, though
such sermons also had not been uncommon. To the
public at large there was little more than a growing sense
of the air thickening round them, until the first flash
shot through it with some phrases used by Mr Walter
Long in moving an amendment to the Address at the
beginning of February ; he spoke of anxiety in the navy
and army, and added that "he believed Unionists,
whenever they had been asked, had advised the members
of the services to do their duty." So this was what had
not been getting into the newspapers ; to the officers of
the armed forces civil war was as near as that, and
the world from which they came and in which they
moved knew it. After this the public cared for very
little else.

The House of Commons could not equally absorb
itself in one thing. Just when the ministerial part
most needed a united front, news from South Africa
started friction again with labour. For some weeks
there had been trouble on the Rand and affrays in
Johannesburg. On 28th January it was announced
that the South African Government had deported ten
labour leaders, and imprisoned a member of the South
African Parliament, Mr Cresswell. Labour in England
was in an ill mood for such an occurrence, and in the
House was openly hostile. The Government stood their

ground ; the deportation had, no doubt, been a high-handed act, but they were not going to interfere with the authority of a self-governing Dominion. They countered the Labour disaffection rather cleverly by taking this Imperialistic line, which prevented the Opposition from making much use of the affair ; and they refused to withhold the Royal Assent to the Indemnity Bill which the deportation had rendered necessary. The arrival of the deportees in England at the end of February, a dinner to them at the House of Commons, and a mass meeting in Hyde Park, kept up a show of vigorous protest ; but it was more to satisfy the rank and file than anything else. The truth came out at a joint meeting a little later of representatives of the Trade Union Congress, the General Federation of Trade Unions, and the Independent Labour Party, which, ignoring taunts, decided by a majority of ten to one to take no action which might turn out the Government.

For the beginning of March had brought serious developments in the Irish situation. First came a peace move which had long been vaguely considered. The obvious suggestion for meeting the case of Ulster—that of some kind of exclusion from the Home Rule Bill —had been made two years before. But it had been put aside by Nationalists and Liberals. It was not as simple as it sounded. Ulster included counties which were politically Nationalist, and even in the distinctly Unionist parts—even in the stronghold of Belfast— there were large Roman Catholic and Nationalist minorities. Was Ulster itself, while protesting against being at the mercy of a Dublin Parliament, and leaving at its mercy Unionists in the other provinces, to keep these minorities at its mercy in its own province ? Unionists had their easy gibe in saying that what the Nationalists really wanted was to make sure that the

only part of Ireland which was industrially wealthy
and "squeezable" should not escape them. But if
some Nationalists did sometimes think of their future
budgets, there was much more depth in their feeling
that it would be deplorable if Ireland, becoming "a
nation once again," could not be whole, but must
always be liable to be rent by difficulties about isolated
minorities, instead of giving them their balancing
interplay in a single representative body. That was, at
least, a vital point of view ; now at the eleventh hour it
gave way in an effort for peace. Mr Asquith produced
on 9th March a scheme of "provisional exclusion."
Any county in Ulster was to be empowered to vote
itself out of the Home Rule Bill, after a preliminary
requisition by a certain proportion of the registered
voters, for a period of six years. Within that time
there must in the normal course be not less than two
general elections in England, in 1915 and 1920. The
excluded counties would then come under the Dublin
Parliament unless the Imperial Parliament confirmed
their exclusion. In other words, the dissident counties
were to be given the chance in at least two general
elections to prove that their exclusion was right. The
scheme had but cool welcome. The Nationalists had
made a forced concession ; Liberals were uneasy about
possible further mutilations ; Unionists disliked the
implication that exclusion was the wrong policy and
would prove itself wrong; Sir Edward Carson called it
"a sentence of death with stay of execution for six
years."

The scheme had hardly begun to be discussed when
it was swept aside by startling reports, ten days later,
that officers at the Curragh were resigning their com-
missions rather than risk having to march against
Ulster. These reports followed close upon an ominous
debate in the Commons. On 19th March Sir Edward

Carson, speaking to a vote of censure on Mr Asquith for
his Irish policy, had asserted that within the previous
two days there had been discussion at the War Office of
mobilisation for active service in Ireland ; and Mr Bonar
Law had remarked that " if it were a case merely of
disorder the army would and ought to obey ; if it were
a question of civil war soldiers were citizens like the
rest of us." The ostentatious manner in which Sir
Edward Carson and eight other Unionists walked out of
the House during the debate suggested crisis ; and now
came this news from the Curragh. With a gasp people
asked themselves if war was actually beginning.

For a week the affair remained cloudy and alarming.
The Prime Minister was both answering questions in
Parliament and dealing with a situation which had yet
to be worked out, so that inevitably information was
piecemeal. First came some reassurance. It was true
that after interviews with General Sir Arthur Paget,
commanding in Ireland, most of the officers of the
Cavalry Brigade at the Curragh—57 out of 70—and the
Brigadier himself, General Gough, had intimated that
they preferred dismissal to obeying orders for service
in Ulster. But upon explanations given at the War
Office, to which they had been summoned, they had
returned to duty, their action having been caused by
" misunderstanding." The Prime Minister authorised
The Times to state on 23rd March that any military
movements contemplated by the Government had been
merely precautionary, and that no general inquiry into
the intentions of officers had been contemplated. A
debate on the same day in a House crowded to the last
inch elicited rather more. The Government had decided
on 14th March to take steps to protect military stores
and munitions in the disaffected parts—a very natural
precaution. General Paget, following a quite usual
course in the moving of troops, arranged meetings at

the Curragh, first with General Gough to work out details, and then with the other officers of the Brigade to make the details clear. Thinking it prudent to make sure of his ground with the senior officers he had intimated that, if any of them were not prepared to obey orders, they should absent themselves from the conference. But his proceedings had gone amiss in two ways. Firstly, the message about senior officers had been misinterpreted, and taken to mean that all officers were being given the choice of obeying orders or not; all that had ever been contemplated by the Government in that direction was that officers actually domiciled in Ulster might be excused from duty there, just as in India and in African territories natives of any rank in the army were always excused from active service in their own home districts. Secondly, General Paget had talked in such a way as to suggest that far more than precaution was in contemplation; he had hinted at movement of troops from England, and of co-operation by the navy, referring to orders which Mr Churchill, it appeared later, had given without the Prime Minister's knowledge, and which were cancelled as soon as possible. The combination of these gravely sounding statements with the choice which by mistake they had been called upon to make, not unnaturally suggested to the officers that the actual coercion of Ulster was to begin; this was the misunderstanding which the War Office explanations had cleared away.

So far the Government had the sympathy at any rate of their own supporters. But the next revelations raised a storm of cross-currents. It came out that General Gough had then received a document from the War Office, signed by Colonel Seely, General French, Chief of the General Staff, and Sir J. S. Ewart, Adjutant-General, which, after a couple of short paragraphs stating the duties of troops in keeping civil order and

the right of the Government to their services, went on to
say that the Government " had no intention whatever
of using this right in order to crush political opposition
to the policy or principles of the Home Rule Bill." The
instant outcry from Nationalists, Liberals and Labour
that this was a sheer surrender to the army elicited the
awkward fact that during the Cabinet discussion of a
document which had contained only the two paragraphs
on the duties of troops Colonel Seely had had to leave
for an audience of the King, and, the discussion being
over when he returned, had on his own responsibility
added the intimation about the Government's intentions.
The Prime Minister stated that all the three signatories
to the document had tendered their resignations, but
these had not been accepted. For a few days more the
affair dragged on, with fresh side-issues. Lord Morley,
it appeared, had had some responsibility for the offending statements. The coincidence of Colonel Seely's
audience of the King with the Cabinet discussion of the
document was used to insinuate some connection of
the King himself with the interpolation. A new Army
Order on discipline, intimating that no officer was to
be questioned by his superior officer as to his probable
attitude in any emergency, and no officer was to ask for
assurances as to orders he might be called upon to obey,
also came in for debate. Mr Bonar Law kept on reading
extracts from officers' letters, showing that they had
been questioned ; the Prime Minister kept on deploring
all this incursion of " hypothetical contingencies " into
the soldier's life ; Mr Lloyd George was scornful about
" optional obedience " ; the Labour members in some
glee harped perpetually on the example officers were
setting of refusing duty in a civil crisis, a lesson which
might have its fruits in the ranks in case of industrial
trouble ; and the general public asked itself what incalculable harm all this confusion might be doing. At

last this whole stage of the excitement about Ireland culminated in a dramatic announcement by the Prime Minister, on 30th March, that Colonel Seely, General French and General Ewart having persisted in their resignations, these had now been accepted, and that he himself was going to take over the War Office. Upon which, as his new post involved vacating his seat, he abruptly left the House.

A breathless fortnight thus ended a breathless first quarter of the year. Yet some other things had been happening. *Parsifal* had for the first time been performed in England at the opera-house in Covent Garden ; and there was much talk of the future of that theatre. Late in 1913 the Duke of Bedford had sold the whole Covent Garden site to Mr Mallaby Deeley, M.P., for £2,750,000. Londoners had been oddly disgruntled by this transaction. They had always known, of course, that the market belonged to the Duke ; they had grumbled at times about the private ownership as responsible for some of the messy inconveniences of the place. But now with a sudden access of concern for it, reading accounts of its strange beauties in the early morning (few of them ever saw it at that time save the strayed revellers from Covent Garden balls, who liked to feel adventurous at the market coffee-stalls in the small hours) when the masses of flowers and fruit for London's day painted its dingy aisles, and even cabbages and carrots, in the quantities in which they came, gave tones to the picture, Londoners felt obscurely hurt by the revelation that such an institution might be sold over their heads and turned into something else. All the talk for and against removing the market—and it was absurdly cramped, reached by narrow streets, and responsible for constant complications of the Strand traffic—was still going on desultorily when, in July, it was announced that the site had changed hands again,

Sir Joseph Beecham having bought it. This turned talk rather to the opera than to the market; for his son, Mr Thomas Beecham, had for some years been prominent in a group of people busily concerned with the future of opera in England. Its art appeal alone certainly had no great hold, as a recent lavish experiment had shown. In November 1911 a large new opera-house, built at great expense in Kingsway by Mr Oscar Hammerstein, a magnate of the New York theatres, had been opened; within a year it had become a music-hall under other management. There had, no doubt, been mistakes in its career, some of which an Englishman might have avoided; it had opened at a period of the year when opera had no place in social habits; its early productions had been rather insignificant. But some fine things had been given, Nikisch and other famous conductors had taken part; and yet it failed. The worst of it was, not the indication that a great city like London would not support two opera-houses, but the suspicion that, if anything happened to the Covent Garden house, and the settled habits which did just keep that going, though very precariously, were broken, London might not even support one. The depressing fact for lovers of music was that the opera would fill only to hear the few first-rank stars, whose fees were so enormous that opera to houses half filled on other occasions with a genuinely musical audience was becoming impossible. This all came back partly to the change in social ideas which affected so many things. The new world of fashion was not necessarily going to preserve any of the habits of the old; it was living its own life and following its own tastes without much regard for tradition; if opera bored it, it was not going to respect—as earlier generations, bored or not, had done—a hallowed institution of the London season. There was, indeed, a fairly successful programme this year; but mainly because of the prominence given to the Russian craze with *Prince Igor*, *Le Coq d'Or*, *Boris Godounov*, and others. Thus, though Sir Joseph Beecham's purchase of the Covent Garden estate seemed to promise some kind of support for Mr Thomas Beecham's energies, it was doubtful whether anything would restore opera in London to its former veneration.

Another portent for the old-fashioned was the issue in March this year of *The Times* at a penny. Only a little while before it had shocked its readers by coming down to twopence and admitting illustrated advertisements ; now it seemed to be forced into bidding for wider circulation, and the last Victorian bulwark might be tottering. At a penny could it help becoming " sensational," and sinking to pictures of the day's news ? These had for some time past crept upwards from the halfpenny Press of the late nineties into sheets of such respectable ancestry as *The Daily Telegraph*, *The Daily Chronicle* and *The Daily News*, which had combined in 1912 with *The Morning Leader*. The news pictures of that period look now coarse and hazy, and were more often than not a day late in appearing ; neither photographers nor block-makers had discovered yet how to do their work well under pressure, and for that reason a rather proud paper like *The Manchester Guardian* confined itself to single pictures of a leisurely kind, and rarely attempted news pictures of the day. Press photographers on public occasions were still liable to be regarded as a rather impertinent intrusion with something undesirably American about them. But a new generation of illustrated weeklies—*The Tatler*, *The Sketch*, *The Bystander*—with their persistent pages of snapshots of people at race-meetings, at shooting-parties, on golf links, or shopping in town, were breaking down this dislike, and the staid older weeklies, *The Illustrated London News* and *The Graphic*, were feeling

dowdy, and beginning to attempt these new habits.
Even those people who resented the impudence of that
sort of publicity were learning to make the best of it.
Not many of such persons were left by now ; the far
more numerous " right " people, who were tolerantly
amused by publicity, and the considerable number who
were beginning to like it, kept the illusion of importance going for the rich social climbers and the arrant
nobodies to whom appearance in these photographs gave
profound gratification. The whole thing was becoming
a hypnotism, very cheapening all round ; at one end
the nobodies destroying by the very crowd of them any
social *cachet* that could ever have been acquired in this
way, and yet greedy for it ; at the other, the working
man and his wife, sensible enough till they turned to
their daily paper, gazing absorbed at pictures of "The
Countess of So-and-so and Friend in the Paddock."
There was one serious effect : no one could believe any
longer in aristocracy. The illustrated Press was helping
to merge all other distinctions in one fairly broad division
between rich people with their hangers-on and the rest.

In some better ways the effect of the illustrated Press
in getting rid of old distinctions was beginning to show
itself. Dress of good taste was no longer the exclusive
property of women comfortably circumstanced. Newspaper photographs and sketches were showing other
women what dress ought to look like ; and the vast
reach of advertisement in the cheaper papers enabled
mass-production of " modes and robes " to be remunerative. Taste of a kind in furniture, too, was spreading,
since the mass-advertisement together with the instalment system, making its first appearance on a large
scale about this time, enabled people of small means to
set themselves up with a kind and a range of furniture
that their fathers and mothers had not commanded.
In neither case was the change altogether admirable.

Being a mechanical mental process it implied no genuine
sense of beauty or elegance. But it got rid of many old
stuffinesses ; it did suggest that there was such a thing
as choice and enjoyment in the appointments of life,
and it did produce an enlivening of outlook which
might well end in a real approach to taste. There was
more and more money for the mass-advertisement to
catch by broadening out the supply of amenities. The
Budget of this year was astounding, with its revenue
surplus of £9,000,000 over the estimate ; the trade returns
continued to flatter us, and prices were showing no more
tendency to rise.

This was an England in which it was difficult to
discern character or opinion of such passionate conviction as the shadow of civil war would seem to imply.
Indeed, the strongest feeling just now of the average
man was that the disastrous element in the outlook
lay not in any insuperable and fatal deadlock anywhere,
but in the growth of a strange tendency to play with
fire. Politicians tempted further and further by their
own extravagances of language, suffragists going always
a little deeper into destructiveness, Labour and Ulster
moulding forces more and more into the machinery of
conflict, and all the while a most dangerous number
of the comfortable classes making up their minds that
something was bound to happen—the whole situation
had the mounting unreality of a nightmare, in which a
man knows himself to be more sane than the creature
he is for the moment being. When peers like Lord
Halifax and Lord Milner, elderly dons like Professors
Goudy and Dicey, eminent clerics and men of letters
were signing, in their comfortable studies, in February
and March, a " British Covenant " declaring their belief
that any action to wreck a Bill they disliked was justified, did they really envisage all the explosive matter
near which they were striking matches ?

But now that the Curragh incident had swept the fog aside, and revealed the very brink of the precipice, would not people come to their senses ? It looked as if they might. When the Commons in the first week of April took up the Home Rule Bill for its third passage there was a much more conciliatory feeling in the House. Mr Balfour disappointingly indulged himself in schoolboy remarks about the " fright " of the Government ; but there was a genuine access of hopefulness when Sir Edward Carson, speaking soberly about the fate which seemed to overshadow Ireland, and the real apprehensions to be overcome in Ulster, turned at the end towards Mr John Redmond and said : " It is worth while your trying. Will you ? " They had not addressed one another for months past ; the phrasing of this appeal was extraordinarily—almost startlingly—simple. Was this the plain natural word, spoken at last, which would break through the nightmare, and let us, if still in some bewilderment, wake up ?

Unfortunately there was another possibility. It was that the Government's back might be to the wall, and with a bit more harrying it might go down. If the way were not made easy for them in Ireland they must go forward to a situation from which they might easily shrink at the last, and ruin themselves. The Naval Estimates might be very dangerous for them, now that Mr Lloyd George had definitely put himself at the head of the considerable mass of Liberalism and Labour determined to restrict that kind of expenditure. Labour's revolt against the arrest of Larkin and the South African deportations, though smothered down, had still possibilities to be exploited. Three-cornered candidatures were already losing the Government an alarming number of seats (they had recently lost one on the South African affair), and Mr Lloyd George was saying that the danger for his party was not Ulster, but the disunion between

Liberals and Labour. So at the very moment of hopefulness all the Government's opponents saw bright chances
in a final assault. For thus, instead of merely saving
Ulster while the rest of Ireland had its way, the whole
field would be won ; an end would be put to all this
subversive legislation and threatening finance (the year's
Budget was once more stiffening up progressive taxation
of incomes) ; and a party going to the polls with its
Parliament Act Bills lost, the suffragists its irreconcilable
enemies, its own left wing and Labour mistrustful, would
certainly not come back to power.

Militant suffragism also seemed to see the Government as with its back to the wall, for outrages broke
out again virulently.   Houses, cricket pavilions and
grand stands, stations, seaside piers and hotels, including a brand-new one at Felixstowe, were being burned ;
a bomb in St John's Church, Westminster, blew out a
stained-glass window just after evening service one
Sunday, another was found under the Coronation Chair
in Westminster Abbey, and another in St George's,
Hanover Square ; Birmingham Cathedral was splashed
with whitewash and stencilled with suffragist mottoes ;
Wargrave Church was burned to the ground.   An
attempt appeared to have been made to break the water
supply of Glasgow.   Pictures which were especially in
the public mind—the Rokeby *Venus* at the National
Gallery because of the high price the nation had paid
for it, the Sargent portrait of Henry James at the Royal
Academy—were damaged, and a case of porcelain
smashed in the British Museum. The authorities once
again closed the great public galleries. The King was
assailed with shouted appeals at a charity matinée ;
and at his own Court a lady being presented dropped
suddenly on her knees and cried : " Your Majesty, won't
you stop torturing women ? " The Home Office Vote
turned again into a debate on militancy ; Mr McKenna

produced figures of the working of the Cat and Mouse
Act ; of 83 persons discharged under it 15 had given
up militancy, and over 20 more had gone abroad. But
figures did not alter recent facts. Mr McKenna was
advised (by Lord Robert Cecil, for instance) to try
deportation ; that, as he replied, would give him no
solution, since any place chosen for deported offenders,
such as the island of St Kilda, would have to be made
in effect into a prison, and the deported would merely
recommence hunger-striking there with added difficulties
for the authorities in looking after them. For the time,
he was proposing to secure lists of the subscribers to
the militant bodies, and take steps to cut off the funds ;
he asserted that most of the outrages now were paid
work. Perhaps the grimmest passage in his speech was
that in which he stated that women were being chosen
to go to prison whose health was so poor that they might
die there.

The momentary hopefulness about Ireland faded
rapidly. Sir Edward Carson's appeal to Mr Redmond
had been made on 6th April. The next news was that
on the night of 24th-25th April the largest and most
defiant piece of gun-running had taken place in Ulster.
The coastguard had been decoyed, telephone and telegraph communication interrupted, and along guarded
roads 25,000 rifles and 3,000,000 cartridges had been
rushed away to points of distribution by lorries and
cars ; the completeness of organisation was revealed in
the fact that no less than 12,000 men had been at work.
The origin of these munitions was not the least of the
nightmare. Unionists who were raising the spectre of
German hostility to foment the discords about the
Naval Estimates were deliberately publishing to Germans
the imminence of civil war by buying rifles and cartridges. It was so open an association that Sir Edward
Carson referred frankly to purchases of " Mausers " ;

and a letter had actually appeared in the newspapers
from certain German professors to warn Ulster that
Protestant Germany did not mean to go quite so far
as taking a share in hostilities. The Curragh incident
revived with the publication on 22nd April of a White
Paper giving the documents which had passed ; the
measures which the Government said they had conceived as purely precautionary were bitterly attacked as
a form of rather subtle and treacherous provocation ;
afraid of what might happen when the Home Rule Bill
became law, they were, it was said, trying to goad
Ulster into a premature explosion which they might
suppress before the country had time to take a stand
about full-blown civil war.

Such accusations were part of a hardening of tone
now in the House. The Opposition was going back to
the demand for nothing less than the complete exclusion
of north-eastern Ireland from Home Rule, and for that
reason made another violent scene when the third
reading of the Home Rule Bill was moved on 21st May.
They objected to the Bill leaving the Commons with no
security for Ulster. But the Bill itself could not be
amended without losing the protection of the Parliament
Act. Mr Asquith's proposal for provisional exclusion
must therefore be in a separate Bill, which, with the
pressure of the Budget and Estimates in the Commons,
was to be introduced in the Lords. Fastening upon this
the Opposition, on the ground that they had a right to
the information before they let the Home Rule Bill go,
asked for details of the Amending Bill, which Mr Asquith
on a plea of respect for the other House refused to give.
Thereupon the now familiar disorder broke out, aggravated when the Speaker, in a well-intentioned but
perhaps not wise effort to awaken a sense of responsibility, asked the leader of the Opposition whether such
conduct had his consent and support. Mr Bonar Law

only too gladly jumped at the chance of a haughty reply, and the House had to be adjourned. When, on 25th May, the Bill received its third reading, the Nationalists might be enthusiastic, Mr Redmond might tell *The Freeman's Journal* that " the Union as we have known it is dead " ; but Sir Edward Carson a week later was in Belfast " to make arrangements," as he said, " for the final scene." And attention now fixed upon Ireland became aware that the Home Rule side in its turn had over 100,000 volunteers enrolled ; and saw the Nationalist party leaders, who had hitherto kept aloof from this reply to Ulster, taking a formal place on its committee in June.

At such a crisis the death of Joseph Chamberlain on 2nd July could be marked by only the briefest turning of thoughts. Time in these urgent sessions had gone quickly, and it was difficult to believe that it was eight years since the political arena had lost that familiar presence, the sharp dominating face with the pointed nose so curiously like the younger Pitt's, the thin figure as full of readiness as a boxer on his toes, the rather harsh, cold voice. One of Mr Chamberlain's distinctions was that all this was so familiar ; the caricaturist had caught at him as eagerly as at Mr Gladstone. What the public which adored him now learned for the first time was, as Lord Morley put it, " his genius for friendship." They had thought of him as a ruthlessly hard hitter, and the very type of a dangerous enemy. But the man who after thirty years of political sword-swinging and Imperialist chauvinism could win that tribute from John Morley must have known something of friendship. He was one of the few people who have been both politician and statesman. Best known in his early years for his genius for party organisation (shrugged at then as " Birmingham caucus work "), he ended by being the first man to make the Colonial Office of front-rank

importance in a Ministry, and Imperial policy a coherent
subject which would hold great popular audiences. He
had made much party history, first in 1886, when the
real question at stake was not whether he would accept
Mr Gladstone's type of Home Rule, but whether the
Liberal party was going in the future to be Gladstonian
or Chamberlainite ; afterwards when his influence was
turning the Conservatives and Unionists into a party
of enterprise and movement ; and finally when he gave
them a new political meaning as Imperial Preference
opened out into Tariff Reform. He never led a Ministry,
and he was not the stuff of which successful prime
ministers are made. Parties, like other compounds, have
their periods of alternate precipitation and crystallisa-
tion. The glorified prime ministers are the crystallisers.
Lord John Russell, Mr Gladstone, Disraeli, at their
zenith, were all the voices of slow political forces coming
to consciousness, and made by them articulate. Peel
is more the analogy for Mr Chamberlain. Both were
precipitating forces, dropping into the compound the
vigorous clarity and energy of some idea which loosens
its inertia and individualises its components for fresh
action ; and, be it remarked, a compound in course of
such a process is unstable. Curiously similar to Peel, for
all their differences of temperament and of intellectual
training, in the business mind which pinned a party's
social policy to a great question of trade and finance,
he would, like Peel, if he had ever led a party, have
had to see it break in his hands.

From paying its tributes to him the House of Commons
went back to the sharp sort of work that he had loved.
The Opposition kept every sort of pressure operating on
the Ministry now. The Naval Estimates had had a
stormy passage, especially in the matter of the measures
taken to ensure a safe supply of oil fuel, since naval
engineering was basing its future upon that. But the

majority had held together. Then the Finance Bill offered an unusual opening for attack. It was, tactically, a very bad one for such a time. The Budget had included some proposals concerning rating which by complicating the Bill and finally compelling a great deal of re-drafting not only produced a distraction of energy disastrous at such a time, but called finally for the first guillotine time-table that had ever been applied to a Finance Bill; so that at the very moment when they most needed to appear conciliatory the Ministry had given another handle for outcries against their over-bearing temper. When the Amending Bill appeared in the Lords, late in June, it was found to be even more conciliatory than Mr Asquith's original scheme; the end of the six years' delay for Ulster was to bring, not automatic inclusion under Home Rule failing other provision, but obligatory reconsideration of the future. Yet even this did not lighten the prospect. The Lords, amending the proposal to the permanent and total exclusion of Ulster, showed that the Opposition were not going to let the Government off. In effect they dared Ministers to drive Ulster to arms; and arrangements were being made for opening English country houses to women and children from there as soon as the fighting should begin.

A last gesture remained. Once already this year Irish affairs had interrupted the King's engagements. In March he and the Queen had been in Lancashire on another of the Royal visits to industry, seeing Port Sunlight and the Cammell Laird shipyards, when the Curragh incident hurried him back to London. They had taken up the round again in April, when they had paid a visit to Paris, less politically intimate than those of which King Edward had the secret, but publicly an enthusiastic success. They had entertained the King and Queen of Denmark in London; and had

returned from a visit to the lace and hosiery regions
of the Midlands late in June, in time for the forms of
sympathy with the Austrian Court in a deplorable
incident in the Balkans, where the Archduke Franz
Ferdinand had been murdered at Sarajevo. On 18th
July the King was to go to Spithead, to review the
assembled fleets. He was late in leaving London, he
took the Prime Minister down with him in the train,
and he came back earlier than he had intended ;
the meaning of all which was that he had invited the
political leaders to a conference on Ulster at the
Palace. The Prime Minister and Mr Lloyd George,
Lord Lansdowne and Mr Bonar Law, Mr Redmond
and Mr Dillon, Sir Edward Carson and Captain
Craig were to try to find some workable scheme of
exclusion.

The political gossips found plenty to talk about.
Constitutional purists remarked upon the dangerous
precedent of the Crown calling into council any but its
Ministerial advisers ; there were scraps of high words
about " a Royal *coup d'état*," and mutterings of the
Ministry being manœuvred into surrenders ; it was
rumoured that the King would not give assent to the
Home Rule Bill without an accompanying Amending
Bill, so that if Unionists could hold up the latter their
game was played for them. It was mainly gossip that
the conference produced, and little hope. No one was
surprised when it broke up quickly. On 24th July
Mr Asquith announced in the Commons that the conference had been unable to come to any agreement
" either in principle or in detail." Two days later, on a
Sunday, Nationalist volunteers pulled off a great gun-
running of their own near Howth, and this time two
or three people had been shot by the regular troops.
The Nationalists were hot for recriminations, and every
thread in the affair was at its highest tension, when on

28th July Sir Edward Grey rose with all his gravity
in the Commons to make a statement concerning the
Austrian rejection of Serbia's reply to an ultimatum
demanding satisfaction for the murder of the Archduke
at Sarajevo.

CHAPTER V

THE WAR YEARS : PART I

THAT last week before the war is extraordinarily
difficult to focus. It is a baffling task to trace
the gradations of national feeling beginning in
a rather relieved turning away from Ulster, moving
through an intensifying consciousness of another crisis
elsewhere, up to the sharp realisation that this crisis
was upon us too. Even to trace a gradation disturbs
the focus. For though that would be historically right,
it is also true that the end had the effect not of a
culmination, but of a sudden shock. Minds had been
moving, but only in a half-light ; what they moved to
blazed as suddenly as if they had been in the dark. So
unbelievable was it that we were in a European war ;
so unmilitary, in spite of all the scares of recent years,
were our habits of thought. At first the clear black-
nesses of the Irish picture were simply " held " ; nothing
else was actually on the screen for us. Then vague grey
shapes flickered, but they might be no more than the
half-seen coincident picture which is often thrown on to
fade and leave the original clear again. Yet they persisted, the original picture dimmed, two pictures hung
there together, until at last suddenly the new picture
stared at us.

Thus Sir Edward Grey's statement on the afternoon
of 28th July evoked only determination to " hang up "
Irish affairs ; a pause of any kind there might save us.
Sir Edward Carson came back from Belfast, and the
Prime Minister announced on 31st July that consideration

of the Amending Bill would be postponed. By that time there were other shadows on the screen; for the ordinary man already had something more in his mind than the feeling that at a time when ultimatums were flying about (and Russia was now emerging behind Serbia) it was unwise for Great Britain to be distracted by a domestic crisis. His newspapers had long familiarised him with the traditional fear among diplomats of any crisis in the Balkans; and their instinctive feeling that, if ever the whole of Europe were to explode, the spark would come from that part of the map. And here was a Balkan incident. He was moreover only too familiar with the idea that Germany was waiting for " der Tag." True, this Sarajevo affair had no more in it essentially than other Balkan incidents to precipitate conflagration; more dangerous incidents had quieted down. But if Great Britain were rent internally, if a Liberal Government, inclined in any case to peace abroad, were in open and notorious difficulty at home, this might be just the touch needed to make Germany snatch at her chance, and use this spark to fire the train. That was to most people what *The Times* meant when it wrote on 29th July of the need to close the ranks at home, and support Sir Edward Grey as the one man able " to limit the area of the war."

There was no great change in the public mind up to the end of that week. The lucky chance that our fleets were all in being for the King's review, and in position to be ordered to stations in the North Sea instead of dispersing for manœuvres, was estimated simply as a happy release from anxiety in a disturbed world, not involving us in anything more than watchful detachment. The week-end is one of the most baffling points of the whole gradation of feeling, for it was, of course, the week-end of the August Bank Holiday; how much of the rising tension was due to a real sense of accumulating peril, and how much to the hypnotised excitement of crowds with little to do but snatch at news ? On the Saturday, 1st August, it was known that Russian mobilisation had brought a declaration of war from Germany ; but this, though it meant that the Balkan incident was threatening, left it Balkan still ; it did not necessarily mean that Germany had taken the tremendous decision. The raising of the bank rate to 10 per cent., a figure it had not touched for fifty years, was merely an item in a general excitement. But on Sunday, 2nd August, the grey shapes really did begin to blur the outlines of what was before us. The drifting crowds of any Bank Holiday Sunday were swollen by hundreds of thousands who found it more exciting to be on the spot in London than to go to the country or seaside. So the event which first threw everything into the high light of " der Tag," the sweeping of France into the war, burst with every possible scrap of its effect. Extra editions of the Sunday papers, with the news that the Germans had crossed the frontiers of France and Luxemburg, were rushed into the streets ; the two meetings of the Cabinet looked far more portentous than the two meetings on Saturday ; and by the evening a vast mass of people were singing the National Anthem and the Marseillaise outside Buckingham Palace.

All the same, they did not quite know what they meant by it. Friendliness and encouragement to France, certainly, and a gesture openly anti-German ; beyond that . . . The British public went to bed that night hardly having yet said those two words. It awoke and, startlingly, the phrase was complete. Beyond that—what ? For the morning papers had the news of the German intention to violate the neutrality of Belgium, and later in the day·it was known that Belgium had appealed to Great Britain. In every city of the kingdom the great crowds drifted as on Sunday ; but less vaguely, because the formless excitement had shaped itself entirely into that great question-mark. For all was uncertainty. Violated neutrality might be a grave outrage ; but no one could gauge the ways of diplomatists or the formulas they might discover. France was at war ; but how much did that mean to us beyond disposition of our fleets ? A Liberal Government was in power which had talked steadily of peace for eight years past ; would they meet the crisis by resignation, or hold on for a way out ? Before people went to bed again the answer was emerging ; it was implicit in the whole of Sir Edward Grey's speech on that afternoon in the House ; it was clear for all who cared to read discerningly in one particular passage, in which, after saying that we had no actual obligations to Russia, no irrevocably *binding* obligations even to France, he went on : " But in view of the Anglo-French friendship let every man look into his own heart and construe the extent of the British obligation for himself." Words like these, from a man who so measured words, could leave little doubt. Even now groups of people, societies and individuals used the few remaining hours to plead for peace. But they availed little ; for everyone had that sense of only a few remaining hours, as soon as it was known that Sir Edward Grey had telegraphed to the German Government for a categorical undertaking to respect Belgian neutrality, and demanding an answer by midnight of 4th August.

Suspense of a kind still existed. We were not taking the broad line of a duty to France ; we were pinning our policy to a specific point, on which it might just conceivably be worth Germany's while to yield, and so allow the peace section of the Cabinet to turn the scale against war. France might well watch us during those twenty-four hours with anxiety and alarm, even if she was a little too impatient with a nation which had lived in so much less familiarity with the idea of war than herself. But there hardly could be said to be a peace section of the Cabinet now, for Lord Morley and Mr John Burns had resigned. And the raising of the specific point proved to be wise; for it was Great Britain's entry into the struggle which made it a world war in the end, and that entry was now to take place, not as a mere tumble into the raw quarrel of France and Germany, but as the defence of international decency. The Cabinet resignations, the prolonging of the Bank Holiday for three days, the taking over by the Government of the railways through a committee of the General Managers, all looked as if the Ministry more than half knew the result of their demand to Germany. No reply came. We were at war.

War. Who can say what the shock of that word meant to the people of Great Britain? On the surface of consciousness a good many things, but none of them approaching in the very slightest to what the reality was to be; and in this, again, France never understood us. She was wholly, instantaneously at war; we were not. We could only envisage confusedly the implications of what had happened. There would be an effort, there would be hard times, and the nation would have to set its teeth and tighten its belt. Many men would have to give up their accustomed lives and fight; we had not supposed, certainly since the Boer War, that our small army could take all the strain; and when the Ministry asked for its first vote of credit of £100,000,000 they had taken authority for enlisting more men. But we had never, in any talk of war, thought of ourselves as providing really great military force; our sphere would be the sea. Yet anyhow the strain must be tremendous. No one could imagine what modern war would cost. And what trade could go on with all Europe ablaze? Only some poor remnant of the marvellous prosperity that we had enjoyed. Some sad loss of life, but far more privation and ruin—unheard-of taxes, idle factories, paralysed ports, and starving people—this was to the majority the extreme spectre of war. It was bad enough ; we had yet to see what our fibre was like after a century since the last real strain ; and we had more to lose, and were in many ways more vulnerable now. We should indeed have to set our teeth. But how few there were who saw any further or could understand Sir Edward Grey's prediction of the ending of the old order over half Europe ; fewer still who guessed for one moment that England as they had known it would never come back again. Yet beneath these surfaces of consciousness, beneath the prospects that could be discerned and put into words, was there not, at least in that first moment, some deeper, more instinctive shock ? For the deeps were stirred. While it may have put the strain it was facing in material terms, what the nation was really thinking of was the spirit it had to meet the strain ; what a great many were thinking of was the fineness that we were going to call upon ; what some at least were confronting was the awful doubt whether such a shattering revelation of mortal impulse could leave any life of the spirit at all. Did not spiritual sensitiveness of so many kinds make an air in which for a few hours something lived that the pressures so soon at work hid again from us ? Was there a strange fleeting vision of a land which, like ancient Egypt, had not a house in which there was not one dead ? Did we, for that moment, catch our breath at something more than the thought of hunger and privation of many sorts ? One can but ask the question now ; what is at least certain is that, however much or little we might be able to express in words, everyone had deep in his mind that it was utterly impossible to say what a war of all Europe might mean. There was more, slight and intangible as it may have been, in the mood of that day than the mere facing of hardship. This could only have brought the days of suspense to a culmination. But they ended in a shock. War. Brief and grim as the word, there was a moment's icy touch upon every soul.

But it was no touch of shrinking or uncertainty. The nation, forgetting everything else, was extraordinarily at one. Very shrewdly the Government issued immediately, on 5th August, a White Paper of information about the recent days. It had all the desired effect on the public mind. There set forth were Grey's strenuous efforts to induce a pause, to assemble a conference, to make Europe think ; there on the other side was the obstinate deafness of Austria. But, far more effective, there set forth was the German Ambassador's conversation with Grey late on 29th July, his cloudy excuses about Belgium, and his suggestion that if Germany made no territorial demands on France in Europe, making colonies the price of defeat, England might agree to come to an understanding and remain neutral. Though the bullying of Belgium soon became the popular justification for war, the first was this attempt to bargain us out of our *entente* with France, the obvious implication that Great Britain would like to dodge the war if she could; and would leave France to fight for her life, if a few diplomatic phrases could be invented to excuse us. The insult may, in the strain of the moment, have been unconscious ; it was none the less real.

The Government had done another shrewd thing. Lord Kitchener, who had in 1911 returned as Agent-General in Egypt to the scenes of his first triumph, happened to be in England in the summer of 1914 making holiday. He was actually at Dover on his way back when, on 3rd August, the Prime Minister stopped him with a telegram. On 5th August it was announced that he had become Secretary of State for War. Nothing

could have more satisfied the public. He had a great
reputation, and the best of it was that he stood for a
master of organisation. His crushing of the Mahdi in
1899 had been said to be the fruit of years of infinite
pains in detail; his clearing up of the South African
war had been attributed to his capacity for creating
a perfect military machine, patiently and persistently
mopping up the guerrilla struggle. The picture of
him in the popular mind—big, strong, impenetrable,
uncommunicative and masterful—was exactly the thing
to create confidence now. A genius at making armies
and keeping them at fighting pitch; uninterested, it
was thought, in anything but the army; above all
entirely clear of politics, his was the very figure to set in
the public eye. Politicians, people felt, might pursue
their ways; if " K " did not like them, they would be
stopped.

The appointment was shrewd in other ways too. It
was so dramatically right that it " blanketed " all the
talk about the necessity now for a Coalition government.
On the Opposition side some newspapers had been
writing as if there could be no doubt; more generally
there was an expectation, without going so far as this,
that the Ministry would make some definite proposal
to Opposition leaders. Nothing of the kind happened.
The Prime Minister received gratefully assurances of
Unionist and Irish support, and carried on. But it
may be questioned whether, without Lord Kitchener,
he could have done so. That stroke by itself put party
feeling aside.

One curious aspect of the beginning of war is the
way in which its coincidence with the August holiday
acted as a piece of good fortune, not only in certain
specific restraints which it imposed, but also in a more
general way by giving time for a reflective pause. The
nation could draw together far better than if war had

come upon it in the midst of its normal occupations ; and it was also an advantage that in any case August is a month in which trade and business are accustomed to running rather slackly. The country thus in its prolonged Bank Holiday watched the first movements, slight as yet, of the machine of war. Railways were taken over with a singular smoothness, which now revealed the fact that the Committee of General Managers acting under the Board of Trade had long existed on paper ; lorries and horse-transport were put under requisition, and official stencil-marks appeared on tradesmen's and farmers' carts and vans. But of course the restraints which a mere prolongation of the holiday imposed were the most important gain. Keeping the banks closed had undoubtedly been intended in the first place to prevent their being caught suddenly by a universal demand for cash ; panic withdrawal of money might have been comparatively small, but since there would have been a natural tendency to think it wise to have a bit more than usual in pocket the banks would have been strained, and the sight of much withdrawing might easily have started panic. That was avoided, and time was given for people to reflect that after all there was no special need for a lot of cash. Also the Government had time to announce and prepare for a substitution of paper currency for gold ; the £1 and 10s. notes, of which the Chancellor of the Exchequer gave notice on 5th August, were ready to be handed over the counters of the banks when they reopened on the 7th ; later in the year the £1 note numbered A000,001 was sold and resold for the Red Cross, reaching a price of about £250.

Quite as important was the fact that the holiday conditions helped to steer us fairly clear, though not quite clear, of panic food-hoarding. Some there was, but as, with banks and shops closed, people could neither get an unusual amount of money, nor do much shopping with what they had, common-sense had time to assert itself. Yet not without a few days of anxiety. There were many cases in every rank of people convinced that there must be a bad pinch, and rushing to buy all the supplies they could lay hands on. Stories were told of houses packed to the attics with provisions, of grocers' shops cleared out, of motor-cars sent round from shop to shop, even from town to town, to pile up reserves in country houses. Nor were the stories only of those with plenty of money to spend. In poorer streets and villages people were doing the same thing on a small scale. The first reaction was the attempt of tradesmen, sincere enough for the most part, though here and there it edged over into profit-making, to conserve their stocks by putting up prices. But that was obviously too rough and ready ; it made the people who had decently re-frained from over-buying suffer for their restraint, and the Ministry hastily set up a Food Prices Committee. This had no power to enforce a scale of prices ; but even the publication of a " recommended " scale had its effect, for the public practically enforced these prices itself ; a sound social spirit had sprung up quite astonishingly. This Committee was the first mild move towards a food control which never became quite complete ; the only compulsion of the moment in this direction was that at this early date the Government did take complete control of the supplies of one foodstuff—sugar.

Of a different kind of commodity they had also taken control—news. There was dead silence about the one fact that everybody wanted to know : had the army crossed to France ? Later on people began to discover that there had been silence about a good many other things. They did not know yet how many of the Territorial Army, mobilised at the time for their annual training (another of the lucky strokes for us of the war coming at the beginning of August) had been moved to posts of defence; nor that the Eastern Counties were already under restrictions; nor that the lighthouses were unlit. A Press censorship had been set up, under Mr F. E. Smith, and the papers were zealous in loyalty to it even before it had quite found its feet. The public, too, was loyal enough in agreeing to silence; but by a very obvious connection grew agitated about other ensurings of secrecy. Since for five or six years past there had been very short intervals without espionage trials on one side and the other, each producing its crop of indignation about the number of Germans and Austrians who had found employment in this country, a strong revival now of expostulation was inevitable. The Government made some reassuring statements of an intentionally vague kind, and the outcry was not as yet virulent.

The far more immediate interest was Lord Kitchener's appeal on 9th August for 100,000 men. Here was something to be busy about, the first definite gesture which the country could make. It had an accompaniment which provided quite as much subject for talk: he had intimated that enlistment would be " for four years or the duration of the war," and that set every tongue wagging. It was from so many points of view extraordinary; true, the Boer War had lasted three years, but only because two of them had dragged out in guerrilla fighting impossible in a European war; how could a clash of trained professional armies last for four years? Again, financially such a prospect was inconceivable. Our first vote of credit was for £100,000,000; if that was to be the scale, mere monetary exhaustion would set in all round within a year at most. Finally everything in the swift German attack, which would not even refrain from violating Belgium, was pointing to tactics and expectations like those of

1870-1871, a rapidly pushed stroke for decision. And yet it was Kitchener, the uncommunicative and the experienced, who was talking of four years. Few people believed him ; this surely was his genius for slow, patient preparation rather over-reaching itself. So " duration " started on its career as a jest, to remain, in the incalculable British way, a jest in dark days when it looked like meaning even more than four years.

The other national response to the crisis besides recruiting was " business as usual." This was not quite as foolish as it came to sound later on. If a rush on the banks had been avoided, and if the public mind was beginning to steady itself about food supplies, there remained the possibility, also in its way a danger, of too much abstention from spending. Under the shadow of the tremendous strain on the Exchequer, and of the rising prices that restriction of supplies must bring, it was thought, people might well decide to go very cautiously, cut down their expenditure, and so, with the best will in the world, make life harder for hands put out of employment. Thus advertising, always eager for a new note, found one in the appeal to enable firms to go on keeping people in receipt of wages, and the old game of commercial competition clad itself in the patriotic mantle of " carrying on " to save labour from distress. The conviction of hard times ahead was so strong that a Relief Fund launched in the names of the Queen and the Prince of Wales met a lavish response, and reached a total of £3,000,000 in a couple of months. The odd thing was that it was very little called upon for its original purpose. Modern war proved to have such utterly unexpected results that, instead of distress, there was almost too much prosperity among those for whom the fund had been intended. Not only did manufacture run into channels demanding more and more, not less and less, labour ; other spectres

of distress turned out to be equally baseless. There was
alarm first about the seaside and holiday places, since
no one would be spending on holidays, and then about
University towns and all lodging-house quarters, losing
the young population that would now go into the army.
No one could possibly foresee how training camps,
hospital and convalescent camps, officers cadet corps
and huge munition settlements would more than make
up the loss. The Relief Fund was in the end mainly
directed to Red Cross purposes.

Our own first war news came, as everyone expected,
from the navy. On 6th August H.M.S. *Amphion* was
sunk by a mine in the North Sea, but she had just been
engaged in sinking a minelayer ; and three days later
H.M.S. *Birmingham* sank a submarine. The first brush
with the enemy was not unsatisfactory. In the next
ten days there was little but the news from Belgium of
the German advance. This was taken as inevitable ;
" little Belgium," gallant as she was, must fall back on
her inner forts, and there could be no attempt to hold
up the grey legions on the frontier ; Namur was the
strong point which would give them pause. Meanwhile
the French had made a counter-stroke across another
frontier and were in Lorraine ; and on the 18th we had
at last the news that the main portion of the British
Expeditionary Force had landed in France without loss
or difficulty. Then suddenly in a new sense the war
began. The French stroke in Lorraine was ineffective ;
the Belgian Government retired to Antwerp, and the
Germans occupied Brussels on the 21st ; by the 24th
Namur, instead of holding out, had fallen. That was
the first real dismay. It was followed within two days
by the accounts of the destruction of Louvain, and this
exploded in a violent outburst all the reports of German
atrocity which had for some days past been gaining
currency. For refugees from Belgium had been coming

into England since the 20th, and had brought with
them stories of their wrecked villages, of ruthless handling of anything that could be called resistance to the
advancing troops, of hasty and wholesale executions of
peasants and townsfolk because some individuals had
been foolishly violent. The burning of Louvain brought
all this to a head, and caught the minds even of those
who had held their judgment suspended about horrors
reported by scared and worn-out fugitives of the type
that had hitherto reached England. The evidence now
was very different ; and that which might have been left
to sink back into its place as mere atrocity-mongering
spread wildly under the appearance of a decent and
righteous indignation. That a few cases of sniping by
civilians, contrary to the laws of war, should be met
by firing a beautiful city, and the destruction of one
of the famous libraries of the world, seemed to leave no
answer to those who had been saying that the Germans
intended to fight with every weapon of brutality, and
to show themselves too clear-headed to bring into war
a civilised mentality. Efficient war must exploit every
frightfulness. That, then, was your great German nation,
and the " Kultur " which was its claim to force its
leadership upon Europe. And *The Times* picked up
another catchword of the bitter and angry passions when
it headed its leading article on Louvain " The March of
the Huns." For a long time nothing was too ghastly for
most of the public to believe. For some reason bitterness
began to fasten upon the Crown Prince even more than
upon the Kaiser. His was the figure most exploited in
cartoons of brutality or looting or bullying, his face in
them growing foxier and foxier as time went on, more
leering, more feebly conceited.

The voices of those who protested against the dreadful readiness to believe anything of the enemy were
drowned. For " stricken Belgium " was the cry to

rouse England, and there was a worried feeling that England was only half-awake. Lord Kitchener, making his first speech in the Lords on 26th August, with a careful adherence to the sheet of paper in his hands, which confirmed everyone's faith in his remoteness from speech-making, amplified but very slightly the news of the army's landing, and announced that the 100,000 men he had asked for were " practically secured." But already they were not nearly enough, and the newspapers had begun to talk about " slackers." Rich people were urged to see that their footmen and gardeners, chauffeurs, gamekeepers and valets went where they were needed, and the hoardings broke out into posters of appeal. A few days later this first wave of worried anxiety rose to its height with the publication on Sunday, 30th August, of the news that the whole French and British forces were in retreat across France and the Germans advancing upon Paris. This was a shocking and awful lifting of the veil. It came, by way of America, without a word of preparation, with no single touch of professional explanation to lighten the " pitiful story," as *The Daily Mail* called it. The next day the Government were hotly assailed : surely there should either have been some preliminary warning that the earliest news might be difficult to understand, or the silence should have been kept a little longer till the news had some kind of perspective ; how had such a baldly grim story been allowed to be our very first vision of our army ? It appeared that the Press Bureau, properly approached before the articles were published, had decided that the shock would be counterbalanced by the stimulus to recruiting, and had therefore permitted publication. Such soothing as the military comments could give the public mind were hastily applied ; by the time the French Government left Paris for Bordeaux on 3rd September people had calmed

themselves to the view that even if the Germans reached
Paris the war was not over, as in 1870-1871, for the
Allied forces were intact, and the moral effect of the
occupation of Paris would be comparatively slight.

All the same, the entirely unfortunate manner of
the first publication of the retreat from Mons had a
disastrous result. Coming on top of the stories of
German atrocities, it must be held very largely responsible for a lamentable embittering of the nation, for the
" hounding " element in the recruiting pressure, for a
state of mind which, if the truth be told, robbed us of
the dignity of France. It had not been ours to meet
the war with the simple and direct movements of a
military nation, the mobilisation *affiches*, the systematic
concentrations of men, the instantaneous change of
front from the mixed civilian life to the clear war-
categories. And now we were not even allowed the
dignity of adjusting ourselves to a supreme crisis in
calmness of mind or confidence. Those first few weeks
must in any case have been weeks of uncertain steps
along strange paths ; they need not have been fretted
as well.

With this sudden exposure of what was going on
behind the official silence came one of the most peculiar
incidents of the war—the epidemic of rumour that
Russian troops had been passing through England for
the Western Front. All along there had been comment
on the vast forces which Russia could bring into play,
and a profound belief in the crushing effect of her sheer
weight if only the necessarily slow-moving bulk could
bring itself to bear before the Germans could free themselves, by an overwhelming rush in the West, to confront
the " steam-roller " in the East. This belief fastened
greedily upon the welcome rumour ; the Russian weight
was coming in on both sides. The astonishing thing
was the highly specific character and unquestionable

authenticity of a very large number of definite accounts
of an occurrence that simply never occurred. People
of the most undoubted veracity and intelligence had
actually seen trains full of troops which were not there.
At first the authorities kept silence ; anything that
cheered up the public was all to the good. Later, as
denials were put about, explanations were attempted :
a train or two of troops from the far north of Scotland,
types strange to English eyes, had undergone an uncontrollable exaggeration. But the whole incident is
really inexplicable ; it amounted to, and must be left
as, a national hallucination. Not even the confirmatory
fact, invented as a joke and widely taken with perfect
gravity, that people had seen the snow of their native
land still on the soldiers' boots, could ridicule the
rumours out of existence.

This was the distraction of a rather blank and anxious
week. Hardly any more news came from France until
the reports on 7th September that the Germans were
" neglecting Paris," and on the 9th that " the tide was
turning." The battles of the Marne and the Aisne had
begun. The publication on the 11th of the first of
General French's despatches certainly turned the tide
at home, with their revelation of the courage and
tenacious skill of the long fighting retreat, their stories
of German masses held up by perfect fire-control, and
of the triumphant steadiness with which highly dis-
ciplined regiments had come through the terribly testing
operations as an unbroken army still. The " pitiful
story " became a magnificent one, the operations, if
alarming, comprehensible and coherent ; there had been
no rout or fatal failure, and a more cheerful energy
could go into all the activities at home.

These were numerous by now. Old organisations of
every kind were finding new work in relieving distress,
in providing temporary employment, in ameliorating

conditions at the hastily run-up training camps for
the recruits. New organisations were few as yet, but
suffragists, responding to the amnesty which had been
declared at the outbreak of war for all suffragists and
other political prisoners, were turning their societies
into Women's Emergency Corps and other such bodies.
Above all, there were two great channels for energy.
One was hospital work. Many great houses had been
promptly offered as hospitals and convalescent homes,
women were flocking in thousands to be trained as
Voluntary Aid Detachments under the Red Cross, and
The Times was starting a fund to provide motor-
ambulances and surgical appliances, and to finance all
the vast expansion of the regular military medical
service that would be called for. The other pressure,
more unexpectedly urgent, was the need for dealing
with the Belgian refugees. They were coming now in a
stream of 300 or 400 a day, and a War Relief Committee
set itself up, with headquarters in some empty premises
in Aldwych, to find them accommodation and food.

For a moment attention went back to politics. The
prolonged session was about to end, and subjects which
had disappeared behind the complete absorption in the
war emerged again. When Mr Asquith announced
that the Ministry did not intend to lose the fruits of the
Parliament Act, and would place the Home Rule and
Welsh Disestablishment Bills on the Statute Book, suspending their operation, however, until after the close
of the war, the House fell back for a day or two into
something like its old inflamed state. Violent things were
said about this taking advantage of the Opposition's
abstention from party action, this " crowning abuse of
the patriotism of the country." Not even the plea of the
wisdom of such a response to the loyalty with which
Nationalist Ireland had on the whole come into the war
could prevent feeling running high ; and it was therefore

a happy inspiration which led Mr Will Crooks, at the moment of prorogation, to ask the Speaker if he would be in order in starting the National Anthem, which he forthwith did. That slight incident was just enough to send members away in a happier and quieter temper.

There was by now a regular, though very small, supply of news from France. Just at the first turn of the tide, Press correspondents had been able to go out to Meaux, and other places close behind the firing line. But as the battle fairly joined the military hand shut down, and nothing came through but a brief daily *communiqué* from French Headquarters, supplemented a little later by descriptive articles from " an eyewitness " at British Headquarters, well-written stuff kept back until a safe interval had passed and the narrative of events could convey no useful information to the enemy. It was not much to have, but it was enough to let people who remembered their Boer War habits buy large maps, and pin little flags here and there upon them when any place was mentioned in the *communiqués*. Maps of the Eastern Front, with all their puzzling names, came also into play, for battle had been joined there too, and the wireless German *communiqués* were fairly ample. Antwerp was holding out, and British marines had been landed at Ostend. The public could take now with some dignity in its sorrow the loss of three cruisers, *Aboukir*, *Hogue* and *Cressy*, in the North Sea ; a submarine had torpedoed one of them, and then got both the others as they stood by to help. More and more, as the news from France told of retreating Germans and advancing Allies, the sting went out of the first shock ; and it was with pride that *The Times* published on 1st October the text of the Kaiser's Army Order, of which there had previously been some reports, giving the Expeditionary Force the name that was to become a cherished distinction—" General French's contemptible little army."

Already the survival of that little army in face of the overwhelming German millions was taking on a touch of the marvellous, and even of the supernatural. From soldiers' letters, from the talk of wounded men at home, there spread gradually a story of heroic shining figures, heavenly figures, who had at a critical moment of the fighting near Mons been seen by our men interposing their immortal mistinesses protectively between the opposing lines and baffling the German advance. Thus, in the twentieth century, the gods and goddesses who saved their chosen heroes on the windy plains of Troy, the " Great Twin Brethren " of the battle of Lake Regillus, came to life again in the persistent legend of " the angels of Mons." Superstition, as the war went on, found plenty of scope in the stories of wayside crucifixes remaining miraculously unharmed when everything round them was shattered and riven by shell-fire ; in the pictures of the *Virgin* of Albert hanging precariously from the top of the battered church steeple, yet never falling, and so on. It began with this profoundly believed legend of angels, which to thousands and thousands of people actually hallowed the exploits of the " Old Contemptibles."

The training camps were alive with the same gay ironic spirit as that which made the old army catch up this name. Luckily the summer and autumn were unusually fine, and the scores of thousands of young men hastily barracked in schoolrooms and institutes, or camped in tents, at first with no uniforms or rifles, and gradually becoming a motley crowd in mingled khaki, plain clothes, and an ugly obsolete blue uniform with a little " fore and aft " cap of which some supplies had been disinterred to serve for the moment, kept up their amazing spirits, drilled and did physical exercises and route-marched all day long, and made the very best of patchy meals and hard and dusty sleeping. The oddest, happiest friendships were made in the mixed ranks of those days, to last till the bloody end which came to nearly all of them ; they were the seeds of the hope that after the war we could never go back to the old mistrust and hostility between classes which had for months shared so cheerily the polishing of buttons, the hungry excitement of " dinner up," the learning of one another's sense of humour, and the long sleepy talks made poignant by the bugles blowing " Last Post " and " Lights Out." Even in the after years, when the pleasant hopes had faded, nothing could spoil the gallant memory of those first recruits. They were the great feature of this autumn in England, the men of Hardy's poem :

> " What of the faith and fire within us,
> Men who march away ? "

For who had not watched them passing, their clouds of dust powdering the green and gold of the hedges ? Few as they were beside the floods of enlisted men of the later years, they seemed to be everywhere ; hardly a village that had not seen some company of them swinging through it ; no town that had not seen its squads marching to the station under some old sergeant. Brown and fit and happy to have " done it," they sang their way along, most often to the neat marching lilt of the sentimental *Tipperary*, sometimes with the irony about themselves they never lost :

> " Send out my mother, my sister and my brother,
> But for God's sake don't send me."

The one thing they never would do was to march to the admirable words and tunes which cultured people provided for them. Where most of the words they sang

came from nobody ever knew; where the tunes came
from was often only too obvious : there are few metres
for which you cannot find a hymn tune.

They were happy men, but they were not enough;
and another bout of bad news early in October led to
fresh recruiting pressures. On the 8th, Antwerp had
been assailed with the first storm of a heavy bombardment. Just as it was known that two naval brigades,
hurriedly constructed by Mr Churchill out of the new
recruits, had been landed there, came the news of the
evacuation of the town, and then of the abandonment
of all its defences. It fell on the 9th; and the naval
brigades after firing hardly a shot could not all be re-
embarked, and large numbers of them had to retreat
to internment in Holland. Mr Churchill was heavily
criticised for this hasty gesture of support for the
Belgians, since it could in any case have done little for
them and ended by losing us some hundreds of men.
An immediate result of these events was a bigger flood
than ever of Belgian refugees, for now that Antwerp had
fallen it seemed doubtful whether any scrap of Belgian
soil would escape the invader. Ostend and the other
coast towns emptied rapidly, and many of the inland
inhabitants, who had felt comparatively safe while
Antwerp held out, waited no longer. The news that
the French Government had offered its hospitality
to the Belgian Court and Government, and that they
had moved to Le Havre, quickened this flight, until
refugees were coming into Folkestone at the rate of
1200 to 2000 a day.

For a week or two the newspapers made the utmost
of the Eastern Front. To the end we never knew much
of the real conditions there, or envisaged easily the vast
areas over which the armies were operating. Moreover
we kept on thinking at this time in terms of " battles."
So the experts who in various newspapers analysed, in

the old Boer War fashion, the daily *communiqués*
worked out visions of German armies on the Niemen
and Austrians round Cracow caught in the vast toils of
the Russian millions, their fronts broken up and their
armies giving way. Hindenburg was being "routed."
Cracow was falling. But attention was soon back in
the West. The Allies were advancing no more, the
Germans were attacking again, and heavy fighting
developing all round Lille. With Ostend in German
hands since mid-October a new idea suddenly illuminated the headlines and the war maps—"The Fight for
the Road to Calais." That was what, to people at
home, the struggle became; if it were lost, a new
Napoleon would be camping his armies by the narrow
Channel for invasion. Or if not for that—if our fleet
still availed to save us, as a century before—there were
perils which we had not faced then. Modern guns would
carry the distance; so near a base for Zeppelins and
aeroplanes would put all England at their mercy. That
danger had become more vivid after the first dropping
of bombs on Paris at the end of September; and this
was why there was such delighted enthusiasm later in
the year when British planes bombed the Zeppelin headquarters at Friedrichshafen. This, too, accounts for the
outbreak just now of a new scare akin to spy-hunting.
There were stories, soon after the German occupation of
Ostend, of the discovery at Dunkirk of concrete beds,
which, laid a few years earlier with a great appearance
of innocence as the floors of villas, were now discovered
to be so immensely solid that they could be nothing but
foundations for big guns, prepared beforehand by the
omnipresent treacherous German. If this had happened
at Dunkirk, it had probably happened at Calais and
Boulogne; indeed it must have, for guns capable of
shelling England would need such bases. And thence
it was but a short step to tales of suspicious concrete

floors in England, awaiting the German invaders who
would know where to find them. The scare had a long
run ; it put Scotland Yard to work, and was not even
damped by the conclusive reports of artillery experts,
who had inspected these places, and tried to make clear
to civilians how impossible it was that the very scientific
and prolonged work of constructing a big-gun platform
could ever be disguised as the mere laying of a concrete
floor. People went on hunting, for it was an irresistible
temptation to ingenuity ; and inevitably the whole spy
scare revived, with endless tales of mysterious use of
lights at night, and with the first hints of wireless
installations concealed in chimneys. The notorious
" Hymn of Hate," of which the words were published
about now, was dragged into the business ; a nation
which went to war like that could not possibly have any
innocent subjects, and every German name must mean
a hidden enemy. More especially the outcry turned
against highly placed or wealthy persons of foreign
origin still allowed to live in London or in such danger-
spots as the Eastern Counties. One result before long
was that Prince Louis of Battenberg, though everyone
who knew anything knew how entirely devoted to his
profession he was, resigned the post of First Sea Lord.
" My birth and parentage," he wrote with dignity,
" have the effect of impairing in some respects my
usefulness on the Board of Admiralty." He was succeeded by Lord Fisher, exactly the man to suit public
opinion, for he was in the popular mind the navy's
counterpart of Lord Kitchener at the War Office. Very
different in character, far from uncommunicative and
impenetrable, he was yet thought of in the same way
as the ruthless genius of organisation, damning all
politicians and caring for nothing but the service.

The possibility of the Germans reaching Calais produced a busy discussion of the position of civilians

under invasion. The presence of swarms of Belgian
refugees, who had actually undergone the humiliation
of helplessly watching an enemy march over their land,
made the discussion full of meaning. What it came to
turn on in the end was the question whether the Government could not give civilians who were still able-bodied,
if unfit for the army, some status which would let them
fight at the last; and that question came down to a
specific point, the recognition of the Volunteer Training
Corps, which had sprung up all over the country. They
were largely scoffed at; what good could they possibly
be, and what chance would they have of ever acquiring
arms ? Masses of the new army recruits were still
without rifles. The place for the more elderly able-
bodied was where thousands by this time were serving,
in the Special Constabulary. That had been organised
since 17th August, the calling up of the Reserves having
depleted the police ranks most seriously, and the enrolled
men were on duty at waterworks, shipyards, gas and
electric-light works, and were beginning to do some
street duty. If an elderly man wanted to serve, this was
his way to give up his time, break his night's rest, and
face weariness and the weather. But though this might
give scope enough in big towns it gave none in small
towns or country places, and the Volunteer Training
movement went on. The War Office authorities were
dead against it; they probably did not desire in any
case to complicate their plans for meeting invasion by
having to include in them great numbers of amateur
soldiers; they strongly objected to any organisation
which might give the shelter of a sort of military service
to men whom they wanted to see in the army, and in
this they had a great deal of public support. So, though
the Central Committee of the V.T.C. succeeded after
a while in extracting a red armlet from the authorities,
they had to wait some time before any kind of uniform

for them was sanctioned, and they never escaped from a certain amount of ridicule.

The recruiting pressure was rising in intensity. Such a figure as 100,000 meant nothing now; the Government were talking about a million. Colonial contingents were already raising our numbers, for the response of the Empire had been swift. Canadian units were in training camps, and many more being recruited. Australians and New Zealanders were on the way. South Africa was to belie magnificently all the apprehension which had been felt when, so short a time after the end of the Boer War, she had been given full self-government. Some echoes of that apprehension had been heard; reviving memories of the Kaiser's telegram to the Boers in 1899 caused some anxiety lest now Boer feeling might turn against us. There was not the least sign of that in the South African Government. They set themselves to the most immediate form of assistance, taking off our hands any concern about the German colonies in Africa; they invaded at once German South-west Africa, and prepared an expedition against German East Africa. Contingents were forming for service in France as well.

The Empire's response was used as one more stimulus to recruiting at home. The life of fit young men in civilian occupations was becoming a burden to them. Newspapers were always wanting the country roused. For though the fight for Calais was losing no ground, the casualty lists were by now beginning to reveal its price. They were small as we came to know casualty lists later, but they were drain enough then on the army as it was : the total loss in killed and wounded was given in mid-November as 57,000, and the worst of the Flanders fighting had yet to show its results. For this was when the great name of Ypres first came into the news, as the scene of a long scattered engagement rising to two intense periods, one just before the end of

October, and the other about 11th and 12th November, with the famous defeat of the Prussian Guard Corps. For some part, at least, of the embittered recruiting pressure there was the excuse that the slaughter was directly or indirectly upon so many people's nerves. Yet much of the pressure in pulpits as well as on platforms was sentimental and often revoltingly complacent; a leading article of this time could actually say : " To some of us elders the war may be a catastrophe. . . . Fortunate are our young men to be young at this time." There in a nutshell is the kind of senseless and cruel pomposity which the younger generation of the war time cannot be expected to forgive.

The truth is that through all the first period of the war to the early summer of 1915 the view of the British public was that the fighting part of the war, so to speak, was a professional business, and that the national part was backing up. The great Red Cross effort to extend the medical services ; the Y.M.C.A. appeal for funds for huts to make training-camp life more comfortable ; working parties everywhere making socks and mufflers for the troops ; " business as usual " pleading that it provided funds for all these activities ; racing as usual, football as usual (though the latter was now being heavily criticised), pleading that they refreshed and amused the workers—this was not a nation at war, but a nation supporting and encouraging part of itself at war. And that accounts for the character and temper of the recruiting pressure ; it was too easy to live in all good faith in the " national " part and push other people into the other part.

It was certainly with every belief in its good faith that the nation settled down to the winter. The line taken by the newspapers for the next few months was that of a great national readiness and determination, if only the Government would understand how to handle

it. " Take us into your confidence," the leading articles
kept saying : " trust us not to be panic-stricken. The
nation offers its whole strength, the truth of the war
situation probably is that you need it ; but until you
bring the truth and the nation together you will not
get the strength." That argument had begun with the
sparseness of news from France ; it might have become
less insistent with the slackening of the fight in Flanders,
which was developing, as Lord Kitchener said when
Parliament met again, into a form of siege warfare. But
it revived vigorously with a trickle of piecemeal information early in November of the loss of a cruiser—two
cruisers—some cruisers—in the South Pacific. When
finally the extent of Admiral Cradock's defeat was
known, the Admiralty became the scapegoat of all the
outcry against over-secrecy. What of the two German
cruisers, *Goeben* and *Breslau,* which, nominally interned
at Constantinople, were at large under the Turkish flag
since Turkey had come into the war ? What about
the converted merchantman, *Emden,* which had suddenly
shelled Madras, and had been sinking shipping all over
the Indian Ocean till she was put out of action, just
about this time, by the Australian cruiser *Sydney* ?
What about the cruiser *Königsberg,* which might or
might not be bottled up by now in an East African
river ? What had held back for so long the casualty
lists after the sinking of *Aboukir, Hogue* and *Cressy* if
not the foolish nervousness which had at one time forbidden the newspapers to mention the opening of the
large supplementary war hospitals, in case the public
should be depressed ? Such was the " unworthy fear
of panic." It happened that the end of November
saw another disaster,. the blowing up of the battleship
Bulwark, in Sheerness harbour, with the loss of about
750 lives, and this intensified the criticism. It was a
startling and inexplicable affair. The authorities might

be positive that it was an accident, and talk about the still unknown dangers in storing modern explosives, but it drove the spy scare to extremes again, clamouring that it was nonsense to pretend that the disaster could not be accounted for while enemy agents were at large; and the Admiralty's real inability to explain was attacked as more evasion and nervousness.

So the national attitude became one of offended dignity in reproach of a Government out of touch with its spirit. It took the first War Budget calmly, with the doubling of the income tax and a heavy stiffening of the duties on intoxicants; and it handsomely oversubscribed the first War Loan of £350,000,000. It greatly modified its tone about the Eastern Front, making much, no doubt, of Hindenburg's defeat at Lodz, and of the capture of Cracow, but warning itself not to exaggerate the effects. It felt no more than the legitimate recovery of its pride when the news came that the German ships which had sunk our cruisers off Coronel had been caught and sunk themselves off the Falkland Islands; in the rapidity and conclusiveness of this riposte the public saw with delight the authentic hand of Fisher.

It was becoming both possible and necessary to envisage a little more clearly the question of the Belgian refugees. At first there had been nothing to do but handle as well as might be the flood of arrivals, just seeing that they did not starve. But by now the stream had ceased. Great numbers were dispersed all over the country, as guests of individual people or occupying empty houses under the care of local committees. Many odd situations developed. The central committee had no time to sort out refugees for the private houses which offered hospitality, and hosts and guests found themselves often with but strained means of contact. Local committees were taken aback by finding their

kindliest efforts accepted as the least that rich England
could do to pay her obvious debt to Belgium ; or were
harassed by discovering that, instead of being all merged
in a common suffering, Belgian class feeling still had
very sensitive toes to be trodden on. There was much
to come of both tragic and comic misunderstanding.
But for the moment what chiefly concerned the central
committee, relieved of much of its pressure, but still
with a great many persons hastily quartered at the
Alexandra Palace, was the effort to find employment
for them, partly as a means of support, but much more
to take up their minds and preserve their self-respect.
Rather ambitious plans of the moment, such as a scheme
for planting a whole Belgian " colony " somewhere,
came to nothing. The refugees, some drifting back
abroad as time went on, many drafted into the Belgian
army, but in the mass continuing under the care of
local committees and finding occupations in the war's
increasing demand for labour, ceased to be an urgent
problem, and became so familiar that we were apt to
forget their weariness of exile.

For the rest, the great preoccupations—the wounded,
the men in the trenches, the men in the training camps—
could not but grow more vivid as Christmas approached.
The illustrated advertisements turned more and more
into displays of what could be bought for them all.
Shopping, indeed, was requiring a stimulus. The diminution of the lighting of London at night (though it was
not yet in darkness) had reacted upon some kinds of
spending ; theatres and restaurants were doing bad
business in this first phase when there were few men on
leave to entertain, and the rest of the nation was not
yet feeling itself so caught into the war that it had a
right to amusement. For the same reasons much other
expenditure had decreased. One of the minor interests
of the time is the sign of change in women's dress ;

elaborate swathings and complicated lines went suddenly
out of fashion ; hats were growing smaller, waists and
hips disappearing ; and altogether, though skirts were
still of ankle-length, the fashion pictures for the first
time begin to be something not wholly fantastic to the
eyes of later young women. It all meant that costly
materials, furs, expensive styles were frowned upon ;
the big department stores and Bond Street itself were
feeling a pinch ; the papers took to' rebuking a little
robustly " ostentatious retrenchments " ; and meanwhile the booming of Christmas presents for the men
might help. Life in the training camps was being made
more vivid by articles about the country in war-time ;
life even in the trenches as vivid as it could be made
by daily columns of extracts from the private letters of
all ranks, and strangely telling these intensely personal
little moments of the army's days and nights often were.
They did much to make us familiar with the soldier's
life, his amiable way of adapting foreign words to his
own tongue, in place-names like " Wipers " and " Plug
Street," and phrases like " Napoo " ; the invincible
spirit which gave nicknames to the shells under which
he suffered, like " Jack Johnson " and " Black Maria "
and " Whiz-bang " ; the imperturbability with which
he made trench life a sort of caricature of life at home,
with London street-names stuck up as guides through
the maze of trenches which could already be described
as " a warren," and his perilous dug-outs called after
luxurious hotels. More curious were the bits of trench
slang now becoming familiar, the origin of which could
never be discovered, like the name " Blighty " for
England, coming in time to have the happy meaning
of a wound that took one home out of the fighting ; or
that expression by which the soldier so subtly eased his
talking of things that often had to be talked about—
" going west." Quantities of ingenious derivations in

the newspapers never really explained these phrases, any more than the French were ever able to explain why their soldiers called the Germans " Bosches " and their wine ration " pinard."

How much more familiarity with the trenches began to mean as Christmas approached ! And then what quiet feelings Christmas might have brought were lost in the storm of anger when, on 16th December, German warships shelled Scarborough, Hartlepool and Whitby for some hours, killing over a hundred people. This was the first loss of civilian life in England, and it added violent fuel to the outcry about German atrocities ; we were now to begin to suffer what the Belgians had been describing to us. For these were harmless " open " towns ; the description of them in the German wireless *communiqués* as " fortified places " was resented as flagrant lying, and the subsequent excuse that there were camps in the neighbourhood mere cowardly quibbling by a navy which would not fight, but only seize a safe opportunity to dash out and murder defenceless people at long range. The attack could be nothing but " frightfulness." At this moment the announcement was made of the appointment of a committee to investigate the charges of atrocity in the German occupation of Belgium ; whatever the committee might ultimately say, the public fastened upon the enemy the bitter name of " baby-killers," and fastened it the more as the early months of 1915 brought the first Zeppelin raids—at Yarmouth, Cromer and King's Lynn, on 20th January, on Tyneside and at Lowestoft in April, and at Southend in May.

All of a piece with this spirit, and taken as justifying it to the whole neutral world, came the German proclamation on 18th February stiffening their submarine warfare. Its original terms were soon much modified, as the result of protests by the United States, for Germany still had hopes of that nation. But even in its modified form the submarine campaign remained in the popular mind as a form of " frightfulness." The feeling was that it was underhand fighting, resorted to because the German navy could not stand against ours openly ; when some German warships were caught in the North Sea, on 24th January, by Admiral Beatty's cruisers, they had lost one ship, the *Blucher*, and two others had only just escaped, badly damaged. In general the use of submarines raised questions of the customs of war which were hotly discussed ; it substituted for the traditional taking of prizes—practically impossible for submarines—sheer destruction of shipping and human lives. " Piracy " it was angrily called, as day after day brought news of vessels sunk round our coasts. There was as yet no grave public alarm about these losses, even though food prices were beginning to rise ; wheat was up from thirty-six shillings to sixty shillings a quarter. The figures given by the Admiralty on 8th April, showing that we had lost thirty-seven merchant-men and six fishing vessels since the German proclama-tion, could not be taken as a serious depletion of our shipping ; and there had been more surprise than any other feeling when it had come out on 9th February that the *Lusitania* had arrived in Liverpool under the American flag ; it was not thought that we needed to employ such subterfuges. Still, if there was no actual alarm, there was a good deal of uneasiness as people noticed where sinking of ships were taking place. The loss of a warship, *Formidable*, on New Year's Day, was only announced as " in the Channel " ; the fact that it was as far down the Channel as off Lyme Regis was not known till much later. But merchantmen were known to have been sunk off Fleetwood and elsewhere along the western and south-western coasts ; and the proof that enemy submarines could operate as freely as that was uncomfortable.

The principal reason for absence of alarm was that, as no one even now had any conception of the duration of the war, this kind of destruction of shipping was not regarded as likely to bring us into real peril; there would not be time for that. We could not get away from old-fashioned views of a war, from what we knew of past wars. There had always been a winter pause; and this, rather than the coming of new conceptions of war, explained the deadlock of the trenches in France and Flanders. Naturally the armies had dug themselves in; it was a kind of hibernation such as we read of in histories of the Crimea. With the spring and summer battle would return, and decisive events supervene. There was, too, something reminiscent of the Crimean War and its institution of the Victoria Cross in the announcement in the New Year Honours list of a new decoration, the Military Cross; but this was to be more freely given, as a decoration for junior officers. Another event of this time was the raising of a regiment of Welsh Guards, to give Wales an honour which the other parts of the kingdom already possessed; they mounted guard for the first time on St David's Day of 1915.

This notion of a mere winter pause accounts for many aspects of the public mind just now. It accounts for the spirit which could still enjoy the extravagant New Year supper-parties of the big hotels, adorned indeed with the flags of the Allies, and accompanied by the playing of various national anthems, as well as for the spirit that angrily criticised this thinly disguised pleasure-hunting. It accounts for the somewhat amused superiority with which many people regarded the innumerable committees and working parties and V.A.D. classes and parcel-sending and writing to lonely soldiers and volunteer drilling; a great deal of useful work was being done, no doubt, but there was also a great deal of fussiness of idle people jumping at anything which could

give them some importance, and hanging, as it were,
on to the skirts of a war which they could not affect
in any way. It accounts, too, for the comparatively
languid interest taken in events in the Near East which
were coming into the war news. The Turks were threatening the Suez Canal, but this was not " the war." It
was thought that across the deserts Turkey could make
no very effective attack, and the Australian contingents
there, stopped on their way to Europe for the defence
of Egypt, could be trusted to deal with them. And
when the first news came of bombardment of the
Dardanelles the comment was that it was " a good
touch of imagination "; it would give the Turks something else to bother them, while the Russians moved
down into Asia Minor, and it gave one of our newest
great battleships, *Queen Elizabeth*, a chance to try her
strength.

Above all, the sense of impending decision tended to
keep up all the fretted, irritable strenuousness of the
people who were convinced that most other people were
behaving as if they did not know that " there was a war
on." The recruiting pressure, part of it growing more
and more explicit as a demand for conscription, continued, in spite of the warnings that all the reproaches
hurled about must be producing in Germany as well as
in France the very poorest impression of our capacities
and determination. One particular form taken by the
pressure just now was the discussion, often in a tone
which seemed hardly civilised at all, whether the younger
clergy should or should not enlist as combatants. The
clergy submitted themselves to the judgment of the
Bishops. Against all the specious phrases about " a
war for civilisation " and " a war against atrocity "
the Bishops held their ground in refusing to sanction
enlistment of men who had taken upon them the peculiar
obligations of the ministry. But unfortunately the result

seemed to be that the ministry was more than ever
anxious to blazon its " patriotism " in ways that were
left to it, the pulpits and recruiting platforms ; and its
peculiar obligations were, with far too few exceptions,
more deeply betrayed than they would have been by
bearing arms. Dr Lyttelton, the Headmaster of Eton,
venturing in a sermon at Westminster Abbey to plead
for less hatred and hounding, had to learn himself what
hounding meant.

In March the people who were so full of patriotism
found a new quarry. With all the cautious phrasing of
the Press censorship information began to appear about
strikes of engineers on the Clyde. Here then, it was
said, were people most flagrantly of all behaving as if
there were no war on, striking in the nation's hour of
need. As another side of the question began to come out,
with the strikers' claim to some share in profits which,
when people thought for a moment, must obviously be
falling to the employers with enormous war contracts,
the patriotic cry shifted into a general indictment of
labour for slackness and bad time-keeping, and drinking
habits largely responsible for those two faults. This new
indignation rose rapidly, and applauded itself as well as
Kitchener when, on 16th March, he made an appeal to
workers to mend all their ways and throw every effort
into the production of what the war required.

By the time he spoke, events had occurred which gave
fresh point to his words. On 11th March had come the
news of the capture of Neuve Chapelle, and " a striking
British advance." For the first few days this had
nothing but a heartening effect. The deadlock was
loosened, all in our favour, and now was the time for
the utmost effort, lest the decisive moment catch us
with our strength not yet deployed ; every possible man
must be in the army by the summer, every ounce of
work put out at home. Mr Lloyd George was meeting

the trade unionists, and his interviews were said to be
" satisfactory," with assurances of full-time work and
no stoppages. When Kitchener in his message to the
workers spoke of having the gravest anxiety about
"the supply of war material at the present time and
for the next few months," his words suggested no acute
difficulty ; for some time past we had been hearing
constantly of artillery duels, and it was natural to
suppose that the beginning of more movement would
require more supplies ; besides, there were the big new
armies to equip. The great thing was that the war
was moving.

Then, about a week later, the tone changed badly.
The fuller accounts of the fighting were coming, and so
were the terrible casualty lists. We had moved forward,
but at a frightful cost for a small advance ; and the
worst of it was that the messages now sent home indicated quite clearly that the war was not " moving "
as people had too hastily thought, and that what had
chiefly been learned was that we were only at the
beginning of the experience of modern war. A sense
of confusion, of a disorganised piecemeal inferno, with
communications all shattered, units left " in the air,"
artillery out of touch, and coherent command impossible,
disengaged itself from the messages ; and all the promise
faded out of the achievement. Worse still, the achievement almost turned into a disaster with its revelation
of the terrible need for shells, and with the very disquieting impression now becoming current that some
people had known of the need all along, and the public
had been kept in the dark again. In a few days little
was left of Neuve Chapelle but the sense of a costly—
some were saying a wickedly costly—lesson ; and the
next two months were full of controversy, exaggerated
and confused statements, angry accusations, culminating, with certain terrible incidents, in a wild rise of the

bitterest of war temper. First of all, people swung to
extremes about the habits of labour. They clutched at
Mr Lloyd George's facile phrase-making when he said :
" We are fighting Germany, Austria, and drink, and so
far as I can see the greatest of these three deadly foes
is drink." The superficiality of this was for the moment
lost in its effects. Patriotic people, of the kind who in
previous years had been the first to dismiss his speeches
as cheaply slashing, now applauded loudly ; labour,
which had enjoyed his abuse of dukes, grew hotly resentful, as well it might, now that his habits of speech
laid them under a wholesale imputation of vicious self-
indulgence, an imputation taken, whatever Mr Lloyd
George may have intended, as applying to their class
alone. A few weeks of heated argument followed. Ideas
of prohibition of intoxicating liquor were in the air ;
they modified into Budget proposals for drastic increase
of duties to check consumption. On the other side grew
a protest against exaggeration, a plea for return to a
sense of proportion, recognising that drink might be an
item, but was no more than that, in the problem of
munitions ; and the voice of common sense, pointing
out that far more harm than good might be done by
suddenly cutting off all liquor from men accustomed
to it in their hard work, besides the certainty that
any such step would throw the country into the worst
possible humour. In the end the taxation proposals
were dropped, and a measure of Government control
in scheduled areas was established ; but for the rest
emphasis turned towards voluntary restraint, and much
was expected from the example set by the King
when, at the beginning of April, he ordered that till
the close of the war no intoxicants were to be served
in the Royal palaces. At the height of the discussion
the Commons found themselves asked to account for
the bland keeping open of their own bars ; and men

on leave from France had biting comments to make on civilians whose one thought, when the taxation proposals were announced, was to rush for stores of whisky before the new duties could be imposed.

Side by side with all this, other conflicts about the production of munitions were being angrily pursued. What, to begin with, was the truth ? Lord Kitchener and Mr Lloyd George had appeared to indicate that Neuve Chapelle had betrayed a terribly perilous defect, an ignorance or stupidity about war conditions which had been murderous to our men at the front. Yet it was recalled that in January Lord Haldane had talked of our " great and increasing progress with regard to artillery " ; now, a month after Neuve Chapelle, Mr. Asquith was denying that our attacks had been crippled by lack of munitions, and that the casualty lists had been swollen by that lack ; and Mr Lloyd George was giving figures of a remarkable development of munition output ; if, he said, our production in September 1914 was taken at the index figure of 20, the figure for March 1915 was 388, and that by a steady growth, not a sudden burst. What were people to believe ? Had there been some gross incompetence which Ministers were now trying to conceal, or was there a deep military disagreement somewhere ? Again the public had the maddening sense of swinging between blank secrecy and most dismaying exposures.

The real trouble, the secret struggle in the Cabinet which was causing all this haziness and inability to get the truth out, was not fully known till long after, when war memoirs began to be published, and Mr Lloyd George's contradictory speeches could be explained in the light of his increasing engrossment with a new war career for himself. But enough was known even at the time to cast a first cloud on Lord Kitchener's popularity. Talk began to leak out of his being too autocratic, keeping too much in his own hands the information from the army commanders, concealing facts out of professional jealousy of civilian interference, so that his colleagues were left to speak in this bewildering way. *The Times* managed to be frank enough : " The War Office," it wrote, " has sought to do too much . . . it cannot hope to organise a nation which its own chief has in many ways curiously failed to understand." The latter phrase hinted at the standing suspicion that news was suppressed or " doctored " for fear of alarming the public. The former phrase summed up the general feeling now emerging from the munitions controversy : it was not merely a question of trade union labour, it was one of properly organising the whole nation. Not only the War Office but the Government as a whole had sought to do too much. Mr Bonar Law had been asking why use was not made of the business man ; newspapers were urging the organising of the employer instead of concentrating on the habits of the wage-earner. The first response was little but a sop to the outcry, when a business man, Mr Booth, was appointed to a new War Office committee on munitions. This would not do. The point was that the War Office must no longer try to keep this matter as purely military ; its business as a department was to organise armies ; for the rest, it should state its requirements and leave them to others to supply. A more adequate response was the appointment on 16th April of an outside committee on munitions, mainly composed of the heads of great engineering firms, with Mr Lloyd George as chairman.

But the public was far too upset to be satisfied by such steps. It was avenging its sense of a general futility partly in carpings at the Government for not telling it what to do, partly in more abject ways. Anger about German methods of warfare, with all the civilian

casualties in the naval and airship raids and the submarine campaign, turned to ill-tempered nagging about
the treatment of German prisoners of war in England ;
a bitter clamour to punish their country through them,
and assertions that they were made more comfortable
than they deserved, finally went as far as accusations
that the Prime Minister and his wife were closely, and
even treacherously, interested in officers interned at
Donington Hall, and no rumour was too ugly for
credence. All that Lord Haldane had done for the
army, and the fact that it was his reorganisation which
had enabled us to enter on the war even as effectively
as we had, was overwhelmed now in the silly reminders
that he had had much of his early education in Germany,
and a phrase he had once used, a phrase to the effect
that Germany was his spiritual home, was flung against
him, with no reference to its context. "Hounding" was
again finding a quarry.

Into all this recrimination fell the news of the landing
of troops at the Dardanelles ; Gallipoli was a word that
we only began to use later. The news was not wholly
a surprise. Since the first bombardment of the forts
at the Narrows there had been plenty of rumour of a
Dardanelles expedition, plenty of rumour too of divisions
in the Cabinet about it. On the whole opinion was
against it, criticising Mr Churchill for being headstrong
again as he had been in the Antwerp expedition, and
forcing through his policy even when Cabinet dissension
had gone far to wreck it. For the news that the landing
had been "strongly opposed" obviously meant that, if
Mr Churchill's plans had been divided and delayed, they
had better have been given up ; the bombardment had
merely given the Turks a couple of months' warning.
And the argument that the expedition was a dangerous
distraction of force from the real theatre of decision
grew very strong when the day that brought the news

of the landing brought also news of another heavy German attack near Ypres. This was "the fight for Calais" again; it might be the decisive fight, and we were throwing away thousands of men.

Then in the week that followed even the terrible cost of the Gallipoli landing, more and more bloodily revealed as the longer accounts came through, was eclipsed by a new horror. The early reports of the renewed fighting round Ypres had given as the main reason for the loss of ground by both the French and ourselves that the troops had been driven out of the trenches by clouds of asphyxiating gas.[1] The immediate outburst of anger at this was strong enough. Here was another proof that the enemy would stick at nothing, another gross rupture of solemn undertakings; for civilised nations had agreed at The Hague Conferences to abstain from the use of poison gases in warfare. Was there no limit to German abominations? But this immediate anger was nothing beside the fury of lacerated feeling when articles began to appear describing the peculiarly dreadful suffering and slow agonised dying that gas inflicted. The terrible thing was that this kind of agony permitted of published detail which would have been impossible in the case of torturing mutilation by shell-fire; so that nothing was spared of the visions of men convulsed, discoloured and ghastly in the appalling and hopeless fight for breath. Never again in the war was there horror quite so rending as that.

Even before the worst descriptions came through, counter-measures had been taken. Dr J. S. Haldane had been sent over instantly to diagnose the nature of the gas, and had reported it as some form of chlorine or bromine. The German troops coming on behind the gas wave had been observed to be wearing respirator-

---

[1] "Eyewitness" had mentioned the expectation of some such thing in a message published about a fortnight earlier.

pads over the mouth, and an appeal was issued for
the provision of similar pads for our men. These were
easily made, and within two or three days an ample
supply had been received. But they were only a primi-
tive precaution, and a week later it was announced that
the War Office was considering forms of defensive equipment, which took shape as the once-familiar " P.H."
helmet of greyish flannel impregnated with protective
solution, and provided with talc eye-pieces. It was an
awkward safeguard, for the long neck-piece had to be
very carefully tucked into the collar all round, and this
was a slow cumbrous job for a man loaded with his
equipment. But it served its purpose while the use of
gas was still occasional and experimental.

Besides the physical horror of the gas attack its
effect had revived all the anxiety about the holding
of our ground and a possible break-through to Calais.
Immediate apprehensions were soon stilled. Trenches
might be cleared in this way, but troops advancing
behind gas had to be slow and cautious; the business
came back to fighting in the end, and then we gave
way no more. The line round Ypres had been bent in
a little; that was all. And again the Germans were
accused of being cowardly quibblers, for in their *communiqués* they were justifying themselves by asserting
that the Allies had been on the point of making use of
poison gas themselves, whereas it must be obvious that
if this had been true we should not have been taken
wholly by surprise and unprovided with the respirator-
pads the Germans had used. But this raised the other
point which was now discussed : were we going to
retaliate in kind, and use poison gas ourselves ? We
were in fact using it a few months later.

Upon the very height of this horror came another—
the sinking of the *Lusitania* on 7th May with the loss of
over a thousand lives. At this the rage against all of

enemy blood broke loose. Mobs in London and other towns attacked hundreds of shops and restaurants which bore German or Austrian names, so thoroughly that for a day or two there was something like a bread famine in East and South London, where very many of the bakers were of these nationalities. Nor was it mob action only; bodies like the Royal Exchange, the Baltic, and other such organisations in London and elsewhere, intimated to members of German or Austrian birth that they had better absent themselves; and every form of exasperated spy-hunting and denunciation was rife. The Government, under attacks in the Commons which revealed the very large numbers of enemy aliens still at large in the country, some 40,000, had just admitted that new circumstances had arisen and called for much stronger action, when the report of the committee on German atrocities in Belgium drove feeling to white heat. The committee, which included men of such cautious minds as Lord Bryce and Mr H. A. L. Fisher, found that there was evidence of indefensible massacres of civilians, looting and rape; and even evidence of what quiet people had been most reluctant to believe— the use of women and children as screens for advancing troops, and murders by crucifixion. The attacks on enemy aliens developed into such violence that troops had to be called out. The Prime Minister spoke of "internment on a huge scale," and plans were immediately announced for incarcerating almost every enemy alien in the country; exemption henceforth would be very jealously granted.

The public mind was at the fever-pitch which ended this first stage of the war. Fighting on all the fronts was acute; at Arras, in the Lens—La Bassée sector, at Festubert, British troops were gaining ground; in Gallipoli we were making good the heroic landing; but on the Eastern Front Mackensen was badly breaking

the Russian lines in Galicia. By mid-May Italy was in
the crisis of decision, and by the 24th she had come in
on the side of the Allies, and declared war. After the
sinking of the *Lusitania* and the killing of so many
and such prominent American citizens what would the
United States do ? This was not a new question ;
common public opinion had been impatient enough
already with what it regarded as the failure of the
other great English-speaking country to rise to its duty.
Now even those who had not these easy views, but
understood something of the mixed character of the
population of the United States, and its traditionally
aloof policy, and could conceive that financially and
in other ways that country might be of far more value
as a non-combatant, began to think that German
submarine warfare might well drive the States into
hostilities.

So an impression of crisis all round, coming on top
of the storm of rage at German methods and of the
revelation from all the fronts of what intense prolonged
effort victory in modern warfare would exact, brought
to a kind of culmination the gnawing sense that we
had gone to war confusedly, weakly, with energies so
ill-directed that they were dislocating, instead of co-
ordinating, the nation's strong limbs. Impulses were
pushing in one direction ; in every phase of life there
were sensible reasons and arguments pulling in another.
Young men were wanted for other work than sitting
on office stools ; but business must not be disorganised
and trade impoverished by hasty recourse to untrained
substitutes; chauffeurs and men-servants would be better
in training camps, many more farm-hands might be
spared, but families must not be suddenly deprived of
wage-earners ; women's capacities on the land could
not reach beyond dairying, and it would be short·
sighted patriotism to take boys from their schooling.

A few women were coming into business ; very few as yet were replacing chauffeurs ; some clubs—even the Athenæum—had made the experiment of introducing parlourmaids into their staff. This mental conflict, the state of mind that could even argue about conscription on a basis of historical constitutional rights of the Crown and the individual, made a poor showing beside the clear-cut drafting of men in a militarist nation ; but then it could be argued that no small part of our contribution to the war was to preserve civilian resources for the war supplies and the finance of the Allies ; and we should therefore fail in our duty, rather than perform it, if we eased our minds impulsively by conscription, and drained our business world as France had had to drain hers. All the difficulties came in the end to the one cry of the moment : the Government had no right to leave the country in this tangle of personal and individual decision ; it must say what people should do ; it must allot the tasks ; it must " mobilise the nation." And this was increasingly the specific loudly urged for the industrial troubles. There was no striking for the time being ; but in certain districts the men were said to be but sullenly and slackly at work. If the nation were mobilised, then industry would be as distinctly active service as the army, war profits would cease and the discontent about them, factories would be under discipline. Granted that our peculiar duty was more complicated than that of France, as being a deliberate mixture of military and civilian effort, new in the world's history, there was all the more need for some new kind of " regimenting " of the nation.

And all the while that these currents of dissatisfaction and uneasiness were concentrating in that single idea other currents of public affairs were concentrating too, and political uneasiness turning in a single direction. The early mishandling of war news in an alternation of dead silence and alarming announcements was being paralleled maddeningly in the fog that overhung the shell controversy. The Dardanelles expedition was suspected, if not known, to have been weakened by disagreements far too vital to the nation to be properly left to a party Cabinet. In the matter of enemy aliens the Government had been far too lenient ; in the matter of national service, far too dilatory. What all this came to was that the first patriotic impulse in Parliament, suspending all opposition, had in fact unwittingly tended to atrophy our central motive power. Everything was in the hands of a single party group, with its far too personal outlook, and with no possibility of adequate criticism, counter-suggestion, or introduction of other points of view : there could be none with so one-sided a control of all the facts. In the earlier stage of the shell controversy the inclination of the Press had been to make of these considerations an urgent demand for complete and frank information. Since this country worked through a Cabinet responsible to Parliament, it could work healthily only if Parliament had all the knowledge necessary for control. And *The Times*, remarking that " the time for a Coalition had gone by," seemed to be playing for the ordinary party change of Government. Then suddenly a new kind of demand became explicit; it dates from the announcement, on 18th May, that " Lord Fisher had not attended at the Admiralty for the last two days." If the Government were falling into open disagreement, then the last possible plea for a party Cabinet, that of cohesion, had gone. So the political uneasiness began to mean the same thing as the other uneasinesses. If the country was to be used as a whole, Parliament must be used as a whole ; and this implied abandoning the practice of one party in office and the other party criticising from outside. That was a division as useless for our present need as the division which we were urgent to obliterate between part of the nation under orders in a war and the rest not under orders. The nation, to work wholeheartedly as one, must be under a Government which politically represented everybody. "Mobilise the nation" meant "mobilise the Government" too.

The latter was easier to effect than the former, and before May was out it was accomplished. A Coalition Government was formed, members of the existing Government standing down for various reasons—some from the simple motive of helping Mr Asquith by placing their offices at his disposal, some with an added reason, such as Lord Haldane's feeling that the attacks on him, grossly ignorant as they were, weakened a Government, or Mr Churchill's acquiescence in a change at the Admiralty without which Unionists would not have joined. When the new Government was announced it was found to include Mr Bonar Law at the Colonial Office, Mr Balfour at the Admiralty, Mr Austen Chamberlain at the India Office, Mr Walter Long at the Local Government Board, Lord Curzon as Lord Privy Seal, and Lord Lansdowne as Minister without Portfolio —this last a novelty in a British Government, conveniently borrowed from foreign practice, but under a title which, also borrowed, was meaningless, the symbol of a British Minister being the Seals of his Office and not a portfolio. Mr Arthur Henderson, taking the Board of Education, brought Labour into the Coalition after some discussion in the party. Sir Edward Carson became Attorney-General; Mr John Redmond, though it was said he had been approached, preferred not to bring in the Nationalist party. The Cabinet now consisted of twelve Liberals, eight Unionists, and one Labour member.

But the vital response to all the agitation lay less in these personal changes than in the first attempt to bring the business strength of the nation straight into the Government. The rudimentary efforts to organise production of war material through two inevitably jealous committees were abandoned, and the heads of the great engineering firms were gathered in the only sensible way into a Ministry of their own, under Mr Lloyd George as the first Minister of Munitions. His appointment was not the least part of the general satisfaction to a public which knew well his energy and " drive," but was not to know till much later what personal manœuvrings for the new Ministry had been helping to befog the shell controversy. People who had most bitterly resented the expressions of his energy in recent years were willing enough now to believe that it could only do good, especially as his power of those years with big working-class audiences might be expected at a crisis to oil the wheels and superheat the steam of the great industrial machine. There was, however, a distinct suggestion that more than a change of Government might be required in the comment of *The Times* on the Coalition as " the last effort we can make under our accustomed conditions of public life."

CHAPTER VI

THE WAR YEARS : PART II

SO ended the first chapter of the war. With all that we now knew about ourselves, with all that these months had taught us of war waged with all the resources of highly developed modern nations, we must make a fresh start. What had come to a head with the change of Government was not merely our particular national sense of rising too sluggishly to the crisis ; it was also the sense that for everyone concerned preconceptions of what the war would be had been falsified. There was, indeed, the belief that the Germans had foreseen its character more clearly than the rest of Europe ; that was part, a large part, of the charge against them now. Every new efficiency of theirs in these conditions was taken as fastening more firmly upon them the guilt of the war ; for it was one more proof of how long and how knowingly they had planned it. But even their purposes had gone astray. The rush of their attack on the West had not succeeded. They were in for a new kind of war as deeply as the Allies ; and the only fear was lest we should not be able to devise the means for meeting critical phases of it in time to catch up with their long start in preparations.

At least we had our chance now, if we made ourselves understand fully what was before us. This was not to be, like all wars hitherto, a clash of armies advancing, retreating, manœuvring, till brought at last by mixed accident and design into some decisive confrontation. It was to be a war of armies more or less immobile testing one another's strength here and there, piling up resources, until after long desultory sparring the opening for an effort at decision with an overwhelming flinging in of force should be found.

So the war maps with the little flags came to hang dusty and neglected ; there was hardly any movement to mark ; the newspaper captions grew shy of the word " advance " and fell to speaking of " biting at the German line." We could but expect at best to hold them pinned until our new measure of the task before us had brought all our resources to bear. The whole attitude to the war news changed. The fears and then the hopes of a great battle in the West, the intense significance which had attached to the fighting on the Marne and the Aisne, and acutely to the battles of Ypres, the confidence in a resistless rolling down of Russia upon Berlin—all this compactness of ideas about the war gave way to the perception of a vast embattled area at any point of which attrition might suddenly begin to tell conclusively. The whole theatre of war had its importance, the Dardanelles campaign with the rest, though there remained the controversy of opinion about either the possibility or the value of any attrition there. The Germans would not make our mistake of distracting their energy. But as we had entered on the campaign, there were arguable sides to it, even for those who did not believe in its wisdom. It would lighten the defence of the Suez Canal; and by easing the Russian advance into Asia Minor it would save them from having to draw off for that purpose any of their forces on the Eastern Front. So the Gallipoli news took an equal place with the news from France ; " Anzacs "— the name compounded out of the initials of the Australia and New Zealand Army Corps—added themselves to war nomenclature ; and the pictures of those stony, barren, sun-stricken hillsides, and of troops in shorts

and khaki shirts crawling among the rocks, grew as
familiar to the imagination as the muddy trenches
and slithering earthworks and half-drowned men of the
war in the West. There was now, too, the Italian
campaign to watch. The Germans had clearly left the
Russian Front mainly to the Austrians, and already at
the cost of some defeats. Cracow had fallen, and so had
Przemysl; much of the fun over that unpronounce-
able name was due to the inspiriting impression that
Germany's principal partner was not up to the job.
Now, with Italy attacking, she must prove less up to it
than ever, and Germany, forced to give more assistance
than Mackensen's stiffening attacks in Galicia, must
weaken her Western armies. Then, if Great Britain put
out her strength, the chance might come.

Thus we began to think of the whole war. And
we could at least feel that we were beginning to see
England's part in it. We looked no longer to Russia to
stagger Germany. France had been at full stretch from
the first. The one thing uncalculated yet was British
man-power. As for the United States, all that the sinking of the *Lusitania* had produced was a succession of
diplomatic Notes in which American feeling was going
to waste like a river in sand; and the best thing to do
was to make up our minds that America would be more
useful as a source of money and munitions than as a
combatant. There again it was Great Britain that could
do most, not only as financially the most stable, but as
holding the sea communications. In yet another way
we took up the war; we, in place of France, had become to Germans the hated enemy. So sure had they
been that, distracted by the Irish situation, and selfishly
absorbed in our world-wide possessions, we should be
blind to the danger to ourselves of their crushing attack
on France, that our entry into the war had driven them
to the pitch of fury. Not content with the "Hymn of

Hate," they were using as a sort of incantation, scattered through their newspapers, appended irrelevantly to all sorts of documents, tagged on to their letters to one another, the appeal " Gott strafe England." The first big Zeppelin attack on London, dropping ninety bombs there on 31st May, though only four deaths were reported, set a kind of seal on the new spirit. Hostilities in this war were not an army business; they overhung all of us.

How best we might all include ourselves in them remained to be worked out; but the strongest note in the fresh start was that this must be the main concern of the Coalition Government. For its very existence was due to the cry of the nation to be organised. In some ways the absence of official organisation actually helped us. People fell so eagerly upon every chance of doing something that private enterprise was alert to find opportunities, and we thus developed some voluntary services of help and comfort to the armies and the munition workers, which were either non-existent or far less effective in the countries more under Government organisation at the beginning, and therefore less fertile in individual undertakings. Thus accounts which came home of the conditions in the Prisoner of War Camps in Germany led to the setting up of a system for supplying them regularly with parcels of food and all the minor necessaries of life. The discovery in the early months of 1915 that men coming home on leave were apt to be landed in London at inhospitable times of night, and forced to spend cold and hungry hours on platform seats, called into being a canteen service at the railway stations to provide them with shelter and hot food. The Y.M.C.A. huts were warm crowded club-rooms of the training camps, and before the next winter had begun to establish themselves near the forward areas in France. All of these activities, with the others that have

31

been mentioned, grew into big auxiliaries and became in varying degrees official; there were enough of them to make a joke of the number of badges of various organisations that people could put on.

But our deep-rooted habit of voluntary service, if it gave us some advantages, had the drawback of making mobilisation of the nation a long and tentative process. Account had to be taken of so much that people were already doing. Not for a twelvemonth yet did we come to compulsory military service, and then only by way of two preliminary stages of continued trial of "voluntaryism." The first, which was all that the new Government actually entered upon now, was a National Registration; Mr Walter Long introduced at the end of June a Bill to compel every individual to state his or her age and occupation, and to state, further, whether the occupation was "serving war purposes." This was a necessary framework for any further action; it left rival opinions of what that further action should be. The information to be compiled from the registration returns might do its own work in stimulating recruiting; it might be used as a handle for much sharper individual pressures upon youngish men to enlist; it might be the basis for conscription. At any rate, it was a piece of organisation. A more immediately active piece was the Ministry of Munitions Bill, which, co-ordinating various powers of control under existing Orders in Council, provided at last a single centralised, and yet elastic, direction of the production of war supplies, laid down special regulations for labour in controlled establishments, and special machinery for dealing with disputes, and aimed at removing a main source of disputes by limiting the profits of all controlled firms to an increase of one-fifth upon the average of the last two years before the war. Yet another measure, the War Pensions Bill, marked our fresh start upon this strange new kind of war. Hitherto no one had thought of those left behind by the army except in terms of the wives and children of the married men. For them a system of separation allowances, made up of a small deduction from the soldiers' pay and a larger grant from public funds, had been working from an early period in the war. But the urgent need for men had drawn into the army hundreds upon hundreds of thousands who, though unmarried, had had others dependent on them—sons contributing to the household expenses, single men supporting relatives or in other ways keeping some family going. The distress of their withdrawal from wage-earning had been becoming serious. Now the fact was faced that " dependents " must be extended in meaning; we must not be grudging, and above all we must not leave anxieties to hamper enlistment. The Bill was delayed by the more pressing haste for the Registration and Munition Bills, and was not passed till late in the year. The organisations which had been stemming the distress—the Soldiers' and Sailors' Families Association and the Patriotic Fund Corporation—had to carry on through the summer distributing what they could through their local representatives. So for some months yet the familiar name of " ring-papers," given to the cards on which separation allowances were drawn, retained its meaning in the minds of the soldiers' wives. They had been called " ring-papers " because of the rings printed on them as in savings-bank books, to take the post-marks recording each payment ; but most of the women associated the name with their wedding-rings.

Meanwhile the second War Loan was being raised. The Government had asked for no specific sum, but were appealing to the country to subscribe all that it could ; and in order to give every class its opportunity small subscriptions could be made through the Post Office. The result was interesting. The Bank of England received subscriptions to the amount of £570,000,000, the Post Office, £15,000,000 ; but the numbers of subscribers by the two methods was almost equal—550,000 through the Bank, and 541,000 through the Post Office.

Yet the tone of this summer is not to be recovered from these efforts to begin a new chapter. There was no spark of encouragement in it. Instead, we had to learn that not all the talk and the warnings of Germany's preparedness for her day of battle had given us any measure of reality. The rest of 1915 seemed to be one long revelation of the strength and resources of the enemy ; and for the first time people began to understand something of the meaning of Lord Kitchener's estimate of the duration of the war. We had to learn how crushingly Germany could fight on one front without losing an atom of her hold on the other. All through the summer and early autumn months—the only possible season for mobile warfare there—the war news was chiefly of the steady defeat of Russia, the hard-fought defence and the fall of Warsaw, a rally at Kovno, the fall of Kovno, the anxiety about Brest-Litovsk with its immense military stores, its capture, and then the invasion of the soil of Russia, the fall of Grodno and of Vilna, the cutting of railway lines, until at last it was the actual defence of Petrograd that was in question. Hindenburg in the north, Mackensen in the centre, had conclusively made nonsense of "the Russian steamroller." And at an early stage the Russian retreat was being used to drive home afresh the lesson of Neuve Chapelle ; they were being beaten by guns and munitions, they had failed for lack of them ; so that there was yet another call for our utmost effort to supply them as well as ourselves. Their lack of equipment grew, in fact, into fantastic stories of troops being sent into the trenches armed with no more than cudgels. As for the Dardanelles campaign, the public was slowly

coming to see that it was not, after all, to be so different
from the Flanders Front; it too was being paralysed
into trench warfare. From time to time news of an
attack on some commanding height like Sari Bair or
Achi Baba, or of the fresh landing at Suvla Bay, with
its illusion of taking the Turks in flank, raised hopes of
decisive action; always the old conditions returned.

So what sense of " lift " there might have been in the
feeling of being taken in hand by the new Government
faded swiftly away. The nation was in a queer puzzled
state, for with all the quickened consciousness of war it
somehow found its old habits very persistent. The newspapers had hardly anything to say except about the war;
and yet a murder case, in which on no less than three
occasions women who had married the man charged
had been found drowned in their baths soon afterwards,
could be followed with much of the old excitement
about such things. War was in everyone's talk, yet
people could meet without its being their own only
thought, and indeed those who could talk of nothing else
seemed to be either bores or tiresomely self-important.
Carefulness was more or less in everyone's mind, yet in
fact there was very little difference in the way we lived.
There was not much " ostentatious retrenchment " to
rebuke. Even Paris, so much more stricken by the war
than we had been at first, was thinking about fashions
again, though of a war kind; it was no wonder that
in England women were spending again on dress, and
finding that the new shortened skirts, very full and
wide, could be as extravagant as the old long swathed
fashions. Compunctions on this score could always
be met with the plea that we must help France commercially as well as in other ways, and that meant
spending on dress. In so many directions we had
recovered from the first violent absorption in the war,
to find that life outside this absorption, as we dropped

back upon it to carry us through a longer struggle, had not yet cut for itself new enough channels. In very many of us this induced, no doubt, a growing forgetfulness; even to the quiet-minded it was uncomfortable, disturbing; vexed reminders that there was a war on had little reason to cease. The timidity of the Registration Act was more and more criticised; and as soon as the " pink forms " containing the personal information were available they were used for recruiting pressures often indefensible; to masses of the more ignorant men they were employed practically as a compulsion to enlist. The Munitions Act had sounded well, but industry was still disturbed. This time it was the South Wales coal-field which was the scene of strikes, again on the question of the war profits of the masters; and though the strike lasted only for a week or two of July, the settlement was due, not to the new machinery of the Act—which had been put into operation and simply defied—but to Mr Lloyd George's personal influence. And when he made a statement, on the adjournment motion a little later concerning the production of munitions, there was far too much hint of difficulties yet ahead for his words to be quite reassuring. He might indeed say that, with the co-ordination of private firms practically complete, and with eighteen large new Government factories being set up, we could hope " in a few weeks " to be able to supply all that was needed for victory. But one vital question remained unsettled —the consent of the trade unions to the wholesale introduction of unskilled labour. Women were urgently pressing for this work; Mrs Pankhurst and others had been to see the munitions factories in France, and had come home full of the magnificent work that women were doing there. In England they were enrolling by thousands in munition bureaux; but until the problem of " dilution " was out of the way comparatively few of them could get to work in the volunteer service which was allowed to keep the factories running over Sunday.

For a day or two at the end of September the rather dreary news from other fronts was lost in the excitement of a successful attack in the West. The newspapers burst out into striking headlines and double-leaded columns describing a joint advance by the British at Lens and the French on their right at Souchez. We had captured Hulluch, Loos and Hill 70; on a five-mile front ground had been gained to a depth of well over two miles; and, above all, the success had been largely due to very heavy artillery preparation. We had learned that lesson, then, and we had the resources for modern war now. Moreover, it was to a great extent a victory of the new armies. There had been some criticism of Lord Kitchener for keeping those armies in England so long; his genius for patient work seemed to be over-reaching itself. Surely with all the winter's training they could have been at the Front long ago, and might, the armchair critics thought, have struck perhaps a fatal blow while the Germans were putting out so much of their strength against Russia; a few hundred thousand fresh men in the Western trenches then might have been just the unexpected stroke. It was something that they were in the fight at last; but it was late in the year, and these particular grumbles continued, especially as once more the advance settled down into the same siege warfare a little farther on.

However, the war news soon went back to the East, with a development startling in its rapidity. In October Bulgaria came in on the German side, the Austrians, relieved of the Russian pressure, attacked Belgrade, the redoubtable Mackensen came on to the scene, and by mid-October Germans, Austrians and Bulgarians were sweeping clean over Serbia. Volunteer ambulance units were rushed out from England to help the wounded and the swarming refugees; a British and French force was hastily landed at Salonica. This piece of the war always remained vague and rather unreal to the people at home. There were some immediate reasons for this. One was that, just at the moment when the full force of the attack developed, the public mind was burning with another burst of passion against Germany. On 16th October there had appeared in the papers a paragraph to the effect that an Englishwoman, Miss Edith Cavell, a nurse who had for some years been living and working in Brussels, had been shot on a charge of assisting war prisoners to escape. The shock was intense and genuine. However unreasonable it may have been to suppose that women who did perilous things in war time could expect different treatment from men, however little Miss Cavell herself had tried to claim any such difference, there was to the ordinary mind something dreadful in the cold-blooded execution of a woman, and not for spying—that, though still dreadful, might be war—but for the very natural impulse of help to her countrymen. Even when it became known that it was not a matter of occasional help but of an elaborate machinery of escape, the punishment still seemed brutal for the offence. As the later accounts revealed the strenuous and frankly horrified efforts of the American Minister in Brussels to obtain reconsideration of the sentence, the British pain and anger felt itself wholly justified. Miss Cavell's death burned deeply into the mind; it fanned to heat again blind and bitter hatred; through all the war it never lost its poignancy; and it remains a martyrdom, for her own nobility in meeting her fate made it that.

The other pressing concern which made the Serbian happening rather remote was that we had entered upon one more of the tentative stages of national service.

On 6th October a new post had come into being, that of Director of Recruiting ; Lord Derby had been appointed to it, and within a few days the " Derby scheme " was announced. So we had come to some kind of climax of the long cry for organising the nation ; what kind of a climax it was depended upon differing opinions. But at least it was organisation of what had been confused before. Instead of the old indiscriminate recruiting, men between 18 and 41 were to be asked to enrol in groups by age, an unmarried and a married group for each year, twenty-three groups of either kind. And instead of the indiscriminate enlisting pressure which had been the first use made of the " pink forms " there was to be discrimination of the work on which men were engaged, with " starred " and " unstarred " occupations, under the supervision of local committees ; so that enrolling in the groups would give the material for a sifting of man-power. The groups would be called up as required, unmarried men first. It was the final phase of the conscription controversy. Those who believed entirely in voluntary effort could maintain that here, for Great Britain at least, was the natural and proper sequel to the Registration Act ; it was volunteering organised and channelled. Those who believed in compulsory service acquiesced in the scheme, for it was voluntaryism's last chance. Lord Derby had said, and the Prime Minister had agreed, that if this did not succeed, conscription must ensue. It was to have until the end of the year to prove itself ; and Lord Derby undertook, if the figures then were unsatisfactory, to inform the public without delay. Controversy sat back, as it were, to await results, and we watched yet another war emblem appear on the scene, the khaki armlet with the red crown on it, which showed that a man had enrolled in his group.

Even if the public mind had had less to occupy it,

the swiftness of events in Serbia would have prevented
their making a real and deep impression. The Allied
forces had been too late. Within a few weeks Serbia
was wiped out more completely even than Belgium.
Nor had we masses of refugees to make the ruthless
story vivid; a few came as far as England, but the
majority found shelter nearer at hand, as in Corsica.
A general sense of horror and suffering in the headlong
rout of a whole nation; a few days when names like
Nish and Monastir and Lake Doiran were added to our
war vocabulary—to most people the fate of Serbia was
little more than this.   Yet, as the first bewildering un-
expectedness of it passed away, and newspapers could
take up the discussions in Parliament about the incursion of Bulgaria, a shadow fell, as in the case of Lord
Kitchener and the shells, upon another great reputation of the early days of the war, that of Sir Edward
Grey. Where had our policy so failed as to throw away
the influence which Great Britain, with all that she
had done for the Balkan nations, ought to have been
able to count upon with them, and how was it that
Germany was being allowed to get hold of them? All the
Dardanelles controversy revived with this, and with the
futility of the deadlock there through all these months
wasting men and strength. Not till after-years was
the story generally known of the long struggles in the
Cabinet and the full scope, crippled in action by one
obstacle after another, of Mr Churchill's plans, his conviction of the immense value of a stroke that should
hold steady the waverings of Bulgaria and Greece, the
difficulties of Sir Edward Grey with Russia obstinately
suspicious of Greek ambitions, the whole succession of
accidents which so fatally co-operated with the hesita-
tions or opposition of Mr Churchill's colleagues to rob
the Dardanelles enterprise of its meaning and its force.
All that the impression at the time amounted to was a

sense that everything in that quarter had been lamentably muddled; that we were trying now with the landing at Salonica to frighten the treacherous "King Tino" from putting Greece also into the pocket of his relative, the Kaiser; and that, as M. Venizelos—of whose patriotic character the British public was perhaps a little too sentimentally sure—had resigned, we were probably too late again.

The public mind turned to a new cry. It had called for organisation; it had called for a Coalition and a business Government; what it must have now was leadership. All the failure to lay hold of the nation firmly, all the friction between War Office and civilian Ministers, Sea Lords and civilian Ministers, all the terrible frittering of plans and counter-plans, came simply to lack of leadership. Too many people were at the job; the Prime Minister must appoint a small War Cabinet of three or five, and they must rule. The demand was more right than most of the public knew; for, whereas in the first months practical decisions had in fact been taken in such a kind of inner Cabinet, the making of the Coalition had brought in so many men too important to be left unconsulted that effective decision was now a matter of debate among a dozen people, with the inevitably disunited habits of long party opposition which had for some years been violent. Even without knowledge of these considerations the public could take up easily enough the cry that only a small compact council of supreme decision could possibly be the right way to win a war. By the beginning of November the Prime Minister had announced the creation of " a strategic Cabinet " of five persons— himself, Mr Balfour, Mr Lloyd George, Mr Bonar Law and the Chancellor of the Exchequer, Mr McKenna.

Not Lord Kitchener. But gossip about him had broken out a few days earlier, for it had been observed that he was not in attendance at the War Office, and rumours of Cabinet dissension were only too ready. They landed an evening paper, *The Globe*, in the distinction of being the first newspaper to fall under the drastic powers of the Defence of the Realm Act ; it was suspended, and not allowed to resume publication till a fortnight later ; even in the stress of war time there was something startling to Englishmen in the suppression of a newspaper—it had always been one of those things that happen abroad. When the truth was known that Lord Kitchener had gone to review the situation in the Near East, it only provoked rumour in fresh directions. For the growing futility of the situation in Gallipoli, especially after the Serbian defeat had saddled us with new responsibilities, was on everybody's mind ; a change of command there, Sir Ian Hamilton being replaced by Sir Charles Monro, added to the gossip. That looked like a new move ; but was any new move possible except withdrawal ? And was that possible ? Putting aside all questions of prestige, could such a movement conceivably be carried out without the most appalling loss of life ? And yet would Kitchener be going except for some very serious purpose ?

Though the Press Bureau might lay a heavy hand on what was published of the other kind of rumours, it could not stop talk. The Cabinet was believed to be working very unhappily, and it was not difficult to find a reason. The Derby scheme was no longer soothing minds ; it was disturbing them. Already it was known that the unmarried groups were not filling as they should ; there was far too much " starring." The conscriptionists were growing confident, the Cabinet more worried. In the country at large the uncomfortable thing was that the pledge given to married men that they should not be called till after all the unmarried groups was being mistrusted now. It had brought the married men in handsomely enough to fill their groups; they were beginning to think they had been too hasty, for if the unmarried groups proved a failure, they would be called immediately.

Thus the second winter of the war threatened to be little less uneasy and restless than the first. Our fresh start had not taken us far. Germany had been able to strike twice heavily in the East, yet, as the check again after the Lens advance showed, could do it without dangerously weakening her line in the West. *Punch* might depict the Kaiser on a rocking-horse with its two ends labelled " East " and " West "; but the sting was that the rocking-horse seemed a very safe mount. Ought it, people began to ask, to be so safe ? The incurable suspicion that our energies were only half-awake turned where it had not turned yet—to the command abroad. For the troops admiration and pride remained undiminished, increased even, as we read of all their ingenious inventiveness in making this new war—the impromptu hand-grenades and shaky trench-mortars, and all the craft of sniping and raids. But some plain things had been said publicly about General Headquarters, about an easiness of life there with constant visitors and ladies among them, and soldier-clerks dropping into their duties about 10.30 A.M. Was it partly easy-going in our higher command which was making the German effort on two fronts so possible to maintain ? Early in December Sir John French handed over the command in France to Sir Douglas Haig, and took up the command-in-chief of the troops at home.

These, too, had lost a little of their early glamour, as the numbers had increased and been swollen by Canadian and Australian contingents under training. Inevitable problems arose with such concentrations of men away from their homes, and in the romance of khaki. It was in the spring and summer of 1915 that people first began to be disturbed about the moral dangers of the training camps, and to discuss the " war babies." A private but influential committee reported in June that there was no foundation for exaggerated rumours of the numbers of such babies. Perhaps the most interesting aspect of the matter was the good sense and the lack of old rigid moralisings which led people to concern themselves more with the problem of the support and care of unmarried mothers and the babies than with the shortcomings of the probable fathers. Earlier generations would not have faced so frankly and reasonably the consequences of throwing together, in an atmosphere of some excitement, crowds of men and the girls of small towns and villages near the camps. The agitation about drinking also had naturally attached itself to the mass of recruits as well as to munition workers. In London special regulations were made restricting drinking facilities near the big railway stations ; and it was partly for military reasons, besides the reasons of general national efficiency and saving money, that the " no treating " order was issued under the Defence of the Realm Act in November; no drink was to be served to any customer not paying for it. Stringent Army Orders were issued about the frequenting of night-clubs by officers in uniform, and there were a few courts martial.

To this second uneasy winter a piece of news just before Christmas Day brought an immense relief, though with melancholy associations. On 21st December it was announced that the whole of the Dardanelles force had been successfully withdrawn in the night of 18th-19th December without the loss of a single life. It was almost beyond belief, and the full accounts, when they came through, made a most exciting story ; the stealing out from the trenches, leaving clock-work and time-fuse arrangements which would go on firing rifles and hurling bombs to give an impression that the trenches were occupied, the smooth embarkation, and the wild scene when at the last moment huge piles of abandoned stores were fired, and the towering blaze along the beaches woke the Turks at last to a bewildered shelling. A burden was off the nation's shoulders, and a weight off its mind ; and the public generally had not the depression of knowing then how, dogged by mishap and disagreement to the very end, the expedition had been robbed of a final effort by the navy, or how near, with the weary exhaustion of the Turks, it was at that very moment of withdrawal to the success which would have justified it. That the enterprise was over, and without a parting massacre to match the slaughter of the landing, was all that people any longer cared about.

More and more, as time passed, a kind of romance, that no other field of battle had, came to hang around Gallipoli. There had been a flash of it at the very beginning, when Rupert Brooke, the radiant young poet, had died on Lemnos. Sir Ian Hamilton, cultured man of letters as well as soldier, had the story of his force told in messages home by Mr Compton Mackenzie, the novelist ; and afterwards Mr John Masefield was to make a prose epic of it. But the expedition had subtler literary flavours. It was fighting hard by the plain of Troy ; it used the Isles of the Ægean to supplement its supplies and camp its drafts ; and the result was that scholars of world-wide fame, the peaceful investigators of long-dead civilisations, were there, unfamiliar figures in their uniforms, attached to this or that fighting force, seconded to mysterious services, turning despised Classical studies to the most useful tricks of modern war, and finding in themselves all kinds of remarkable capacities, from piracy in motor-launches to observing from aeroplanes. And it was just like them that Oxford and Cambridge Common Rooms heard after a time a little, the public nothing at all, of all their surprising achievements.

But these were only the most picturesque of a great company of men who turned from their books to strange new occupations. The war seemed to be calling perpetually for more knowledge of a thousand things—of peoples all over the world, of climates and industries, of products and raw materials. Either because they had, in some of their peaceful habits, learned of these things, or because they had the minds that could find out about them, dons and researchers were at work in the oddest ways for the Foreign Office, the Admiralty, or the War Office.

Another withdrawal at this time was that of the Indian troops from France. People had liked in the early months of the war to think that men of whose age-long warrior traditions they had read so much, the men whom Kipling had made familiar, had brought over to our need their fighting qualities. Many of them we had seen, for they had their own hospital at Brighton, giving to George IV.'s Pavilion, perhaps for the first time, a population not out of accord with its domes and fantasies. As time went on there had been rumours that in the European climate, and the strange conditions of the new and so largely mechanical warfare, the Indians were rather cruelly out of their element ; and there was no surprise when they were sent home. Their return might also liberate for active service territorial units which, at the beginning of the war, had been sent to garrison India.

This Christmas of 1915 remains in the mind as the great parcel-sending time. For by now, after another twelve months' recruiting, the army was in millions, and there was no house in the country that had not some relative or friend to remember. In most places the parcel-sending was organised to some extent by an informal committee, for the sake of seeing that the parcels of poor people and country folk, ill-accustomed to such tasks, were made up securely and properly addressed. In most places, too, money had been collected to send a parcel to every man of the place who was serving, so that no one should be so poor or friendless as not to have his token of remembrance ; and the committees were all busy assembling in little piles a plum-pudding, chocolate, cigarettes and so on for each man, and sewing each pile up into a neat canvas package. There was never quite such a distribution again, for one thing, because by the time the next Christmas came round men in the army were rather better off for food and tobacco than the people at home.

The time had now come for the Derby scheme to publish its results and show us whether or no we must take the final step of compulsion. Just before 12th December, the last day of voluntary group enlistment, there was a heavy rush of unmarried men who had been hanging back ; it remained to be seen whether that had saved the scheme. But of this there was little expectation. Before the end of the year it was being said that enough was known of the Derby figures to make compulsion certain ; and it was noticed that Sir John Simon, the only convinced opponent of conscription in the Cabinet, was not attending Cabinet meetings. He resigned on 4th January, and on the 5th the figures were published. They were complicated, but what emerged from them was that, when all possible allowances had been made for " starred " men, and men who were medically unfit, there were over 650,000 single men who had simply evaded enrolment. This, after all that had been said, could only mean one course of action. And indeed from many angles opinion was coming round to compulsion. One strong argument, for instance, could be derived from the growing burden of separation

allowances. The war was costing by now about £5,000,000
a day. It was absurd to be enlisting married men
and paying the heavy separation allowances for wives
and families while there were hundreds of thousands
of young men, the vast majority of whom would have
either no dependents to claim allowances, or dependents
entitled to far less of an allowance than a wife and
family. But the argument which was gaining more and
more hold was that nothing but compulsory service
could possibly be fair all round. Besides the general
unfairness of leaving national service to individual
decision and individual pressures, specific unfairnesses
were increasingly apparent. It had been seen how
unfairly a voluntary group-system might work for the
married men. There was too the unfairness of patching
up wounded and sick men and returning them to the
front while hundreds of thousands were avoiding going
out at all. There was the unfairness of leaving the
employer who had let his men go to carry on with
substitutes in face of competitors who would give up no
men until they were compelled. And to compulsion the
Government came.

" The turning point of the war," said the newspapers.
Perhaps ; but not for some months even yet did we
round it completely. All along, one main motive for
reluctance had been the fear of a deep division of the
nation ; Mr Bonar Law had been expressing this only a
month or two earlier. And the attitude of Labour was
a grave difficulty in the way. Wage-earners had the
strongest suspicion that conscription for active service
would soon mean conscription for all the industrial
service at home, and this they would not have. It would
be folly to antagonise them, and their disaffections were
known to be far from appeased. Indeed rumour, obscure
because of the muzzling of the newspapers, was hinting
at disaffection worse than any yet, in that it was openly

revolutionary. The greatest care was taken to keep secret the fact that Mr Lloyd George's famous wizardry, sent to charm the Clyde in December, had proved a shocking failure ; but the facts came out in the Commons early in January 1916, when questions were asked concerning the suppression of *Forward*—an advanced Labour paper which had published accounts of his abortive efforts—and drew from him statements that " a powerful organisation " was at work which made conciliatory approaches quite useless. There were, of course, many who saw in all this only a reason the more for conscription. To the Government, however, it could only be a reason for caution ; and the famous decision for compulsion turned out, when the Bill was introduced on 5th January, to be no more than a compulsory supplement to the Derby scheme. Unmarried men between the ages of 18 and 41 who had not attested were to be treated as attested ; otherwise the enrolled groups remained the basis of recruiting.

This was immediately seen as only one more deplorable half-measure. But for a while two other subjects caught the watchful minds of the people who were always screwing the nation up to the mark. One was the strenuous appeal for war savings. The second War Budget had estimated for an expenditure of £1,590,000,000, and that meant asking for every possible penny. To catch all small savings War Savings Certificates were now invented, and issued at post offices at the price of 15s. 6d., to become of the value of £1 in seven years' time. A War Savings Committee was added to the many other committees ; and to its propaganda about cheap and nourishing breakfasts, food-values of the simple dinner, avoidance of unnecessary travelling, and so on, the zealous people added their own activities in denouncing the fashions, in indignation about the elaborate menus at the big hotels, about motoring to race-meetings, about the long lines of cars and taxis ironically parked outside a Guildhall meeting to preach economy.

This was the period at which Zeppelin raids took on the aspect of a systematic bombing campaign. In the early months of 1916 they were coming frequently and in fleets, and were penetrating much farther inland, reaching some Midland counties. Ever since a big raid on London, in October 1915, when over forty people had been killed, there had been complaint of the apparent helplessness of the authorities. Now the complaint rose loudly. Sir Percy Scott had been appointed to command the air defence of London; but the glamour which hung about the hero of the naval guns at Ladysmith in 1899, and all his reputation in warship gunnery since then, could not conjure up out of nothing men, material, and staff work for the job. This year was to see far more extensive air-raiding; but there had been enough of it already to work up a storm of popular impatience during February at the immunity of the raiders. As a by-election happened to occur just then in East Hertfordshire—which was on the line of airships making for London over the East Anglian coast—Mr Pemberton Billing, standing as an Independent candidate on the outcry of the moment, was swept into Parliament early in March as the first " member for better air defence." He found an ally in Mr Joynson Hicks, who was making his first reputation in the House by taking up this subject. It widened out into a vigorous agitation for fresh methods over the whole of our air service. Aeroplanes were taking a part in the war far greater than the observation duty which was all that they had been expected to perform; they were going to be a fighting force, and as such must have an organisation which would give the service perfectly free development. To the attack on the immediate question of air defence the

Government had but a feeble reply to make. The Prime
Minister rather unfortunately suggested that the best
defeat of Zeppelin raids would be " darkness and
composure." Courage enough there was ; composure
was a thing the Government hardly had the right to
ask for until they induced confidence. Darkness we had
already in London, the early lighting restrictions had
been much stiffened, and before long the streets were
entirely unlighted ; most other large towns were now
kept as dark as the East Coast towns had been from the
beginning. Shops had to indicate by some transparency
device in their blinds (which survived here and there
long after the war) whether they were open or closed ;
special constables acquired a new duty in watching for
careless streaks of lights from house windows on their
rounds ; and town dwellers generally discovered with
some surprise, to the amusement of country people, that
a moonless night can be so dark that no one can see
his way about. Incidentally a few of them were much
uplifted by finding that there are far more stars in the
sky than they had ever supposed.

In the middle of February the war in the West caught
all minds again. A heavy German attack was launched
at Verdun. From the outset, long before anyone could
foresee the tremendous saga that it was to become, it
was anxiously watched. It seemed to have an instant
significance : once again, was this the great battle of
the war ? The drastic German dealing with the Eastern
Front in 1915 would of course be followed by some
terrific turning upon the Allies in the West ; and here
it was. Then, as it became known that this was " the
Crown Prince's battle," and that the Kaiser was there,
and the *communiqués* told of the masses and masses of
troops thrown into the assaults, it looked indeed like the
bid for victory. As the days passed, and the attack was
seen to be no mere winning of trenches and consolidating

a new piece of ground, that impression increased. Into the long war of position had come after all a pitched battle of something like the óld kind, though heightened with all the immensity of modern warfare ; it was a deliberate and gigantic trial of strength, and such a thing might well be conclusive. Eagerly, but very anxiously, the British people heard the echoes of the heroic French cry, " Ils ne passeront pas," and watched the awful fury of the fight for Fort Douaumont.

Just as the fight began there died one who had known well and loved both England and France, and had made of his knowledge something new in literature—Henry James. Even the preoccupation with the war did not rob him of his tributes, for he had identified himself with the war in a gesture of sympathy that had been deeply valued ; he had abandoned his American citizenship, and been naturalised as an Englishman, because at such a time he would not be in any respect less English than those among whom he had passed nearly all his life. In the New Year Honours list of this very year he had received the Order of Merit ; and it was sad that he did not live longer to enjoy it. But he had at any rate lived to enjoy in his later years the kind of reputation that meant most to him, and some recognition of what the modern novel owes to his conception of his art—a recognition which had led him to expound that conception in a series of prefaces to his books, fascinating to other writers. The modern artistic method of " the stream of consciousness," though the phrase was not then current, and though he fastened upon consciousness in a narrower way than the moderns, is in fact a method which derives largely, if not principally, from his view of the novel as a presentation of life by intense imaginative concentration upon the minds of the characters ; and he had suffered the fate of all pioneers of an art in being regarded at one time as " too difficult."

It was not long before we had an anxiety of our own to divide the war news with Verdun. Little notice had so far been taken of an expedition up the Tigris, composed of troops from India, which was designed to be another distraction of the Turkish forces from Egypt and from the Russians in Asia Minor. The latter object certainly seemed to be achieved; February brought news of the fall of Erzerum and hopes of a Turkish collapse. But the Tigris expedition had gone wrong. General Townshend was besieged in Kut-el-Amara, and a relieving force was being held up, now by floods, now by persistent fighting; till Mesopotamia, with alternations between " nearly there " and " another check," came only too near our familiarity with the endless alternations of the Western Front. Endless—but it was difficult to believe that such a fight as that at Verdun in its immense persistence could fail to bring the smash. Week after week it went on, dying down now for a day or two and blazing up again into some new frightful passage of attack and defence, unlike anything hitherto in the war. Fort Douaumont, the fort and village of Vaux, the Bois des Corbeaux, the Mort Homme, Malancourt—place after place in the circle of defences rang with a blood-stained glory in the *communiqués*, till it seemed as if not even the Germans could stand this drain of men. Nor, for all the bitter suggestions to that effect, would they be suffering it for nothing more than the Crown Prince's conceited obstinacy. They must surely be meaning to make it the final effort for which no cost could be too high. And if so, with the French holding on magnificently, the enemy might crack. Yet the incessant trench-fighting on our front showed no weakness in them; and the best that we could do to help at the moment was to take over from the French more of the line, and use our slowly increasing numbers in that way.

But was this all we could do, while France was at what might be a death-grip? Could anything, people asked, show more clearly how fatally we had shilly-shallied, to find ourselves now with volunteer recruits not nearly ready, when, if we had faced compulsory service at the beginning, we might have had by this time the sort of army that côuld have turned the scale for good with the Germans so desperately engaged? The great chance was going by, and we still lost in the wretched half-measures. Recruiting was "a chaos." The unmarried groups had been called up on 10th February; within a month, by two proclamations, on 4th and 11th March, the whole of the married groups were called, and the storm of criticism broke. Had it ever been expected, when the Derby scheme began, that the older married men would be called like this? Nor was there much hesitation in pointing out where the scheme had gone wrong. Tacking it on to "voluntaryism" had made it far too weak all through, and the possible exemptions had been so numerous that the professed compulsion of the unattested unmarried men had turned out almost a dead letter. The whole scheme must go, and straightforward conscription take its place.

We were coming to that late in April, when for a week minds were violently wrested away in a new direction. On 25th April the papers were full of "an armed raid" on Ireland. A German ship carrying munitions had been captured, a convoying submarine had got away, but two men landed from her in a boat had been traced to hiding and arrested. One of them was Sir Roger Casement. It was a wild episode, and yet in a strange way, when it happened, it came as a more than half-expected thing. The ghost of Lazare Hoche hung about it. England at war had always had to fear that her enemy would strike through Ireland. There was bound to be some such desperate enterprise as this, and in its passionate futility it was a sheer wraith of the old, unhappy, far-off things ; the modern touch of the submarine could not really bring into our own day that vision of the two men landing from a boat on a desolate shore, not finding the friends they had hoped to meet, and walking off alone to set fire to Ireland. The fact that it was Casement who had come over in the submarine shocked many people, for he had been in British Government service as a consul. He had made his reputation first when sent to inquire into statements about abominable labour conditions in the Congo rubber trade, and later into similar statements about the rubber trade on the Putumayo ; it had not occurred to anybody to reflect what gleams of the age-long Irish sense of oppression, working in his mind, may have lain hidden in the words of his reports. There had been rumours about him since the early days of the war, but only now did the general public learn how he had been all the time in Germany, working bitterly against England, and endeavouring with the connivance of the German authorities to persuade Irish soldiers in prison camps to join him on this raid.

And after all only to make this solitary landing. Only ? The next day Dublin was echoing with the crackle of rifles and the slamming thud of field guns, and no one knew what the rebellion might be. For a day or two there was hardly any news. In Dublin the rebels had seized the Post Office and the Four Courts, and there were signs of rising elsewhere. Then on 1st May came the statement that " the back of the rebellion was broken," and the rebels surrendering ; and long accounts of the fighting, the perilous street battles from house to house, windows and roof parapets deadly with snipers, Sackville Street in flames, the Four Courts battered, the Post Office and Liberty Hall, the headquarters of Irish labour republicanism, shelled to pieces.

"A man named Collins" had been prominent in it all ;
James Connolly, who had been Larkin's colleague in the
strike of 1913, was reported killed. By 2nd May it
was over ; about 1000 of the Irish had surrendered,
489 had been deported for trial, including one Eamonn
de Valera, and England was asking angrily how it had
all happened. For it had given a very real alarm. On
the day the rebellion broke out German ships had
again shelled some East Coast towns ; and it might well
look as if, at the crisis of Verdun, Germany had contrived to stab us in the back. One part of the storm
of nerves was soon over. Mr Birrell, the Irish Secretary,
could look for no mercy. All the bitter resentment in
the years just before the war of the Home Rule measure
lived again when he had to face the House on 3rd May
with the admission that, though he had known of the
new movement in Ireland, Sinn Fein—that we now first
heard of—he had entirely miscalculated its purpose and
determination ; and with the confession that he had
utterly failed in his duty. Whatever was felt by those
who heard him in the House, who saw his face as he
spoke of the three executions of leaders that morning,
people in general spared nothing of their scornful anger
against a smooth literary amateur who had taken
Ireland in war as triflingly as, to their minds, he had
taken the struggle over Home Rule, and had bungled
her into this useless bloodshed.

He resigned, of course, at once ; and his public life
was over. But the storm of nerves was not appeased.
It was too acute to pause, except with a resentful
surprise, at Sir Edward Carson's plea that there should
be no taking of vengeance now. Day after day came
statements of more executions, but there was, side by side
with the alarmed exasperation, a sense of how terribly
wrong we must have been going with Ireland, to make
such men die in desperation. Just as that was turning

to a sense of how terribly wrong we were going now, with drawn-out executions, the climax of those nerve-ridden days came with the reports of the death of Mr Sheehy Skeffington. No one who knew anything of him could believe for a moment that he had had arms in his hand, yet he had been shot ; and as, piecemeal, came the miserable story of a British officer, judged in the end insane by a court martial, ragingly putting him and others to death in a yard, bitterness against the rebellion felt the chill of some shame, and there were no more executions. That last incident silenced, if it did not convince, those who could not even now believe that there had been too many executions already.

The Dublin rising masked to a great extent the final stage of the question of compulsory service, and took the interest out of one more event of war time strange to English ideas, the first secret session of Parliament. After some days in late April, during which it was pretty well known that the Cabinet was at a crisis, the announcement was made that Parliament would sit in secret to hear the Government's statement, and that powers under the Defence of the Realm Act would be drastically used in the case of any leakage of information. Too much, in fact, had been known in the last few months of Cabinet affairs. Ministers themselves had not been able at such a time to remember strictly their traditions ; Mr Churchill, departing from office to service in France, had, in October 1915 and since, revealed a good deal of his relations with Lord Fisher. Mr Lloyd George had found the success of his capture of a leading rôle in the shell controversy rather clouded by some things Lord Haldane had said about Cabinet negotiations with great engineering firms in the autumn of 1914. Much besides had become known in less public ways. So strong measures were threatened against any printing of information about the secret session other than what might be officially communicated after it ; and this was not a time at which people would pay much attention to the invasion of privilege implied in a decision by the Executive, not by Parliament itself, as to the publication of proceedings. Lord Salisbury expressed a formal protest in the Lords ; the Commons, in a way that would have distressed a seventeenth-century member, hardly seemed to be aware of the invasion.

The secret session took place on 25th April, and no detail of the Ministerial statement was given. But for events in Ireland the next incident would not have escaped as lightly as it did—the fiasco on 27th April, when the Government's first proposals, outlined on a motion by Mr Long for leave to introduce a Bill, were so promptly pulled to pieces that they never became a Bill at all. The Prime Minister simply withdrew the motion. After all the recent crisis, the proposals were still half-hearted ; they applied compulsion to all youths as they reached the age of 18, but otherwise only concerned the men already enrolled. In the absence of any specific information as to what the Ministry had said to the secret session, no one could imagine on what basis of numbers serving and required it could ever have been supposed that compulsion for the future at the age of 18 would supply enough men. Above all, the proposals did nothing to remedy the irritating tangle of unfairnesses. But before the public mind had grown easy enough about Ireland to round upon Ministers, they faced their fence. On 3rd May, the date of Mr Birrell's statement to the Commons, the Compulsory Service Bill was introduced, applying to all men between the ages of 18 and 41 ; the tribunals in every National Registration area which had been working under the Derby scheme were to continue to consider applications for exemption, whether on the grounds of the nature of

the civilian occupation of the applicant (though these
were to be much more strictly considered) or on that
of conscientious objection to military service.

After nearly two years we had come to conscription.
It had been discussed to weariness, and the old controversies trailed on even now into the question whether
such a surrender of principle should have been made
when it might well be too late to have any real effect.
For however we might have modified our views of the
war into methods of attrition, it was always possible
that attrition might reveal itself in a sudden cracking
somewhere, not necessarily in a slow wearing-down.
And there was big fighting enough to make the possibility of a sudden cracking. All this time the terrific
concentration of Verdun was continuing with varying
fortunes. A violent Austrian attack on the Italians in
the Trentino, the first time for nearly a year that that
front had come much into the news, was countered by
a strong Russian revival on Austria's Eastern Front
early in June which brought back, as the Eastern Front
always did, old ideas of sweeping movements and vast
results ; General Brusiloff's armies captured Lutsk and
Czernowitz, and were numbering their Austrian prisoners
in hundreds of thousands. By the end of the month the
attack in the Trentino had died away, and the Italians
had on the whole held their ground. The conviction
grew that the comparative quietness on the British
Front meant some gathering of our new armies for a
blow which, falling on German armies appallingly
strained by their Verdun effort, and weakened badly
by the double Austrian collapse, might break them
down completely.

Not that this early summer of 1916 had much that
was exhilarating for us. On 1st May we learned that
Kut-el-Amara had fallen, and General Townshend and
his men were prisoners—the relief force had not got

through. Zeppelin raids were almost nightly occurrences, and though one or two failed to get back to their base we seemed to be still very helpless against them. Then a great flaming of headlines on 3rd June startled the whole country. At last the big naval battle had come ; instead of the long exasperating vexation of cruisers slipping out to shell coast towns, submarines slipping round to sink ships, the main German fleet had been caught at sea, and tremendous broadsides of those gigantic guns had had their chance. Eagerly people began to read, and gravely they read on ; worry had come where we had most hoped for nothing but pride and security. The result had been no smashing glorious blow. After hours of action off Jutland, the German fleet had vanished home in night and fog ; and, as far as the Admiralty announcement went, we could not be sure that we had not suffered more than they. We had lost six cruisers and eight destroyers, and knew of the sinking of only one German battle-cruiser, one light cruiser, and an unspecified number of destroyers. Next day certainly brought better news—two German battle-ships as well as two battle-cruisers had been sunk and we had lost no ships of those classes ; the respective losses were now put, ours at 14 vessels, the Germans at 18. But German *communiqués* were putting their losses very differently and claiming the engagement as a victory. We, with the best will in the world, were taking it after all our high hopes as little better than virtually a defeat. At the very best, granted it a drawn battle, it was a kind of defeat to have had the German main fleet at sea and not finished the business.

The truth was, perhaps, that we had to learn about the sea what we had already learned about the land— that modern warfare was utterly unexpected and gave us none of the old compact decisive actions. Swift vessels, fighting at immensely long range, could not hold one another to blows in the old Nelson way ; and across the great distances engagements must always be uncertain and results unsure. But we had not learned this ; and it was not easy to get over the shock of the first Admiralty announcement : it had perhaps better have been less honest. Endless argument arose, hints of some lack of co-ordination between Admiral Jellicoe and Admiral Beatty, in command of the battle-cruisers which had first made contact with the German fleet, talk too of some failure of the Admiralty to keep in wireless touch with the fleets, and, contrarily, of too much Admiralty interference by wireless.

Controversy about the battle in all its aspects, with precisely careful calculation of minutes here and minutes there at which things happened, was to drag on for long ; and indeed, like much else, could not possibly be cleared up until the end of the war should give us facts on the German side. Now discussion was cut across sharply. The afternoon of 6th June struck everyone aghast with the news that Lord Kitchener, starting on a visit to Russia, had been drowned ; the ship in which he had embarked had been sunk off the Orkneys, probably by a mine. In its abrupt suddenness the news was as shocking as anything in the war. The public had not even known of his journey ; and he was dead. Every single frct of strained war minds leapt into life and fastened upon this calamity. The spy scare first ; secret the departure might seem to have been, but was it conceivable that by mere mischance that ship, of all ships, should have been sunk ? Spies must have learned of his departure, and it would be found that it was a submarine, and not a mine, that had blown up the ship. Then bitterness of the meanest kind : the Government had not wanted Kitchener ; they had quarrelled with him, found him too strong ; or else they had come round to the view that he was really standing in the way of victory now, obstinate, clinging to old ideas because he had no active service in this war and would not learn from those who had ; the Russian visit had been a mere excuse to get rid of him, and he had been exposed to this useless and now fatal risk. Then even a kind of national hallucination, like that over the supposed passage of Russian troops through England ; Kitchener was not dead at all ; it was some elaborate piece of secrecy, misleading the enemy, so as to make sure that he did get to Russia ; all the time he had been taking some other route. There was even a stranger hallucination still, the queer outbreak of a superstition one would have thought extinct for centuries, reviving the Merlin and Arthur legends in a belief that, apparently dead, Kitchener was really awaiting in some magical spot a moment for his return. Amid all these swaying excitements of mind the truth of his achievement, the real value of his work and his personality, had to abide its final estimation ; too much of it was still behind official veils. But from all the wild rumours, even more from the reluctance to believe that he could be dead and England without him, one thing at least emerged—the hold he had upon his countrymen's imagination to the last.

CHAPTER VII

THE WAR YEARS : PART III

WE were moving again into a new chapter of the war. Its opening was not so definitely marked as the opening of the second one had been, both by our fresh envisaging of what the war was to mean, and by the making of the Coalition Government. No particular event dates the third phase. Yet it is very distinct, though at the time we passed into it half unconscious of the transition. Mainly it is marked by a far quieter temper and a real unity of feeling. In the first phase we had been violently roused, but very wrong in our conceptions of what was before us ; in the second, wiser in some ways, we had been energetic, anxious, but still so caught in the tangled cross-currents of our old habits of doing things that the new start was, after all, much farther off than we thought, and we were not even sure that we had made it. Now a kind of quietness of mind which, for all the rending personal apprehensions, all the hard exhausting work, did replace the recriminations and the rasped nerves, showed that the new start had been made for months past, little as we had noticed it. If the mental change is the broad sign of it, the lesser signs are a number of changes which, coming gradually upon us, had in the sum of them made us a nation at war. There was little need in June 1916 for the old fretted cry that most people were living as if there were no war on.

For one thing, those first six months of 1916 saw the great entry of women into the war tasks. Their own special spheres—nursing, and V.A.D. work of all kinds, and canteen work at stations, at the camps, at munition works—had been growing enormously; but now they were everywhere. They were in every form of business, from the big banks to the tiniest city office ; they were in every industry, even as navvies in gas-works; they were ticket collectors and porters, tram and bus conductors, guards on the Underground railways ; they had replaced chauffeurs, gardeners, footmen, hunt servants and club servants. By June there were probably 150,000 on munition work, very many of them women who had never done any physical work in their lives, but now endured the full stretch at the lathes and in the filling-shops. The " dilution " difficulty had been largely overcome by a formula of the Prime Minister's in January ; and the only check on a much greater employment of women was the lack as yet of the big new Government factories to put them in. There was, too, a new recruiting of women that was very popular, for it put them into the army. From an early stage of the war there had been suggestions that one most obvious way of using women to liberate men would be to give them that part of the army's life which in civil life was always regarded as a woman's job—cooking, catering, and other such services. It was absurd to be keeping men at them, and there was also the argument that women would probably do them much more economically. Experiments in this direction had been made, but only piecemeal, until the beginning of 1916 the Adjutant-General decided upon the formation of the Women's Auxiliary Army Corps. Within a few months the Waacs were 50,000 strong, and became familiar figures in France as well as at home in their short khaki skirts and neat little feminine versions of the military cap. They ranged widely, from the trim smart chauffeuse of a War Office car, or the waitresses of the Officers'

Club at Montreuil dressed in the G.H.Q. colours, to the fatigue-parties of the Base camp cook-houses. All this work of women seemed to come with a rush. It had been long talked of, here and there women tram conductors, ticket collectors and so on had been noticed. Now, no doubt with the calling up of the Derby groups, this change in the aspect of daily life was suddenly unmistakable.

Then again, the whole nation was beginning to be more careful. It had to be, for several reasons. The broad general one was that the Exchequer was not going to let us off with war loans ; it was quite properly determined also to do all that could possibly be done out of income, and the revenue was being screwed up to a point that would a few years earlier have appeared quite fantastic. Mr Gladstone had once in warning depicted what he thought the impossible bogey of a Budget of £200,000,000. Now in 1916 the Chancellor was budgeting for over £500,000,000 ; the graduated income tax (Mr Gladstone thought a sixpenny one matter for apology) ran now from 3s. to 5s., an entertainments tax was imposed, and a tax on matches which led to a boom in mechanical lighters. All this meant a real check in spending, for as yet the new flood of war wealth was spreading but slowly. There were other limitations too. The submarine sinkings of ships were still far from the real menace of twelve months later. But tonnage was urgently needed by the Government for war material, and some of the habitual cargoes of peace days were being ruled out. Wood-pulp was the first, Sweden having put an embargo on its export in January ; and the result was that there must be economy in the use of paper. Shops were no longer generous with paper bags and wrappings, and before long would wrap up nothing at all ; ingenious methods were invented for using envelopes over and over again,

and the true " patriot " acquired another of his eagerly
sought distinctions in the unseemly scraps on which he
wrote his letters. Restrictions soon followed on imports
of timber and of tobacco. By the end of June the
growing indignation about careless use of motors—one
case was quoted of two people who in 1916 used petrol
on a drive of 150 miles to buy a pet dog—was met by
a system of control, petrol being obtainable only on
permits, though these were for some time too easily
granted ; it was not difficult to find some small war job
for a car that would be good enough excuse for a permit.
Besides these first definite restrictions of supplies there
was at least a beginning of much other carefulness.
Households were having " meatless days," and were
glad to have them, for with the heavy demand of the
army and of the allied nations, and with higher freights,
meat was rising seriously in price. Bread was not sold
new, and last crusts not thrown away. We had early
been asked to be careful with potatoes. This spring and
summer of 1916 saw a great effort at vegetable-growing.
Something had been done in the year before ; but now
the Food Supplies Committee was making a more pressing appeal. In many ways it did good. Thousands
of bits of waste land and odd corners were put into
cultivation ; middle-aged amateurs took over the allotments which wage-earners gone to the war had had
to give up; suburban gardens everywhere, which had
prided themselves on their roses or their hardy annuals,
prided themselves now on carrots and runner-beans.
But inevitably there was much waste labour and breaking up of ground really useless. And it was absurd
that even in a matter like this there had to be a kind
of ostentatious patriotism; people who had plenty of
flower beds to convert to vegetable-growing could not
be content without the added gesture of digging up a
tennis lawn for planting potatoes. It seemed to comfort

them to make it so very plain that they were doing every kind of duty, and preventing lawn tennis as well as increasing food supplies.

But above all, what drew people together now was the growing consciousness that, for all the outcry about the chaos of recruiting, evasions of service and so on, there were vast armies in being which had sprung from every town and every village in the kingdom. There was no place so small that it could not show in some windows the cards, familiar then, with a representation of the Victoria Cross on them, and the name of a man who had gone to serve. Gone, indeed ; the men were in France. That change, too, seemed to have come with a rush. In spite of the fact that the autumn battles had been to some extent battles of the new armies, that for months they had been steadily going away, the mass of them had been still at home for the Christmas of 1915. Now, all of a sudden, they were the B.E.F. And this helped towards the quietness of mind in a community of anxiety and pride.

And in the early days of July a fresh hope with the pride. At last the big engagement on the British Front had begun, as the long struggle at Verdun wore itself out ; the battle of the Somme was sweeping forward. It stood out most curiously, that battle. One reason was that, much as we had read by this time of the fury of modern shelling, the Somme first made really vivid the vision of square miles of country, mere torn and cratered devastation from which even the kindly soil had vanished ; of whole villages which, though they had names in the *communiqués* and were talked of as captured, were nothing but conventional marks of an advance, and in themselves not even stumps of ruined houses, but actually ground down till they were no more than patches of the devastation slightly more hummocky than the rest. Secondly, the battle was a

very real advance; day after day the lines on the war
maps in the papers kept altering their curves and
putting more of France behind our lines. Rightly or
wrongly, there came the heartening impression that
munitions were adequate, that staff work, training,
preparation, were at last up to the measure of the new
gigantic kind of war, control and coherence in an attack
achieved, as far as they ever could be achieved, in
modern conditions. Again, this, far more than Hulluch
and Loos, was to people at home the battle of the new
armies; somehow we knew that the men who fought
over Guillemont and Thiepval and the rest were the
battalions with the familiar double numbering—1st/4th,
2nd/4th — which marked the legions of the civilian
soldier. Within a week or two we were knowing it in
the one more way that made this battle stand out. No
one who lived through that time will ever forget the
casualty lists of the Somme. In daily batches of ten
thousand they struck at the endless little villas in
suburban roads which had, so short a while before,
been warm with pride in the trim young officer, or the
budding sergeant with his stripes fresh on his sleeve;
at the schools which junior masters had so lately been
visiting in their new Sam Brown belts; at the universities — terribly heavily there — where name after
name in the lists meant that some undergraduate would
chatter no more in the college lodge or cross the quad in
shorts and sweater, some young don would look no more
from his windows upon the gardens; at the country
houses which, growing suddenly still and stricken, remembered in their fine tradition the cottages in the
village which would have grown still too. From that
time the armies were England.

   This latter half of 1916 had in it a sincerity of purpose
fine enough to take its place beside so much sorrow. If
some of the exaltation of early days of the war had

faded, much that was sentimental, and even hysterical, had faded too. And the puzzled mind of 1915 was past ; the old life which seemed to entangle so persistently our wish to live in the war had gone. All habits were upset. Middle-class households woke at unearthly hours to get a daughter off to a factory ; and kept a running meal going in the evening for the return of that daughter and the one working overtime in an office, and a mother fitting in hours at a surgical-dressing depot, and a father going on special-constable duty at midnight. Working-class homes in village and in town made up a dinner now for the wife as well as for the husband to take out to the day's labour. Fashionable women, who had hardly heard of such things, ran their households according to shifts in factories and hours of duty at canteens ; and if some of them laid themselves open to cynical comment by the frequency with which they appeared in the illustrated papers in becoming uniforms that looked like fancy dress, this was not altogether their fault ; the modern Press must have its public characters to exploit. Evenings and nights carried on the business of the day. Long and light now the evenings were ; for with the new sense of its value in war time, especially for the amateur food production that was being so vigorously urged, the Daylight Saving Bill, rather scoffed at in earlier years, had gone through Parliament in May in a single week. People were discovering what Mr Willett, its patient promoter, had so often told them, that the ingenious device of putting clocks forward would perfectly simply work a kind of miracle. Time-tables and meal-hours and all our other fixed points could remain fixed, and yet we should find our days longer, and that by more than one hour in the effect which the change had on the mind. The experiment had its amusing accompaniments in the stories of those who thought it a blasphemous interference with the divine order of sunrise and sunset. Nor was it of use in all his work to the farmer ; dew would not dry off an hour earlier, nor cows change their milking habits. But in the gardens and on the allotments the hour more of daylight made all the difference to work ; and it was no small thing either that tired people from heavily working businesses had that much more air and light to enjoy when they came home. As for the working nights, they brought experiences which will never be quite forgotten. Thousands of people made the discovery of the uncanniness of occupations carried on when the life of day and sun has gone out of the world ; the shadowiness of figures moving and work going on in the windy black spaces of goods yards and amid the lurid gleams of gas-works, the ghostly hollow sound of dark and empty streets, the queer solitariness which somehow clings to work at night, even when one is not alone.

The quieting sense of unity in being about the nation's business was helped and widened by sense of unity with the armies. Even at the time people were aware, though never quite as fully as they should have been, how remarkably the postal service of the army worked ; in retrospect it seems miraculous. Vague as might appear an address to no more precise a place than a certain unit, " B.E.F., France," letters and parcels reached their manifold and wild destinations with extra-ordinarily little delay, and went up with the rations into the trenches. Soldiers serving abroad had no need to use postage stamps, and the replies came back as quickly, with the triangular stamp of the Field Censor in a corner. The armies were not hopelessly far away. In many ways, now that the early months were over, and experience had shown us more clearly what things we still must be cautious about and what did not matter, people at home, though nothing could ever convey the realities of the Front, had increasingly a kind of familiarity with it.

The strictness which had kept all accounts of the fighting to the official " Eyewitness " had broken down ; and the newspapers had been allowed to send their own correspondents to France. They had not the romantic chances of the old-time war correspondent. They were brigaded, as it were, in a château reserved for them, did their work under supervision, and saw just as much of the Front or its near neighbourhood as the authorities permitted. But at least they could introduce a variety and vividness of their own into the war story ; and as time went on they saw more and more of the real thing. Then, again, there were a good many visitors to the battle area now, politicians useful in keeping up war spirit at home, labour leaders who might influence war industry, notable personages among the Allies, or even more among neutrals whom we wished to conciliate. Visitors also were brigaded in a château, close to the field of Agincourt, and taken on selected journeys to the Front—sometimes, if malicious rumour were true, to places which were not the Front at all, but only looked like it. Photographs and drawings of the battle area were numerous. A sort of conscientiousness, very odd in some aspects, made the Government feel it a duty to send out distinguished artists, lest posterity might be unaware of the insane nightmare mankind at war can make for itself. Volumes of drawings by Mr Muirhead Bone were published ; Sir William Orpen, besides his sketches of the Front, made studies of the innumerable types of the armies. War posters by him, Mr Brangwyn, and others, for a while gave unusual interest to the hoardings.

Besides all this, the armies now were full of men not only sharply alive to all their surroundings, and to the infinitely various human reactions to them, but also able to tell in letters the things which could be told, the trifles of the daily life and companionship, the unconquerable humanity of the whole inhuman existence out there. Mostly, no doubt, they falsified it; in part from necessity, for the truth about much of the life of the Front would have come too near things that would not pass the Censor; in part from their own courageous simplicity which liked to keep the tones down to simple levels. " Ole Bill " and his " better 'ole "; all the war jokes, with the pictures of patient bewildered soldiers in a landscape of savage shell-bursts indifferent to everything except some irrelevant trifle, and that as absorbing or exasperating as it would have been if they were waiting for a bus on some street corner at home—this kind of thing may have had a certain falseness. But it had its truth too, and its value. It had its share in getting rid of sentiment and hysteria. If we talked less now of " little Belgium " and " the Hun," it was largely because we were picking up both the ironies and the genialities of the fighting soldier. And it had the value of making between home and the Front the only possible link, for none could ever have been made of the grim realities. Those who were out there had that in their souls which could never be approached by even the utmost effort of imagination by those who were not.

This was part of a poignancy of the occasional meetings without which, after all, pictures and letters would not have meant so much. When men came home on leave, near as they brought the war in some ways, in the other, deeper ways, these meetings seemed rather to make more impassable that dark chasm between the Front and home. To parents and to wives aching with expectation of their man, his coming at last and the hours of companionship were shot through with a vein of sadness, however they might struggle against it, the sadness of feeling that the inmost centre of his life, that in which he was really and truly living, was shut away, incommunicable. In the vast majority of cases the men did not want to talk about it; they left it "over there," and the longing, when they came home, was for the placid familiar things—the tidy bathroom (that always first), sheets and a bed, meals on a table-cloth, and idle hours, like a week-end of the old civilian days. But the real barrier was not in these wishes of theirs; it was more subtle and impenetrable. It was simply the fact that the world of the Front was not this world at all; it might have been on another planet; and no talk, no effort of sympathy and love, could bring the one world into the other.

Indeed even in the most external ways it was from another world that they came, the men who crowded Victoria Station through the last half of the war. The thronging ghosts which to older generations will always haunt those platforms have uncouth shapes which are hardly human. Distorted with pack and equipment, bayonets and entrenching tools, mess-tins and haversacks, and rifles slung on a shoulder, clumsy in their heavy greatcoats, mediæval in the sleeveless leather jerkins and the flattish steel helmets which they were wearing since the early summer of 1916, they looked entirely creatures of some other life. It was hardly like a mere difference of clothes and belongings; it was as if that half-secret, underground world of the front line, which grew, in place of grass and hedges, sordid stumps and rusty wire and rotting rags of men, had produced a new race of the right shape to live in it, ponderous little dinosaurs of the battle slime. How much easier if they could have been thought of so! But they were our men. Strapped and belted into all that weight and cumbrousness were the infinite patience and cheeriness and courage of our men, living their perilous lives with no more of their own than they could carry. So it all had to come with them, to be laughed over and cried over by their women as they tumbled noisily out of the leave train ; to be laboriously mustered again in a few days and make once more the fighting man who tramped off down a platform suddenly grown dreary and cruel to the silent little groups left by the gateway. The leave trains at Victoria never found their poet.

They did much to help the quieter, more unified spirit of the nation through the winter of 1916 and the early months of 1917. After the Somme battle the Front had gone back to the old trench warfare, and the leave turns could work fairly smoothly. It was much, too, that when the soldiers came they found that the strangeness was not all on one side ; home was very different. This was not merely because of all the war work. People were beginning to do without many things they had been accustomed to, even if it were only in a lack of constant hot water, sugar, and a certain amplitude of meals. To London, at least, air raids had in the summer and autumn brought something of the reality of war. A good many suburbs now had known bombardment, the frightful noise, the stabbing flash of explosions and the glare of burning houses.; had seen shattered buildings and the ghastliness of torn bodies in blood and mud. But no longer quite helplessly. They had seen another kind of glare on the night of 2nd September, when a Zeppelin was brought down in flames near Enfield by a fighting aeroplane, and had flocked out eagerly next day to see its charred and twisted ruin. Then as, three weeks later, two more were brought down in Essex, and a week after that another at Potters Bar, confidence began to grow. This was not mere raiding at the enemy's pleasure ; it was part of the war over here, and that was a very different thing to bear. Whatever the enemy's fleet of Zeppelins might

be, our dealing with them could not but become more
and more effective; and they must take long, and be
very costly, to replace. In fact, after one more raid in
November, when two airships were brought down at
sea on their return journey, the country hardly saw
Zeppelins again. They killed many—thirty to forty
deaths had become an average casualty list—but the
material damage done was never anything like what the
Germans were induced by their authorities to believe.
One of the exasperations in England of the raids was
that the Government, for fear of giving information
about a raid which might act as a guide to subsequent
raiders, suppressed facts, and we had to see the enemy's
communiqués convincing the rest of the world that all
kinds of serious things had happened to us. Neutrals
visiting London were said to be amazed to find so much
of it standing.

But the first battling with Zeppelins was not the
only excitement of the autumn. There was a much
bigger one—the tanks. On 15th September the first
of these grotesque monsters had lumbered across the
Somme trenches—an utter and complete surprise. Not
the least of the excitement was that at last we were
ahead in a device for modern war, at last we had done
something that the Germans had not invented first.
Zestfully people read of the queer things—how they
could waddle across pits and trenches, and wade through
barbed wire; how they rose like some ungainly beast
against walls and tree stumps and pushed them over on
their way; how they bore down invulnerably, spitting
fire, upon German strong-points and machine-gun nests,
and cleared them out. Then came the wonder of how
such things could ever have been kept secret. For
obviously they must have taken months of experiment,
months to construct. How had it been done, where had
it been done, without a word getting out? The thrill

was extraordinary and immensely exhilarating. We had indeed waked up about munitions, if our workshops, besides making possible the devastating days of gun-fire on the Somme, and the incessant shelling now along all the Front, could turn out in the mass wholly new war engines like these. And we must be growing vastly more efficient in war ways to have kept the secret. The name had done it, people said : " Tanks " was such an innocent reply to questions about what might be being made in a place where steel plates and rivets were going in large quantities. Somehow the armies might need quantities of tanks, for one of the odd aspects of the war now was that no one would be surprised at a mass supply of anything for the troops ; and it was much more ingenious to have a perfectly prompt reply to questions than to provoke curiosity by refusing an answer. Even when the need for secrecy was over, the name was too good to lose ; it was taken up with an almost affectionate glee. Whatever the authorities may have intended to call their new armoured cars, as tanks they appeared, and tanks they remained so persistently that, when they had to have a corps of their own, it could be nothing but the Royal Tank Corps. Rumour began to tell, after the event, of how they had been made and tested somewhere in open desolate parts of Norfolk, but little was really known at the time. Nor did people want to know much: The great thing was that they had been made, and had sprung a vast sur-prise. The public was far too pleased to pay much attention to the critics who said that we had only bungled things again by bringing the tanks into action on a small scale, and so giving the secret away, instead of waiting to send them over upon the enemy in masses that might quite possibly have finished the war.

The nation in these months was not feeling critical. It had the sense of finding its feet in the war, and did

not expect the results of its pulling together to appear
too soon. Next year, surely. And because it was as a
whole so busy, it paid little heed to those who were
still unappeasably critical. They had not, in this new
phase, been leaving the nation alone. They had had
a fresh mouthpiece in the summer. Mr Hughes, the
Prime Minister of Australia, was in England, and he
had been very busy " spellbinding " up and down the
country on the iniquities of Germany and the civilising
force of the British Empire, and on the plain duties
which these propositions laid upon his audiences. Much
had been made of him, even to creating for him a brand-
new constitutional precedent ; he was the first Dominion
Prime Minister to take part in a meeting of the Cabinet.
He had also been one of the Government delegates to a
conference in Paris in June, which was heavily coloured
by the kind of spirit he represented. This was an
Economic Conference of the Allies, to envisage the
possibilities of an agreement by which, after the war,
their trade should become a kind of mutual possession,
excluding Germany. Economists may have had their
own views about such a mirage, but they kept quiet.
For of course behind all the war spirit there was the
long jealousy in Great Britain of German trade, indeed
the conviction that " der Tag " had been designed,
whatever the German war-lords might think, to capture
a world supremacy in commerce, and that " Kultur "
was a blind for wholly material motives. All the fear
of German trade methods, the alarm about her cheap
efficient production, the talk about slavery to work and
money-making which made this possible, about their
insinuating commercial travellers, " dumping," and the
undermining of our markets, concentrated on the flattering vision of liberation from this rivalry. Germany had
staked her all, and we must see to it that she did not
contrive to get the most important part of her stake

back off the table while we were not looking. The war must not be taken as a merely military affair, to end when a military decision should be reached. We must not be fools enough to defeat Germany's armies, and then leave her with the trade victory she really coveted.

Every autumn and winter of these years brought, perhaps naturally, some kind of uneasy movement of the national mind, some kind of worry about our war life; and the better mood of 1916 did not escape this. When Parliament met in the autumn it began at once to ask whether we were taking seriously enough the subject of food supplies. Some carefulness there had been, but it was not by any means general, and it was not spreading. In fact, habits of economy were rather declining than increasing, for one or two reasons. To a certain extent economy had been involuntary—the restraint of rising prices. But two things were by now happening to counteract this : first, an enormous expansion of war work at piece-rates or at good wages with bonus additions, and secondly, an addition of war bonuses to most fixed salaries. The circle was beginning to revolve which was to prove so calamitous after the war—high prices, due in a minor degree to the hampering of trade, but much more to the creation of money by the Government's huge credits for its needs, and then the distribution of more money in salaries and wages to meet the prices. Another reason was that as people became more and more occupied in war tasks they felt themselves freed from the stinting and care which had once been the only kind of contribution most of them could make to the demands of the crisis. Now they were contributing service and might justly feed their tired bodies ; they could mostly afford to do so, and they thought the agitation about supplies rather fussy. Forced over and over again to recognise how much better the Germans had done most things since the war began, this was the one point on which the British public felt superior. It had always regarded as fussy the way in which at the very start of the war Germany, under the military thumb till it had no life left to call its own, had had some of its main food supplies rationed. Later on, seeing the reproduction in our newspapers of bread cards and meat cards in use over there, people had interpreted them hopefully as signs of a danger from which we were free. The German might vaunt his security from air raids, his towns cheerfully ablaze with light while we groped in darkness ; but if he could still sit at his ease at café tables, there was precious little on them, and that chiefly unappetising substitutes, like acorn coffee. Leave him his hungry satisfaction in his street lamps ; we had good sound food behind our carefully drawn blinds. Here lay the Government's difficulty. Much as they needed the first call on food supplies, much as they had to control freights and cargoes, they must not risk such a discouragement as a system of food control might induce. That step, in view of the feeling that food was the one thing in which we were more comfortable than Germany, might shake unpleasantly the nation's *moral*. Yet the matter could not be left quite untouched. A compromise was found in the announcement in mid-November of the appointment of a Food Controller, Lord Devonport, but not of any system of control. All that was said on the latter point was that he would have his system ready, if and when it should be necessary. For the moment he did no more than restrict, in December, restaurant and hotel meals to two courses at luncheon and three at dinner. So the situation was met as well as it could have been at the moment ; the existence of a Food Controller might make people a little more heedful ; and his first action had dropped on a carelessness which everyone could impugn, without coming too close home.

For those who were still conscientiously on the alert for miserable half-measures, here was another. We had not got out of the habit of them, even in the old troublesome matter of recruiting. The Compulsory Service Act, after all, had not satisfied the zealous patriots. To them it was far too heavily tainted with the relics of voluntaryism in the provisions about exemptions and the tribunals. There were two lines of attack : first, that far too many " indispensables " were still managing to keep out of the army ; and secondly, that avoidance of military service on conscientious grounds ought never to have been allowed. In the former matter the Government was in another dilemma : they needed an ever-increasing industrial effort ; they needed increased food supplies ; and though women's work was becoming more and more effective it was only slowly releasing men. This was especially true of agriculture, the difficulties on either side being made plain enough in the House of Lords by Lord Derby, as Director of Recruiting, and Lord Selborne, as Chairman of the Committee on Food Supplies. There was a steady appeal for the breaking up of more land for crops, which was no work for amateur labourers ; and in general, agriculture, if depleted too seriously of its men, could at the best only maintain existing production, and could certainly not increase it. For the first time England began to learn that agricultural labour was not the unskilled occupation which an ex-aggeratedly industrial age had thought it. Slightly bewildered by this discovery, the tribunals remained always weak in dealing with rural " indispensables." They did in time become more strict about labourers ; they were always frightened of the farmer, and to the end far too many fit men of that class managed to stay at home. In the matter of conscientious objection there was not so much a dilemma as a flat contradiction of views, a much more bitter thing. If exemption on this ground had been confined to the Society of Friends, with their unbroken tradition of refusal of every kind of conflict, it would have been generally accepted. But this would have been a sectarian provision out of accord with modern ideas. No spiritual tenet could now be given an exclusive institutional connection, and it had to be recognised that a point of conscience might be common to men outside as well as inside organised communities. The door was thus opened, however, to objections to military service which, though they might be " conscientious " in a wide sense, were more political than religious, and had never been contemplated when the exemption clauses of the Act were passed. The question was naturally raised whether the words " military service " should not be strictly interpreted in relation to the individual conscience as meaning the bearing of arms ; and whether, in face of the vast field of occupations only nominally military—the Pay Corps, the Medical Corps, office work on the lines of communication and in the back areas, Base camp duties of all kinds—the tribunals ought to pay any attention to objectors who refused to do anything of that kind, refused even work on the land, because it contributed to the bearing of arms by other people. This kind of argument was strengthened by the fact that even many of the Quakers had not held back from ambulance-driving and hospital service ; and a Non-Combatants Corps had been formed for various duties in France.

A further point of criticism was gaining ground, though it was not yet as vigorous as it became in the following year. Mr Churchill, after retiring from office, had more than once spoken in the House of an evasion of which France was much more aware than England (it was on his return from service there that he had spoken of it)—the *embusqué* in uniform. There were, he said, far too many people who had indeed gone into the army, but had not been, and meant never to be, in the fighting. They were in all kinds of secure employment in France, they could be seen at home in trains and buses safe, in their khaki, from criticism, but no more doing their duty, and far less honourable, than the men who refused to put on khaki at all.

Late in September the appointment was announced of a Man-Power Distribution Board. It did not appease all the criticism. Would it be more than a kind of super-tribunal, subject probably to all the weaknesses of the ordinary tribunals ? What was needed was not multiplication of duties, but a new forcefulness and determination behind the existing duties. That brought us to another change of Government. It proved to be a far bigger event than the making of the Coalition in the spring of 1915. It was no mere change of Ministers, but an attempt to make at last the sort of Ministerial machine that a war called for, with new offices and new functions as well as new men. Unfortunately it happened in a way that tarnished all its good aspects with associations of intrigue, and turned a sound reconstruction of ideas into the similitude of a rather mysterious scramble. This was largely due to the fact that the impulse came, not from a more or less spontaneous tide of opinion, as in the case of the Coalition, but from a deliberate newspaper agitation working on the public mind ; and at a time when the Press was under a control which had in other cases been prompt to suppress criticism and rumour, the openness and impunity of this agitation looked like connivance in some high places. The agitation began towards the end of 1916, directing itself upon the Prime Minister. It did not, indeed, revive the worst of the earlier calumnies about him and Mrs Asquith, but it was in a key which in fact played upon all the wanton bitterness that had inspired them. The suggestions that Mr Asquith was not the man to

lead a War Cabinet—whether they were based upon
his age, or upon his mental habits and his lawyer-like
precision, with all its limitations, in a situation often
requiring a certain recklessness of speech and even of
decision—could merge too easily in many minds into
hints that it was not merely inaptness for a time of
war, but a deep and serious alienation from the war
which was hampering him and the country. Whatever
the hints were, the broad implication was clear, that the
country needed now someone much more sharply and
determinedly *in* the war; it needed someone able to
put aside all else till the war was won, to see the war in
relation to nothing but the war; it needed above all
someone who had proved his capacity to be rousing,
stimulating, dynamic. If the reference was not obvious
enough, care was soon taken to make it so. On 1st
December was published a letter from Mr Lloyd George
to the Prime Minister, saying that he could not remain
in the Government unless the machinery for directing the
war were " drastically overhauled," and proceeding to
propose a War Committee which excluded Mr Asquith.
The smooth reason given for this proposal was that, as
the War Committee must sit every day, and the Prime
Minister had other work to do, it would be better for
him not to be a member of it, but to attend it occasionally in consultation. Even at a time like this, when a
good many questions of taste had long given way to
the urgency of war, a newspaper campaign culminating
in such a letter had to cover itself in a very lavish
cloaking of patriotism—and it need hardly be said that
to a great part of the nation no amount of cloaking
availed.

A letter of this kind communicated to the Press
could not be answered. On 5th December Mr Lloyd
George resigned, and a few hours later the Prime
Minister resigned also. The King went through the

constitutional form of sending for Mr Bonar Law, and he went through the form of failing to construct a Ministry. On 6th December Mr Lloyd George was sent for, and the new Government was quickly made. There were several important changes of office besides the retirement of Mr Asquith. Sir Edward Grey, who had become Viscount Grey, went with him, and Mr Balfour took the Foreign Office. Lord Derby's work as Director of Recruiting was rewarded with the War Office, which Mr Lloyd George had held since Lord Kitchener's death. Mr Bonar Law became Chancellor of the Exchequer. But more important than these appointments was the new type of Government machine which now revealed itself. The experiment of a small War Cabinet constructed inside a Government gave way, by a slight but significant change, to the idea of a distinct War Cabinet of Ministers without Departments at the head of a largely increased Ministerial body. The principle of a compact supreme group having been established, the rest of the Government could be fully expanded to cover the needs of the war without the old fear of cumbrousness and slowness of action. Four new Departments appeared. Three of them carried on wholesale the success of the Ministry of Munitions in bringing the business man straight into Government, with the offices of the Shipping Controller, the Food Controller, and the Ministry of Blockade, which, though to the end the public knew little of it, worked by enlisting the skill of big industrial and commercial men, with their lifelong experience of the habits of the world's trade, and of the movements of crops and manufactures, to interfere with Germany's supplies in a way that Government officials or the navy could never have achieved by themselves. The business man was also brought straight in by such appointments as those of Sir Albert Stanley, chairman of the London Underground Railways, to the Board of

Trade, and Sir Joseph Maclay as Controller of Shipping ; neither of them was a politician. The fourth new Department, the Ministry of Labour, was largely a gesture, the delimitation of its functions and the question of its relation to all the industrial duties of the Home Office and the Board of Trade being rather vague. But there had for years past been a growing opinion that we should recognise, as other nations had done, the necessity in a great modern community of a separate Government Department for labour ; and the very wide control of industry now by the Government made a good opportunity for the innovation.

Disquieting aspects of the change of Government did not pass without comment. The strong public opinion in its support had been too openly organised by the determination of a powerful owner of newspapers to effect a change, and put the man of his choice at the head of affairs ; it was a very ostentatious proof of the ease with which a vast newspaper-reading public could be manipulated. Moreover Mr Lloyd George's letter to Mr Asquith took on an unpleasant appearance of plausibility when it was seen that the reasons he then suggested for a Prime Minister's surrender of the War Cabinet to other people did not apply in his own case. Beyond entrusting the leadership of the House of Commons to Mr Bonar Law, he apparently found in the "general duties" of a Prime Minister none of those obstacles he had formerly perceived to membership of the War Cabinet, which he now constructed of himself, Lord Curzon, Lord Milner, and Mr Arthur Henderson. Mr Henderson's membership was interesting. Whatever crevasses might have opened in Mr Lloyd George's reputation with the world of labour, he was still able to placard the support of the official party and the trade union leaders. Beyond question, too, he had the public mind with him. Points of scruple counted for little in the general feeling that he possessed a combination of force or personality and tireless flexibility of mind, ready to turn instantly in the vital direction of the moment, which were pre-eminently the qualities required in the supreme charge of a nation at war. The country had struggled long for unity of purpose, and had more or less achieved it. It had then called out for leadership, and had now achieved that. The new Prime Minister was easily the most stimulating figure in public life. His significance had the queerest kind of illumination a month or two later, when some people living in Derby, a mother, her daughter, and her son-in-law, were arrested on a charge of conspiracy to murder Mr Lloyd George and Mr Henderson. They were said to be anarchists, but of a most bizarre turn of mind, for they had been devising as their weapons darts poisoned with strychnine and curare. They were sentenced to heavy terms of penal servitude.

For the rest, it was a winter of no vivid impressions. The New Year of 1917 brought with it a 50 per cent. increase in railway fares, war bread—to economise wheat supplies by the compulsory use of parts of the grain which in peace time were removed from flour—a limitation of the use of sugar for sweets, and an experimental fixing of future prices of potatoes, which provoked an outcry from the big growers. A terrible explosion at a munition factory in East London, killing 69 people and injuring about 450 others, and half-wrecking several streets, was a reminder, if any had been needed, that volunteering for this work meant more than hard toil; it meant real peril. Not the least, perhaps, of the minor successes of the war was that with so much dilution of the labour there were not far more accidents of this kind. A War Loan was raised during January to an accompaniment of much propaganda from pulpits. The most obvious interest of it was that it showed how we were beginning to think in the new terms of money; the Loan produced, besides a good deal of conversion of bonds, £1,000,000,000 of fresh subscriptions, and one single big business, the Prudential Assurance Company, put itself down handsomely for £20,000,000. In another event of the month—the Allies' reply to a tentative Peace Note from the United States—no one was much interested. The restatement of the only terms the Allies would contemplate—complete liberation and restoration of the small states which had been overrun, and full reparation to France, Russia, and other invaded countries—was little more than a formality. In so far as the public generally took any notice of the affair, it was to wonder, rather caustically, whether America was ever going to do anything more energetic than the sending of Notes.

She was going to, quite soon now. At the end of January 1917 the German High Command took the fatal step which brought the United States into hostilities. The exchange of Notes in 1915 on the submarine campaign had ended in the Germans undertaking not to sink merchantmen without warning to enable passengers and crew to leave a ship; and after the sinking of the *Sussex* the American Government had insisted that this must apply even to armed merchantmen. But now, on 31st January, the German Government issued a notice to neutrals of unrestricted submarine warfare. Within a "barred zone," which they laid down, all vessels would be liable to be sunk without warning. Whatever its unwisdom from some points of view, this was for Germany the plainest way of bidding for a decision. Submarines had become most formidable vessels. Like aeroplanes, they had undergone the forced concentration of skill and inventiveness aroused by the war needs, which had developed them within two years to a point they might hardly have reached in twenty years of peace. They were no longer small diving boats, firing torpedoes only, with a narrow range of cruising; they were powerful under-water ships, able to take long voyages (one, the *Deutschland*, peacefully equipped, had actually crossed the Atlantic and appeared sensationally in New York harbour), and armed with guns protruded from below when the boat was running on the surface. With a large fleet of this kind, and methods of either locating or fighting them in a most rudimentary state as yet, the Germans, ahead of us again—for we had never thought of our commerce being attacked in a way that the navy could not deal with—might well think of bringing England to her knees. No longer hampered by having to expose themselves in giving warning, which had meant letting many ships go by when breaking surface would have been dangerous, submarines keeping down for their work of destruction could increase it enormously.

The Government, still deciding that voluntary food control, like voluntary recruiting, must be tried to its utmost limits, saw the new German menace not as justifying systematic rationing, but as a means of extra pressure on private action. They started to publish prominently statistics of the weekly sinkings of ships, as a warning; the form, however, in which they were published, not giving the totals of tonnage, but the number of vessels, had no very alarming appearance, and did not press aside other interests. One of the most comforting at the moment was a long statement by Mr Barnes in February on the subject of pensions. This was a matter which by now touched thousands of homes, with all the men who had " done their bit," and found themselves back in civilian life, so handicapped by wounds or gassing that the future was dark to them and their families. They were by this time wearing the little silver badges with the Royal monogram

in the centre which protected them against the people
who were still hunting for shirkers. In its larger responsibilities to them it was never supposed that the
country would fail. But there was great reassurance
when Mr Barnes's statement promised to co-ordinate
properly the whole business of these responsibilities in
a Government Department of its own. He detailed,
besides the actual pensions, schemes for training in new
trades men disabled for their old occupations. A great
and admirable private effort had already given life and
hope, in a measure no one would have believed possible,
to one whole class of the tragically disabled—the blinded
men. For many years blind men of courage had been
setting themselves to bring to an end the old frightful
isolation of the blind from the normal activities of life.
It happened that shortly before the war a prominent
newspaper proprietor, Mr Arthur Pearson, had gone
blind, and he brought unimpaired into this new life of
the blind world the energy and the power of "getting
at" the public which a successful newspaper proprietor
must have. Under his leadership the men blinded in
the war (and modern warfare made far more of these
casualties than the old campaigns) were not allowed for
a moment to feel themselves hopelessly disabled or even
excessively handicapped. A pleasant enclosed place in
Regent's Park—St Dunstan's—had been generously
given for his work, and its name became a household
word ; Mr Pearson saw to that. By his own courageous
example, and great wisdom in his training methods, he
wrought miracles. This was one of the happiest of the
many ways in which development of ideas was immensely
quickened by war needs. At the same time a refuge
was being brought into being for others whose wounds
cut them off from normal life quite as much as the blind.
A fund had been raised for buying the " Star and Garter "
at Richmond and erecting on its fine site a new building

to be presented to the Queen as a permanent home for the hopelessly disabled.

Marvels of surgery were being done for them. But indeed the whole medical service of the war was wonderful. There had never been anything like it. The prophylactic work kept these millions of men in camps, in the frightful conditions of the trenches, and the none too sanitary conditions of rest billets, without a single serious outbreak of enteric or other such diseases. Nor was it only the hopelessly disabled for whom the marvels of surgery were available ; these were almost as common in the war area as in the great hospitals at home. Out there badly wounded men passed into the hands of the most famous of surgeons : the shell-shocked into the care of the most brilliant brain and nerve specialists. Yet the great men could have done little had it not been for the thousands of general practitioners who, making what arrangements they could for their practices, went out to lavish in the advanced dressing stations and the casualty clearing stations the skill without which most of the bad cases would never have lived to come into the specialists' hands. That service was perhaps the only one of the war in which the armies never lost confidence. For all the tragedy, a kind of happiness seems to hover about the memory of the crowds of men who became so familiar a sight in the ill-fitting blue uniforms and pink ties which, when the men were out of doors, looked even uglier with the khaki caps. There were times when there seemed to be almost as much of that blue about as there was of khaki.

Though less open, perhaps, than in the earlier years, when it had time and again been disappointed, the persistent looking to the next year for a decision had really been as strong as ever through the winter of 1916. Yet the first big news of the war in 1917, at the end of February, was almost too startling. The Germans along a wide section of the British Front, from Arras to Soissons, were retreating. What weakness did this mean, what admission of the strain of Verdun and the whole past year on the German armies? And was it going to be sprung upon and turned into a disastrous opening of their lines? That kind of hope was short-lived. The movement had been too secretly prepared, too swiftly carried out, to be taken advantage of, and it was also too large. To occupy along that length of Front ground to a depth of about eight miles at the narrowest point, and as much as twenty miles at the widest was so huge a task that the advancing troops never really harried the retreat; prisoners and captured guns were in disappointingly insignificant numbers. In the end the Germans were discovered to have retired to a far more effectively fortified line, shorter by some forty miles than the old line they had had to defend; it was "the Hindenburg line," which now became part of our war talk. After his smashing campaign on the Eastern Front, Hindenburg had come West to the appointment which virtually, though not formally, was the Command-in-Chief; and this strategic retreat was his first work. It had been too successful for us; but it was a retreat, and this fact, and the capture immediately afterwards of Vimy Ridge, the epic day of the Canadians, with its 20,000 prisoners and 250 guns, might well mean that strain was telling on the Germans.

This was the great hope. It saw no check to itself in the event now which was a few months later to destroy it. As suddenly as the German retreat came the news of the Russian Revolution. Unexpected in one sense, it was in another, people began to find, something that they had more than half expected after all. In the first shock of the war Russia had lost all her old associations in the minds of the British, and had signified only a force which we hoped might be gigantic. Then, as common sense came with better understanding of the war, we began to wonder how, after the long years of indignation against absolutist Czardom and sympathy with Russian exiles and their passion for liberty, we could ever have imagined that Russia would be anything but a very lame giant. Her checks, and soon her heavy defeats, had emphasised the lesson; the Allies had all been caught, no doubt, less fully armed than the Germans, but Russia had had besides a corrupt oligarchy to make even what preparation there had been largely a sham. Her people must know it ; and it was impossible to think that after such a murderous betrayal of them they would after the war endure the old tyranny. Yet they had, Russian literature had always told us, their intense personal loyalty; the Grand Duke Nicholas had led them well, and when, in the summer of 1916, the Czar announced that he was taking over the command of his armies, people had thought that this might be the way of the great change : he and people together might free themselves from the soulless engine that Czardom had become. This was not easy to believe ; the Czar's own qualities and capacities seemed too insignificant. Yet the blind faith of the Russian masses in " the little Father " might hold firm. The news of the Revolution, therefore, was strangely compounded of the expected and the sudden. But the expectedness prevailed over the suddenness, and long familiarity with the idea of revolution in Russia took all alarming quality from the news, and coloured the English mind to accept it without any grave anxiety about its effects on the war. The Government telegraphed to Prince Lvoff, welcoming the change which made Russia a democratic partner of democratic allies.

There was anyhow little time to think about it, for the United States declared war. Unappeasable grumblers said it was too late, and people in general doubted whether, apart from a certain tightening of the blockade pressure on Germany, the entry of America now could have much more than a moral effect. She was not wasting time; she had watched our experiences and went straight to conscription. The millions of men which that must mean might be an impressive thought, but we had learned how long it took to make a fighting soldier for this war; we could not let the thought impress us much as we faced again, at a time when any month might be critical, the unending question of our own man-power. Compulsory service had procured for the army since the beginning of the year 100,000 men less than the estimate, and controversy over exemptions, never quite stilled, revived sharply. It had the effect of stiffening the action of the tribunals. They began interpreting " conscience " in a much stricter way. They refused to allow it to include objections to service which were either politically or religiously humanitarian in a broad sense. They reduced valid objection almost entirely to membership of the Society of Friends, or bodies as secure as they in a long tradition. The result was that other objections to service became now mere refusals to serve, and therefore law-breaking; the bulk of applicants for exemption on conscientious grounds were sent to prison. This line of action embittered hopelessly a conflict of views which could never be reconciled. Nothing could bring together those who believed with all that was best in them that the individual conscience was inviolable, and the moral law explicit, and those who, in varying degrees and from varying angles, believed that the social need was paramount. The conscientious objectors themselves, if religious, accepted their sufferings; if politically extreme, made of them fuel for their own fire; the deeper wound was dealt to those who, not themselves coming under the tribunals, had no expiation to offer for the darkening of the whole moral conception of the world they knew.

But stiffer action by the tribunals, and the other step which the Government now took—the introduction of a Bill enabling the authorities to call up for re-examination men who had been rejected on medical grounds before conscription was introduced—were alike hampered by the two problems which persistently dogged recruiting. The first was the temper of the labour world, whose resentment of compulsory service might always break out at any fresh stage of it. There was acute trouble in the air with a strike of engineers at Barrow, which defied the efforts both of trade union officials and of the Minister of Labour. It lasted from 21st March to 4th April, ending then in a nominal concession by the Government recognising the right of the men to negotiate through their shop stewards (the new portent of the industrial unrest) instead of through the union officials. But the truth was that the strike had been forcibly stopped by threats of drastic use of the Defence of the Realm Act and conscription ; and this was a situation which could not lightly be further irritated. The other problem—the old dilemma of the concurrent need for men in the army and in production at home — had become worse than ever with the submarine campaign, which was rapidly taking its graver form as the submarine menace. It had been pressing steadily on us in losses every week of some 12 to 20 ships of over 1600 tons, apart from the smaller ones. In the third week of April these figures leapt terrifyingly to 40.

Warnings and exhortations poured out from the Food Controller. Some were addressed to tradesmen ; grocers, for instance, were meeting the shortage of sugar by a device of their own—refusing to sell sugar except to customers making other purchases—and this had to be forbidden. Others were addressed to the rich, who were asked to eat no potatoes and the least possible quantity of bread in order to leave those food-stuffs to people who depended more upon them. For general use a " recommended " ration scale was issued. But again the only definitely imposed restrictions were upon meals in restaurants. These naturally caused most criticism, from the mere fact of their publicity, and newspapers had been publishing angry letters about " food-hogs." The restrictions imposed in December had been ineffective. An Order was now issued rationing the supply of bread and meat to hotels and restaurants, and compelling them to one meatless day a week and five days a week without potatoes ; the Order did not apply to restaurants in which the total charge for a meal, including drink, did not exceed 1s. 3d. An Order was also issued concerning cakes and pastry, limiting the quantities of sugar and flour used for those purposes ; and forbidding the serving in a restaurant of any afternoon tea costing more than 6d. or including more than 2 oz. of bread, cake or biscuits.

Another and more far-reaching result of the anxiety was the Corn Production Bill. This established fixed prices for corn to encourage especially the breaking up of ground which would not at first produce remunerative crops without a bounty. It also enabled the authorities to supervise cultivation, and to prosecute occupiers of land who were neglecting it, or not making adequate use of it. Most important of all, the Bill dealt with labour conditions which, owing to the inevitable weakness and difficulties of the trade union idea among the scattered and remote agricultural workers, had been lamentably left aside by the great industrial movements. A minimum wage was established for farm labourers, with a statutory weekly half-holiday. What was even more valuable was the appointment of a Central Agricultural Wages Board, with Wages Boards in every

33

county, consisting of an equal number of farmers and labourers with a few independent " appointed members " nominated by the President of the Board of Agriculture, under an impartial chairman. These Boards in their working proved to be far more than mere wage machinery. They had powers of inquiry which, since they were for adjusting the minimum wage in cases of physical or other defects, let a flood of light into labour conditions on farms, especially in the more backward counties.

This was one of the measures of the time which were producing a curious result of the war upon men's minds. They caught sight of a marvellously encouraging vision. Just in the same way as the urgent national need had stimulated beyond all conceptions the pace of advance in flying, for example, so it seemed to have brought on at a bound social and ameliorative action by the State which in peace time made way so slowly and against such dead-weight of mistrust and vested interests. Government control of railways had worked from the very first day of the war, and old vexatious complications of the movement of goods had disappeared. Control of mines had followed. The big industries, textiles, boots, engineering, shipbuilding, steel and iron, without losing all the elasticity of private ownership, were under regulation as to profits on capital, wages and hours, and the handling of industrial disputes. Moreover, a whole vital region of industrial life, which the State had only been able to penetrate inch by inch against the employer's view of his rights, had suddenly been thrown wide open to supervision and direction. The notion of factory and workshop inspection widened out amazingly into the most sweeping conceptions of duty towards the welfare of workers. War needs provided plausible overriding of still reluctant employers on two broad grounds. Factories must not only be kept running, but running

smoothly, with ample labour and maximum efficiency.
This meant, firstly, that conditions must be as attractive as possible to ensure the stability of the labour ;
and secondly, that there must be provision for more
than formal healthiness, there must be also precautions
against fatigue, possibilities of recreation and change of
mind to keep up energy. So trained welfare workers
and nurses, rest-rooms and educational classes, enlarged
the sphere of factory inspectors. It was, of course, only
in new Government factories (except for the few enlightened firms which had introduced all these activities
long before the war) that the fresh ideas, with their
accompaniments of model housing and so on, could be
put into operation at their best. But over the whole of
large-scale industry they had their influence, not least
because war necessities made far more public the study
of industrial fatigue and impairment of output, which in
peace time an enterprising employer would see to have
lessons for his pocket. Supervision of industrial conditions could never, it was thought, return to the old
narrow limits.

Legislation was taking its strides too. There was not
only the Corn Production Bill. The report of the
Speaker's Conference on Electoral Reform had issued
in a new Representation of the People Bill, simplifying
the whole franchise, and including women—the com-
prehensive Bill which had been so insuperable a problem
of the militant suffrage days. The war had solved it.
Women had taken a place in the national life which
swept away for good all the old notions of their disqualifications for plenary citizenship ; it was in pride
now, not in any need of proof of their case, that they
paraded, in a deputation to the Prime Minister at the
end of March, the multiplicity of uniforms they were
wearing. In April the new President of the Board of
Education, Mr H. A. L. Fisher, introduced a Bill so

wide alike in its immediate proposals and in the ultimate
prospects it opened that again a movement was made
which only years of effort in peace conditions could have
commended to the House. Beholding all this assertion
of the right and the power of the State, observing, too,
that control produced none of the disastrous results,
the fear of which would never have given way except
to an overmastering crisis, how could the social enthusiast fail to hope that the country could not now
go back to the old unorganised, uncontrolled conflict of
private interests ?

Nor was it only Government control of which he was
thinking. The country had learned more than that.
It had seen, in spite of all the industrial trouble which
persisted, some recognition of what could be achieved
by capital and labour pulling together instead of apart.
Why should that effort of understanding not leave its
effects behind ? The Report of the Whitley Committee
on Industrial Conciliation, published in June of this year,
promised help, especially as, if not fully aware of the
significance of the shop-steward movement, it did grasp
the tendency towards decentralising union methods,
in proposing a hierarchy of councils from a National
Industrial Council down through Regional Councils to
Shop Councils. Composed of employers and employed,
the councils were to act, not merely on the appearance
of a matter of dispute, but continuously, as in some
degree a joint consideration of interests, which might
grow very near to joint management of industry. The
report was to prove too optimistic. But at the time it
was welcomed. For the air was full of that without
which all these hopes for the future, whether of Government control or of a better private outlook in industry,
would never have been as strong as they were. The
great foundation must be the new comradeship of
the army and the munition works, the vast friendly

acquaintance of classes with one another, and the good sense which must surely spring from that. There lay the hope that, once the country had begun to learn— even if driven into it—what a really national social consciousness might be, it could never quite lose sight of it again.

Even in the most material ways it had learned a great lesson. It had found out that it could spend immensely more than had been conceived of as possible. No one would for a moment want the war level of taxation to remain. But if we could at extreme need screw the year's revenue up, as we were doing in 1917, to over £638,000,000, then obviously even in peace our old figures of £200,000,000 or so were far too timid. Income tax at 5s. and 6s. in the £ could not be permanent, but 9d. or 1s. was unnecessarily lenient. The Excess Profits Duty was a form of control of capitalistic interests too useful to give up ; and the Entertainments Tax, and some at least of the increase of duties on intoxicants and tobacco, were clearly impositions the public would stand rather than go without these things. The country was discovering, therefore, not only what social effort it might put out, but how much it could afford. The Education Estimates, under Mr Fisher's new Bill, showed an advance of £4,000,000. Moreover, Ministers were learning to spend courageously, and get rid of the false idea that niggling is economy.

But of course there were two sides to that matter. Bold spending, admirable enough in business enterprise, was apt to look reckless when the big business men now in Government Departments had their hands on public money. Did unstinted provision of actual war supplies involve all the costliness of much that was going on ? Complaints in the House of Lords that within two years the Government had taken over in London alone eight large hotels, two clubs, a town hall, and fifty other more

or less public buildings for office work, subject to ultimate compensation and liabilities for repair, made only
one item of the indictment. All over the country huts
had sprung up like a plague. It was hardly credible
that in the early days there had been reason to complain
of the slowness with which shelter had been provided
for the first recruits. Now standardisation of pattern
and mass-production of the material allowed the merest
wave of any official wand to plant somewhere a dozen
of the long low huts, with their iron stoves, which must
frame so many memories in the minds of the war
generation—army memories of barrack-rooms with rows
of bedding and kit, orderly-rooms and company offices
with weak-legged tables and piles of army forms, the
nests in which sergeant-majors and soldier-clerks led
lives enviably remote from parades and fatigues ;
civilian memories of incessantly clicking typewriters,
incorrigible draughts, and the exasperating clatter of
feet upon the thin floors. Huts invaded the open spots
of London ; those built on the ground of the lake in
St James's Park—drained to prevent its reflection
locating the Whitehall neighbourhood to enemy aircraft
—had a sort of fame of their own ; huts to the extent
of positive cities settled down upon Salisbury Plain and
the Aldershot sandhills, Catterick and Cannock Chase ;
creeping lines of huts ran out at some point from almost
every town of any size ; pools of huts spread in all
manner of quiet places which for any reason might be
convenient for troops. Huts had become an immense
business, and they made some big fortunes.

A related subject of complaint was the enormous
increase of clerical staffs. The Ministry of Munitions
was said to have grown in numbers by 100,000 in the
space of two months. During the first rush of impromptu effort to meet the strain, staffs might reasonably have had to be increased without stopping to

think. But had not the time come for more careful organisation and saving of labour ? That line of argument was to gain in vigour during the next twelve months, with every reconsideration of our man-power. In the summer of 1917, with all the old Departments still adding fresh work to themselves, and the new Departments—Shipping Control, Food Control, Munitions, Labour, Pensions, Blockade—still discovering what they had to do, the civilian army was piling up its millions like the fighting army. Indeed there was no real pressure for economy ; the country had not yet had to ask itself very seriously where the money was coming from, and did not much want to ask. The ironies aimed at the " dug-outs " (another piece of war vocabulary) who had found remunerative jobs, and the vastly important young women, who made Government offices acquire the afternoon-tea habit and powdered their noses on the most august hearthrugs, remained as yet indulgent jests. For the money was flowing about in a pleasantly universal fashion. Some might wonder what was going to be the effect after the war of the " flapper " who had drawn a weekly salary as good as her father had earned before the war, of households formerly dependent on one man's earnings which now had three or four daughters in munitions. Some might wonder, too, what kind of a post-war life was likely to be faced by young men who were now drawing officers' pay with next to no responsibilities and plenty of amusement to be bought.

There was little hesitation in buying it, either. The tendency to feel that, when nearly everyone had a war job of some kind, or at least a war pressure on the old civilian job, one was free to amuse oneself, had increased rapidly ; and 1917 was a strange mixture of moods and behaviour. Strain, anxiety, the imminent shadow of death were there ; food and drink were costly, if not actually restricted; streets were dark at night Yet all the time people were dining and dancing as never before, the theatres full (*Chu Chin Chow* was at the height of its popularity, and *The Bing Boys* was rivalling it), cinemas beginning to grow into more spacious shape. If there was restlessness in the spending of money there were obvious reasons for this. Nearly everyone was extraordinarily at a loose end, millions away from home, and those still nominally at home conscious that the drain on men and women and the new independences had broken up completely the old settled ties. There was also the grimmer reason, too familiar now for pretence of concealment. Why should anything be grudged to the men who could never know, when a leave ended, whether they would see another ? If they felt they could waste no minute, if money seemed insignificant to them, who had any right to criticise them ? Who, indeed, had much right to say what life meant beside those who carried theirs in their hands ?

Conduct could have little significance except in its relation to the war. In that relation it might have the fullest possible range, from selfless idealism to the mere snatching at the immediate moment ; but it depended almost entirely upon the fibre of the individual character. Of authority there was next to none. That which had been the most vigorous side of English religious life in recent years, its efforts to make of faith less a duty in itself than an illumination of strenuous and robust social service, unfortunately ensnared it now. Honourably ashamed of their alienation from the national existence, through a century of torpor followed by a century of rather formal revivification confronted by strong movements of secular thought, the churches had endeavoured to find their way back into that existence by many paths—such as the growing political zeal of the Free Churches, the revaluation by Broad Churchmen of tradition and belief, devoted effort in slum missions and clubs. But all this meant that the national existence was colouring the mind of the churches rather than the other way round ; and they had little to bring to the war except what they had been giving for years in peace. Not that this was valueless ; example and influence did not fail. The Rev. G. A. Studdert-Kennedy, " Woodbine Willie," was only the best known of many of his kind ; Talbot House at Poperinghe was the home of a spiritual sincerity of effort which was to survive after the war in the organisation of " Toc H." But again it was far too much a question of the individual fibre of the chaplain, not the panoply of a church. Save for some admirable exceptions the army chaplain was to the mass of the soldiers a kind cheery person, who saw to their needs in cigarettes and chocolate, often served them in canteens, and gave them occasionally a bit of the old lost civilian life in some hearty hymns and a brief address. He wore not only an officer's uniform, but the mind of the officers' mess as well. The Roman Catholic chaplains were, of course, in wholly different case ; but in the army as a whole there were few of them. And to the bulk of the world at home, less near the ultimate realities, authority had become even more shadowy ; the doing of jobs and having a good time in the intervals made up the simple formula.

As the summer advanced, the check which the first few months of the new submarine campaign had administered tended to lose its hold. The alarm of the third week of April died down, as it was seen that that sudden big rise in the number of sinkings was not going to set the pace of destruction. Though the mere steadiness of the weekly total at a much lower figure might be a serious enough concern to the authorities, the country at large did not really grasp its meaning. It was, besides, convinced that much of the shortage and high prices was due to a profiteering "ramp"; and thought so the more when, on the retirement of Lord Devonport in June, his successor, Lord Rhondda, initiated at once a policy of limitation of prices. Lord Devonport, though he had the merit of bringing to the work of the Food Controller the expert knowledge of one who in his business days had been the head of a great firm of wholesale provision merchants, had brought to it also a reputation, from the days of the Port of London strike, of complete lack of sympathy with the classes which were suffering most from high prices. Lord Rhondda's change of policy, therefore, was the more marked. A fixing on 20th July of maximum prices for live cattle was followed by the control of all flour mills of any importance, and the fixing of prices for bread and potatoes. The year's crop of the latter promised so well, and the appeal for potato-growing had been so successfully answered, that the potatoless days were cancelled. Cheered, perhaps a little too easily, by seeing a restriction removed, and believing that fixed prices would bring out held-up supplies, the public lost much of its alarm of the spring.

Again the Government were in one of their frequent dilemmas. Anxious as they might be, in their clear understanding of the gravity of our losses of tonnage, they dared not impose too many restrictions. They had had a fresh warning in the report of an inquiry they had set on foot into the causes of industrial dis-affection. Engineers had been striking again, and arrests had had to be made; a railway strike had threatened and had only been averted by Sir Albert Stanley's promise that Government control should continue after the war long enough for a thorough consideration of the hours of work. Apart from actual stoppages of work there was an uneasy sense that labour conditions in general were dangerously restless, and output all the

while precarious. Mr Lloyd George had set committees
to work in different areas, and these now reported
that, besides the vexed questions of labour dilution and
conscription, disaffection was largely due to high prices
and the growing number of restrictions. Obviously,
then, a policy of fixed prices was to be preferred as
long as possible to any more restrictions of purchase by
rationing.

In one affair of the summer the Ministry had the
labour world on the whole with them. An International
Socialist Congress was to be held at Stockholm, and a
sudden storm arose in the Commons about the question
of granting passports to certain prominent Labour Party
members, Mr Ramsay MacDonald and Mr Jowett among
them, to attend the Congress. The Government's line
at first was to issue the passports on an understanding that no communication should be held with enemy
members of the Congress. But an unforeseen incident
altered the whole face of the matter. The Seamen's
and Firemen's Union, which had just previously brought
into the I.L.P. Conference some energetic views about
the war from the men who faced the submarine campaign, now refused to allow any ship to sail which was
to carry British Labour representatives to a Congress
including delegates of the enemy. At the annual conference between the Labour Party and the Trade Union
Congress Mr Arthur Henderson set himself to persuade
the meeting that British representatives should go to
Stockholm on the ground that the peoples of the Allies
could there present their case to the enemy peoples,
and perhaps open their eyes. But the conference was
not easy to persuade, and though after an adjournment
it did pass a resolution approving of the Stockholm
Congress, this was by so small a majority as to be
ineffective. There ensued a rather obscure controversy
between Mr Henderson, the Prime Minister and Mr

Bonar Law. Mr Henderson had just come back from a visit to Paris, where he had met representatives of French and Russian labour. What the Cabinet had or had not understood beforehand as to his intentions and the opinions he meant to express became simply a matter of point-blank contradiction, beyond solution. The personal upshot was that he resigned from the Cabinet, and Mr Barnes took his place ; the general upshot seemed to be that labour, however restless under war control, was not going to dissociate itself from the war. The Trade Union Congress in September passed a resolution against the attendance of British representatives at Stockholm.

The summer and autumn of 1917 were the gravest time of air raids. These were not only a night infliction, now that aeroplanes, instead of airships, were making them. With their swiftness of flight and smallness of mark the planes could raid boldly in the daytime. People were still slow to realise their danger ; during a big raid on 7th July, by a fleet of twenty planes, the general impulse was to be out watching the glittering things manœuvring in the sky. But as the raids increased, and perhaps especially because of the killing on 7th July of a number of children in an East End school (Mr Will Crooks, coming from the pitiful scenes of the inquest, had made a fiery speech in the House), it dawned upon the public that daylight raids had one serious aspect which night raids had not. At night people were mostly at home, in the daytime they would normally be moving about in the open. So the question arose of some system of warning on the approach of a raid, to give time for taking cover. There was some hesitation about doing this, mainly on the ground that it might lead to panic ; but after a rapid succession of raids at the end of September arrangements were made for giving warning, first by police and messengers in cars and on bicycles, with large notices, illuminated at night, and then, for greater efficiency and certainty, by sound signals instead of notices—whistles for the " Take cover " and bugles for the " All clear." Boy Scouts immensely enjoyed being used for the " All clear." To most people taking cover meant no more than staying in the safest part of their home or their office building. But from the flimsy crowded two-storey streets of the poorer quarters people flocked into the tubes, which were open to them for the purpose ; on moonlit nights these were often crowded as early as half-past five by mothers, with their families camped round them.

Under the Food Controller local committees were set to work in August and September, looking after his scale of limited retail prices, which had now extended to most cereals and some kinds of tea. They had also to attend to the first approach to real rationing. On 3rd August sugar supplies were put upon a new system ; everyone had to register with a particular retailer, and no supplies could be obtained except as a registered customer at one shop. This meant that instead of the irregularity of stocks, which had been leading since early in the year to queues at any shop which happened to have a supply, the Government could direct its distribution of sugar with some certainty of supplying every household. But queues, though undesirable, had had a certain salutary effect. The too easy reassurance of the public under fixed prices was calling now for a renewed economy campaign, and this led to a new post under the Food Controller, the Director of Food Economy, to which Sir Arthur Yapp was appointed. In effect it meant using, as a second line to Lord Rhondda's price policy, the system of recommended rations. Sir Arthur Yapp set to work to organise it through the local Food Committees.

There was another organisation too. Some of it did not mean very much to the ordinary man. The changing of the War Cabinet into the Imperial War Cabinet was more than a mere change of name. It enabled Mr Lloyd George to give himself and the nation the services of extra and unpaid Ministers, free for all sorts of impromptu duties, in the shape of distinguished Colonial leaders. In 1917 General Smuts took his place in this Cabinet. The South Africans' own peculiar part of the war was over. They had speedily secured German Southwest Africa; and though the campaign in German East Africa had been longer—the German Commander there, Von Lettow-Vorbeck, proved to be a great leader at the Boers' elusive kind of warfare—it had, for all practical purposes, finished. General Smuts came to England with a reputation made up partly of memories of the Boer War, partly of his very efficient work in this war, and partly of what South Africans said of his straightness, his good sense, his quiet clear-headedness. He was soon believed to be exerting a great influence behind the scenes.

No one was very clear as to the functions of the post of Director of Information under the Prime Minister (Mr John Buchan was its first holder) which seemed to turn later into a kind of Department under Lord Beaverbrook. Nor was it quite clear what the Ministry of Reconstruction was to do when the Bill establishing it was passed in November. It fitted in, however, with the general faith that the country after the war was not going back to old haphazard ways; and it occupied itself in collecting a mass of information and studying a wide range of questions. Much more obviously satisfactory was the other new Ministry now set up—the Ministry of Air. In one way it made little change; the Air Board, housed mainly in the Hotel Cecil, had already proved itself a sound outcome of all the criticism of our air policy, and there was little complaint now of our position in the air-fighting which was developing so astonishingly on the Western Front. But the creation of the Ministry put the whole subject on to the right level of importance. It led to one uncomfortable incident. Lord Cowdray was at the time head of the Air Board. He was left to discover from the publication of correspondence in the newspapers that the post of Air Minister had, without reference to him, been offered to Lord Northcliffe. Lord Northcliffe refused it, preferring to keep his newspapers free from any such limitation of action as his acceptance of a Ministry might have imposed ; his brother, Lord Rothermere, became the first Minister for Air.

CHAPTER VIII

THE WAR YEARS : PART IV

ONCE more, by imperceptible degrees yet very distinctly in the end, the nation's mood was changing. Through the latter part of 1917 the final phase of the war temper was creeping upon us. The war went on, work went on, discomforts went on; but some quality had faded out of it all. The endurance was not breaking, but it had gone numb. We had come to the time of setting our teeth.

There were serious reasons why we must do so. The first was that Russia was collapsing utterly. We could see now how fatuously we had at first responded to the news of the Revolution, how foolish it had been to suppose that any new regime could smoothly take the place of the old. For a few months it had been possible to believe that. A single figure, Kerensky, seemed to emerge, dominating the situation, keeping unity in the giant system, able to give orders. Then the truth began to appear, and we wondered how we could have expected anything else. The vast mass, once its tradition had gone, once it had stirred, was bound to disintegrate; and that it was doing through all the late summer. Armies were simply melting away, trudging off by whole divisions to board trains and go home. As yet we knew next to nothing of the names which were later to throw this first Revolution into the background—Lenin, Trotsky and the rest. We did not know that definite new purposes were shattering the nation. We saw what we thought only the inevitable crumbling of a people that had risen blindly against its sufferings, and had not found its new direction. By the autumn, Russia, for all practical purposes, was out of the war ; by December an armistice had been concluded, and the Germans were freeing themselves at Brest-Litovsk, in the meetings with the Russian delegates, from any more need for large forces on that Front. Their troops must be pouring westward.

Before this collapse was quite complete there came what looked like the beginning of another. In October the Italian armies were caught by a surprise, long and carefully prepared in the recesses and concealed valleys of the mountain Front on the Upper Isonzo, and had crumpled terribly. It was the disaster of Caporetto, which cost them nearly 3000 guns and 250,000 men taken prisoner, and drove them back from all their victorious advances to defence of the Piave. This might well mean still more enemy troops liberated for the Western Front. Yet the French and British had to draw on their own armies to reinforce Italy, lest she too should be driven to an armistice.

On our own Front yet another year was to end leaving us much where it had begun, and that in spite of two big attacks. The capture of Messines Ridge in October, beginning with an enormous explosion of mines, which was said to have been heard in London, had had no great results after all ; the Ridge had not given the commanding position over the German lines which had been expected. That battle had been followed by the long effort of Passchendaele, which seemed to give us some ground only at the cost of a new front line, which was far worse to hold than the old one. Two exhausting battles, and of the other Allied Fronts one gone and the other most dangerously shaken. The looking ahead to the next year had a different tone this time ; it could not but be a sober reckoning of the weight that must be going to fall on the French and British Fronts.

A sober reckoning, but not nervous. The Front must hold, the finish must be fought. The man-power must be found; and, as far as the Government's statements went, it was going to be found. There was to be no more divided authority in this matter, and no more frittering of decision among local bodies. The Ministry of National Service, in its original form as a sort of civilian counterpart of the military directorship of recruiting, had not been a striking success. When Mr Neville Chamberlain resigned, the control of the whole man-power of the nation was unified, the Director of Recruiting, Sir Auckland Geddes, becoming Director of National Service. The Geddes brothers were just then reaching the high curve of their rather surprising appearance in our public affairs. Sir Eric Geddes, by way of a post in the Ministry of Munitions and then the Directorship of Military Transport, had become First Lord of the Admiralty in the summer of 1917. He, coming from a vigorous career in the railway world, was — and looked — one of the captains of industry for whom the country had been clamouring, to bring some business courage and imagination into the conduct of the war. Sir Auckland Geddes, coming from—and looking like—an academic career, which had taken him to the principalship of a Canadian university, was less immediately explicable, but he must be, it was supposed, another of Mr Lloyd George's happy discoveries.

At any rate he was energetic enough in his promises when, in December, he made his statement about man-power. That question had changed its nature. It was no longer a matter of how to find more men to draft into the army or into munitions. More men were not there to find. Man-power meant now getting everyone into the place where he was wanted; the end of the *embusqué* must come, wherever he was. This was what Sir Auckland Geddes promised. With the whole affair under his single hand—conscription, medical inspection, exemption, indispensable occupation, and so on—he could start on the one course left to us now, a searching and continuous " comb-out." He announced in the Commons that his Department was already card-indexing every man of the forces kept in England, and that the back areas in France would be combed too, as well as all the huge Departments at home. He had in mind returning men to civil work, especially on the land and for building aeroplanes, as well as putting every fit man into the fighting line ; and, indeed, the two were bound to go together. There was vigour in the statement. There needed to be, for if man-power slipped through the comb there was nothing left.

That was one of the marked elements in this ultimate mood of the war. There was no untried effort to turn to, no new inspiration for our strength. The machine must do it now. It was fully made, we were all in its grip, from the smallest civilian job at home to the remotest and most forgotten " cushy job " in France. There was nothing now to be magnificently achieved ; there was only a determined grinding along towards something that we must make ourselves reach. Determined it remained ; the purpose somehow held ; but it had grown, when tired men and women could stop to think about it, soulless and mechanical. Through months and months, as the scope and pressure and the unpredictable developments of the war revealed themselves, people had thought incessantly of the way to meet them, method, machinery. They had it now. The machine worked. And the life had gone out of it. The impulse was no strong, common flame any longer. It had become—what had it become ? No one who asked that question now could quite answer it.

There lay, on both sides of the struggle, the insidious anxiety of the final phase. The only open recognition of this by the Government was an energetic promotion of propaganda in enemy countries; the best way to counter any numbing of the war spirit at home was to suggest that weakening of purpose on the other side had reached a point at which it might be worked upon to produce collapse. So there were now areoplanes at the Front, dropping bundles of pamphlets instead of bombs into the German trenches (Mr Punch's title-page for 1918 depicted him so engaged); and flights of tiny, gay-coloured balloons were liberated, when the wind was favourable, to spread pamphlets all over the enemy's back areas. Another new Department came into being, the Directorship of Propaganda, which Lord Northcliffe did not refuse. However, there was another picture in the same issue of *Punch*, which implied very clearly that public opinion in the enemy countries was not the only thing to think about. It showed a British soldier and sailor appealing to the people at home to "stick it"; and we were hearing again an echo of a cry of the moment in France, " Que les civiles tiennent."

Naturally the anxiety concerned itself most acutely with the civilian population. They were not under discipline, and there were so many ways—evasion of restrictions, slackening of effort, resignation of jobs, and open striking—in which failure of the war-feeling might take form. This accounts for the peculiarly heated resentment provoked by the Lansdowne peace letter. Lord Lansdowne wrote to *The Daily Telegraph* at the end of November a letter suggesting that the time had come to make efforts for a peace by negotiation. That was one way of recognising the chance of playing upon German feeling. But it was the last way desired by the British leaders. Mr Lloyd George at once replied that there was "no half-way house between defeat and victory," and denounced as a public danger anyone who thought there was. "Defeatism" had become the bogy of public men, and Lord Lansdowne suffered for it. Distinguished as his career had been in foreign affairs, he had always been remote from the ordinary man, and it was only too easy now to hustle his proposals out of sight. He never took a prominent place in the national life again ; this brave and serious gesture was the last act of a long and faithful service to the State.

With regard to the armies, anxiety had not to be so watchful and persistent. They were under discipline and the rigid military law. There was only one way in which a weakening of resolve could show among them ; and only then if it were disastrously widespread and deep. Yet the mind of the armies too had changed, and the authorities knew it. Indeed, it is probably true that the armies, always living under the machine in an entirely different way from the civilian, had felt before the civilians the creeping in of that numbing mechanicalness. In part it was due to the very excellence of all the military arrangements now. Here also the whole thing *worked* about as smoothly as it could. From the depots and training camps and officer cadet corps at home, out to the big Base camps of Le Havre or Étaples, along the whole gradation of the lines of communication, through rest camps, detail camps, army and corps schools of drill, gunnery, bombing, gas, through the belt of corps and divisional headquarters, up to the rest billets, the forward area and the line the machine worked. Not only that, but the High Command had seen to it that it worked to give the soldier all the health and comfort, all the casual amusement and distraction that was possible. From the dirt and " minor horrors," as they were called, of the trenches troops went back to divisional baths, ingeniously installed in ruinous chateaux and sugar factories, and got a complete change of under-clothes, instead of retiring to draughty rest billets to hunt lice. Expeditionary Force canteens supplemented generously the old Y.M.C.A. huts. Pay had been improved and men had money to spend in estaminets. Concert-parties were encouraged among the men themselves (and how good they were, with all the talent that had so unexpectedly found itself in uniform!), and concert and theatrical parties from England were always at the Base camps and were taken into the rest-billet areas. Night and day, in every weather, tearing along the back-area roads and steeplechasing wildly through the forward areas, the despatch riders shuttled to and fro in an incessant racket of open exhausts, knitting closer the whole enormous fabric.

It worked, through every careful gradation; and there lay its danger. One of the civilian soldiers of those days, looking back afterwards to the change of mood in 1917, has said that what happened seemed to be that, whereas earlier they had felt they were fighting *for* something, fighting too *against* something, they now felt that they were merely fighting.[1] The mechanism was so good, its construction had taken so much pains and energy and attention, that men were beginning to wonder whether anybody in authority was still asking himself what it was all for, whether it ever would occur to anybody to stop it. As long as there was strain and awkwardness in the management and the life generally of these vast armies, there might remain the saving sense of temporariness, of effort for an emergency. But now that the war world was so completely a world, might it not take on a dreadful kind of permanence? This was, in its way, the same as the civilian feeling; we were grinding along in a hazy sense that there was something we must do, and no one pulling up for a minute to examine with anything like a free mind *what* we

[1] Mr R. H. Mottram, in *Ten Years After*. This seems to have been true of both sides. Much the same kind of feeling is discernible in, for instance, *The Case of Sergeant Grischa*, by Arnold Zweig.

thought we must do. True, it was only at a later date that the feeling could be put as reflectively as that ; at the time it was much more vague. But it was there, and the concern about war-weariness in the army and the *moral* of the troops is the proof of it.

It might even be put in a rather paradoxical way ; the fighting armies were wondering if they were not a bit too good at their job. They did it so well that they had become the kind of instrument which the authorities could use confidently. And they began to feel simply like an instrument, and to wonder about the people who handled them. For the fighting armies had become entirely new, a made thing, very efficient. One of the strongest impressions of that time is that their job was both entirely new and yet also thoroughly practised and accustomed. They learned little but the new war-fare now : the minimum of drill, more for discipline and a habit of unity in action than for anything else ; for the rest, gas drills, bombing and bayonet-fighting, sniping and machine-gunning, the technique of trench raids, and craft in keeping alive, made up their training. Their ranks were new ; very few now of the old army survived among them, even in the old army battalions, except as those king-pins of the military unit, regimental and battery sergeant-majors, and company sergeant-majors. Their officers were new, except, again, for some regimental and a few battalion commanders. The ranks and the officers' messes alike were making their own traditions. The days were gone when the first sprinkling of the new officers into the old messes, with their particular code of conduct, had produced its crop of jokes about " temporary gentlemen." The phrase might still be heard. An officer of the old army, coming carefully groomed from corps or divisional headquarters, or from even more august regions, might think in that way of the groups in dug-outs, where stockbrokers,

schoolmasters, city clerks, undergraduates and promoted
sergeant-majors made up what would be unrecognisable
to him as an officers' mess. Pernickety A.P.M.'s at the
Base, or embarkation officers at Boulogne, might be
exasperated by the sight of captains and lieutenants in
worn khaki, shapeless caps and high boots out of
ordnance stores, looking, with their packs and haversacks and muddy trench-coats, far more like the men
they commanded than like the old idea of men in command. The fighting officers did not mind. They drew
together in their own little groups on the leave-boats or
in cafés, for they had their own pride and a new tradition
which they were certainly not afraid, if need were, to
set confidently beside the tradition that now lived on
mainly in the Staff.

Here, too, lay an insidious danger. They knew their
job, these men of the new army. But what if they began
to question whether those who kept them at it really
knew what they were doing, or had any policy that
mattered now ? They could fight, and fight well ; but
that had made them very open-eyed. Small wonder if
the interminable mud-choked struggle of Passchendaele
made the armies begin to ask themselves whether the
masters of the machine had any clear ideas. Hanging
on to the edges of craters captured and recaptured over
and over again, slipping into shell-holes to drown, sucked
down, wounded, into liquid mud, bombing and machine-
gunning along a line that was a mere spasmodic string
of holes, always changing shape under the shelling—
small wonder if men began to be aware of a suspicion
that the war was turning into an immense futility. Yet
the deepest futility of all, curiously enough, rooted itself
in the feeling that the whole thing was unescapable ; it
must go on. Whatever the soldiers might think, they
had not the slightest intention of letting the country
down.

So it is in recalling these last two years of the war that one catches sight, dimly, perhaps, of what full-grown heroism is like. Round those armies hung none of the panoplied glamour of the " Old Contemptibles," lit by the great tradition of Waterloo, Lucknow, Kandahar. They were simply the new civilian armies. From them had even departed the romantic gleam of " the First Hundred Thousand." They were serving under no beguiling illusion of glory or lofty sacrifice. Soldiers would not swallow any longer the kind of thing that had sent men gaily to war in 1914. They had their own opinion of the ruthless war views of elderly patriots, and devoted suppliers of war material, and administrative indispensables, so safe and so voluble at home. That opinion was not often expressed, but it found words occasionally, as in Mr Siegfried Sassoon's poems ; and action occasionally, as when in the spring of 1918 the troops at Étaples broke out in anger against the complacent newspapers, which shrieked about the dropping of bombs there upon hospital huts, and had nothing to say of the gross stupidity of imperilling wounded men and nurses by placing big hospitals alongside a notoriously large Base camp for combatants. Expression of these kinds might be rare, but the disillusion behind them was universal. And yet these fighting men, with no belief in politicians jostling one another obscurely in and out of office, or in the cheap stuff which passed for public opinion, stuck grimly to their faith in one another and in something that must be their country behind all the tawdry " patriotism." That is why one can see, in the time when no one talked of heroes, what heroism, not impulsive and bedecked and dazzled, is like. Those huge numbers of men, each with a quiet, peaceable place in life at home which he had had to leave, went to and fro to the fighting line with very little delusion about their chances of ever getting back.

Night after night they were marching up to the trenches,
transport drivers and despatch riders were starting
along the shell-blasted roads, gunners crouching under
camouflages, quite sure that sooner or later "their
number would be up." No romantic nonsense about war
was left ; only a racking familiarity with the morning
and evening " stand to," the periodical " strafes " and
"hates " of the artillery (we had not given up that
kind of ironical war vocabulary), wiring, the sudden
murderous infernos of trench raids, and death, ugly and
revolting. They faced death as no armies in the world
had ever faced it. And instead of heroics they sang :

> " Oh, my, I don't want to die,
> I want to go home."

At home those who waited had to reach in some way
the same sort of heroism grown out of romantic trap-
pings. It had long ceased to be something fine and
distinguishing to have one's man or one's sons at
the war. That was the common lot, its dead-weight of
apprehension a mere flat monotony now.

Towards the end of 1917 a fresh breath of interest
blew through the war news. General Allenby, taking
command in Egypt, had turned the situation there from
a defence of the canal into a new attack on the Turks,
and had moved across the deserts into Palestine. There
was one strange and interesting feature of this campaign.
The soldiers' letters home, which had had so little to
say of places, however wonderful in their way, that
struck no chord in their minds, like the classic spots of
the Ægean or the Nile, suddenly sprang into vividness
when they wrote of places in Palestine. Whatever might
be said of the emptiness of churches and the failing hold
of Christianity, the Bible story now proved to be so deep
in the ordinary English mind that, as the army moved
among the Bible place-names—Beersheba, Gaza, Jaffa,

the Dead Sea, the Jordan—the soldiers wrote almost
as if they were in some sense at home. It was with a
naïve kind of surprise and affection that they came close
to the most sacred spots, Bethlehem, the Mount of Olives,
Jerusalem itself. Even at this late and disillusioned
stage of the war, when no one could think much of the
Christianity of Europe, there was a rather anxious
pause as Jerusalem was approached. Would that city,
of all cities, have to be blown to pieces, and filled with
blood and death ? The news that this had not happened
was received with real relief. But it was the religious
feeling of the Turks, rather than of the Christians, that
saved Jerusalem ; when on 8th December Allenby had
it obviously at his mercy, it was peacefully surrendered.
The British occupied it on 11th December.

Interesting it was, but it was all remote, and retreating
Turks could make little difference. There was only one
real area of the war now. Just as in the winter of 1915
our first concentrated ideas had opened out, and we
began to see the war as a vast embattled ring all round
Europe, so now ideas narrowed again, and we could see
it pressing only more and more intensely upon us. This
was not merely a vague feeling ; it was becoming a daily
experience in the December of 1917 and the January of
1918, with a sudden sharpening of difficulty in getting
food. To be a registered customer no longer meant
that one was sure of supplies. Queues had grown again
for butter, margarine and tea ; and then, just as they
began to grow for meat and bacon, they were rather
startlingly stopped by a complete and visible emptiness
of the butchers' shops. There was always miscellaneous
stuff in a grocer's shop, so that shortage of a few things
did not necessarily discourage queues. But shortage of
meat left nothing in a butcher's shop to make a queue
for, and in January butchers quite frequently did not
open at all. The big wholesale meat markets were also

visibly empty. Rationing at last had to come. It began
with a General Order that registered customers were to
be entitled to no more than ¼ lb. of butter, 1½ oz. of tea,
and ½ lb. of sugar per head per week ; this was not as
yet enforced by ration cards. Next came a new Order
about meals in restaurants. Two days a week, Wednesday and Friday, were to be meatless ; no meat on any
day was to be served at breakfast ; no milk to be served
as a beverage except to children ; the quantity of bread
or cake at tea was cut down to 1½ oz. ; and customers
were not to be provided with any sugar. People had to
carry their own little packet of sugar about with them
(they had long done this when paying calls), or the phials
of saccharine tablets that now became so familiar. The
meat ration of the army was reduced for all units mainly
engaged in office and depot work ; and it began to dawn
upon the public that, as the soldiers were now far more
secure in food supplies than the civilians, common sense
had better replace enthusiasm in canteens, and make a
less lavish provision of food in them. Before January
was out, compulsory rationing of meat, on a card system,
was announced. The cards were being issued to every
household early in February and became operative on
25th February.

They gave the conscientious housewife some distracted
thinking to do, but the newspapers set to work to help
her by simplifying the phraseology of official regulations,
and giving specimen lists of purchases to show how the
system worked. Every section of a card entitled to so
much meat-stuff ; but it might be so much money value
of butcher's meat, or so much weight of poultry or game,
or cooked or canned or potted meat. The planning of a
week's supplies became a complicated problem of fitting
together joints with bones, chicken without feathers,
rabbits without skins, sausages with them, and occasional long shots at improbable things like venison. The

popular restaurants rose to the occasion at once, with
meals devised to cost exactly a coupon or two ; busy
waitresses' duties had to be simple, and people out to
lunch from business needed simplicity too, in order to
know exactly how many of their coupons they would
have to subtract each week from the household pool.
The great hotels and expensive restaurants involved
their customers—or, at any rate, their waiters—in more
intricate coupon performances at the end of a meal.

People were good-humoured about it, and the Government were careful to say cheering things at the same
time. They were announcing in January that the submarine menace was now " held " ; there was not the
least need for alarm, only for care and system. New
construction of ships was overtaking the losses, and
new ways of warfare were tackling the submarines.
There was, in fact, little real alarm, for there had been
for some months rumours of what was going on. We
had heard talk of improvised shipyards doing marvellous
things in rapid construction, and even of concrete ships,
swift and simple to build ; we had heard, too, of hydro-
phone " listeners," which located submarines, depth-
charges which crumpled and buckled and holed them,
and then, more thrillingly, of the mystery ships which,
looking like tramp steamers and full of navy men playing
at being rag-tag crews, let themselves be torpedoed on
the heroic chance that the submarine would be tempted
up to the surface in time for their concealed guns to
destroy her before they went down themselves.

Thus for the last eighteen months of the struggle sea-
fighting, like everything else, as it seemed, in this war,
went in unexpected ways, and stimulated heroism which
no one had foreseen. The glamour was not, after all, to
spread at its brightest over those immense battleships
and swift battle-cruisers, with the long guns nosing
out at their sinister turrets, which had been so great a

pride, as year by year before the war they took the water. True, the real effect of the battle of Jutland had by now emerged more distinctly. Dubious as the results may have been on paper, the German main fleet had never come out again; and the thought of our own fleet away in the misty remoteness of Scapa Flow gathered once more associations of power and mastery. But just as modern war on land had turned from the old spectacular clash of great moving armies into the tireless, watchful activities of trench-fighting and "pushes," so the sea war passed from the big fleets to the submarines and the destroyer flotillas, to the mine-sweepers and the motor-launch patrols. The old navy had become, as the old army had, the highly trained professional core of the fighting, radiating out like the main threads of a spider's web through a vast network of civilian service; and at sea, as on land, the war had become a tangled conflict of impromptu ingenuities and inventiveness, cold courage at insignificant jobs, and relentless endurance. People never knew as much of the sea service as they knew of the land-fighting; there were not the millions engaged in it to make it so familiar. But they heard something of the yachtsmen and amateurs who largely made up the motor-boat patrols; of the plain and homely tugs and steam-trawlers which went about the perilous business of mine-sweeping as simply as they had gone about their old affairs; of the crews of the lesser mercantile marine and tramp steamers, whose hard and dangerous lives, always close enough to death, had been made even more deadly. The shock of the battle of Jutland had been gradually lost in the sense that even in the strange ways of this strange war we were still the island nation, at home upon the sea, and its born masters.

Air raids were beginning to be defeated too. They were constant throughout this winter on moonlight

nights. A fresh kind of outcry about aliens arose from
these raids. Those possessed of money—" Jews " was the
common description of them—were said to be moving out
of London, and swarming, the richer ones to Maidenhead
and other up-river places, the rest into Slough and its
neighbourhood; about the latter there was particular
indignation, because one of the big Government depots
of war material was known to be growing up there, and
workers at it were being crowded out by these fugitives
from London. Aliens of the poor class were accused of
being responsible for the real panics that raids now
brought in the crowded quarters of East London and
south of the river, and for the wild rushes to the overcrowded tubes. Raids had indeed become far more
terrifying experiences, not only in the casualties inflicted
(death-rolls of forty or fifty, with eighty or a hundred
injured, were frequent), but also in their nerve-shattering
noise. The alarm was now given by heavy explosions of
maroons, and London had by this time such a force of
anti-aircraft batteries that the succeeding hour or two
became one continuous appalling uproar, punctuated
with the splitting crash of bombs. But at least the uproar did mean defence ; raiders were at last finding it
occasionally impossible to attack London itself, and had
to turn back and drop their bombs elsewhere. All this
made more rumours of new devices, and mysterious
headquarters in London, where sound-observations of
approaching planes were worked out, and the line of
the raid watched till the time came for orders to be
telephoned to searchlight stations and batteries and
gun-carrying lorries.

At this stage of the war it was only from time to
time that the country paid any attention to politics. In
general it was inclined to think that Parliament might
as well cease to meet, for it was apt to do harm. Attacks
on Ministers were considered to be more likely to give

away secrets to the enemy (for they usually concerned some war event) than to help us. In December the House had gone into secret session again, the sixth occasion, because one of these attacks, by Mr Joseph King, was putting into words matter which had to be kept out of print. In January the Franchise Bill, with the vote for women, and the Education Bill, which, besides its general enriching of the educational system, abolished the " half-timer " and drastically restricted the employment of children, passed into law. But another of the long problems of politics was still unsettled—Ireland. The placing of the Home Rule Act on the Statute Book in September 1914 had been at the best little more than a gesture ; feelings that had been on the verge of civil war in the July of that year had only gone into suspension when the greater war began. The rising of April 1916 had shown that even the gesture was useless ; and at intervals there were bits of news in the papers which showed how fiery the embers of that rising still were, breaking out into flames of murderous attack here and there, especially in County Clare, where Mr de Valera had won a by-election for Sinn Fein. But people had not yet learned what those two words really meant, and Parliament had gone on busying itself in the belief that it could still deal with the Irish question. A Convention had been gathered in Ireland in 1917 to propose a scheme for Parliament to consider, in the hope, or the delusion, that this would be a way of getting Ireland to solve her own problems. Sinn Fein, however, had simply held aloof from it ; and now, just as in the old days Mr Gladstone had had to suppress the Land League with one hand while offering Home Rule with the other, Mr Lloyd George was devising a scheme on the Convention's lines and trying to suppress Sinn Fein. We had not advanced at all ; after all the hopes of recent years we were back in the old impasse with only the names of things changed. It must have been in sorrow of heart that at this juncture, early in March, Mr John Redmond died. With tactics so different from Parnell's, a nature so different, liked by the House yet never beguiled by its liking, he had been as single-minded and as persistent as his predecessor in the leadership of the Irish party. He used opportunities differently, but he never missed or wasted them. He had seen a Home Rule Bill become an Act at last, only to become also a dead letter. He had led his party to that victory, only to feel Ireland slipping from him into far other hands.

A current of politics hardly observed at the time, but of no small significance, was the revision of the Independent Labour Party's constitution. In the autumn of 1917 membership of it—hitherto a group membership of trade unions and other societies—was made individual. What this meant, of course, was the passage of the party from the position of an industrial entity to the position of a national political party, from representing the wage-earner in his groups to representing a distinct and separate outlook upon politics in general, with which many were ready to associate themselves who had under the old rule no possible means of joining the party, because they could belong to no labour organisation. This was emphasised in the spring of 1918 by a change altering the party's professed purpose to that of furthering the interests of workers " by hand or brain." With these changes the further resolution could be taken to establish a Labour Party in every constituency. Instead of being merely a Parliamentary instrument for the industrial vote, and therefore not much seen outside industrial areas, the party was now to take its place beside the two great traditional parties as in the widest sense a third alternative for the general voter. All this was thoroughly in the spirit of the British

Labour movement, politics instead of the class war, a vertical section of the nation instead of a horizontal one, a recognition that there were Conservative and Liberal wage-earners, so that it was a pity not to open the Labour Party to people of means who might be Socialists. The change would probably have come in any case; but here again was a development hastened by the war. The breaking down of some old barriers, the presence of Labour in the War Cabinet, the new sense of Labour in the national life, must all have worked to hasten the change.

Yet in some ways it was an unfortunate moment for such a move. A bid by the Labour Party to rank as a national party came rather ill at a time when their rank and file were constantly repudiating their leadership in industrial disputes, and were laying themselves open, by striking in war time, to the accusation that they were too incurably sectional in outlook ever to have a national appeal; they could not think nationally even in the direst need the nation had ever faced. Mr Henderson was warning the Government and Parliament in February that "at no time during the war had the industrial situation been so bad." The new "comb-out" was reviving the double resentment against conscription and dilution; skilled men were threatening a huge strike if the comb were not so directed that dilution labour was taken first. Besides, wage-earners of all kinds resented the beginnings of rationing. They felt more than other people the puzzles of trying to arrange the weekly budget; they suspected that distribution of supplies was, as their men had taught them about so much in the army, a matter of "wangling," and that the shops in their own streets came off badly in comparison with the rich folk's shopping quarters; and they remained convinced, to the end of the war and beyond it, that the whole pressure was more due to profiteering than to any real shortage of food-stuffs. The new restrictions in mid-March—the closing of all places of entertainment at 10.30 P.M. for the saving of fuel in heating and light, and the prohibition of any cooking in restaurants between 9.30 P.M. and 5 A.M. the next morning—did not perhaps affect the wage-earners very much, but they were suffering from what had caused the new restrictions—difficulties in the supply of coal—and anyhow restrictions in general were becoming an increasing exasperation to them. They felt badgered and put about, and senselessly caught in the machine.

Suddenly upon all the uneasiness at home fell the thunderclap of the March disaster. There had been from the latter part of February statements now and then in the papers about information of a coming German Offensive, gathered from prisoners. Everyone had known in a vague way that the collapse of Russia must mean a concentration of German forces in the West for a desperate struggle there. Mr Lloyd George, on the first receipt of the news, was taking the line in Parliament that it had all been allowed for, and that the British retreat was a foreseen necessity; but the newspapers did not look like that. They looked as if we had been caught very badly by surprise, and there was a wild outcry for a scapegoat. On 21st March, in the blind thickness of a densely misty morning, masses of troops had flung themselves startlingly, without any artillery preparation to give warning, on the Fifth Army, and the Front had given way completely. Someone must suffer for that, and the Army Commander, General Sir Hubert Gough, was relieved of his command. All the scattered feeling that not the nation itself, but the way in which it was being handled, was our weakness concentrated upon him and his staff. The men had been heroic enough; they had fought desperately; every available man, down to the cooks and the transport and the labour companies, had rallied to the shock and held up the rush wherever for a little while it was possible to stand firm. The frightful failure lay in the complete surprise, and that came back to the Staff. The anger rose with the violent tension of anxiety for the next ten days. The Front had broken as no Front had broken yet in the West. This was no short costly effort. Along something like fifty miles, from the Scarpe to the Oise, our line had gone, and day after day it gave ground more. By the 24th we were back to the Somme, and the thrusting German salient on the maps went stretching forward still. The papers were urgent against panic ; those that had most vented the bitter outcry at first steadied themselves down to telling the country that this was the crisis bound to come, the last effort, the supreme moment for holding on ; it was the winning or losing of the war.

And well it might be, as the effect of the thrust grew daily clearer. The enemy was coming appallingly close to Amiens, and if he reached that, he could cut the French and British apart, and utterly disorganise the whole of the vital railway communications to the line. Albert was lost ; the enemy got Montdidier, and Amiens was within gun-range. But by then hope had begun to glimmer again. The rush was slackening ; the line was beginning to hold. By 1st April the news was definite that the German Advance was stemmed, and by 3rd April the intensity of battle was dying down. In the pause that followed, the Prime Minister made an announcement which strengthened enormously the great sense of relief. In the future the Allied armies were to be in one single command ; Marshal Foch was to be supreme. Sir Douglas Haig, generously effacing himself, had agreed. It was a piece of good sense that comforted nearly everybody. There had been attempts in 1917 to bring about unity through an Allied War Council at

Versailles ; but no one had been much interested in it, or in the complicated incidents in February 1918 which led to the resignation of Sir William Robertson and the appointment of Sir Henry Wilson as Chief of the Imperial General Staff. There had been controversy about this in Parliament, but it had only wearied people with the sense that all this personal quarrelling was not getting on with war. The single command pleased them, not simply as a strategic soundness, but as a kind of promise that there would be less of all this half-political wrangling mixed up with the job of war.

The pause of relief was very short. There was just time to take in the pressing appeals to the munition workers to make good the heavy losses of material, and give up their Easter holidays ; to hear how the King had hurried over to France for his armies to see him at the crisis ; to read of the amazing things that the airmen (they became the Royal Air Force early in March) did nowadays, swooping low to pour bombs and machine-gun bullets upon trenches, and transport and moving batteries. There had just been time, too, to introduce on 5th April a new Man-Power Bill, putting the age for conscription up to 50, and providing for drastic withdrawal of exemption from young men, when, on 9th April, another piece of the Front broke. Again on a thick misty morning, and again without preliminary bombardment, the Germans attacked just south of Ypres, where some Portuguese troops were in the line, drove in a salient of three and a half miles, and started to soak Armentières and Bailleul with gas-shelling till they had to be evacuated. Fighting had begun again, too, in front of Amiens. " The sternest and most critical hour of the war," as *The Times* called it, was going to be a terribly long one. The rush in the north was never so sweeping as the first had been ; but it was every bit as alarming, for it showed how tremendous the German

bid for victory was going to be. Haig's message was
the grimmest truth : " There is no other course open
to us but to fight it out. Every position must be held
to the last man ; there must be no retirement." It
was longer now before the news was allowed to be
reassuring. The Messines Ridge, won so few months
before, was lost again by 16th April, and a terrific fight
began for Mont Kemmel. Gas-soaked, like the ruined
towns, the small heights round Ypres were growing
more and more difficult to hold ; and we were soon back
in the fears of the early days of the war, and " the
fight for Calais." But it was a stern fight, and the
single command showed itself now in the bringing up
of fresh divisions from the French reserves to take over
the struggle for Kemmel.

This was still going on when, with the abruptness
with which all big war news, good or bad, was wont
to come, the St George's Day raid by the navy on
Zeebrugge rang out gallantly. To dash the Germans'
last hopes of their submarine campaign while they were
pouring men into their immense effort on land was
good ; and as far as we could know it had been done.
Though a shift of wind had rather spoiled the smoke-
screen, the concrete-filled ships which had been meant
to block the submarine harbour, if not sunk quite in
the right spot, seemed at least to have made the use of
the harbour almost impossibly awkward. Anyhow, the
story was a great one, the swoop of the fighting ships,
the reckless laying of the *Vindictive* alongside the mole,
the sailors leaping ashore in the hand-to-hand way of
an old-time boarding, the blowing-up of the connecting
link between the mole and the pier, the flare-lit, gun-lit
devilry and courage of the whole thing. It sufficed to
carry us over the last few anxious days around Ypres,
the final loss of Kemmel Hill on 26th April, the fear of
the thrust coming right through ; and on to the second

pause of relief when on 1st May the papers could announce the defeat of a heavy German attack towards Ypres itself, the stemming of the rush, and the new line holding firm.

During those days the most famous of Germany's fighting airmen was killed, Captain von Richthofen. His name was almost as well known in England as in Germany. For air-fighting had been taking a larger and larger place in the news, and it always kept a character of its own which marked it off from the rest of the war. One reason was that it had such fresh power to stir the imagination—the clash in the air of these swirling, diving, flashing things, droning like vicious wasps, swooping in a sudden silence, and bursting into a savage roar again, while the machine guns rattled spasmodically across the sky. It was so amazing, too, that in these three or four years men, who had so lately been so cautious in the air, took it now so casually that they could fling their machines right and left, sideways and upside down, with no more anxiety than a bird has. It all meant, of course, that the flying officers were specially chosen men, put through the most searching tests of body and nerves, out to take any and every risk. An aerodrome officers' mess was like no other in the army, for they hardly ever sat down in the evening as they had been in the morning, and there was a queer loneliness in the deaths they died. Most of all, air-fighting— perhaps because it alone in this vast impersonal war kept the glamour of personal combat—maintained a real chivalry. So we had known of von Richthofen, who added to skill and daring notable even among airmen a piratical touch by painting scarlet the machines of his squadron—" Richthofen's Circus," as our men called it. The air chivalry was strong when he was buried with full honours behind our lines, and the planes of both sides dropped wreaths upon his grave.

Attention was too strained in other directions to be concerned about the Budget, though this year the revenue was put at the astounding figure of £842,000,000. In one sense there could be by now no real comparison with pre-war Budgets : the value of money had so completely altered. Letter post at 1½d. and postcards at 1d. —two of the imposts of this year—were, in fact, no more than an adjustment of revenue figures to this new value. Income tax at 6s., spirit duty at 30s. a gallon and beer duty at 50s. a barrel represented certainly stiffish increases of taxation, but not the enormous increases that pre-war values would suggest. To those who could stop to think about it, finance was almost the greatest of the many staggering ways in which all prediction had gone wrong. It had been so conclusively proved before the war that the appalling cost and money destruction of a modern war simply could not go on for more than a few months. Pacifist writers had even convinced many people that, in face of an inevitable stalemate ending, war could not be worth any nation's while. Yet here we were, well into a fourth year of war, and the money was there. The ordinary public knew nothing but the plain fact that salaries and service pay and wages went on, aware only of queer prices and pressures that made them demand rises and bonuses. Economists knew more, but could not yet see effects clearly. Bankers were showing that there was something behind it all which warned them to remould the credit structure. In the latter part of 1917 and the early part of 1918 those banking amalgamations took place which have put the control of money and credit into the hands of " The Big Five." This policy was watched with some jealousy, though it was not until after the war that it came in for heavy criticism. The amalgamations were the natural application to the rather dimly apprehended new finance of a process which had long been going on. Steady increase, alike in the quantity of money and in the banking habits of the people, had for many years before the war induced a stabilising of the system by continual absorption of the old private banks into great joint-stock concerns, and a " run " on a bank had become a thing relegated entirely to past days. The Mortiboys and Ovendens and Doughtys of the early nineteenth century had been such familiar human personages in their communities that credit had meant their own individual circumstances and reputation, which panic could throw down. But it was next to impossible to have anxieties about the wealth of a great ramified joint-stock bank. Now, with a swift and violent expansion of currency, the manageability of which might well appear very doubtful, the credit structure had to be made even more taut against possible strain, and put into few enough hands to ensure co-operation and mutual understanding at a crisis. Criticism was on the same lines as that aroused by the earlier absorptions of local banks. The ill effect of these, inevitable, perhaps, but hard, had been that the old elasticity of credit to a local customer was lost. A private banker would constantly take the risk of giving credit in a time of need on his own faith in his client; big centralised banks could do it only by uniform rules. On a much bigger scale the anxiety now was of the same kind; credit would become more and more a matter of bank policy, pure and simple, with the elimination of a competition between banks which had forced them to some courting at least of their customers' interests.

Another subject which, like the Budget, was obscured by the acute anxiety of the war news was the Government's scheme, based on the report of the Convention, for Ireland. All the labour and controversy of the years just before the war became sheer waste. The new proposals gave up the idea of a separate Ulster, meeting the

case of that province and the Southern Unionists partly
by a retention of 42 Irish members at Westminster,
partly by a guarantee of a minimum membership of
at least 40 per cent. of the Irish House of Commons
for the Unionists, made up of additional members for
Ulster and nominated Unionist members for other parts
of Ireland. Sir Edward Carson had resigned from the
War Cabinet early in the year, to have his hands
free.

The only aspect of the Irish situation which went
into the mind of the country at large was that these
proposals were accompanied by the question of extending
conscription to Ireland. The Man-Power Bill introduced in all the anxiety of the German rushes raised
the conscription age to 50, and made a clean cut of all
exemptions for men under $23\frac{1}{4}$, wherever they were—in
Government Departments, in munition works, or on the
land. An England so drained of men looked angrily
across at an Ireland keeping her men to make murderous
trouble. May of this year was to see the Lord-Lieutenant
(General French had gone to that post) issuing proclamations about treasonable correspondence with Germany,
and arresting and deporting Sinn Feiners just in time, it
was said, to stop another armed rising, which de Valera
was to have commanded. But even the hot-heads, who
were blind enough to think that conscription might be
as useful a weapon against disorder in Ireland as they
thought it to be against strikes in England, could hardly
suppose that to draft the rankest disaffection into the
army could be very helpful. Those who pressed for conscription for Ireland did so mainly on the unconvincing
ground that it was derogatory to her to suppose that she
would wish to be kept apart from Great Britain's need.
In the end the Government watered down their proposal
to a provision that the new Bill *might* be extended to
Ireland by Order in Council.

With the slackening of anxiety in May came some ugly reverberations of certain aspects of the first onset of anxiety in March. A scapegoat had been found them ; now came assertions that that had been nothing but scapegoat-hunting of a wholly dishonourable kind, and that the real responsibility had by this means been conveniently pushed out of sight. Sir Frederick Maurice, a distinguished soldier who had been Director of Military Operations in the first two years of the war, wrote for *The Daily Chronicle* an article making the most serious accusations. The blame for the disaster to the Fifth Army lay, he said, at the door of the British representatives on the Allied War Council, who had agreed, against military advice, to take over from the French more of the line than we could properly hold, and had forced General Gough to thin out his Front beyond the point of safety. When the smash came, not only had no one of them had the honesty or courage to tell the truth, and share the burden, but they had even been guilty of deliberate misstatements in order to save themselves. The pity was that just at this time it was far too easy for the Prime Minister to evade this fine attempt to remedy a wrong. It followed soon upon the disputes about the Chief of the General Staff, and also upon another matter which raised the question of military officers using in public their professional knowledge to attack Ministers—the debate in the Commons on the resignation of Sir Hugh Trenchard, Chief of the Air Staff. It was easy, when Sir Frederick Maurice's charges came up in the Commons, to take advantage of the public's impatience with all these recriminations about the High Command, its irritated sense that the only thing to do was to get on with the war. The debate, manœuvred off into rambling attempts to decide between inquiring into the charges by Select Committee or by appointing for the purpose two of the judges, never forced the Government to the point of a definite and honest reply.

The fright that the whole affair had given to Mr Lloyd George was to be made fully apparent at the end of the year, when the test of a candidate's fitness for official support in the General Election was the attitude he had taken in the Maurice debate. The only immediate action, however, was the placing of Sir Frederick Maurice on retired pay, for his breach of Army Regulations by putting a professional matter into the public Press. That was unworthy, for the whole subject of Army Regulations in this connection had been rendered absurd, since the salutary provision which prevents officers on the active list from sitting in Parliament had necessarily during the war become a dead letter. The consequence was that in the debate on Sir Hugh Trenchard's resignation an officer of the Air Force who was also a distinguished Member of Parliament — Lord Hugh Cecil — could, by a speech in the House, get matter into print which, conveyed in an article by an officer not a Member of Parliament, like Sir Frederick Maurice, could be made an excuse for retiring him.

In these ways, and by General Gough's loyal dignity, the Fifth Army controversy was only too easily shelved. The nation was, besides, deep in its immediate worries and the very real pinch of its food allowance. Mr Clynes became Food Controller in June, on the resignation of Lord Rhondda, who had worked to his utmost limit, and died at the beginning of July. Mr Clynes was optimistic in speeches about the passing of the submarine menace and better prospects. Actually there was a small increase of the meat ration in June, and there were more ample supplies of bacon from America. But these ameliorations were too slight to cure the growing fret and strain of the restrictions. It was not mere irritation. Lightly though we came off in comparison with German civilians, health was by now suffering appreciably. Children were starved of sugar-stuffs, and even jam at this stage had far less than its proper quantity of sugar. The war bread was to large numbers of people most indigestible. Fats of all kinds were so meagrely allowed (a mechanised chemical warfare made vast demands for them) that practically none could be used in cooking, and what could be obtained for use in other ways was inadequate for health. Nor was the shortness of allowance the only trouble. Constantly it was impossible to obtain the due allowance, and in poor quarters queues had begun again to weary the housewives, and exasperate them often with disappointment in the end. People had begun here and there to learn how households could co-operate in the preparation of meals, so as to use food allowances to the best advantage; but enterprise and organisation of this sort were far too rare. For the most part, households struggled along individually with the war-cookery hints which the writers on such subjects in the Press produced with much fluency, if not much ingenuity. In the summer an effort was set on foot to help the poorer households over some of the discomforts of rationing. On the model of a public kitchen which had been wisely started in Poplar, national kitchens were opened—four more in London, and others in Leeds, Glasgow, Birmingham, Newcastle, Cardiff, Bristol, and other big towns. Using food-stuffs on the large scale they could prepare meals, in exchange for coupons, far more appetising and nourishing than a wage-earner's household could manage for itself.

The reason for Mr Clynes's anxious optimism was the old trouble, the fear of the temper of industrial workers, but he did little good. His reassurances about submarines only encouraged workers in their rooted belief that profiteering had most to do with their troubles. Food shortage was bad enough. But there were all the other exasperations. Beer and spirits, heavily advanced in price by taxation and weakened in strength by the restriction of malt supplies, were " no good to anybody." Tobacco was not only dear but difficult to get; the authorities kept the army " issue " going fairly well (though often with brands of cigarettes that nobody had heard of before or ever heard of again), but only by depleting civilian supplies. Now even matches were often unobtainable. Nothing could persuade the workers that no one was making money out of all this. Railway travelling came under drastic restrictions in June. Coal was short, labour was short, rolling stock and locomotives were short, for quantities had been sent over to France, where familiar types of engines were to be seen " doing their bit," with huge white numbers on them; even stretches of permanent way were said to have been sent over. Yet people with high and easy wages, officers and men in the luxury of leave passes, would not listen to any appeals to travel less; nothing but severe restriction would avail. Thus a mass of minor vexations gathered, as it were, on the surface of the serious troubles, and the national temper grew irritable.

One outbreak of it was another clamour against enemy aliens. This seemed to be precipitated by some sensational articles in a weekly paper—the notorious *Black Book* articles—which, giving a war twist to the commonplace kind of attack on the vices of Society, asserted that certain forms of moral viciousness were to be associated with pro-German mentality. That was only the most flagrant piece of the outcry, which became very general. East End borough councils, especially that of Stepney, indignantly laid at the door of aliens the panics during air raids. The Royal Society passed a resolution for expelling enemy aliens from membership. The spy scare waked again in the Commons; and, though the Home Secretary revealed the truth that the dangerous spies were quite as often neutrals as enemy aliens, a committee recommended that all enemy aliens without exception should be dealt with, the males over eighteen interned and the females deported. Mr Lloyd George helped the scare by saying that at every reverse of the Allies he received many anonymous letters from aliens crowing over England, and was reminded that enemy aliens were still in Government offices.

In the more serious ways temper began to snap again in July among munition workers. The incessant smothered friction about combing-out was worked upon by new regulations, limiting the number of skilled men that each firm might employ. The object was simply to see that each firm had its fair proportion of skilled men ; but it looked too much like combing out more skilled men for the army. Coventry began a strike, and it spread alarmingly to Birmingham, Manchester and Lincoln. This time not only the trade union leaders but the shop stewards themselves were thrown over. Just as the strike was threatening to spread to Leeds the Government announced that every worker absent from his work on a given day would be deemed to have placed himself voluntarily outside the exempted industries, and would be called up for the army. That was effective for the moment, and the strike collapsed.

By that time rationing had become fully systematised at last. Every individual had now a ration-book, with leaves for meat, bacon, sugar, butter, margarine and lard. Spare leaves allowed for the rationing by local committees of tea, cheese and other articles which could be left to local discretion. Special books were issued for children, for growing boys, and for men on heavy manual labour, adjusting the rations to those cases. Coal consumption was, in a looser sense, rationed too, by the cutting down of retailers' supplies by 25 per cent.

By that time, too, the war news had grown strained

again. The badly bent lines in the Salient and opposite
Amiens were holding; but now the French were giving
way to another desperate German rush on the Soissons
and Aisne Front. It began on 27th May, and throughout June thrust itself steadily down towards Château
Thierry. Yet there was not the same acuteness of
anxiety as before. For one thing, this new thrust had
not the obvious and immediate alarm of the threat to
vital communications in the Amiens attack; or of the
renewed attempt on Ypres and Calais. Nor was it so
swift; it hesitated more, moved with more difficulty.
But, above all, there was an unaccountable feeling in
the air that Foch was just waiting for some chance the
enemy might give him, a curious kind of conviction that
he was far more sure of himself than the Germans knew,
with more than they knew up his sleeve. Rumours flew
about of his fresh unwearied divisions held on the
leash; and besides, the Americans were pouring in.
Some had, in fact, been in action in the Salient during
the April rush, General Pershing having agreed to their
being brigaded with British troops, and our worn-out
men had watched them going up in their clean uniforms
and brand-new equipment. They had arrived in force
since then, and in pleasant French places had been
passing the weeks of that sunny summer, still under the
flush of the pleased heroism which British and French
troops had long grown out of. Mr Lloyd George announced in July that 305,000 Americans were already
in France, and other large convoys on the way. So that
it was not the unrelieved apprehension of the March
and April days which watched the new attack. Side by
side with the anxiety was this strangely prevalent confidence that Foch was on the verge of his stroke. The
new German salient looked tempting for him, narrow
and peaked, traplike. Would this be the chance for
which he was waiting? It was. Ludendorff made one

more effort, from 15th to 17th July. On 18th July
Foch struck back. With the Germans' new tactics of
no artillery preparation, the French counter-attacked on
the Château Thierry salient, then the English on the
Amiens Front. At last! Once again came a cry from
France, the cry of triumph—" On les aura ! "

But the ways of this war had gone too deep into the
country's mind for any over-confidence. The newspapers
had for three years past warned us against thinking
largely of " breaking through," of crumpling up lines,
and so on. They had kept rigidly to talk of " pushes "
only. These great German efforts themselves, which
had at first looked like breaking through after all, had
petered out in the end to no more than pushes of an
exceptional kind. Large as were the bulges they had
made in our lines, the enemy had come to the familiar
standstill, and turned more or less immobile again.
So there were no extravagant hopes of Foch's counter-
attack. It was doing well on both the French and
the British Fronts; the bends in the line were being
flattened out again. Germany would know now that
she could not defeat the Allies. But in so far as the
mind went further than that, it was only to think
that this was a necessary readjustment of the lines while
we waited for the final stage. It would put an end to
anxiety about Amiens or Ypres or Calais, and stabilise
the Front until the American armies could be thrown
in, full force, in the spring.

There was certainly nothing of the complete change
of temper and mood which any thought of victory now
would have brought. There was no more fear that our
Front might smash. But there was no sudden alert
rousing of the mind such as would have come with any
hint that this was the beginning of the end. Germany
had given us such a sense of her power that we thought
we should need a couple of million Americans for that.

People went on with their jobs, a little less wearily perhaps, a little more eager again for the war news in the papers—but that was all the difference. Tempers remained what they had been, ticklish and precarious, when no overwhelming pressure of war news was upon them; and the result in August and September was a disheartening epidemic of strikes. They began with the women employees of the bus and tram services demanding equal pay with the men and the same war bonus; women on the tube railways followed. Then the miners came out; and in the last days of August, queerest of all, the Metropolitan and City Police. War had done very odd things to us when we had to see the police, not in their familiar places keeping a strike procession orderly, but forming one themselves, to demand better pay, and marching in fours to that very Tower Hill where strikers had so often fought them. London was so astounded and amused that somehow it managed to run itself for a day. A certain number of Special Constables were on duty at crossings, regulating the traffic, not unsuccessfully, and good-humouredly greeted by the strikers on their march as blacklegs. It was altogether a good-humoured strike, but it was probably as well that it lasted only a day. The task of negotiating was given to General Smuts—a clever move, because on the one hand the strikers could meet him more amiably than they might have met the Departmental authorities, and on the other hand he could be more conciliatory than the usual authorities. He came quickly to a settlement, conceding with slight modifications the men's demands. All of these strikes were on the old troubles of high prices and profiteering, and the immediate demands were all for higher pay. The police were out also, as their strike opponents in old days had so often been, for recognition of their union. A police trade union—it was a topsy-turvy world. But for the time

· being it was a world in which money was easier to come by than in the peace world. So when cotton operatives came out on 1st September, railwaymen a little later, shipwrights on the Clyde, and a number of smaller industries, the easy money cured most of the troubles. Anything to keep things going.

For those were deeply uneasy weeks. Nerves were all on edge. Among those who seemed, perhaps, to mind the strain of the war least—indeed even to find it something that ranged from a zestful excitement to a great opportunity—nerves were on edge with the perpetual swing from hard work to eager amusement, from scrubbing ward floors or trying for some record in fuse-caps to dinners and dances and cinemas and men. The mass of people at no spectacular job, but holding things together as best they could, were worn with the length of the strain, the dull incessant fear of the fatal War Office telegram, the slaughter or the shattered exhaustion of their men in the big retreats, and now with the conflict of mind which longed wearily to think the end might be coming, and yet obstinately refused to think so. Nerves were on edge, too, in all high places, with the fear that, in the very last lap, the nation's mind might uncontrollably relax, and the tension snap too soon. There was sharp disagreement among military authorities between those who felt strongly that the men's *morale* had come to need something to think of besides the interminable war, some looking forward, some thought of what they would do in civilian life again ; those who would not go so far as that, but felt equally strongly that it would be insane, with this army of 5,000,000 in being, to make no plans for its demobilisation, no classifying of men for their return to civil life ; and those who were dead against anything and everything which might put into the soldier's head any ideas whatever except of going on fighting. Of the people at

home the authorities had not quite the same sort of
fear. Munition workers might be restless, but the mass
of them, drawing very large wages, would not be in a
hurry to stop. Yet, with what was now known about
the state of things inside Germany, who could tell when
or how some "rot" might set in disastrously among
civilians, some final refusal to endure any longer the
waste and the blankness and the grinding slaughter ?

Then, slowly, through all the disintegrating nerviness
began to creep a kind of unity again. What was really
happening was that the war news suddenly began to
take on an arresting kind of continuity. It had for so
long been either quite static, or a brief alternation of
pushes and counter-attacks for a few days at a time.
But now, half unconsciously, people became aware of
a new kind of persistence in the news; nerviness and
strain lost themselves in a gradual turning away of
the whole national mind from its own affairs at home.
These went on mechanically, but attention was no
longer on them. It was on the other side. The great
rousing of the mind was coming at last. In the third
week of August the British advance had begun to be
startling ; and then at the end of the month came the
news which really suggested for the first time a possible
German collapse. All through the counter-attack, even
when it was pressing forward most steadily, people had
said carefully that we were only recovering the battered
ground lost in the retreats ; we had to reach the
Hindenburg Line yet. On their old Front the Germans
would stand fast again. The strength of that position,
all the careful preparation of it long before, would make
it still impregnable. We came to it—and in the last days
of August the point which was reputed the most formidable, commanding the whole position, the Drocourt-
Quéant switch, was carried by the Canadians ; the great
Hindenburg Line had gone. That did mean something ;

not even the most wary could go on being wholly
guarded in their expectations. After this anything
might happen, even victory.

Life at home did not notably change. There was not
the least slackening of the machinery, not a minute less
of any kind of war work. The great thing now was not
to give the slightest chance of a pause, to put in every
ounce of effort. The push, glorious as it was, might not
be beyond the possibility of dragging to a standstill
again. In fact, what actually was operating at home
was such a perfection of the organising of munitions
that every kind of war supply was being produced on a
scale to smother the enemy utterly in the spring. For
a month more the balance hung. Mid-September brought
the first completely American battle, the attack on the
Saint-Mihiel salient which had jutted into the French
line since the earliest days of the war, and now crumbled
before the newcomers. Finally, on 28th September, the
last piece of the line began to move. The British and
Belgians attacked in the extreme north, and within the
very first day Messines Ridge, fought over for a week
earlier in the year, had been recaptured. Quite clearly
the German power of resistance was past. The whole
Allied line had caught fire now; the whole German
line was yielding. From that moment even the most
obstinate doubts broke down. German prisoners were
being taken by tens of thousands a day, guns at the
rate of a thousand a week. October was one long tale,
almost monotonous but for all the individual anxieties,
of advance and of capture of the places so long watched
from our lines, then of the further unattainable places,
Saint-Quentin, Cambrai and Le Cateau, Lille, Ostend,
the whole Belgian coast. The collapse had come.

The England that watched it was not feeling high-
spirited. It was, in any case, tired, rather underfed,
even now incredulous. Besides, one of the gravest

influenza epidemics was sweeping the country. By the end of October the deaths in London alone were up to 750 a week. Services everywhere were devastated ; police, fire brigades, telephone exchanges, the big hospitals, the huge Government Departments, were paralysed. The story of those last few days of the war is curiously different from the story of the days of its beginning. In spite of the news there was no strongly rising tide of excitement, nothing in the aspect of the streets to mark what was going on. In grey weather people went about their drearily familiar jobs, and home of an evening in the same pitch-dark streets, though not since the early summer had there been any air raids. Even the announcement that the Germans had asked for a safe-conduct for the discussion of terms of an armistice could hardly rouse the mind to much more than a numb recognition that the war was over. This request—the impregnable Germans, the Germans who had seemed to have every kind of command of war method that we had not, reserves that had never failed them, ruthless persistence—the Germans coming across with the white flag—surely that should have been a vivid, tense moment. It was not. Imagination could hardly whip itself up to picture those few figures, so enormously significant, somehow making their way through the huge welter of armies to come face to face with Foch and Haig. It could not grasp the amazing fact that somewhere on that colossal, impersonal battle-front a little personal path had opened through the rifle-fire and the shelling, to enable men to do what no one had done for more than four years—drive calmly from one side to the other. The end, like the beginning, was too immense to grasp.

Too immense, and also too unexpected and too sweepingly complete. The Armistice terms to the Germans were the terms of sheer defeat : the withdrawal of all

their forces ; the surrender to the Allies of the bridge-
heads of Cologne, Coblenz and Mainz—of the Rhine,
that is, their pride ; of 5000 guns, 30,000 machine
guns and 2000 aeroplanes ; of all their submarines,
50 destroyers, 8 light cruisers, 6 battle-cruisers, and
10 battleships. And we now knew why. The whole
German structure had suddenly smashed in revolution.
The Kaiser had abdicated, and he and the Crown Prince
had taken refuge in Holland. There had been, it was
said, a mutiny at Kiel, when the naval command had
tried to order the fleet out for one desperate fight
before the end ; Soldiers' and Workmen's Committees, of
the type which had made the Russian Revolution, were
raising the red flag in Berlin, and all the big German
cities, and working on the troops. It was too complete.
We might have been fighting all these years to end
Kaiserism and Prussianism, but it was staggering,
bewildering, to see them crumple like this, the Kaiser
and Crown Prince feebly giving in to the first breath of
the storm (though there was bitterness ready enough to
feel that this was just what they would do), the haughty
and iron-willed High Command helpless, the mail and
the eagle helmets a heap of tinsel. Too unexpected also
in its way of happening. People had been thinking
vaguely that the great drive forward of the armies must
go on, Germany be invaded, Berlin reached. With
success had come a return to old notions of war—the
beaten country, the triumphal entry into the enemy's
capital, the flags and drums, the steel and glitter of a
conquering march past of fighting men. But the end
had come with an abruptness as queer and as drably
impromptu as almost everything in the war had been :
armies in no particular array, pulled up to a standstill
anywhere and everywhere, just stopped. A victorious
end, with absolutely nothing to make the authentic
blaze and thrill of victory.

And to its final minute the war was to keep its insane quality. The enemy had surrendered ; there were the Armistice terms, signed by the Germans, and everyone knowing that they were signed. Yet because of the enormous area of the fighting, because of the tremendous range orders had to cover, men must go on killing one another till a fixed hour—till 11 o'clock on the morning of 11th November. Actually, the end already reached, men were being killed the very last half-hour. Could anything have shown more clearly the crazy mechanicalness of it all ? Not even the knowledge that the terms had been signed disintegrated the Western fighting ; not even the knowledge that within a few hours they would be at peace with one another could make the opposing armies spontaneously give up killing. The machine fixed a limit ; till then they doggedly pounded along. No doubt something of the same sort acted upon civilian minds. Till the hour struck they could not leave their grooves.

This, at any rate, made Armistice Day stand out, as indeed it should have done, sharp and clear. In this alone the end was like the beginning. Though for three or four weeks it had been approaching, and for some days past had been certain, it came at last with a shock, suddenly. In London it was startling. The firing of the maroons which signalled the suspension of hostilities seemed to explode the whole of that enormous hive. Instantly from every building in every quarter people poured into the streets. It was like an extraordinary piece of symbolism, as if, coming out of the war, coming out of the long relentless pressure, they had to come out of everything, come out of wherever they happened to be, drop everything, forget everything except that they were alive and released. In every town, in all the big hut settlements where war needs had gathered people in crowds, the same instinct held : to crowd together.

In the country places, where even the Great War itself had brought no new-fangled signals and the church bells still did the duty they had done after Waterloo, men and women clustered by cottage gates and in little market-places. London, as the day wore on, grew wilder and wilder. Into the central streets, crowded in any case with the masses of people who had left every office empty, streamed the suburbs; and packed motor-buses, taxis ragged with people on the roof, private cars with their running-boards stormed by casual passengers, ploughed through solid rivers of humanity. The crowds had had the King and Queen out on the balcony of a window of the Palace in the middle of the morning, and fairly mobbed the Royal carriage driving along the Mall in the afternoon. They drifted to and fro hour after hour, increasing as the evening came. For the lights were on, and people, with that sense of coming out of everything, loved to give themselves the feeling of coming out of the dismal war-darkness too. Lighted shop windows and restaurants which could once more look gay were too good to miss. Till far into the night streets swarmed and were noisy. The mood lasted over the next day, when the King and Queen made a more formal drive through their capital.

But this kind of excited jubilation was not typical of the country as a whole. Indeed even in London, the place of crowds and shows, it was, after the first hour or two, shallow and forced in tone. The moment's impulse, on the stroke of the hour of release, to be out and to feel the sense of liberty rising in one glorious exhilaration, was genuine enough, and almost universal. But that was soon over; there was no great swelling burst of victorious pride which could sweep the nation into days of exuberant festivity. Relief was the one strong feeling, not triumph; and it was for the most part a dull relief, which wanted only to get away from

everything to do with the war, even from the ending
of it.[1] Later on we heard how strangely the final hour
had come upon the armies, the complete absence of
any excitement at all, the bewilderment of the sudden
cessation of every sound, the emptiness left by the
abrupt stopping of everything they were there to do.
People at home had not that strange drop into blankness; but after the first hour of excitement something
of the same sort happened to them. There was no war
on any longer; but what else was there? They were
tired, listless, devitalised. And though the first night
or two of peace had given, by contrast with the black
nights of war time, an impression of light and gaiety,
those winter weeks were really cold and dreary and dark.
Coal supplies had fallen off badly; retailers had, at the
best, only 75 per cent. of their normal supplies, and
in fact had very often far less than that. Gas and
electric-light companies were working on heavily curtailed stocks of fuel. In every way the tides of life were
running too low for celebrations or rejoicings. British
civilians had not suffered as German civilians had. But
they had had their privations; and now crouching,
underfed, over miserable fires in ill-lighted rooms,
with a foggy dampness outside and influenza lowering
their spirits, they could rise to little more than telling
themselves that anyhow the war was over.

[1] It is curious and interesting to observe how very little the Armistice
or the end of the war figures in the pages of *Punch* at this time.

CHAPTER IX

1919 : DEMOBILISED

OFTEN enough since August 1914 Parliament had been accused of being out of contact with the real life and the real feelings of a nation at war. Its members appeared to be so inextricably bound in the old habits of politics that no crisis could shake them out of being politicians. Its debates were so preponderantly a useless, if not actually dangerous, raking over of controversial or unfortunate events that people asked themselves what good purpose at all its sessions were serving. The plea that in a war for the liberty of peoples representative institutions should least of all abdicate, that Parliamentary government must prove that it could meet this supreme ordeal of Western civilisation, was plausible.[1] But had it proved any such thing ? It is true that, at the outset, not only had party strife been suspended, but in the formation of the Parliamentary Recruiting Committee and the Food Prices Committee there were suggestions that Parliament might envisage for itself, as the rest of the country had to, a wholly new conception of its functions, achieve leadership in new directions, and embody the people at war. But it carried no further this early approach to the ways in which the Revolutionary Convention of 1793 in France had risen to the needs of " la patrie en danger," this tentative move towards something like the Committees of the Convention and the " représentants

[1] Mr Winston Churchill, for instance, advances this plea in *The World Crisis : the Aftermath.*

en mission." Parliament was soon back in the old
ways, with debates, divisions, party prejudices, harrying
of Ministers. People uprooted from all their old
habits, absorbed in the exacting details of their new life
in the army or elsewhere, saw with amazement that
at Westminster alone nothing seemed to have changed.
Parliament, instead of being in the front of the nation,
foreseeing and controlling, was trailing behind, endlessly
discussing decisions taken in fact over its head, and
events it had done nothing to guide. Instead of riding
the main current of the nation's life, it was anchored
in a side-channel, stirred only by back-wash from the
stream.

Now the House of Commons capped its poor record
throughout the war with the most unpardonable failure
of all. Its first thought at the end of the war was
apparently for.itself alone, and its own position in the
new circumstances. Just when the nation was going to
need very badly to keep its head, and Parliament should
have been most free in its own mind to help, members
gave their whole attention to themselves and their seats.
A few days before the Armistice a document had been
circulated among members, urging the maintenance of
the Coalition Government in power. That had not been
very eagerly signed ; immediately after the Armistice,
on 16th November, a large meeting of members was
called at the Central Hall, Westminster, to listen to the
Prime Minister, Mr Bonar Law and Mr Barnes on the
need for giving to the Coalition, which had brought the
war to a successful end, a fresh mandate for the transition to peace. Preparations for an immediate General
Election were hurried forward on lines which, under
the guise of being still patriotic abstention from party
strife, were really something far lower. Five hundred
candidates took the field with the express sanction of
the Coalition leaders. Labour kept its hands free, and

entered the fray along its own lines. But any other
candidate stood for election under most unfair imputa-
tions—he had not the blessing of Mr Lloyd George, so
he must have hindered the war.

Such was " the Coupon Election." In those critical
weeks, with history under their hands, the nation's
leaders were wire-pulling. Excuses have been made for
them. They were tired ; they had been making enough
history. Nor could they, or anyone perhaps, grasp at
the moment the fact that, because everyone else was
tired too, their vast war machine was going to run down
to a stop as abruptly and as confusedly as the fighting.
People were not going to wait to be arrayed in any
particular posture for peace, any more than the armies
had been arrayed for the cease-fire. They were going to
turn away from the war just anyhow. Presumably the
calculation of the statesmen was that, while they busied
themselves about a new Parliament, the country would
carry on without much change of mind. Then, with
their refreshed authority from a General Election, they
would begin to make the country's peace-mind. This
was a perfectly false calculation. Long before they
had their fresh authority—even before they had fairly
started to ask for it—the country had tumbled higgledy-
piggledy into the shallowest kind of peace mentality ;
and instead of guiding and setting the tone, statesmen
had to pick up what tone there was, and pretend it was
theirs.

It can, of course, be argued that the tone was inevitable, that no effort of guidance could have made any
difference. But it can also be said that, at the moment
of the Armistice, and for a few days afterwards—only
a few days, but that might have been long enough—
the country was not, as a whole, in a bitter or revengeful
frame of mind. There had been bitter elements throughout the war ; there were very many whom their personal

griefs and losses had made only more bitter. But there were other elements in plenty. There were those who had never failed of the sense of the suffering on the other side as well, who found in the poems of Lady Margaret Sackville, for instance, the truest burden of the war. There were the masses and masses of simple people who, because they were simple and saw things in the plain terms of their own homes and not in large patriotic phrases, knew always in their inexpressive way that there were humble villages and mean streets and swarming working quarters in Germany as desolated as their own. There were the masses, again, who, however loosely warlike at the beginning, had learned from their men in the army to think of the enemy not as " the Hun " of the newspapers, but as " Jerry " and " Fritz," in the tolerant way of the soldiers. Was there not enough here to have responded to any touch of vision given at the right moment ? For those few days the nation hung suspended. The war was over ; it had no particular feeling one way or the other about the peace. Surely it might, with its cherished pride in being a nation of sportsmen, taking success like gentlemen, as well as defeat, have been swung into a quiet generous frame of mind. There would have been, of course, angry dissentients, clamorous for revenge and the uttermost farthing. But the broad popular mind, at any rate, might easily have been lifted into the calmer atmosphere which, to do them justice, statesmen on the whole wished for.

Too unsure of themselves to risk the great gesture, they let the chance go by. The vision was not given. It could not belong to election programmes. Parliament, in its hurry to think about itself, set the nation also upon thinking solely about itself. In its hurry to make promises it filled the air with expectations of what we could get, not what we could give, of the fruits of

victory, not of peace. As the poised balance of the first
few days began to swing it came down heavily towards
self-interest. The moment's chance of strength and
generosity had vanished.

The result was seen only too plainly in the coarsening
of tone during the next week or two. The Coalition
manifesto, issued jointly by the Prime Minister and
Mr Bonar Law on 22nd November, had, even if narrow
and too immediately political in its outlook, a measure
of gravity. It had little to say except about our own
problems, but it was full of hope of the happier future
before a country which had so tried its mettle, and
before the returning soldier who had earned so much.
" A land fit for heroes to live in " was the only right
monument for the heroes who would live there no more.
But the manifesto was followed by the hectic spate of
platform speeches — the election was to be rushed
through to send the political leaders to the Peace Conference, with the country behind them—and in the turgid
banality of political meetings only the poor resentments
and angers, not the dignity and patience, of war suffering
found voice. Responsibility for the cruel devastation
of these years, indemnities, our attitude for the future
to enemy countries—these subjects needed discussion.
But they could only deteriorate miserably in the slap-
dash generalities of an election campaign. On the eve
of the poll Mr Lloyd George substituted for the manifesto a poor kind of hoarding poster, a coupon bid for a
Coupon majority : Trial of the Kaiser ; punishment of
those responsible for atrocities ; the fullest indemnities
from Germany ; Britain for the British, socially and
industrially ; rehabilitation for those broken in the war,
and a happier country for all.

It carried the day. The new House of Commons, when
the returns came in, numbered 478 Coalition members,
59 Labour members, and a mere scrap of Liberalism

which had refused to label itself with the precious coupons, 27 members. But in the very process of consolidating its position the Ministry took solidity out of everything else. They had let loose a vociferous haste, and in the rush of it the whole nation, civilian and military alike, slipped rapidly out of hand. All the careful plans for gradual and systematic demobilisation of war industry and the armies began to go wrong, and fell within a few weeks into the angry confusion of wholesale methods, which were the very thing the authorities had most wanted to avoid. Soldiers clamoured to go home, their people at home clamoured to have them back. Prewar labour clamoured for a clean sweep of all dilution labour, and especially of the women who had taken men's jobs. Dilution labour and the women hotly resented this brushing aside of all they had done ; and, now that women had votes, politicians did not find this phase of the difficulties easy to deal with. Ugliest of all, a great part of the labour world which had stayed comfortably at home all the time actually wanted to prevent the men who had gone from coming back ; they were jealous and frightened about the flooding into the labour market of those millions of men.

Armistice feelings had evaporated pitifully. Discomforts and strains, which even while the war was on had not been patiently borne, grew more and more exasperating in those discouraging winter days. The papers were full of complaints of the still rising prices—eggs, for instance, were costing 9d. each. They were full also of complaints of the bullying manners of shopkeepers, taxi-drivers, bus and tube attendants, and so on—the implication being that these had so much enjoyed their dictatorial position under war emergencies and restrictions that they would not now give them up in peace time. The fault, in truth, was on both sides. People were in an obstinate hurry to have everything just as it used to be, all their old ways back again, and those with whom they dealt in this impatient mood lost their tempers, or grew morose and discourteous. Moreover, most of these servants of the public had their own troubles in uneasiness about the keeping of their jobs, which would not help them to be genial under difficulties. Above all, few had yet grasped the fact that money, at least, was never going to be just as it used to be. The result was that prices not only terribly high, but actually still rising, with the war over, no submarines about, no more need for tonnage for munition material, roused acutely the conviction that a wicked amount of profiteering was going on. Every kind of payment, from the grocer's and butcher's bills to the taxi-driver's fare, was tainted with this suspicion. Efforts were even made, by wholly unauthorised local committees and a kind of boycotting, to force prices down.

London had its shows now and then to distract it and remind it that, after all, the war had been won. The Mall was lined from end to end with ranks of captured German guns, huge heavy artillery pieces, squat howitzers, field guns, long, thin anti-aircraft guns, with trench-mortars and machine guns filling the odd spaces. Men rambled curiously round the things that had once roared death at them; children climbed on the gunners' seats and worked every handle that was movable. On 1st December Clemenceau and Foch were in London, a visit mainly for preliminary business of the Peace, but a chance for the crowds to see them; and on 19th December Haig and the army commanders came home to cheering streets. Even they were hardly so fêted as was President Wilson, when he arrived on 26th December with Mrs Wilson. He was the man of the hour. Under him America had come into the war; upon his "Fourteen Points" the Germans had based their surrender; and he was coming now not merely to take his part in the making of the

35

Peace, but to impose the Covenant of the League of Nations. In all the fading of early idealism as the war dragged on, the loss of all the fine feelings of fighting for free peoples against international brutality, one ideal had survived—that this must be " the war to end war." It might not always be idealistically expressed ; it had in masses of men taken the plainer shape of saying to themselves : " We have got to finish this job—but never again." Yet with peace revived the higher sense that the worst betrayal of the youth which had been slaughtered would be to leave in the world any chance that future generations of youth should have to face the same hell again. And for that, above all men, President Wilson stood now. He came from a land free of the age-old rivalries of Europe, from a land that could be sane and sensible. His coming, quite rightly, was not merely a London show. He went to pay a pious visit to Carlisle, the home of his forbears, and thus some of the big northern cities also had their chance to see him, tall and thin and austere, a typical figure for the hopes he represented.

One of the earlier visits of December—the arrival of the Emir Feisul—let loose a cloud of the most wildly romantic rumour, which gradually spread till the man at the heart of it became a popular hero, decked in all the story-book excitement for which grim modern war seemed to have no place. Bit by bit, from the people who had known about it, came the tale of a young Oxford don, who, in archæological work in the Near East before the war, had discovered his gift for getting on with Arabs, understanding them and their ways, able, as far as a European ever is able, to live their life in mind as well as in body. Colonel Lawrence was the most extraordinary of all the cases of quiet-seeming scholars who walked straight out of culture into war with the most brilliant success. Practically single-handed he had instigated and manipulated a revolt of Arabs against

the Turks, which had been of most material assistance
in the later stages of Allenby's advance. He had known
how to manage his headstrong and erratic levies and to
use them in skirmishes and railway-cutting and transport-
harrying. Under his hand a new kingdom had arisen;
and the tale had all the right picturesque accompaniment
of burnouses and camels, tents in the desert, and swooping, sudden raids handled by the mysterious white leader.
Even what was known then, before he had written his
book, was more exciting than any Kipling story of the
lone Englishman turning into a chieftain of warrior
nomads. Stimulus to the interest in Lawrence was given
by his own profound dislike of notoriety. He would not
be seen or interviewed, or lionised in any way at all. No
one even seemed to know where he was. That put the
finishing touch : he was not only the story-book Englishman come true ; he was the silent, strong man as well.

The new year opened uncomfortably. In the armies
six weeks of bored waiting, of dreary fatigues on clearing-
up jobs, of useless and tedious formal drill, with which
commanding officers tried to keep discipline, were producing discontent on the verge of mutiny. The hope
that educational and technical classes, which might give
the men a better chance when they returned to civil life,
would interest them and keep them occupied while a
calculated and classified demobilisation went on, had
gone to pieces. A new branch at the War Office had
come into being in the previous September to organise
educational work among the troops. This work had
been going on since the spring of 1918 as a method of
keeping up *morale*, and through the later months of the
war it had had some success. After the war the system
was to become established, as a means of saving the army
from what had always been one of its blemishes—the
fact that it was a " dead-end " occupation for a man,
giving him but limited prospects of employment at the

end of his service. But in this interval, as a steadying force during a gradual demobilisation, the idea failed. Men wanted only to be at home again, and wanted that intensely. Demobilisation bases in France grew more and more difficult to handle, even when they did not break out into actual disorder; in England too the early days of January brought riots in camps at Dover, Folkestone and Osterley, and angry demonstrations of troops outside the War Office. There was nothing to do but to scrap practically all the careful plans for returning men to civil life. They would not stand being classified for return according to the state of the labour market. For that meant seeing men go home after perhaps six months' service and no fighting, because their trades were not overstocked, while men with two or three years of fighting service were still kept back. The troops demanded one simple principle—demobilisation according to length of service and at the utmost speed at which the necessary documents could be issued. Belatedly the Government recognised how remote from human nature their neat paper plans had been. In a week or two demobilisation centres were working men off at the rate of 50,000 a day. Most of them would not wait for the standard civilian suits which the authorities offered, and trudged off just as they were; for a long time khaki, with the military buttons cut off, made a working dress for men in factories and in the fields. Even at this new pace of demobilisation the worst case of disorder in a camp was yet to come. Colonial troops had, in addition to other demobilisation difficulties, to await transport and their own governments' arrangements. They were delayed for too long, and in March Canadian troops at Kimmel Park mutinied. Five were killed and over twenty injured before order was restored; and a few days later there was a riot near an American Y.M.C.A. hut in London.

The new Ministry was announced on 10th January. It was still almost the swollen Ministry of war time. The Food Control and Shipping Control Departments naturally had to continue. But the Ministry of National Service was combined with the Ministry of Reconstruction under Sir Auckland Geddes; and the Ministry for Air, by a mistaken policy which subsequently had to be abandoned, was combined with the Secretaryship of State for War. The Ministry of Munitions survived under a more peaceful name as the Ministry of Supply. In this there was a hazy suggestion that we might carry on into peace some of the large-scale purchasing system and organisation of the war. But the real reason for the continuance of this Ministry was that the control had been too complete, and the mass of employed persons too vast, to permit of a sudden throw-back to normal conditions; the Ministry was necessary for softening the return to ordinary wage competition. In personnel the new Government was the old one, with a few changes of Department. Sir Eric Geddes became one of the Ministers without Portfolio; Mr Churchill went to the War Office (the scrapping of demobilisation plans fell to him); Sir F. E. Smith became Lord Chancellor and Lord Birkenhead. The only mild sensation was the appointment of Sir S. P. Sinha as Under-Secretary for India; he was the first native of India to become a member of a British Government, and was very soon the first native of India to take his seat in the House of Lords. His appointment served as a reminder that one of the Liberal policies interrupted by the war had been a further experiment in self-government for India, which was to take shape later in this year.

In January came also—but two months too late to have any healing generosity in it—concern for the starved condition of the defeated countries. In both of them the war collapse had been collapse into revolution.

The Austro-Hungarian Empire was not destroyed by the Peace Treaties: it ceased to exist at the moment of the cessation of hostilities. What left the battle area was not an Austro-Hungarian army, nor even Austro-Hungarian regiments; in the very process of going, those military shapes melted uncontrollably into new coalescences, and only racial groups of Czechs, Slovaks, Poles, Croats, Magyars and Slovenes filled the home-bound trains. The young Emperor Karl of Austria had had to abdicate and leave his country, like the Kaiser. Both countries seemed likely to avoid the plight of Russia—the passing of a constitutional revolution into the hands of social revolutionaries: Germany was settling down into a bourgeois republic, Austria-Hungary into a number of nations which would find different forms of constitution. The Soldiers' and Workmen's Committees in Germany, which had looked at first like a reproduction there of the Soviet spirit, had not gained a hold on the sober German mind. Little more than an unhappy echo of a conflict already over was in the news now that Karl Liebknecht and Rosa Luxemburg, whose notoriously extremist opinions had made them leaders of the Spartacists (the name class-war fanatics in Germany gave themselves), had been killed in Berlin. Liebknecht was reported to have been shot while trying to escape after arrest, Rosa Luxemburg to have been shot by someone firing from an infuriated crowd.

Naturally, perhaps, as being the real end of the war—the disappearance from Europe of the Austrian Empire which had so long, and the German Empire which had so disturbingly, occupied their places on the map—these revolutions had been watched without much thought of the other conditions the war had produced in those countries. Still, there had been many concerned also for the effects of the long blockade. Here again, it seemed, the United States must do what we could not.

Relief in food supplies on an enormous scale was necessary, and a Mr Hoover emerged rather suddenly as the
organising genius for the purpose. He was announcing
in January that 1,500,000 tons of food-stuffs would be
needed to pull mid-Europe through until the next harvest,
and he was at work co-ordinating effort, securing transport, constructing the machinery for distribution. In
an England still thinking of enemy countries the only
public effort that could hope for success was an appeal to
the sentiment for children, with the "Save the Children
Fund."

The new House of Commons met, and a strange body
the election returns had produced. The sensational fact
was that, except for the Irish Unionists, hardly an Irish
member was present. The old Nationalist seats had
gone solidly to Sinn Feiners, and they, instead of
coming to Westminster, were holding a Convention, a
Republican Convention, in Dublin. But few understood
at all how sinister this was; it was taken as a rather
childish ill-natured gesture. Another thing dismissed as
a gesture was the Labour Party's announcement that, in
view of the virtual obliteration of independent Liberalism,
they would regard themselves, and act, as the official
Opposition. This was seizing the opportunity to put the
seal on their recent moves towards becoming a third
national party. To act as the official Opposition laid a
claim to be regarded, not as a specialised group outside
the normal play of politics, as the Irish Nationalists had
been, but as a party which meant some day to be in
office. Not that this appeared to most people anything
more than a piece of pomposity; only in such a freak
of a House could a group of 59 members give itself these
airs.

There was deep irritation behind this criticism, for the
industrial world was stormy and threatening. Political
labour leaders who had to spend half their time trying

vainly to keep labour following them only gave an
impression of impertinence when they pretended to
office. It looked as if labour in the mass was growing
less, and not more, political in purpose. " Direct action "
was the catchword again, as it had begun to be just
before the war, as it had not ceased to be—though the
Press censorship had largely blindfolded the public—
during the war; and it was a more threatening catchword now. For a good many people had been asking
themselves nervously, for some time, what was going
to be the effect of passing millions of men through
the ghastly schooling of the war. How could they be
expected to come back with the old restraints, the old
values of human life, from years of familiarity with
killing at close quarters ? In actual crime far more
murderous methods must be expected; and in strikes
the violence which had been becoming more and more
common might take a terrible new character. What of
a strike in which half of the workmen and half of the
police might have learned how to fight from house to
house along a street, and clear out a strong-point with
bombs ? In fact such apprehensions proved to be
baseless : the war left no widespread infection of
brutality. But during these months direct action was
a phrase with peculiarly alarming associations. Apart
from this, labour demands were much more disturbing
after four years in which over and over again workers
had apparently only had to strike to get what they
wanted. This was one more of the ways in which failure
to grasp what the financing of the war had really involved was deplorable. The readiness with which
advances of pay and bonus had been granted was partly,
no doubt, especially in the later stages of the war, due
to the urgent need of keeping things going ; but it had
also been due to the fact that, with money values
changing so completely, the advances were largely a

mere adjustment to prices, and therefore proper. This, however, was not the way in which they appeared either to labour or to the rest of the community. Each side drew a false conclusion, embittering to any industrial dispute. People who were always ready to be impatient with strikes thought they had a far better case for indignation now, when wages generally were at a figure which, on paper and by pre-war standards, looked like sheer luxury for those who earned them; there were ironic stories about working-class wives buying things in provision shops which a middle-class wife had just decided she could not afford. The impression given to the mass of labour by its wage advances was no more reasonable. They had simply deduced that there was, as they had always suspected, far more money due to them than they had ever been able to get, until the war gave them their chance really to frighten a government. This lesson they proposed to carry over into peace time, and it was of little use for Mr Clynes to urge upon them lawfulness and political action, worse than useless for Mr Lloyd George to talk about " Prussianism in the industrial world." Another epidemic of strikes had broken out, among shipwrights and engineers, with rioting in Glasgow, among gas and electricity workers, with the threat to plunge London into darkness on a given night. Here was direct action, plainly enough. The Government made no terms with it. They still had the Defence of the Realm Act to strengthen their hands, and they announced that, if the threat were carried out, they would imprison every striker. That was enough to " postpone " this strike, and the others had been composed by the early days of February.

But a bigger difficulty loomed—the coal mines. Miners were determined to bring their grievances to a head, and to make the country face the circumstances of their industry, unlike any other staple industry in the squalor of its housing, the danger and unnatural conditions of the work. They demanded a 30 per cent. advance in wages, a six-hour instead of an eight-hour day, and nationalisation of the mines.

This last demand was based partly on the general principle that minerals should not be allowed to be private property, and partly on the practical view that many of the worst grievances in mining—inadequate equipment, fluctuations and discrepancies in wages, bad housing—had their roots in the private ownership of mines, encouraging a sluggishness in adopting new ideas and preventing a pooling of resources whereby the good mines might help to keep up wages in the less profitable ones. The demand for a shorter day, again, was based, first, on the general principle that the conditions inseparable from mining should be imposed only in short shifts, and secondly, on the practical view that shorter hours would mean the employment of many more men. This latter plea had particular force at the time when thousands of miners would be returning from the army, who could only very slowly go back into employment, and a great number of whom would probably never be reabsorbed at all. In the drain of men, workings had been closed which would take time to reopen, and the poorer ones might not be opened again. Hence the miners added to their demands, for the moment, the payment from State funds of full wages to all demobilised miners until they were reabsorbed.

The Government had to come to terms, and quickly. The necessities of the war had badly crippled coal production ; it was an industry that neither women nor dilution labour could help. Now with the country needing every possible energy of production, and the fullest possible employment of industry, a check in coal supplies—which at best were very seriously below the normal—would be fatal. The Government offered an immediate advance of a shilling a day on wages, and in proposing a Royal Commission to consider the more general demands they agreed to the insistence of the miners' leaders that its report must be prompt. After some discussion of dates it was laid upon the Commission, of which Mr Justice Sankey was appointed chairman, to report by 20th March. On these terms the miners' strike notices were postponed till 22nd March.

Other troubles of the Government did not smooth their path with labour. The pace of demobilisation which had been forced upon them had given them for a short time something like a panic that they might be left without an army at all. For the war army had been a "duration" army, save for such small remnant as might be left (and very little of that in the ranks) of men enlisted on the pre-war service terms. From having 5,000,000 soldiers they might even find themselves without the necessary number for the Army of Occupation. And they needed more than that. For we had forces still campaigning in Russia. During the last year of the war there had been too much to occupy our minds with France for anyone to pay much attention to the minor business of trying to help Russian leaders who had kept some troops together, and refused to accept the Bolshevik peace with Germany. It had been worth while to send reinforcements to them, for any chance, however slender, of keeping Germany from drawing at her ease on the grain resources of the Ukraine and other Russian districts, to escape the stranglehold of the blockade, was not to be missed. But this had involved supporting armies which in refusing to accept the Bolshevik peace refused also to accept the Bolshevik regime. That made every kind of trouble now. For the Government, feeling it dishonourable to leave these armies to face the Bolsheviks alone, the moment that we had no interests of our own to serve, were anxious to

keep in strength our forces at Murmansk and Archangel
in the north, and along the Batum—Baku line in the
south. Yet it could not be denied that, in the circumstances, a defensible piece of war policy had become
political intervention in the internal affairs of another
country, and controversy was only too ready to grow
heated. Labour in its disaffected mood was fulminating
against an attempt to crush a social revolution. But
there were plenty of people thoroughly approving of the
attempt. The Bolshevik Government not only refused
to be responsible for debts of the Tsarist regime, or
for trading or other concessions granted under it;
they also announced that, not content with making a
Communist State for themselves, they intended to force
Communism on all other States. They thus roused, as
well as the financiers and commercial men with interests
in Russia which had become a dead loss, everyone who
feared or mistrusted the growing power of labour and
the increasing insistence of its demands. Indeed, the
Bolsheviks justified the hostility to them; declaring war
on the social order in all other States, they could not
complain of intervention in their own. The result in
Great Britain was that for months to come a lot of the
smothered class-feeling flew about in angry talk of White
and Red armies, Koltchak, Wrangel, Denikin, Lenin and
Trotsky. Labour accused the Government of wasting
money in a financiers' war; others accused labour of
being so swollen with war wages that it was losing its
head altogether.

There seemed to be any number of subjects to nag
about, and any amount of readiness to nag. The peace
mood was as queer and fretted as any of the war moods
had been. It was made up of many currents. There
were all the people who could not stand having any more
difficult things to face or think about, and just wanted
to be done with the abnormal. There were the de-

mobilised men wanting their jobs back, and the people
who did not want to lose them. There were people in
all sorts of businesses distended by war needs, in old
Government Departments which had had to take on
new functions, and in the huge new Departments. There
was the outcry against all of these, the clamour for
instant retrenchment, and vexed irritation at the undiminished swarm of " dug-outs " and clerks and typists
hanging on to salaries they could never hope for in the
competition of normal life. The too-familiar mood of
contemptuous impatience with the Government was
helped now by one of the strange results of the nation
having been plunged so completely into the war. Everyone—the soldiers pre-eminently, but civilians hardly
less—was coming back to his ordinary life with some
degree of scorn for Government institutions. Millions
who had never had any contact with Administration
before had come immediately under it, or even become
a part of it. With no conception of the complexity of a
Department's work, or of the real need for much of the
over-carefulness, which appeared mere fussy formality,
they lumped together the mistakes and failures inseparable from the terrific strain of such a war on any
Government, the makeshift quality of much that it had
had to do, the stiffnesses of a great many people trying
to cling to the proper authorised ways in the midst of
a raging torrent of events, the real incompetence and
unimaginativeness of a great many more, and decided
that the war had been a frightful revelation of what
Administration was, once you got inside it. And they
came out of it with one universal feeling—that the war
had been won not by Ministers and War Office generals,
tail-coated permanent officials and red-tabbed colonels,
who had been supposed to manage affairs, but by the
ordinary man : by big business running munitions, by
clerks and brokers and bank cashiers and schoolmasters

and lawyers and junior partners commanding companies
and platoons, by the huge mass of commonplace folk who
had filled the ranks.   In its bitterer forms the feeling
went so far as to suggest that we now knew what a
" ramp " all the governing we had accepted before the
war must have been ; these superior people, with their
supposed experience, were of far less use 'than the
average man taken out of the competitive market.   To
all this was added the talk of the demobilisèd men, and
their sense that the national job was done a lot better
when it depended upon them than it was being done
now.

So there was a self-assured and dictatorial tone in
all the nagging of the Government.   They must do
something about industry and stop the extravagant
unemployment dole.   They must get prices down and
remove that excuse for high wages.   They must draw in
their own tremendous expenditure, sell off surplus stores
and their big improvised factories.   They must set about
removing rationing, restriction of hours of drinking, and
other tedious survivals of the D.O.R.A.   They must do
something about the appalling lack of housing accommodation and not leave men who had done their bit
jostling one another for lodgings—miserable enough
when they could be got at all.   And they must do all
this quickly.   A popular newspaper, whose cartoonist
invented just now the two moss-grown complacent
incapables labelled " Dilly " and " Dally," exactly hit
the mood of the moment, and was never at a loss for
some new field of muddle and waste in which to depict
them displaying incompetence.

Irritation concentrated on the delay in the making of
peace.   Half of these worries, and all these lingerings
of war expenditure and war typists and war motor-cars,
were because we were not yet formally at peace.   What
were the people doing in Paris ?   The discussions there

were secret, but there was, of course, talk about the
complexity of the decisions which had to be taken,
the assessing of Germany's ability to satisfy the Allied
demands, and the delimitation of the frontiers of new
nationalities. " Self-determination " was a blessed word,
but it did not draw plain lines on a map. However,
excuses did not appease impatience. Had not the delegates taken to Paris experts enough to get on with this
work ? There they were, more of these enormous staffs
of officials, clerks and typists, housed in great hotels,
hanging on to the skirts of peace-making, as they had
hung on to the skirts of war, and in no more of a hurry
that it should be over. This particular irritability was
shot through with suspicion that the delay must be due
to some whittling down of peace terms. About these,
passing months had brought no more plain sense. In
the din of the General Election the profound difficulties
of the question of indemnities had degenerated into
" making Germany pay " and into Mr Lloyd George's
" Search their pockets." He might have regretted that
phrase since, and the fatal tendency to bid for the roar
of a delighted audience which betrayed him into it.
But he was not going to be let off. In the unpleasant
surprise of prices going higher than ever, and life in
general being so uncomfortable, the least suspicion that
Germany was not going to pay through the nose, pay for
everything, disgorge wealth to ease our pockets, roused
an outcry.

Mr Lloyd George was leading a divided life, oscillating
between Paris and the House of Commons. He had to
keep in touch with the debates, for the House was busy
with all the subjects about which the public was impatient. It was tackling the housing question along two
lines : first, a Rent Restriction Bill, to prevent landlords
from profiteering out of the wild demand for houses, by
forbidding any raising of the rent of houses below a

certain rental and forbidding also eviction of tenants ; and, secondly, a Housing Bill giving large powers to local authorities, to which was subsequently added a subsidising of private enterprise. The problem was colossal, and it had taken the country as a whole badly by surprise. There was more than one reason for it. The rate of house-building before the war had not been adequate to the demand, so that there was a shortage to start with. When the war broke out, house-building, which would in any case have slackened, had soon been forbidden entirely : building labour and building material had to be restricted to Government purposes alone. To the normal shortage was added a complete stoppage of supply. The official estimate, putting the deficiency at 350,000 houses, was certainly not over the mark. Upon this supervened a quite unusual demand for houses at the end of the war. Many, in the pressure of work, had given up those they had ; and there were thousands and thousands of couples who, quite rightly in those tragically uncertain years, married while they could, but being, save for leave times, separated had not had need for a house till the war was over.

Another effort in this direction—well meant, but more futile in the end—was a Land Settlement Bill. There had been much talk about the effect that army life would have upon men in making them unwilling to go back to town streets and office stools. Surely great numbers of them would want to find open-air occupation, and would rejoice to put their gratuities into some kind of small-holding enterprise. Besides, encouragement of this would help to relieve the rush back into the employment market. Some large tracts of agricultural land were bought, training centres established on them and small-holding colonies sketched out. The measure was criticised heavily : was it sensible to spend money in putting raw men on to the land when all kinds of

agriculture had been more or less insolvent for years ?
Sentiment had its way, and the Bill went through ; but
the colonies never showed any indication of success, and
were soon abandoned.

The House was tackling also some of the ramifications
of Government expenditure. The worst of it was that
it was just in the last year or so of the war that organisation of supplies had reached its full strength, and
there were huge establishments barely finished, or just
at high pressure, when the Armistice came. There were
great aeroplane works (we had at the end been building
4000 planes a month and equipping 200 squadrons in
place of the 6 with which we began the war), and aero-
dromes with acres of concrete floors and hangars. There
was Gretna, a complete town of munitions, and all the
other factories which had enabled us to fire on one
single day towards the end of the war—the day when
the Hindenburg Line was broken—950,000 shells, costing
nearly £4,000,000. There was the very " hush-hush "
establishment at Richborough, of which the public
hardly knew anything, but which was rumoured to have
turned that ancient relic of a place into the most modern
kind of port for a train-ferry service which would marvellously hasten delivery to the armies. The two places
most prominent in discussion in the House were the
Cippenham motor depot near Slough and the Chepstow
shipyards. About the latter the Government made the
interesting suggestion that, if some labour organisation
could be formed to take them on and work them co-
operatively, they might have the site and the plant ; it
seemed a pity to scrap works which, unlike the munition
factories, might well find a place in peace production.
But no one was ready for such an experiment and the
idea was dropped. The Cippenham depot was for cen-
tralising in one spot the vast business of war motor-
transport. It was seized upon as a piece of expenditure

which could most easily be cut off at once; but again the Government hesitated about scrapping works that might still have their use. A Select Committee was appointed to consider plans, and meanwhile there was a good case for retaining a depot at which the mass of transport vehicles could be collected for disposal.

At the beginning of the session the House had started on two Bills of government organisation. The Ministry of Health Bill was merely reconstructive; it gave, besides a new name, a new shape, a better meaning, and powers more in accordance with modern notions, to the old Local Government Board. The Ministry of Transport Bill, an effort to carry on one of the easiest of the war's lessons of organisation, was more jealously scrutinised. It gave the new Minister drastic powers of regulation (this was the first Bill to go far towards that surrender of the powers of Parliament which later fell under criticism) and most unusual powers of expenditure. As it was quite generally known that Sir Eric Geddes's position of Minister without Portfolio was a waiting-room until the new Ministry should be established, the apprehension about these powers was strong. Business autocrats— with their swift taking of decisions and their imaginative flights in expenditure—had been exactly what a war called for; but to launch one with unprecedented powers upon the country in peace time was quite another matter. In the end, the Minister's authority in expenditure was curtailed and made much more subject to Parliamentary sanction.

The Mines Commission duly reported on the fixed date. There were, however, three separate reports. The chairman, with the independent members, reported in favour of a wage advance of 2s. a day, the reduction of hours to 7 until July 1921, and then the establishment of the 6-hour day, and a levy of 1d. a ton to raise a fund for improving housing. The mine-owners on the

Commission reported for a wage advance of 1s. 6d. and
for a 7-hour day without any future reduction to 6 hours.
The miner members reiterated their demand for a 30
per cent. wage advance, an immediate 6-hour day and
nationalisation of the mines. On this the Government
offered the miners the terms of the first of these reports,
adding to them some provisions for giving miners a
voice in management, and a promise of progressive reorganisation of the whole industry. The miners, under
Mr Smillie's leadership, were steadily growing more
insistent on this last point. Nothing, they kept on saying, could make lasting peace in the industry until the
mines were nationalised. Their great point was that the
constant reply of the mine-owners to their demands—
that the industry could not afford to grant them—could,
no doubt, be proved true as things stood ; but that was
no answer to the argument that a nationalised industry,
pooling output and using boldly every modern idea for the
scientific exploitation of coal, would soon show what the
industry could really afford. For the moment the miners
agreed to the Government's offer, and left this larger
question to further consideration by the Commission.
Meanwhile Mr Smillie on the one side, and on the other
the Duke of Northumberland, showing himself an
acute as well as an irreconcilable maintainer of private
rights, carried on a duel over nationalisation in print
and on platforms, as slashing in phrase as it was good-
tempered on the whole in spirit.

It was gradually becoming apparent that much of
the nagging and grumbling which had been filling the
air was part of a general hurry and impulsiveness quite
as ready to find vent in many other ways, rushing back
to pre-war amusements or keeping the headier distractions of the war time spinning. In that mixed
way people grumbled at the packed crowding of buses
and tubes, and yet enjoyed the bustle and energetic

life of it after the brooding dull weariness, the loose
individual scramble after so long marching in ranks.
They grumbled about their jobs or their lack of them,
yet enjoyed the tolerance that did not expect the
" demobbed " to do very much for a while. They
grumbled about profiteering and the cost of drinks, and
enjoyed the equal tolerance they extended to themselves
not to begin anxieties about money just yet. This gayer
side of the restlessness and hurry grew until, for the
few months of summer, it almost swept irritation out
of the national temper. Partly this was because warmth
and beauty came with a rush over the country that year.
The cold dreary winter, as it happened, had lasted
very long, and bitter winds had held everything back.
The late spring came with extraordinary loveliness of
leaf and flower all at once ; and the country seemed to
shake off the war. The soldiers were all home, except
those whom tempting increases of pay and promise of
generous leave had secured for the Army of Occupation ;
and they were home with gratuities to spend. There
had been lavish out-of-work donation, and there was
a good stock of savings from the high war wages of
whole families. It was as if people, cheered by the
sunshine, suddenly grew sick of worrying and fussing,
and plunged into a sort of playtime after the hard
years. Everyone was out and about. Men after years of
camps and billets, women after the busy communal life
of hospitals and munitions and motor units and offices,
did not settle down as thankfully as they thought
they would in the days when home was only a thing to
long for. Besides, thousands upon thousands had but
makeshift homes, and little to keep them indoors. There
was an immense boom in small cars and motor-cycle
combinations, a demand that no supply could overtake,
even when the surplus war-stuff of that kind was thrown
on the market. There was a revel of dining and dancing,

theatre-going, cinema-going. Cinemas, stimulated by
the war-time amusement-hunting, were arising now as
big comfortable places, the very thing for the rapid
methods and flamboyant style of the reinforced-concrete
architecture which particularly distinguished them.
Dinner-dancing was no longer dining first and dancing
afterwards, but dining round a dancing floor and dancing
between courses. Jazz bands swarmed ; it was an
occupation jumped at by groups of demobilised friends
with gratuities to pool for a bit of capital.

The post-war world let itself go, and had a look at
itself. The most obvious change, at first sight, was in
the women. Short skirts and bobbed hair, taken to for
practical reasons during the war, had grown more and
more familiar sights, but only now did people begin to
see how universal they were. The new fashion outline
meant a new mind also ; war work and the breaking of
home ties had quickened enormously the casual, rather
flippant, independence of the young generation. But
there were other changes as well. In the mixed life of
the new armies' messes, and of all the ways in which
women had worked together, with the odd mixing, too,
that war-made fortunes had induced, a certain kind of
exclusiveness in amusements had vanished. It was no
longer the comparatively few who came out to spend
money of an evening. Men and women of a kind who
had thought but sparsely of entertainment before the
war had learned, in leave times and so on, of the many
amusing things there are to do ; and they turned this
first summer of peace into a long and cheery leave.
Nothing great or even very interesting on the stage or
in literature was stimulated into life. Nothing great was
called for. The eagerness was only for amusement, and
revues and dancing and night-clubs answered it.

There was a disturbing and ugly flash from the night-
club life early in the year, when a young actress, Miss

Billie Carleton, died of drug-taking, and a man, escaping the charge of manslaughter which had been the inquest verdict, was sentenced to eight months' imprisonment for conspiring to procure cocaine. This was the first case that brought cocaine-taking sensationally into the papers. There had been, quite early in the war, some prosecutions of Colonial soldiers for procuring cocaine, but they had been more or less hushed up. In the later war years, however, there had been talk about cocaine habits growing in the feverish pleasure-hunting and nerve strain ; Miss Carleton's death produced indignant comment on the traffic.

By mid-June, people were amusing themselves far too successfully to pay much attention to the Peace when at last it was signed. The terms were known in May, when they were communicated to the Germans ; and if the indemnity figures were far smaller than those which had been tossed about in December they were big enough to look impressive. The German delegates, protesting strongly, had taken the terms back to Germany to lay before the Reichstag. But they had had to accept them, and the signature of the Peace Treaty was about to take place. The popular mind in England had half forgotten this business of dictating terms to Germany when a strange almost crazy piece of news flung it back into strong feeling again. On 23rd June the Germans scuttled their surrendered ships lying in Scapa Flow, and all had gone to the bottom, except one of the battle-ships and five of the light cruisers. There was a wave of amazed disgust. It looked like such a childish gesture of spite, or worse. *Punch's* cartoon depicted the top of a mast sticking out solitary from the waves, flying the signal : " Germany expects every man this day to do the dirty." Admiral von Reuter took full responsibility. He explained that, the surrender of the fleet having been part of the terms of the Armistice, and the

Armistice terms being superseded by the acceptance of
the Peace terms, he had regarded himself as free to
carry out the orders given at the beginning of the war
that no German ship was ever to be surrendered. But
the explanation seemed as childish as the act ; the fleet
had been surrendered, and it was incredible that German
naval men could really feel the bitterness of that fact
cured by such action as this.

The incident made much more lively than it would
otherwise have been the concentration at the final
moment on the scene at Versailles—the long line of the
delegates of the Allied Powers, the fateful document
which might or might not hold a new world in it, and
the entry of the German delegates to sign it under those
watching eyes. There had been more magnificent and
glittering ends to other wars, the gold-laced, high-
collared, beribboned splendours of Vienna, the helmeted
militarism of 1871 on this same spot. Here was only
commonplace civilian garb, almost a pose of democratic
plainness. But that was the right note. Pomp of
uniforms might be in place when a clash of professional
armies had brought their masters, kings and marshals,
face to face in the end. This war had not been like
that. It had been the war of the ordinary man ; and
that plain-garbed grouping of the victors and the solitary
entry of the vanquished made its right end. For this
was not only a peace—it was a giving of sentence.

The cheap ideas of a more specific act of judgment,
which had inspired the " Hang the Kaiser " cry at the
election, still survived. Mr Lloyd George announced
in the House on 3rd July, in his formal statement on
the Peace, that it had been agreed at Versailles that a
Tribunal of the Allied Powers to conduct the trial of the
Kaiser should sit in London, and that requisition would
be made of Holland for his surrender. And the House
of Commons cheered ! It is no wonder that months

were even now to pass before the clap-trap of the whole notion finally revealed itself. It was not until early in 1920 that *Punch* published its cartoon of the conversation between Holland and the Entente Policeman :

HOLLAND : " So you'd like me to surrender the Kaiser ? "

ENTENTE POLICEMAN : " Well, I didn't go so far as that. I only asked you for him."

Concentration on the scene at Versailles was brief. Not even Mr Lloyd George could get any importance out of it, or control the bored sense that the Peace was an anti-climax, when the " demobbed " feeling had had hold of people for weeks and had been breaking out in so many exuberant directions. There had been a week of tense excitement in May over the first attempt to fly the Atlantic, made by Mr Hawker and Commander Mackenzie-Grieve. Flying had made such enormous advances during the war that the public rather hastily assumed that there was nothing which could not now be achieved. The check was all the sharper when no more news of the airmen came after their start. Days went by—a whole week—and then with immense relief people read that the two had been picked up in mid-Atlantic by a small steamer, transferred to H.M.S. *Revenge*, and had just been landed at Thurso. They travelled up to a tremendous reception in London, to be decorated by the King, and lunched by *The Daily Mail*, which had offered a prize of £10,000 for the first successful Atlantic flight. The excitement of the gallant opening bid for the prize had hardly died down when it was won. In June, Captain Alcock and Lieutenant Whitten-Brown flew over, in 16 hours 12 minutes, and there was quite enthusiasm enough left to rise to the occasion. The King knighted them both, and Mr Churchill, whose Department included now the Air Service, made the presentation of *The Daily Mail* cheque.

The Peace celebrations in London—the march of troops, headed by General Pershing and the Americans, then Lord Beatty leading the navy detachments and Lord Haig the army, with Marshal Foch riding beside him—were too belated to mean very much. Peace had been uncomfortable, far from the blissful coming right of everything which had been expected. There had been too much that made us talk of winning the war and losing the peace. The march was just a show, a day's excitement for the crowds, a stirring of memories for the demobilised, but no great climax of triumph.

The tide of high spirits was, in fact, already beginning to run down. Before the House adjourned in August it had to pass hurriedly a Bill attempting to soothe the outcry against high prices. There was still no real grasping of the fact that all our conceptions of prices would have to be changed ; people were clinging incurably to the expectation of the return of pre-war prices. There was ceaseless complaint of profiteering, and talk of tradesmen and farmers and market-gardeners actually destroying their goods rather than let prices down. Rationing and the registration of customers were still in operation—the Food Controller was talking about keeping them on through the coming winter—and caused mixed feelings. It might be dangerous to take them off, and yet they meant absence of competition for custom, which might well be part of the profiteering game. The new Bill set up local tribunals for controlling prices, with county appeal tribunals. Economists might be wise about it, and dismiss it as a mere sop ; the tribunals would soon find how little they could effect. But something had to be done, in a state of feeling so violent that Lord Milner could warn the House of Lords, in the debate on the Bill, that there would be a revolt unless some action were taken.

The main interest of the adjournment was Mr Lloyd

George's statement on the mines. The Sankey Commission had issued further reports at the end of May. There were four of them. One, by the chairman alone, was in favour of immediate nationalisation of the coal royalties. The miner members and one or two of the independent members were for complete nationalisation. The mine-owners reported, of course, completely against it. Sir Arthur Duckham reported in favour of the State taking, with due compensation, the mineral rights, but not ownership of the mines. Three out of the four reports were thus in favour of some measure of nationalisation. But it was not a fortunate moment for the idea. Just when the country was in a mood of disillusioned contempt for Government Departments it was not likely to agree with the miners' assertion that Government management 'would cure their troubles. Nor, when it was galled by the running on of the vast war expenditure and the swollen Ministries, was it likely to take kindly to the prospect of one more Ministry. It had just accepted two new bodies, the Ministry of Transport and the Electricity Commissioners, but one to work the mines would be much more speculative. Besides, the country was peevish again with industrial unrest. Railwaymen had been demanding the promised consideration of their conditions[1] ; police forces had been striking again (the Home Secretary gave the Metropolitan Police short shrift, but there was more trouble in Manchester, and in Liverpool even rioting) ; and, above all, the new conditions for the miners agreed upon in March had been made the reason for an advance of six shillings a ton in the price of coal. Altogether it was no favourable time for a policy of nationalisation ; and unusual as it might be to set aside flatly the majority of a Royal Commission, anxious as some might be about the closing of the door to the one thing the

[1] See page 1034.

miners were set upon, Mr Lloyd George informed the
House that the Government had definitely rejected that
policy.

The whole question was not nearly so urgently on the
public mind as the need for economy. That was the one
popular cry of the autumn and winter. Just before
the adjournment the Chancellor of the Exchequer,
Mr Austen Chamberlain, had been very gloomy and apprehensive about the national finances. Budget figures,
like prices, were still rising instead of falling; the
estimated revenue now was £1,160,000,000. With all the
hot suspicion of profiteering, this looked at any rate like
taking money off the war fortunes; and there was a
touch of the same kind of view in Sir Thomas Whitaker's
contention that the income-tax authorities ought to be
very strict and inquisitive about wage-earners' incomes.
A "Victory Loan" in June raised £250,000,000. But
by July the Chancellor was taking depressed views.
Speaking on the Consolidated Fund Bill, he said that
the position was turning out far worse than he expected.
Revenue was proving to be badly below his estimate,
and expenditure had been over it. One accompaniment
of the strain was that the famous Liberal finance of the
pre-war years began to wear thin. Talk about import
duties, which would have roused the strongest feeling in
1912 or 1913, slid into the debates, and Free Traders,
doing their best not to look foolish, hung on to saving
phrases about "key industries"—a helpful catchword
starting on its career at this time. But, even when so
many handsome dogmatisms of those earlier years were
tottering, there was something altogether too bland in
the placid announcement that land valuation and
the taxation of unearned increment — the core and
pith of the great "People's Budget," the policy for
which it had been worth while to challenge the Lords,
the bulwark against Protection, the rich resource for

social welfare, the banner that Mr Lloyd George had carried so assuredly through a lurid battle-smoke of Limehouse speeches and a whirlwind election — had proved unremunerative and unworkable, and would now be reconsidered with a view to their extinction.

But across the gulf the war had dug between 1919 and the fierce political battles of 1909 not many people reached back for stones to throw. The country did not want that kind of bickering. It wanted—and more than ever after the Chancellor's anxious warnings—economy. There was no excuse for more delays, now the Peace had been signed. Again, something had to be done which might be soothing, and directly after the adjournment Mr Lloyd George issued instructions for every Department to overhaul its work and its personnel, and produce a scheme for cutting down its costs.

He, with one or two other prominent people, Mr John Burns among them, received just now a testimonial of a kind unusual in public life. Mr Andrew Carnegie died at the beginning of August; and among his bequests were one of £2000 a year to Mr Lloyd George and one of £1000 a year to Mr John Burns. Mr Carnegie had been a multi-millionaire with a reputation all his own. The story of his rise to enormous wealth in the Pittsburg steel factories was one not often to be told of a Britisher; and there was a sort of national pride taken in his having come back to buy a Scottish castle and settle down over here to spend his money. He had for many years been making for himself a special place in the national life, by giving and equipping public libraries, large and small, and later by the foundation of the Carnegie Trust for various educational purposes. Though he was said to have once been worth £70,000,000, he left now only £5,000,000 to be disposed of by his will.

September brought an odd little distraction to the newspapers. One of the grievances left by the Peace

Conference in re-drawing the map of Europe had been
the rejection of the Italian claims to certain ports on the
eastern coast of the Adriatic. Now Signor d'Annunzio,
with a romantic writer's mind made even more romantic
by war service, putting himself at the head of the more
violent section of the protesting Italians, organised a
military expedition of his own, descended on Fiume, and
annexed it. This condottiere gesture provided exciting
news for some days.

A dashing figure of quite another kind, yet also
romantic, was lost to English life in that month by the
death of Lord Beresford. Marked out early in his career
by a courageous exploit with the gunboat *Condor* during
the Egyptian campaign of 1884, he had come to impress
himself upon the public imagination in the way of Lord
Fisher at a later date, as the breezy sailor carrying the
interests of the service through the short-sighted and
dusty tangles of politics. The people loved his Irish
humour, his downright speech, and his buoyant ways,
even though, as he grew older, his appearances in politics
had been apt to become a little acrid.

In the autumn another kind of complaint began to
grow up beside the economy cry. It was that no one was
working hard enough. That pleasant "demobbed"
feeling must come to an end. It was, in fact, dying out.
Uniforms, which had lingered about for months, were
disappearing fast, and people were discovering that no
one wanted any longer to listen to anything about the
war. Better settle down again, and get on with jobs. But
that, said the newspapers, was what nobody was really
doing. They began to lecture the public on elementary
economics ; the great fact to face was that for all
the four years of war we had made no fresh wealth,
and had blown away much of what we had had before.
This was what we were suffering from, and no amount
of economy in Government or anywhere else could help,

if we did not understand that we had to work, not merely as hard as before, but far harder, to make up for the missed wealth-production of those years. Yet there were the mines, held up by disputes about pay and hours, and coal production disastrously below the normal. There were railwaymen, striking in September, causing a return of war regulations, and a call for volunteer service for food supplies and for a vast milk depot in Hyde Park—a grave disturbance of all sorts of industry just when our railways should, like everything else, have been more, and not terribly less, busy. There was the Trade Union Congress, angry still about the war with Russia (though by that time the withdrawal of the Murmansk and Archangel forces had been decided upon, and was being organised), and insisting upon nationalisation, instead of facing the urgent need to get industry on its feet again.

Out of all the dissatisfaction grew a movement for founding a Middle-Class Union. The idea was that, between organised labour on the one side, and a swollen well-entrenched Government on the other, the black-coated salary-earners and the drawers of modest dividends were going to be badly squeezed. Wages constantly forced up, hours forced down, and output restricted, were going to keep price-levels high ; and it was notorious that earned salaries moved far less easily, if they moved at all, to meet higher prices than wages did, with the union organisation behind them. Incomes from investment did not move at all, so that rising prices simply halved them automatically. At the same time it was upon salaries and incomes of this kind that the tax collector fastened most ruthlessly. It would be wise, then, for the middle classes to take a leaf out of the wage-earners' book, and have their own organisation. But, of course, middle classes are not an entity, like a trade ; they could never have a true union existence ;

and even if they approximated to it they could not act as sharply and menacingly as a trade could upon the national life. The idea never came to much.

Though the war was by now boring as a topic of ordinary talk, there was plenty of interest in some war books which came out in the autumn. The most piquant was General French's book, *1914*, which aroused some very strong feeling. The sensational part of it was French's revelation of the fact that he had deliberately set going the newspaper campaign against Lord Kitchener which dragged into publicity the shell controversy in 1915. Over this action, as a matter of personal conduct, of service etiquette, of military loyalty, of a real duty to the nation over-riding all these considerations, argument raged—on the whole, not to French's credit. There had been already too much gossip about his period as Commander-in-Chief. Free though they were of personal implications of this kind, the memoirs of Lord Fisher and Lord Jellicoe were published too soon ; the acuteness of certain differences of opinion during the war was still too strong. Memoirs that were widely read for quite other reasons were those of Tirpitz, Ludendorff and Falkenhayn. People were eager for the chance of seeing the war, for the first time, from the other side, and finding out a little of what we had been able only to guess at during those years. The main burden of these three books was to throw the blame for Germany's collapse upon the civilian population and the civilian leaders, who had, according to these writers, let the fighting spirit down. The other main impression left by them, rightly or wrongly, was that they justified all we had felt about Prussianism : they were the very voice of a rigid military caste regarding the whole German Empire in the spirit of a drill-sergeant.

But that, surely, was to be the voice of a completely buried past now, whether in Germany or anywhere else.

The first anniversary of the Armistice was marked by the launching of the League of Nations Union at a great meeting in London. From the moment of the cessation of hostilities Lord Robert Cecil had been devoting himself to a movement for making the League of Nations an active reality in the public mind. Few people knew then that the Covenant which President Wilson had made his own peculiar task in the Peace settlement was in origin largely Lord Robert's work. But they had come to know that there was a man in England who was not going to let us decline upon the vague assurance that the Covenant existed, any more than he was going to allow us to say that the League was a piece of idealism, which would crumble into futility at the first national quarrel. He was going to make public opinion constantly aware that the Covenant was an instrument for use, not an automatically acting preventive, a means by which nations could avoid wars if they wished to strongly enough, not a heaven-sent guarantee against their own foolishnesses ; he was not going to let us, as it were, hang it up somewhere as a lifebelt, forget about it, and then, grabbing at it when we had navigated into some disaster, curse it because it would not save us from drowning. He had spoken, with the Archbishop of Canterbury and Lord Grey of Fallodon,[1] at a great meeting in the Albert Hall in June, just before the signing of the Peace Treaty. The Armistice meeting was to start the League of Nations Union as an organisation for keeping the League in the public mind, and making us follow its work. At the moment there was enthusiasm enough. It was to be Lord Robert's greatest achievement that he was not misled by the ease of the start.

A remarkable new subject of conversation appeared in November. There had been an eclipse of the sun at the end of May, with statements in the papers that the

[1] Sir Edward Grey had accepted a peerage, with this title.

usual astronomical expeditions to take observations had
a special interest and importance, because a new theory,
the Einstein theory, which the public vaguely understood to have something to do with the transmission of
light, and of which a total eclipse would provide a
possible test, might be either verified or disproved. It
was said informally, when the expeditions returned,
that the theory had been proved to be sound, but the
full calculations necessary were not available until
November. It turned out that the whole business was
entirely beyond even the sketchiest comprehension by
the ordinary man. All that he gathered was that the
shortest way between two points is not necessarily
what we call a straight line, that Newton's theory of
gravitation was only of partial validity, that Euclidean
geometry had little relation to the facts of the universe,
that generally speaking we had forgotten to allow for
the whole universe being on the move—a number of
very dim notions. To mathematicians and scientists of
the first order, it appeared, the Einstein theory was one
conclusive step of a prolonged recent remaking of human
conceptions of the universe. The ordinary man looked
at the equations blankly, and decided he could never
really know anything about it.

On 1st December the House of Commons received its
first woman member. One of the last acts of the war
Parliament had been to hurry through a Bill supplementing the grant of the vote to women by enabling
them to sit in the House. The General Election had
been too hasty for the candidature of women to begin
then. But it is curious that the first woman's candidature, when it did take place, was not the concerted
action of any feminist movement celebrating a great
advance. On Mr Astor's succession to the peerage his
wife stood for the vacated seat. So rapidly had we
taken to the idea of women in politics that Lady Astor's

election roused little discussion except in the form of entertaining questions of how a woman member might be expected to conform to the sober costumes of the House, whether she would retain her hat, and if so how she could comply with certain customs in debate. Lady Astor appeared, led up by the Prime Minister and Mr Balfour to take the oath, in costume that suited very well the ordinary masculine town clothes, and was altogether an admirable introducer of a new age. Her arrival coincided happily with the last stages of a Bill removing sex disabilities in the profession of the law.

The most important piece of work of this autumn session was the Bill making reforms in the Government of India. The reforms initiated in 1909, when Mr John Morley was Secretary of State and Lord Minto Viceroy —the first marked step away from purely official government, giving natives of India elective seats on the Provincial Councils and the opportunity of bringing criticism to bear — had done little to placate Indian Nationalist feeling. That had received formidable re-inforcement of late. Beside the original movement, violent in word and often in action, had arisen one far more difficult to handle, a non-resistance movement aiming at its object by complete dissociation from every-thing Western, and intended to become one gigantic boycott. At its heart was a revered and gentle figure, Gandhi, who knew how to give to Nationalism the fire, not of violence, but of that austerity and abstinence which can be so invincible an inspiration to Eastern minds. Disappointed by the failure of the Morley-Minto reforms, the Liberal Government had sent out Mr Montagu, when he was Secretary of State; and he, in conjunction again with the Viceroy, Lord Chelmsford, had drawn up a long and elaborate report, on which the new Bill was now based. The report had been criticised as making, in an enthusiasm for self-government, the

mistake which Mr Morley had avoided—that of thinking
that the demand of the peoples of India, with all their
conditions of sharp religious hostilities, widely differing
racial characters, and vast masses of extremely poor
and ignorant peasantry, must necessarily be met by a
representative system of a wholly Western type. Mr
Morley had given powers of criticism and advice. The
Montagu-Chelmsford Report introduced a measure of
control over Ministers in the manner of Western
Parliaments. The system which the new Bill set up
was a dyarchy. It divided power in two ways : first by
reserving some subjects of administration wholly to the
Central Government, and second, by dividing the subjects of provincial governments into " reserved " and
" transferred " subjects. The latter were placed in the
hands of a body of Ministers responsible to the elected
Chamber of the provincial assembly, and in this branch
the attitude of the Lieutenant-Governor of a Province
to the Ministers was to be that of the head of a Western
State to a Cabinet dependent on a majority. The former
branch remained in the hands of the Lieutenant-Governor
and his Executive Council. The other large change
made by the Bill was that in place of the Viceroy's
Council was set up a bi-cameral Central Assembly, an
elected Chamber and a Council, in neither of which was
there an official majority.

Other associations attached themselves to the return
of the Prince of Wales from a tour to the United States
and Canada in the battleship *Renown*. He brought
with him the beginnings of a reputation for making a
charming success of such affairs, which later years were
to increase. He had captivated New York ; and sport
and camping and ranching in Canada had captivated
him. His return now was his first real entry upon popularity at home. The country had liked the simplicity
with which he had been sent to Oxford and the stories

of the frankness with which he had lived an undergraduate's life, enjoying most what was least hedged
about by his princedom, like games and dinners in hall.
That had been abruptly ended by the war ; and it says
much for the impression he had made on the public
mind that the strongest feeling for him then was one
of sympathy with him in his inability to make the
authorities let him fight exactly as all the rest of his
generation.

Before the year was over Ireland was beginning to
take that place in the news which was to make the
next eighteen months so tragic and dreadful. Absorbed
in their own affairs, English people had thought little
of what was happening over there. There had been a
moment of mixed vexation and amusement in March,
when Mr de Valera, who had been one of the Sinn
Feiners arrested in 1918, had escaped from Lincoln gaol.
The amusing part of it was in the stories of two
beguiling Irish girls, who had used their good looks to
help the escape. Since then there had been constantly
recurring accounts of attacks upon police barracks and
upon post offices, and the ambushing and killing of
constables. But to people in general this meant little
more than a bad phase of the unhappily usual state of
Ireland, a recurrence of the old " moonlighter " days.
By December, however, the seriousness of what was
going on became apparent. The sporadic attacks were
growing more frequent, more determined ; and then came
a murderous attack on General French, the Viceroy ;
his car was ambushed on a road, and his escape was
extraordinary. That was just before Mr Lloyd George
produced yet one more scheme for Home Rule and the
difficulty of Ulster—a system of two separate Parliaments, with a single Federal Council of forty for the
whole of Ireland, elected in equal proportions by the
two legislatures. The scheme was said to be the work

of a new genius at constitution-making, Mr Lionel
Curtis. The main comment on the proposal at the
moment was that it was a pity it had been so long delayed. For a whole year the Sinn Feiners, keeping away
from Westminster, had had their hands on Ireland,
with disaffection growing more organised the whole time.
However, here was the new Home Rule at last, and a
fresh start on the old road of conciliatory proposals and
coercion of lawlessness.

CHAPTER X

1920–1922 : THE PAINFUL TRUTH

THE history of the next three years belongs to this volume only in summary, as a concluding chapter. In detail those years are the beginning of a new time, of the discovery that the post-war world was not the pre-war world crippled yet recovering, but something totally new. All that is in place here is a brief recounting of the disappearance of much that we had carried over, in hope, from war time into peace— forms of government control and national organisation, and coalition of parties ; the fading of the belief that we had been, as a people, so soundly and healthily shaken together that we could not fall again into the old lack of understanding ; the gradual discovery that, instead of having been helped forward, in spite of all its pain and horror, by the war, we had been very badly knocked down by it. To the next period, rather than to the one here related, belongs the fact that the great majority of people worried about all this less than might have appeared, and got along quite well in casual detachment from solemn people who had made such a mess of life, and were so unsuccessfully trying to clear it up.

One of the baffling aspects of the time is its maze of contradictions. Although by every showing people ought to have been leading a rather uncomfortable, pinched and hampered existence, it was difficult to see any signs of this. There was talk about " the new poor," the old aristocratic and society families falling upon hard times, giving up their country houses and town mansions to make way for the war-wealthy and the profiteers. Changes of that sort there were, but not to any marked degree. The movement from large houses had many other reasons behind it. One was that domestic servants were becoming difficult to get or to keep, partly because war work had given young women much more independent ideas of employment, partly because even without the war influence they had begun to revolt against an occupation which employers had done nothing to adapt to new times. Another reason was that people were finding that in the many amusing ways of spending money the pomps and solemnities of a big house were a dull form of costliness. A large and pleasant flat solved the servant problem, and left money for restaurant dinners, bridge-parties, cars and race-meetings. The same kinds of adjustment were going on all through the professional classes.

The truth, perhaps, is that most of the talk about the new poverty was in the early half of 1920, when the effect of the war on prices was at its worst, and the index-figure of comparison with pre-war prices rose to 176. The Budget for this year, too, was as depressing as that of the year before ; the revenue to be raised was over £1,340,000,000 ; letter postage went up to 2d., telegrams to 1s., and spirits and beer were more heavily burdened than ever ; the Excess Profits Duty was raised again, and a Corporation Tax on limited liability companies was imposed. Moreover the railways added a further 25 per cent. to the 50 per cent. increase of fares.

Yet even so it would have been difficult for a casual visitor to observe any striking signs of narrowed resources. He would not have seen the universities and public schools less full (they were, in fact, more crowded), the restaurants emptier, the golf-courses less populated at a week-end, less cars on the road, or expensive shops beginning to look seedy. People were

convinced that the financial pressure was largely unnecessary, and that it was not for them but for the
Government to economise. A good deal had been done.
The Food Control and Shipping Control Departments,
and the renamed Ministry of Munitions, had been dis-
banded in the latter part of 1919; and the sale of surplus
stores had begun. Quantities of linen, tons of wire, had
been put on the market at bargain prices; Mr Mallaby
Deeley rushed into fame by making a great business of
selling the standard suits of clothes which had been prepared for demobilisation, and left on the Government's
hands in hundreds of thousands; outfitters secured
masses of army shirts and socks and other garments,
good money's worth at the few shillings asked for
them. But no one believed that economising had
made more than a beginning. Budget figures would
have to come down a lot more. Behind that conviction
people comfortably sheltered themselves in going on
much as usual with their own personal expenditure.

So the newspapers still had plenty to lecture the
nation about. We were all too frivolous. Dress was
becoming a scandal; this was the time when *Punch* had
a picture of a girl whose nightmare was that she had
gone to a dance in her nightgown, and found herself
embarrassingly overdressed. Dancing was more than
a craze; people had their inseparable partners, danced
with them alone, and would not go to parties except
in couples. The music was more jazz than ever; the
dancing more lugubrious. It was no longer a pursuit
for the young, either; the war had made a difference
there; the older generation, finding itself not so old
after all, no longer sat about bored and yawning. The
theatre was frivolous; true, *Abraham Lincoln* had had
its success in 1919, but the great hit of 1920 was *The
Beggar's Opera*. Every class of society was frivolous,
for cinemas, with their cheap seats, were packed to

watch Charlie Chaplin, Douglas Fairbanks and Mary
Pickford, the trio who first became film idols over here.
With the summer began the loud complaints about
chars-a-bancs invading the countryside. In the intervals
of frivolity depression awaited us. We might know,
unhappily enough, that a nation could not send its
youth to death for four years and keep its vitality.
Yet we had still to learn that what was left of the
younger generation was seared and, as it seemed, indifferent and unresponsive. The bored disillusion of
young novelists betrayed the truth of new movements
in painting and music as no stirring of fresh life, but only
an impulse of scorn for the old. The elder generation
had made a mess of the world; the younger seemed to
be too contemptuous to mind about it. Every month
some nation defeated us in one sport or another; the
question of the wife in *Punch*, seeing her husband
unusually interested in the paper—" What is it, dear ?
Has England won something ? "—summed up the
situation.

This was not a public mind likely to be judicious
about any of its national affairs. It was snappy about
all of them, and not even Mr Lloyd George could conjure
with it any longer. He was leading a strenuous life, still
to and fro across the Channel, or holding conferences
with French Ministers at Sir Philip Sassoon's place,
Lympne, or with his own Ministers at Chequers, the
lovely Buckinghamshire house which Lord Lee had
given to be a permanent country house for Prime
Ministers, handy to London in this age when week-
ending had become a necessity of life. The gift had
been made during the war, but only now had the Prime
Minister been able to begin to make much use of it.
The French conversations were growing sharp in tone ;
and the British public, allowing too little for the fact
that the French had had the war for four years on their

own outraged soil and we had not, was inclined to be hurt and vexed. About Russia the popular mind was merely hot-tempered, and abusive of Bolshevism. It was growing peevish with America, seeing the pound sterling drop actually below four dollars in the exchange; hearing gloomy predictions about the likelihood of New York, with the immense stores of gold which she had drawn during the war, taking the place of London as the world's money market; reckoning up the debt to America, and beginning to hint that as, in the end, she had had to do so little fighting, she might at least, by cancelling some of the loans, make up her due contribution to the effort that others had borne bloodily for four years.

Worst of all our national affairs was Ireland. By the summer of 1920 conditions there were atrocious. Against Sinn Fein, so much more sheer and open rebellion, so much better armed, than the old movement had been, the Government fell back upon its own men who had not forgotten their fighting. They reinforced the Royal Irish Constabulary by enlisting demobilised men who had not settled down again in civil life. Wearing with their khaki the dark caps of the R.I.C., they were attaining a grim notoriety as " the Black and Tans." For some months the conflict did not differ much, except in extent and persistence, from the old conditions of a period of coercion in Ireland. But a bitterer spirit crept in. The police and the Black and Tans were sick of meeting, in the old restrained ways, the perpetual ambushing and murder, and they took to reprisals. They might not be able to bring proper legal evidence against individuals of murder or complicity in murder, or of harbouring rebels, but they knew well enough houses and people that were giving secure refuge to Sinn Fein gunmen. They began their own raids, ambushings and killings : so many policemen killed, so many Irish to die

in retaliation. Late in the year the situation seemed one
of absolute despair. Rebellion was not being weakened,
yet the Government, engaged in its new Home Rule
proposals, tried to forbid reprisals, and to bring conditions back to a struggle of law against disorder. In
November, speaking in the City, Mr Lloyd George chose
to be optimistic; we "had murder by the throat." But
we had not. The Irish news grew bloodier, more brutal
every week. In the very month in which Mr Lloyd
George spoke, English officers, dragged out of bed one
morning in hotels in Dublin, were shot in cold blood
before the eyes of their wives.

Throughout the first six months of 1921 it had to be
recognised that the state of affairs was no longer the
suppression of a lawless element. It was full rebellion,
working through the most difficult kind of guerrilla
fighting, which reminded people of the last two years of
the Boer War. Uniformed British forces were opposed to
an elusive enemy, armed men at one moment, the next
moment indistinguishable among the people of a little
street, or scattered in farms. There was discussion of
the possibility of using the methods of the later stages
of the Boer War, lines of block-houses, and sweeps of
region after region, interning women and children, and
rounding up the men. That is, no doubt, what the war
would have come to, had not the Irish question fallen,
with many others, into the mood of wholesale change
of mind, withdrawal, stopping short for a fresh start,
which so curiously and distinctly marks the year 1921.
It is the coming of that mood which justifies the inclusion of a brief summary of these years as the final
chapter of the war period.

In many ways it was a melancholy, and even tragic,
giving up of high hopes; an end to all notions that the
ordeal had shown us new paths for the national life.
The Government took its hand off every kind of control

or organising supervision which had seemed to offer
fresh prospects of managing our affairs, and shut down
all of its immediate "betterment" schemes. The
reason for this was, indeed, not openly a denial of the
ideals ; it was the urgent and material reason of money.
We could not afford what we were doing and what we
had hoped to do. Budgets could remain at their present
figures only by sending prices still higher, for they continued to involve the creation of Government credits.
And that, by now, opened prospects of the gravest alarm,
for warnings were under our eyes on the Continent.
Austrian and German currency was beginning to go
mad. Money had been manufactured for credits until
prices had lost any relation to a fixed standard. People
were going about with wads of notes drawn fresh from
the banks every morning, which might, when drawn,
buy them breakfast, but would be most unlikely to
buy them supper. We were not near that kind of total
collapse yet ; but in a world of staggering currencies
(French francs and Italian lire were none too steady) no
risks should be run. That meant creating no more credits,
but balancing the Budget on the year's revenue. The
revenue in turn depended upon trade, upon output,
upon the production of marketable wealth ; and we
could not be perfectly clear-headed about the amount of
wealth we were producing till we removed all the dis-
guising influences of Government control, subsidy of
enterprise, or privileged output of any kind. Only by
being sure of the net reality of trade figures could we
genuinely balance Budgets.

So the last Government enterprises were wound up,
and buildings and plant put on the market. The subsidy
for housing was cut off, and the local authorities left to
do what they could by housing bonds or other devices.
Control was taken off articles of food and drink, off the
mines, and then off the railways. There was a despairing

plea for keeping it on agriculture. The war had given us
a fright about food supplies ; and there were many who,
genuinely anxious for the chance of reviving a rural life
which the last forty years had been steadily strangling,
did not want it thrust into a neglected corner again.
So strong was this feeling that, in their election manifesto, Mr Lloyd George and Mr Bonar Law had found it
worth while to promise definitely that the agricultural
minimum wage and the Wages Boards should survive.
Now this promise went the way of the high hopes in
general. Control was taken off there too, and the agricultural labourer left to take his chance. The land,
vivified for this brief time by a Government concern for
it at last, was thrown back into its old apathy. What
made this worse was that another industry, one which
could still frighten the Government, could not be so
treated. The anger of the miners at being dropped back
into decontrol promptly issued in a strike. They did
not get control back, but they wrung from the Prime
Minister a subsidy of £10,000,000 for the maintenance of
the wage-level.

These withdrawals mounted up to a fairly complete
abandonment of rosy electioneering promises. The process itself may have been inescapable ; the sadder fact
was that the temper in which it was done showed hardly
a remnant of that kindliness and sympathy between
classes of which the war idealists had seen visions,
hardly a trace of that concern for the less fortunate of
the community which the comradeship of the armies
was supposed to have produced. It cost too much. We
went back to the old unregulated scramble with an
absence of regrets about doing so which would have
looked like treachery if it could have been foreseen in
1915 or 1916. In some definite organisations—regimental
associations, Old Comrades associations, the British
Legion—links were kept with some, at least, of the

feeling of those days.   But there had been no rebirth
of the nation.

The Government could not scrap all its promises and
do nothing about clearing up its own extravagances.   A
committee was set up to overhaul the Civil Service
expenditure, since the Departments seemed unable to
do it themselves.   There was cynical comment at first
when its chairman appeared in the person of Sir Eric
Geddes, the notorious " big business " spender during
the war.   But " the Geddes axe " turned out to be a
fairly drastic lopper.   It did not do all that was asked
of it.   Sir Robert Horne, who had had another of the
meteoric careers from business to high office, becoming
Chancellor of the Exchequer after only two years'
membership of the House, had asked for a reduction
of £130,000,000 in Civil Service Estimates ;   what he
got in the Geddes Committee's recommendations was
£100,000,000 ;   what he actually achieved in his next
year's Estimates was £52,000,000.   But with that, and
with some use of the axe in the fighting services, Budgets
did begin to come down substantially.   The millions in
them dropped back into three figures.

It was in July that Ireland came into this Government mood of reconsidering fundamentally most of what
it was doing.   In effect what Ministers did was to give
up the idea that we were governing Ireland.   That had
been behind all the long drawn-out policy of mixed
coercion and conciliation, based on the view that we
must ourselves impose order there, whatever else we
might do.   When conversations took place between
Government representatives and Sinn Fein leaders in
prison, when Sir James Craig met Mr de Valera (a
courageous act in those days of kidnapping and murder),
Ministers were approaching the position of treating
with Sinn Fein as the Provisional Government of another
nation.   True, at the stage which followed, when General

Smuts (there was almost the suggestion of an invaluable
mascot about his undefined but powerful place in our
affairs) went over to Ireland to enter on negotiations,
the Government professed some detachment from his
proceedings. In March Mr Asquith had been suggesting
that " Dominion status " for Ireland might meet the
case ; and this gave added significance to the intervention of General Smuts, who had himself helped to
bring a people long in racial antagonism to Great Britain
to a successful Dominion status. There was a hard
struggle yet before the end was reached. Mr de Valera
was refusing to consider any status but that of a wholly
independent republic. Ministers obviously could have
nothing to do with that. Finally, by not insisting on
the claim for independence being openly abandoned
before the Conference met, a way was found for getting
the Sinn Fein delegates to London to treat. Difficulties
even then were far from over. A group of irreconcilable
Conservatives were violently attacking in Parliament the
very idea of negotiations. Mr de Valera and Mr Michael
Collins were holding out to the last for independence.
Ministers forced the end. They gave the Sinn Fein
representatives point-blank the prospect of ruthless
and full-scale war. A few hours later, under the formula
of loyalty to the King " in virtue of the common citizenship of the British Commonwealth of Nations," the Irish
Free State was born.

To the country at large this was a relief. Again,
something had had to be done, and was at last done.
But the strain of carrying it through, and of the following weeks in which the Treaty was under debate in
Parliament, made very visible the beginning of the end
of the Coalition. It had suffered for three years from
the disappointments of peace, from the bewildered impatience at the thronging difficulties of recovery, from
the delays and frictions with our Allies which beset the

remaking of Europe. No one could see what increased strength of purpose or vigour in action the continued suspension of party politics could be said to have produced. It did not appear to give the representatives of the nation any unusual kind of authority abroad. Nor could it be said that the fact that there was a Coalition Government in power really made much difference to the settlement of the Irish question. The situation over there had grown so bloodstained that, if the House of Commons had been constituted on normal party lines, the irreconcilables would not have been able to persuade it to refuse a settlement of any kind which would leave Ireland a part of the dominions of the Crown.

The continuance of the Coalition had involved the idea that the establishment of peace was some definite effort, occupying a more or less definite time, which would command something of the same sort of national unity as the war had commanded, and should therefore be in the hands of a political unity. Now we knew that peace and recovery were not effects to be produced, things to be done, but an existence to be lived. We had better begin to live it as normally as we could. All the decontrol had been recognition of this. Politics must be decontrolled as well. As early as January 1922 Unionist disaffection was active, Sir George Younger, their Whip, pressing for an immediate election. Mr Lloyd George held on for some months, which only made the Coalition plight worse. Those months brought into the open a factor new and dangerous in British politics, the existence of a huge election war-chest in the single control of Mr Lloyd George ; there were acrimonious debates on the sale of honours and other methods by which election funds had long been accumulated. Those months landed us also in the most acutely anxious stage of our post-war relations with France, over the disastrous advance of Greece into Asia Minor, which ended in a

few days of the gravest anxiety, when we hovered on
the brink of renewed war with Turkey, and were saved
only by the fine character of the man on the spot,
Sir Charles Harington.

That unpardonable muddle brought the end.   In
October 1922 Mr Lloyd George resigned.   It may be
taken, perhaps, as a tribute to the place he had filled in
the national life during the years before the war, to the
unmatched energy and flexible readiness of mind with
which he had held the nation during the war, to the
dominance of his personality throughout the crisis, that
not till the moment of his resignation can this volume
be properly closed.

INDEX

Wales, Edward, Prince of (afterwards Edward VII.), 19, 293; suggests the foundation of Imperial Institute, 190; wins the Derby, 399; suggests the hospital fund for London, 414; a pall-bearer at Mr Gladstone's funeral, 437; proclaimed King, 562. (See also Edward VII., King.)

Wales, George, Prince of (afterwards King George V.), 575; meets Lord Kitchener, 600; visits Quebec, 743. (See also George V., King.)

Wales, radical county councils in, 662; university college for, 146; riots in, 195

Walkley, A. B., 240, 580

Wallace, Alfred Russel, 885 (note)

Wallace, Sir Richard and Lady, 426

Walsall anarchists, the, 342

Walter, John, 705

Wanklyn, Mr, a phrase coined by, 548

War, the Great: declaration of war, 4th August 1914, 903; railways taken over by Government, 913; White Paper issued on 5th, showing Sir Edward Grey's efforts for peace, 915; Kitchener appointed to War Office, 915; paper currency issued, 917; Food Prices Committee set up, 918; Press censorship under F. E. Smith, 919; first vote of credit for £100,000,000, 919; "Business as usual," 920; Relief Fund started by Queen and Prince of Wales, 920; H.M.S. *Amphion* lost, 921; Namur falls, 921; French and British forces in retreat across France, 923; widespread and general belief in the rumour of Russian troops in England, 924; found to arise from troop trains bearing Highland regiments, 925; battles of the Marne and Aisne, 925; General French's despatches hearten the public by showing retreat from Mons orderly and unbroken, 925; "Eyewitness's" reports,

War—*continued*
927; loss of *Aboukir, Hogue* and *Cressy*, 927; "the angels of Mons," 928; Mr Churchill's attempt to relieve Antwerp with two naval brigades fails, 930; "the fight for the road to Calais," 931; new scare about "concrete beds," 931; not dissipated by reports of artillery experts, 922; Prince Louis of Battenberg resigns as First Sea Lord, and succeeded by Lord Fisher, 932; Volunteer Training Corps, 933; swift response of Empire in sending troops, 934; Ypres, first battle of, 934; embittered recruiting pressure, 935; Red Cross and Y.M.C.A. work, 935; fight developing in Flanders into a sort of siege warfare, 936; battle of Coronel, 936; *Bulwark* blown up at Sheerness, 936; spy scare again, 937; first War Loan, 937; battle of Falkland Islands, 937; Scarborough, Whitby and Hartlepool shelled, 940; committee appointed to investigate charges of atrocity, 940; first Zeppelin raids, 940; Germans stiffen up their submarine warfare, 940; modified by protests from U.S.A., 940; Admiral Beatty captures the *Blucher*, 941; food prices begin to rise, 941; loss of the *Formidable*, off Lyme Regis, 941; institution of new decoration, M.C., 942; bombardment of the Dardanelles, 943; recruiting pressure, 943; Neuve Chapelle terrible casualties, 944, 945; the drink question, 946; secret struggles in Cabinet not known till later, 947; munitions' controversy, 948; German prisoners in England reported too well treated, 949; divisions in Cabinet about Dardanelles, 949; renewed fighting at Ypres, 950; first poison-gas attack, 950; sinking of the *Lusitania*, 951, 953; mobs attack alien shopkeepers, 952; report of

PRINTED IN GREAT BRITAIN BY
LOWE AND BRYDONE (PRINTERS) LTD., LONDON.